2022 and 2023 Selected Papers from *Algorithms* Editorial Board Members

2022 and 2023 Selected Papers from *Algorithms* Editorial Board Members

Editor

Frank Werner

MDPI

Basel • Beijing • Wuhan • Barcelona • Belgrade • Novi Sad • Cluj • Manchester

Editor
Frank Werner
Otto-von-Guericke-University
Magdeburg
Germany

Editorial Office
MDPI
St. Alban-Anlage 66
4052 Basel, Switzerland

This is a reprint of articles from the Special Issue published online in the open access journal *Algorithms* (ISSN 1999-4893) (available at: https://www.mdpi.com/journal/algorithms/special_issues/2022_EBM).

For citation purposes, cite each article independently as indicated on the article page online and as indicated below:

Lastname, A.A.; Lastname, B.B. Article Title. *Journal Name* **Year**, *Volume Number*, Page Range.

ISBN 978-3-7258-0641-6 (Hbk)
ISBN 978-3-7258-0642-3 (PDF)
doi.org/10.3390/books978-3-7258-0642-3

Contents

About the Editor

Frank Werner

Frank Werner studied mathematics from 1975 to 1980 and graduated from the Technical University Magdeburg (Germany) with distinction. He received a Ph.D. degree (with summa cum laude) in Mathematics in 1984 and defended his habilitation thesis in 1989. From this time on, he worked at the Faculty of Mathematics of the Otto-von-Guericke University Magdeburg in Germany, and since 1998 as an extraordinary professor. In 1992, he received a grant from the Alexander von Humboldt Foundation. He was a manager of several research projects supported by the German Research Society (DFG) and the European Union (INTAS). Since 2019, he has been the Editor-in-Chief of the journal Algorithms. He is also an Associate Editor of the International Journal of Production Research since 2012 and of the Journal of Scheduling since 2014 as well a member of the editorial/advisory boards of 18 further international journals. He has been a guest editor of Special Issues in ten international journals, and has served as a member of the program committee of more than 140 international conferences. Frank Werner is an author/editor of 14 books, among them the textbooks 'Mathematics of Economics and Business' and 'A Refresher Course in Mathematics'. In addition, he has co-edited three proceedings volumes of the SIMULTECH conferences and published more than 300 journal and conference papers, e.g., in the International Journal of Production Research, Computers & Operations Research, Journal of Scheduling, Applied Mathematical Modelling, or the European Journal of Operational Research. He received Best Paper Awards from the International Journal of Production Research (2016) and IISE Transactions (2021). His main research subjects are scheduling, discrete optimization, graph theory, and mathematical problems in operations research.

Preface

This is the printed edition of a Special Issue published in the journal Algorithms. After the great success of two previous Special Issues published in the same journal, where Editorial Board members of the journal present their latest research, the third edition covers submissions from the two years 2022 and 2023. This book contains the Editorial and 16 research papers. Among the subjects addressed in this book, I can mention neural networks, machine and deep learning approaches, optimization of agricultural processes, cloud-based eye-monitoring, algorithms for heart disease diagnosis or time-series clustering, to name a few.

Finally, thanks are given to all who contributed to the success of this issue: authors from 19 countries, many referees from all over the world, and the journal's staff. I hope that the readers of this book will find many stimulating ideas for their own future research and that we obtain many interesting submissions also for the next edition of this special issue type covering the years 2024 and 2025.

Frank Werner
Editor

algorithms

MDPI

Editorial

Special Issue: "2022 and 2023 Selected Papers from Algorithms' Editorial Board Members"

Frank Werner

Faculty of Mathematics, Otto-von-Guericke University Magdeburg, P.O. Box 4120, D-39016 Magdeburg, Germany; frank.werner@ovgu.de; Tel.: +49-391-675-2025

This is the third edition of a Special Issue of *Algorithms*; it is of a rather different nature compared to other Special Issues in the journal, which are usually dedicated to a particular subject in the area of algorithms. In particular, the first edition of such an issue from 2020 [1] contained 8 papers, and the second edition from 2021 [2] contained 12 papers. Over the last few years, the Editorial Board of the journal has been considerably extended. Currently, my work as Editor-in-Chief is supported by 2 Associate Editors, 5 Section Editors-in-Chief, and 135 further members of the Editorial Board. Since these scientists cover a huge spectrum of research fields related to the development of algorithms, the journal decided to set up Special Issues of this type, in which our Editorial Board Members can present their latest work to the readers of *Algorithms* so that they can have an overview of our Editorial Board Members' current research. The current issue considers submissions from the past two years, 2022 and 2023.

After a careful review process, 16 papers were selected for this issue. As a rule, all submissions have been reviewed by two (and often even more) experts from the corresponding area. Subsequently, for this special issue, the published research papers were surveyed in the order of their publication dates.

The first accepted research paper by Leone and Cohen considers a rendezvous game, where players move at different speeds and markers can be left by one of the players on the infinite line. For its solution, an LP-based formulation is suggested. The authors showed how the search space can be reduced to a space of significantly smaller dimensions by making the enumeration of all elements realistic.

The next paper by Sangaiah et al. presents a method for tackling fault detection and diagnosis in a cellular network. The authors use two datasets made up of performance support system data and drive test data. They also present a framework for identifying the need for handovers. By applying the dynamic neural network method, great accuracy was achieved.

Then, Cordero et al. present a study on the generalization of a known family of multi-point scalar iterative processes for approximating solutions of non-linear systems. A convergence analysis under different smooth conditions is given. They also investigate stability, analyze the fixed and critical points of the resulting rational operator, and present graphical analyses of dynamical planes, parameter lines, and bifurcation planes. Finally, numerical tests are produced for various non-linear systems in order to check the obtained theoretical results and to compare the proposed schemes with existing ones.

In the next paper, Maniezzo and Zhou deal with the setting of hyperparameters in optimization algorithms and propose a novel learning scheme. Their approach differs from existing ones and exploits the learning and generalization capabilities of artificial neural networks, with the goal of adapting a general setting using automatic configurators. The suggested approach is tested on two algorithms: one algorithm that is very sensitive to parameter settings applied to instances of the generalized assignment problem, and a robust tabu search algorithm applied to instances of the quadratic assignment problem. In both cases, the approach turned out to be effective.

Citation: Werner, F. Special Issue: "2022 and 2023 Selected Papers from Algorithms' Editorial Board Members". *Algorithms* **2024**, *17*, 65. https://doi.org/10.3390/a17020065

Received: 1 February 2024
Accepted: 1 February 2024
Published: 3 February 2024

The paper by Efrimov et al. deals with the optimization of the formation and use of a machine and tractor fleet within a crop farming enterprise. The authors discuss the concepts and indicators that characterize the process of agricultural operations related to said machine fleet. In particular, after presenting the problem and context in detail, an optimization model for executing a complex of mechanized works in agricultural production is presented. Then the authors present a general scheme consisting of five stages. It includes a heuristic algorithm for performing a set of agricultural works, the results of which are compared with those obtained by the GAMS solver. In particular, the authors present results for real data in an agricultural enterprise alongside interpretations of the obtained results.

Then, in contribution 6, Belousov et al. present a neural network package which has been optimized for the use on a high-performance computing cluster for a future compressed baryonic matter (CBM) experiment at a research facility in Germany. The package has been developed in C++. To identify events containing quark–gluon plasma, fully connected and convolutional neural networks have been created. The tests show the superiority of convolutional neural networks over fully connected networks, and achieved high accuracy with the considered dataset.

In the next paper, Gursesli et al. introduce a system which makes the collection, processing, real-time streaming, and storage of eye tracking data possible. For the development of this system, the Java programming language, WebSocket protocol, and Representational State Transfer were used. The results were obtained under two sets of test conditions, namely local and online scenarios. The results show that this system can significantly support the research community by providing real-time data transfer and storage.

Then, Tetteh et al. present a Multi-Genome Grammatical Evolution which is better suited to treating multi-output problems, in particular for digital circuits. They adapt genetic operators, mappers, and initialisation routines to work with the new genome representation. The authors also develop custom grammar syntex rules and a new wrapping operator. The approach is tested on combinatorial circuit benchmark problems. It turns out that the developed approach outperforms standard Grammatical Evolution.

In contribution 9, Belousow et al. present a second paper within this issue; they discuss a neural network-based competition between short-lived particle candidates in the CBM experiment at the same research facility mentioned in contribution 7. The authors replace the existing particle competition between K_s-mesons and Λ-hyperons of the Kalman Filter Particle Finder with a neural network approach, which provides a raw classification performance with an error of less than 2 %. They also demonstrate that their approach improves the quality of the physics analysis.

Leon et al. deal with improving the efficiency of warehouse operations and explore the possibilities of combining simulation with reinforcement learning, with the goal of developing effective mechanisms for the quick acquisition of information in complex environments (occurring, for instance, in manufacturing and logistic systems). In particular, the paper showcases the integration of the FlexSim commercial simulator and the RL OpenAI Gym library in Python. The effectiveness of the suggested method is evaluated by several experiments.

In the paper by Halawi et al., a new multi-objective anonymization approach is suggested. It generalizes the known-degree anonymization problem and intends to model data security and privacy more realistically. Their model guarantees a convenient privacy level. The resulting multi-objective graph realization approach is derived and solved by means of Integer Linear Programming

In the paper by Manescu and Dumitrescu, a novel global optimization approach is developed, which is based on differential evolution combined with two other approaches based on the Sparrow Search Algorithm and Bald Eagle Search, respectively. As a high-level online learning mechanism, a genetic algorithm is adopted. The proposed methods are compared with 10 state-of-the-art heuristics and well-established algorithms based on a set of 12 difficult problems. It turns out that the performance of the main algorithm, called HyperDE, is superior to that of the existing heuristics.

The paper by Belcastro et al. deals with a cryptocurrency problem and suggests a strategy for maximizing profits through identifying when it is advantageous to buy or sell cryptocurrencies. The authors combine various statistical, text analytical, and deep learning techniques to produce recommendations for a trading algorithm. The resulting trading algorithm is tested on historical data and turns out to be very successful.

Dell'Amico et al. deal with a minimum-cost arborescence problem with precedence constraints and waiting times. For this NP-hard problem, compact models of polynomial size are discussed, which turned out to be essentially smaller than earlier ones. These models are experimentally evaluated. As a result, the authors were able to close 7 previously open instances; they were also able to derive better lower bounds on the optimum cost for 71 instances and improved upper bounds for 80 instances among 88 open instances.

Shokouhifar et al. present an ensemble heuristic–metaheuristic feature fusion learning algorithm for the prediction of heart disease. The construction of the ensemble learning model comprises seven base learners. The objectives are to identify the most pertinent features for each base learner and to aggregate the decision outcomes of the particular base learners through ensemble learning. The performance of the developed EHMFFL algorithm is evaluated using different measures for the Cleveland and Statlog datasets, and the new algorithm turns out to be superior to existing state-of-the-art algorithms.

In the last paper, Fotakis et al. deal with sharp-based time-series clustering using Dynamic Time Warping distance. A two-stage framework is presentedm which is based on Sparse Gaussian Modeling. An extensive computational evaluation is carried out using datasets from the UCR Time Series Classification Archive. The proposed framework generates results that can compete with those of a standard k-means algorithm but also has considerable advantages in clustering quality, CPU utilization, and memory requirements.

As the current Editor-in-Chief, it is my pleasure to thank all the Editorial Board Members for their support for *Algorithms* over the last few years. I hope that the Editorial Board Members of the journal will also submit their most recent high-quality works to Special Issues of this type in the future.

Conflicts of Interest: The author declares no conflict of interest.

List of Contributors

1. Leone, P.; Cohen, N. Rendezvous on the Line with Different Speeds and Markers That Can Be Dropped at Chosen Time. *Algorithms* **2022**, *15*, 41.
2. Sangaiah, A.K.; Rezaei, S.; Javadpour, A.; Miri, F.; Zhang, W.; Wang, D. Automatic Fault Detection and Diagnosis in Cellular Networks and Beyond 5G: Intelligent Network Management. *Algorithms* **2022**, *15*, 432.
3. Cordero, A.; Maimo, J.G.; Rodriguez-Cabral, A.; Torregrosa, J.R. Convergence and Stability of a New Parametric Class of Iterative Processes for Nonlinear Systems. *Algorithms* **2023**, *16*, 163.
4. Maniezzo, V.; Zhou, T. Learning Individualized Hyperparameter Settings. *Algorithms* **2023**, *16*, 267.
5. Efremov, A.A.; Sotskov, Y.N.; Belotzkaya, Y.S. Optimization of Selection and Use of a Machine and Tractor Fleet in Agricultural Enterprises: A Case Study. *Algorithms* **2023**, *16*, 311.
6. Belousov, A.; Kisel, I.; Lakos, R.; Mithran, A. Neural-Network-Based Quark-Gluon Plasma Trigger for the CBM Experiment at FAIR. *Algorithms* **2023**, *16*, 344.
7. Gursesli, M.C.; Selek, M.E.; Samur, M.E.; Duradoni, M.; Park, K.; Guazzini, A.; Lanata, A. Design of Cloud-Based Real-Time Eye-Tracking Monitoring and Storage System. *Algorithms* **2023**, *16*, 355.

8. Tetteh, M.; de Lima, A.; McEllin, J.; Murphy, A.; Dias, D.M.; Ryan C. Evolving Multi-Output Digital Circuits Using Multi-Genome Grammatical Evolution. *Algorithms* **2023**, *16*, 365.
9. Belousov, A.; Kisel, I.; Lakos, R. A Neural-Netwok Based Competition between Short-Lived Particle Candidates in the CBM Experiment at FAIR. *Algorithms* **2023**, *16*, 383.
10. Leon, J.F., Li, Y.; Martin, X.A.; Calvet, L.; Panadero, J.; Juan, A.A. A Hybrid Simulation and Reinforcement Learning Algorithm for Enhancing Efficiency in Warehouse Operations. *Algorithms* **2023**, *16*, 408.
11. Halawi, O.N.; Abu-Khzam, F.N.; Thoumi, S. A Multi-Objective Degree-Based Network Anonymization Method. *Algorithms* **2023**, *16*, 436.
12. Manescu, A.-R.; Dumitrescu, B. HyperDE: An Adaptive Hyper-Heuristic for Global Optimization. *Algorithms* **2023**, *16*, 451.
13. Belcastro, L.; Carbone, D.; Cosentino, C.; Marozzo, F.; Trunfio, P. Enhancing Cryptocurrency Price Forecasting by Integrating Machine Learning with Social Media and Market Data. *Algorithms* **2023**, *16*, 542.
14. Dell'Amico, M.; Jamal, J.; Montemanni, R. Compact Models to Solve the Precedence-Constrained Minimum-Cost Arborescence Problem with Waiting Times. *Algorithms* **2024**, *17*, 12.
15. Shokouhifar, M.; Hasanvand, M.; Moharamkhani, E.; Werner, F. Ensemble Heuristic-Metaheuristic Feature Fusion Learning for Heart Disease Diagnosis Using Tabular Data. *Algorithms* **2024**, *17*, 34.
16. Fotakis, D.; Patsilinakos, P.; Psaroudaki, E.; Xefteris, M. Efficient Timne-Series Clustering through Sparse Gaussian Modeling. *Algorithms* **2024**, *17*, 61.

References

1. Werner, F. 2020 Selected Papers from Algorithms' Editorial Board Members. *Algorithms* **2021**, *14*, 32. [CrossRef]
2. Werner, F. 2021 Selected Papers from Algorithms' Editorial Board Members. *Algorithms* **2021**, *14*, 357. [CrossRef]

algorithms

MDPI

rticle

Rendezvous on the Line with Different Speeds and Markers That Can Be Dropped at Chosen Time

ierre Leone * and Nathan Cohen

TCS-Sensor Lab, Centre Universitaire d'Informatique, Battelle Batiment A, Route de Drize 7, CH-1227 Carouge, Switzerland; nathan.cohen@etu.unige.ch
* Correspondence: pierre.leone@unige.ch

Abstract: In this paper, we introduce a linear program (LP)-based formulation of a rendezvous game with markers on the infinite line and solve it. In this game one player moves at unit speed while the second player moves at a speed bounded by $v_{max} \leq 1$. We observe that in this setting, a slow-moving player may have interest to remain still instead of moving. This shows that in some conditions the wait-for-mummy strategy is optimal. We observe as well that the strategies are completely different if the player that holds the marker is the fast or slow one. Interestingly, the marker is not useful when the player without marker moves slowly, i.e., the fast-moving player holds the marker.

Keywords: asymmetric rendezvous on the line; markers; asymmetric speeds

itation: Leone, P.; Cohen, N. endezvous on the Line with ifferent Speeds and Markers That an Be Dropped at Chosen Time. gorithms **2022**, *15*, 41. https:// oi.org/10.3390/a15020041

cademic Editor: Frank Werner

eceived: 15 December 2021
ccepted: 26 January 2022
ublished: 27 January 2022

1. Introduction

The problem that we discuss in this article revolves around the problem faced by two parachutists dropped from an airplane on an island and who need to rendezvous. In order to reduce the dimension of the search space, the two can move to the coastline and restrict their search by moving along the coastline. The two parachutists facing the sea can move to right or to the left. However, going to the right or the left is not a common sense of direction. In an island, depending on where the parachutists are located (north or south) a motion to the right can lead to go eastward or westward, and the two cannot agree on a common direction, for instance, by observing where the sea is flowing (as it would be possible if they were moving along a river). The distance separating them initially may not be known. To formalize the problem, the distance may be assumed a random variable or, this is the approach taken here, the distance is assumed to be bounded and an upper bound on the rendezvous time are searched for. Two novel parameters are considered for this problem. We assume that the two parachutists may move at different speeds and we assume that the parachutists can drop off a marker at the position they are and it may be subsequently found by the other as they pass by the same position. Finding the marker is very useful since it indicates in which direction to go to rendezvous with the other.

More formally, we introduce a variation of the asymmetric rendezvous problem on the line that was introduced by Alpern and Gal [1]. In the original setup, two players are placed on a line at a known distance D and move on the line to rendezvous. The player's strategies may be different and start at the same time, and both players move at the same speed $v = 1$. At the start and while moving, the players look in a fixed direction, say, right or left. The directions are chosen randomly each with probability $1/2$. It results that players move either in the direction they look to or the other one, i.e., forward or backward. A strategy is a succession of forward and backward moves. The optimal solution of this problem is shown to be $13D/8$. Many variations have been proposed showing that even a simple topology such as the infinite line leads to interesting problems. Among the hardest seems to be the symmetric rendezvous on the line where the two players have to play the same strategy. Partial solutions of this problem were obtained. In [2], a strategy was proposed that ensured the rendezvous time satisfied $R \leq 5D$. Subsequent strategies were proposed in [3,4] that used the same technique as in [2] and reduced the rendezvous time to $R \leq 2.28338D$ and $R \leq 2.2091D$, respectively. Ref. [5] generalized the technique ar improved the bound to $R \leq 2.19653D$. The best known bound $R \leq 2.1287D$ is given in [

Some papers deal with the problem where the initial distance between the players unknown, see for instance [7–10]. Usually, the distance is characterized by a probabili function. Note that if the players use strategies tailored for a known distance D wi rendezvous time R to a problem where it is only known that the distance is bounded by then the rendezvous time for this problem is bounded by R.

The way time enters the game leads to relevant variations as well. The constrai that the players start at the same time may be relaxed and this leads to asynchrono rendezvous problems [11,12]. Asynchronous rendezvous problems may assume that a adversary chooses the starting delay or the clocks are assumed to drift with different speed There are relations between problems where clocks drift at different speeds and ones whe players move at different speed [12].

A problem where players move on the line and share similarities with the rendezvo problem is the group search problem on the line [13]. This problem is motivated by th evacuation problem where players must simultaneously gather at some point. One ma imagine that people need to leave a building and are helped with a line drawn on the flo but do not know the right direction to follow. When players move at different speed interesting strategies can be found where a fast player move to help slower players.

Problems where players move on a circle share similarities with problems on th line [14–18]. Compared to the infinite line, the ring is a compact topology, but symmetr breaking has to be solved as well to ensure rendezvous. Tokens may be left by pla ers [19–21]. For rendezvous problems on the line, Refs. [22,23] present results whe markers are used by players. With a more robotic and computer science flavor som problems encompass faulty agents [24,25].

Rendezvous problems are far from being limited to the infinite line or a ring. Proble may be stated for agents moving on a plane, on graphs, on a torus, on networks and s on, see for instance [26–28]. These problems are different from the ones considered i this paper.

Markers can have different effects. For instance, the game may end at the time th marker is found, i.e., rendezvous occurs or the marker is found. This would be the case a phone number is written on the marker. With such a marker, the game would be clos to a version of a search-and-rescue game [29]. This may be seen as a mix of rendezvou and search games, see for instance [30–32] for search games on graphs and [26,33,34] fo general references.

2. Our Contributions

In this paper, we consider the (synchronous) rendezvous problem on the line wit known initial distance D where players move at different speeds and where a marker ca be left by one of the players. Without loss of generality, we assume that one player move at speed 1 while the second player moves at speed $v \leq 1$. We show that investigations ca be conducted with linear programming techniques to identify optimal strategies. This i not the conventional approach in the literature where the results are usually guessed an optimality is subsequently proved. The reduction of rendezvous search game to anoth formalism to be solved appears in the literature, see for instance [35]. Here, the reductio to parametric linear programming has the further advantage that the same method ca be applied to compute different measures of optimality. For instance, the optimization the last rendezvous time. Actually, any linear combination of the rendezvous times ca be optimized.

In [23,36], a similar problem with markers is considered. The parametric linear pr gramming approach of this article leads to more precise results than the ad hoc approa of [23]. Moreover, here we accommodate to players with different speeds, extending th results of [23,36].

3. Problem Formulation

We begin by presenting the formalization of the problem as given in [1]. Two players, I and II, are placed at distance $D = 1$ (although the results depend linearly on the initial distance and are stated for a general D). apart on the real line, and faced in random directions which they call "forward". Their common aim is to minimize the expected amount of time required to meet. They each know the distance 1 but not the direction the other player is facing. It is not a restriction to assume that player I's starting point is located at position 0 of the line and their speed is bounded by $v \leq 1$. Their position is given by a function $f(t) \in \mathcal{F}(\alpha)$, where

$$\mathcal{F}(\alpha) = \{f : [0, T] \to \mathbb{R},\ f(0) = 0, |f(t) - f(t')| \leq \alpha|t - t'|\}, \quad (1)$$

for some T sufficiently large so that the rendezvous will have taken place.

What are unknown are the initial position of player II that may be ± 1 and the forward direction of player II that may point to the positive or negative side of the infinite line. Again, without restriction of generality, we assume that the speed of player II is bounded by 1. Hence, depending on the initial conditions of player II their position at time t is given by $\pm 1 \pm g(t)$ with $g \in \mathcal{F}(1) = \mathcal{F}$.

The rendezvous times are defined by:

$$t^1 = min\{t : f(t) = 1 + g(t)\}, \quad (2)$$

when player II is originally located at $+1$ and their forward direction points to the positive side of the line.

$$t^2 = min\{t : f(t) = 1 - g(t)\}, \quad (3)$$

when player II is originally located at $+1$ and their forward direction points to the negative side of the line.

$$t^3 = min\{t : f(t) = -1 + g(t)\}, \quad (4)$$

when player II is originally located at -1 and their forward direction points to the positive side of the line.

$$t^4 = min\{t : f(t) = -1 - g(t)\}, \quad (5)$$

when player II is originally located at -1 and their forward direction points to the negative side of the line.

It is common in the literature to speak of four agents (of player II) located at positions ± 1 and with forward direction ± 1 and moving concurrently. Player I needs to rendezvous with the four agents to end the game [26]. Concretely,

- Agent 1 is located at $+1$ with forward direction $+1$ and its rendezvous time is t^1,
- Agent 2 is located at $+1$ with forward direction -1 and its rendezvous time is t^2,
- Agent 3 is located at -1 with forward direction $+1$ and its rendezvous time is t^3,
- Agent 4 is located at -1 with forward direction -1 and its rendezvous time is t^4.

We show in Figure 1 the configurations of the four agents and the optimal solution of the problem without marker. We observe on this figure that the speeds of both players are always maximal (equal to 1). Then, a complete description of the optimal strategy is provided by the order with which player I rendezvous with the agents, i.e., agent $2, 3, 1$ and finally 4.

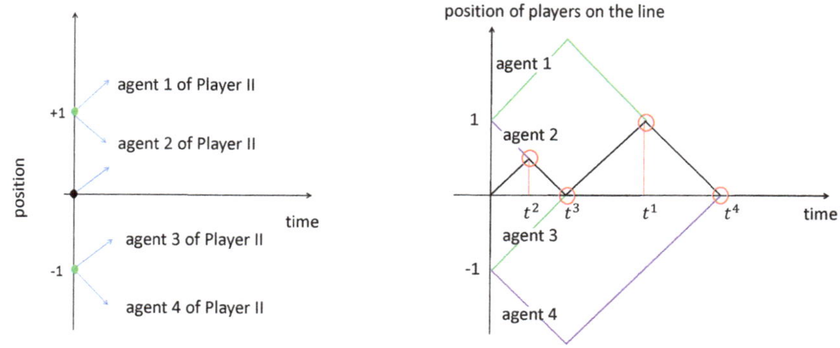

Figure 1. (**On the left**):the four agents of player II. Each one corresponds to a particular initial position and direction of the forward move. (**On the right**): the optimal solution of the game without marker. Player I goes forward for time $\frac{1}{2}$, then backward for time $\frac{1}{2}$, then forward for time 1 and backward for time 1. Player II goes forward for time 1, then backward for time 3. The rendezvous occur successively with agents 2, 3, 1 and 4 at times $t^2 = \frac{1}{2}$, $t^3 = 1$, $t^1 = 2$ and $t^4 = 3$.

Definition 1. *We introduce the notation $t_1 \leq t_2 \leq t_3 \leq t_4$ to denote the rendezvous times in the order they occur, (o_i, b_i) denotes the agent with origin $o_i = \pm 1$ and forward direction $b_i = \pm 1$. The order of the rendezvous times is given by the index i, t_1 is the rendezvous with agent (o_1, b_1), t_2 is the rendezvous with agent (o_2, b_2), t_3 is the rendezvous with agent (o_3, b_3) and t_4 is the rendezvous with agent (o_4, b_4). When necessary, we use the convention $t_0 = 0$*

For instance, for the solution in Figure 1 it holds that $t_1 = t^2$, $t_2 = t^3$, $t_3 = t^1$, $t_4 = t^4$ and $(o_1, d_1) = (1, -1)$, $(o_2, d_2) = (-1, 1)$, $(o_3, d_3) = (1, 1)$, $(o_4, d_4) = (-1, -1)$,.

We do not make any assumptions on how the functions $f(t)$ and $g(t)$ are computed. A different formalism than what we are proposing here may be possible. For instance, as in differential games [37–39], $f(t)$ and $g(t)$ may be bound to be solutions of ordinary differential equation. Our approach here is different. We first show that the functions $f(t)$ and $g(t)$ that may be optimal have the restricting feature of being of constant derivative between two rendezvous. Then, we enumerate all possible solutions. Notice that pursuit-evasion games are usually modeled as differential games. Compared to pursuit–evasion, our rendezvous game is cooperative and this makes possible the enumeration of all efficient strategies (player I rendezvous with the four agents and what is to be discovered is the order leading to the shorter average of the rendezvous times).

The rendezvous value $R(f, g)$ is defined to be the average value

$$R(f,g) = \frac{1}{4}\left(t^1 + t^2 + t^3 + t^4\right).$$

Finally, the rendezvous value of the game is defined by

$$R = \min\left\{R(f,g) : f \in \mathcal{F}(v), g \in \mathcal{F}\right\}. \tag{6}$$

A first remark that simplifies the problem is that the functional spaces $\mathcal{F}(v)$ and $\mathcal{F}$ may be reduced to consider only functions $f \in \mathcal{F}(v)$ and $g \in \mathcal{F}$ *lwhose speed is constant between the rendezvous times*. Indeed, if the speed is not constant, moving at the average speed between rendezvous times leads to the same rendezvous value. Moreover, similarly to Lemma 5.1 of [1], Theorem 16.10 of [26] or Proposition 3 of [23], we have the following result for $g \in \mathcal{F}$.

Proposition 1. *If $v \leq 1$, then, for the optimal strategies, the function $g \in \mathcal{F}$ is of constant slope equal to ± 1 between the rendezvous, i.e., the speed of the fast player is always maximal.*

Proof. Let us assume that player II, whose position is given by function $g \in \mathcal{F}$ and initial position is known, does not move at maximal speed between rendezvous times $t_{i-1} < t_i$. This means that player II can reach the rendezvous position at a time $t_i - \epsilon$ with $\epsilon > 0$. By moving faster, it may happen that player II rendezvous with player I before time t_i, reducing the rendezvous time t_i. If not, we modify the trajectory of player II in the following way. After reaching the rendezvous point at time $t_i - \epsilon$, player II continues in the same direction for a period $\epsilon/2$ and then goes the other way for a period $\epsilon/2$, back to the rendezvous position at time t_i. At time $t - \epsilon/2$, player I must be at a distance less than $v\epsilon/2$ from the rendezvous position and because player II is at a distance $\epsilon/2$ and $\epsilon/2 \geq v\epsilon/2$, the rendezvous must occur before time t_i. To summarize, by moving at full speed, player II always reduces the rendezvous time t_i. After time t_i player II follows the original strategy and the remaining rendezvous times are not changed. In total, the modified strategy reduces the rendezvous value showing that the original strategy is not optimal. We emphasize that the fast-moving player moves at maximal speed while the slow-moving player can move at any speed in $[0, v]$. □

Corollary 1. *We assume here that the speed of player I is bounded by $v \leq 1$ and the speed of player II by 1, i.e., $f \in \mathcal{F}(v)$ and $g \in \mathcal{F}$. The sets of optimal strategies (f, g) for players I and II, respectively, are given by*

$$f(t) = \begin{cases} v_1 \cdot t, & t \in [0, t_1] \\ v_1 \cdot t_1 + v_2 \cdot (t - t_1), & t \in [t_1, t_2] \\ v_1 \cdot t_1 + v_2 \cdot (t_2 - t_1) + v_3 \cdot (t - t_2), & t \in [t_2, t_3] \\ v_1 \cdot t_1 + v_2 \cdot (t_2 - t_1) + v_3 \cdot (t_3 - t_2) + v_4 \cdot (t - t_3), & t \in [t_3, t_4] \end{cases} \tag{7}$$

$$g(t) = \begin{cases} d_1 \cdot t, & t \in [0, t_1] \\ d_1 \cdot t_1 + d_2 \cdot (t - t_1), & t \in [t_1, t_2] \\ d_1 \cdot t_1 + d_2 \cdot (t_2 - t_1) + d_3 \cdot (t - t_2), & t \in [t_2, t_3] \\ d_1 \cdot t_1 + d_2 \cdot (t_2 - t_1) + d_3 \cdot (t_3 - t_2) + d_4 \cdot (t - t_3), & t \in [t_3, t_4] \end{cases} \tag{8}$$

where $v_i \in [-v, v]$, $d_i = \pm 1$ and $t_1 \leq t_2 \leq t_3 \leq t_4$ are the rendezvous times.

Proposition 1 and Corollary 1 are not new and are constantly used in the literature, see for instance Chapter 17.1 of [26]. We stress that player I having the smallest speed bound may move at a slower speed than the maximal one. Indeed, we will observe that for v small, the optimal strategy for player I is to not move before t_2. The "wait for mummy" strategy is then optimal for starting the game.

We consider that player I has at their disposal a marker that may be left at a chosen time. The marker helps player II, who stops following the strategy after finding the marker and continues in the same direction at maximal speed until rendezvousing with player I. The same arguments as the ones in Proposition 1 and Corollary 1 or Proposition 3 of [23], which show that player I move at a constant velocity before and after dropping the marker. There are four different cases to consider for the formulation of the problem depending on which interval, $[0, t_1]$, $[t_1, t_2]$, $[t_2, t_3]$, $[t_3, t_4]$ player I drops off the marker at. This leads to the following proposition that characterizes the optimal strategies.

Corollary 2. *When player I has a marker that can be dropped off at chosen time z, the set of optimal strategies f for player I are given by*

$$f(t) = \begin{cases} v_0 \cdot t, & t \in [0, z] \\ v_0 \cdot z + v_1 \cdot (t - z), & t \in [z, t_1] \\ v_0 \cdot z + v_1 \cdot (t_1 - z) + v_2 \cdot (t - t_1), & t \in [t_1, t_2] \\ v_0 \cdot z + v_1 \cdot (t_1 - z) + v_2 \cdot (t_2 - t_1) + v_3 \cdot (t - t_2), & t \in [t_2, t_3] \\ v_0 \cdot z + v_1 \cdot (t_1 - z) + v_2 \cdot (t_2 - t_1) + v_3 \cdot (t_3 - t_2) + v_4 \cdot (t - t_3), & t \in [t_3, t_4] \end{cases} \tag{9}$$

if $z \in [0, t_1]$.

$$f(t) = \begin{cases} v_1 \cdot t, & t \in [0, t_1] \\ v_1 \cdot t_1 + v_0 \cdot (t - t_1), & t \in [t_1, z] \\ v_1 \cdot t_1 + v_0 \cdot (z - t_1) + v_2 \cdot (t - z), & t \in [z, t_2] \\ v_1 \cdot t_1 + v_0 \cdot (z - t_1) + v_2 \cdot (t_2 - z) + v_3 \cdot (t - t_2), & t \in [t_2, t_3] \\ v_1 \cdot t_1 + v_0 \cdot (z - t_1) + v_2 \cdot (t_2 - z) + v_3 \cdot (t_3 - t_2) + v_4 \cdot (t - t_3), & t \in [t_3, t_4] \end{cases}$$

if $z \in [t_1, t_2]$.

$$f(t) = \begin{cases} v_1 \cdot t, & t \in [0, t_1] \\ v_1 \cdot t_1 + v_2 \cdot (t - t_1), & t \in [t_1, t_2] \\ v_1 \cdot t_1 + v_2 \cdot (t_2 - t_1) + v_0 \cdot (t - t_2), & t \in [t_2, z] \\ v_1 \cdot t_1 + v_2 \cdot (t_2 - t_1) + v_0 \cdot (z - t_2) + v_3 \cdot (t - z), & t \in [z, t_3] \\ v_1 \cdot t_1 + v_2 \cdot (t_2 - t_1) + v_0 \cdot (z - t_2) + v_3 \cdot (t_3 - z) + v_4 \cdot (t - t_3), & t \in [t_3, t_4] \end{cases}$$

if $z \in [t_2, t_3]$.

$$f(t) = \begin{cases} v_1 \cdot t, & t \in [0, t_1] \\ v_1 \cdot t_1 + v_2 \cdot (t - t_1), & t \in [t_1, t_2] \\ v_1 \cdot t_1 + v_2 \cdot (t_2 - t_1) + v_3 \cdot (t - t_2), & t \in [t_2, t_3] \\ v_1 \cdot t_1 + v_2 \cdot (t_2 - t_1) + v_3 \cdot (t_3 - t_2) + v_0 \cdot (t - t_3), & t \in [t_3, z] \\ v_1 \cdot t_1 + v_2 \cdot (t_2 - t_1) + v_3 \cdot (t_3 - t_2) + v_0 \cdot (z - t_3) + v_4 \cdot (t - z), & t \in [z, t_4] \end{cases}$$

if $z \in [t_3, t_4]$. *The optimal strategies for player II are still of the form of Equation (8). In any cas the parameters are constrained to* $v_i \in [-v, v]$ ($v \leq 1$) *and* $d_i = \pm 1$, *and* $t_1 \leq t_2 \leq t_3 \leq t_4$ *are t rendezvous times.*

Corollaries 1 and 2 are very useful in making the rendezvous value of the game give by Equation (6) computable. Indeed, the set of functions (f, g) to be considered is finit Notice that for the problem with marker, the set is finite provided that v is fixed.

It is crucial to point out that in Corollary 2, the optimal strategy of player II is of th form of Equation (8), but if the marker is found at some time, player II no longer follow the strategy but continues in the same direction thereafter. For instance, if the marker found in the interval $[0, t_1]$ at time t_z we must have $z \leq t_z$ and the condition

$$o + d_1 b t_z = v_o z,$$

must be satisfied, where o is the original starting point of player II ($o = \pm 1$) and b is th forward direction of player II ($b = \pm 1$). Indeed, the condition states that player II startin at position o at time 0 is at the marker's position at time t_z, i.e., the marker is found. Th coefficient d_1 is given by the strategy followed by player II and $d_1 \cdot b$ is the effective motio depending on the forward direction b. Thereafter, player II does not follow the strategy bu continues in the same direction, i.e., we substitute d_1 for d_i in Equation (8). Hence, if th rendezvous does not occur in $[0, t_1]$, player II's motion is given by

$$o + d_1 b t_z + d_1 b (t_1 - t_z) = o + d_1 b t_1.$$

If no rendezvous occurs in the next time interval $[t_1, t_2]$, the motion of player II is given b

$$o + d_1 b t_1 + d_1 b (t_2 - t_1),$$

(compare with the second line of Equation (8)). The same reasoning applies for the ne time intervals, $[t_2, t_3]$ and $[t_3, t_4]$.

4. Solution of the Problem without Marker

The optimal strategies of the problem without marker are given in Corollary 1. There are eight unknowns v_i and d_i, the rendezvous time being a consequence of these variables. To reduce the problem to a family of linear programs we rewrite the strategies to remove the products $v_i \cdot t$ by introducing new variables vt_i with the bounds $0 \le vt_i \le v \cdot (t_i - t_{i-1})$, where v is the maximal speed of player I. To take into account that the speed of player I may be negative (when player I is going backward), we introduce new variables $a_i = \pm 1$ and the motion is computed relatively to $a_i \cdot vt_i$. Notice that a_i is a parameter that is fixed before calling the LP-solver (hence, the problem is still linear).

To define the meeting times t_i, we need to specify in which order they occur. Ordering the meeting times amounts to choosing a permutation σ of $\{1,2,3,4\}$ such that $t_i = t^{\sigma(i)}$ where t^i are defined by Equations (2)–(5). For this, we introduce new variables (o_i, b_i) with $o_i = \pm 1$ and $b_1 = \pm 1$ to refer to specific agents of player II. Concretely,

- Agent 1 is referred by $(o_i = +1, b_i = +1)$ and the rendezvous time t^1 is defined by (2),
- Agent 2 is referred by $(o_i = +1, b_i = -1)$ and the rendezvous time t^2 is defined by (3),
- Agent 3 is referred by $(o_i = -1, b_i = +1)$ and the rendezvous time t^3 is defined by (4),
- Agent 4 is referred by $(o_i = -1, b_i = -1)$ and the rendezvous time t^4 is defined by (5).

The rendezvous always occur in the order $(o_1, b_1), (o_2, b_2), (o_3, b_3), (o_4, b_4)$. The values of o_i and b_i are given by:

$$
\begin{aligned}
&\min_{\Delta_i}\; t_1 + t_2 + t_3 + t_4 \\
&o_1 + d_1 b_1 t_1 = a_1 vt_1 \\
&o_2 + d_1 b_2 t_1 + d_2 b_2 (t_2 - t_1) = a_1 vt_1 + a_2 vt_2 \\
&o_3 + d_1 b_3 t_1 + d_2 b_3 (t_2 - t_1) + d_3 b_3 (t_3 - t_2) = a_1 vt_1 + a_2 vt_2 + a_3 vt_3 \\
&o_4 + d_1 b_4 t_1 + d_2 b_4 (t_2 - t_1) + d_3 b_4 (t_3 - t_2) + d_4 b_4 (t_4 - t_3) = a_1 vt_1 + \\
&\qquad\qquad\qquad\qquad\qquad a_2 vt_2 + a_3 vt_3 + a_4 vt_4 \\
&0 \le vt_1 \le v \cdot t_1 \\
&0 \le vt_2 \le v \cdot (t_2 - t_1) \\
&0 \le vt_3 \le v \cdot (t_3 - t_2) \\
&0 \le vt_4 \le v \cdot (t_4 - t_3) \\
&a_i, b_i, o_i, d_i \in \{0,1\} \textstyle\sum o_i = 0, \sum d_i = 0,\; o_i = o_j \Rightarrow d_i \neq d_j. \\
&t_1 \ge 0, t_2 \ge 0, t_3 \ge 0, t_4 \ge 0
\end{aligned}
$$

For the computation of the solution, we use the variables o_i, b_i, d_i, a_i as parameters. For each set of values, we solve the corresponding linear program. The number of linear programs solved was 1536, which was solved in a few seconds using the Python Gurobi library [40]. Notice that by symmetry, we fixed $a_1 = 1$ and $d_1 = 1$.

The plot of the results are shown in Figure 2, where the optimal rendezvous value is plotted versus the maximal speed of player I for discrete values $n/1000$, $n = 0, 1, \dots, 1000$.

Besides the computation of the optimal rendezvous values, we recorded the corresponding optimal strategy. We observe that for $v \le 0.618$ the optimal strategy is ($a_1 = 0$, $a_2 = 0$, $a_3 = 1$ and $a_4 = -1$) for player I and ($d_1 = 1$, $d_2 = 1$, $d_3 = -1$, $d_4 = -1$) for player II as illustrated in Figure 3. In terms of the optimal strategy of Corollary 1, the speeds of player I are $v_1 = 0, v_2 = 0, v_3 = -v$ and $v_4 = v$. Notice that player I can play the symmetric strategy ($a_1 = 0$, $a_2 = 0$, $a_3 = 1$, $a_4 = -1$) as well, which is not illustrated.

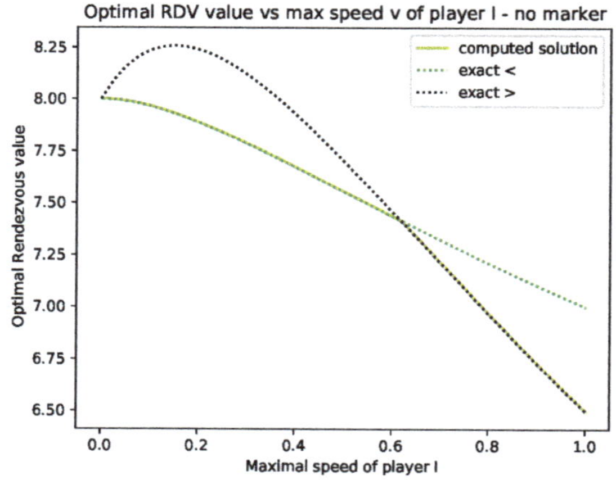

Figure 2. Plot of the solution of the rendezvous problem vs. the maximum speed of player I. The computed solution is a plot a 1001 points evaluated at $n/1000$, $n \in [0, 1000]$. The exact solution has two algebraic forms for $v < (\sqrt{5}-1)/2$ (exactl<, (13)) or $v > (\sqrt{5}-1)/2$ (exact >, (14)).

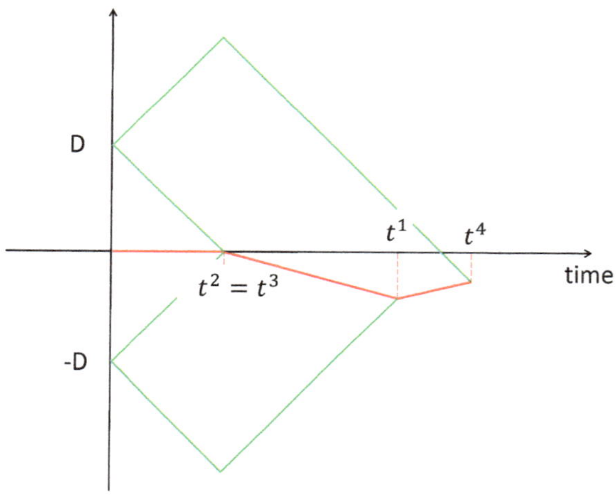

Figure 3. Optimal strategy for $v \in [0.001, 0.618]$.

It is relevant to observe that until $t^2 = t^3$ the wait-for-mummy strategy is the optimal strategy for player I, as motion starts only after. For this strategy the expressions for the rendezvous times and the rendezvous value of the game are given by:

$$t_1 = 1, t_2 = 1, t_3 = \frac{3+v}{1+v}, t_4 = \frac{v^2+8v+3}{(1+v)^2},$$

$$R = \frac{4v^2+16v+8}{(1+v)^2}. \tag{13}$$

Since $v = 0.619$ the optimal strategy is a switch to $a_1 = 1, a_2 = -1, a_3 = 1$ and $a_4 = -1$ for player I and $d_1 = 1, d_2 = 1, d_3 = -1$ and $d_4 = -1$. In terms of the optimal strategy of Corollary 1 the speeds of player I are $v_1 = -v$, $v_2 = v$, $v_3 = -v$ and $v_4 = v$. The speed of player I is large enough to allow the improvement of the rendezvous value by moving from the start. The expressions for the rendezvous times and rendezvous value of the game are given by:

$$t_1 = \frac{1}{v+1}, t_2 = \frac{3v+1}{(v+1)^2}, t_3 = \frac{5v+3}{(v+1)^2},$$
$$t_4 = \frac{7v^2+14v+3}{(1+v)^3}, R = \frac{16v^2+28v+8}{(1+v)^3}. \tag{14}$$

With direct computations, we see that (13) is better that (14) for $v \leq (\sqrt{5}-1)/2$, see Figure 2.

It is stated in [26], Chapter 17.1, that the optimal solution is given by (13) for $v \leq (\sqrt{5}-1)/2$ and by (14) for $v \geq (\sqrt{5}-1)/2$. With our linear programming approach we first conclude that (13) is optimal for $v = n/1000 \leq (\sqrt{5}-1)/2$ and by (14) for $v = n/1000 \geq (\sqrt{5}-1)/2$, $n = 0, 1, 2, \ldots$ (discrete values).

However, we can say more. Let us denote $opt(v)$ the function that returns the optimal value of the game when the speed of player I is bounded by v and $nextToopt(v)$ the function that returns the next-to-optimal value of the game when the speed of player I is bounded by v. These two functions are decreasing since a strategy for v is always a strategy for $v' \geq v$. Hence, if we have that $opt(v) < nextToopt(v+dv)$ and the strategy at $opt(v)$ is the same as that at $opt(v+dv)$, it must be that this strategy is optimal in the interval $[v, v+dv]$. By computing $opt(n/1000)$ and $nextToopt(n/1000)$, $n = 0, \ldots, 1000$, we detect that the condition stated above is satisfied for $v \in [1/1000, 0.618]$ and for $v \in [0.619, 0.990]$. To summarize, we have proved the following theorem.

Theorem 1 ([26], Chapter 17.1). *For $v \in [1/1000, 0.618]$, the rendezvous value of the game is given by (13) and the optimal strategy is plotted in Figure 3 and for $v \in [0.619, 0.990]$ the rendezvous value of the game is given by (14) and the optimal strategy is plotted in Figure 4.*

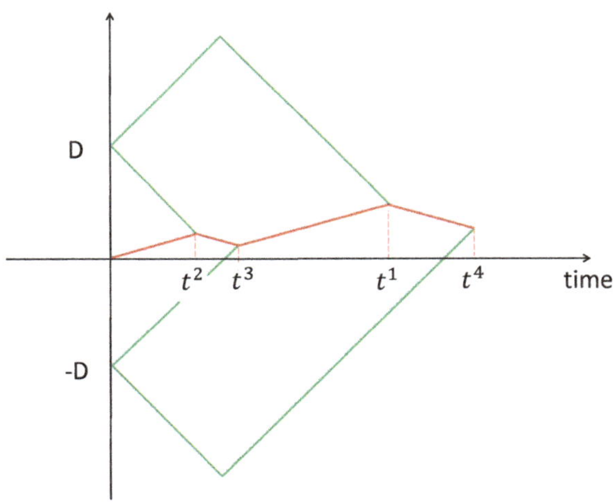

Figure 4. Optimal strategy for $v \in]0.619, 0.990]$.

The interval in which Theorem 1 is stated to be true may be enlarged by computing the numerical solutions on a finer mesh, i.e., increasing the number values of n for which we solve the LP.

5. Solution of the Problem with a Marker Held by the Slow Player

The marker is held by one of the players and may be dropped off at any given time. Once dropped off, the marker is to be found by the other player when is passes at the location. Once found, the player stops following the original strategy and continues in the same direction until rendezvous occurs. We first assume that the marker is held b player I, who moves with the lowest speed bounded by $v \leq 1$, and denote z as the droppin time. There are four possibilities, $z \in [0,t_1], z \in [t_1,t_2], z \in [t_2,t_3]$ and $z \in [t_3,t_4]$, each on leading to a family of linear programs to solve. It happens that only the first case $z \in [0,t$ is relevant. For all other cases the optimal solutions do not make use of the marker and a given in Section 4.

The strategy of player I is now given by $(a_0,\ a_1,\ a_2,\ a_3,\ a_4)$ where a_i indicates wheth v_i is positive or negative, i.e., the speed v_i are always assumed positive and the motion are depending on the product $a_i \cdot v_i$. With respect to Section 4, the only novelty is th introduction of a_0, see Equation (9) (compare with (7) with no marker).

Agents of player II can find the marker or not. Hence, for each agent we must genera two linear programs each one assuming the agent finds the marker or not. Actually, fo the first agent rendezvousing (agent (o_1,d_1)), we do not need to differentiate wheth the marker is found or not, as the equations are the same. We use the new variable k_1 t indicate that agent (o_2,d_2) finds the marker $k_1 = 1$ or not ($k_1 = 0$), in the interval $[0,t$ Again if the marker is found by (o_2,d_2) in the interval $[t_1,t_2]$, the equations do not chang The variable k_{21},k_{22} indicate that agent (o_3,d_3) finds the marker in the interval $[0,t_1]$ o $[t_1,t_2]$, respectively. Finally, the variables k_{31},k_{32} and k_{33} indicate that agent (o_4,d_4) find the marker in the interval $[0,t_1]$, $[t_1,t_2]$ or $[t_2,t_3]$, respectively.

This leads to the family of linear programs shown in Equations (15)–(17) (we deno $\Delta t_i = (t_i - t_{i-1})$ and t_{iz} the time at which the marker is found by (o_i,b_i)).

$$\min_{\Delta_i}\ t_1 + t_2 + t_3 + t_4$$

$$o_1 + d_1 b_1 t_1 = a_0 v z + a_1 v t_1 \qquad (*$$

$$\begin{aligned}
&k_1(o_2 + d_1 b_2 t_1 + d_2 b_2 \Delta t_2) + \\
&(1-k_1)(o_2 + d_1 b_2 t_{1z} + d_1 b_2 (t_1 + \Delta t_2 - t_{1z})) = a_0 v z + a_1 v t_1 + a_2 v t_2 \\
&(1-k_1)(o_2 + d_1 b_2 t_{1z}) = (1-k_1) a_0 v z
\end{aligned} \qquad (**$$

$$\begin{aligned}
&k_{21}k_{22}(o_3 + d_1 b_3 t_1 + d_2 b_3 \Delta t_2 + d_3 b_3 \Delta t_3) + \\
&(1-k_{21})(o_3 + d_1 b_3 t_{2z} + d_1 b_3 (t_1 + \Delta t_2 + \Delta t_3 - t_{2z})) + \\
&(1-k_{22})(o_3 + d_1 b_3 t_1 + d_2 b_3 t_2 z + d_2 b_3 (\Delta t_2 + \Delta t_3 - t_{2z})) = \\
&a_0 v z + a_1 v t_1 + a_2 v t_2 + a_3 v t_3 \\
&(1-k_{21})(o_3 + d_1 b_3 t_{2z}) + (1-k_{22})(o_3 + d_1 b_3 t_1 + d_2 b_3 t_{2z}) = \\
&(1-k_{21})(1-k_{22}) a_0 v z
\end{aligned} \qquad (15) \quad (***$$

$$\begin{aligned}
&(1-k_{31})(1-k_{32})(1-k_{33})(o_4 + d_1 b_4 t_1 + d_2 b_4 \Delta t_2 + d_3 b_4 \Delta t_3 + d_4 b_4 \Delta t_4) + \\
&(1-k_{31})(o_4 + d_1 b_4 t_{3z} + d_1 b_4 (t_1 + \Delta t_2 + \Delta t_3 + \Delta t_4 - t_{3z})) + \\
&(1-k_{32})(o_4 + d_1 b_4 t_1 + d_2 b_4 t_{3z} + d_2 b_4 (\Delta t_2 + \Delta t_3 + \Delta t_4 - t_{3z})) + \\
&(1-k_{33})(o_4 + d_1 b_4 t_1 + d_2 b_4 \Delta t_2 + d_3 b_4 t_{3z} + d_3 b_4 (\Delta t_3 + \Delta t_4 - t_{3z})) = \\
&a_o v z + a_1 v t_1 + a_2 v t_2 + a_3 v t_3 + a_4 v t_4 \\
&(1-k_{31})(o_4 + d_1 b_4 t_{3z}) + (1-k_{32})(o_4 + d_1 b_4 t_1 + d_2 b_4 t_{3z}) + \\
&(1-k_{33})(o_4 + d_1 b_4 t_1 + d_2 b_4 \Delta t_2 + d_3 b_4 t_{3z}) = \\
&a_0 v z (1-k_{31})(1-k_{32})(1-k_{33})
\end{aligned} \qquad (16) \quad (****$$

In this set of equations, the first one is the minimization problem to be solved. Notic that we minimize the sum of the rendezvous time while the number given in the Introdu tion and Results sections are the average of the rendezvous times. There are four sets o equations, (*), (**), (***) and (****). Equation (*) is the constraint that player I rendezvou with agent (o_1, b_1) at time t_1. Agent (o_1, b_1) may find the marker before time t_1. However, in this case, the optimal solution is to continue in the same direction, i.e., the equation would be

$$k(o_1 + d_1 b_1 t_1) + (1-k)(o_1 + d_1 * t_{0z} d_1 b_1 (t_1 - t_{0z}) = a_0 vz + a_1 vt_1,$$

where $k = 1$ if player II does not find the marker and $k = 0$ else, and t_{oz} is the time at which player II finds the marker. This equation reduces to (*). In (*), if a player finds the marker in the interval $[t_1, t_2]$ the optimal strategy is to continue in the same direction and the marker is useless, and so on for (***) and (****) if the marker is found in the interval $[t_2, t_3]$ and $[t_3, t_4]$, respectively.

The three remaining sets of equations (**), (***) and (****) are composed of two equations. The first one accounts for the rendezvous of agent (o_i, b_i) with player I and the second one is valid only if the marker is used (k_1, k_{21}, k_{22}, k_{31}, k_{32}, k_{33} equal 1) and we define the times when the marker is found as t_{1z}, t_{2z}, t_{3z}.

The next set of equations is composed of the speed constraints. The variable vz is the product of the speed of player I and the time z at which the marker is dropped; this product is bounded by $v \cdot z$ since the speed of player I is bounded by v. In the results, we observed that the speed of player I is v (maximal) or 0 but we obtaind no solution with v in between.

$$\begin{aligned} &0 \le vz \le v \cdot z \\ &0 \le vt_1 \le v \cdot (t_1 - z) \\ &0 \le vt_2 \le v \cdot \Delta t_2 \\ &0 \le vt_3 \le v \cdot \Delta t_3 \\ &0 \le vt_4 \le v \cdot \Delta t_4 \end{aligned} \tag{17}$$

The family of linear programs was generated by assigning values to the parameters of Equations (15)–(17). These values must satisfy the constraints (the constraints $t_i \ge 0$ were included in all linear programs)

$$\begin{aligned} &a_i, b_i, o_i, d_i \in \{0,1\} \sum o_i = 0, \sum d_i = 0,\ o_i = o_j \Rightarrow d_i \ne d_j, \\ &t_1 \ge 0, t_2 \ge 0, t_3 \ge 0, t_4 \ge 0. \end{aligned}$$

The families of linear programs were solved for a maximal speed of player I ranging from 0 to 1 with a step size of $1/1000$, i.e., the optimal solutions $opt(v)$ were computed for $v = n/1000$, $n = 0, 1, \ldots, 1000$. The result was that the same strategy was used, see Figure 5. The speed of player I was maximal along the trajectory and the best solution was obtained for $z \in [0, t_1]$. With respect to the notation of Corollary 2 the speeds of player I were ($v_0 = -v$, $v_1 = v$, $v_2 = -v$, $v_3 = v$). The marker reduced the rendezvous value even when the speed of player I was very slow.

The rendezvous times are given by:

$$\begin{aligned} &z = \frac{1}{v+3},\ t_1 = \frac{3}{v+3},\ t_2 = \frac{5v+3}{(v+1)(v+3)}, \\ &t_3 = \frac{7v^2+12v+9}{(v+1)^2(v+3)},\ t_4 = \frac{9v^3+27v^2+35v+9}{(v+1)^3(v+3)}, \end{aligned} \tag{18}$$

$$R = \frac{24v^3+68v^2+76v+24}{(v+1)^3(v+3)}.$$

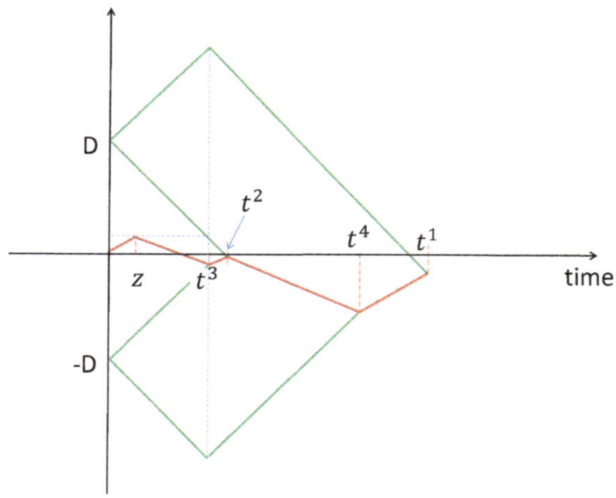

Figure 5. Optimal strategy when player I holds the marker and is the slower player.

The optimal solution function $opt(v)$ is decreasing because a strategy for v is a strategy for $v' \geq v$ as well. Hence, if the value of the next-to-optimal strategy $nextToopt(v + dv)$ for a speed $v + dv$ is larger than $opt(v)$, the strategy that leads to $opt(v)$ is optimal for speeds in $[v, v + dv]$. With our mesh size of $1/1000$, we numerically observed that this occurred since $v \geq 17/1000$. Hence, we have a computer-assisted proof summarized in the following Theorem.

Theorem 2. *For $v \in [17/1000, 1]$, the rendezvous value of the game is given by (18). The optimal strategy is plotted in Figure 5 and the optimal rendezvous values in Figure 6.*

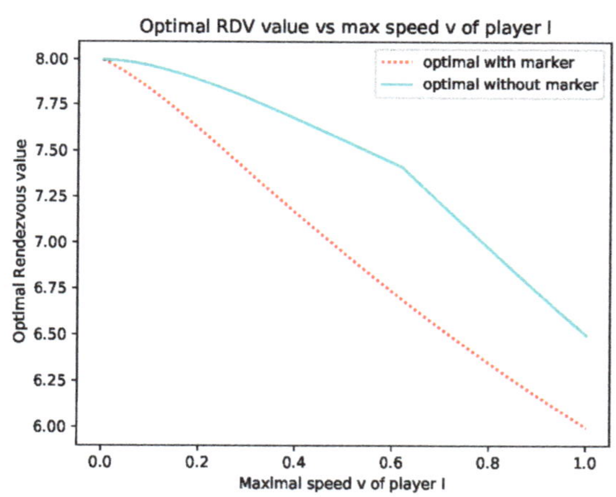

Figure 6. Optimal solutions with (18) and without marker. The slow player holds the marker.

The interval in which the Theorem is stated to be true may be enlarged by computing the numerical solutions on a finer mesh. It is relevant to point out that for the optimal strategy, the time at which the marker is found is t_1, i.e., the same time as the first rendezvous occurs.

6. Solution of the Problem with Marker Held by the Fast Player

The family of linear programs to be solved when the marker is held by the fast player (I) is very similar to the one defined by Equations (15)–(17). The changes are that the coefficients a_i are no longer multiplied by the maximal speed v, as are now the coefficients d_i. The system of equations is not reproduced here to save some space.

The results are plotted in Figure 7. We observe that for speeds slower than $v \approx 0.805$ the marker is not useful and the optimal solution is given by the optimal solutions without marker stated in Theorem 1. For speeds faster than $v \approx 0.805$, the marker starts to be useful and the strategy is similar to the optimal one when the marker is held by the slow player, see Figure 5. When the fast player holds the marker, we obtain that the rendezvous times are given by:

$$z = \frac{1}{3v+1}, \ t_1 = \frac{3}{3v+1}, \ t_2 = \frac{3v+5}{(v+1)(3v+1)},$$
$$t_3 = \frac{9v+5}{(v+1)(3v+1)}, \ t_4 = \frac{3v+7}{(v+1)^2}, \tag{19}$$
$$R = \frac{24v^2+52v+20}{(v+1)^2(3v+1)}.$$

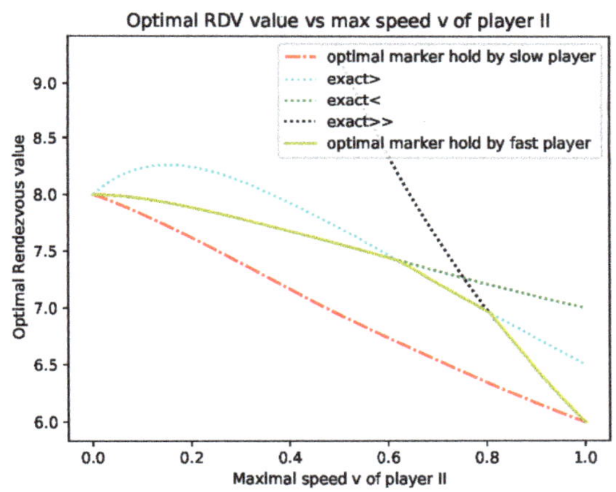

Figure 7. Optimal solutions with marker, i.e., (13) for $v \leq (\sqrt{5}-1)/2$, (14) for $v \geq (\sqrt{5}-1)/2$, (19) for $v > 0.805$, and without marker. The fast player holds the marker.

The optimal rendezvous value is decreasing with the maximal speed v because a strategy for maximal speed v is a strategy for maximal speed $v' \geq v$. Moreover, if we denote $opt(v)$ the optimal rendezvous value for maximal speed v, and $nextToopt(v)$ the next-to-optimal rendezvous value, it follows that if $nextToopt(v+dv) \geq opt(v)$ and the strategy leading to $opt(v)$ and $opt(v+dv)$ is the same, then the strategy is optimal on the entire interval $[v, v+dv]$. By numerical computation and using the two stated observations we obtain the following Theorem.

Theorem 3. *For $v \in [1/1000, 0.618]$ the rendezvous value of the game is given by (13) and the optimal strategy is plotted in Figure 3; for $v \in [0.619, 0.805]$, the rendezvous value of the game is given by (14) and the optimal strategy is plotted in Figure 4; for $v \in [0.807, 0.966]$, the rendezvous value of the game is given by (19), the rendezvous values are plotted in Figure 7 and the optimal strategy is plotted in Figure 8.*

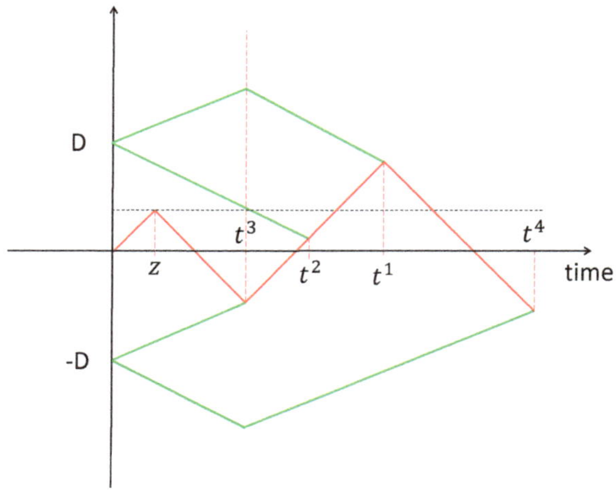

Figure 8. Optimal solutions with marker, i.e., (19) for $v > 0.805$; for lower speeds the optim solutions are the ones without marker (Theorem 1). The fast player holds the marker.

It is relevant to point out the difference between the optimal strategies when th marker is held by the slow (Figure 5) or fast player (Figure 8). After the rendezvous time in Figure 5 the slow player (who holds the marker) turns, while in Figure 8, the fast play (who holds the marker) continues on their way. The transition from the two strategies "continuous" in the sense that when the speeds are equal at time t_2, the two remainin agents to be found are at equal distance from player I. Hence, both strategies are optim (turning or continuing).

7. Conclusions

In this paper, we presented variations and solutions of the classical rendezvous pro lem on the line. In particular, we considered that players moved at different speeds an made use of markers as communication channels. We showed, for instance, that in som conditions the slow player had better waiting still for the fast one.

We showed how the search space $\mathcal{F}$ given by (1) can be reduced to a space of muc smaller dimension making the enumeration of all elements realistic, in order to find the one leading to the optimal solution of our problem. The reduction follows from Proposition This new formulation is compatible with mixed-integer linear programming and is show to lead to a solution efficiently using the Gurobi solver [40].

Author Contributions: Writing—original draft preparation, P.L. and N.C. All authors have read an agreed to the published version of the manuscript.

Funding: This research received no external funding.

Data Availability Statement: Data sharing is not applicable to this article as no datasets wer generated or analyzed during the current study.

Conflicts of Interest: The authors declare no conflict of interest.

References

1. Alpern, S.; Gal, S. Rendezvous search on the line with distinguishable players. *SIAM J. Control Optim.* **1995**, *33*, 1270–127 [CrossRef]
2. Alpern, S. The Rendezvous Search Problem. *SIAM J. Control Optim.* **1995**, *33*, 673–683. [CrossRef]
3. Anderson, E.J.; Essegaier, S. Rendezvous Search on the Line with Indistinguishable Players. *SIAM J. Control Optim.* **199** *33*, 1637–1642. [CrossRef]
4. Baston, V. Note: Two rendezvous search problems on the line. *Nav. Res. Logist.* **1999**, *46*, 335–340. [CrossRef]

5. Uthaisombut, P. Symmetric Rendezvous Search on the Line Using Move Patterns with Different Lengths. Citeseer. 2006. Available online: http://citeseerx.ist.psu.edu/viewdoc/summary?doi=10.1.1.59.6033 (accessed on 15 December 2021).
6. Han, Q.; Du, D.; Vera, J.; Zuluaga, L.F. Improved Bounds for the Symmetric Rendezvous Value on the Line. *Oper. Res.* **2008**, *56*, 772–782. [CrossRef]
7. Baston, V.; Gal, S. Rendezvous on the Line when the Players' Initial Distance is Given by an Unknown Probability Distribution. *SIAM J. Control Optim.* **1998**, *36*, 1880–1889. [CrossRef]
8. Alpern, S.; Beck, A. Rendezvous Search on the Line with Limited Resources: Maximizing the Probability of Meeting. *Oper. Res.* **1999**, *47*, 849–861. [CrossRef]
9. Alpern, S.; Beck, A. Pure Strategy Asymmetric Rendezvous on the Line with an Unknown Initial Distance. *Oper. Res.* **2000**, *48*, 498–501. [CrossRef]
10. Ozsoyeller, D.; Beveridge, A.; Isler, V. Symmetric Rendezvous Search on the Line With an Unknown Initial Distance. *IEEE Trans. Robot.* **2013**, *29*, 1366–1379. [CrossRef]
11. Stachowiak, G. Asynchronous deterministic rendezvous on the line. In Proceedings of the International Conference on Current Trends in Theory and Practice of Computer Science, Špindleruv Mlýn, Czech Republic, 24–30 January 2009; pp. 497–508.
12. Czyzowicz, J.; Killick, R.; Kranakis, E. Linear rendezvous with asymmetric clocks. In Proceedings of the 22nd International Conference on Principles of Distributed Systems (OPODIS 2018), Schloss Dagstuhl-Leibniz-Zentrum fuer Informatik, Hong Kong, China, 17–19 December 2018,
13. Chrobak, M.; Gąsieniec, L.; Gorry, T.; Martin, R. Group search on the line. In Proceedings of the International Conference on Current Trends in Theory and Practice of Informatics, Pecpod Snežkou, Czech Republic, 24–29 January 2015; pp. 164–176.
14. Howard, J.V. Rendezvous Search on the Interval and the Circle. *Oper. Res.* **1999**, *47*, 550–558. [CrossRef]
15. Kranakis, E.; Santoro, N.; Sawchuk, C.; Krizanc, D. Mobile agent rendezvous in a ring. In Proceedings of the 23rd International Conference on Distributed Computing Systems, Providence, RI, USA, 19–22 May 2003; pp. 592–599.
16. Flocchini, P.; Kranakis, E.; Krizanc, D.; Santoro, N.; Sawchuk, C. Multiple mobile agent rendezvous in a ring. In *Latin American Symposium on Theoretical Informatics*; Springer: Berlin/Heidelberg, Germany, 2004; pp. 599–608.
17. Kranakis, E.; Krizanc, D.; Markou, E. The mobile agent rendezvous problem in the ring. *Synth. Lect. Distrib. Comput. Theory* **2010**, *1*, 1–122. [CrossRef]
18. Di Stefano, G.; Navarra, A. Optimal gathering of oblivious robots in anonymous graphs and its application on trees and rings. *Distrib. Comput.* **2017**, *30*, 75–86. [CrossRef]
19. Czyzowicz, J.; Dobrev, S.; Kranakis, E.; Krizanc, D. The power of tokens: Rendezvous and symmetry detection for two mobile agents in a ring. In Proceedings of the International Conference on Current Trends in Theory and Practice of Computer Science, Nový Smokovec, Slovakia, 19–25 January 2008; pp. 234–246.
20. Flocchini, P.; Kranakis, E.; Krizanc, D.; Luccio, F.L.; Santoro, N.; Sawchuk, C. Mobile agents rendezvous when tokens fail. In *International Colloquium on Structural Information and Communication Complexity*; Springer: Berlin/Heidelberg, Germany, 2004; pp. 161–172.
21. Das, S.; Mihalák, M.; Šrámek, R.; Vicari, E.; Widmayer, P. Rendezvous of mobile agents when tokens fail anytime. In Proceedings of the International Conference on Principles of Distributed Systems, Luxor, Egypt, 15–18 December 2008; pp. 463–480.
22. Baston, V.; Gal, S. Rendezvous search when marks are left at the starting points. *Nav. Res. Logist.* **2001**, *48*, 722–731. [CrossRef]
23. Leone, P.; Alpern, S. Rendezvous Search With Markers That Can Be Dropped at Chosen Times. *Nav. Res. Logist.* **2018**, *65*, *6–7*. [CrossRef]
24. Das, S.; Luccio, F.L.; Markou, E. Mobile agents rendezvous in spite of a malicious agent. In Proceedings of the International Symposium on Algorithms and Experiments for Wireless Sensor Networks, Patras, Greece, 17–18 September 2015; pp. 211–224.
25. Das, S.; Focardi, R.; Luccio, F.L.; Markou, E.; Squarcina, M. Gathering of robots in a ring with mobile faults. *Theor. Comput. Sci.* **2019**, *764*, 42–60. [CrossRef]
26. Alpern, S.; Gal, S. *The Theory of Search Games and Rendezvous*; Springer: Berlin/Heidelberg, Germany, 2006; Volume 55.
27. Alpern, S. Ten open problems in rendezvous search. In *Search Theory*; Springer: Berlin/Heidelberg, Germany, 2013; pp. 223–230.
28. Pelc, A. Deterministic Rendezvous Algorithms. In *Distributed Computing by Mobile Entities*; Springer: Berlin/Heidelberg, Germany, 2019; pp. 423–454.
29. Lidbetter, T. Search and rescue in the face of uncertain threats. *Eur. J. Oper. Res.* **2020**, *285*, 1153–1160. [CrossRef]
30. Baston, V.; Kikuta, K. Search games on a network with travelling and search costs. *Int. J. Game Theory* **2015**, *44*, 347–365. [CrossRef]
31. Baston, V.; Kikuta, K. A search problem on a bipartite network. *Eur. J. Oper. Res.* **2019**, *277*, 227–237. [CrossRef]
32. Baston, V.; Kikuta, K. Search games on networks with travelling and search costs and with arbitrary searcher starting points. *Networks* **2013**, *62*, 72–79. [CrossRef]
33. Hohzaki, R. Search games: Literature and survey. *J. Oper. Res. Soc. Jpn.* **2016**, *59*, 1–34. [CrossRef]
34. Alpern, S.; Fokkink, R.; Gasieniec, L.; Lindelauf, R.; Subrahmanian, V. *Search Theory*; Springer: Berlin/Heidelberg, Germany, 2013.
35. Alpern, S.; Beck, A. Asymmetric rendezvous on the line is a double linear search problem. *Math. Oper. Res.* **1999**, *24*, 604–618. [CrossRef]
36. Leone, P.; Buwaya, J.; Alpern, S. Search-and-Rescue Rendezvous. *Eur. J. Oper. Res.* **2021**, *297*, 579–591. [CrossRef]
37. Isaacs, R. *Differential Games: A Mathematical Theory with Applications to Warfare and Pursuit, Control and Optimization*; Courier Corporation: Chelmsford, MA, USA, 1999.

38. Mehlmann, A. *Applied Differential Games*; Springer: Berlin/Heidelberg, Germany, 2013.
39. Friedman, A. *Differential Games*; Courier Corporation: Chelmsford, MA, USA, 2013.
40. *Gurobi Optimizer Reference Manual*; Gurobi Optimization, LLC: Houston, TX, USA, 2021.

algorithms

MDPI

rticle

Automatic Fault Detection and Diagnosis in Cellular Networks and Beyond 5G: Intelligent Network Management

run Kumar Sangaiah [1], Samira Rezaei [2], Amir Javadpour [3,*], Farimasadat Miri [4], Weizhe Zhang [3] nd Desheng Wang [3]

1 International Graduate Institute of AI, National Yunlin University of Science and Technology, Douliu 64002, Taiwan
2 Leiden Institute of Advanced Computer Science, University of Leiden, 2311 EZ Leiden, The Netherlands
3 Department of Computer Science and Technology (Cyberspace Security), Harbin Institute of Technology, Shenzhen 150001, China
4 Computer Science Department, Ontario Tech University (UOIT), 2000 Simcoe St N, Oshawa, ON L1G 0C5, Canada
* Correspondence: a.javadpour87@gmail.com

Abstract: Handling faults in a running cellular network can impair the performance and dissatisfy the end users. It is important to design an automatic self-healing procedure to not only detect the active faults, but also to diagnosis them automatically. Although fault detection has been well studied in the literature, fewer studies have targeted the more complicated task of diagnosing. Our presented method aims to tackle fault detection and diagnosis using two sets of data collected by the network: performance support system data and drive test data. Although performance support system data is collected automatically by the network, drive test data are collected manually in three mode call scenarios: short, long and idle. The short call can identify faults in a call setup, the long call is designed to identify handover failures and call interruption, and, finally, the idle mode is designed to understand the characteristics of the standard signal in the network. We have applied unsupervised learning, along with various classified algorithms, on performance support system data. Congestion and failures in TCH assignments are a few examples of the detected and diagnosed faults with our method. In addition, we present a framework to identify the need for handovers. The Silhouette coefficient is used to evaluate the quality of the unsupervised learning approach. We achieved an accuracy of 96.86% with the dynamic neural network method.

Keywords: cellular network management; network optimization; cellular network troubleshooting; data mining; unsupervised learning; supervised learning; self-healing networks

itation: Sangaiah, A.K.; Rezaei, S.; vadpour, A.; Miri, F.; Zhang, W.; 'ang, D. Automatic Fault Detection nd Diagnosis in Cellular Networks nd Beyond 5G: Intelligent Network lanagement. *Algorithms* **2022**, *15*, 32. https://doi.org/10.3390/ 15110432

cademic Editor: Frank Werner

eceived: 26 September 2022
ccepted: 15 November 2022
ublished: 17 November 2022

1. Introduction

Cellular networks' future is in heterogeneous networks. These networks consist of different radio and architecture technologies. On the other hand, the growing services and technologies increase the complexity of these networks and the internet of things (IoT) daily. For operators' survival in today's competitive world, it is necessary to use a new strategy to manage these networks. Using self-organizing networks (SONs) is the most common solution to achieve this goal. The architecture of SONs consists of three general parts: self-configuration, self-healing, and self-optimization [1,2].

Self-regulating networks include different phases, including designing, updating, or developing the network. Transmitter stations, base receivers, nodes, and other network terminals need to set related parameters, especially with the emergence of LTE networks based on IP and with flat architecture [3,4].

With the increase in the complexity of cellular networks, self-healing networks have become more popular. However, the rate of published studies and articles in this field is much more limited than in other areas. These networks can manage faults and system failures by automated detection and identify their causes. Finally, the self-optimizir network calculates and values the network parameters that need to be reset, according the network status, traffic, and services used by the users [5].

Therefore, actions related to self-regulating networks are in the development phas or any activities related to resetting the network are in the operational stage. The se optimization starts working in cases where there is no apparent problem in the networ but the cell performance is average. Finally, the measures related to the network's se healing capability are used when the quality and efficiency of the network severely declir Our focus in this paper is on self-healing networks. This research seeks to find som solutions to improve the process that is currently used in the industry to detect faults ar identify the cause of faults. Therefore, all assumptions and modeling have been mad according to the needs of the sector and consultation with experts in this field. In additio according to experts in this field, it improved the quality of operational work.

1.1. Innovation, Importance, and the Value of Research

Considering the importance of cellular networks in everyday life and the fact th they are becoming an inseparable part of modern lives, paying attention to the faults the network, trying to reduce the time a fault affects the network through early detectic of the fault, and, also, the correct identification of the fault caused in the network so as expedite a return to the network's normal mode are of particular importance.

The difference between this work and other similar works in this field includes th use of accurate data for modeling the behavior of the network in the face of variou types of faults, and examination of all the characteristics and critical statistical indicato that optimization engineers use in the operators to analyze the faults that occur in th network. All features are reviewed simultaneously. Therefore, the effect these indicato have on each other, and the impact of combining the values of different indicators o the network's performance, are studied in this research. In addition, unlike most of th proposed methods, the construction of the proposed model in this field was achieve without the intervention of human resources and experts. Since there is a possibility human fault in setting model parameters and the assigned values are highly dependent o the expert's experience, the fact that different experts may value the parameters in differer ways, under the same circumstances, is pertinent. For this reason, the use of a method th rejects human intervention is significant. Finally, this research used three available source of information in troubleshooting and optimizing the networks, which, according to ou study, is the first case of research considering all sources. In other words, all related wor in this field composed our first source of information, namely, the performance suppo system data. In the second section, these data are introduced in detail.

1.2. Global System for Mobile Communications (GSM) Architecture

The GSM network is a digital cellular communication system that operates by th cellular making of a geographic area and reusing frequencies for non-contiguous cells. Th network consists of some components, such as the network and switching subsystem (NSS base station subsystem (BSS), and operation support system (OSS). Figure 1 shows th GSM network architecture [6].

As seen above, the base station subsystem includes all the related radio capabilities the GSM network and is responsible for establishing communication between the networ subsystem and network users. Therefore, the BSS is composed of several base statio controllers that manage the operations at base transceiver stations (BTSs) through the Ab interface. Each transmitter and receiver of the base station is responsible for serving th users of its coverage area through the A (air) interface [7,8].

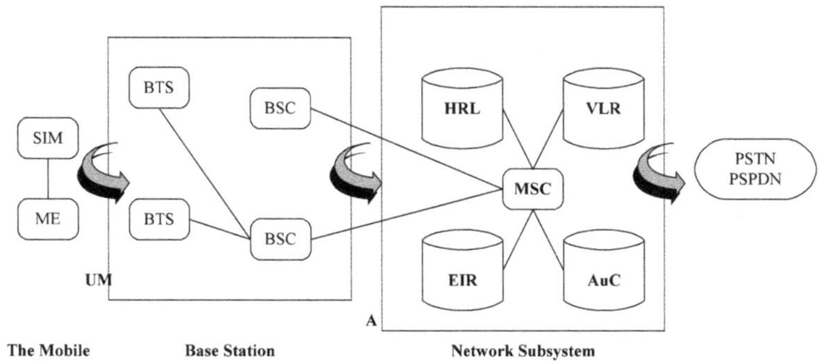

Figure 1. The architecture of the GSM network.

There are three types of data sources to analyze and check the quality of these networks and identify and troubleshoot the faults that occur in the networks. The most critical data used in the fault management of these networks is the statistical data reported from the BTS side, which indicates the status of various statistical indicators from different traffic and signaling perspectives. The second category of used data results from an experiment in the areas covered by the networks through human power. This test is a method to measure and check the coverage status, capability, and quality of the networks. This test is conducted by making a call with a mobile phone that can record the reported measurements and parameters from the BTS side. The name of this test in the industry is the driving test. In the third section, some detailed information about this category is given. Finally, the last category of used data in improving the network performance is the use of collected information from subscriber complaints. Section four reviews the registered reports of the Mobile Telecommunication Company of Iran (Hamrahe Avval).

In general, our main goals in this research are as follows:

- To use accurate data to identify the cause of a fault that occurred in the network (the required data was obtained in cooperation with the mobile telecommunication company, Hamrahe Avval.)
- To appropriately use available data sources to improve the accuracy of fault diagnosis systems
- To analyze different indicators' values and how they affect the occurrence of faults
- To model events and unpleasant events (faults) in the network
- To have a comprehensive view of the network and the fault types that occur in the network
- To provide a model that has a minor dependency on expert opinion.

1.3. An Introduction to Decision Support Systems

Decision support systems, as is evident from their name, are decision support methodologies. A DSS requires a knowledge base, a user interface, and a mechanism for processing the data in the database. A DSS is an information system that facilitates the decision-making process for managers using an interactive user interface. DSS uses online analytical processing (OLAP). Therefore, it requires analyzing a large amount of data related to the organization's past [9].

This project deals with the organization of different components of a DSS system that can correctly detect a fault and identify the cause of the obtained fault. Therefore, one of this project's goals is to provide a knowledge base and a mechanism for processing faults in the system.

1.4. Problem Definition

There are some significant problems with the existing methods for self-healing networks. First, most of the studies have used a simulator to model the system, and the dynamics characteristic of radio networks are the most apparent features of this type o network. Therefore, if a simulator is used, the events that happen for these networks ma be ignored in reality. On the other hand, as mentioned before, the number of publishe articles in the field of self-healing networks is less than in other areas. Thus, the researcher have not paid enough attention to one of the most critical issues in the field of cellula networks, due to the competitive ethos among operators and the need to keep customer satisfied in this industry. On the other hand, according to our studies, all conducted studie in this field are limited to using performance support system data that include key perfo mance indicators. In this research, we tried to use other available resources to improve th accuracy of the presented model for fault detection and to identify the cause of the faults i the system [10].

1.5. *Self-Healing Networks*

As mentioned, the number of published articles in self-healing networks is less tha in other fields. There are several main reasons for this. First, it is difficult to specif the common faults and the corresponding causes in these networks, due to the networ dynamics and their dependence on the behavior and services used by the users. Whe different experts face a specific fault, they may have different opinions. On the other hanc there is no valid document in the literature in this field to correlate the fault and the caus of the fault in the network. The second reason is the complexity and difficulty of simulatin faults and modeling the network mode in simulators. In addition, it is almost impossible t have an acceptable quantity of faults during the lifetime of a network. Due to the reason mentioned, less investigative research has been conducted in this area than in other area

As was mentioned before, this research aimed to solve various challenges in the fiel of cellular networks' fault detection, to categorize different types of faults according t varying values of performance evaluation indicators, and to investigate the impact of eac fault on these indicators. In other words, our research was conducted in the framewor of self-healing networks. In general, the nature of a cellular network's components an systems is not immune to faults and failures. In the old methods, faults were detecte by activating alarms. When remote methods could not solve the faults, radio networ engineers were sent to the site to identify the fault. As expected, this process is very tim consuming, and sometimes it takes more than a week for the system to return to its norma status [10].

On the other hand, some problems cannot be traced through alarms and are onl identified if a complaint is reported to the operator by the customer. The future of thes systems is improving with the use of self-healing methods. In general, self-healing method address the process of remote fault detection, identify the cause of the fault, and, finall set up the fault compensation system, or repair activities, to minimize the effects of th fault on the equipment and network components. For this purpose, in this section, we firs present the available views and methods in the fault detection field and in the diagnosi of causes of faults in cellular networks. The logical flow of self-healing systems is give in [10]. This flow consists of three logical parts: identifying the fault, analyzing the caus of the fault, and, finally, setting up the fault compensation system. In the following, w briefly review the studies conducted, according to the categories presented in this study.

1.5.1. Fault Detection

This section is responsible for identifying faulty cells. Self-healing mechanisms con tinue to function only on these cells. Identifying defective cells is the most superficial aspec of the work, which may be assessed using alarms and indicator values. If the efficienc graph of a cell has a steep decreasing slope, that cell is considered disabled. Establishing threshold for index values is a straightforward, but typical, method in this area [11]. Fo instance, a cell is recognized as faulty if the value of an index is less than (or greater than the predetermined threshold. Other approaches, such as in [12], consider a profile for eac index, which depicts the indicator's normal state. The issues with employing a thresh old are avoided since the fault detection stage continuously measures each indicator's divergence from its profile. A solution is offered in [13] to issues like personnel needing to correctly configure the parameters for profile building and deviation detection [14]. The Kolmogorov–Smirnov test compares the index's distribution with its ideal state as the functional approach. Each index's profile contains a record of the statistical distribution of the index in normal mode [14].

One of the current issues is that alarms may not detect all network faults. As a result, the network problem might not be discovered for several hours or days. Finding cells that are referred to as sleeping cells, and which are unable to send an alert to the center, is the key issue in this subject. On the other hand, it is impossible to guarantee the presence or absence of faults in the system by looking at the value of just one index. So, it is essential to assess multiple indicators' values [13], simultaneously.

It is possible to implement an intelligent and dynamic fault detection mechanism. According to the study in [15], defective cells can be divided into three categories: deteriorated cells that are still functional while having subpar quality, paralyzed cells, in which a severe fault occurred, but the fault has little to no negative impact on the user experience, and does not result in disgruntled customers, and network cells that eventually shut down and cannot carry traffic.

In [16], the process of detecting disabled cells is carried out by creating observation graphs, binary classification, and a list of nearby cells. Along with classifier quality, accuracy in recognizing the frequency pattern of network issues should also be considered. It was demonstrated that, despite the classifiers' high sensitivity in diagnosis, they produce many false alarms, making them unsuitable for industrial use.

Network faults have been found in [7] utilizing the Self-Organization Map (SOM) and K-means clustering methods. SOM is not only used in the scenario mentioned above. By creating the techniques for cell categorization, the researcher in [17] improved the control of the state of the cells in the cell network. An anomaly is defined as a significant data disagreement with SOM nodes. The use of a local threshold to identify abnormalities distinguishes this study from similar ones, because local approaches improve diagnosis accuracy and decrease the production of false alarms. The distribution of deviations in the network can be used with the adaptive threshold in this investigation [18].

Garc sets, categorization, and SOM are three data mining techniques that have been used to measure the performance of mobile networks [19]. These techniques are used to discretize the value of the indicators and to categorize the status of a network into good, normal, bad, and unacceptable network states.

In [20], data vectors representing the system's normal state were employed to perform the learning step of a neural network used to construct the normal state profile. The confidence interval for the normal/non-normal state was established through experimental analysis. To determine the reason for the fault, inference rules were produced using the trained network.

One of the tasks that may be mentioned in the context of fault detection is using the alarm correlation technique and delivering fewer alarms to operators. These algorithms are sensitive to minimum support and confidence levels for pattern identification methods. The method finds a high number of patterns when these parameters are set to small values and a low number of patterns when these parameters are set to large values. Since this research did not investigate the correlation of alarms, other pertinent details were avoided [7].

It should be emphasized that after recognizing the fault, factors, including its duration and the effect it has on the operation of the system, should be examined. If the observed fault fits the prerequisites, the process of determining its source and compensating for it begins.

1.5.2. Identifying the Cause of Fault

- This section suggests remedies for a cell's aberrant and dysfunctional condition. As a result, it is crucial to start by limiting the fault within a cell. The nearby cells should

work together to reduce the fault's detrimental impact if it cannot be swiftly fixe Corrective actions must be conducted to eliminate the fault when the fault's root cau is identified. The following section goes into more depth about this phase.
- Hardware and software issues may be causes of cell faults, and other potential caus include incorrect configuration, inadequate coverage, and interference. As previous stated, alarms alone cannot identify the source of an issue and additional data, suc as the values of the indicators, must also be examined.
- The following categories serve as a general summary of the current methods used this field. Here, the primary focus is on techniques based on data mining and findir significant patterns in the data to identify the cause of the fault.
- Methods based on data mining
- Statistical methods

Data mining techniques are among the approaches adopted in the automation network fault detection, due to the enormous and growing volume of data accessible f the evaluation of the quality of cellular networks. The absence of a database of classifie instances, highlighted in the introduction section, is one of the most significant issues this sector. Moreover, this area is separated from other areas related to identifying the cau of faults, due to the continuous nature of the performance evaluation indicators and th existence of logical faults that are not dependent on the physical parts of the equipmer and are probably related to the wrong settings of the equipment. For instance, Rule-Base Systems (RBSs), which are a subset of Expert Systems employing a set of "if–then" rules [1 did not gain enough success in cellular communication networks because they did n perform successfully in cases with both large and unpredictable ranges. Making rules dynamic and unpredictable contexts has its own set of issues.

The two main divisions of data mining methods are unsupervised and supervise methods. The following sections review the methods used in these two types.

1.5.3. Methods Based on Data Mining

- **Supervised Methods**

Due to the issues that exist in this domain, and have already been referred to, th present methods in the area of supervised methods primarily investigate in a restricte way. The techniques employed are often limited to Bayesian networks. The most effecti techniques in this area are discussed in the following sections.

There has been much interest in using Bayesian networks to represent network even and communicate between faults and their causes [21]. The primary distinction betwee these approaches depends on the structure used for identifying the cause of the fau and the various fault indicators and reasons that the suggested solution can look int A model for locating defects in cellular networks using the Naive Bayesian classificatio method was introduced in [21]. The fault causes are treated as classes, and the values various indicators are treated as features. The introduced model, providing the knowledg base used for classification, is divided into two primary categories: quantitative an qualitative. The quantitative section comprises the links between these components, an the qualitative part includes the model's components. This article demonstrated ho the average beta density function parameters could be used to thoroughly specify th relationships between the model's parts. By discretizing the index values and using th Spartan Bayesian classification approach, [22] was able to identify the fault source. Th entropy minimization discretization (EMD) method was applied to boost the effectivene of the proposed model. Utilizing this technique resulted in the best possible selection useful indications from the input parameters.

The study in [23] aimed to improve a network's accuracy by considering the contin ous nature of the index values. Giving them discrete values decreased the precision of th results produced. As a result, the Smooth Bayesian network was employed with varyin state uncertainty. On the other hand, as these parameter values were considered, mor data was required to calculate the parameter values. The findings of the applied metho which used Bayesian law, are displayed in [24], utilizing a dynamic simulator system on the UMTS network. The architecture for employing these networks' troubleshooting tools was provided. It is always necessary to strike a balance between the precision and complexity of a model. The DCR index calculated the number of disconnected calls, which was the fault detection criterion in [20] (thoroughly explained in the second section). The system experienced a fault if the value of this index exceeded the threshold, and the causes of the fault were determined by looking at the simplified Bayesian network and utilizing the Independence of causal impact (ICI) approach between the indicators and the faults' causes. The simplified Bayesian technique was dealt with using the ICI method, and each fault source was employed as an independent node with two true or false states in the modeling. The outcomes of the simulations demonstrated that the effectiveness of these two approaches was equivalent but that the ICI approach was more complex. As a result, the simplified Bayesian model was given precedence. These techniques employed reverse engineering to create faults under particular circumstances. In other words, the methodologies utilized in the paper attempted to model the fault using the value of the key performance indicators when the fault occurred, even though the source of the issue was previously known.

The absence of a database of classified instances that can be utilized to estimate the parameters of the suggested model is one of the issues in this subject. A technique for developing a statistical model using expert knowledge was provided in [25]. In this method, knowledge acquisition was accomplished in two stages: first, with the assistance of experts, knowledge was gathered, and then models were built. Information about the various types of faults, variables that influence the various types of faults, the relationship between the types of faults and the influencing variables, the threshold for each variable, the likelihood that each variable influences faults, and, finally, comparison of the information obtained were all related to the data collection stage. Finally, this method constructed the model via the Bayesian network approach. It was proved that when parameter values were calculated using statistical features, rather than expert judgment, systems to detect the causes of faults performed more accurately.

In [26] a strategy for locating the fault's root cause, that combined neural network and law-based techniques, was offered. The rules matrix and a hierarchical and distributed multi-dimensional structure were employed to gain the capacity for parallel reasoning. However, the author concentrated on the Internet network and did not estimate the accuracy of this method on cellular networks. Due to the neural network's high power in detecting data behavior, it was also employed in research in [27] in such a way that the criteria for determining the cause of a fault were applied to each type of fault that the neural network specified. These rules could use other available data to check network efficiency and deviation of neighboring cells to ensure that one did not affect the other.

- **Unsupervised Methods**

Among the unsupervised techniques, the Self-Organization Map (SOM) is the most popular one. This neural network-based technique is usually utilized for data presentation. This process transforms high-dimensional data into two- or three-dimensional data, preparing it for presentation [28]. According to [29], the SOM algorithm was given a predetermined set of features, and after clustering the data, each cluster was utilized to identify the various fault types, their sources, and the times when they occurred. This technique was only used in regard to the difficulties of signaling channel capacity and traffic flow analysis. The study's researcher in [29] began by using SOM to decrease the dimensions of the data to two or three dimensions. After applying clustering techniques, such as hierarchical approaches, and division methods, such as k-means, to the data, the clusters were then assessed using the Davies–Bouldin index.

1.5.4. Statistical Methods

Identifying the cause of faults in [30] was done by comparing the values of numerous indicators and taking appropriate corrective action, based on expert judgment. The operational approach involved ranking the causes of the set of indicators that strayed from their profile in decreasing relevancy. The scoring system employed in this approach determined the likelihood of a specific cause for an occurred fault, using the set of indicators that deviated from the baseline.

In [31], the network status was examined using the characteristic vector of the network status, which was as long as the number of the analyzed indicators. This characteristic vector considered the threshold limit for the six most significant indications. The Hamming distance was used to determine how various records differed. As a result, the fault cause was the same for records that belonged to the same category. The expert specified the number of categories.

A multilayer hierarchical structure was used in [32,33] for fault-cause couples. The collection of current criteria was classified according to the knowledge of industry professionals. Counters were utilized in this study as an alternative for key performance indicators.

1.6. Compensating the Occurred Fault

The purpose of this section is to suggest relevant action to solve problems. In [10], these measures were divided into simple and parametric. Simple activities are those that can be executed without additional arguments. In other words, there is a direct relationship between the cause of the fault and the necessary measures to fix it. For example, if the cause of the fault is, in part, a hardware problem, the corresponding action is to send a technician to the site and replace that part. On the other hand, parametric measures are not easily determined and require the implementation of different algorithms. For example, if it is necessary to change the parameter value, its new value should be calculated. Since the number of parametric measures is large, it would be valuable to introduce an algorithm to identify the standards. To compensate for the fault in the study in [34], changing and resetting the parameters of neighboring cells, and optimizing the covered area by them, was utilized. Things such as filling the space of the disabled cell, resetting the antennas' power consumption, and choosing the correct value of the parameters through fuzzy logic and reinforcement learning were performed in this study. In general, the necessary measures in correcting the occurred fault depend entirely on the detected fault in the first step and the cause of the detected fault in the second step. Among the measures to fix the fault are resetting the parameters, reducing the angle of the antenna, or increasing the strength of the received signal by the user.

The distinctive feature of all past works is the limited view of the faults in the network because, by considering this field's data complexity and the uncertainty in the number of parameters assigned by experts for a model's relationships, it was difficult to consider a large number of network events. On the other hand, the accuracy of the obtained model from this method strongly depends on the expert's knowledge and the assigned value to each parameter. Thus, this article focuses on designing a model that can perform the initial stages of model construction with minimal dependence on expert opinion and only using available statistical information. In addition to reducing the model's dependency on humans, the accuracy of the produced model is increased by removing the effects of human error. The general framework of the conducted work of this article is illustrated in the following figure. As seen in Figure 2, this paper uses three types of data: performance support system data, drive test data, and customer contact center data. This paper's second and third sections discuss the first two sources of information. These three sources of information on the network mode can determine the existence of a problem in an area. In addition, using the information fusion methods, this system can automatically identify the fault causes in cellular networks with the help of three different data types.

The structure of this article is as follows. In the second section, after getting familiar with the indicators used in the qualitative assessment of the network condition and the types of faults affecting the value of each indicator, the essential source of available data, called the performance support system, is examined in detail. The results are evaluated to analyze the cause of a fault. The third section introduces another source of available fault diagnosis: drive test data. In the fourth section, after submitting the third source of data, subscriber complaints, the results of the previous two sections are reviewed and examined. Finally, in the fifth section, we summarize, conclude and provide a perspective for future work.

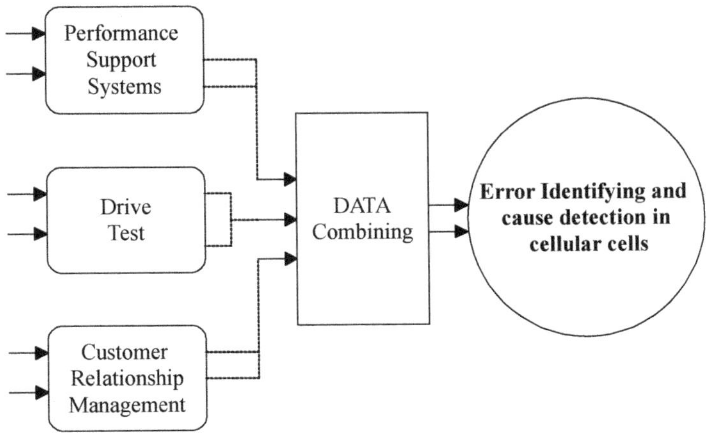

Figure 2. An overall framework of the conducted works in this paper.

2. Performance Support System

As mentioned in the previous section, one of the used data sources in troubleshooting cellular networks is the available data in the performance support system. This system collects statistical data reported from transmitter and receiver base stations. This data examines the network mode from various aspects. Key indicators are calculated using counters that record all the events that have occurred in the network. These key indicators, comprehensively explained below, are evaluated to troubleshoot in the performance management part of cellular networks. The values of these indicators determine the cause of the fault in the system, and help industry experts improve the system's performance. The data we used was supported by the Mobile Telecommunications Center (Hamrahe-Avval). These data were related to Tehran's eighth district and included 50 primary transmitter and receiver stations.

In the following, we first make a preliminary statement about the channels used in the cellular network and the process of making calls in these networks. We examine the measured indicators in the performance support system in detail, and, finally, we describe the applied method in regard to these data.

2.1. Definitions, Principles, and Theoretical Foundations

The first step in troubleshooting cellular networks is to identify faulty cells. A problem in the network refers to a situation that hurts the quality of network service. Different operators use different methods to identify issues in the network. It is first necessary to know the cellular network and the key performance indicators in troubleshooting in the network to identify its network faults.

2.1.1. Standalone Dedicated Control Channel (SDCCH) Signaling Channel

This channel is dedicated to subscriber signaling activities. Among these activities, we can mention the basic steps to making a call, updating the physical location of subscribers, and sending and receiving short messages. Each subscriber occupies a capacity of the signaling channel before making a call in the network.

2.1.2. Traffic Channel (TCH)

This channel, accounting for about 75% of the radio resource range, is used to transm sound in the network. The network signaling channel provides about 25% of the netwo resource capacity.

2.1.3. Key Performance Indicator (KPI)

The key performance indicators in the cellular network management literature a measures that can be used to measure the quality of a network at different levels. Some these indicators depend on time or user behavior, such as the number of downlinks to th user. Other indicators, such as the channel quality indicator (CQI), random channel acce attempts (RCATs), or the percentage of dropped calls, due to lack of dependency on th user program used on the user side, are less related to the user's behavior, so the indicato of this category are more suitable for evaluating the network condition. Telecommunicatic networks are changeable, and there are several key performance indicators to asse network condition. Using manual methods to solve network problems does not meet th management needs of these networks.

Many indicators are used to evaluate the quality of radio networks, and by saving th fault-free behavior of each KPI, its deviation from its normal behavior can be identifie The high number of these indicators, and the related counters to each one, have mad it impossible to check all the indicators and the impact of each one on the quality of th network. In the following, we examine the steps of establishing a call in a cell networ Then we introduce the most important indicators affecting the network mode, submitte by experts in this field.

2.1.4. Procedures for Making a Call

From the moment the subscriber initiates a call to when the traffic channel is su cessfully assigned to him or her, various steps are performed in the network. In Figure the different stages are illustrated, along with the indicators used to measure the stati tical status of the network. These indicators are fully explained in the following part this section.

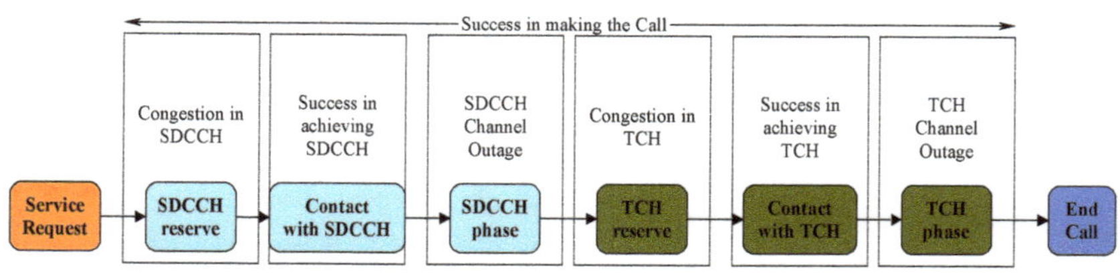

Figure 3. The steps of making a call in the GSM network with the network performance measur ment indicators.

2.1.5. Introducing the Most Important Key Performance Indicators

As seen in the above figure, several indicators measure the network quality fro different aspects. For this purpose, before identifying faults in a network, it is first necessar to thoroughly examine these indicators and the factors that affect them.

1. **SDCCH Congestion**

Traffic channels in radio networks carry the main network load, while control an signaling channels are used to achieve this goal. These channels are used to control th behavior of mobile phones, to communicate, to control established calls, to facilitate ca handover, etc. If subscribers' demands exceed the available resources, congestion occurs i this channel. One solution to this problem is adding more resources and physical capacit to the network resources.

2. **SDCCH establishes success rate**

This indicator shows the percentage of successful requests to take over SDCCH. One of the reasons for a negative value for this index is downlink interference, which occurs when there are too many subscribers' location updates, due to network design issues, and hardware issues.

3. **SDCCH drop**

When a network user makes a request to communicate with another subscriber, or when a network user is called by another network subscriber (through an incoming call), there is a need to take over the SDCCH. Some reasons, such as the timing advanced (TA) timer, low strength of the downlink or uplink signal or both, or low quality of the downlink or uplink signal, affect the SDCCH drop. In addition, if the traffic channel is congested, the requested call is returned on the SDCCH.

4. **SDCCH means holding time**

This index indicates the required capability of the SDCCH for high-speed access. That is, it measures the mean time the channel is held due to switching between services. The longer this time, the worse the service provided.

5. **TCH Congestion**

Congestion in the network means insufficient resources are available to make calls on the network. Congestion in the traffic channel is one of the most critical problems of the radio network, and it strongly affects the quality of the network. Congestion leads to higher subscriber dwell time in the SDCCH. One of the ways to reduce congestion in the network is to use more radio resources. Unfortunately, there are many limitations in terms of economy, lack of space for installing resources, etc. Therefore, it is recommended to use other methods, such as using the "half rate" technique. In this method, each period is assigned to two subscribers instead of serving one subscriber. Although the use of half-rate improves the network congestion situation, it reduces the quality of the received signal by the user. Another way to deal with congestion is to share the traffic load of the cell and transfer calls to neighboring cells. Like the half-rate technique, this method has the problem of reducing service quality.

6. **TCH Assignment Success Rate**

This indicator directly affects the user experience and shows the TCH assignment success rate percentage. If there is congestion in the traffic channel, the value of this index decreases. Other factors, such as the amount of coverage, interference, and hardware problems, also reduce the percentage of this index.

7. **Call Setup Success Rate**

This indicator, one of the most important key performance indicators used by all mobile phone operators, indicates the successfully launched call rate. There is no single standard method for measuring this index; therefore, every operator can calculate it differently. High values of this attribute indicate good network performance because a high percentage of calls are successfully established. Many reasons can be listed for inappropriate values of this index, including weakness in signal strength, congestion in the traffic and signaling channels, disconnection in the SDCCH, and failure in the appointment of the TCH.

8. **Call drop Rate**

Once the user has successfully taken over the traffic channel, due to various reasons, he or she may lose connection with the network during the call. The most important reasons that lead to the interruption of a call within a network are weak power and poor signal quality. Improper coverage of the radio path, hardware faults, and non-optimal setting of parameters affect the signal strength. Interference, issues related to coverage and handover (neighbor loss, incorrect settings in positioning algorithms), and, finally, the wrong set c parameters, can also cause deterioration of the quality of the signal received by the user.

9. **Handover**

The handover process is conducted by controlling positioning algorithms. Each BS(measures some information, such as the downlink signal strength and quality of th mobile user and the downlink signal strength and quality of the user's six best neighbor when making a handover decision. The "Handover failure Rate" index provides valuabl information, such as the efficiency between two neighbors, the strength or weaknes of the typical radio path between two neighbors, issues related to interference at th border between two neighbors, etc. In addition, to identifying weak neighbors in th radio path, handover optimization is used to improve the call failure percentage due t handover failure. Therefore, the incorrect design of neighborhoods, traffic congestio at the destination, and the fault of swapped sectors in implementing antennas lead t handover failure.

10. **UL/DL (UpLink/DownLink) Signal Quality**

This indicator, which has been introduced in the previous sections as one of the reason for success or failure in the most important network quality assurance indicators, calculate the quality of the sent signal through the base transmitter and receiver station to the use (the downlink signal), as well as the sent signal from the user to the station (the uplin signal). If the received signal strength by the user is less than the amount specified i the existing settings of each operator, the user's call is disconnected. In addition to signa quality affecting the increase or decrease of the call disconnection rate, other factors. suc as access to the traffic channel and signaling interrupted in the signaling channel, etc. ca also play a part.

11. **The amount of half-rate capacity usage**

There is no such measurement indicator in the base transmitter and receiver statio Still, in the transmitter and receiver station, the network's transmission traffic is measure at the total and half rate. The half-rate capacity is the high number of call requests in a area, which cannot increase the power in that area. Therefore, they reduce the call quality i such areas by converting the full-rate channel to half-rate to cover more calls and suppor more calls. This article uses this feature to identify the amount of network load.

For each KPI, it should be determined whether it functions similarly to its profile o whether it has a specific statistical change compared to it. One of the available ways t check this situation is to define a threshold on the KPI values and divide the range of thei values into two categories: above the threshold and below the threshold. More advance techniques for fault detection involve checking whether each KPI passes the threshol value continuously for a specific time or passes the threshold value a certain number o times. All threshold-based methods face the problem of quantizing the range of KPI value into a binary space below the threshold and above the threshold. However, this mean other helpful information is lost, and it is impossible to reliably detect faults from thes data. In the following, the architecture of the proposed method, in regard to these data is explained.

2.2. Architecture of the Proposed Method

To achieve the goal of this research, which was to detect a fault and identify its cause we used the following framework. In the next part, we explain this architecture's differen aspects in detail (Figure 4). The work process entailed preparing the available data, whic was the raw data received from a BSC in Tehran, for the next operation. To ensure dat validity, it was necessary to consider only the high traffic hours of the day. Since the data were, in fact, statistical characteristics of the network condition, they were reliable and valid only if the frequency of the used network was acceptable [10].

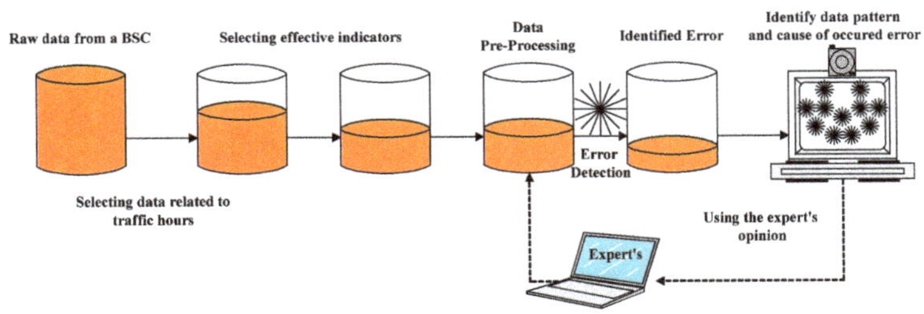

Figure 4. Architecture of the proposed method with performance support system data.

Among dozens of measured characteristics in network equipment, only some indicators, having the most significant impact on achieving the goal, were considered. Then, data preprocessing and cleaning operations were performed. After that, for fault detection in the system, a criterion for evaluating the quality of the network was introduced to detect the unfavorable network mode by examination of this value. Identified faults were entered into the next stage of the model to identify the cause of a fault. We tried to determine the cause of a fault that occurred in the network by using clustering algorithms. Finally, the obtained results were shared with an expert for evaluation. According to the expert's opinion, any necessary changes were applied to the model, and the process was repeated [35].

2.3. Feature Selection

After selecting the valid data, the first step to working with the data was to choose the effective indicators and features to achieve the goals. There are two ways to do this. One makes use of feature selection algorithms, and the other uses expert knowledge to select the most practical features. Since our available data was not marked to identify the cause of faults in the network, the only known solution was to use unsupervised algorithms and methods. Due to the problems in the field of feature selection in unsupervised methods, expert knowledge was used to select compelling features. In addition, since the foundation of this research was based on the industry and experts' opinions, trusting the experts' views, and following the industry's applied policies, could help us achieve the goals of this research. Therefore, the selection of features in this research was based on expert opinion.

2.4. Data Preprocessing

Since our method was based on data and all the results of our work were the result of working on the data, it was necessary to prepare the data for operations to increase the method's accuracy. The management of the missing values and the identification and removal of outliers were among the actions taken to clean the data before performing other operations on the data. Thus, all records containing missing values and outliers were removed from the data to simplify the work.

In addition, because the value of the analyzed indicator occurred in different intervals, it was necessary to replicate the index interval before applying any operation to the data. For this purpose, we used the minimum–maximum normalization method. Thus, the set of values of each index would be in the range of zero and one. To normalize each index with the minimum–maximum plan, after obtaining the minimum and maximum values of each index, the value of the index in each record was subtracted from the minimum value, and the result divided by the effect of removing the maximum values from the minimum, which indicated the data range. The following relationship shows this method [4,36,37].

Equation (1): normalizing data by the minimum–maximum method:

$$Normalized\ Value = \frac{the\ value - min(values)}{data\ range} \tag{1}$$

2.5. Fault Detection

Cellular networks are not immune to faults due to equipment, weather conditions, ar user behavior. Various faults reduce the quality of network service. An alarm is generated the system for any abnormal situation in the network. The high volume of generated aler in network management systems has dramatically reduced the possibility of using the alerts in a targeted and effective way. They are used only in unique and rare cases. The ke performance indicators discussed in detail in the previous section were the basis of our wo and, in fact, the origin of the work of the operators' performance management departme Since our method was completely designed based on the industry and operators an related industries' needs, and was completely practical, it was used to detect faults in term of the standard used by Iranian operators.

2.5.1. Defining the Network Quality Assessment Criteria

Fault detection is the most straightforward step in self-healing systems and network The complete, correct call rate (CCC) was the method used in the first mobile operat for fault detection and was the basis of our work. Therefore, only one criterion wa used to check the network status. As mentioned in the previous section, there are mar indicators to measure the quality of the network in different sectors and parts, each which examines the network from only one perspective and the statistical informatio provided by each index is based on one of the aspects of the network. The research tea of Sofrehcom Company provided a measure using indicators and criteria to evaluate th network condition. This criterion was obtained as the product of the following indicato

1. Congestion percentage in the signaling channel (SD-Cong)
2. Success in signaling channel adjustment (SDestab)
3. Certain percentage in the signaling channel (SDdrop)
4. Traffic channel congestion percentage (TCHcong)
5. Traffic channel assigning failure rate (TCHAssignFR)
6. Mean uplink and downlink signal quality (RxQual)
7. Disconnection in traffic channel (DCR)

Equation (2): Calculating the qualitative measure of network performance:

$$\begin{aligned} \text{CCC} &= (1-\text{SDcong}) * \text{SDestab} * (1-\text{SDdrop}) * (1-TCHcong) \\ &\quad * (1-TCHAssignFR) * RxQuality * (1-DCR) \end{aligned} \quad (2$$

As can be seen, the CCC index consisted of the product of the seven most importar indices. Therefore, if only one index had an unfavorable situation, its value would affe the result and the value of the CCC index. Therefore, by examining the importance of onl one index, the status of the most important indicators of the network could be acquire The fault detection process was performed by checking the value and behavior of th index during one month of available data. In this process, a histogram diagram of th index's monthly behavior was drawn in the investigated area, and the knees of the grap were evaluated as characteristic points in the behavior of the index. This method wa used to discretize the performance of an index in a period into general categories, such a good, normal, bad, and unacceptable in [38]. Our priority was to work on a set of record that were in worse condition. This meant that network performance management an optimization departments had to first check the network parts in a worse situation. Afte troubleshooting these parts, other parts of the network could be inspected and evaluate Therefore, we focused on the worst aspects and cells of the network. Other analyses an reviews were conducted on this part, and we reviewed different parts of the network.

2.5.2. Indicators' Analysis

As discussed in the previous section, we considered parts of the network as havin faults and unacceptable status using the CCC index. We investigated the parts of th network that needed quick reaction and action to improve the conditions. Therefore, ou data was divided into fault and non-fault categories. As a result, we could use classification algorithms, including a decision tree, to analyze the network status and check indicators. The questions we sought to answer in this section included the following [10]:

1. Which indicators play a more effective role in fault detection?
2. Which combination of values of indicators leads to faults in the system?
3. The value of which indicators have a higher impact on creating faults in the network?
4. In general, what are the indicators of network faults caused by violations?

2.6. Identifying the Fault Cause

Identifying the cause of the fault was the most crucial goal of this research. It was necessary to perform several actions on the data to achieve this goal. Therefore, at first, the list of effective indicators was selected, according to expert opinion, from dozens of measured indicators in operators. In the next step, the non-deterministic relationship between the causes of fault and the values of the considered indicators was checked. The non-deterministic relationship meant that, for a specific cause of fault, the value of an index might be different at different times and in other cells.

On the other hand, the variance of the values of an index for a specific fault caused at different times and in different cells might be significant. Therefore, it would be challenging to find an index that had an unusual behavior for a particular cause of fault [39]. The figure below shows the probability distribution of different index values in the face of other faults in the network. As can be seen in Figure 5, it was impossible to deduce the fault caused by only considering the index value.

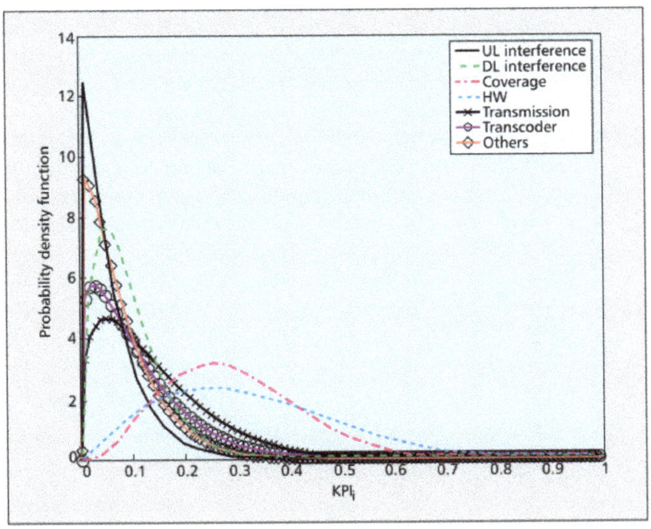

Figure 5. The possible distribution of different indicator values facing different faults.

In addition to identifying the necessary action to fix the fault, sometimes it is essential to consider the cost of doing so. Sometimes it is possible to do a replacement at a lower price. For example, if there is a hardware problem and the solution is to replace that part, it is better to restart it due to its low cost. Cost can include the cost of implemented time, the cost of executed action, its price on the network, etc. In the following, we review the steps to identify the fault caused.

2.6.1. Examining the Data Tendency to Clustering

The most important and main step in self-healing networks is identifying the cause of the fault. Since the available data were raw data, not labeled for the reason faults occurred, it could be said that the information was unsuitable for classification methods. It was necessary to prepare the data for clustering methods.

Since the data of cellular networks have not been used in clustering methods in these dimensions, it was necessary to ensure the clustering capability of the data. For this purpose the Hopkins coefficient was used. The Hopkins coefficient quantitatively indicates the data's tendency to cluster [40]. In this process, some random points are generated among other issues in the data and the distance between the random points and the fundamental points of the data is compared with the distance between two actual points in the data. In this way, it tries to ensure the non-randomness of the data pattern and the possibility of finding clusters that show the behavior of the data. The following relationship shows how to calculate this coefficient.

Equation (3): Hopkins' coefficient:

$$H = \frac{\sum_{i=1}^{n} q_i}{\sum_{i=1}^{n} q_i + \sum_{i=1}^{n} w_i} \quad (3)$$

where q_i represents the distance between the generated random points and the nearest real data records, and w_i represents the distance between the real records and the closest real neighbor in the data. In this way, the closer the value of the Hopkins coefficient to one, the more the data tends to be clustered.

2.6.2. Classification of Indicators

As mentioned before, it was necessary to select several indicators to perform operations on the data from dozens of indicators measured in managing cellular networks. Considering the characteristics of the cellular network, such as the dynamism and high variability of these networks, the simultaneous use of all these features would not lead to proper clustering of the data. On the other hand, since the steps of making a call and using the cellular network are two separate parts of receiving the signaling channel and receiving the traffic channel, these indicators have good separation capability. Therefore, the segmentation of the feature space was achieved according to expert opinion to increase the accuracy of the clustering algorithms and to obtain more favorable results from a practical point of view. Table 1 represents the list of indicators used according to the division.

Table 1. The list of indicators used in the traffic channel.

Signaling Part	
The indicator's name	the Persian equivalent
SD-Congestion	SD channel congestion percentage
SD-Drop	Communication percentage on SD channel
SD-Estab	SD channel selection success rate
CDR	Communication percentage on TCH channel
TCH-Congestion	The percentage of congestion on the TCH channel
TCH-Assign-FR	TCH channel adoption failure percentage
RxQuality	Average uplink and downlink signal quality

2.6.3. Data Clustering

The purpose of this step was to find meaningful clusters in the data. This meant trying to estimate the cause of faults in the system by finding meaningful patterns of network behavior in the data. Since any fault occurring in the network affects the value of one or more features simultaneously, the fault's cause could be estimated by considering the distribution of indicators in each cluster. The results obtained at this stage were provided to the expert to evaluate and interpret the distribution of data in each cluster, as well as to take a comprehensive look at the values of all indicators related to each category. In the next section, we discuss the obtained results from experts in detail. So, our goal at this stage was to find clusters that could model the behavior of the data well.

Among the clustering methods, various methods were applied to the data. Among these methods, the Expectation-Maximization process provided a more suitable answer to our data. The details of the results obtained in evaluating different clustering methods are described in the next section. In the following, we explain the mechanism and working method of the EM algorithm.

The Expectation-Maximization algorithm, or EM method, is an iterative algorithm that estimates maximum likelihood. This algorithm starts with an initial estimate of θ and iteratively improves this initial estimate toward the observed data. This algorithm should be continued until the difference between the two estimates, 1 + t, and the estimate number, t, is less than the threshold limit (Algorithm 1). Otherwise, the convergence condition is satisfied, and the algorithm ends. In the following, we review the steps of this algorithm, where i represents the ring index, θ represents the estimate, and T represents the threshold limit for the algorithm to end [41].

Algorithm 1 Expectation-Maximization method 1 begin initialize θ^0, T, i = 0

Architecture of the proposed method with performance support system data:

```
Start
Raw data from a BSC
        Selecting effective indicators
        Data Pre-Processing
        Selecting data related to traffic hours
        Identified Fault
        Identify data pattern and cause of occurred fault

  begin initialize θ^0, T, i = 0
            do i → i + 1
            E step: compute Q (θ ; θ^i)
            M step: θ^{i+1} → argmax Q (θ ; θ^i)
            until Q (θ^{i+1} ; θ^i)–Q (θ^I ; θ^{i−1}) ≤ T
  return θ̂ θ^{i+1}
  end
```

By experimenting with the data set, the detailed results of which are given in the next section, the EM method was selected from other clustering methods to categorize the available data. Due to the complexity and dispersion of data in this field, to achieve quality clusters, parts of the data that were not well clustered were re-clustered with the EM algorithm, and the results obtained were provided to the expert for final evaluation.

2.6.4. Evaluation of Produced Clusters

In this step, we evaluated the obtained clusters. Due to the lack of access to the gold data, we used intrinsic measures to evaluate the clustering results with the correct mode. Intrinsic measures assess the quality of obtained clusters without the need for external information. For example, the criteria that check the degree of adhesion or separability of the data in a cluster are among the internal criteria for evaluating clusters. On the other side are external measures. These criteria, which are supervised methods, are used when gold data are available, and the quality of clustering algorithms can be evaluated by comparing them with the target data [42]. In the following, we consider the internal methods that were compatible with the limitations of the work in this project and were used to evaluate the produced clusters. It should be noted that the same coefficients were used to obtain the optimal number of clusters, and the value of these coefficients was calculated for different numbers of clusters. The optimal value of these coefficients indicated the optimal number of clusters.

The Davies–Bouldin method is one of the most common ways of internally evaluating clusters obtained in clustering algorithms. The problem with this algorithm is that its excellent evaluation value does not use all the hidden information in the data and does not recover all the information [43]. The Silhouette coefficient, another internal evaluation measure of clustering methods [44], was used in this research. Both of these methods are based on the stickiness of the data in one cluster and the separability of the data with respect to other clusters. In the following, we review the details of these two methods.

✓ Silhouette Coefficient Method

The Silhouette coefficient is one of the most common ways of internally evaluating clusters obtained in clustering algorithms, and is based on calculating data adhesion and separability. Unlike the Davies–Bouldin method, which considers only the centers of the clusters, this method performs its calculations on all the points of the clusters. The general relationship below shows how to calculate the Silhouette coefficient.

Equation (4): The general formula for calculating the Silhouette coefficient:

$$S(o) = \frac{b(o) - a(o)}{max\{a(o), b(o)\}} \quad (4)$$

where *a(o)* indicates the cluster stickiness containing record o and is calculated through the following relationship.

Equation (5):

$$a(o) = \frac{\sum_{o' \in C_i, o' \neq o} dist(o, o')}{|C_i| - 1} \quad (5)$$

And

Equation (6):

$$b(o) = \min_{C_j : 1 \leq j \leq N} \left\{ \frac{\sum_{o' \in C_j} dis(o, o')}{|C_j|} \right. \quad (6)$$

where $dis(o, o')$ calculates the Euclidean distance between two points of o and o'. Therefore $a(o)$ calculates the average distance of point o with all the points that are in the same cluster with o. The value $b(o)$ also calculates the average distance for all clusters from point o with all points that are not in the same cluster with o. Finally, for each cluster, the Silhouette coefficient value is obtained by averaging the values of S_i in each cluster. The following figure shows an interpretation of Silhouette coefficient values for two clusters. In fact, the value of this coefficient is between -1 and 1. If b_i which indicates the distance of each point from other points that are not in the same cluster, is smaller than a_i, which indicates the distance of points within a cluster, the result of the Silhouette coefficient is smaller than zero and has negative values. The closer the value of this coefficient to 1, the more correct is the assignment of each point to the cluster similar to itself. If the value of this coefficient is zero, it means that the point is located on the border between two clusters (Figure 6).

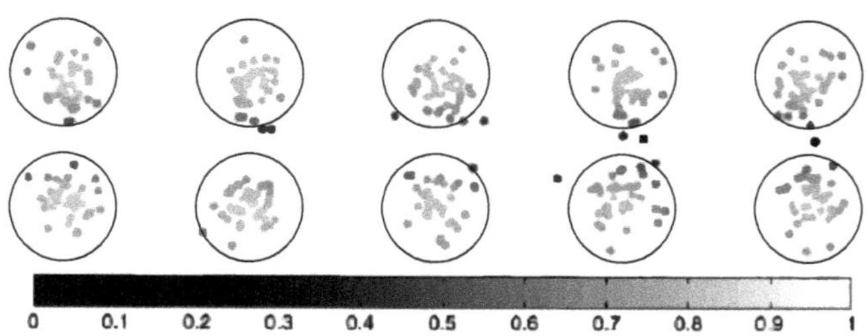

Figure 6. The Silhouette coefficient values' interpretation.

3. Results

In this part, we examine the obtained results from the data analysis of the performance support system. For this purpose, we first introduce the used data in this research and then report the obtained results.

3.1. Introduction of the Data Set

This data set, which included the most essential and central part of our work, contained statistical indicators of the quality mode of the network, which were collected by the transmitter and receiver base stations in real time. These data were averaged every hour and sent to the operators. The available data for conducting this research was the result of an hourly average of the events and the statistical status of the network, which was made available to the researcher in cooperation with the mobile telecommunication company (Hamrahe Avval).

These data contained statistical information on network quality measurement indicators at the covered points. Since the cellular network was very dynamic and complex and the volume of generated data was very high, we started the work by choosing one of the worst base station controllers in Tehran. This controller is located in District 8 of Tehran and covers a considerable part of this area. The data contained 64,114 records. Among the 70 indicators and features of this data, 14 indicators were selected by experts to achieve the goal of this research. The characteristics and impact of each on the network's quality and the cause of the occurred fault in the network were investigated.

Table 2 provides the evaluated the statistical characteristics of these indicators. Since the values of different indices have different distributions, the minimum–maximum normalization method was used to normalize the data.

Table 2. Statistical status of the used indicators.

The Indicator's Name	Mean	Standard Deviation
CSSR	0.950793	0.106
CDR	0.0412	0.068
HSR	0.832	0.2735
HTr-Rate *	0.3408	0.4048
SDCCH-Congestion-Rate	0.0555	0.18109
TCH-Congestion-Rate	0.0401	0.11137
SDCCH_DR	0.0448	0.1404
SDCCH-MHT	0.0707	0.076
SDCCH-Assign-Success-Rate	0.4676	0.4249
TCH-ASSIGN-FAIL-RATE	0.0478	0.0672
RX-QUAL-DL	0.8485	0.1394
RX-QUAL-UL	0.4080	0.4847
Random-Access-Success-Rate	0.6765	0.4295
TCH-Availability	0.9366	0.1233

* The HTr_Rate feature is the ratio of the traffic carried on the half-rate channel to the total traffic of that station.

The histogram of the CDR call drop rate indicator, which shows the drop rate in calls, is shown in Figure 7. As is clear in the figure, for some samples, the value of this index was higher than the threshold and, therefore, it indicated a problem in the records.

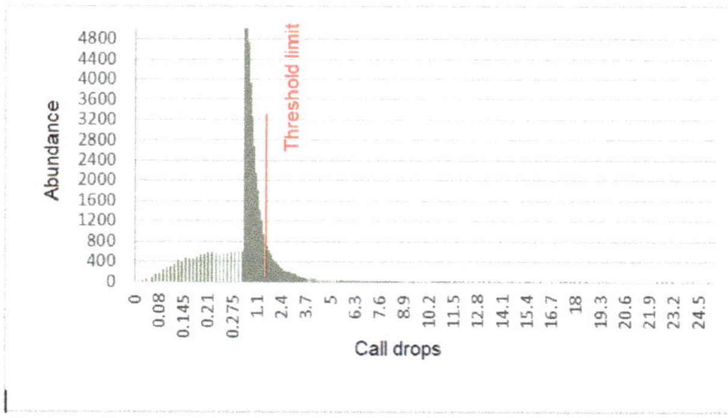

Figure 7. The histogram of the dropped calls in the data.

3.2. The Definition of Quality Criteria and Indicators Analysis

After selecting the features and pre-processing the data, the criterion for checking the quality status of the network was introduced. The evaluation criterion was the CCC index which is obtained from the multiplication of a number of the most important indices. The histogram of this index was derived from 64,115 records and is illustrated in Figure 8.

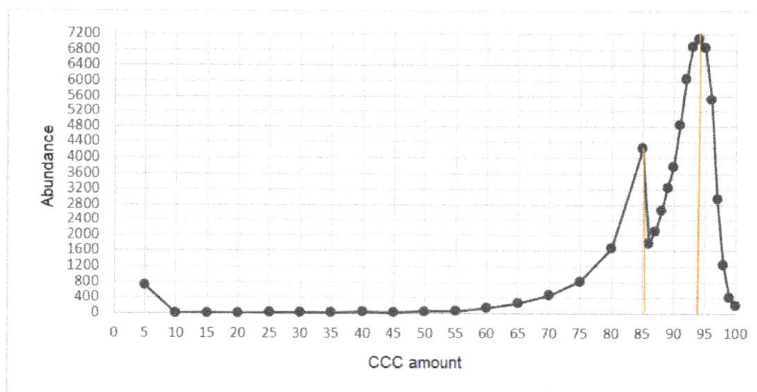

Figure 8. The histogram of CCC index value in one month of the examined data.

As expected, and as can be seen in the above diagram, the range of numerical values of CCC was between 0 and 100. Values close to 100 indicated higher quality. In Figure 8 there are two knees. Therefore, we divided the network status into three discrete categories. The first category had a CCC value higher than 94 and represented excellent quality. The second category had a CCC between 94 and 85 and represented acceptable quality. Several records fell into the third category, having a CCC less than 85. This category represented unacceptable quality of the network, and, therefore, our work priority was to focus on the data of the third category, the unacceptable category. From now on, we considered the records with CCC less than 85 as faults and identified the cause of the fault in these records.

Before addressing the issue of identifying the cause of the fault, an analysis of the values of these indicators was conducted. To do this, we used classification algorithms and, especially, a decision tree. The reason for using the decision tree algorithm is this method's display ability and its good interpretation ability. In decision tree algorithms the Quest method is used. This method had high accuracy for our provided data and this accuracy was obtained at a lower tree depth. Therefore, it avoided the problem of overfitting the model on the training data. The following tree separated the test data with 93.66% accuracy. The results were obtained with the help of Clementine software. It can be seen that among the 14 features used by experts in these networks to analyze the quality status, and among the seven indicators used in defining the quality criteria of the network, only three indicators, those of call interruption, interruption in the signaling channel, and the success rate in achieving the signaling channel, could estimate the network status (Figure 9).

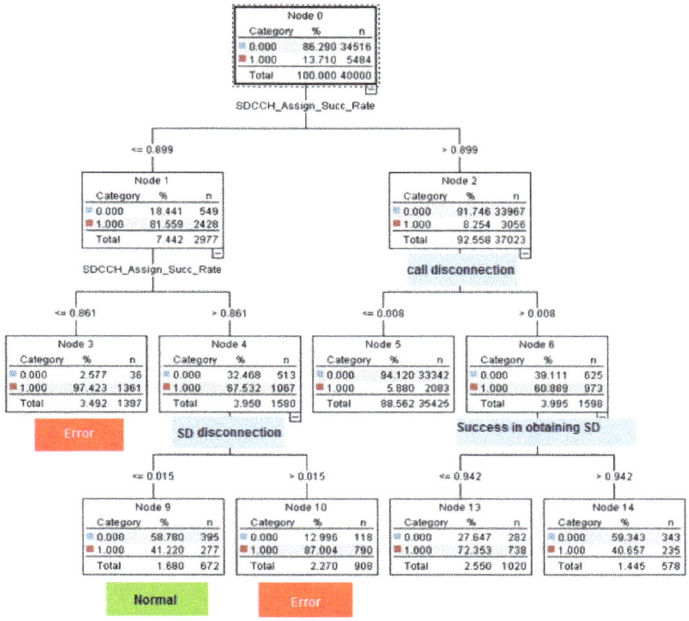

Figure 9. A schematic of the data production tree with two fault and non-fault categories by the use of Quest algorithm.

3.3. Clustering Analysis and Fault Cause Identification

In this section, we examine the results obtained from the clustering performed on the performance support system data. In clustering, the data is generally divided into traffic and signaling data categories. The results of each type and their analysis are given in the following. First, the traffic clusters were checked, and then the signaling clusters were studied. As mentioned before, the characteristics used in the traffic section included:

- The percentage of communication failure in the TCH channel.
- The percentage of congestion in the TCH channel.
- The percentage of loss in adopting the TCH channel.
- The average quality of the uplink and downlink signals.

The clustering results of different methods are shown in Figure 10.

As illustrated in the above figure, the Expectation-Maximization clustering method provided a better response to the data than other methods. In addition, the optimal number of clusters was 5. Therefore, the EM method was applied to the data with several 5 clusters. The information related to this clustering was provided to the expert, and the expert comments, confirming the correctness of the obtained clusters, are given below, along with a view of the data distribution in each cluster. The data detected as faults were divided into traffic and signaling categories, and, as mentioned, the optimal number of clusters for the traffic data under consideration was 5. Therefore, one of these clusters indicated a favorable situation in the traffic cluster, which meant that the problem was only in the signaling data, and the system had no problem in terms of traffic.

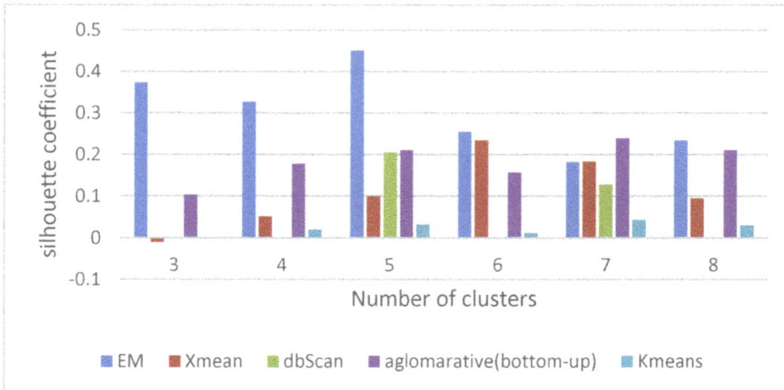

Figure 10. Silhouette coefficient according to the number of clusters for different clustering method traffic section.

A similar situation existed for signaling data. The problem was that some records on had traffic issues (Figure 11). The allocated records in (c) suffered from high outliers i the SD channel and the capacity problem. SD channel congestion and outages are of gre importance, due to their direct impact on the shared network experience. Some influenti factors in increasing the absolute value of this channel are the coverage level, interferenc low quality, and instability of communication links in the Abis interface. Since there wa a congestion problem in this cluster, the probability of a coverage problem in this are was less than the probability of other reasons. On the other hand, the cut-off value in th cluster was much higher than the threshold. Therefore, the cause of the problem might b hardware problems. The congestion problem was very critical in (d). The behavior of th channel access success indicator was also unacceptable. Therefore, this cluster's record ha the problem of inadequate coverage, as well as low signal strength. Furthermore, thes sites should be checked for interference. Cluster (e) had the same problems as (d), in term of high cut-off value and failure to access the channel, but the difference was that there wa no congestion problem in this cluster. Finally, cluster (f) had a hardware problem, due t the wildly inappropriate success rate of reaching the signaling channel.

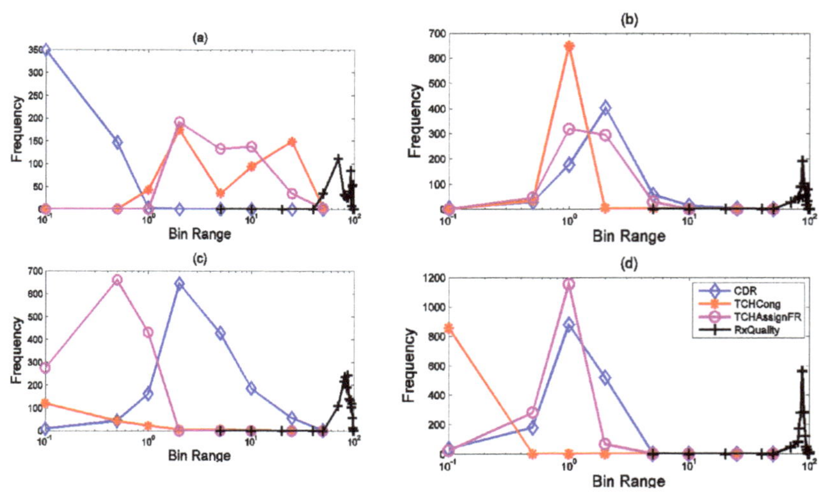

Figure 11. Indicators of statistical distribution of the signaling sector. Each cluster represents a moc of the network.

3.4. Evaluation of the Results

The expert was asked to label the new data records according to the obtained clusters to evaluate the results from the records clustering. For this purpose, traffic and signaling data documents were provided to the expert separately. Having the labels for the obtained clusters in the previous step, it was now possible to test the accuracy of the clustering results by running different classification algorithms and using the test data labeled by the expert.

Therefore, different classification algorithms were applied to the data in both traffic and signaling data parts. The evaluation results of the other models on the test data are given in Table 3. It should be noted that, due to the lack of balance in the training data in the records related to each class, Clementine software was used to balance the records of each type. This software was also used to apply different classification methods to the data. The number of training set records was 8006, and the number of traffic and signaling data test set records was 53.

Table 3. Evaluation of obtained clusters for traffic data.

Band Category Type	The Accuracy on Data Test
Neural Network–Rapid	86,54
Neural Network–RBFN	78,85
Neural Network–Dynamic	80,77
Quest decision tree	59,62
Support vector machine	82,69
Regression- band category tree	57,69

By obtaining the different classification methods' results, accuracies of 90.38%, 86.54%, and 78.85% for traffic data were obtained from some forms of summarizing opinions, such as voting, weighted voting concerning model confidence, and the highest confidence method. The standard voting method worked better on our data. The results of the used methods for the data of the signaling section are shown in the following table. The voting method is the best way to collect opinions, with an accuracy of 92.31. Other practices, including weighted voting, had an accuracy of 88.46 and 80.77 in relation to model confidence and the highest confidence (Table 4).

Table 4. Evaluation of obtained clusters for signaling data.

Band Category Type	The Accuracy on Data Test
Neural Network–Rapid	80,77
Neural Network–RBFN	88.46
Neural Network–Dynamic	78,85
Neural Network–General prune	80,77
Quest decision tree	59,62
Support vector machine	90,38
Decision tree categorizer–regression	71,15

3.5. A Comprehensive List of Identified Fault Causes of the Performance Support System Data

In the following part, a summary of the causes of faults in the cellular network is provided. The results obtained from numerous conversations with industry experts in the mobile network optimization department of the Mobile Communications Company (Hamrahe Avval) were collected.

Reason number 1: hardware problems, including transmitter failure, antenna feede failure, and combiner failure: the impact of these types of fault can be seen in call an indicator interruption in the signaling channel, failure rate in traffic channel assignmen and in the signal quality.

Reason number 2: hardware problems related to the link, containing several mode The first case is when the connection is completely disconnected, and the site is turned of The second mode refers to the time when the link is momentarily down and, therefore, ha a negative impact on the traffic channel availability index. The third case is related to type of problem in the system that cannot be traced by the value of the indicators and ca be identified according to the drive test (which is examined in detail in the next section In this case, the channel availability indicator does not indicate a problem, but the signa quality suffers due to the high Bit fault rate (BER). In some cases, this problem may also b reported by subscribers.

Reason number 3: Hardware problems caused by Abis interface failure. This happen when the number of signaling channels is insufficient compared to the region's demand and subscribers' demand. Therefore, the impact of this problem can be seen in the SDCCH Assign index.

Reason number 4: problems caused by overshooting. Overshooting is caused b improper design of sites and inappropriate coverage of a place in remote areas, and can b found by checking the value of the advanced timer. To solve this problem, it is necessary t change the physical characteristics of the antenna, such as its angle, height, and direction

Reason number 5: frequency interference, including interference in the BCCH channe and traffic channel. If the interference is in the BCCH channel, the traffic parameters ar also affected in addition to the signaling parameters. If the interference is in the traffi channel, only the traffic parameters are damaged.

Reason number 6: lack of capacity problems in the traffic and signaling channel. Th solution is to increase the capacity and define relevant features in the settings of cellula networks to allocate dynamic capacity to the required channels according to the networ traffic situation.

In this section, the method used to detect the fault and identify the cause of the faul in the network is examined in detail. The difference between this work and other simila works in this field can be divided into the following. First, unlike the vast majority o similar works, our method used actual data to identify the cause of the fault in the network Other similar works cannot model the mode of the network. Our proposed model consider all the essential statistical characteristics and indicators of the network at the same time This means that, unlike all the mentioned methods in the literature review section, it has a comprehensive view of the network and the fault types that occur in the network. Finally the proposed model has the most negligible dependence on expert opinion. This is even though most of the proposed methods depend on the expert to build the model and adjus the parameters. The expert's opinion in setting the parameters of the model may have a significant impact on the results obtained. Due to its negligible dependence on exper opinion, our model has the advantage of avoiding such significant impacts.

3.6. Drive Test

As mentioned in the first section, the second category of the used data in this research is the data related to drive test measurements. The drive test is a real test of the network to obtain detailed information about the location of the fault, how the antennas around the location signal, and to check the redistribution status in the routes. To perform this test the operators send a group of human resources to the site. The responsibility of human resources is to check the network quality from different perspectives. Various scenarios such as short calls, long calls, and non-calling mode or idle mode, are proposed by human power. The non-calling mode analyzes the mobile device's signal exchanges with the receiving station. The test is a method to measure and check the coverage status, network capability, and quality from a common point of view. The test is conducted by making a call through several mobile phones with software to control and record the reported measurements and parameters from the BTS side and the Global Positioning System (GPS). The measurements are transferred from the mobile phone to the computer. The measurements only report network mode from different perspectives and cannot identify the fault type and cause. In general, the drive test process consists of the following steps:

1. Setting the devices for the required measurements
2. Defining routes
3. Determining the testing time and type
4. Performing the test
5. Collecting data and related reports

Figure 12 shows the scope of conducting a drive test according to the division of urban areas and the boundaries between the central controller stations.

Figure 12. Drive test route map according to the division of urban areas and the border between base controller stations. The blue lines illustrate the 8 urban areas, the yellow lines illustrate the border between the base control stations, and the red lines illustrate the drive test route.

By analyzing the conducted measurements in the drive test, some results, such as determining blind spots and non-coverage, determining the displacement of the sector or the feeder, determining an area with interference, interruption of conversation, and failure in the transfer, are determined. In general, the identified faults list in the drive test is as follows:

1. Problems related to sector and feeder changing
2. Call interruption problems caused by interference and sector signal overshooting.
3. Interference problems that require checking assigned frequencies to nearby cells.
4. Problems related to outsourcing, which can be traced by adequately setting the neighborhoods, coverage area, and related parameters to outsourcing.
5. Problems related to the coverage area, which, by adjusting the height, power, and angle of the antenna, lead to a change in the design and, finally, the installation of a new site.

3.7. Definition of Different Scenarios in the Drive Test

In general, three different scenarios test the network condition in a drive test. Each of these three scenarios examines the network status from particular aspects, and various faults are identified in these scenarios. In the following, we describe each of the three scenarios.

Scenario number 1: Idle mode: In this situation, the responsible person for the test puts the mobile phone in idle mode. This means that phone calls cannot be made. This is to test the network in serving cell reselection when moving the mobile phone. In addition, the received signal level is measured at different points of the network, and the locations wi suitable signal levels are provided to the optimizer for further investigations.

Scenario number 2: Short calls: The short call scenario means evaluating the netwo in terms of call establishment parameters. That means assessing whether the mobile pho subscriber can easily make a call, and what the problems in the process of making a ca are, including access to the signaling and traffic channels. Call blocking parameters ar thriving network access rate are investigated in this scenario.

Scenario number 3: Long calls: The long call, unlike the short call, may be maintaine continuously during the drive test. This scenario aims to test the network in terms of ca interruption rate, conversation quality, received signal quality, and check reassignments

This article examines the problems affecting network service quality by reviewing a three scenarios. In the following, we first introduce the measured parameters in the driv test and then describe the process of identifying network problems in these three scenaric

3.8. Introducing the Measured Parameters

This section introduces the essential measured parameters in the drive test that for our feature vector. This information is used to design the network; for example, to achiev the correct redistribution and to control the radio signal's power.

1. Signal quality:

In some systems, such as UMTS, the signal quality parameter is directly dependent c the signal-to-noise ratio [45]. In other methods, such as GSM/GPRS, the signal quality is Bit or symbol fault rate function.

2. Signal level:

The received signal level is a measure to control the power of the received sign and the transmission at the place of receiving the signal. The accepted signal range b the mobile user is between −110 dbm and −48 dbm. The low level of the received sign can have several reasons. For example, consider a rural area where the distance to th base transmitter and receiver station is not suitable. This area receives a weak signal, du to the long distance to the BTS, and installing a new station is impossible due to hig cost. Another reason for the decrease in the signal level can be the presence of harmfu interference with other received signals in the area. In addition, some tall buildings cause rapid attenuation of the signal strength and, therefore, the signal inside the building is nc strong enough. An unacceptable signal level can lead to call termination [46].

3. Speech quality:

The literature on cellular networks measures speech quality with the SQI-MOS p rameter. In its calculation, an algorithm is used to consider the network mode, such a frame fault rate (FER), and bit fault rate. The algorithm can also calculate the coding typ used in speech transmission, which affects the speech quality level and the highest possib quality, by calculating the difference between the analyzed sound quality on the side of th transmitter and the receiver. The result is shown as a number between 1 and 5.

4. Carrier-to-Interference (C/I) Ratio:

One of the most effective and accurate methods for analyzing interference in comm nication channels is measuring the Carrier-to-Interference (C/I) Ratio. Route design an equipment design are two critical factors affecting the interference level. The neighborhoo of nearby systems that use the same frequency band is one of the apparent reasons fc interference, due to the wrong design of routes.

5. Advanced Timing:

In the literature in this field, advanced timing refers to the time it takes for the mobi phone signal to reach the base station. Since GSM uses multiple access technology, base on time division, to share a frequency band between different users and considering tha the users are located at an extra distance from the base station, this criterion can be used t estimate the distance of the user to the base station used.

3.9. The Architecture of Working with Drive Test Data

As mentioned in the previous section, to review the architecture of working with performance support system data and use the received data through field testing, it was necessary to take measures to identify the meaningful patterns from the data, according to the illustrated architecture in the following figure. Therefore, after collecting the raw data of the drive test, through the TEMS Investigation software, which was used to analyze these data, a report of the network mode was prepared, based on the scenario type and the characteristics and effective indicators by the use of expert opinion. These features were fully introduced in the previous section. To use the extracted data from this software, it was necessary to convert the data format into a usable format for the next steps. At this stage, we used MapInfo software to transform data into a.csv format for data mining and meaning recognition algorithms. The obtained data needed to be pre-processed. Therefore, it was necessary to clear this data before performing any operations. Then, appropriate algorithms were applied to the data to identify the meaningful patterns in the data, and, finally, the results were validated according to expert opinion. If there was a need to make changes in the model, the changes were applied, and again we used the expert to evaluate the results (Figure 13).

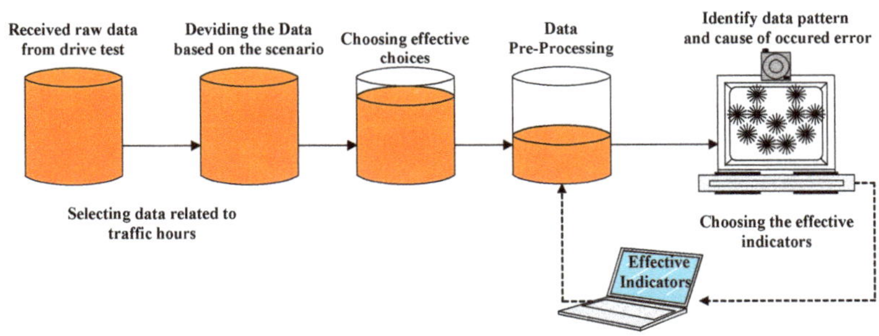

Figure 13. Architecture of working with drive test data.

3.10. Data Preprocessing

As mentioned in the previous section, there was a need for data pre-processing to obtain results with higher accuracy. Missing values and records containing outliers were removed from the data. Outliers were removed from the data by identifying the allowed values for each attribute. The used data in this section were ordinal data types. Ordinal discrete numbers are the same as categorical data, with the difference that the states in ordinal variable values have a meaningful order. To manage ordinal data, it is necessary first to establish correspondence between each data value and its corresponding rank so that the data falls in the interval of [1, Mf], where Mf is the number of different modes in the ordinal data for feature f. Since there are many other states for ordinal data, it is necessary to normalize the data to the interval [0,1] to prevent all features from having the same effect. So, if the i-th data rank in attribute f is rif, we have:

Equation (7): Normalization of ordinal data

$$z_{if} = \frac{r_{if} - 1}{M_f - 1} \tag{7}$$

To calculate the degree of similarity between two data records, it is possible to do the same for continuous data [10].

It should be noted that the available data that indicate the overall situation in a network are usually unbalanced because the network works well in most areas. There is a smaller percentage of points that have problems. Since the optimal range of all the used features in this research was included in the standard, we could separate the records in which the optimal degree of all variables were observed from the other data and label them as fault-free to investigate the problem of data imbalance. Therefore, by doing this, a significant amount of data was reduced, and would be more suitable for analyzing the cause of a fault in the network.

3.11. Identifying the Data Pattern and Identifying the Fault Cause

To divide the data into meaningful categories, it was necessary to apply different clustering algorithms to the data, according to the examined scenarios and the results obtained from the evaluation of the clusters. The best separating algorithm should be identified from the drive test data. Since the data of this part was similar to the data of the last section, it was raw data, and it was impossible to use external criteria to evaluate the correctness of the obtained results. It was necessary to use internal performance evaluation criteria to assess the obtained clusters. The standard for evaluating the clustering of the drive test data was also similar to the performance support system data, namely, the Silhouette coefficient. It should be noted that to ensure the ability to cluster the data, the Hopkins coefficient was applied to the data of each scenario. The obtained result for the scenario of the idle mode was 0.88%, and for the long call it was 0.94%. Therefore, the data had good capability for clustering. The analysis of the obtained results, according to different scenarios, is given in the following part. Table 5 summarizes the related information to the features examined in this test.

Table 5. A summary of the statistical information of the used features.

Feature's Name	Minimum	Maximum	Optimal Interval (Standard)
Carrier-to-interference ratio	5	25	≥25, <35
Signal level	−101	−31	More than −65
Signal quality	0	7	Less than 3
Call quality	0	4.1	Equal to 3.9
Advanced timing	0	3	Less than 1

Scenario number 1, Idle mode: This tests the received signal level at different points of the network. Locations with inadequate signal levels are reported to the optimizer for further investigation. According to the characteristics that were considered in this scenario including the signal level, the ratio of the carrier power to the interference and the advanced scheduler, and the number of optimal clusters, which were of three numbers, according to the expert's opinion, after data pre-processing, we had the results indicated in Figure 14.

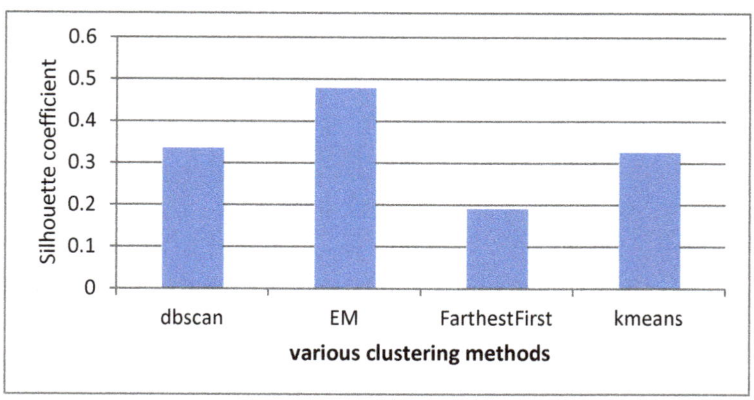

Figure 14. Silhouette coefficient on the idle mode scenario with the number of 3 clusters.

Therefore, on the drive test data in the idle state scenario, the estimation maximization (EM) method provided a more suitable answer than other methods. A more complete description of the obtained clusters' characteristics is given in Table 6.

Table 6. The details of Clusters and Feature's name.

Feature's Name	Cluster 1	Cluster 2	Cluster 3
Signal level	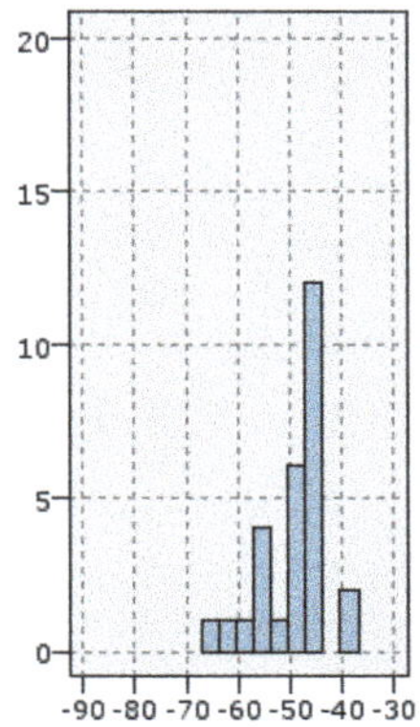	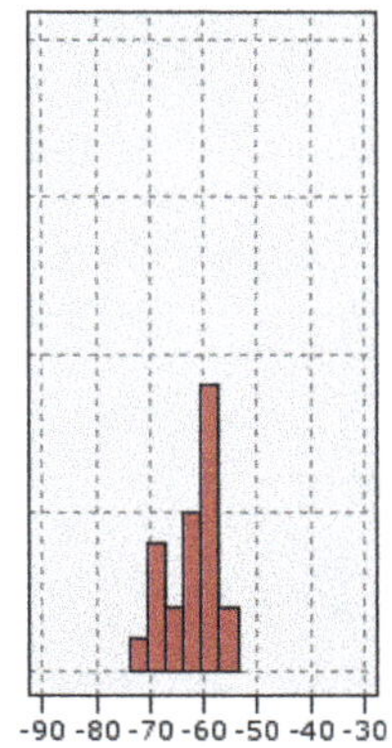	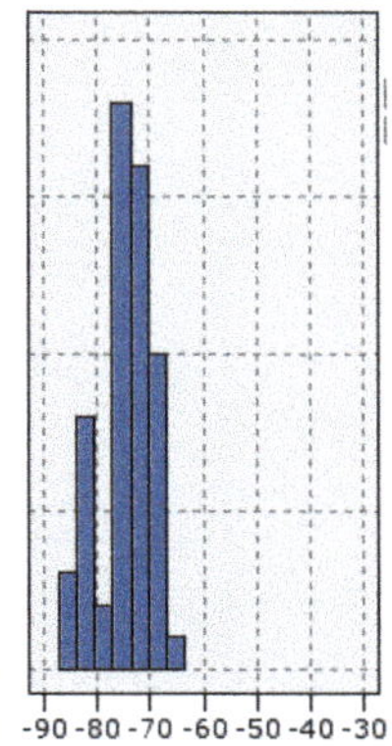
Carrier-to-interference ratio	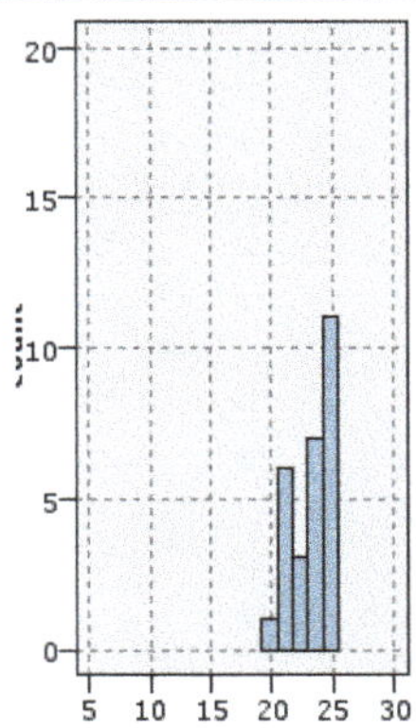	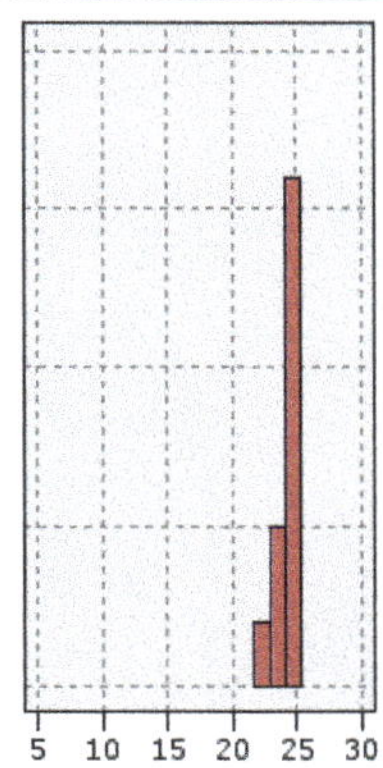	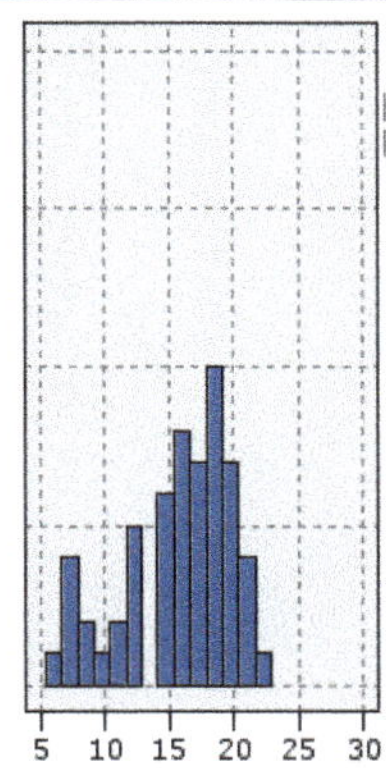
Advanced timing	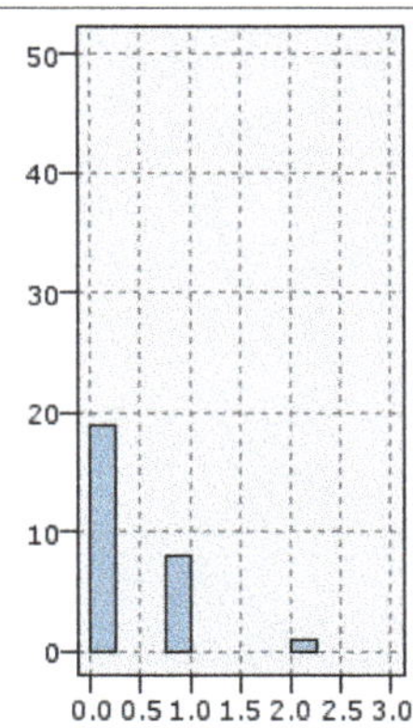	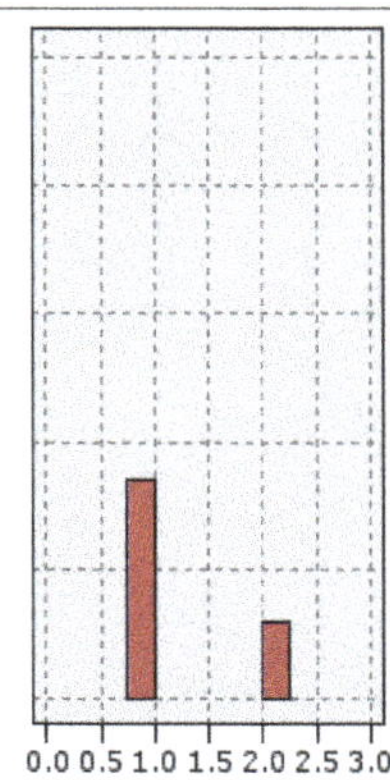	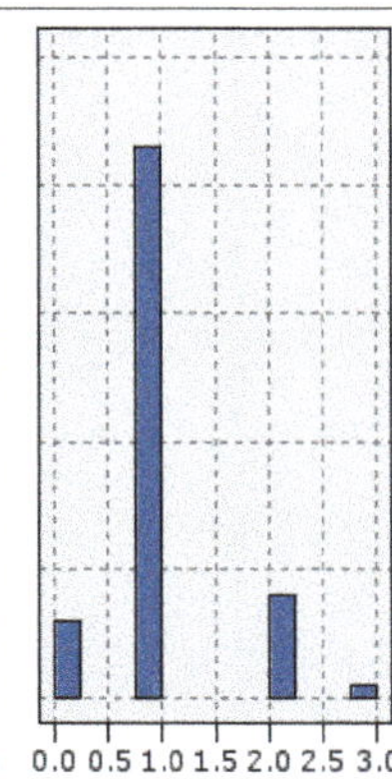

Each of the obtained clusters indicated good, average and unfavorable network conditions in terms of the received signal characteristics of the mobile phone in the idle mode. In cluster number 1, according to the statistical information table of the used features, all records were in a suitable and optimal condition. In cluster number 2, although the interference in the environment was negligible, the signal level was weaker than the optim mode. The low signal level in the records included in this category was due to the relative large distance between the base transmitter and receiver station. Since there was very litt interference in this category, these areas did not have the problem of improper frequen design of adjacent cells or the problem of interfering signals from neighbors. Therefore, tl records of this cluster did not report a specific problem in the network. If a new antenr was installed to improve the signal level in this area, it would interfere with the receive signal in the neighboring points. The third cluster contained records that were not far fro the service station and had an unacceptable level of interference and signal. This mea that the path obstacles might reduce the signal strength. The interference caused by th signals of the neighboring cells should be corrected by resetting the site parameters, suc as the height and angle of the antenna in the adjacent cell.

Scenario number 2, short call: The purpose of this scenario was to check the network terms of its access success rate. Many calls were attempted in this scenario. In the availab data of this research, there were 8 blocked calls out of 349 calls in the short call scenari These results showed high interference in these areas, and the signal level was insignifica Further investigation of the reasons for blocked calls was available in performance suppo system indicators and is covered in Section 4.

Scenario number 3: Long-term call: This scenario, which was the most critical scenar in the field test, measured signal quality, conversation quality, carrier power to interferen power ratio, and advanced timing. The purpose of this scenario was to identify the state the system on call interruptions and handovers.

As seen in the following figure, among the different clustering methods applied this data, the k-means method achieved a higher Silhouette coefficient than other metho Therefore, we first briefly overview the k-means clustering method. The details of th results are given later in this section.

The k-means method is among the best cluster partitioning methods. This mear that, according to the number of clusters, there is an attempt to optimize the data divisic according to the similarity or distance criterion (Figure 15). Several algorithms with different number of clusters were tried on this data. For the k-means method, the numb of 4 clusters had the best answer. The Silhouette coefficient value for this cluster was 0.62

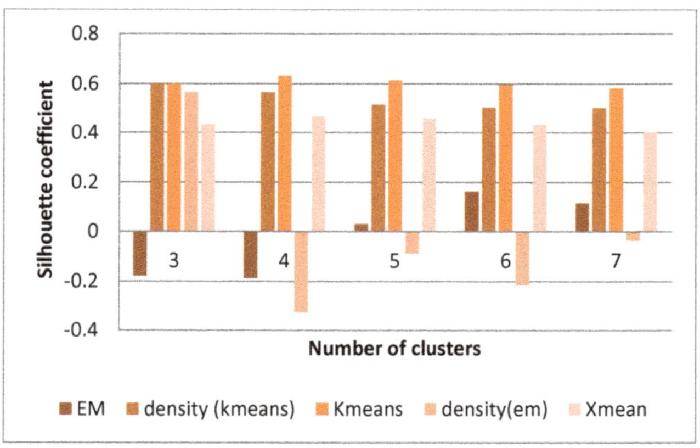

Figure 15. Silhouette coefficient value of different clustering methods–long call scenario.

Table 7 illustrates the obtained histogram of the features in 4 categories.

The signal quality in cluster number 1 was inadequate. Low signal quality was du to low power and signal level. Paying attention to the characteristic value signal powe interference power ratio showed significant interference in the system due to the sign level. On the other hand, since the value of the advanced timer parameter was low, th decreased signal level was not the long distance from the transmitter station. Therefore, th problem could be seen in the voltage standing wave ratio (VSWR). The problem, expressed as a loss in signal strength, was due to hardware problems in the antenna or its incorrect installation. Another reason for the problem was the wrong tilt of the antenna angle. It could be seen that in this situation the quality of the signal was not good, and the received sound in the receiver had good quality. This problem could be seen in the audio coding type used in this network.

Table 7. The histogram of different features in the obtained clusters–long call.

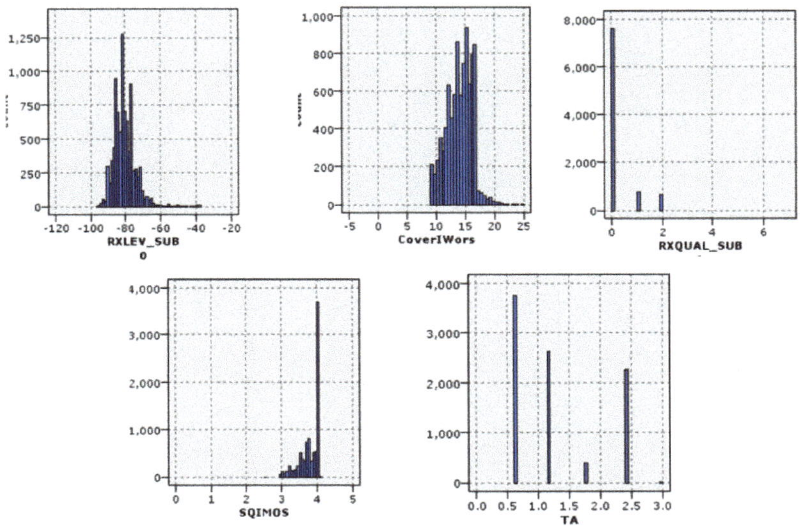	First category
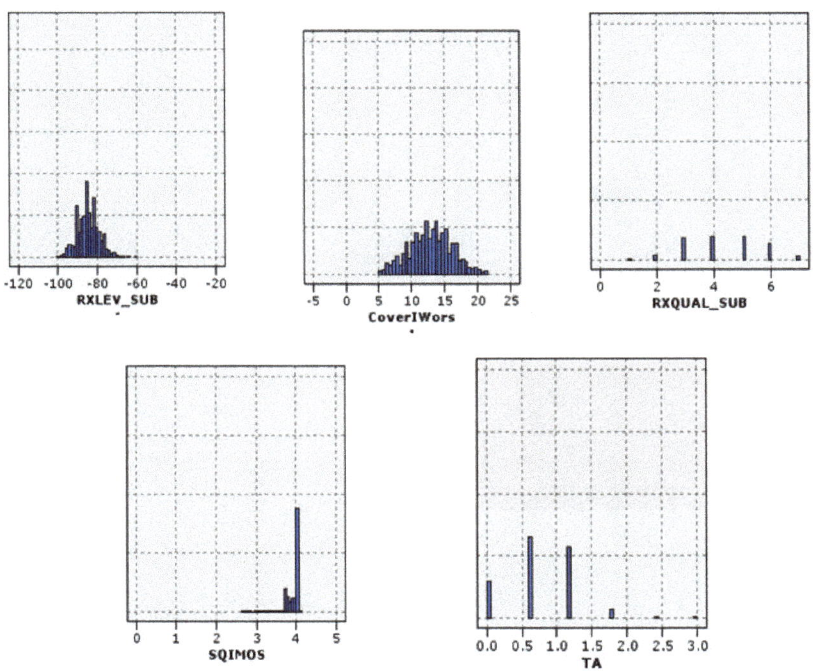	Second category

Table 7. *Cont.*

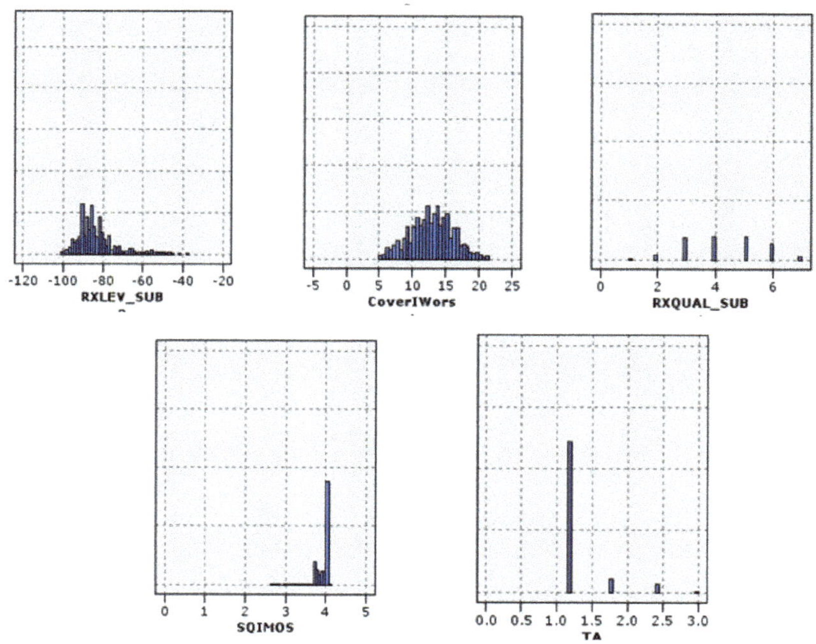	Third category
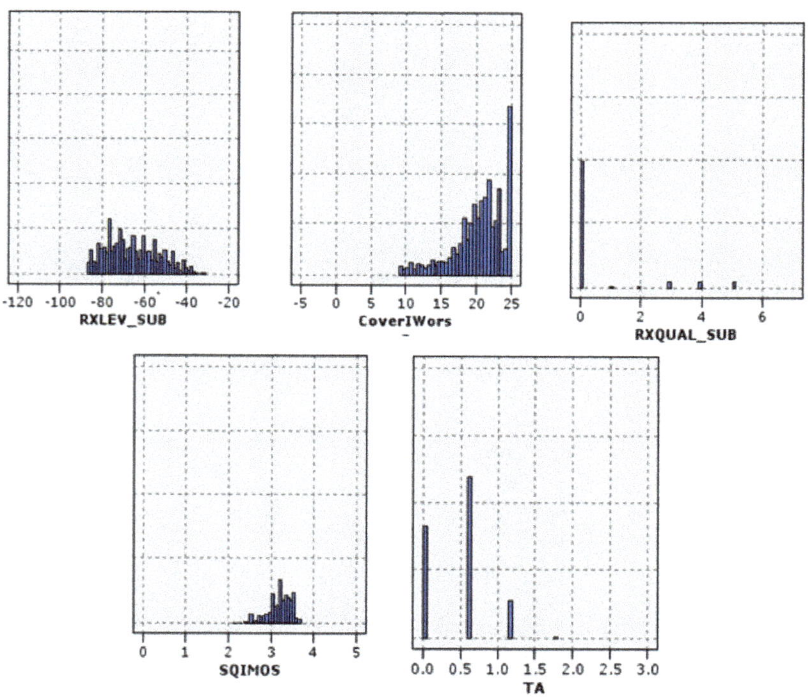	Forth category

In cluster number 2, the signal level was low. A high value of the advanced timer confirmed the presence of a problem in the standard received signal. This meant that this signal reached the subscriber from a long distance, and, therefore, the service site's signal was out of range. Thus, site design parameters, such as antenna height and angle, should be considered to reduce the coverage area or the antenna power.

In cluster number 3, all features were in good condition. This cluster showed the proper state of the network.

In cluster number 4, the bad quality of the signal was not caused by the power reduction and signal level or interference. On the other hand, the value of the advanced timer also showed the system's status. Therefore, according to the expert, the reason for this was hardware problems in one of the sources of sending and receiving information in antennas called TRX.

Cluster number 5 showed high interference in the system. On the other hand, the signal level in this cluster was suitable. Therefore, the interference strength could be seen in the low power of the carrier signal. In this cluster, the advanced scheduler also had an acceptable value. Therefore, the reason for the existence of this problem could be attributed to the presence of interference from external sources, such as signals from other operators, or incorrect installation of sectors and the need to swap them.

3.12. Review the Handover

As mentioned before, one of the issues addressed in the long call scenario is the handover issue. Our model investigated this issue separately. By reducing the quality of the signal received by the user, which is a function of the bit fault rate, the network is obliged to transfer the user's call to a better cell. Sometimes, outsourcing may happen later than the appropriate time, and this phenomenon leads to common dissatisfaction with the network.

To solve this problem, the proposed solution is to use a time window to detect the quality and level of the signal received by the user in a long call. The time window length and the threshold value were considered on the quality and level of the signal according to the expert's opinion. If the subscriber received signal quality worse than, or equal to, 5 and the signal level was less than −75 within six times of receiving information from the central transmitter station, our system requested retransmission in the network because otherwise the user's call would be disconnected, which would lead to user dissatisfaction. Figure 16 shows the signal quality and level at different network points.

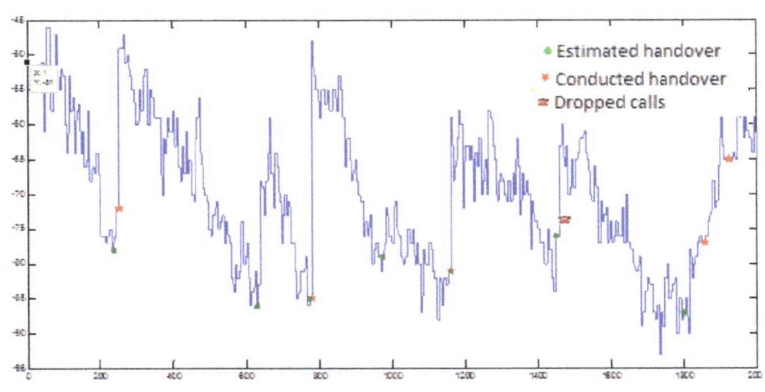

Figure 16. Silhouette coefficient value of different clustering methods–long call scenario.

This section introduces the drive test, one of the scientific and engineering methods for identifying the location of the fault and the cause of its occurrence. Different scenarios performed in a drive test by a team of experts were investigated separately in this research. For the scenario of idle mode, three separate signal strength categories were considered for the subscriber, which divided the network mode into three categories: good, average, and bad. In the short call scenario, where the network mode was examined in terms of the call establishment parameters, after identifying the exact location of the blocked calls and the state of the received signal, the characteristics of the indicators of the performance monitoring system were used to analyze the cause of the problem. Finally, the long call contact of four categories was obtained for the most critical scenario. Their interpretatic is available in detail in Section 3.7 To evaluate the clustering method, in addition to tl Silhouette coefficient, data classification using the cluster number label was used, tl accuracy results of which are given in the training and test data at the end of Section 3 Relocation, one of the most important goals of long call scenarios, was also examine separately in this section. The results of the handover evaluation are given.

3.13. Combining Data Sources

The purpose of this section is to combine the results of the second and third sectior In other words, in this section, we wanted to complete the architecture of automatic fau detection and detection in cellular networks by examining the results of these two sectior As mentioned in previous sections, two critical data sources for fault detection in cellul networks are performance support system data and field test data. Each of these two da sources examines the network status from different aspects. Therefore, the qualitati issues of the network were discussed from two different perspectives related to these tw data sources. To identify faults and problems in the network, it was necessary to examir these data sources separately.

Another data source that we used in this section to more precisely identify the fau cause was data related to subscriber complaints. These data, which were collected fro the communication center with the subscribers of the mobile telecommunication compar (Hamrahe Avval), indicated the problems reported to the operator by the subscribers of th network. In the following, we briefly explain customer complaints' data and then introdu the data combination methods. The results of combining these three data sources are give at the end.

3.14. Subscriber Complaints Dataset

Investigating customer complaints is one of the essential activities of customer-oriente organizations. Considering the competitive world among operators, it is necessary manage customer complaints and adequately satisfy customers. The block diagram the communication of subscribers' complaints with different departments of the mobi telecommunication company (first companion) is shown in Figure 17.

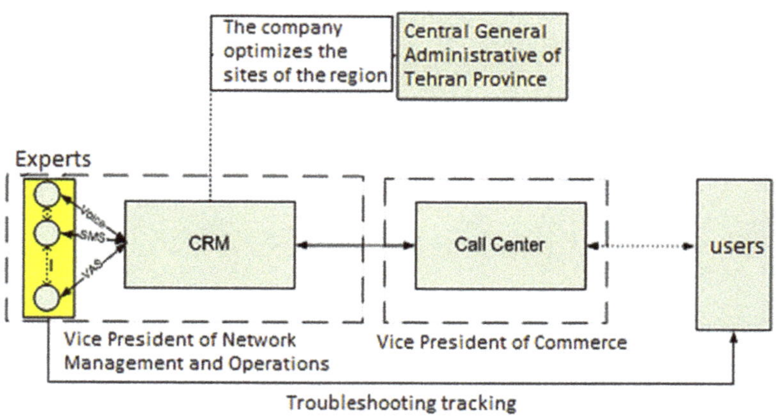

Figure 17. Silhouette coefficient on idle mode scenario with 3 clusters.

After the customer communicates with the call center, the user report is separate from other calls based on the communication with the technical department. At th stage, complaints related to a similar incident are consolidated before being sent to th technical department and, finally, sent to the customer relations department of the technic department. The received reports in the technical department are re-checked and divide into categories, such as Voice, SMS, etc. Problems related to the optimization of region sites and the maintenance of BTS sites are sent to the Central General Administration of Tehran Province. After investigating the problem, the expert's report is transferred to the call center and the call center contacts the subscriber if necessary. The available data collection we used of to complaints from mobile telecommunication center subscribers related to technical problems, and was reported in October and November of 2020. The number of records of this data was 3200 in total. Table 8 below shows the features in this data.

Table 8. The data characteristics of subscribers' complaints.

Feature Name	Feature Type
Registration time	Time
Request type	Text
Request description	Text
Site ID	Text
BCS ID	Text
Explanation	Text

Among the reported problems by subscribers, temporary network disruption, echoing, receiving false messages during calls, coverage problems, disconnection, and antenna weakness were mentioned. The total number of these problems was divided into 6 general categories; about 80% of the reported issues was related to antenna and network coverage problems.

This category's data was used to help better identify network faults, especially those not specified in the other two data categories. Therefore, by adding this information to the previous data, this information could be used to increase the accuracy of the proposed model. Our observations showed that about 1% of all calls raised as technical complaints to the mobile telecommunication company were unrelated to the technical department. The problem was related to the subscriber himself or herself, for reasons such as problem registration by non-technical personnel in the operator, as well as issues associated with the user, such as problems related to some types of mobile phones (for example, some mobile phones cannot support the AMR feature), wrong settings on the shared telephone (for example, call transferring to the wrong number), the existence of a hardware problem in the phone that led to poor quality audio, etc.

Among the remaining 99% of complaints, about 35% of these calls stated problems were not worth taking any appropriate action, for technical and economic reasons. Calls were mostly related to the lack of antenna in remote areas or certain parts of a private house; for example, a user in a village with a relatively small population may contact the customer complaint center for lack of coverage in the network. Since there would be economic problems in installing a new site in that area, the mobile telecommunications company cannot take action to satisfy the customer. According to discussions with the experts, no specific action is taken to improve the network situation for this category of reports. Finally, 65% of the subscribers' complaints reflected a real problem in the network.

It is important to note that all customer complaints should be investigated. After investigating a common complaint, according to the amount of other data available, such as performance support system data and field test data, appropriate actions are taken for that data if necessary. In other words, if both other data sources are available, if the other two data sources confirm the absence of a problem in the area, that problem is not transferred to the next step. In the case of a severe problem in the network, one of these two data sources could transmit this problem.

Our reviews of the data confirmed the validity of customer complaint data. For example, on the 15th and 16th of October, several subscribers' complaints were recorded in the system for a specific cell in the network. The received information from the performance support system for this particular cell confirmed the occurrence of a problem in the are because the average CCC of this cell was below 85 during high traffic hours, and our mode detected the problem. Therefore, paying attention to subscribers' complaints is one of th critical issues in identifying causes offaults.

3.15. Fault Detection

According to the conducted studies and the results presented in the second and thir sections, which specifically focus on the performance support system and drive test dat we offer a mechanism to combine this information to complete the architecture of automati detection of recorded fault.

All three of our data sets were unavailable at all times, and, due to drive testin limitations and subscriber complaints, the methods used to combine information differec according to the types of available data for each region.

There are different ways to combine information from these three categories of dat The simplest of these methods is the use of majority opinion voting. If all three data source are available, this method identifies a record as a fault when at least two of the thre information sources confirm the occurrence of a fault in a specific cell and at a particula time. Another method is to use weighted voting. The basis of this method is the unequa accuracy of different data sources in fault detection. Therefore, assigning more weight t methods with higher precision is necessary. In this way, decisions are made about new dat based on each method's ability to correctly identify faults in the network and consider th system's threshold.

As we mentioned earlier, all data sources may not exist simultaneously in this frame work. In addition, according to conversations with field experts, who emphasize th necessity of checking all the reported faults from the performance support system an drive test sources, all the reported faults from these two sources should be checked. I both of these sources report the absence of a problem for a region and at a particular tim and there is a subscriber complaint for this region, this complaint is ignored. Otherwis the common complaint is used to improve the accuracy of diagnosis of the fault's caus (Table 9).

Table 9. Checking different situations in combining information according to available data source

The Number of Available Data Sources	Used Method
Only source number 1 reports an fault. Source number 1 and 2 report an fault	Check the problem
Source number 1 and 3 are not available	Trust first source
Source number 1, 2 and 3 are available	Trust first and second sources

3.16. Fault Identification

Since the first and second data sources have two different views of the network an the events within the network, the type of detected fault from these two sources diffe Drive testing accurately identifies fault location and cause when a data source (performanc support system) cannot respond appropriately. These two data sources are complementar to each other. When there are complaints from subscribers in an area, an expert is used t improve the accuracy of the solution provided.

As mentioned in the third section, it is necessary to examine the key performanc indicators discussed in the second section for the short call scenario. Identifying the reaso for blocking a call request using measurable parameters and features is not achieved i the drive test. Therefore, according to the findings of the second section, it is necessar to comment on the problems of the traffic sector and signaling sector for the desired are Related indicators to request blocking in the signaling sector include congestion in the traffi and signaling channels, the success rate in accessing the traffic and signaling channels, an interruption in the signaling channel.

Among the drive test data, there were eight blocked call requests. The results of comparing these requests with the indicators of the busiest hours of the same day are shown in the Table 10.

Table 10. Comparison of drive test information and performance support system for blocked calls.

ID	C/I	RxLe	RxQual	TA	SDCong	SDDrop	SDestab	TCHCong	TCHAssign
1	11.4	−91	7	2	0.42	0.79	96.71	2.2	2.77
2	17.9	−79	0	1	6.61	0.53	97.56	0	0.49
3	13.2	−76	4	2	1.41	0.38	98.11	0	1.09
4	8.7	−79	7	3	0	0.27	88.11	0	0.34
5	11.7	−77	4	3	0	3.71	88.20	0	1.39
6	12.5	−82	5	1	0.43	0.46	96.17	1.81	14.54
7	13.1	−83	6	1	0	1.27	89.18	0.24	22.16
8	15.4	−91	7	2	0	1.31	96.86	0	5.11

It is evident that records 1, 6, and 8 did not have signaling problems, and the reason for the call blocking problem was related to the indicators of the traffic department. Thus, records 2, 3, 4, and 5 were almost healthy in establishing traffic department calls, and there was no need to perform traffic checks on the blocked calls. It was possible to identify the fault by the method of determining the cause and using the performance support system data.

In this section, after introducing the third category of information, called subscriber complaints, we discussed the issue of combining different available information sources to identify the fault and also to analyze its cause. In this process, the main focus is on two sources of information, performance support systems and drive testing to identify the fault. A significant percentage of the complaints raised by subscribers is not a priority in solving network problems, and, from an economic pint of view, and even a technical point of view, are not cheap to resolve. Complaints from subscribers are only used to help the expert in identifying the cause of a fault that occurred in the system. Further investigations and analysis of subscribers' complaints to determine their importance in expressing the problem and helping to solve it are proposed as one suggestion for future work in this research. As mentioned before, the two information sources of drive test and performance support system data complement each other in fault detection and identify its cause. The combination of these two sources of information to identify the reason for the blocking of a call request in the drive test was investigated in this section, and how to find the cause of the fault in the field test, by using the method of identifying the fault caused in the data of the performance support system, was discussed.

4. Discussion and Conclusions

Troubleshooting in cellular networks is essential due to the nature of the networks' components, hardware, and software problems. Considering the competitive world among cellular network operators, the need for automatic fault detection and identification of the causes of faults, so as to restore the network to its normal mode, have become increasingly apparent. This article aimed to provide a framework for automatic fault detection and investigation of the cause of a fault to help the human resources in this field. This article was based on scientific principles and sought to solve problems in the industry, and its modeling was performed in consultation with experts in the field. Unlike other research conducted in this field, this research had different data sources, and by using the ability of the data to check the network mode from different perspectives, it identified faults with higher accuracy and exhibited greater ability to analyze the cause of fault. In addition, the proposed model had the most negligible dependence on experts in building the model and its initial assumptions. Therefore, it was immune to human faults and experts' taste.

Finally, in responding to the needs of experts, this model had a minor dependency c human resources and could continue to work without human resources' intervention. I this paper, the general framework of the activities was shown in "Fault! Reference sour not found". The considered input sources were performance support system data, driv test data, and data related to customer complaints. Fault detection in the case of the fir two categories of data, performance support system data and drive testing, was performe by methods fully explored in the second and third sections. Faults identified from the da sources were entered into the "combining data" section, along with potential subscrib complaints. In this part, faults were collected together with the knowledge extracted fro the previous steps, and a decision was made for an area. Therefore, the input of the thre parts, "performance support system," "drive test," and "subscriber complaints", was th available data from the three types of sources, and in the output port, the detected fau characteristics were entered into the information combination part. Finally, the detecte fault was sent to the output and cause.

The performance support system is one of the most important sources of informatic in identifying network problems. The data of this system were examined in detail i the second section. The CCC quality criterion was used for fault detection. The recorc identified as faults by this criterion were entered into the next step of the algorithm t determine the cause of the fault. These data were divided into traffic and signaling da categories, and the related problems to each section were identified separately. Since th available data were only unlabeled raw data, the clustering algorithm method was use By implementing different algorithms with different numbers of clusters, 5 clusters with Silhouette coefficient of 0.4509 for traffic data and 6 clusters with a Silhouette coefficient c 0.503 were obtained for signaling data. Each of these clusters represented a specific caus for a fault in the network. Finally, different classification algorithms were applied to th labeled data through clustering to better evaluate the results. For traffic and signaling dat combining the effects of different classifiers through opinion voting had the best accurac in test data. In fact, 90.38% accuracy was obtained for traffic data and 92.31% for signalin data, which was a significant improvement compared to the accuracy of other simil tasks. Drive test data were collected in three short, long and idle mode call scenarios. Th short call identifies network problems in call setup, the long call identifies issues relate to handover and call interruption, and, finally, the idle mode ascertains characteristic of the standard signal in the network. This research used performance support syster data to solve the problems of blocked calls in short calls, long calls, and idle mode an used clustering algorithms to identify the cause of existing problems. For the accuracy c this method, in addition to the Silhouette coefficient, various classified algorithms wer performed on the training and test data in the case of long call scenarios. In the best cas an accuracy of 96.86% was obtained with the dynamic neural network method. In additio the time window was used to provide a framework for identifying points that neede handover, and its results were presented in the third section of the outsourcing revie section. As mentioned in the first section, the number of studies conducted in this fiel has been minimal, and this study can be expanded to various areas. Examining subscrib complaint data in more detail, including identifying the importance of the reported proble for operators, is one of the essential activities to reduce the time spent by experts in th industry. In addition, according to the record that the subscriber registers in the syste and the explanations that they provide to the subscriber complaints center, it is possible t identify the fault type and analyze its cause.

Author Contributions: Conceptualization, A.K.S.; Software, A.K.S., S.R. and A.J.; Formal analysi S.R., A.J., F.M., W.Z. and D.W.; Investigation, F.M. and W.Z.; Resources, A.K.S., F.M. and D.W.; Da curation, A.K.S., S.R. and A.J.; Writing—original draft, A.K.S., S.R. and A.J.; Writing—review editing, A.J.; Visualization, A.J.; Supervision, A.J. and W.Z.; Project administration, A.J. All autho have read and agreed to the published version of the manuscript.

Funding: This work was supported in part by the Fundamental Research Funds for the Central Universities under Grant No. HIT.OCEF.2021007, the Shenzhen Science and Technology Research and Development Foundation under Grant No.JCYJ20190806143418198, the National Key Research and Development Program of China under Grant No. 2020YFB1406902, the Key-Area Research and Development Program of Guangdong Province under Grant No. 2020B0101360001, the Guangdong Provincial Key Laboratory of Novel Security Intelligence Technologies under Grant No. 2022B1212010005. Professor Weizhe Zhang is the corresponding author.

Data Availability Statement: The data that support the findings of this study are available from the corresponding author, upon reasonable request.

Conflicts of Interest: The authors declare no conflict of interest.

References

1. Papidas, A.G.; Polyzos, G.C. Self-Organizing Networks for 5G and Beyond: A View from the Top. *Future Internet* **2022**, *14*, 95. [CrossRef]
2. Sumathi, A.C.; Javadpour, A.; Pinto, P.; Sangaiah, A.K.; Zhang, W.; Mahmoodi Khaniabadi, S. NEWTR: A multipath routing for next hop destination in internet of things with artificial recurrent neural network (RNN). *Int. J. Mach. Learn. Cybern.* **2022**, *13*, 2869–2889. [CrossRef]
3. Loskot, P. Mobile Networks. In *Emerging Computing Paradigms: Principles, Advances and Applications*; John Wiley & Sons Ltd.: Hoboken, NJ, USA, 2022.
4. Sangaiah, A.K.; Javadpour, A.; Pinto, P.; Ja'fari, F.; Zhang, W. Improving Quality of Service in 5G Resilient Communication with THE Cellular Structure of Smartphones. *ACM Trans. Sens. Netw.* **2022**, *18*, 43. [CrossRef]
5. Parameswaran, S.; Bag, T.; Garg, S.; Mitschele-Thiel, A. Cognitive Network Function for Mobility Robustness Optimization in Cellular Networks. In Proceedings of the 2022 IEEE Wireless Communications and Networking Conference (WCNC), Austin, TX, USA, 10–13 April 2022; pp. 2035–2040.
6. Borwankar, S.; Pandya, R.; Sharma, R. Unacknowledged Mode LAPDm Protocol Development at MS Side of GSM Network. In Proceedings of the Fifth International Conference on Microelectronics, Computing and Communication Systems, Ranchi, India, 7 November 2020; pp. 413–421.
7. Bratman, J.; Fabbri, D.; Zimmerman, A. Reinforcement Learning Approach to Managing Distributed Data Processing Tasks in Wireless Sensing Networks. *Eecs. Umich. Edu.* **2009**, 1–10.
8. Nisar, F.; Baseer, S. A Comprehensive Survey on Mobile Communication Generation. In Proceedings of the 2021 International Conference on Innovative Computing (ICIC), Lahore, Pakistan, 9–10 November 2021; pp. 1–6.
9. Peng, Y.; Yang, X.; Xu, W. Optimization research of decision support system based on data mining algorithm. *Wirel. Pers. Commun.* **2018**, *102*, 2913–2925. [CrossRef]
10. Rezaei, S.; Radmanesh, H.; Alavizadeh, P.; Nikoofar, H.; Lahouti, F. Automatic fault detection and diagnosis in cellular networks using operations support systems data. In Proceedings of the NOMS 2016—2016 IEEE/IFIP Network Operations and Management Symposium, Istanbul, Turkey, 25–29 April 2016; pp. 468–473.
11. Fotouhi, A.; Qiang, H.; Ding, M.; Hassan, M.; Giordano, L.G.; Garcia-Rodriguez, A.; Yuan, J. Survey on UAV cellular communications: Practical aspects, standardization advancements, regulation, and security challenges. *IEEE Commun. Surv. Tutor.* **2019**, *21*, 3417–3442. [CrossRef]
12. Hasanshahi, Z.; Azmi, P.; Gholizadeh, M.H.; Khajezadeh, M. The Flexibility of the Generalized Gamma Distribution in Modeling the Fading Based on Kullback-Leibler and Kolmogorov-Smirnov Criteria. *IEEE Access* **2020**, *8*, 8393–8404. [CrossRef]
13. Alekseeva, D.; Stepanov, N.; Veprev, A.; Sharapova, A.; Lohan, E.S.; Ometov, A. Comparison of Machine Learning Techniques Applied to Traffic Prediction of Real Wireless Network. *IEEE Access* **2021**, *9*, 159495–159514. [CrossRef]
14. Guo, P.; Fu, J.; Yang, X. Condition monitoring and fault diagnosis of wind turbines gearbox bearing temperature based on kolmogorov-smirnov test and convolutional neural network model. *Energies* **2018**, *11*, 2248. [CrossRef]
15. Yang, H.; Wang, B.; Yao, Q.; Yu, A.; Zhang, J. Efficient hybrid multi-faults location based on hopfield neural network in 5G coexisting radio and optical wireless networks. *IEEE Trans. Cogn. Commun. Netw.* **2019**, *5*, 1218–1228. [CrossRef]
16. Mishra, D.; Natalizio, E. A survey on cellular-connected UAVs: Design challenges, enabling 5G/B5G innovations, and experimental advancements. *Comput. Netw.* **2020**, *182*, 107451. [CrossRef]
17. Fourati, H.; Maaloul, R.; Chaari, L.; Jmaiel, M. Comprehensive survey on self-organizing cellular network approaches applied to 5G networks. *Comput. Netw.* **2021**, *199*, 108435. [CrossRef]
18. Wang, S.; Ferrús, R. Extracting cell patterns from high-dimensional radio network performance datasets using self-organizing maps and K-means clustering. *IEEE Access* **2021**, *9*, 42045–42058. [CrossRef]
19. García, A.J.; Toril, M.; Oliver, P.; Luna-Ramírez, S.; Ortiz, M. Automatic alarm prioritization by data mining for fault management in cellular networks. *Expert Syst. Appl.* **2020**, *158*, 113526. [CrossRef]
20. Asghar, A.; Farooq, H.; Imran, A. Self-healing in emerging cellular networks: Review, challenges, and research directions. *IEEE Commun. Surv. Tutor.* **2018**, *20*, 1682–1709. [CrossRef]

21. Barco, R.; Lázaro, P.; Wille, V.; Díez, L.; Patel, S. Knowledge acquisition for diagnosis model in wireless networks. *Expert Sys Appl.* **2009**, *36*, 4745–4752. [CrossRef]
22. Khanafer, R.M.; Solana, B.; Triola, J.; Barco, R.; Moltsen, L.; Altman, Z.; Lazaro, P. Automated Diagnosis for UMTS Network Using Bayesian Network Approach. *IEEE Trans. Veh. Technol.* **2008**, *57*, 2451–2461. [CrossRef]
23. Barco, R.; Díez, L.; Wille, V.; Lázaro, P. Automatic diagnosis of mobile communication networks under imprecise parameter *Expert Syst. Appl.* **2009**, *36*, 489–500. [CrossRef]
24. Sathya, V.; Kala, S.M.; Bhupeshraj, S.; Tamma, B.R. RAPTAP: A socio-inspired approach to resource allocation and interferenc management in dense small cells. *Wirel. Netw.* **2021**, *27*, 441–464. [CrossRef]
25. Song, K.; Zeng, X.; Zhang, Y.; De Jonckheere, J.; Yuan, X.; Koehl, L. An interpretable knowledge-based decision support system and its applications in pregnancy diagnosis. *Knowl.-Based Syst.* **2021**, *221*, 106835. [CrossRef]
26. Saeed, U.; Jan, S.U.; Lee, Y.-D.; Koo, I. Fault diagnosis based on extremely randomized trees in wireless sensor networks. *Relia Eng. Syst. Saf.* **2021**, *205*, 107284. [CrossRef]
27. Tan, M.; Lafond, C.V. PERFEX: A cellular performance support expert. *Expert Syst. Appl.* **1996**, *11*, 449–454. [CrossRef]
28. Wang, Y.; Ruan, Y.; Tang, Y. Intelligent Fault Diagnosis Method for Mobile Cellular Networks. In Proceedings of the 2021 IEE Globecom Workshops (GC Wkshps), Madrid, Spain, 7–11 December 2021; pp. 1–6.
29. Nouioua, M.; Fournier-Viger, P.; He, G.; Nouioua, F.; Min, Z. A survey of machine learning for network fault management. I *Machine Learning and Data Mining for Emerging Trend in Cyber Dynamics*; Springer: Cham, Switzerland, 2021; pp. 1–27.
30. Szilágyi, P.; Nováczki, S. An Automatic Detection and Diagnosis Framework for Mobile Communication Systems. *IEEE Tran Netw. Serv. Manag.* **2012**, *9*, 184–197. [CrossRef]
31. Riaz, M.S.; Qureshi, H.N.; Masood, U.; Rizwan, A.; Abu-Dayya, A.; Imran, A. Deep Learning-based Framework for Multi-Faul Diagnosis in Self-Healing Cellular Networks. In Proceedings of the 2022 IEEE Wireless Communications and Networkin Conference (WCNC), Austin, TX, USA, 10–13 April 2022; pp. 746–751.
32. Moulay, M.; Leiva, R.G.; Maroni, P.J.R.; Diez, F.; Mancuso, V.; Anta, A.F. Automated identification of network anomalies and thei causes with interpretable machine learning: The CIAN methodology and TTrees implementation. *Comput. Commun.* **2022**, *19* 327–348. [CrossRef]
33. Eli-Chukwu, N.C.; Aloh, J.M.; Ezeagwu, C.O. A systematic review of artificial intelligence applications in cellular network *Eng. Technol. Appl. Sci. Res.* **2019**, *9*, 4504–4510. [CrossRef]
34. Saeed, A.; Aliu, O.G.; Imran, M.A. Controlling self healing cellular networks using fuzzy logic. In Proceedings of the 2012 IEE Wireless Communications and Networking Conference (WCNC), Paris, France, 1–4 April 2012; pp. 3080–3084. [CrossRef]
35. Javadpour, A.; Wang, G.; Rezaei, S.; Li, K.-C. Detecting straggler MapReduce tasks in big data processing infrastructure by neura network. *J. Supercomput.* **2020**, *76*, 6969–6993. [CrossRef]
36. Han, J.; Pei, J.; Tong, H. *Data Mining: Concepts and Techniques*; Morgan Kaufmann: Burlington, MA, USA, 2022.
37. Javadpour, A.; Rezaei, S.; Li, K.-C.; Wang, G. A Scalable Feature Selection and Opinion Miner Using Whale Optimizatio Algorithm. In *Advances in Signal Processing and Intelligent Recognition Systems*; Springer: Singapore, 2020; pp. 237–247.
38. Aymen, A. New traffic modeling for IoV/V2X in 5G network based on Data Mining. In Proceedings of the 2021 IEEE 93r Vehicular Technology Conference (VTC2021-Spring), Helsinki, Finland, 25–28 April 2021; pp. 1–7.
39. Riaz, M.S.; Qureshi, H.N.; Masood, U.; Rizwan, A.; Abu-Dayya, A.; Imran, A. A Hybrid Deep Learning-based (HYDRA Framework for Multi-Fault Diagnosis using Sparse MDT Reports. *IEEE Access* **2022**, *10*, 67140–67151. [CrossRef]
40. Yuan, K.-H.; Guarnaccia, C.A.; Hayslip Jr, B. A study of the distribution of sample coefficient alpha with the Hopkins sympton checklist: Bootstrap versus asymptotics. *Educ. Psychol. Meas.* **2003**, *63*, 5–23. [CrossRef]
41. Elbatal, I.; Alotaibi, N.; Alyami, S.A.; Elgarhy, M.; El-Saeed, A.R. Bayesian and non-Bayesian estimation of the Nadaraj ah Haghighi distribution: Using progressive Type-1 censoring scheme. *Mathematics* **2022**, *10*, 760. [CrossRef]
42. Chakraborty, S.; Islam, S.K.H.; Samanta, D. *Data Classification and Incremental Clustering in Data Mining and Machine Learning* Springer: Berlin/Heidelberg, Germany, 2022.
43. Zafarani, R.; Abbasi, M.A.; Liu, H. *Social Media Mining an Introduction*; Cambridge University Press: Cambridge, UK, 2014; p. 38 [CrossRef]
44. Javadpour, A.; Saedifar, K.; Wang, G.; Li, K.-C.; Saghafi, F. Improving the Efficiency of Customer's Credit Rating with Machin Learning in Big Data Cloud Computing. *Wirel. Pers. Commun.* **2021**, *121*, 2699–2718. [CrossRef]
45. Barik, D.K.; Mali, S.; Ali, F.A.; Agarwal, A. Design and Analysis of RF Optimization in 2G GSM and 4G LTE Network. I *Innovation in Electrical Power Engineering, Communication, and Computing Technology*; Springer: Singapore, 2022; pp. 11–18.
46. Abdelazez, M.; Rajan, S.; Chan, A.D.C. Signal Quality Assessment of Compressively Sensed Electrocardiogram. *IEEE Trans Biomed. Eng.* **2022**, *69*, 3397–3406. [CrossRef] [PubMed]

algorithms

MDPI

rticle

Convergence and Stability of a New Parametric Class of Iterative Processes for Nonlinear Systems

licia Cordero [1,*], Javier G. Maimó [2], Antmel Rodríguez-Cabral [2,3] and Juan R. Torregrosa [1]

1 Instituto de Matemática Multidisciplinar, Universitat Politècnica de València, Camino de Vera, s/n, 46022 Valencia, Spain
2 Instituto Tecnológico de Santo Domingo (INTEC), Av. Los Procéres 49, Santo Domingo 10602, Dominican Republic
3 Escuela de Matemáticas, Universidad Autónoma de Santo Domingo (UASD), Ciudad Universitaria, Av. Alma Mater, Santo Domingo 10105, Dominican Republic
* Correspondence: acordero@mat.upv.es

Abstract: In this manuscript, we carry out a study on the generalization of a known family of multipoint scalar iterative processes for approximating the solutions of nonlinear systems. The convergence analysis of the proposed class under various smooth conditions is provided. We also study the stability of this family, analyzing the fixed and critical points of the rational operator resulting from applying the family on low-degree polynomials, as well as the basins of attraction and the orbits (periodic or not) that these points produce. This dynamical study also allows us to observe which members of the family are more stable and which have chaotic behavior. Graphical analyses of dynamical planes, parameter line and bifurcation planes are also studied. Numerical tests are performed on different nonlinear systems for checking the theoretical results and to compare the proposed schemes with other known ones.

Keywords: nonlinear systems; convergence order; iterative processes; stability analysis

itation: Cordero, A.; G. Maimó, J.; odríguez-Cabral, A.; Torregrosa, J.R. onvergence and Stability of a New arametric Class of Iterative rocesses for Nonlinear Systems. gorithms 2023, 16, 163. https://oi.org/10.3390/a16030163

cademic Editor: Frank Werner

eceived: 8 February 2023
evised: 10 March 2023
ccepted: 14 March 2023
ublished: 16 March 2023

1. Introduction

Many papers deal with methods and families of iterative schemes to approximate the solution of nonlinear equations $f(x) = 0$, with $f : I \subseteq \mathbb{R} \to \mathbb{R}$ as a function defined in an open interval I. Each of them has a different behavior due to their order of convergence, stability and efficiency. Of the existing methods in the literature, in the present manuscript, we focus on the family of iterative processes (ACTV) for approximating the solutions of nonlinear equations, proposed by Artidiello et al. in [1]. This family was constructed adding a Newton step to Ostrowski's scheme, and using a divided difference operator. Then, the family has a three-step iterative expression with an arbitrary complex parameter α. Moreover, its order of convergence is at least six. Its iterative expression is

$$
\begin{aligned}
y_k &= x_k - \frac{f(x_k)}{f'(x_k)}, \\
z_k &= y_k - \frac{f(y_k)}{2f[x_k, y_k] - f'(x_k)}, \\
x_{k+1} &= z_k - [\alpha + (1+\alpha)u_k + (1-\alpha)v_k]\frac{f(z_k)}{f'(x_k)}, \ k = 0, 1, \ldots
\end{aligned} \tag{1}
$$

where

$$u_k = 1 - \frac{f[x_k, y_k]}{f'(x_k)} \quad \text{and} \quad v_k = \frac{f'(x_k)}{f[x_k, y_k]}, \quad k = 0, 1, 2, \ldots$$

The divided difference operator is defined as

$$f[x,y] = \frac{f(x) - f(y)}{(x - y)}, \quad \forall x, y \in I.$$

By using tools of complex dynamics, the stability of this family was studied b Moscoso [2], where it was observed that there is good dynamic behavior in the case $\alpha = 1$. In Section 2, we present the multidimensional extension of family (1) and prove i convergence order.

In the stability analysis (Section 3), we determine whether the fixed points of th associated rational operator are of an attracting, repulsing or saddle point nature; on th other hand, we search for which values of the parameter-free critical points may appear. I the bifurcation analysis of free critical points (Section 4), we calculate the parameter line which we generate from the mentioned free critical points, then we generate the bifurcatio planes for specific intervals of parameter α, and as a consequence of these studies, w generate the dynamical planes for members of the family with stable and unstable behavio In Section 5, some numerical problems are considered to confirm the theoretical result The proposed schemes for different values of parameter are considered and compared wit Newton's method and some known sixth-order techniques, namely $C6_1$, $C6_2$, $B6$, $PSH6$ $PSH6_2$, $XH6$, introduced by Cordero et al. in [3], Cordero et al. in [4], Behl et al. in [5 Capdevila et al. in [6], and Xiao and Yin et al. in [7].

The iterative expressions of these methods for solving a nonlinear systems $F(x) = 0$, F $\Omega \subseteq \mathbb{R}^n \rightarrow \mathbb{R}^n$ are shown below. Newton's scheme is the most known iterative algorithm

$$x^{(k+1)} = x^{(k)} - \left[F'\left(x^{(k)}\right)\right]^{-1} F\left(x^{(k)}\right), \quad k = 0, 1, \ldots, \quad (2)$$

where $F'(x)$ denotes the Jacobian matrix associated to F.

The following sixth-order iterative scheme (see [3]) is named $C6_1$. It uses three evalu tions of F and two of F', per iteration:

$$\begin{aligned} y^{(k)} &= x^{(k)} - F'\left(x^{(k)}\right)^{-1} F\left(x^{(k)}\right), \\ z^{(k)} &= y^{(k)} - F'\left(x^{(k)}\right)^{-1}\left[2I - F'\left(y^{(k)}\right) F'\left(x^{(k)}\right)^{-1}\right] F\left(y^{(k)}\right), \\ x^{(k+1)} &= z^{(k)} - F'\left(y^{(k)}\right)^{-1} F\left(z^{(k)}\right), \quad k = 0, 1, \ldots \end{aligned} \quad (3)$$

The following scheme, introduced in [4], is a modified Newton–Jarratt compositio with sixth-order convergence and evaluates twice F and F', per iteration. It is denote by $C6_2$:

$$\begin{aligned} z^{(k)} &= x^{(k)} - \frac{2}{3} F'\left(x^{(k)}\right)^{-1} F\left(x^{(k)}\right), \\ y^{(k)} &= x^{(k)} - \frac{1}{2}\left[3F'\left(z^{(k)}\right) - F'\left(x^{(k)}\right)\right]^{-1}\left[3F'\left(z^{(k)}\right) + F'\left(x^{(k)}\right)\right] F'\left(x^{(k)}\right)^{-1} F\left(x^{(k)}\right), \\ x^{(k+1)} &= y^{(k)} - \left[-\frac{1}{2} F'\left(x^{(k)}\right) + \frac{3}{2} F'\left(z^{(k)}\right)\right]^{-1} F\left(y^{(k)}\right), \quad k = 0, 1, \ldots \end{aligned} \quad (4)$$

Algorithm (5) was constructed by Behl et al. in [5] and it is denoted by B_6.

$$y^{(k)} = x^{(k)} - \frac{2}{3}F'\left(x^{(k)}\right)^{-1}F\left(x^{(k)}\right),$$

$$z^{(k)} = x^{(k)} - \left[a_1 I + a_2\left(F'\left(y^{(k)}\right)^{-1}F'\left(x^{(k)}\right)\right)^2\right]F'\left(x^{(k)}\right)^{-1}F\left(x^{(k)}\right), \quad (5)$$

$$x^{(k+1)} = z^{(k)} - \left[b_2F'\left(x^{(k)}\right) + b_3F'\left(y^{(k)}\right)\right]^{-1}\left[F'\left(x^{(k)}\right) + b_1F'\left(y^{(k)}\right)\right]F'\left(x^{(k)}\right)^{-1}F\left(z^{(k)}\right),$$

where $k \geq 0$, $a_1 = -a_2 + 1 = 5/8, a_2 = 3/8, b_2 = 1 - b_3 + b_1 = (-1/2)(1 + 3b_1)$, $b_3 = (1/2)(3 + 5b_1)$ and b_1 is a parameter. This is a class of iterative processes that achieves convergence order six with twice F evaluations and F', per iteration. For our comparison, we will use two versions of method B_6, one of them with $a_2 = \frac{3}{8}$, $a_1 = \frac{5}{8}$, $b_1 = -\frac{3}{5}$, $b_3 = 0$, $b_2 = \frac{2}{5}$ and the other one with $a_2 = \frac{3}{8}$, $a_1 = \frac{5}{8}$, $b_1 = 1$, $b_3 = 4$, $b_2 = -2$.

Capdevila et al. in [6] introduced the following class of iterative methods that we call $PSH6_1$. The elements of this family have an order of convergence of six and they need three evaluations of function F, one of the the Jacobian matrix F' and a divided difference $[x, y; F]$ per iteration:

$$y^{(k)} = x^{(k)} - \left[F'\left(x^{(k)}\right)\right]^{-1}F\left(x^{(k)}\right),$$

$$z^{(k)} = y^{(k)} - \left[I + 2t^{(k)} + \frac{1}{2}\alpha t^{(k)^2}\right]\left[F'\left(x^{(k)}\right)\right]^{-1}F\left(y^{(k)}\right), \quad (6)$$

$$x^{(k+1)} = z^{(k)} - \left[I + 2t^{(k)} + \frac{1}{2}\alpha t^{(k)^2}\right]\left[F'\left(x^{(k)}\right)\right]^{-1}F\left(z^{(k)}\right), \quad k = 0, 1, \ldots,$$

where α is free and $t^{(k)} = I - \left[F'\left(x^{(k)}\right)\right]^{-1}\left[x^{(k)}, y^{(k)}; F\right]$. For the numerical results, we will take $\alpha = 0$ and $\alpha = 10$.

Introduced also by Capdevila et al. in [6], we work with the following scheme, denoted $PHS6_2$, with the same order of convergence and the same number of functional evaluations per iteration as $PSH6_1$:

$$y^{(k)} = x^{(k)} - \left[F'\left(x^{(k)}\right)\right]^{-1}F\left(x^{(k)}\right),$$

$$z^{(k)} = y^{(k)} - \left[I + 2\left(I + \alpha t^{(k)}\right)^{-1}t^{(k)}\right]\left[F'\left(x^{(k)}\right)\right]^{-1}F\left(y^{(k)}\right), \quad (7)$$

$$x^{(k+1)} = z^{(k)} - \left[I + 2\left(I + \alpha t^{(k)}\right)^{-1}t^{(k)}\right]\left[F'\left(x^{(k)}\right)\right]^{-1}F\left(z^{(k)}\right), \quad k = 0, 1, \ldots$$

In this case, we take $\alpha = 10$.

Finally, we use the method called XH_6 introduced by Xiao and Yin in [7]. In this case, we need twice F evaluations and F' on $x^{(k)}, z^{(k)}$ and $x^{(k)}, y^{(k)}$, respectively, per iteration.

$$y^{(k)} = x^{(k)} - \frac{2}{3}F'\left(x^{(k)}\right)^{-1}F\left(x^{(k)}\right),$$

$$z^{(k)} = x^{(k)} - \frac{1}{2}\left[-I + \frac{9}{4}F'\left(y^{(k)}\right)^{-1}F'\left(x^{(k)}\right) + \frac{3}{4}F'\left(x^{(k)}\right)^{-1}F'\left(y^{(k)}\right)\right]F'\left(x^{(k)}\right)^{-1}F\left(x^{(k)}\right), \quad (8)$$

$$x^{(k+1)} = z^{(k)} - \frac{1}{2}\left[3F'\left(y^{(k)}\right)^{-1} - F'\left(x^{(k)}\right)^{-1}\right]F\left(z^{(k)}\right), \quad k = 0, 1, \ldots$$

Multidimensional Real Dynamics Concepts

Discrete dynamics is a very useful tool to study the stability of iterative schemes for solving nonlinear systems. An exhaustive description of this tool can be found in the book [8]. A resource used for the stability analysis of iterative schemes for solving nonlinear systems is to analyze the dynamical behavior of the vectorial rational operator obtained to apply the iterative expression on low degree polynomial systems. This technique generally uses quadratic or cubic polynomials [9].

When we have scalar iterative processes, the tools to be used are of real or complex discrete dynamics. However, here, we handle a family of vectorial iterative methods, so real multidimensional dynamics must be used to analyze its stability, see [6]. We proceed by taking a system of quadratic polynomials on which we will apply our method in order to obtain the associated multidimensional rational operator and perform the analysis of the fixed and critical points in order to select members of the family with good stability.

Some concepts used in this study are presented, see for instance [10].

Let $G : \mathbb{R}^n \to \mathbb{R}^n$ be the operator obtained from the iterative scheme on a polynomial system $p(x)$. The set of successive images of $x^{(0)}$ through $G(x)$, $\left\{x^{(0)}, G\left(x^{(0)}\right), \ldots, G^m\left(x^{(0)}\right), \ldots\right\}$ is called the orbit of $x^{(0)} \in \mathbb{R}^n$. $x^* \in \mathbb{R}^n$ is a fixed point of G if $G(x^*) = x^*$. Of course, the roots of $p(x)$ are a fixed point of G, but there may be fixed points of G that are not solutions of system $p(x)$. We refer them as strange fixed points. A point x that satisfies $G^k(x) = x$ and $G^{k-p}(x) \neq x$, for $p < k$ and $k \geq 1$ is called a periodic point, of period k. For classifying the stability of fixed or periodic points, we use the following result.

Theorem 1 ([8], pg. 558). *Let $G : \mathbb{R}^n \to \mathbb{R}^n$ be of type C^2. Assuming that x^* is a periodic k-point, $k \geq 1$. If $\lambda_1, \lambda_2, \ldots, \lambda_n$ are the eigenvalues of $G'(x^*)$, we have the following:*

(a) *If all eigenvalues λ_k verify that $|\lambda_k| < 1$, then x^* is an attracting point.*
(b) *If an eigenvalue λ_{k_0} is such that $|\lambda_{k_0}| > 1$, then x^* is unstable, that is, repulsor or saddle.*
(c) *If all eigenvalues λ_k verify that $|\lambda_k| > 1$, then x^* is a repulsive point.*

The set of preimages of any order of an attracting fixed point of the multidimensional rational function G, x^*,

$$\mathcal{A}(x^*) = \left\{x^{(0)} \in \mathbb{R}^n : G^m\left(x^{(0)}\right) \to x^*, m \to \infty\right\},$$

is the basin of attraction of x^*, $\mathcal{A}(x^*)$.

The solutions of $G'(x) = 0$ are called the critical point of operator G . The critical points different of the roots of $p(x)$ are called a free critical point. The critical points are important for our analysis because of the following result from Julia and Fatou (see [11–13]).

Theorem 2 (Julia and Fatou). *Let G be a rational function. The immediate basin of attraction of a periodic (or fixed) attractor point contains at least one critical point.*

2. Family ACTV for Nonlinear Systems

Taking into account the iterative expression of family (1), we can extend, in a natural way, this expression for solving nonlinear systems $F(x) = 0$. We change scalar f' by vectorial F' and $f[x, y]$ by the divided difference operator $[x, y; F]$. The resulting expression is

$$
\begin{aligned}
y^{(k)} &= x^{(k)} - \left[F'\left(x^{(k)}\right)\right]^{-1} F\left(x^{(k)}\right), \\
z^{(k)} &= y^{(k)} - \left(2\left[x^{(k)}, y^{(k)}; F\right] - F'\left(x^{(k)}\right)\right)^{-1} F\left(y^{(k)}\right), \\
x^{(k+1)} &= z^{(k)} - \left[\alpha F'\left(x^{(k)}\right)^{-1} + (1-\alpha)\left[x^{(k)}, y^{(k)}; F\right]^{-1}\right] F\left(z^{(k)}\right) \\
&\quad - (1+\alpha)\left[I_n - F'\left(x^{(k)}\right)^{-1}\left[x^{(k)}, y^{(k)}; F\right]\right] \cdot F'\left(x^{(k)}\right)^{-1} F\left(z^{(k)}\right),
\end{aligned}
\tag{9}
$$

where I_n is the $n \times n$ identity matrix.

Mapping $[\cdot, \cdot; F] : \Omega \times \Omega \subset \mathbb{R}^n \times \mathbb{R}^n \longrightarrow \mathcal{L}(\mathbb{R}^n)$ such that

$$[x, y; F](x-y) = F(x) - F(y), \text{ for any } x, y \in \Omega,$$

is the divided difference operator of F on $\mathbb{R}^n$ (see [14]).

The proof of the main result is based on the Genochi–Hermite formula (see [14]),

$$[x, y; F] = \int_0^1 F'(x + t(x-y))dt, \text{ for all } (x, y) \in \Omega \times \Omega.$$

By developing $F'(x+th)$ in Taylor series around x, we obtain

$$\int_0^1 F'(x+th)dt = F'(x) + \frac{1}{2}F''(x)h + \frac{1}{6}F'''(x)h^2 + \mathcal{O}\left(h^3\right). \tag{10}$$

Denoting by $e = x - \xi$, where ξ is a zero of $F(x)$, and assuming that $F'(\xi)$ is invertible, we obtain

$$
\begin{aligned}
F(x) &= F'(\xi)\left(e + C_2 e^2 + C_3 e^3 + C_4 e^4 + C_5 e^5\right) + O\left(e^6\right), \\
F'(x) &= F'(\xi)\left(I + 2C_2 e + 3C_3 e^2 + 4C_4 e^3 + 5C_5 e^4\right) + O\left(e^5\right), \\
F''(x) &= F'(\xi)\left(2C_2 + 6C_3 e + 12C_4 e^2 + 20C_5 e^3\right) + O\left(e^4\right), \\
F'''(x) &= F'(\xi)\left(6C_3 + 24C_4 e + 60C_5 e^2\right) + O\left(e^3\right),
\end{aligned}
$$

where $C_q = \frac{1}{q!}[F'(\xi)]^{-1}F^{(q)}(\xi), q \geq 2$. Replacing these expressions in the Genocchi–Hermite formula and denoting the second point of the divided difference by $y = x + h$ and the error of y by $e_y = y - \xi$, we obtain

$$[x, y; F] = F'(\xi)\left[I + C_2(e_y + e) + C_3 e^2\right] + O\left(e^3\right).$$

Particularly, if y is the Newton approximation, i.e., $h = x - y = [F'(x)]^{-1}F(x)$, we obtain

$$[x, y; F] = F'(\xi)\left[I + C_2 e + \left(C_2^2 + C_3\right)e^2\right] + O\left(e^3\right).$$

Convergence Analysis

Theorem 3. *Being $F : \Omega \subseteq \mathbb{R}^n \to \mathbb{R}^n$ differentiable enough in an open convex neighborhood Ω of ξ, root of $F(x)$. Consider a seed $x^{(0)}$ close enough to the solution ξ and that $F'(x)$ is continuous and invertible in ξ. Then, (9) has a local convergence of order six, for all $\alpha \in \mathbb{R}$, with the error equation*

$$e^{(k+1)} = \left[(5+\alpha)\left(C_2^5 - C_2^2 C_3 C_2\right) - C_3 C_2^3 + C_3^2 C_2\right] e^{(k)^6} + O\left(e^{(k)^7}\right),$$

being $C_k = \frac{1}{k!}[F'(\xi)]^{-1}F^{(k)}(\xi), \quad k = 2, 3, \ldots, \quad e^{(k)} = x^{(k)} - \xi$.

Proof. From

$$y^{(k)} = x^{(k)} - \left[F'\left(x^{(k)}\right)\right]^{-1} F\left(x^{(k)}\right), \quad (1$$

We perform the Taylor series of $F\left(x^{(k)}\right)$ and $F'\left(x^{(k)}\right)$ around ξ,

$$\begin{aligned} \mathrm{F}\left(x^{(k)}\right) &= F'(\xi)\left[e^{(k)} + C_2 e^{(k)^2} + C_3 e^{(k)^3} + C_4 e^{(k)^4} + C_5 e^{(k)^5} + C_6 e^{(k)^6} + C_7 e^{(k)^7}\right] \\ &\quad + \mathrm{O}\left(e^{(k)^8}\right), \end{aligned} \quad (1$$

$$\begin{aligned} \mathrm{F}'\left(x^{(k)}\right) &= F'(\xi)\left[I + 2C_2 e^{(k)} + 3C_3 e^{(k)^2} + 4C_4 e^{(k)^3} + 5C_5 e^{(k)^4} + 6C_6 e^{(k)^5} + 7C_7 e^{(k)^6}\right] \\ &\quad + O\left(e^{(k)^7}\right). \end{aligned} \quad (1$$

We suppose that the Jacobian matrix $F'(\xi)$ is nonsingular and calculate the Tayl expansion of $\left[F'\left(x^{(k)}\right)\right]^{-1}$ as follows:

$$\begin{aligned} \left[F'\left(x^{(k)}\right)\right]^{-1} &= \left[I + X_2 e^{(k)} + X_3 e^{(k)^2} + X_4 e^{(k)^3} + X_5 e^{(k)^4} + X_6 e^{(k)^5} + X_7 e^{(k)^6}\right]\left[F'(\xi)\right]^{-1} \\ &\quad + \mathrm{O}\left(\left(e^k\right)^7\right), \end{aligned} \quad (1\cdot$$

where $X_2, X_3, X_4, X_5, X_6, X_7$ are unknowns such that

$$\left[F'\left(x^{(k)}\right)\right]^{-1} F'\left(x^{(k)}\right) = I.$$

Then, it can be proven that

$$\begin{aligned} &\left[F'\left(x^{(k)}\right)\right]^{-1} = \Big[I - 2C_2 e^{(k)} + \left(4C_2^2 - 3C_3\right)e^{(k)^2} + \left(6C_3C_2 + 6C_2C_3 - 4C_4 - 8C_2^3\right)e^{(k)^3} + \\ &\left(16C_2^4 + 9C_3^2 - 12C_3C_2^2 - 12C_2C_3C_2 - 12C_2^2C_3 + 8C_4C_2 + 8C_2C_4 - 5C_5\right)e^{(k)^4} + \\ &\left(-32C_2^5 - 18C_3^2C_2 + 24C_3C_2^3 + 24C_2C_3C_2^2 + 24C_2^2C_3C_2 - 16C_4C_2^2 - 16C_2C_4C_2 + 10C_5C_2\right. \\ &\left. - 18C_3C_2C_3 - 18C_2C_3^2 + 12C_4C_3 + 24C_2^3C_3 - 16C_2^2C_4 + 12C_3C_4 + 10C_2C_5 - 6C_6\right)e^{(k)^5} \\ &+ \left(64C_2^6 + 36C_3^2C_2^2 - 48C_3C_2^4 - 48C_2C_3C_2^3 - 48C_2^2C_3C_2^2 + 32C_4C_2^3 + 32C_2C_4C_2^2 - 20C_5C_2^2\right. \\ &+ 36C_3C_2C_3C_2 + 36C_2C_3^2C_2 - 24C_4C_3C_2 - 48C_2^3C_3C_2 + 32C_2^2C_4C_2 - 24C_3C_4C_2 - 20C_2C_5C_2 \\ &+ 12C_6C_2 - 48C_2^4C_3 - 27C_3^3 + 36C_3C_2^2C_3 + 36C_2C_3C_2C_3 + 36C_2^2C_3^2 - 24C_4C_2C_3 - 24C_2C_4C_3 \\ &\left. + 15C_5C_3 - 24C_3C_2C_4 - 24C_2C_3C_4 + 16C_4^2 + 32C_2^3C_4 - 20C_2^2C_5 + 15C_3C_5 + 12C_2C_6 - 7C_7\right) \\ &e^{(k)^6}\Big]\left[F'(\xi)\right]^{-1} + O\left(e^{(k)^7}\right), \end{aligned} \quad (1\colon$$

and multiplying expressions (12) and (15), we obtain

$$\begin{aligned} &\left[F'\left(x^{(k)}\right)\right]^{-1} F\left(x^{(k)}\right) = e^{(k)} - C_2 e^{(k)^2} + 2\left(C_2^2 - C_3\right)e^{(k)^3} + \left(3C_3C_2 + 4C_2C_3 - 3C_4 - 4C_2^3\right. \\ &e^{(k)^4} + \left(-6C_3C_2^2 - 8C_2^2C_3 + 6C_3^2 - 6C_2C_3C_2 + 6C_2C_4 + 4C_4C_2 + 8C_2^4 - 4C_5\right)e^{(k)^5} + \\ &\left(-16C_2^5 - 9C_3^2C_2 + 12C_3C_2^3 + 12C_2C_3C_2^2 + 12C_2^2C_3C_2 - 8C_4C_2^2 - 8C_2C_4C_2 + 5C_5C_2\right. \\ &\left. - 12C_3C_2C_3 - 12C_2C_3^2 + 8C_4C_3 + 16C_2^3C_3 - 12C_2^2C_4 + 9C_3C_4 + 8C_2C_5 - 5C_6\right)e^{(k)^6}. \end{aligned}$$

Taking into account $e^{(k)} = x^{(k)} - \xi$, the expansion of the error at the first step of family (1) is

$$\begin{aligned} y^{(k)} - \xi = & C_2 e^{(k)^2} - 2\left(C_2^2 - C_3\right)e^{(k)^3} - \left(3C_3C_2 + 4C_2C_3 - 3C_4 - 4C_2^3\right)e^{(k)^4} \\ & - \left(-6C_3C_2^2 - 8C_2^2C_3 + 6C_3^2 - 6C_2C_3C_2 + 6C_2C_4 + 4C_4C_2 + 8C_2^4 - 4C_5\right)e^{(k)^5} \\ & - \left(-16C_2^5 - 9C_3^2C_2 + 12C_3C_2^3 + 12C_2C_3C_2^2 + 12C_2^2C_3C_2 - 8C_4C_2^2 - 8C_2C_4C_2 + 5C_5C_2\right. \\ & \left. -12C_3C_2C_3 - 12C_2C_3^2 + 8C_4C_3 + 16C_2^3C_3 - 12C_2^2C_4 + 9C_3C_4 + 8C_2C_5 - 5C_6\right)e^{(k)^6}. \end{aligned}$$

For $z^{(k)}$, we calculate $\left[x^{(k)}, y^{(k)}; F\right]$ up to order six using the Genochi–Hermite formula seen in (10), obtaining

$$\begin{aligned} = & F'(x)\left[I + C_2 e^{(k)} + \left(C_2^2 + C_3\right)e^{(k)^2} + \left(C_4 + C_3C_2 + 2C_2C_3 - 2C_2^3\right)e^{(k)^3}\right. \\ & + \left(C_5 + C_4C_2 + 3C_2C_4 + 2C_3^2 - 3C_2C_3C_2 - 4C_2^2C_3 - C_3C_2^2 + 4C_2^4\right)e^{(k)^4} \\ & + \left(C_6 - 8C_2^5 + 6C_2C_3C_2^2 + 8C_2^3C_3 + 6C_2^2C_3C_2 - C_4C_2^2 - 6C_2^2C_4 - 4C_2C_4\right. \\ & \left. C_2 - 6C_2C_3^2 - C_3^2C_2 - 2C_3C_2C_3 + 2C_4C_3 + 3C_3C_4 + C_5C_2 + 4C_2C_5\right)e^{(k)^5} \\ & + \left(C_7 + 16C_2^6 + 9C_2C_3^2C_2 + 12C_2C_3C_2C_3 + 12C_2^2C_3^2 - C_3C_2C_3C_2 - C_3^2C_2^2\right. \\ & - 12C_2C_3C_2^3 - 12C_2^2C_3C_2^2 - 12C_2^3C_3C_2 - 16C_2^4C_3 + 4C_3C_2^4 + 8C_2C_4C_2^2 \\ & + 8C_2^2C_4C_2 + 12C_2^3C_4 + C_4C_2^3 - 8C_2C_4C_3 - 9C_2C_3C_4 - 3C_3C_2C_4 - C_3C_4C_2 \\ & - C_4C_3C_2 - 2C_4C_2C_3 + 5C_2C_6 + C_6C_2 - 2C_3^3 + 4C_3C_5 + 2C_5C_3 + 3C_4^2 \\ & \left.\left. -5C_2C_5C_2 - 8C_2^2C_5 - C_5C_2^2\right)e^{(k)^6}\right] + O\left(e^{(k)^7}\right). \end{aligned} \quad (16)$$

Following a similar procedure to the one used in (14) and (15), we have

$$\begin{aligned} & \left(2\left[x^{(k)}, y^{(k)}; F\right] - F'\left(x^{(k)}\right)\right)^{-1} = \left[I + \left(C_3 - 2C_2^2\right)e^{(k)^2} + \left(2C_4 - 2C_3C_2 - 4C_2C_3 + 4C_2^3\right)e^{(k)^3}\right. \\ & + \left(-4C_2^4 + 6C_2^2C_3 + 6C_2C_3C_2 - 6C_2C_4 - 2C_4C_2 + 3C_5 - 3C_3^2\right)e^{(k)^4} + \left(-2C_4C_2^2 + 8C_2^2C_4\right. \\ & + 8C_2C_4C_2 - 2C_4C_3 - 4C_3C_4 + 8C_3C_2^3 - 4C_2C_3C_2^2 - 8C_2^2C_3C_2 - 4C_2^3C_3 - 2C_5C_2 - 8C_2C_5 \\ & \left. -2C_3C_2C_3 + 8C_2C_3^2 + 4C_6\right)e^{(k)^5} + \left(8C_2^6 - 4C_2^4C_3 + 8C_2^2C_3C_2^2 - 4C_2C_3C_2^3 - 24C_3C_2^4 + 4C_2^3C_3C_2\right. \\ & - 10C_2^2C_3^2 - 2C_2C_3C_2C_3 + 10C_3^2C_2^2 + 12C_3C_2C_3C_2 + 16C_3C_2^2C_3 - 10C_2C_3^2C_2 + 10C_2C_4C_3 - 6C_4 \\ & C_2C_3 - 2C_4C_3C_2 - 4C_3C_2C_4 + 10C_2C_3C_4 - 4C_2C_4C_2^2 + 10C_4C_2^3 - 4C_2^3C_4 - 12C_2^2C_4C_2 - C_5C_3 \\ & \left.\left. -5C_3C_5 - 10C_2C_6 - 2C_6C_2 - 3C_3^3 + 10C_2C_5C_2 + 10C_2^2C_5 - 4C_5C_2^2 - 2C_4^2\right)e^{(k)^6}\right] + O\left(e^{(k)^7}\right). \end{aligned} \quad (17)$$

Now, we obtain the expansion of $F\left(y^{(k)}\right)$,

$$\begin{aligned} \left(y^{(k)} - \xi\right)^2 = & C_2^2 e^{(k)^4} + \left(-4C_2^3 + 2C_2C_3 + 2C_3C_2\right)e^{(k)^5} + \left(12C_2^4 - 11C_2^2C_3 + 4C_3^2 + 3C_2C_4\right. \\ & \left. -4C_2C_3C_2 + 3C_4C_2 - 7C_3C_2^2\right)e^{(k)^6} + O\left(e^{(k)^7}\right), \\ \left(y^{(k)} - \xi\right)^3 = & C_2^3 e^{(k)^6} + O\left(e^{(k)^7}\right), \end{aligned}$$

$$\begin{aligned}F\left(y^{(k)}\right) =& F'(\xi)\left[\left(y^{(k)}-\xi\right)+C_2\left(y^{(k)}-\xi\right)^2\right]+O\left(\left(y^{(k)}-\xi\right)^3\right)\\ =& F'(\xi)\Big[C_2e^{(k)^2}+2\left(C_3-C_2^2\right)e^{(k)^3}+\left(3C_4+5C_2^3-3C_3C_2-4C_2C_3\right)e^{(k)^4}\\ &+\left(4C_5-6C_2C_4+10C_2^2C_3-6C_3^2-4C_4C_2+8C_2C_3C_2-12C_2^4+6C_3C_2^2\right)e^{(k)^5}\\ &+\left(28C_2^5-27C_2^3C_3+16C_2C_3^2+15C_2^2C_4-9C_3C_4-8C_2C_5+5C_6-16C_2^2C_3C_2\right.\\ &+9C_3^2C_2+11C_2C_4C_2-5C_5C_2-18C_2C_3C_2^2+8C_4C_2^2-12C_3C_2^3-8C_4C_3\\ &\left.+12C_3C_2C_3)e^{(k)^6}\Big]+O\left(e^{(k)^7}\right).\end{aligned} \quad (18)$$

Considering the results obtained in (16)–(18), the second step has as the error equation

$$\begin{aligned}z^{(k)}-\xi =& \left(C_2^3-C_3C_2\right)e^{(k)^4}+\left(-2C_4C_2+2C_2^2C_3+2C_2C_3C_2+4C_3C_2^2-2C_3^2-4C_2^4\right)e^{(k)^5}\\ &+\left(10C_2^5-5C_2^3C_3-8C_2^2C_3C_2-8C_2C_3C_2^2-9C_3C_2^3+4C_2C_3^2+6C_3^2C_2+8C_3C_2C_3+3C_2^2C_4\right.\\ &\left.+3C_2C_4C_2+6C_4C_2^2-3C_3C_4-4C_4C_3-3C_5C_2\right)e^{(k)^6}.\end{aligned}$$

To obtain the error equation of the third step, we need the calculation of $[x^k, y^k; F]^{-1}$ and $F\left(z^{(k)}\right)$ since the other elements were previously obtained. Following a process similar to that seen in (17) and developing only to order two, we have that

$$[x^k, y^k; F]^{-1} = I - C_2e^{(k)} - C_3e^{(k)^2} + O\left(e^{(k)^3}\right).$$

For the calculation of $F\left(z^{(k)}\right)$, we are only interested in the terms up to order six, so applying what we see in formula (18), we obtain

$$F\left(z^{(k)}\right) = F'(\xi)\left[\left(z^{(k)}-x^*\right)\right]+O\left(\left(z^{(k)}-\xi\right)^2\right).$$

The resulting error equation for the family of methods (9) is

$$e^{(k+1)} = \left[(5+\alpha)\left(C_2^5-C_2^2C_3C_2\right)-C_3C_2^3+C_3^2C_2\right]e^{(k)^6}+O\left(e^{(k)^7}\right).$$

□

Once the convergence order of the proposed class of the iterative method is proven, we undertake a complexity analysis, taking into account the cost of solving the linear system and the rest of the computational effort, not only of the proposed class but also of Newton's and those schemes presented in the Introduction, with the same order six. In order to calculate it, let us remark that the computational cost (in terms of products/quotients) of solving a linear system of size $n \times n$ is

$$\frac{1}{3}n^3 + n^2 - \frac{1}{3}n,$$

but if another linear system is solved with the same coefficient matrix, then the cost increases only in n^2 operations. Moreover, a matrix–vector product corresponds to n^2 operations. From these bases, the computational effort of each scheme is presented in Table 1. As the ACTV class depends on parameter α, we consider $\alpha = 1$, as this value eliminates one of the terms in the iterative expression, reducing the complexity.

Table 1. Computational cost (products/quotients) of proposed and comparison methods.

Method	Complexity C
Newton	$\frac{1}{3}n^3+n^2-\frac{1}{3}n$
$C6_1$	$\frac{2}{3}n^3+5n^2-\frac{2}{3}n$
$C6_2$	n^3+4n^2-n
B_6	n^3+8n^2-n
$PSH6_1$	$\frac{1}{3}n^3+11n^2-\frac{1}{3}n$
$PSH6_2$	$\frac{5}{3}n^3+9n^2-\frac{2}{3}n$
$XH6$	$\frac{2}{3}n^3+7n^2-\frac{2}{3}n$
ACTV$\alpha=1$	$\frac{2}{3}n^3+5n^2-\frac{2}{3}n$

Observing the data in Table 1, there seems to be a great difference among Newton's and sixth-order methods, with $PSH6_2$, B_6 and $C6_2$ being the most costly, in this order. Our proposed scheme ACTV for $\alpha=1$, stays in the middle values of the table. However, this must be seen in contrast with the order of convergence p of each scheme. With this point of view, the comparison among the methods is more clear.

With the information provided by Table 1, we represent in Figures 1 and 2 the performance of the efficiency index $IO=p^{\frac{1}{C}}$ of each method, where p is the order of the corresponding scheme. This index was introduced by Traub in [15], in order to classify the procedures by their computational complexity.

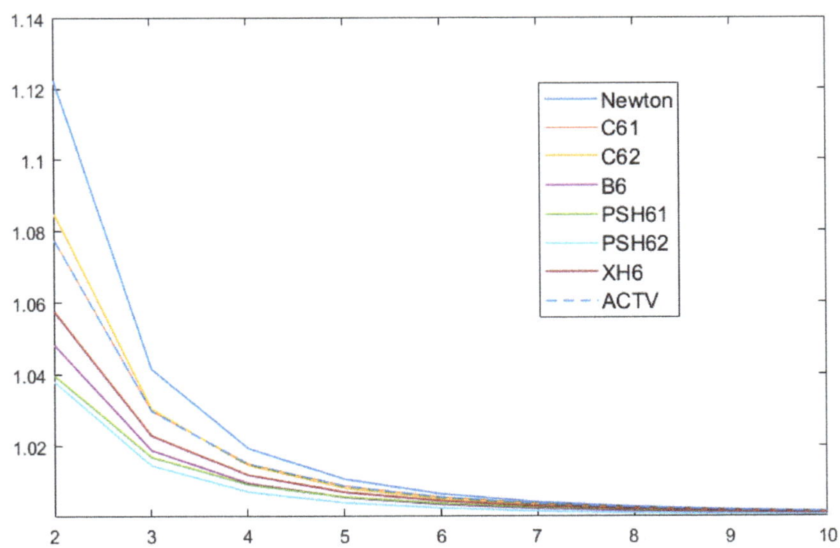

Figure 1. Efficiency index IO for systems of size $n=2$ to $n=10$.

In Figure 1, we observe that the best scheme is that of Newton, being that our proposed procedure (dashed line in the figure) is third in efficiency. This situation changes for bigger sizes of the system (see Figure 2), as ACTV for $\alpha=1$ achieves the second best place, very close to Newton's, improving the rest of schemes of the same order of convergence. Our concern now is the following: is it possible to find some values of the parameter α such that this performance is held or even improved? The improvement can be in terms of the wideness of the set of converging initial estimations. This is the reason why we analyze the stability of the class of iterative methods.

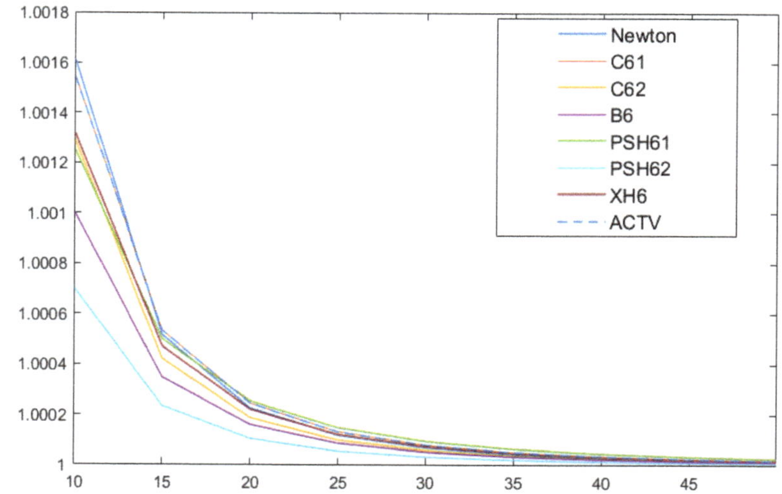

Figure 2. Efficiency index IO for systems of size $n = 10$ to $n = 50$.

3. Stability Analysis

Let us consider a polynomial system of n variables $q(x) = 0$, $q : \mathbb{R}^n \to \mathbb{R}^n$ wher $q_i(x) = x_i^2 - 1$, $i = 1, 2, ..., n$ and we denote by $K(x)$ the associated rational functio From now on, we denote by $ACTV^6(x, \alpha) = \left(actv_1^6(x, \alpha), actv_2^6(x, \alpha), \dots, actv_n^6(x, \alpha)\right)$ th vectorial function obtained when class (9) is applied on $q(x)$. As $q(x) = 0$ is uncouple all functions $actv_j^6(x, \alpha)$ are analogous, with the difference of the index $j = 1, 2, ..., n$. The expressions are

$$actv_j^6(x, \alpha) = \frac{p(x, \alpha)}{128 x_j^5 \left(1 + x_j^2\right)^2 \left(1 + 3x_j^2\right)}, \quad j = 1, 2, ..., n, \tag{19}$$

where,

$$\begin{aligned} p(x, \alpha) \;=\; & 1 + x_j^6(404 - 20\alpha) + x_j^{10}(782 - 6\alpha) + \alpha + x_j^{12}(77 + \alpha) - 2x_j^2(1 + 3\alpha) \\ & + 5x_j^8(155 + 3\alpha) + x_j^4(11 + 15\alpha). \end{aligned}$$

There are values of α for which the operator coordinates are simplified; we show th particular case when $\alpha = 1$.

$$actv_j^6(x, 1) = \frac{1 - 7x_j^2 + 34x_j^4 + 90x_j^6 + 125x_j^8 + 13x_j^{10}}{64 x_j^5 \left(1 + x_j^2\right)^2}, \quad j = 1, 2, ..., n. \tag{20}$$

By determining and analyzing the corresponding fixed points of the operator, w present a synthesis of the most relevant results.

Theorem 4. *Roots of $q(x)$ are the components of 2^n superattracting fixed points of $ACTV^6(x, \alpha$ associated to the class of iterative methods (9). The same happens with the roots of $l(t) = -1 - \alpha$ $(1 + 5\alpha)t^2 - (10 + 10\alpha)t^4 + (10\alpha - 286)t^6 - (421 + 5\alpha)t^8 + (\alpha - 307)t^{10}$ depending on α:*

- *(a) If $\alpha < -1$ or $\alpha > 307$, there are two real roots of $l(t)$, denoted by $l_i(\alpha)$, $i = 1, 2$. Fixe points $(l_{\sigma_1}(\alpha), l_{\sigma_2}(\alpha), \dots, l_{\sigma_n}(\alpha))$ where $\sigma_i \in \{1, 2\}$, are repulsive points. However, if any c $l_{\sigma_j}(\alpha) = \pm 1$, $j \in \{1, 2, \dots, n\}$, then they are saddle points.*
- *(b) $ACTV^6(x, \alpha)$ has no strange fixed points for $-1 \leq \alpha \leq 307$.*

Proof. To calculate the fixed points of $ACTV^6(x,\alpha)$, we solve $actv_j^6(x,\alpha) = x_j$,

$$-\left(x_j^2-1\right)l(t) = -1-\alpha+(1+5\alpha)t^2-(10+10\alpha)t^4+(10\alpha-286)t^6-(421+5\alpha)t^8 + (\alpha-307)t^{10}, \tag{21}$$

for $j = 1,2,\ldots,n$, that is, $x_j = \pm 1$ and roots of $l(t)$, provided that $t \neq 0$.

At most, two of the roots of $l(t)$ are not complex, depending on α. The qualitative performance of $ACTV^6(x,\alpha)$ is deduced from the eigenvalues of $ACTV^{6'}(x,\alpha)$ evaluated at the fixed points. Due to the nature of the polynomial system, these eigenvalues coincide with the coordinate function of the rational operator:

$$Eig_j(l_j(\alpha),\ldots,l_j(\alpha)) = \frac{\left(-1+l_j(\alpha)^2\right)^5\left(5(1+\alpha)+3l_j(\alpha)^6(77+\alpha)+3l_j(\alpha)^4(65+17\alpha)+l_j(\alpha)^2(49+37\alpha)\right)}{128l_j(\alpha)^6\left(1+l_j(\alpha)^2\right)^3\left(1+3l_j(\alpha)^2\right)^2} \tag{22}$$

We calculate the absolute values of these eigenvalues only where fixed points are real; it is clear that those fixed points $l_j(\alpha) = \pm 1$ are super attracting.

We proceed to plot some of the eigenvalues; if $\alpha < -1$, the eigenvalues of $\left(ACTV^6\right)'(x,\alpha)$ at any strange fixed point are named saddle points when their combinations have some component +1,-1 and the combinations of real roots coming from $l(t)$ are named repulsors because all eigenvalues are greater than 1 (see Figure 3a); if $\alpha > 307$, a similar behavior is observed (see Figure 3b). □

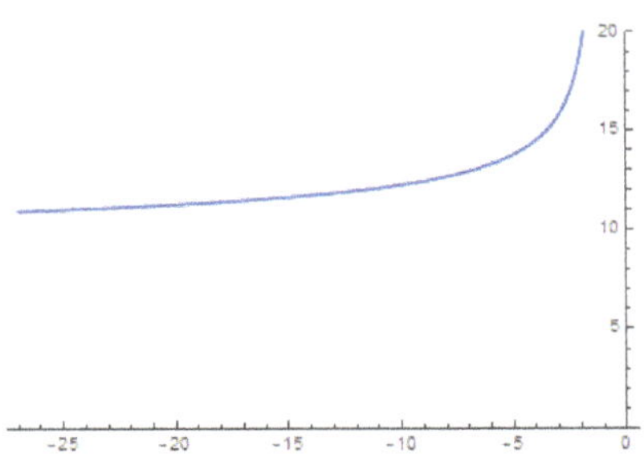

(a)

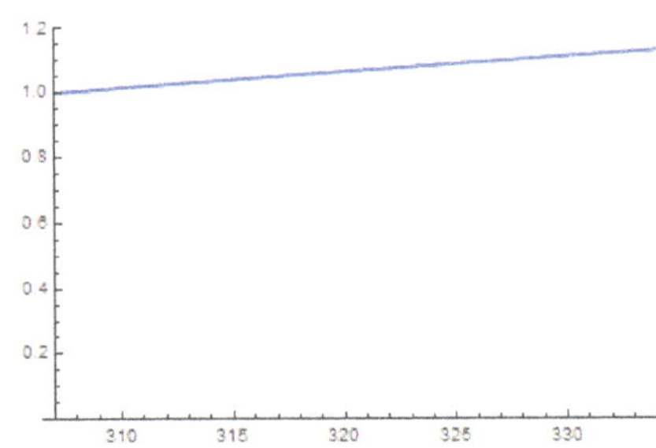

(b)

Figure 3. Eigenvalues associated to the fixed points. (**a**) $Eig_j(l_1(\alpha),\ldots,l_1(\alpha),\alpha)$ for $\alpha < -1$. (**b**) $Eig_j(l_1(\alpha),\ldots,l_1(\alpha),\alpha)$ for $\alpha > 307$.

Once the existence and stability of strange fixed points of $ACTV^6(x,\alpha)$ is studied, our aim is to show if there exist any other attracting behavior different from the fixed points.

4. Bifurcation Analysis of Free Critical Points

In the following result, we summarize the most relevant results about critical points.

Theorem 5. *$ACTV^6(x,\alpha)$ has as free critical points*

$$(cr_{\sigma_1}(\alpha), cr_{\sigma_2}(\alpha),\ldots,cr_{\sigma_n}(\alpha)),\ \sigma_i \in \{1,2,\ldots,m\},\ m \leq 6,$$

make null the entries of the Jacobian matrix, for $j = 1,2,\ldots,n$, being $cr_j(\alpha) \neq \pm 1$, $\forall j$, that is,

(a) If $\alpha \in (-\infty,-77] \cup \{-5\} \cup [-1,\infty)$, there not exist free critical points.
(b) If $\alpha \in (-77,-5) \cup (-5,-1)$, then two real roots of polynomial $k(x) = 5+5\alpha+(49+37\alpha)x^2+(195+51\alpha)x^4+(231+3\alpha)x^6$ are components of the free critical point.

Proof. The not null components of $ACTV^{6'}(x,\alpha)$ are

$$\frac{\partial a\,\text{ctv}_j^6(x,\alpha)}{\partial x_j} = \frac{\left(-1+x_j^2\right)^5\left(5(1+\alpha)+3x_j^6(77+\alpha)+3x_j^4(65+17\alpha)+x_j^2(49+37\alpha)\right)}{128x_j^6\left(1+x_j^2\right)^3\left(1+3x_j^2\right)^2}, \quad j=1,2. \tag{23}$$

Then, the real roots of $5(1+\alpha)+x_j^2(49+37)\alpha+3x_j^4(65+17\alpha)+3x_j^6(77+\alpha)$ are fre critical points, provided that they are not null. □

4.1. Parameter Line and Bifurcation Plane

Now, we use a graphical tool that helps us to identify for which values of parameter there might be convergence to roots, divergence or any other performance. Real parametri lines, for $n=2$, are presented in Figures 4 and 5 (see Theorem 5). In these figures, a differen free critical point is employed as a seed of each member of the class, using $-77<\alpha<-$ and $-5<\alpha<-1$ to ensure the existence of real critical points.

To generate them, a mesh of 1000×1000 points is made in $[0,1]\times]-77,-5[$ for th first figure and $[0,1]\times]-5,-1[$ for the next. We use $[0,15]$ in Figure 4a to increase th interval where α is defined and $[0,1]$ in Figures 4a and 5, allowing a better visualizatio So, the color corresponding to each value of α is red if the corresponding critical poin converges to one of the roots of the polynomial system, blue in the case of divergenc and black in other cases (chaos or periodic orbits). In addition, we use 500 as the limit o iterations and tolerance 10^{-3}.

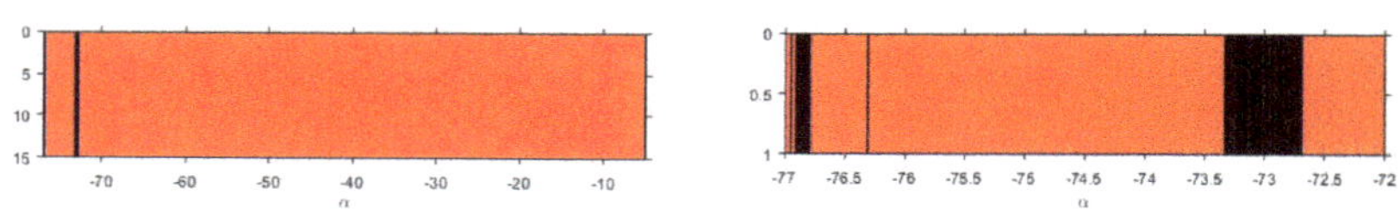

(a) (b)

Figure 4. Parameter line of $ACTV^6(x,\alpha)$ in $\alpha\in(-77,-5)$. (**a**) $\alpha\in(-77,-5)$. (**b**) $\alpha\in(-77,-72)$.

The global performance of each pair of free critical points is similar, so only $(cri_1(\alpha),cri_1(\alpha))$ is shown in Figure 4. In Figure 4a, only a small black region shows non-convergence to th roots (red color) . Now we show the parameter line for $\alpha\in(-5,-1)$.

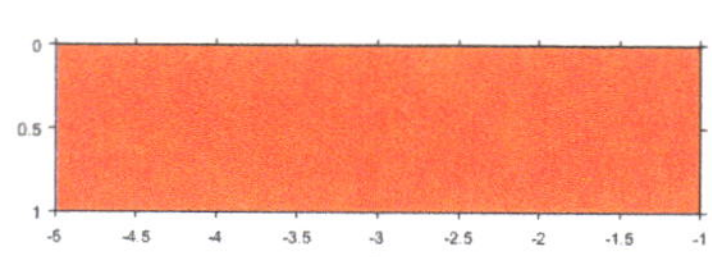

Figure 5. Parameter line of $ACTV^6(x,\alpha)$ in $\alpha\in(-5,-1)$.

In the line shown in Figure 5 it is observed that the zone shows global convergence t the roots. Therefore, it is a good area for choosing α.

The concept of bifurcation is important in nonlinear systems since it allows us to stud the behavior of the solutions of a family of iterative methods. In reference to dynamica systems, a bifurcation occurs when a small variation in the values of the system parameter (bifurcation parameters) causes a qualitative or topological change in the behavior of th system. Feigenbaum or bifurcation diagrams appear to analyze the changes of each clas of methods on $q(x)$ by using each critical point of the function as a seed and observing it performance for different ranges of α. By using a mesh with 4000 subintervals in each axi and after 1000 iterations, different behaviors can be observed.

Figure 6 shows the bifurcation diagrams in the black area of the parameter line Figure 4b, specifically when $\alpha \in (-73.5, -72.5)$. In Figure 6a, a general convergence to one of the roots appears. However, a quadruple-period orbit can be found in a small interval around $\alpha = -73$. It includes not only periodic but also chaotic behavior (strange attractors, blue regions).

To obtain the strange attractors, we plot in Figures 7 and 8 the orbit of 1000 initial guesses close to point $x = (0.36, 0.36)$ in the (x_1, x_2)-space by iterating $ACTV^6((x_1, x_2), \alpha)$. The value of the parameter used is $\alpha = -73.25$, laying in the blue region. For each seed, the first 500 iterations are ignored; meanwhile, the following 400 appear in blue and the last 100 in magenta color. We see in Figures 7 and 8 that a parabolic fixed point bifurcates in periodic orbits with increasing periods, and therefore falls in a dense orbit (chaotic behavior) in a small area of (x_1, x_2) space.

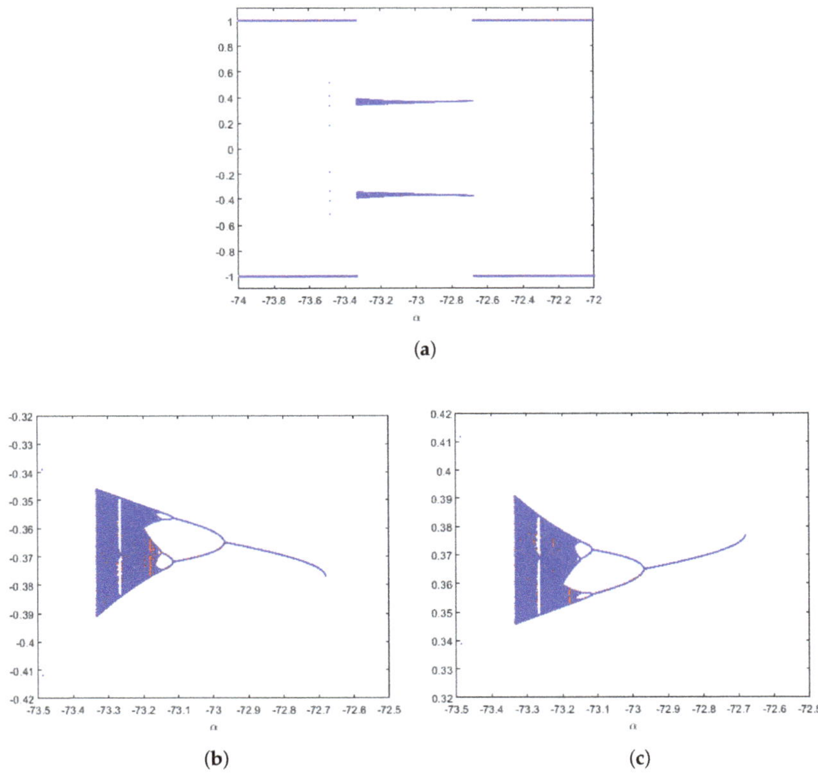

Figure 6. Feigenbaum diagrams of $ACTV^6(x, \alpha)$, for $-73.5 < \alpha < -72.5$, from different critical points. (**a**) $(cri_1(\alpha), cri_1(\alpha))$ and $(cri_2(\alpha), cri_2(\alpha))$. (**b**) $(cri_1(\alpha), cri_1(\alpha))$ a detail. (**c**) $(cri_2(\alpha), cri_2(\alpha))$ a detail.

For values of $\alpha \in (-76.9, -76.5)$, the bifurcation diagrams can be observed in Figure 9. It is related to the black region of Figure 4b. In addition, it can be observed a general convergence to one of the roots, but a sixth-order periodic orbit appears in a small interval around $\alpha = -76.8$. It includes chaotic behavior (blue regions) beside periodic performance. Strange attractors can be found in them. To represent it, we plot in Figure 10 the (x_1, x_2)-space the orbit of $x^{(0)} = (0.0001, 0.0001)$ by $ACTV^6((x_1, x_2), \alpha)$, for $\alpha = -76.9$, laying in the blue region.

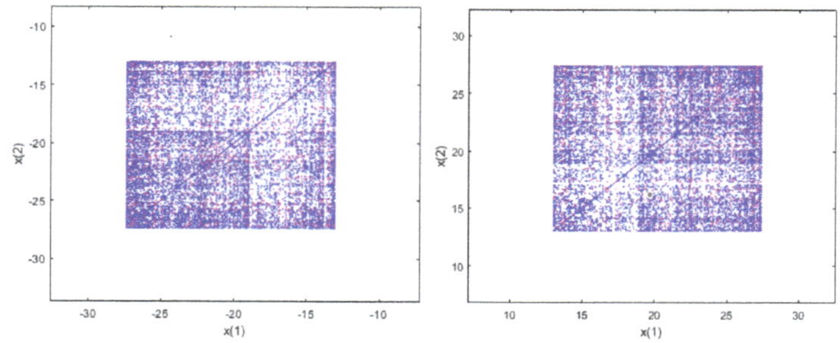

(a) (b)

Figure 7. Strange attractors of $ACTV6(x, \alpha)$ for α in blue quadruple-period cascade. (**a**) $\alpha = -73.2$ (**b**) $\alpha = -73.25$.

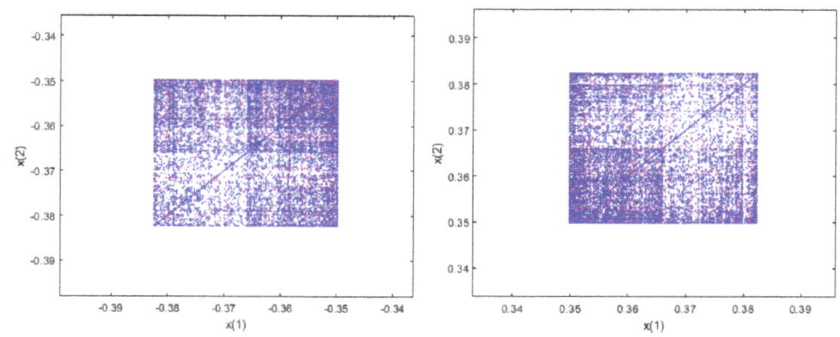

(a) (b)

Figure 8. Details Strange attractors of $ACTV6(x, \alpha)$. (**a**) $\alpha = -73.25$, a detail. (**b**) $\alpha = -73.25$, a deta

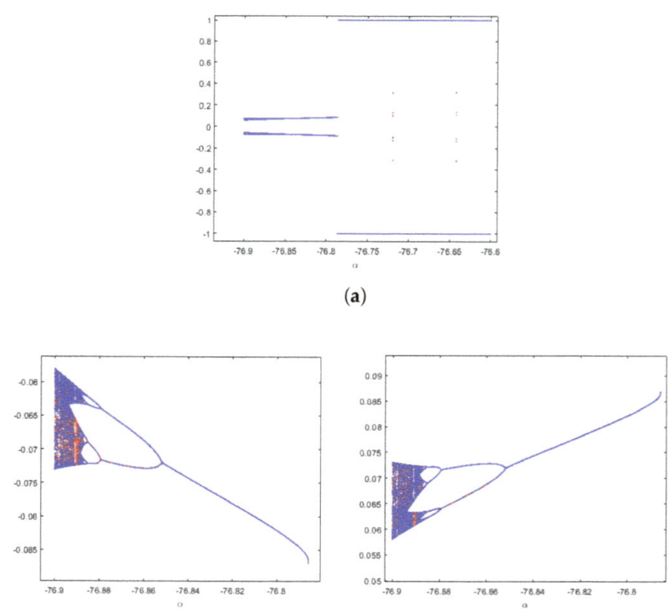

(a)

(b) (c)

Figure 9. Feigenbaum diagrams of $ACTV^6(x, \alpha)$, for $-76.9 < \alpha < -76.6$, from different critical point (**a**) $(cri_1(\alpha), cri_1(\alpha))$ and $(cri_2(\alpha), cri_2(\alpha))$. (**b**) $(cri_1(\alpha), cri_1(\alpha))$ a detail. (**c**) $(cri_2(\alpha), cri_2(\alpha))$ a detail

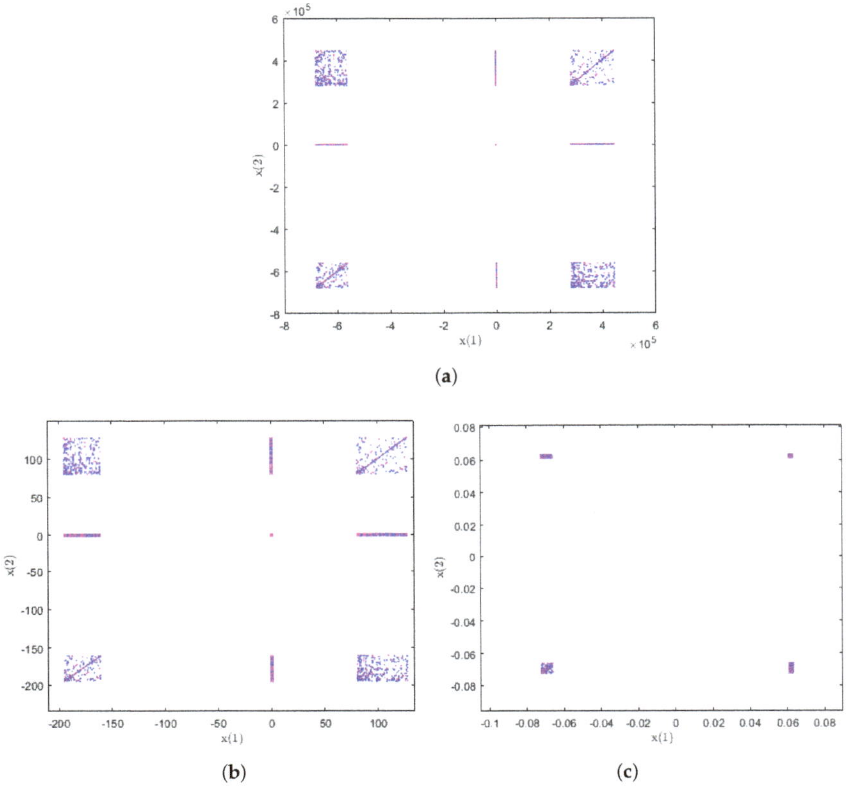

Figure 10. Strange attractors of $ACTV6(x, \alpha)$ for α in blue quadruple-period cascade. (a) $\alpha = -76.89$. (b) $\alpha = -76.89$ a detail. (c) $\alpha = -76.89$ into the detail.

4.2. Dynamical Planes

The tool with which we can graphically visualize most of the information obtained is the dynamical planes; in these, we represent the basins of attraction of the attracting fixed points for several values of parameter α. The above mentioned can only be done when the nonlinear system has a dimension of 2, although the results of the dynamical analysis are valid for any dimension.

To calculate the dynamical planes for the systems, a grid of points is defined in the real plane, and each point is used as an initial estimate of the iterative method for a fixed α. If the iterative method converges to some zero of the polynomial from a particular point of the grid, then it is assigned a certain color; in particular, if it only converges to the roots of $q(x)$, the predominant colors are orange if it converges to $x = (1, 1)$, blue if it converges to $x = (-1, 1)$, green if it converges to $x = (-1, -1)$ and brown if it converges to $x = (1, -1)$. If, as an initial estimate, a point has not converged to any root of the polynomial in 100 iterations at most, it is assigned as black. The colors in certain basins are darker or not, indicating that the orbit in certain initial estimate will converge to the fixed point of the basin with greater or fewer iterations, with the lighter colors causing fewer iterations.

For α with stable behavior, we elaborate our graph that has a grid with 500 × 500 points, with 100 as the maximum number of iterations and limit of $[-5, 5]$ for both axes (see Figure 11), for values of α in unstable regions the interval is $[-40, 40]$ in both axes in Figure 12 and $[-30, 30]$ in Figure 13. Periodic orbits are also observed in Figure 13.

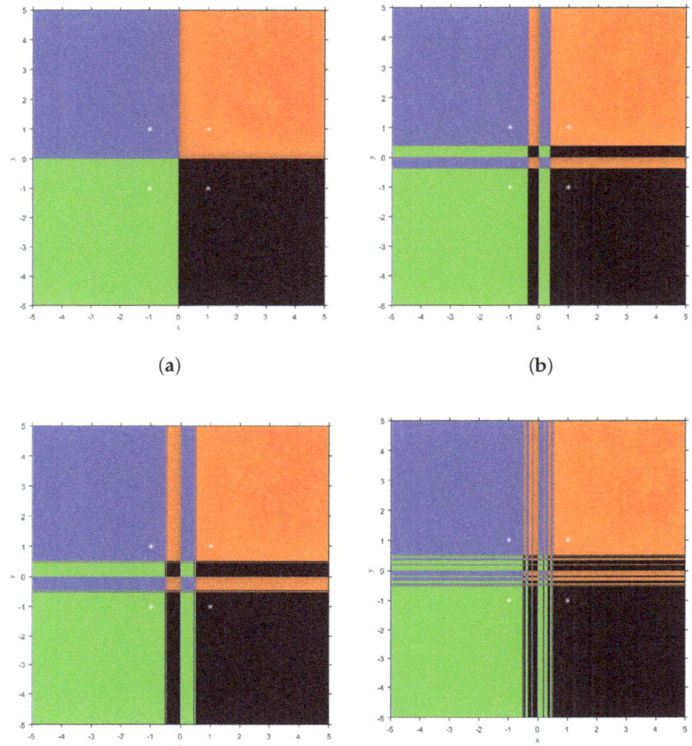

(a) (b) (c) (d)

Figure 11. Dynamical planes for some stable values of parameter α. (**a**) $\alpha = 1$. (**b**) $\alpha = -5$. (**c**) $\alpha = -40$. (**d**) $\alpha = -72$.

In Figure 11a, we see four basins of attraction that correspond to the roots of polynomial system, with a very stable behavior. However, each basin of attraction has more than one connected component for $\alpha = -5$ and $\alpha = -40$, as can be seen in Figures 11b,c respectively. This performance increases for lower values of α close to the instability zones seen in the parameter lines Figure 4b, as seen in Figure 11d.

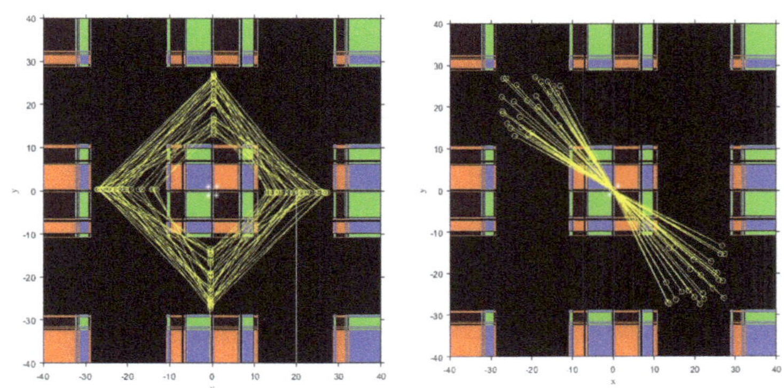

(a) (b)

Figure 12. Unstable dynamical planes of $ACTV^6(x, \alpha)$ on $q(x)$. (**a**) $\alpha = -73.25$. (**b**) $\alpha = -73.25$.

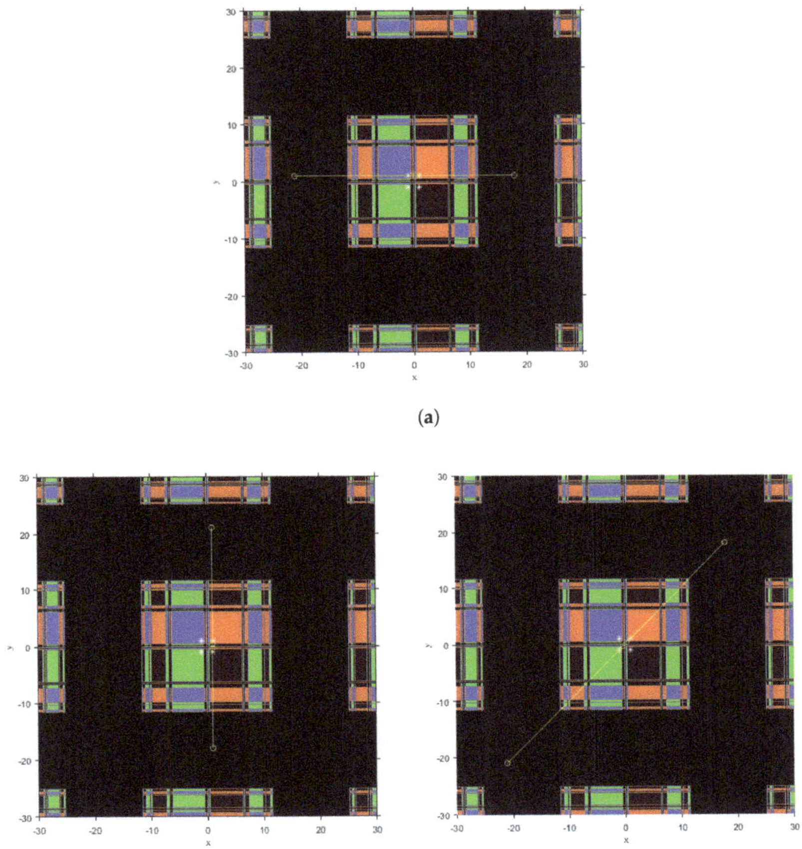

(**a**)

(**b**) (**c**)

Figure 13. Periodic orbits for parameter $\alpha = -73$ for different initial values. (**a**) $x^{(0)} = (0.361236, 1)$. (**b**) $x^{(0)} = (1, 0.361236)$. (**c**) $x^{(0)} = (-21.0469, -21.0469)$.

In Figure 12, we can see a chaotic behavior (chaos) when we take initial estimations in the black zones, producing orbits with random behavior that do not lead to the expected solution. Finally, in Figure 13, the phase space for $\alpha = -73$ is plotted. In them, the following 3-period orbits are painted in yellow:

- $\{(-21.0469, 1), (-0.368161, 1), (0.361236, 1), (17.9769, 1)\}$,
- $\{(1, 17.9769), (1, -0.368161), (1, 0.361236), (1, -21.049)\}$,
- $\{(-21.0469, -21.0469), (-0.368161, -0.368161), (0.361236, 0.361236), (17.9769, 17.9769)\}$,

We can observe three attracting orbits, whose coordinates are symmetric.

5. Numerical Results

We are going to work with the following test functions and the known zero:

(1) $F_1(x_1, x_2) = (e^{x_1} e^{x_2} + x_1 \cos(x_2), x_1 + x_2 - 1)$, $\bar{\xi}_1 \approx (3.46750,\ -2.46750)$.
(2) $F_2(x_1, x_2, x_3) = (\sin(x_1) + x_2^2 + log(x_3) - 7,\ 3x_1 + 2^{x_2} - x_3^{-3} + 1,\ x_1 + x_2 + x_3 - 5)$, $\bar{\xi}_1 \approx (-2.21537,\ 2.49969,\ 4.71567)$.
(3) $F_3(x_1, x_2) = (x_1 + e^{x_2} - \cos(x_2), 3x_1 - x_2 - \sin(x_2))$, $\bar{\xi}_1 \approx (0,\ 0)$.
(4) $F_4(x_1, x_2, x_3, x_4) = (x_2 x_3 + x_4(x_2 + x_3),\ x_1 x_3 + x_4(x_1 + x_3),\ x_1 x_2 + x_4(x_1 + x_2)$, $\bar{\xi}_1 \approx (0.57735,\ 0.57735,\ 0.57735,\ -0.28868)$.

(5) $F_5(\xi_i) = \arctan(x_i) + 1 - 2\left[\sum_{k=1}^{20} x_k^2 - x_i^2\right] = 0, i = 1, 2, \ldots, 20, \bar{\xi}_1 \approx (0.1757, 0.1757, ..$ $0.1757), \bar{\xi}_2 \approx (-0.1496, -0.1496, ..., -0.1496)$.

The obtained numerical results were performed with the Matlab2022b version, wit 2000 digits in variable precision arithmetic, where the most relevant results are shown i different tables. In them appear the following data:

- k is the number of iterations performed ("-" appears if there is no convergence or exceeds the maximum number of iterations allowed).
- $\bar{x}$ is the obtained solution.
- ρ is the approximated computational order of convergence, ACOC, defined in [16]

$$\rho = \frac{\ln \frac{\left\|x^{(k+1)} - x^{(k)}\right\|}{\left\|x^{(k)} - x^{(k-1)}\right\|}}{\ln \frac{\left\|x^{(k)} - x^{(k-1)}\right\|}{\left\|x^{(k-1)} - x^{(k-2)}\right\|}}, \quad k = 2, 3, \ldots,$$

(if the value of ρ for the last iterations is not stable, then "-" appears in the table).

- ϵ_{aprox} is the norm of the difference between the two last iterations, $\left\|x^{(k+1)} - x^{(k)}\right\|$.
- ϵ_f is the norm of function F evaluated in the last iteration, $\left\|F\left(x^{(k+1)}\right)\right\|$. (If the erro estimates are very far from zero or we get NAN, infinity, then we will place "-").

The iterative process stops when one of the following three items is satisfied:

(i) $\left\|x^{(k+1)} - x^{(k)}\right\| < 10^{-100}$;
(ii) $\left\|F\left(x^{(k+1)}\right)\right\| < 10^{-100}$;
(iii) 100 iterations.

The results obtained in the tables show that, for the stable values $\alpha = 1$ and $\alpha = -$ the expected results were obtained. For the parameter values that present instability i their dynamical planes ($\alpha = -73.25$ and $\alpha = -76.89$), in some examples, the convergence i a little lower than expected; Tables 2–5 have a higher number of iterations than methods o the same order shown in Table 6. There is behavior that is not out of the normal for Table

If the initial point is selected in the black area, these unstable family members do no converge to the solution, Table 4. In this last table, we observe that Newton's method doe not converge to the desired solution with the initial estimate $x = (-17.76, -17.78)$ contrar to the stable members of the ACTV family.

Table 2. Results for function F_1, using as seed $x^{(0)} = (2.5, -1.5)$.

Iterative Method	k	ρ	ϵ_{aprox}	ϵ_f	$\bar{\xi}$	Cpu-Time
$ACTV^6, \alpha = 1$	4	6.0038	8.580×10^{-76}	0	$\bar{\xi}_1$	3.5022
$ACTV^6, \alpha = -5$	4	6.0001	$8.576 \times 10^{e-110}$	0	$\bar{\xi}_1$	3.5053
$ACTV^6, \alpha = -73.25$	4	5.883	$1.015 \times 10^{e-38}$	$1.299 \times 10^{e-229}$	$\bar{\xi}_1$	3.8991
$ACTV^6, \alpha = -76.89$	4	5.874	6.0584×10^{-38}	6.1856×10^{-225}	$\bar{\xi}_1$	3.4959
Newton	9	2.0000	7.299×10^{-146}	1.964×10^{-291}	$\bar{\xi}_1$	1.2855
$C6_1$	4	6.0011	3.393×10^{-101}	0	$\bar{\xi}_1$	1.6573
$C6_2$	4	6.0011	1.044×10^{-88}	0	$\bar{\xi}_1$	1.5505
$B6, b_1 = -3/5$	4	6.004	2.675×10^{-75}	0	$\bar{\xi}_1$	1.7605
$B6, b_1 = 1$	4	6.0008	6.720×10^{-92}	0	$\bar{\xi}_1$	1.5495
$PSH6_1, \alpha = 0$	4	6.0101	3.503×10^{-65}	0	$\bar{\xi}_1$	3.6422
$PSH6_1, \alpha = 10$	4	6.0000	1.013×10^{-125}	0	$\bar{\xi}_1$	3.5589
$PSH6_2, \alpha = 10$	4	6.159	2.556×10^{-34}	8.874×10^{-203}	$\bar{\xi}_1$	3.9764
$XH6$	4	6.0026	1.161×10^{-80}	0	$\bar{\xi}_1$	1.6411

Table 3. Results for function F_2, with initial estimation $x^{(0)} = (-2, 2, 4)$.

Iterative Method	k	ρ	ϵ_{aprox}	ϵ_f	$\bar{\xi}$	Cpu-Time
$ACTV^6, \alpha = 1$	4	6.0096	7.045×10^{-158}	0	$\bar{\xi}_1$	6.4105
$ACTV^6, \alpha = -5$	4	6.0214	5.875×10^{-179}	0	$\bar{\xi}_1$	6.1329
$ACTV^6, \alpha = -73.25$	4	6.0161	1.622×10^{-106}	0	$\bar{\xi}_1$	6.2416
$ACTV^6, \alpha = -76.89$	4	6.0162	1.447×10^{-105}	0	$\bar{\xi}_1$	6.0655
Newton	8	2.0004	9.136×10^{-113}	3.933×10^{-225}	$\bar{\xi}_1$	1.4579
$C6_1$	4	5.995	7.360×10^{-143}	0	$\bar{\xi}_1$	2.4032
$C6_2$	4	6.0076	3.126×10^{-188}	0	$\bar{\xi}_1$	2.1022
$B6, b_1 = -3/5$	4	6.007	2.544×10^{-149}	0	$\bar{\xi}_1$	2.3387
$B6, b_1 = 1$	4	5.9824	4.643×10^{-201}	0	$\bar{\xi}_1$	2.2433
$PSH6_1, \alpha = 0$	4	6.0048	5.895×10^{-119}	0	$\bar{\xi}_1$	5.7749
$PSH6_1, \alpha = 10$	4	5.9613	2.647×10^{-165}	0	$\bar{\xi}_1$	6.0901
$PSH6_2, (\alpha = 10)$	4	5.9973	5.492×10^{-46}	2.478×10^{-273}	$\bar{\xi}_1$	7.0308
$XH6$	4	6.0019	9.690×10^{-153}	0	$\bar{\xi}_1$	2.5955

Table 4. Results for function F_3 and initial guess $x^{(0)} = (-17.76, -17.78)$.

Iterative Method	k	ρ	ϵ_{aprox}	ϵ_f	$\bar{\xi}$	Cpu-Time
$ACTV^6, \alpha = 1$	10	5.9096	1.148×10^{-35}	4.953×10^{-211}	$\bar{\xi}_1$	8.2697
$ACTV^6, \alpha = -5$	79	6.0503	1.697×10^{-177}	0	$\bar{\xi}_1$	65.9107
$ACTV^6, \alpha = -73.25$	-	-	-	-	-	-
$ACTV^6, \alpha = -76.89$	-	-	-	-	-	-
Newton	-	-	-	-	-	-
$C6_1$	-	-	-	-	-	-
$C6_2$	-	-	-	-	-	-
$B6, b_1 = -3/5$	6	5.9119	1.353×10^{-35}	2.050×10^{-210}	$\bar{\xi}_1$	2.4022
$B6, b_1 = 1$	-	-	-	-	-	-
$PSH6_1, \alpha = 0$	-	-	-	-	-	-
$PSH6_1, \alpha = 10$	-	-	-	-	-	-
$PSH6_2, \alpha = 10$	26	5.994	7.5229×10^{-84}	0	$\bar{\xi}_1$	26.0787
$XH6$	-	-	-	-	-	-

Table 5. Results for function F_4 and initial approximation $x^{(0)} = (1, 1, 1, 1)$.

Iterative Method	k	ρ	ϵ_{aprox}	ϵ_f	$\bar{\xi}$	Cpu-Time
$ACTV^6, \alpha = 1$	4	6.0917	6.448×10^{-61}	0	$\bar{\xi}_1$	9.0684
$ACTV^6, \alpha = -5$	4	7.0212	5.485×10^{-75}	0	$\bar{\xi}_1$	9.1124
$ACTV^6, \alpha = -73.25$	4	4.7204	2.972×10^{-41}	3.558×10^{-239}	$\bar{\xi}_1$	8.6135
$ACTV^6, \alpha = -76.89$	4	4.3741	3.677×10^{-41}	6.341×10^{-236}	$\bar{\xi}_1$	8.8727
Newton	9	2.0083	2.927×10^{-144}	4.469×10^{-290}	$\bar{\xi}_1$	2.0165
$C6_1$	4	6.3232	1.707×10^{-91}	0	$\bar{\xi}_1$	2.5118
$C6_2$	4	6.2666	4.519×10^{-110}	0	$\bar{\xi}_1$	2.4156
$B6, b_1 = -3/5$	4	6.3173	4.001×10^{-93}	0	$\bar{\xi}_1$	2.4766
$B6, b_1 = 1$	4	6.2481	5.909×10^{-118}	0	$\bar{\xi}_1$	2.3827
$PSH6_1, \alpha = 0$	4	5.7907	5.398×10^{-50}	2.505×10^{-292}	$\bar{\xi}_1$	8.5868
$PSH6_1, \alpha = 10$	4	7.0301	1.819×10^{-70}	0	$\bar{\xi}_1$	8.7981
$PSH6_2, \alpha = 10$	4	4.726	3.477×10^{-37}	7.995×10^{-207}	$\bar{\xi}_1$	8.9312
$XH6$	4	6.3144	5.747×10^{-94}	0	$\bar{\xi}_1$	2.5340

Table 6. Results for function F_5 using as initial estimation $x^{(0)} = (1, 1, \ldots, 1)$.

Iterative Method	k	ρ	ϵ_{aprox}	ϵ_f	$\bar{\xi}$	Cpu-Time
$ACTV^6, \alpha = 1$	5	6.000	3.605×10^{-128}	0	$\bar{\xi}_1$	427.4885
$ACTV^6, \alpha = -5$	5	5.9965	1.036×10^{-181}	0	$\bar{\xi}_1$	411.3637
$ACTV^6, \alpha = -73.25$	7	6.0011	4.997×10^{-81}	0	$\bar{\xi}_1$	625.0273
$ACTV^6, \alpha = -76.89$	16	6.000	8.800×10^{-139}	0	$\bar{\xi}_2$	1367.1656
Newton	11	2.000	5.758×10^{-148}	2.829×10^{-294}	$\bar{\xi}_1$	24.0160
$C6_1$	5	5.9999	2.773×10^{-113}	0	$\bar{\xi}_1$	42.2095
$C6_2$	5	6.000	9.4818×10^{-155}	0	$\bar{\xi}_1$	35.5499
$B6, b_1 = -3/5$	5	5.9999	1.685×10^{-116}	0	$\bar{\xi}_1$	45.1993
$B6, b_1 = 1$	5	6.000	1.018×10^{-173}	0	$\bar{\xi}_1$	40.3692
$PSH6_1, \alpha = 0$	5	5.9991	2.420×10^{-87}	0	$\bar{\xi}_1$	482.4615
$PSH6_1, \alpha = 10$	5	5.9627	2.360×10^{-162}	0	$\bar{\xi}_1$	598.1063
$PSH6_2, \alpha = 10$	5	5.9723	1.127×10^{-48}	2.564×10^{-285}	$\bar{\xi}_1$	593.7798
$XH6$	5	5.9999	6.072×10^{-118}	0	$\bar{\xi}_1$	59.5617

Although Newton's method (except in case of F_3) is faster than sixth-order methods its error estimation is improved by the stable members of our proposed family. Moreover there exist cases where Newton fails because the initial estimation is far for the searched roots. In this cases, the stable proposed methods are able to converge.

6. Conclusions

In this manuscript, we extend a family of iterative methods, initially designed to solve nonlinear equations, to the field of nonlinear systems, maintaining the order of convergence. We establish, by means of multidimensional real dynamics techniques, which members of the family are stable and which have a chaotic behavior, taking some of these cases for the numerical results.

On the other hand, the dynamical study reveals that there are no strange fixed points of an attracting nature; however, in a very small interval of values of parameter α we find some periodic orbits and chaos. By performing the numerical tests, we compare the method with some existing ones in the literature with equal and lower order, verifying that the proposed schemes comply with the theoretical results. In short, the proposed family is very stable.

Therefore, we conclude that our aim is achieved: we selected members of our proposed class of iterative methods that improve Newton and other known sixth-order schemes in terms of the wideness of the basins of attraction.

Author Contributions: Conceptualization, A.C. and J.R.T.; methodology, J.G.M.; software, A.R.-C.; validation, A.C., J.G.M. and J.R.T.; formal analysis, J.R.T.; investigation, A.C.; resources, A.R.-C.; writing—original draft preparation, A.R.-C.; writing—review and editing, A.C. and J.R.T.; visualization, J.G.M.; supervision, A.C. and J.R.T. All authors have read and agreed to the published version of the manuscript.

Funding: This research received no external funding.

Data Availability Statement: Not applicable.

Acknowledgments: The authors thank the reviewers for their corrections and comments that have helped to improve this document.

Conflicts of Interest: The authors declare no conflict of interest.

References

1. Artidiello, S. Design, Implementation and Convergence of Iterative Methods for Solving Nonlinear Equations and Systems Using Weight Functions. Ph.D. Thesis, Universitat Politècnica de València, Valencia, Spain , 2014.
2. Cordero, A.; Moscoso, M.E.; Torregrosa, J.R. Chaos and Stability of in a New Iterative Family far Solving Nonlinear Equations. *Algorithms* **2021**, *14*, 101. [CrossRef]

Cordero, A.; Hueso, J.L.; Torregosa, J.R. Increasing the convergence order of an iterative method for nonlinear systems. *Appl. Math. Lett.* **2012**, *25*, 2369–2374. [CrossRef]

Cordero, A.; Hueso, J.L.; Martínez, E.; Torregrosa, J.R. A modified Newton-Jarrat composition. *Numer. Algorithms* **2010**, *55*, 87–99. [CrossRef]

Behl, R.; Sarría, Í.; González, R.; Magreñán, Á.A. Highly efficient family of iterative methods for solving nonlinear models. *J. Comput. Appl. Math.* **2019**, *346*, 110–132. [CrossRef]

Capdevila, R.; Cordero, A.; Torregrosa, J. A New Three-Step Class of Iterative Methods for Solving Nonlinear Systems. *Mathematics* **2019**, *7*, 121. [CrossRef]

Xiao, X.Y.; Yin, H.W. Increasing the order of convergence for iterative methods to solve nonlinear systems. *Calcolo* **2016**, *53*, 285–300. [CrossRef]

Clark, R.R. *An Introduction to Dynamical Systems, Continous and Discrete*; Americal Mathematical Society: Providence, RI, USA, 2012.

Geum, Y.H.; Kim, Y.I.; Neta, B. A sixth-order family of three-point modified Newton-like multiple-root finders and the dynamics behind their extraneous fixed points. *Appl. Math. Comput.* **2016**, *283*, 120–140. [CrossRef]

). Devaney, R.L. *An Introduction to Chaotic Dynamical Systems Advances in Mathematics and Engineering*; CRC Press: Boca Raton, FL, USA, 2003.

1. Gaston, J. Mémoire sur l'iteration des fonctions rationnelles. *J. Mat. Pur. Appl.* **1918**, *8*, 47–245.

2. Fatou, P.J.L. Sur les équations fonctionelles. *Bull. Soc. Mat. Fr.* **1919**, *47*, 161–271. [CrossRef]

3. Fatou, P.J.L. Sur les équations fonctionelles. *Bull. Soc. Mat. Fr.* **1920**, *48*, 208–314. [CrossRef]

4. Ortega, J.M.; Rheinboldt, W.C. *Iterative Solution of Nonlinear Equations in Several Variables*; Academic Press: Cambridge, MA, USA, 1970.

5. Traub, I.F. *Iterative Methods for the Solution of Equations*; Prentice-Hall: Englewood Cliffs, NJ, USA, 1964.

5. Cordero, A.; Torregrosa, J.R. Variants of Newton's method using fifth-order quadrature formulas. *Appl. Math. Comput.* **2007**, *190*, 686–698. [CrossRef]

algorithms

MDP

Article

Learning Individualized Hyperparameter Settings

Vittorio Maniezzo [1,*,†] and Tingting Zhou [2,†]

[1] Department of Computer Science, University of Bologna, 47521 Cesena, Italy
[2] Department of Economics and Management, University of Science and Technology Beijing, Beijing 100083, China; b20190402@xs.ustb.edu.cn
[*] Correspondence: vittorio.maniezzo@unibo.it
[†] These authors contributed equally to this work.

Abstract: The performance of optimization algorithms, and consequently of AI/machine learni solutions, is strongly influenced by the setting of their hyperparameters. Over the last decades, a ri literature has developed proposing methods to automatically determine the parameter setting fo problem of interest, aiming at either robust or instance-specific settings. Robust setting optimization already a mature area of research, while instance-level setting is still in its infancy, with contributio mainly dealing with algorithm selection. The work reported in this paper belongs to the latt category, exploiting the learning and generalization capabilities of artificial neural networks adapt a general setting generated by state-of-the-art automatic configurators. Our approach diffe significantly from analogous ones in the literature, both because we rely on neural systems to sugge the settings, and because we propose a novel learning scheme in which different outputs are propos for each input, in order to support generalization from examples. The approach was validated c two different algorithms that optimized instances of two different problems. We used an algorith that is very sensitive to parameter settings, applied to generalized assignment problem instanc and a robust tabu search that is purportedly little sensitive to its settings, applied to quadrat assignment problem instances. The computational results in both cases attest to the effectiveness the approach, especially when applied to instances that are structurally very different from tho previously encountered.

Keywords: optimization algorithms; inductive learning; parameter setting; neural netwo generalization; data abstraction; combinatorial optimization

Citation: Maniezzo, V.; Zhou, T. Learning Individualized Hyperparameter Settings. *Algorithms* **2023**, *16*, 267. https://doi.org/10.3390/a16060267

Academic Editor: Frank Werner

Received: 5 May 2023
Revised: 24 May 2023
Accepted: 24 May 2023
Published: 26 May 2023

1. Introduction

Most optimization algorithms, and consequently most AI/machine learning (M solutions, have an effectiveness that depends heavily on the values imposed on high-lev guiding parameters, usually called *hyperparameters*. Choosing a bad setting can result anything from needing more time to reach the solution to being denied any success in th search. Therefore, the identification of an effective hyperparameter setting is configured a higher-level optimization task, instrumental in obtaining a successful application of th search algorithm of interest.

Over the last few decades, a rich literature has developed proposing methods for aut matically estimating parameter settings, using approaches ranging from purely statistic to tailored heuristics. Two main lines of research have emerged, one aiming at identifying robust setting that makes an algorithm of interest effective on all (most) instances of th problem to be optimized, and one tailoring the setting to each specific instance. In fact, is a common practical awareness that different instances of the same problem can requi very different computational efforts to solve, even if their dimensions are the same. Th computational complexity theory justifies such diversity among problems, but it cannot b declined at the instance level, while the "no free lunch" theorem is valid even among i stances [1]. More efficient solution processes could therefore benefit from different setting tailored at the individual instance level, but the marginal benefits must be weighed against the costs of achieving them.

This work considers both objectives, building upon automatic configurators but taking into account the large diversity among instances of the same problem. The approach we follow differs from that usually proposed in the literature of individual settings in that we adapt prelearned settings to each specific instance, relying on neural networks, specifically multilayer perceptrons (MLPs), to obtain the adapted settings in real time. Specifically, the methodology we present makes use of state-of-the-art automatic algorithm configurators to generate datasets of instance/setting pairs to be processed by the neural module. The generalization and abstraction capabilities of the neural component are used to obtain instance-specific hyperparameter settings for out-of-sample instances.

We assume that the different computational requests coming from different instances are due to different structures in the data distribution at the instance level and use this assumption to derive a pipeline that allows us to tailor the parameter setting of a given search algorithm to single, previously unforeseen instances.

It is clearly ineffective to propose raw instances as learning bases, so we rely on sets of descriptive statistics computed on both in-sample and out-of-sample (i.e., train and test) instances and pass them as input to the neural module. The pipeline starts by computing a set of descriptive statistics on the available instances, possibly filtering them, and applying a state-of-the-art configurator to different subsets of structurally similar instances. This produces a dataset of instance/setting pairs that can be used to instantiate learning. The learning module consists of a multilayer perceptron, whose abstraction and generalization capabilities are well known, and which is used in this case to abstract the mapping between instance statistics and setting, so that when a new instance is proposed, its statistics are computed and fed as input to the MLP, which in turn outputs the individualized setting.

We applied this pipeline to two different well-known combinatorial optimization heuristic algorithms whose code was made available by the authors and used it to solve two different problems. First, we considered a Lagrangian matheuristic [2,3], an algorithm that is very sensitive to its settings, and applied it to generalized assignment problem (GAP) instances. Second, we tested a robust tabu search [4], an algorithm that is considered robust precisely because of its relative insensitivity to hyperparameter settings, and applied it to quadratic assignment problem (QAP) instances.

The paper is structured as follows. Section 2 provides an overview of the state of the art in robust and instance-level parameter setting optimization. Section 3 details the problems we considered in this study and the algorithms we used to solve them and introduces the parameters of these algorithms that need to be set. Section 4 describes the pipeline we propose, including the stages of feature selection, possibly data augmentation, MLP learning, and parameter setting generation. Finally, Section 5 contains the computational results obtained in our study, and Section 6 draws some conclusions from the results obtained.

2. Related Literature

State-of-the-art optimization algorithms typically have a large number of parameters that need to be modified to ensure their performance. Traditionally, the identification of an effective setting has been achieved through a manual, experimental approach, mostly guided by the experience of the algorithm designers. However, manual exploration of the combinatorial space of parameter settings is tedious and tends to produce unsatisfactory results. Expectedly, the manual search can be less efficient than automatic procedures, so automatic configurators have been proposed for use when very high performance is required. Automatic or at least computer-assisted configuration has evolved along a line that tries to identify robust settings to be used on all problem instances, and along a second line that tries to propose individualized settings. There are several surveys that cover these topics [3,5–7].

Configurators of the first type [8–12] typically assume that an instance set of divers representative instances is available, and specific methods are applied to the set to deriv a robust setting that is effective on all of them, and thus hopefully on other instance of the same problem. Widely used systems in this group include ParamILS and irac besides generic nonlinear optimization algorithms such as the Nelder–Mead simple swarm optimization [13], Bayesian optimization [14], or a random search [15] applied t this specific task.

ParamILS [11] is an iterated local search (ILS) algorithm that works in the searc space of the parameters. It works on categorical parameters; therefore, real and intege parameters must first be converted to discrete values. After a possibly random initializatio a local search is started. The local search in ParamILS is a first-improvement local searc based on a one-exchange neighborhood, which can only change one parameter at a tim Each time a move finds a new improvement, it takes it and continues the search until a neighborhoods are examined or the budget is exhausted. At that point, the better of th current or previous local minima is kept, and the last solution is perturbed to reinitializ the search. ParamILS can be used for run-time configurations because it implements procedure called adaptive capping, which prunes the search early to evaluate potentiall poor-performing configurations, greatly reducing computation time.

The irace package [12] implements the so-called iterated race method, which is generalization of the iterated F-race method for the automatic configuration of optimizatio algorithms [16]. irace is based on three successive phases. In the first phase, it generate candidate configurations using an appropriate statistical model. In the second phase, i selects the best candidate configurations using a race method based on either F-race or paired Student's t-test. Third, it updates the system's probability model to give the mos promising configurations a higher probability of being used. The general process starts b generating configurations within the user-specified value intervals for each parameter an subjecting them all to a race. In the race, configurations are evaluated on a first instanc of the provided instance set, then on the second, and so on. As soon as a configuration i judged to be bad, it is eliminated, and the search continues until a small subset, by defau four, of configurations survive, which are proposed in the output.

These algorithms represent the state of the art for robust setting optimization. Th literature on individualized configuration uses them as a module of a more complex proces as our approach suggests as well.

Individualized tuning itself has different goals and follows different approache One approach is adaptive configuration, where parameter values are adjusted during th optimization process based on the performance of the algorithm [5]. This was pioneere by evolution strategies [17,18] and has received considerable attention since then but fall outside the scope of our research.

Even if we narrow the focus to static settings that do not change values during th search, there is a second subdivision to be made, namely between configurators that selec the most promising solution algorithm, or part thereof, from a portfolio of candidat algorithms [19], and those that work on a single algorithm and optimize its parameters.

Individualized *algorithm selection* has been more extensively studied and has prove to be able to significantly improve the state of the art in some notable combinatori problems, including propositional satisfiability [20] and the traveling salesman problem [21 Prominent systems in this area are hydra [22] or llama [23], which are primarily algorith portfolio selection systems, where the included automatic parameter configurator passe the task to optimizers such as ParamILS. Another interesting effort in the area of algorith selection is the instance space analysis for algorithm testing [24], a proposal to structure th analysis of instance complexity and the degree of coverage of the universe of instances of given problem guaranteed by the available test sets.

Research on optimizing parameters of a single algorithms, which has been named *per instance algorithm configuration* (PIAC) [6], has seen less contributions. It typically involve two phases: an offline phase, during which the configurator is trained, and an online phase in which the configurator is run on given problem instances. The result of the second phase is a parameter configuration determined on the features of the specific instance to be solved. We remark the difference from a standard algorithm configuration, which typically produces a single configuration that is then used on all presented instances.

The state of the art in PIAC is currently represented by ISAC (instance-specific algorithm configuration) [25]. Its general approach is the same as that described above or in instance space analysis, and as the one we adopted in our proposal as well. First, the available benchmark instances are clustered into distinct sets based on the similarity of their feature vectors as computed by a geometric norm. Then, assuming that instances with similar features behave similarly under the same algorithm, some kind of search is used to find good parameters for each cluster of instances. Finally, new instances are presented, and the optimized settings are used to determine the one to use for that instance. The way this is done may vary across systems. ISAC uses a *g-means* algorithm to cluster the training instances, and when a new instance is shown, it checks if there is a cluster whose center is close enough to the feature vector of the input. If so, the parameters for that cluster are used, otherwise a robust setting optimized for each problem instance is used. Our proposal differs in that it relies on the generalization ability of neural networks, which allows the adaptation of the learned settings to any new instance.

A final note is in order here. We found a contribution that seems to overlap with ours [26], but unfortunately it was presented only as an abstract with no details nor reported results, so it was hard to understand the extent of the overlap, let alone compare the results.

3. Algorithms and Problems

Two algorithms from the literature with the authors' code available from the Internet [27,28] were tested for individualized parameter setting: a Lagrangian heuristic applied to the GAP and a robust tabu search applied to the QAP. In the following, we present some details on them.

3.1. Lagrangian Heuristic and the GAP

Lagrangian heuristics, as the name suggests, are rooted in Lagrangian relaxation, a largely used decomposition technique providing bounds to the optimal solution values of combinatorial optimization problems (COP) but also usable as a basis for effective heuristic approaches [3].

The general structure of a Lagrangian code, whose pseudocode is provided in Algorithm 1, is aimed at finding the optimal, or at least a *good* feasible solution $\mathbf{x}_{UB}$ of a problem that can be modeled as $\min\{c^T x : \ Ax \geq b, \ Cx \geq d, \ x \in \mathbb{Z}^n_+\}$, where the constraints $Ax \geq b$ are "hard" and the constraints $Cx \geq d$ are "easy". The method requires to remove the hard constraints and penalize them in the objective function by means of a penalty vector $\boldsymbol{\lambda}$ of *Lagrangian multipliers*, then to decompose the problem into a master problem and a subproblem. The subproblem LR(λ), $\min\{c^T x + \lambda^T(b - Ax) : \ Cx \geq d, \ x \in \mathbb{Z}^n_+\}$, provides a (lower, in case of minimization) bound as a function of $\boldsymbol{\lambda}$. The solution of the subproblem can be infeasible for the whole problem, but a *fixing* heuristic (which is a driven heuristic, hence the denotation of metaheuristic for the whole procedure) can turn it into a feasible solution $\mathbf{x}^{\mathbf{h}}$. The last element to mention is the penalty update procedure that hopefully drives the process toward better and better lower and upper bounds; this can be done in different ways, the most common being a *subgradient optimization* [29].

In the pseudocode of Algorithm 1, step 4 solves the subproblem, obtaining a solution $\mathbf{x}^{\lambda}$ which is possibly infeasible for the whole problem but whose cost z_lambda is a lower bound to the problem's optimal cost. Step 6 checks its feasibility and returns a vector $\mathbf{s}$ of subgradients, which is null in the case of a feasible solution. Step 7 is the optimality check and step 8 is the call to the fixing heuristic. Finally steps 10–11 implement the penalty update heuristic and step 12 implements Polyak's rule [30] that ensures the convergence of the series of penalty vectors.

Algorithm 1: Lagrangian heuristic

1 procedure LagrHeuristic;
Input : Control parameters (see below)
Output: A feasible solution $\mathbf{x}_{UB}$ of value z_{UB}
2 Initialize α, z_{UB}, z_{LB} and the penalty vector λ;
3 **repeat**
4 $\quad \mathbf{x}^{\lambda}$ = solve subproblem LR(λ) ;
5 $\quad z_{LB} = max(z_{LB}, z_{\lambda})$; `// Lower-bound update`
6 $\quad$ check for unsatisfied constraints, return subgradient vector $\mathbf{s}$;
7 $\quad$ **if** ($\mathbf{s} = \mathbf{0}_{1,m}$ *and* $\lambda(Ax - b) = 0$) **then** solution is optimal; **stop**;
8 $\quad$ construct heuristic solution $\mathbf{x}^{\mathbf{h}}$ using $\mathbf{x}^{\lambda}$ and λ ;
9 $\quad z_{UB} = min(z_{UB}, z_h)$; `// Upper-bound update`
10 $\quad$ compute steps as $\theta = \alpha(\frac{z_{UB} - z_{LB}}{\sum_i \mathbf{s}_i^2})$;
11 $\quad$ update the penalty as $\lambda_i = max(0, \lambda_i + \theta \mathbf{s}_i)$;
12 $\quad$ **if** *(step reduction condition)* **then** decrease α; `// α decrease`
13 **until** *end_condition*;

The specific problem we applied the Lagrangian heuristic to is the GAP. This problem asks to uniquely assign n clients, index set $J = \{1, \ldots, n\}$, to m servers, index set $I = \{1, \ldots, m\}$, so that a cost function gets minimized while satisfying capacity constraints. Assignment costs are specified by a cost matrix $\mathbf{C} = [c_{ij}]^n_m$, server capacities by a vector $\mathbf{Q} = [Q_i]_m$ and client requests to servers by a request matrix $\mathbf{q} = [q_{ij}]^n_m$. Partial assignments are not allowed, thus the mathematical formulation of the GAP is as follows.

$$z_{GAP} = \mathbf{min} \sum_{i \in I} \sum_{j \in J} c_{ij} x_{ij} \tag{1}$$

$$\mathbf{subject\ to} \sum_{j \in J} q_{ij} x_{ij} \leq Q_i \qquad i \in I \tag{2}$$

$$\sum_{i \in I} x_{ij} = 1 \qquad j \in J \tag{3}$$

$$x_{ij} \in \{0, 1\} \qquad i \in I, j \in J \tag{4}$$

It is possible to relax in a Lagrangian fashion either constraints (2) or constraints (3) (or both), thus obtaining two (three) different subproblems to solve at step 4.

Algorithm 1 when applied to the GAP has six parameters to set, which are:

- *alphainit*: initial α value for penalty updates;
- *alphastep*: step reduction (step 12);
- *minalpha*: minimum step length value (step 12);
- *inneriter*: internal iteration number before changing $alpha$ (step 12);
- *maxiter*: maximum number of iterations (terminating condition, step 13);
- *algotype*: which subproblem is used (step 4) (see [2] for details).

The GAP is a very well known and studied problem, and several benchmark instance sets exist. The online collection from which we downloaded our test set was the GAPLIB instance library [31], which contains most instances from the literature.

3.2. Robust Tabu Search and the QAP

Tabu search is a very well-known metaheuristic, originally proposed in [32,33], that basically extends a local search by forcing a move to the best neighbor solution at each iteration, even if it is worse than the incumbent one. To avoid cycling, a memory structure is used that keeps track of the last explored solutions, or abstractions thereof, and forbids going back to them by declaring them "tabu". The number of iterations when an element is considered tabu, corresponding to the length of the tabu list, is also called the "tenure" of the tabu elements. Several details in the algorithm can be varied, giving rise to a rich specific literature [34]. We used a specific variant called *robust* tabu search [4] which, despite its simplicity, proved to be effective on the QAP. The pseudocode is presented as Algorithm 2. The label robust was given because it "requires less complexity and fewer parameters than earlier adaptations", further specifying that it "has a minimum number of parameters and is (...) capable of obtaining solutions comparable to the best previously found without requiring (...) altered parameter values" [4]. This focus on parameter independence makes this algorithm particularly well suited for validating our approach to individualized settings.

Two specific elements make this version of tabu search robust. The first is that the tenure of the tabu items is a random variable instead of a static value. A maximum and minimum tenure is given, and a value is generated iteratively within that interval.

The second feature is a long-term diversification method that favors moves that have not been performed for a long time. If a move has not been tested for a long number of iterations, the move is executed regardless of its quality. This is included in an "aspiration" test, which otherwise dictates that if a move generates a solution better than any previous one, it will be executed even if it is tabu.

Algorithm 2: Robust Tabu Search

function TabuSearch();
Input : Control parameters (see below)
Output: A feasible solution $\mathbf{x}_{UB}$ of value z_{UB}
for *nrep times* **do**
    Generate a feasible solution $\mathbf{x}$;
    Set $\mathbf{x}_{UB} = \mathbf{x}$ and $TL = \emptyset$;
    Generate a feasible solution $\mathbf{x}' \in \mathcal{N}(\mathbf{x})$ such that
    $z(\mathbf{x}') = min\{z(\hat{\mathbf{x}}), \hat{\mathbf{x}} \in \mathcal{N}(\mathbf{x}), \hat{\mathbf{x}} \notin TL$ or $z(\hat{\mathbf{x}}) < z(\mathbf{x}^*)$ or *test diversification*$\}$;
    `// aspiration condition`
    Set $\mathbf{x} = \mathbf{x}'$, $TL = TL \cup \{\mathbf{x}\}$;
    if $(|TL| > TT)$ **then** remove from TL the oldest element;
    if $(z(\mathbf{x}_{UB}) > z(\mathbf{x}))$ **then** set $\mathbf{x}_{UB} = \mathbf{x}$;
    if *(tabu tenure update condition)* **then** update TT;   `// Tabu tenure update`
    if *not(terminating condition)* **then go to** 5;
end
return $\mathbf{x}_{UB}$;

The heuristic was applied to the QAP, whose formulation can be described as follows. We are given an index set F of n facilities to be assigned to an index set L of n locations. Let $\mathbf{D} = [d_{ih}]_n^n$ be the distance matrix from each location $i \in L$ to each location $h \in L$, and let $\mathbf{F} = [f_{jk}]_n^n$ be the expected flow from facility $j \in F$ to facility $k \in F$. Finally, let c_{ik} be a fixed cost for assigning facility k to location i, for each $i \in L$ and $k \in F$. By using binary variables $x_{ik} = 1$ iff facility k is assigned to location i, the QAP can be stated as the following quadratic 0-1 problem:

$$z_{QAP} = \mathbf{min} \sum_{i \in L} \sum_{j \in F} \sum_{h \in L} \sum_{k \in F} d_{ih} f_{jk} x_{ij} x_{hk} + \sum_{i \in L} \sum_{k \in F} c_{ik} x_{ik} \tag{5}$$

$$\textbf{subject to} \sum_{i \in L} x_{ik} = 1 \qquad k \in F \tag{6}$$

$$\sum_{k \in F} x_{ik} = 1 \qquad i \in L \tag{7}$$

$$x_{ik} \in \{0, 1\} \qquad i \in L, k \in F \tag{8}$$

Considering all possible hyperparameter choices actually embedded in the downloaded code, the robust tabu search was run with 7 parameters to set, which were:

- *maxcpu*, maximum total CPU allowed time (terminating condition, step 10);
- *maxiter*, maximum number of iterations (terminating condition, step 10);
- *iter2resize*, number of iterations before resizing the tabu list (step 9);
- *minTLlength*, minimum tabu list length (step 9);
- *maxTLlength*, maximum tabu list length (step 9);
- *iter2aspiration*, number of iterations before unconditional acceptance (test diversification, step 5);
- *nrep*, number of search restarts (step 2).

The QAP is a well-known and studied problem; there is an online repository, the QAPLIB library [35], which has collected most of the instances from the literature over the years. We downloaded our test set from that site.

4. Learning Configurations

Both formulations, GAP and QAP, assume that the instances are described by matrices of coefficients, two 2D matrices and a 1D vector in the case of GAP and three 2D matrices in the case of QAP. The use of a single data repository for the GAP and a single one for the QAP allowed us to take advantage of a common format for each of the two problems and, more importantly, to know exactly how each subset of instances contained in the repositories was generated. We had access to the underlying structural characteristics that led to the input data, and we were able both to generate new instances structured according to the repository instances and to design generative procedures that produced structures very different from those that appear in the literature instances. In the following subsections, we first describe how we obtained the learning examples to present to the neural network from the matrices and then, for each algorithm, how we constructed the corresponding training/validation/test sets.

4.1. Feature Selection

To abstract the details of each instance and to make instances with different dimensions compatible with a same learner, we used sets of descriptive statistics computed on each matrix, the same statistics for all matrices. We also computed sets of correlation statistics between matrices. The descriptive statistics included basic ones such as mean, standard deviation, IQR, etc., but also distribution fits for uniform (chi-square, Kolmogorov–Smirnov), for normal (chi-square, Shapiro–Wilk, Kolmogorov–Smirnov, Anderson–Darling), and for gamma (chi-square, Kolmogorov–Smirnov) distributions. Correlations quantified the average request vs. average capacity, cost/request correlation, etc. We are aware of contributions that have identified particularly significant complexity predictors for specific problems, such as ruggedness and flow dominance for the QAP [36], but we wanted to present here a general methodology that can be applied to any combinatorial optimization problem of interest, so we computed the same statistics on all matrices, regardless of the problem they referred to.

This resulted in about 100 different statistics for each instance in the case of the QAP and about 70 in the case of the GAP, which were preprocessed for relevance and only the surviving ones were to be used as input for the learning module. Data filtering was done first by removing all statistics that varied too little over the training set (*low variance filter*), then we ran a PCA which suggested that 7 variables could account for more than 97% of the variance, both in the case of the GAP and QAP, but we could not use the principal components as we wanted to keep the original statistics. However, following the decreasing relevance order and the analysis of the heat map of the correlations between the variables, we were able to shortlist the set and reduce it to 11 variables in the case of the GAP and 14 in the case of the QAP. Figure 1 shows the heat map of surviving descriptive statistics for the case of the Lagrangian heuristic; blue balloons outline the subsets of highly correlated variables that were eventually represented by a single variable of each subset.

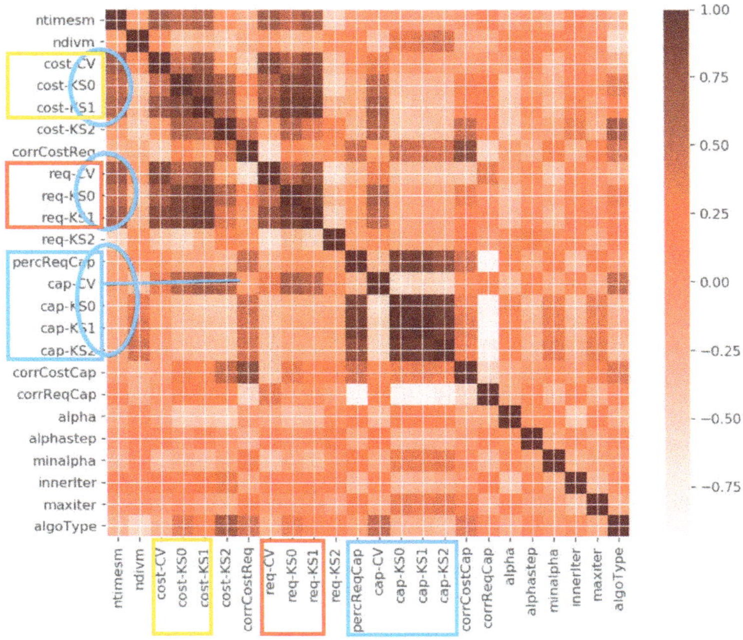

Figure 1. Descriptive statistics correlation, heat map.

4.2. Learning Lagrangian Heuristic Setting

All instances from the GAPLIB repository were generated under controlled settings and already separated into subsets of structurally similar instances. The main benchmarks from the literature, both included in the GAPLIB, are Yagiura's [37] and Beasley's OR-library [38]. Both authors generated instances that were supposed to range from easy to difficult. We independently optimized the parameter setting on 4 different subsets, 2 derived from the biggest OR-library instances (sets 11 and 12) and 2 consisting of the hardest Yagiura instances (sets D and E) by means of the automatic configurator *irace* [12]. The other sets from these literature benchmarks were composed of instances too easy to solve and would have biased the parameter choice toward values of little interest for more complex tasks.

Beasley's OR-library instances were generated with costs c_{ij} as integers from the uniform distribution U(15, 25), requests q_{ij} from uniform distribution U(5, 25), and capacities were computed as $b_i = 0.8 \sum_{j \in J} q_{ij}/m$. Set 11 had $m = 10$ and $n = 50$ ($r = n/m = 5$) while set 12 had $m = 10$ and $n = 60$ ($r = n/m = 6$).

Yagiura's instances of type D had requests q_{ij} from uniform distribution U[1, 100], costs computed as $c_{ij} = 111 - q_{ij} + e_1$, where e_1 is from uniform distribution U[−10, 10] and $b_i = 0.8 \sum_{j \in J} q_{ij}/m$. Type E instances had requests $q_{ij} = 1 - 10 ln\ e_2$, with e_2 from uniform distribution U(0, 1], costs $c_{ij} = 1000/a_{ij} - 10e_3$, with e_3 from uniform distribution U[0, 1] and capacities $b_i = 0.8 \sum_{j \in J} q_{ij}/m$.

This detailed knowledge of the generation procedure allowed us to generate additional instances that were structurally similar to the benchmark ones.

4.2.1. Data Augmentation

The chosen benchmark sets consisted of a total of 31 instances, which were too few for effective generalization. However, we were able to extend the training dataset without losing the knowledge of the instance structures. The data augmentation resulted from two contributions.

The first augmentation stemmed from the observation that learning in our syste used a feature that distinguished it from standard supervised learning. Typically, learnir is implemented by defining a training set, possibly a validation set, and then a test s It is assumed that the input–output pairs presented with the training set are learned shown, and that the network works as much as possible as an associative memory c them, reproducing the output when the training input is re-presented. In our case, we we much more interested in supporting abstraction and generalization, and we did this al by means of a feature offered by irace. This configurator proposes, for each set of instanc on which parameters are optimized, up to 4 best settings it can find. We used them all the training set, which was therefore composed of records that associated the same input different outputs, making it impossible for the network to reproduce exactly the trainir set after learning. We experimentally noticed that including all suggested settings in th training set permitted a more effective generalization than generating only a record fro the best one. This resulted in 77 records derived from the automatic configurator.

However, that set was still a small one, so we artificially enlarged it. This was possib because the authors described the generators used for producing the instances of th subsets, along with the parameter values they used. We reimplemented the generators an obtained 28 further instances similar to the examples used by the configurators, and w associated each of them with the best parameter configurations obtained for the publishe instances. The final complete training composed by literature-related instances set consiste of 105 records.

4.2.2. Neural Learning

Finally, the subset of relevant statistics was separately related to each parameter be set, in order to determine which of the statistics were relevant to each parameter. Th allowed us to reduce the search space because we could compute further correlations wi respect to each specific output.

The final parameter settings were generated by neural networks, specifically fee forward MLPs. The network input consisted of arrays containing the selected statistic values computed on each instance, and the output was the corresponding parameter valu The networks, all composed of 3 dense layers, had the structure reported below, where fo each parameter, we detail the number of input neurons, the number of hidden neurons, an the number of output neurons (always one, since each network is tailored to one paramete of the corresponding network. The activation function was a sigmoid for the hidden lay and a ReLU for the output layer. The number of hidden neurons was determined b checking the effectiveness of all values in the interval $[n/2, 2n]$, where n is the number input neurons, and keeping the best one, the smallest in case of ties. Comparable resul were also obtained with n-4-4-1 architectures, which were discarded because they require more connections.

- *alphainit*: 5-10-1 network (71 weights);
- *alphastep*: 7-7-1 network (64 weights);
- *minalpha*: 8-5-1 network (51 weights);
- *inneriter*: 5-10-1 network (71 weights);
- *maxiter*: 6-4-1 network (33 weights);
- *algotype*: 8-7-1 network (71 weights).

In the case of the GAP, network learning could also have been modeled as a multiva ued, multioutput regression with 11 inputs and 6 outputs. However, given the limited siz of the training set and the limited correlation among parameter values, the resulted searc was more effective when optimizing a specific network for each parameter as described.

4.3. Learning Tabu Search's Heuristic Setting

The structure of the experiment for the QAP was the same as for the GAP. The QAP ha more diverse instance sets, often derived from real-world applications, and QAP instanc can be very challenging, even at relatively small dimensions. Therefore, for our tests, w removed the instances that were too small, which would be too easy to solve anyway, and those that were too large, which would require a long CPU time to optimize. Furthermore, we also removed the instances from the sets that, after the above selection, were left with too few items and those for which we were uncertain about the generation procedure. The available QAPLIB benchmark sets that met these requirements consisted all of midsized instances (n between 12 and 50) of the sets BUR, CHR, ESC, HAD, LIPA, NUG, and TAI. Collectively, they amounted to 85 instances that, after the inclusion of the best configuration for each group proposes by irace (up to 4), generated a training set of 305 records.

In that case, there was no need for data augmentation because we considered the dataset to be of sufficient size. However, even in that case, we independently optimized an MLP network for each of the control parameters, according to what we did in the GAP case. We separately optimized the tabu search control parameters on each of these sets using irace. The number of hidden neurons was determined as for GAP, resulting in the following architectures.

- *maxiter*: 5-4-1 network (29 weights);
- *minTLlength*: 6-8-1 network (65 weights);
- *maxTLlength*: 6-7-1 network (57 weights);
- *iter2aspiration*: 5-9-1 network (64 weights);
- *iter2resize*: 7-5-1 network (46 weights);
- *maxcpu*: 6-7-1 network (57 weights);
- *nrep*: 7-8-1 network (73 weights).

5. Computational Results

All computational tests were conducted on a Windows 10 machine with 16 GB of RAM, and all computations were performed on a single CPU, in a single thread. Notwithstanding that MLP backpropagation-based learning is a standard procedure, network training was tested on four different frameworks based on four different languages to verify this assumption. The frameworks were: accord.net (C#) [39], ANNT (C++) [40], tensorflow (python) [41], and nnet (caret) (R) [42]. The efficiency and effectiveness were indeed comparable between all frameworks, possibly because the learning task was very simple, so a few seconds of CPU time were sufficient to achieve the final good performance in all cases. In the following, results were produced by the python/tensorflow implementation. We remark that the training time was incurred only once per algorithm per problem, so each new instance did not incur any additional training time for its solution.

5.1. In-Sample Validation

A first set of tests verified whether individualized settings improved over problem-wide ones on the training set. To this end, a base setting S_0 was obtained by running irace on a subset of 20 instances, uniformly chosen among all instance subsets, first for the GAP, then for the QAP. Each instance of the test set was optimized either by LagrHeu or by a tabu search, both with the S_0 setting and with the S_n setting suggested by the network. Finally, for each problem, we computed how many times S_0 or S_n was better. A configuration was considered better than another on a given instance if it produced a better solution, or if it produced a solution of the same quality as its counterpart but in less CPU time. When solution quality was equal and cpu times differed by less than 10%, S_0 was considered better, breaking ties in favor of the null hypothesis. While a simple numerical comparison could determine relative performance, a statistical significance test based on the binomial distribution was used to assess the significance of the difference, with hypothesis H0 assuming that all differences were due to chance alone ($p = 0.5$). Note that the results reported in the S_0 column correspond to the results obtained by irace alone; therefore, the table shows a comparison of the results obtained by the individualized settings against those obtained with a state-of-the-art automatic configurator.

We did not report the CPU times needed for obtaining the individualized setting because they corresponded to the time needed to propagate the input in a small three-leve MLP, therefore less than 1 ms.

In the case of the GAP, the in-sample validation produced the results shown in Table The individualized setting produced more dominating results on all instance subset although statistical significance ($\alpha = 0.05$) was never reached, albeit close for the Yagiura subset, possibly because it counted a larger number of instances.

Table 1. GAP, in-sample validation.

Type	n	S_0	S_n	p (*Binomial*)
Beasley 11	5	1	4	0.188
Beasley 12	5	2	3	0.500
Yagiura D	6	2	4	0.344
Yagiura E	13	4	11	0.059

In the case of the QAP, the in-sample validation reported in Table 2 was, as expected less conclusive, as can be seen from the higher values of the binomial probabilities. Al though the individualized setting produced dominating results in almost all rows, statistica significance was again never reached. This is not surprising, since the robust tabu search was explicitly designed to be insensitive to the parameter setting, so tuning it should no have much effect. Another possible reason for the failure to reach significance is the low numerosity of the instance sets. Given these obstacles, the consistently higher number o better results obtained with individualized settings is noteworthy. Note that the Lagrangian heuristic is deterministic, while the robust tabu search has a random component, so the results in Table 2 are six-run averages. However, it is worth noting that the robust tabu search proved to be very stable in its results, in most cases producing identical results in al repetitions.

Table 2. QAP, in-sample validation.

Type	n	S_0	S_n	p (*Binomial*)
BUR	8	3	5	0.363
CHR	14	4	10	0.090
ESC	18	8	10	0.407
HAD	5	3	2	0.813
LIPA	6	2	4	0.344
NUG	13	4	9	0.133
TAI	17	5	12	0.072

5.2. *Out-of-Sample Validation*

In out-of-sample tests, the optimized problemwide setting and the neural-suggested setting were applied to instances not used by irace in the optimization phase. This was done in two steps, first using the full datasets from the literature and then augmenting them with newly generated benchmarks.

5.2.1. Full Datasets

In the first step, a test set was used for the GAP that included all literature instances of the chosen subsets, not just a sample of them, although the simplest sets were quickly solved to optimality in all cases. Each instance was solved with both the global setting and the individualized setting. The results are given in Table 3 and are consistent with those of Table 1. We can see that the significance was slightly improved, mainly due to the increased cardinalities, but the relative performance was basically the same. The comparatively higher number of instances better solved by the global setting was mainly due to the fact that the tie-breaking policy acted on instances that were quickly solved to optimality.

Table 3. GAP, full literature test sets.

Type	n	S_0	S_n	*p (Binomial)*
Beasley	60	23	37	0.046
Yagiura	39	14	25	0.054

Similarly, we constructed a test set including all QAPLIB instances with n between 12 and 50. This resulted in the inclusion of the sets ELS (one instance), KRA (three instances), ROU (three instances), SCR (three instances), SKO (two instances), STE (three instances), THO (two instances), and WIL (one instance). This brought the total number of instances to 103 but the added sets being so small, we present in Table 4 the results grouped by size rather than by name.

Table 4. QAP, full literature test sets.

Size	n	S_0	S_n	*p (Binomial)*
12–15	19	11	8	0.820
16–20	31	14	17	0.360
21–30	27	9	18	0.061
31–40	19	7	12	0.180
41–50	7	2	5	0.227

The results of Table 4 were consistent with those of Table 2 in that individualized settings outperformed global settings in all but one row, without reaching statistical significance. The only subset where global settings performed better, modulo the tie-breaking policy, was that of the simplest instances, where both codes could quickly solve all instances.

5.2.2. New Instances

In order to better evaluate the abstraction power of the neural adaptation, we generated some new instances either according to the literature generators or based on data distributions that were clearly different from the literature ones. In particular, since we had to generate data matrices for both problems, we generated them according to a gamma distribution, which is both very flexible and possibly very different from the uniform distribution that is usually at the core of the generation of the literature benchmarks.

In the case of the GAP, we generated 15 instances structurally similar to Beasley's OR-library ones, 18 similar to Yagiura's E ones, and 30 instances based on the gamma distribution. The literature-like instances were generated in order to achieve a clearer significance, while the gamma ones were to assess the abstraction power of the trained networks. All instances are available from [31] and validation results are reported in Table 5.

The table shows that the number of instances better solved with the individualized settings was higher than with the global setting in all rows. In this case, statistical significance at $\alpha = 0.05$ was reached for two subsets, the Yagiura-like and the newly generated gamma. The results for the Yagiura were consistent with those of Table 5, which already bordered significance, but in that case, from the nonsignificance side. The results on the gamma instances confirmed that a setting optimized for a subset of the instance space can be suboptimal when applied to instances from a different subset, and that neural abstraction can help to constrain the problem. Indeed, we see that the significance of the difference was greatly increased on these instances, and we interpreted this result as consistent with the assumption that motivated the generation of these instances, i.e., that a setting optimized for a given instance set can be suboptimal when applied to instances that are structurally very different from those on which it was optimized.

Table 5. GAP, generated instances.

Type	n	S_0	S_n	p *(Binomial)*
Beasley-like	15	4	11	0.059
Yagiura-like	18	5	13	0.048
gamma	30	7	23	0.003

Finally, we also generated instances for the QAP, both replicating the generatic procedure for the subsets where it was reproducible (i.e., the CHR, NUG, and TAI subse and using the gamma generator to generate the QAP matrices. The results are show in Table 6. Again, compared to the results of their GAP counterpart in Table 5, the results outlined a smaller impact of the individualized approach, and this testified to th robustness of the robust tabu search, i.e., the low sensitivity to parameters as indicate by the name of the method. However, even in that case, the highest significance wa achieved on the new gamma instances. This was consistent with the results presented Table 5, where the gamma instances also had a greater significance. We thus have furth confirmation that unexplored instance subspaces can limit the effectiveness of setting optimized elsewhere in the instance space, and that the MLP abstraction can help mitiga this problem, possibly biasing the setting in a direction related to the properties of th vector of statistics of structural properties.

Table 6. QAP, generated instances.

Type	n	S_0	S_n	p *(Binomial)*
CHR-like	15	5	10	0.151
NUG-like	15	6	9	0.304
TAI-like	15	5	10	0.151
gamma	30	11	19	0.100

6. Conclusions

This work reported on results obtained by exploiting the abstraction capabilitie of neural networks, in particular multilayer perceptrons, when attempting to identi optimized instance-level parameter settings for an algorithm of interest applied to a give problem. Our proposal did not cover adaptive parameter optimization or algorith portfolio selection, but it is a contribution to the relatively unexplored area of instance-lev continuous parameter optimization.

We proposed a generic pipeline from feature identification through feature selectio possibly data augmentation, and neural learning, where standard supervised learning wa adapted to favor abstraction over precision. Computational results on different algorithm and different problems confirmed the effectiveness of the method.

Future work includes a quantitative analysis of the improvement in solution qualit that can be achieved by individualized settings. In this paper, we committed to using code from the literature, codes that were unaware of our target use. This entailed the problem to which they were applied and resulted in differences in solution quality between glob and individualized settings usually well below 5%, a position that did not change muc using larger instances. An analysis of codes and problems that allows for larger difference in solution quality due to different settings can take this research beyond the analysis rankings presented in this work.

Author Contributions: Conceptualization, V.M.; Methodology, V.M. and T.Z.; Writing—origin draft, V.M. and T.Z. All authors contributed equally to this work. All authors have read and agree to the published version of the manuscript.

Funding: This research received no external funding.

Data Availability Statement: The data presented in this study are openly available in the repositories cited in the text.

Conflicts of Interest: The authors declare no conflict of interest.

References

1. Wolpert, D.; Macready, W. No Free Lunch Theorems for Optimization. *IEEE Trans. Evol. Comput.* **1997**, *1*, 67–82. [CrossRef]
2. Boschetti, M.A.; Maniezzo, V. Benders decomposition, Lagrangean relaxation and metaheuristic design. *J. Heuristics* **2009**, *15*, 283–312. [CrossRef]
3. Maniezzo, V.; Boschetti, M.; Stützle, T. *Matheuristics*; EURO Advanced Tutorials on Operational Research; Springer International Publishing: New York, NY, USA, 2021.
4. Taillard, E. Robust taboo search for the quadratic assignment problem. *Parallel Comput.* **1991**, *17*, 443–455. [CrossRef]
5. Aleti, A.; Moser, I. A Systematic Literature Review of Adaptive Parameter Control Methods for Evolutionary Algorithms. *ACM Comput. Surv.* **2016**, *49*, 1–35. [CrossRef]
6. Kerschke, P.; Hoos, H.; Neumann, F.; Trautmann, H. Automated Algorithm Selection: Survey and Perspectives. *Evol. Comput.* **2018**, *27*, 1–47. [CrossRef] [PubMed]
7. Talbi, E.G. Machine Learning into Metaheuristics: A Survey and Taxonomy. *ACM Comput. Surv.* **2021**, *54*, 1–32. [CrossRef]
8. Bartz-Beielstein; Flasch, O.; Koch, P.; Konen, W. SPOT: A Toolbox for Interactive and Automatic Tuning in the proglangR Environment. In *Proceedings 20. Workshop Computational Intelligence*; KIT Scientific Publishing: Karlsruhe, Germany, 2010.
9. Birattari, M.; Stützle, T.; Paquete, L.; Varrentrapp, K. A Racing Algorithm for Configuring Metaheuristics. In Proceedings of the GECCO 2002, New York, NY, USA, 9–13 July 2002; Langdon, W., Cantú-Paz, E., Mathias, K., Roy, R., Davis, D., Poli, R., Balakrishnan, K., Honavar, V., Rudolph, G., Wegener, J., et al., Eds.; Morgan Kaufmann Publishers: San Francisco, CA, USA, 2002; pp. 11–18.
10. Hutter, F.; Hoos, H.; Leyton-Brown, K. Automated Configuration of Mixed Integer Programming Solvers. In Proceedings of the CPAIOR 2010, Bologna, Italy, 14–18 June 2010; Lodi, A., Milano, M., Toth, P., Eds.; Lecture Notes in Computer Science; Springer: New York, NY, USA, 2012; Volume 6140, pp. 186–202.
11. Hutter, F.; Hoos, H.H.; Leyton-Brown, K.; Stützle, T. ParamILS: An Automatic Algorithm Configuration Framework. *J. Artif. Intell. Res.* **2009**, *36*, 267–306. [CrossRef]
12. López-Ibáñez, M.; Dubois-Lacoste, J.; Pérez Cáceres, L.; Birattari, M.; Stützle, T. The irace package: Iterated racing for automatic algorithm configuration. *Oper. Res. Perspect.* **2016**, *3*, 43–58. [CrossRef]
13. Bacanin, N.; Bezdan, T.; Tuba, E.; Strumberger, I.; Tuba, M. Optimizing Convolutional Neural Network Hyperparameters by Enhanced Swarm Intelligence Metaheuristics. *Algorithms* **2020**, *13*, 67. [CrossRef]
14. Filippou, K.; Aifantis, G.; Papakostas, G.; Tsekouras, G. Structure Learning and Hyperparameter Optimization Using an Automated Machine Learning (AutoML) Pipeline. *Information* **2023**, *14*, 232. [CrossRef]
15. Esmaeili, Z.A.; Ghorrati, E.T.M. Agent-Based Collaborative Random Search for Hyperparameter Tuning and Global Function Optimization. *Systems* **2023**, *11*, 228. [CrossRef]
16. Birattari, M.; Yuan, Z.; Balaprakash, P.; Stützle, T. F-Race and Iterated F-Race: An Overview. In *Experimental Methods for the Analysis of Optimization Algorithms*; Bartz-Beielstein, T., Chiarandini, M., Paquete, L., Preuss, M., Eds.; Springer: Berlin/Heidelberg, Germany, 2010; pp. 311–336.
17. Rechenberg, I. *Evolutionsstrategie—Optimierung Technischer Systeme Nach Prinzipien der Biologischen Evolution*; Frommann-Holzboog-Verlag: Stuttgart, Germany, 1973.
18. Beyer, H.G.; Schwefel, H.P. Evolution Strategies—A Comprehensive Introduction. *Nat. Comput.* **2002**, *1*, 3–52. [CrossRef]
19. Rice, J.R. The Algorithm Selection Problem. *Adv. Comput.* **1976**, *15*, 65–118.
20. Xu, L.; Hutter, F.; Hoos, H.; Leyton-Brown, K. SATzilla2009: An Automatic Algorithm Portfolio for SAT. 2009. Available online: https://www.cs.ubc.ca/~hutter/papers/09-SATzilla-solver-description.pdf (accessed on 4 May 2023).
21. Kerschke, P.; Kotthoff, L.; Bossek, J.; Hoos, H.H.; Trautmann, H. Leveraging TSP Solver Complementarity through Machine Learning. *Evol. Comput.* **2017**, *26*, 597–620. [CrossRef] [PubMed]
22. Xu, L.; Hoos, H.; Leyton-Brown, K. Hydra: Automatically Configuring Algorithms for Portfolio-Based Selection. *Proc. AAAI Conf. Artif. Intell.* **2010**, *24*, 210–216. [CrossRef]
23. Kotthoff, L. LLAMA: Leveraging Learning to Automatically Manage Algorithms. *arXiv* **2013**. [CrossRef]
24. Smith-Miles, K.; Muñoz, M.A. Instance Space Analysis for Algorithm Testing: Methodology and Software Tools. *ACM Comput. Surv.* **2023**, *55*, 1–31. [CrossRef]
25. Kadioglu, S.; Malitsky, Y.; Sellmann, M.; Tierney, K. ISAC—Instance-Specific Algorithm Configuration. *Front. Artif. Intell. Appl.* **2010**, *215*, 751–756.
26. Dobslaw, F. *A Parameter Tuning Framework for Metaheuristics Based on Design of Experiments and Artificial Neural Networks*; World Academy of Science, Engineering and Technology: Istanbul, Turkey, 2010; Volume 64.
27. Maniezzo, V. LagrHeu Public Code. Web Page. 2018. Available online: https://github.com/maniezzo/LagrHeu (accessed on 9 February 2023).

28. Taillard, E. Éric Taillard Public Codes. Web Page. 1991. Available online: http://mistic.heig-vd.ch/taillard/ (accessed on February 2023).
29. Shor, N.Z. *Minimization Methods for Non-Differentiable Functions*; Springer: Berlin/Heidelberg, Germany, 1985.
30. Polyak, B.T. Minimization of Unsmooth functionals. *USSR Comput. Math. Math. Phys.* **1969**, *9*, 14–29. [CrossRef]
31. Maniezzo, V. GAPlib: Bridging the GAP. Some Generalized Assignment Problem Instances. Web Page. 2019. Available online: http://astarte.csr.unibo.it/gapdata/GAPinstances.html (accessed on 9 February 2023).
32. Glover, F. Tabu Search—Part I. *ORSA J. Comput.* **1989**, *1*, 190–206. [CrossRef]
33. Glover, F. Tabu Search—Part II. *ORSA J. Comput.* **1990**, *2*, 14–32. [CrossRef]
34. Glover, F.; Laguna, M. *Tabu Search*; Kluwer Academic Publishers: Dordrecht, The Netherlands, 1997.
35. Burkard, R.; Çela, E.; Karisch, S.E.; Rendl, F.; Anjos, M.; Hahn, P. QAPLIB—A Quadratic Assignment Problem Library—Problem Instances and Solutions. Web Page. 2022. Available online: https://datashare.ed.ac.uk/handle/10283/4390 (accessed on February 2023).
36. Angel, E.; Zissimopoulos, V. On the Hardness of the Quadratic Assignment Problem with Metaheuristics. *J. Heuristics* **2002**, *8*, 399–414. [CrossRef]
37. Yagiura, M. GAP (Generalized Assignment Problem) Instances. Web Page. 2006. Available online: https://www-or.amp.i.kyoto-u.ac.jp/members/yagiura/gap/ (accessed on 9 February 2023).
38. Cattrysse, D.; Salomon, M.; Van Wassenhove, L.N. A set partitioning heuristic for the generalized assignment problem. *Eur. J. Oper. Res.* **1994**, *72*, 167–174. [CrossRef]
39. Accord.net. Web Page. Available online: http://accord-framework.net/ (accessed on 9 February 2023).
40. ANNT. Web Page. Available online: https://github.com/cvsandbox/ANNT (accessed on 9 February 2023).
41. Tensorflow. Web Page. Available online: https://www.tensorflow.org/ (accessed on 9 February 2023).
42. Nnet (caret). Web Page. Available online: https://cran.r-project.org/web/packages/nnet (accessed on 9 February 2023).

algorithms

rticle

Optimization of Selection and Use of a Machine and Tractor Fleet in Agricultural Enterprises: A Case Study

ndrei A. Efremov [1], Yuri N. Sotskov [2,*] and Yulia S. Belotzkaya [1]

[1] Department of Economic Informatics, Belarusian State University of Informatics and Radioelectronics, 6 Brovki Street, 220013 Minsk, Belarus; efremov@bsuir.by (A.A.E.); grigoreva@bsuir.by (Y.S.B.)
[2] United Institute of Informatics Problems of the National Academy of Sciences of Belarus, 6 Surganov Street, 220012 Minsk, Belarus
* Correspondence: sotskov48@mail.ru; Tel.: +375-17-249-61-20

Abstract: This article presents a realized application of a model and algorithm to optimize the formation and use of a machine and tractor fleet of an agricultural enterprise in crop farming. The concepts and indicators characterizing the processes of agricultural operations of the machine fleet in the agrarian business are considered. A classification of approaches for optimizing the implementation of a complex of mechanized agro-technical operations is given. We systemize different views on the problems under study and possible solutions. The advantages of the proposed model and algorithm, as well as the problematic aspects of their information and instrumental support are discussed. The problem of choosing the optimality criterion when setting the formal problem of optimizing agricultural operations by a fleet of machines in the agricultural field is considered. A modification of the economic and mathematical model for optimizing the structure and production schedules of the machine and tractor fleet is developed. The model is applied in a numerical experiment using real data of a specific agricultural enterprise, and the economic interpretation of the results is discussed. We apply an approach for determining the economic effect of the use of the developed model and algorithm. The possibilities for practical application of the obtained results of the study are substantiated.

Keywords: scheduling; agricultural machinery; management; nonlinear model

itation: Efremov, A.A.; Sotskov, N.; Belotzkaya, Y.S. Optimization of election and Use of a Machine and actor Fleet in Agricultural nterprises: A Case Study. *Algorithms* **23**, *16*, 311. https://doi.org/ .3390/a16070311

cademic Editor: Jean-charles Billaut

eceived: 4 May 2023
evised: 14 June 2023
ccepted: 19 June 2023
ublished: 21 June 2023

1. Introduction

To increase the efficiency of agricultural production, it is important to optimally distribute agricultural machines and tractors between agricultural operations when performing the spring sowing campaign and harvest drive. The machine and tractor fleet (MTF for short) performs one of the main tasks in agricultural enterprises, specifically, the implementation of mechanized work according to certain, clearly established agro-technical criteria, while complying with optimal quality parameters and minimum cost requirements. The technical and economic efficiency of mechanized agricultural production largely depends on the capacity and structure of the machine and tractor fleet which is available to the agro-industrial enterprise. As a result, it becomes necessary to design scientifically based integrated algorithms for determining the optimal quantitative composition of the machine and tractor fleet of agricultural enterprises. The most important stage in solving agricultural problems of optimal organization of production is achieved with the help of computers and is described in modern scientific, practical and operational research literature. It is the development of economic and mathematical models that take into account the specifics of the agricultural production process, as well as the most important interrelations between technical and economic factors [1].

The machine and tractor fleet is designed to ensure the execution of agricultural works with the most acceptable agro-technical terms. Due to the universal nature of most agricultural machines, determining the optimal replacement schedule for the MTF and assessing the economic effectiveness of the operations of machine-tractor aggregates different brands and formations should be carried out not for only individual crops, b also comprehensively for the whole complex of crops that are cultivated on a farm. It necessary to consider the calendar dynamics and coincidence (parallelization) of differe technological and auxiliary processes in the agricultural production [1,2].

We must consider the key concepts needed to develop algorithms for optimizir the formation and use of the MTF of an agricultural enterprise. Field cultivation, beir one of the main branches of crop production, involves production directly in the fiel mainly of annual spring and winter crops, such as grains, potatoes, industrial crops, e Agro-technology is a set of technological operations that are performed in the cultivation a certain crop. Machine-tractor works are operations that are performed on a certain fie at specific time intervals in the implementation of a specific agricultural technology (e. harrowing a field) using specialized machines and tools. There are specific interrelatio and interdependencies between machine-tractor works which determine the clearly defin chronology of their implementation and the intervals between them. An agro-technic period of work (agro-term) is the normative period of work for the agricultural operatio (e.g., the agronomic period of chiseling from 5 April to 10 May).

A machine-tractor (MT for short) unit is a set of a certain number of units of agricultur machinery, which are combined into one whole to perform an agricultural operatic that has a mechanized character. The following combinations can act as a MT unit: tractor equipped with an agricultural machine; and a combine mounted with specialize equipment (e.g., when pressing hay, one requires a tractor MTZ-82 equipped with a bal PRF-750). For the uniformity and formalization of the problem, it can be assumed th the equipment that performs some agricultural operation by itself, without combinir with other equipment (device), is still an aggregate of the type "self-propelled equipme equipped by fictitious trailer equipment". Based on this assumption, in the process a numerical experiment, the initial value of the number of such fictitious units is set some sufficiently large number (e.g., 10,000). The same unit can perform agricultur operations in different parts of the field, but at the same time have different operation characteristics (e.g., fuel consumption and production rates). The latter indeterminac can be determined by introducing digital twins of the agricultural machinery taking in account the individual characteristics of specific pieces of equipment.

Natural and production conditions are a set of factors that determine the operatin conditions and efficiency of the MT unit operations. These factors include the space co figuration of the field, the conditions for the movement of the aggregates, the type of so in the field, the conditions of remuneration, etc. It should be noted that such conditior can also be emulated using digital twins, including modules of neural network analys econometric and simulation modeling, etc. The planned task is the mandatory minimu volumes of gross harvest of agricultural crops established by the person making manag ment decisions at the enterprise or by a higher management body. The MT unit schedule a formalized plan for the implementation of a complex of mechanized agricultural work and provides the most rational distribution of the MT unit in time, ensuring the fulfillme of the planned tasks.

The rest of this article is organized as follows. The related literature is surveyed i Section 2. The problem setting is presented in Section 3. A mathematical model is describe in Section 4. A general schema for choosing the machine and tractor fleet and algorith is presented in Section 5. The numerical experiments are described in Section 6. Th computational results are discussed in Section 7. Future research directions are outline in Section 8, and concluding remarks are given in Section 9. The computational resul obtained for the agricultural complex "Novy Dvor-Agro" are presented in Appendix A.

2. Related Literature

The article [3] deals with production planning in agricultural systems with scarc water resources in arid regions. The farmers' profits were increased by reducing machiner transportation costs based on optimal schedules. Farm production planning and machinery scheduling for perennial crops were introduced to maximize the net value. The optimization method allowed for production planning, machinery scheduling and crop rotation. The optimal machinery transportation routes were determined and the irrigation water requirements were analyzed. The model yielded a mixed-integer linear optimization that was assessed on two case studies.

The paper [4] presents an optimization method for farm management during a planning horizon. The model features were the incorporation of crop rotations and the consideration of crop impacts on the environment by environmental constraints. The decision tool produces a crop rotation plan which maximizes profits while satisfying the specified constraints and requirements. The proposed method was formulated as a mixed-integer linear programming optimization. The authors of [4] investigated the impact of various environmental constraints, aiming to limit the environmental impacts of farm activities to below given levels. Some constraints were derived by adopting life cycle assessment algorithms, which were illustrated using the agriculture system data available from Luxembourg. The impacts of a variety of environmental constraints, including greenhouse gas emissions, were investigated.

Agricultural works can be performed by different sets of machines belonging to different brands characterized by different sizes, prices and interchangeability. Machines with different productivity result in uneven time and costs of performing work. Since mechanized works and their implementation conditions differ, each set of machines will be effective when performing one agricultural operation and less effective or completely unprofitable when performing another. When first scheduling the implementation of a complex of works, sets of machines can be assigned to specific operations in certain agro-technical periods with a given composition of MT units that are available to the enterprise. The initial plan for solving an optimization problem, especially a nonlinear one, largely determines the final result of the model calculations [5]. In this regard, the task is to determine the distribution of mechanized works according to the methods of execution (sets of machines) within a given fleet (possibly with the option of its replenishment), in which all works are performed during the planned period in the best possible way in accordance with the established optimization criteria. A technically and economically feasible way of performing a specific list of works should be determined. In order to increase the efficiency of the use of an MTF in an agricultural business, it is required to determine its rational composition with the help of economic and mathematical modeling [6].

Field operation planning is critical for the efficiency of agricultural activities. This planning problem was addressed in [7], where particular algorithms were developed based on discrete event simulation and computer programming. The developed model captured the equipment and tracks for the evolution of its movement across the field via so-called state transition tables. The validity of the model was tested by comparing its performance with empirical data collected from harvesting equipment.

In the paper [8], an asymmetric multi-depot vehicle routing problem for the maintenance of a farm machinery was studied. To provide a door-to-door service for farm machinery maintenance, a node service and arc service were used. Multiple constraints included the customer's time window, maximum repair work duration, fleet size and vehicle capacity. A mathematical programming problem was formulated with the criterion to minimize total costs. A discrete firefly algorithm with compound neighborhoods and presenting neighborhood procedures was developed to solve the problem heuristically. Procedures with reduced computational complexity to evaluate the duration infeasibility were suggested. The computational results demonstrated that the proposed algorithm performed better than CPLEX solver for most large instances. The algorithm was superior to others for solving benchmark instances of multi-depot vehicle routing problems with specified time windows.

Olives are one of the most important agricultural products. However, the traditional harvesting methods fail to fulfill the current need for olive harvesting mechanization. To expedite the olive harvesting mechanization process, engineers have designed various machines and types of equipment. The considered challenge is to select the best olive harvesting machine to improve the economic conditions in agricultural production and thereby maintain the product's demand. The authors of [9] describe a decision support system to aid decision making about olive harvesting machines. They evaluated six agricultural machines according to nine criteria to classify them into three groups: beneficial, non-beneficial and target-based criteria. For these weighted criteria, the best-worst method was applied. Due to having a target criterion in the selection problem, the decision matrix was normalized by the target technique. Using the proposed algorithms, the best harvesting machine was selected. A dominance algorithm was developed to integrate the resultant rankings of harvesting machines.

The authors of [10] describe a computer program developed for selecting agricultural machinery for a group of farms. The computer program was based on mixed-integer linear programming linked to several databases contained in spreadsheets. The program selects the machinery set for an individual farm, which corresponds to the low annual mechanization cost of the multiform through the specified time. The input data include the variable and fixed costs for twelve years, the schedule of agricultural operations, various combinations of equipment and the farm area. The program is capable of calculating the number of working days required for each tractor and is implemented at a farm level in the different periods. The program allows studying the effect of changing values on fixed and variable costs through time. A case in Guanajuato for farms cultivating wheat and sorghum was used to demonstrate the model and program application. The mechanization costs were reduced during the passage of time. The optimal solution of the machinery park selected for the first year was not the same as that selected through other years. For the machinery, the solution was below the quantity of tractors available on the tested farms.

The introduction of intelligent machines with autonomous vehicles to agriculture enables increases in efficiency and reduced environmental impacts. Innovative sensing and actuating technologies with improved communication technologies provide potential advancements. A full exploitation of engineering advances requires the agricultural machinery management process to be revisited. Traditional agricultural operations planning algorithms for job-shop scheduling may be supplemented with better features. The objectives of the review paper [11] were to outline the required advances in agricultural machinery management to achieve sustainable operations in agriculture. Five key management tasks in agricultural machinery management were selected that span the various management phases. These tasks include capacity planning, task planning, job-shop scheduling, route planning and evaluation. For each of these tasks, a definition was provided and the related literature was discussed in [11].

Different precision agricultural technologies revolutionized the way farmers grow crops. The paper [12] presented a wide overview of the modern management practices including a soil preparation, crop fertilization, proper irrigation, pest management, disease management and storage of potato crop using these technologies. The authors of [12] reviewed the environmental and economic aspects of the technology using major research engines including Science Direct, Scopus and Web of Sciences. They discuss the challenges faced by potato farmers in increasing yields, improving quality and reducing production costs. The use of yield monitoring systems, precision planting, variable rate application of inputs and remote sensing was discussed. They summarize the state of the art in precision agricultural technologies. The review [12] highlighted the benefits of using precision agricultural technologies in potato crop management.

The paper [13] addresses the problem of assigning agricultural machines in multi-machine navigation. Agricultural machines need to complete multiple agricultural jobs together. To realize the management of agricultural machinery cooperation, studies on job assignment based on the ant colony algorithm were conducted in [13]. A job assignment model of agricultural machinery cooperation was established by combining dynamic job assignments. A job assignment process based on the ant colony algorithm was established by considering the match between real supply and a real demand, the job capacity of the agricultural machinery, and the job cycle and cost. The dynamic and static job assignments of agricultural machinery cooperation based on the ant colony algorithm were realized on MATLAB. Based on the static job assignment, the dynamic job assignment was realized with different possible scenarios, including new jobs and malfunctioning harvesters, thus laying a foundation for solving the scheduling problem under a farmland job environment.

In farmland operations, multiple agricultural machines complete multiple jobs together. In the paper [14], studies on path conflict detection based on topographic maps and time windows were conducted to solve the conflict-free path problem for agricultural machinery in a farmland environment. The path preplanning was performed based on a topographic map and the algorithm proposed by Dijkstra. The global path conflict was detected based on the given time windows. The global path conflict detection algorithm was simulated on MATLAB with the topographic map of Zhuozhou Farm (Chine). The computational results showed that the path optimization and path conflict detection of agricultural machinery can be realized based on the topographic map and time windows. A conflict resolution strategy requiring the least time was obtained to achieve a conflict-free path when using multiple agricultural machines.

Farmers are faced with the problem of increasing yields with limited resources. The extensive use of agricultural machinery is one of the most efficient methods to achieve this. Since agricultural machinery is expensive, it is economically impractical for small-scale farmers. Instead, farmers can submit a usage request to an agricultural machinery company, and the company will dispatch their machines to farmers to provide an operational service. This business model has shown promising benefits. The authors of [15] developed a two-step dispatching algorithm for shared agricultural machinery for specified time windows. At the first step, a spatiotemporal clustering algorithm was used to cluster farmlands according to their location, time windows and crop strain. The shortest route within each given cluster of farmlands was also determined. At the second step, the shared agricultural machines were routed across the clusters to minimize the dispatching costs. Both these steps were formulated as a mixed-integer linear programming problem. The two-step heuristics based on CPLEX were proposed to solve the problem. Computational experiments were conducted with large data from a real-world agricultural machinery company. The computational results demonstrated the efficiency and abilities of the developed algorithms.

The socio-economic situation stimulates the need for accelerated development of agricultural production in the Russian Federation. Therefore, it is necessary to use more new technologies to ensure uninterrupted high-quality operation of the machine and tractor fleet. The paper [16] analyzes the dynamics of Russian Federation imports and exports of agricultural machinery based on data from the Federal State Statistics Service and the Ministry of Agriculture of the Russian Federation. The geographical structure of exports and imports of the different types of a machinery and tractor fleet were examined. Against the background of the revealed trends in Russian exports and imports, it was noted that the export of agricultural machinery should increase by 1.8 times by 2025. It was predicted that the share of the Russian equipment of all major types (i.e., tractors, combines, tillage equipment, and sowing equipment) would reach 80% by 2025. Other types of equipment would exceed 50%.

It is important to design a service system with optimal locations of maintenance facilities to guarantee a rapid response to failures of busy agricultural machinery during harvest time. The paper [17] aims to optimize the location and relocation of hierarchical levels of facilities consisting of maintenance stations and mobile service fleets over multiple periods of a harvest season to support the operation of agricultural machinery. The authors of the paper [17] formulated a multi-objective covering location problem for the hierarchical facilities that maximizes the total demand covered within response radii while minimizing the modification to facility locations between different time periods. The ε-constraint algorithm uses lexicographic optimization to obtain a set of non-inferior solutions that allow a decision maker to evaluate the trade-off between multiple decision objectives. Th algorithm was applied to a real-life problem to illustrate the effectiveness of the decisio model and algorithms. Based on the obtained computational results, the optimal facili locations for a practical implementation were recommended. A sensitivity analysis of th selected parameters was applied. It compared the solution obtained from the model wit period-specific solutions that took no account of the changing locations of facilities betwee the time periods.

Optimal capacity planning is very important for improving the efficiency of agricu tural operations and reducing the operating cost for maintenance service providers durin the harvesting season. Many published studies present scheduling approaches that d not account for downtime. However, the published methods are not applicable in som fields of agricultural operations because of the high failure rate during a harvesting seaso Only a few studies include allocation methods and related models between planning level especially for the uncertain demand in agricultural machinery maintenance. The paper [1 includes a two-stage analytical algorithm that connects the data between planning leve and aims to develop a dynamic capacity scheduling algorithm of maintenance servic for agricultural machinery fleets. The authors of the paper [18] developed a schedulin model and algorithm for agricultural machinery fleets based on the time window of ha vesting. A service mode and a dynamic covering model based on the scheduling resul were proposed, in which queuing theory was used to find the service parameters. Th research satisfies the needs of service providers to find an optimal balance between servic quality and service costs. A real-life agricultural problem was described to illustrate th applicability of the model and the effectiveness of the designed algorithms.

The paper [19] is devoted to the dynamic facility location problem with respect to th agricultural machinery maintenance network that is designed to ensure prompt and reliab responses to agricultural machinery during a harvest period. A busy farming season wa divided into several time periods in which the problem was to determine where to loca temporary maintenance stations. This problem was formulated as a mixed-integer linea program to minimize the total service mileage between maintenance stations and deman points. To solve the mixed-integer program, an algorithm based on Benders decompositio was developed. The model and algorithms were illustrated by application to of a real-worl problem in China. The computation determined an optimized facility location-allocatio plan and demonstrated the advantage of implementing contiguity constraints.

The paper [20] presents the potential for using software for optimization of machiner park equipment in sustainable agriculture. The developed algorithms enable selection o agricultural equipment to perform planned agricultural works. Using this software, th desired economic effects and advantages can be achieved, and the possible risk related t the purchase of agriculture equipment can be minimized. Agricultural producers mo frequently rely on computer programmers to support their activity. The frequently use software consists of different applications assisting current activity by producing fina cial and reporting documents. The software enables producers to record the operation performed, the inputs purchased, and the levels of agricultural production. Compute programs for scheduling, planning and designing production are less used. This is b cause there are more programs available for reporting and balancing than for plannin and scheduling. The use of applications belonging to the latter group may give farmer competitive advantages and help them to avoid mistakes in their decision making. Th increased availability of agricultural technology programs, whose basic function is to sele machinery park agricultural equipment, would allow producers to carry out simulation and check the results of the planned decisions.

Summarizing the above survey, one can conclude that planning of the machine flee is important for sustainable agriculture. Its basic objectives are as follows: ensurin the suitable selection of crops and crop rotations, planning fertilization, and controllin fertilization and livestock density. The realization of these objectives and maintainin appropriate production profitability is possible with suitably selected agricultural machine

One can assume that in the future, the significance of algorithms and programs for the management and scheduling of agricultural machinery will increase.

3. A Statement of the Problem

In Belarus, an agro-industrial enterprise usually has its own machine and tractor fleet, i.e., a fixed set of tractors, combines and agricultural machines of certain brands. In accordance with the plans of the spring sowing campaign, the enterprise must perform a set of interrelated mechanized operations of a given size and within the specified agro-technical terms. The main tasks of the decision maker are formulated as follows:

- Determine whether the available production capacity is sufficient to implement the crop production plan.
- In the case of lack of production capacity, draw up a scientifically based plan for expanding the MTF through the lease or purchase of new equipment.
- Draw up an optimal schedule for the implementation of a complex of field works, in which the value of the total costs quoted will be minimal, taking into account the fact that the depreciation depends on the planned operating time of each specific type of equipment.

It is clear that the quality of the initial data plays an important role in the reliable implementation of the optimization algorithms in practice. Today, in the context of the digital transformation and intellectualization of agricultural production, it is possible to automate the collection, storage and processing of primary data. A digital twin technology can be used for this purpose. A digital twin of the machine and tractor fleet of an agricultural enterprise is a virtual copy of physical tractors, combines and agricultural machines with all their technical characteristics.

A digital twin of the field contains information on the condition of the soil and crops, updated in real time using a system of sensors and analysis of images obtained using drones and other devices. A digital twin of the staff contains accurate information about the number and qualifications of free and employed machine operators. A digital twin of weather conditions provides data on temperature and its dynamics during the planning period, as well as on the nature and intensity of precipitation. All these digital twins are components of a single information system (a digital platform), which must necessarily include a module for managing the operation of the machine and tractor fleet, a part of which will be described in this article.

An important aspect in the modeling process is the fact that machine and tractor units tend to fail from time to time. To take this factor into account in the developed model, one can enter the so-called technical readiness factor. It can be enlarged, i.e., it can relate not to a specific unit of technology, but to a group. For example, for tractors, this is equal to 0.9, for combines, 0.85. The latter coefficient may be interpreted as follows: the average harvester has a probability of 0.85 of being serviceable at some point in time. However, in order to simplify this study, the coefficient of technical readiness for all types of equipment is assumed to be equal to 1 in the developed and tested model.

To reduce the size of the mathematical model, we divided the planning period into a number of time intervals, which are called periods of constant conditions in the sense that during each such time period, the set of mechanized operations performed by the machine and tractor fleet remains fixed. Note that one could assume that each working day is a separate period of unchanged conditions, but in this case, the size of the model would increase significantly and the calculations would become quite cumbersome.

The source for compiling a price matrix of one hour of operation of machine and tractor units is the calculations made by the economists of the enterprise, which take into account the entire list of resource costs, including the salary of the machine operator (as well as the assistant machine operator, if any), deductions from wages, and the cost of fuels and lubricants (but not including the depreciation of equipment, which is accounted for separately in our model). The matrix of hourly productivity of agricultural machinery can be obtained either on the basis of regulatory and reference documentation or from aggregated data on the work of the MT unit in past periods.

4. A Mathematical Model

We next describe a mathematical model of the problem of optimizing the formation and use of the MTF of an agricultural enterprise when performing a complex of mechanized works in agricultural production.

4.1. Model Variables

We use the following variables in the mathematical model:

$X = \left[x_{ijkt}\right]$ denotes the number of MT units in the combination of a tractor (or combine) of grade j and an agricultural machine (implement) of grade k on the performance of mechanized work i in the t-th period of constant conditions $\left(i = \overline{1, I}, j = \overline{1, J}, k = \overline{1, K}, t = \overline{1, T}\right)$;

$Y = \left[y_{ijkt}\right]$ denotes the operating time of an MT unit consisting of a tractor j (or combine) and an agricultural machine (implement) of grade k on the performance of work i during the working day (in hours) in the t-th period of unchanged conditions;

$L = [l_j]$ denotes the number of purchased tractors (or combines) of grade j;

$R = [r_k]$ denotes the number of purchased agricultural machines (implements) of grade k;

$L^0 = \left[l_{j^0}\right]$ denotes the number of j-grade tractors (or combines) received by the enterprise under leasing agreements;

$R^0 = [r_k^0]$ denotes the number of agricultural machines (implements) of grade k received by the enterprise under leasing agreements.

4.2. Model Parameters

The following parameters are used in the mathematical model:

D_t denotes the duration of the t-th period of unchanged conditions, during which, according to the plan, it is necessary to perform the agro-technical work in question (in working days);

T_{max} denotes the maximum duration of the working shift, i.e., the longest possible time that can be used for performing agricultural operations during the day by one tractor or combine (in hours);

V_i denotes the total volume of mechanized work of type i (in the relevant units of measurement: tonnes, hectares, etc.);

l_j^+ denotes the number of available tractors (or combines) of grade j;

r_k^+ denotes the number of available agricultural machines (implements) of grade k;

a_j denotes the average annual costs for the purchase of a tractor (or combine) of grade j;

b_k denotes the average annual costs for the purchase of agricultural machinery (tools) of grade k;

a_j^0 denotes the leasing payments for a tractor (or combine) of grade j (for one year);

b_k^0 denotes the leasing payments on agricultural machinery (gun) of k grade (for one year);

f_j is the annual normative fund of a tractor (or combine) of grade j (in hours);

$P = \left[p_{ijk}\right]$ denotes the performance matrix of the MT unit as a part of a j-grade tractor (or combine) and an agricultural machine (implement) of grade k when performing mechanized work i;

$U = \left[u_{ijk}\right]$ denotes a price matrix of one hour of MT unit operation consisting of a tractor (or combine) of grade j and an agricultural machine (implement) of grade k when performing mechanized work i;

$C = \left[c_{ijk}\right]$ denotes a matrix of the cost of work i by the equipment of grade j with an agricultural machine of grade k, taking depreciation into account.

The objective Function (1) with Equality (2) determine the total average annual cost of performing the entire complex of mechanized works calculated in monetary units:

$$F\left(X,Y,L,T,L^0,R^0\right) = \\ = \sum_{i=1}^{I}\sum_{j=1}^{J}\sum_{k=1}^{K}\sum_{t=1}^{T} x_{ijkt}\cdot y_{ijkt}\cdot c_{ijk}(X,Y)\cdot D_t + \sum_{j=1}^{J} l_j\cdot a_j + \sum_{k=1}^{K} r_k\cdot b_k + \sum_{j=1}^{J} l_j^0\cdot a_j^0 + \sum_{k=1}^{K} r_k^0\cdot b_k^0 \rightarrow min \quad (1)$$

where $c_{ijk}(X,Y) = u_{ijk} + a_j\cdot g_j(X,Y)$ and the following equality hold

$$g_j(X,Y) = \begin{cases} 1, \; if \sum_{i=1}^{I}\sum_{k=1}^{K}\sum_{t=1}^{T} y_{ijkt}\cdot x_{ijkt}\cdot D_t \le f_j\cdot l_j, \\ \tau, \; if \sum_{i=1}^{I}\sum_{k=1}^{K}\sum_{t=1}^{T} y_{ijkt}\cdot x_{ijkt}\cdot D_t > f_j\cdot l_j, \end{cases} \left(j = \overline{1,J}\right) \quad (2)$$

where τ denotes a coefficient that takes into account the intensity of an operation of the equipment ($\tau > 1$ when agricultural machines (tools) are utilized in an intensive regime). The economic meaning of the coefficient τ is as follows. If the total actual output of tractors (or combines) of this brand exceeds the normative time fund, then depreciation deductions should be adjusted upwards.

4.3. Four Conditions Restricted the Mathematical Model

The following conditions were used in the model.

Condition 1. *For the available number of tractors (or combines):*

$$\sum_{i=1}^{I}\sum_{k=1}^{K} x_{ijkt} \le l_j^+ + l_j + l_j^0, \; j = \overline{1,J}, \; t = \overline{1,T}.$$

At any time, the total number of j-grade tractors (combines) operating simultaneously on all agro-technical operations should not exceed their available number (including those purchased in the current year).

Condition 2. *For the acquisition of tractors (combines) with agricultural machines (implements):* $\sum_{i=1}^{I}\sum_{j=1}^{J} x_{ijkt} \le r_k^+ + r_k + r_k^0, \; k = \overline{1,K}, \; t = \overline{1,T}.$

At any time, the total number of agricultural machines (implements) of grade k operating simultaneously on all agro-technical operations should not exceed their available quantity.

Condition 3. *For the output during the shift:* $y_{ijkt} \le T_{max}, \; i = \overline{1,I}, \; j = \overline{1,J}, \; k = \overline{1,K}, \; t = \overline{1,T}.$

The number of hours worked by one tractor (or combine) should not exceed the maximum allowable duration of the working shift. The total amount of work performed by the MT unit assigned to a specific mechanized work should not be less than the volume according to the plan. It is assumed that exceeding the plan is also possible.

Condition 4. *For the economic content of variables:* $x_{ijkt} \in Z_+$, $y_{ijkt} \in R_+$, $l_j \in Z_+$, $r_k \in Z_+$, $l_j^0 \in Z_+$, $r_k^0 \in Z_+$.

The number of tractors (combines), agricultural machines (implements) and lorries should be expressed in an integer non-negative number (zero is also allowed). The number of hours of operation during the shift of each tractor (combine) shall be expressed as a real non-negative number.

4.4. Remarks for Restricting a Possible Application of the Mathematical Model

We next provide the following remarks on the model.

Remark 1. *The annual costs for the purchase of a tractor (or combine) of grade j are calculat according to the following formula:*

$$a_j = \frac{A_j}{T_j}, \quad (3)$$

where A_j determines the initial cost of purchasing a tractor (or combine) of grade j; and T_j determin the standard useful life of a tractor (or combine) of grade j.

Remark 2. *The annual costs for the purchase of agricultural machinery (tools) of grade k a calculated according to the following formula:*

$$b_k = \frac{B_k}{t_k}, \quad (4)$$

where B_k determines the initial cost of acquiring an agricultural machine (tool) of grade k; and determines the normative useful life of an agricultural machine (tool) of grade k.

The Formulas (3) and (4) are based on the linear method of calculating depreciation. O should take into account that there are more approaches which may be more precise and can be us if required.

Remark 3. *If for some reasons the purchase of certain brands of tractors or other agricultur machines is not possible or their parameters (price and service life) are not known, then the val of the a_i (b_k) for these brands is taken to be equal to some large number (for example, 10^{10}). The due to the fact that the target function tends to a minimum, these brands will not be among tho recommended for purchase.*

Remark 4. *If the agricultural enterprise does not have the opportunity to conclude a leasi contract for the supply of a specific brand of a tractor or other agricultural machinery, then the val of a_i^0 (b_k^0) for these brands is taken to be equal to some large number (for example, 10^{10}). Then, d to the fact that the target function tends to a minimum, these brands are guaranteed not to fall in the optimal plan.*

Remark 5. *The question of choosing a monetary unit in which all the cost parameters of the mod will be expressed is quite important. Given that the planning period in this task is one year, it possible either to make calculations in Belarusian rubles (BYR) and take into account the inflatio factor by multiplying all cost parameters by the projected price index, or to use in the calculations nominally more stable monetary unit, for example, USD or EUR. Note that this issue is importa only for determining the costs associated with the formation and use of the MT unit, but does n affect the structure of the fleet and the schedule of mechanized work.*

Remark 6. *An important role is played by the correct determination of the values of costs a_i, b_k, and b_k^0. To select their correct values, the marketing service (a specialist or a subdivision replaci it) must conduct a study of the market for agricultural machinery. For this purpose, specializ catalogs, websites of manufacturers and distributors of tractors and agricultural machines, as w as information from exhibitions, forums, etc. can be used.*

It should be noted that at the current stage of development of economic science, mo seriously applied tasks in the field of economics are characterized by a large quantity input data and numerical parameters. Dealing with thousands of variables and hundre of constraints manually is extremely difficult. In this regard, there is a need to emplo specialized software products to solve optimization problems. However, even this do not guarantee the desired results, since the vast majority of optimization packages a based on the use of the method of generalized reduced gradient or its analogues. To app this approach correctly, both the objective function and the functions involved in writing constraints must be smooth. At the same time, in certain cases, in the process of optimizing the use of the MTF of an agricultural enterprise in agricultural production, there may be objects and processes in the description of which specialists have to use discontinuous functions, i.e., functions that have breaks (of the first or second type).

The economic meaning of the gaps in the objective function can be interpreted as follows. If the total actual output of tractors (combines) of this type exceeds the normative output, then depreciation deduction should be adjusted upwards (by multiplying by the corrective coefficient g_0). For example, if the regulatory annual fund of the combined operating time, according to technical requirements, is 900 h, and it has worked 1000 h, then depreciation should be written off from the cost of finished products at an increased rate, for example, 8% more than in a normal operation. It is especially important to use this approach in intense agro-technical periods. The considered problem belongs to the class of non-smooth optimization problems, since there are gaps of the first type in the objective function. In this regard, it is required to select such tools that are able to successfully solve problems of this type. At the present stage of development of specialized software designed to solve optimization problems, there are a number of problems associated with the processing of non-smooth functions. Algorithms and computer programs that are capable of solving this kind of problem are usually distributed on a commercial basis. Thus, not every agricultural enterprise can afford to purchase such a software product and periodically allocate considerable funds for its renewal. Moreover, modern software products, even the most powerful, have limitations on the dimensionality of the problem being exactly solved.

To apply the above mathematical model to the optimization of the MTF of real organizations of the agro-industrial complex, the problem must be brought into a form that can be solved by standard means, in particular, by the Solver package included in the MS Excel environment or by a free version of software products such as GAMS (e.g., version 24.5). There are several ways to solve such problems. It is possible to divide a problem with gaps into a finite number of sub-problems, each of which is considered at a continuous scope of definition in the absence of gaps. Having solved each of the sub-problems, it is possible to choose the best solutions obtained and it may be practically sufficient for the original problem with gaps.

In the Equation (1), τ denotes a given constant whose value is greater than 1. Note that according to Equation (1), the coefficient of g_j is a discontinuous function that depends on the variables x_{ijkt} and y_{ijkt}. It is required to select a continuously differentiated function $\tilde{g}_j$ of variables x_{ijkt} and y_{ijkt} that would accurately approximate the change in the coefficient of g_j. To do this, we transform the objective function so that it becomes smooth, i.e., we eliminate the gaps of the first type. To construct such a function $\tilde{g}_j$ we propose to use the following logistic function:

$$\varphi(z) = \frac{1}{1 + \exp(-z)} \tag{5}$$

The graph of the Function (5) is shown in Figure 1.

Let $f(X)$ denote a function that depends on the multidimensional array X. The value of this function is denoted as y. Let $h(y)$ denote a function dependent on the scalar y (which describes the values of the function $f(X)$) given by the formula:

$$h(y) = \begin{cases} c, \ if\ y \leq a, \\ d, \ if\ y > a. \end{cases} \tag{6}$$

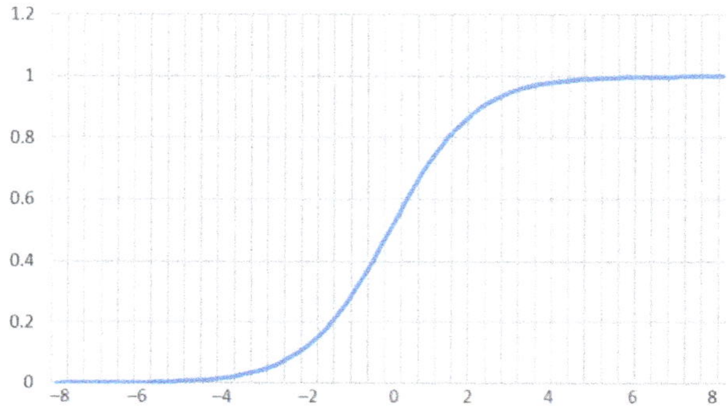

Figure 1. The graph of the logistic function.

Ultimately, it is necessary to obtain a functional dependence of the form $h[f(x)]$. By means of elementary transformations (compression, stretching and parallel transfer), it is possible to select a function $\tilde{h}(y)$ such that it can be used for the approximation of the function g_j. In the considered case, when the function g_j is determined by Formula (4), one can assume that

$$f_j(X) = \sum_{i=1}^{I}\sum_{k=1}^{K}\sum_{t=1}^{T} y_{ijkt}\cdot x_{ijkt}\cdot D_t - f_j\cdot l_j, j = \overline{1, J}, \tag{7}$$

where the parameters a, c and d are equal to 0, 1 and g_0, respectively:

$$a = 0,\ c = 1,\ d = g_0 \tag{8}$$

In this case, array X consists of variables x_{ijkt} and y_{ijkt}. According to Equations (7) and (8), the Formula (4) can be written as follows:

$$g_j = h\left[f_j(X)\right] \tag{9}$$

In the next step, the task is, in some way, to approximate the discontinuous function $h(y)$ with the continuous function $\tilde{h}(y)$ in order to be able to approximate the discontinuous Function (4) by the following smooth function:

$$\tilde{g}_j = \tilde{h}\left[f_j(X)\right] \tag{10}$$

As a basis for the approximation of the function $h(y)$, one can take the logistic Function (5). Note that $\varphi(-\infty) = 0$ and $\varphi(\infty) = 1$. Moreover, with a sufficiently large value of s, it can be assumed that $\varphi(-s) \approx 0$ and $\varphi(s) \approx 1$. For example, for $s = 6$, the values of $\varphi(-s)$ and $\varphi(s)$ are already close enough to 0 and 1, respectively, as can be seen from Figure 1, namely, $\varphi(-6) = 0.0025$ and $\varphi(6) = 0.9975$.

We take the value $b > a$. Then, based on the Function (5), we define the function $\psi(y)$ such that $\psi(a) = \varphi(-s)$ and $\psi(b) = \varphi(s)$. Therefore, $\psi(a) \approx 0$ and $\psi(b) \approx 1$. As a result, we build a linear function that corresponds to the values a and b of the values of $-s$ and s, respectively. Such a linear function is given by the following formula:

$$z = \frac{2y - a - b}{b - a}s \tag{11}$$

In Function (11), the variable y acts as an argument. Substituting the Formula (11) into the Equality (5), we obtain the desired function $\psi(y)$ as follows:

$$\psi(y) = \frac{1}{1 + \exp\left(-\frac{2y-a-b}{b-a}s\right)} \tag{12}$$

Based on Function (8) (such that $\psi(a) \approx 0$ and $\psi(b) \approx 1$), we construct the function $h(y)$ such that $\tilde{h}(a) \approx c$ and $\tilde{h}(b) \approx d$. To do this, one can build a linear function that corresponds to the values 0 and 1 of the variables c and d, respectively. Such a function is determined by the following equality:

$$\chi = (d - c)\psi + c \tag{13}$$

In Function (13), the variable ψ acts as an argument. Substituting the Formula (12) into the Equality (13), we obtain the desired function $\tilde{h}(y)$ as follows:

$$\tilde{h}(y) = (d-c)\psi(y) + c = \frac{d-c}{1+\exp\left(-\frac{2y-a-b}{b-a}s\right)} + c = \frac{d + c\cdot\exp\left(-\frac{2y-a-b}{b-a}s\right)}{1+\exp\left(-\frac{2y-a-b}{b-a}s\right)}$$

Thus, we obtain the following equality:

$$\tilde{h}(y) = \frac{d + c\cdot exp\left(-\frac{2y-a-b}{b-a}s\right)}{1+exp\left(-\frac{2y-a-b}{b-a}s\right)} \tag{14}$$

Note that in accordance with the above smoothing procedure used, Function (14) is increasing, and the following conditions hold:

$$\lim_{y\to-\infty} \tilde{h}(y) = c,\ \lim_{y\to\infty} \tilde{h}(y) = d,\ \tilde{h}(a) \approx c,\ \tilde{h}(b) \approx d \tag{15}$$

Therefore, Function (14) approximates Function (6). In such a case, the accuracy of the approximation increases when the value of the parameter b decreases (recall that a value of the parameter b must be greater than a value of the parameter a). In the case of interest (i.e., when performing Equalities (7) and (8)), by virtue of the Formula (14), Equality (10) takes the following form:

$$\tilde{g}_j = \frac{g_0 + \exp\left[-\frac{2\left(\sum_{i=1}^{I}\sum_{k=1}^{K}\sum_{t=1}^{T} y_{ijkt}\cdot x_{ijkt}\cdot D_t - f_j\cdot l_j\right)-b}{b}s\right]}{1+\exp\left[-\frac{2\left(\sum_{i=1}^{I}\sum_{k=1}^{K}\sum_{t=1}^{T} y_{ijkt}\cdot x_{ijkt}\cdot D_t - f_j\cdot l_j\right)-b}{b}s\right]},\ j = \overline{1,J} \tag{16}$$

In Equality (16), b denotes the step of the smoothing procedure and s is a scale factor. It should be noted that in accordance with the above arguments, the accuracy of the approximation increases with an increase in the value of the parameter s and a decrease in the value of the parameter b, where $s > 0$ and $b > 1$.

5. A Schema and Algorithm for Selection and Use of a Machine and Tractor Fleet

In this section, we present a general schema for choosing a machine and tractor fleet and a heuristic algorithm for optimizing the set of agricultural works.

5.1. A Schema for Choosing a Machine and Tractor Fleet

Figure 2 presents a general scheme for constructing a set of models for the formation and use of a MTF at the meso-level and micro-level of agricultural production. At the heart of the work of the model complex at the meso-level, which covers a group of enterprises that are united by their geographical location and the dominant line of activity, is the following provision. If one enterprise with a given set of resources is able to provide a certain economic result and maintain it at a constant level, then another enterprise with the same set of resources and other characteristics being equal, has the potential to achieve no less economic result than the first enterprise.

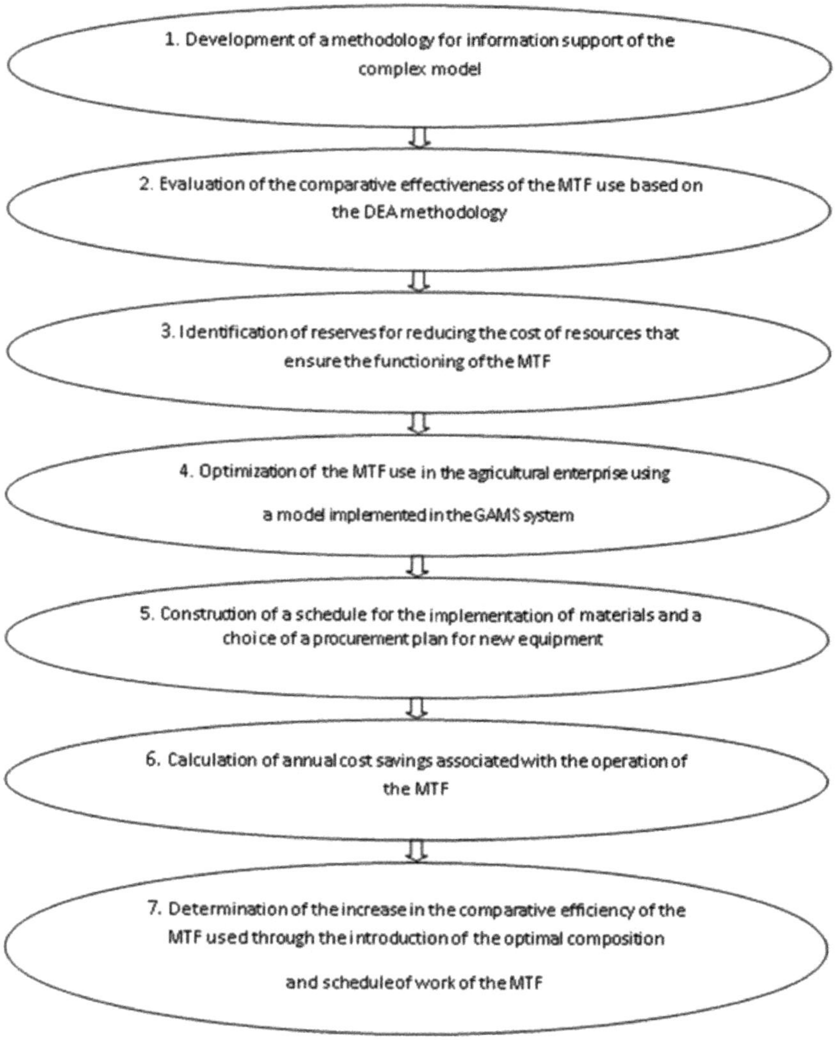

Figure 2. A general schema for choosing machine and tractor fleets.

The formalization of the process of MTF functioning at the meso-level presuppose an assessment of the comparative effectiveness of its use by a group of enterprises. To d this, one should refer to the procedure for constructing and analyzing the Data Envelop Analysis (DEA), which is based on fractional linear programming and duality theory.

The optimization model developed in Section 4 is connected with stage 4 of th scheme presented in Figure 2, which is a core of the whole optimization process for th MTF operations at the meso-level and micro-levels in the agro-industrial complex. Not that there is an opportunity to improve this approach by adding into the model uncertaint factors presented in most agricultural frameworks.

Ensuring the competitiveness of agricultural production in modern conditions i impossible without an accurate and scientifically sound system of production organizatio an integral element of which is the planning of mechanized agro-technical work. Th existing models for optimizing the use of a company's machine and tractor fleet in fiel production are based on the mathematical apparatus of linear programming and greatl simplify reality. Sections 3 and 4 examine the possibility of applying nonlinear models to solving the problem of optimal planning of spring field operations.

In Section 5.2, special attention is paid to the heuristic algorithm for obtaining an initial reference plan close to the optimal one and the algorithm for obtaining an integer solution. The described heuristic algorithm can be successfully applied in practice in the operational and production planning concerning the use of the available machine and tractor fleet in the field. An example of calculations according to the proposed methodology for a specific agro-industrial enterprise is given Sections 6 and 7.

5.2. A Heuristic Algorithm for Optimizing the Execution of the Set of Agricultural Works

Note that the task of drawing up an optimal schedule of a complex of machine and tractor works is not trivial. It requires a deep understanding of the essence of the simulated process (object) and should take into account its individual features. Therefore, to search for the initial plan, it is impractical to use a greedy algorithm [21] as this involves making locally optimal decisions at each stage, assuming that the final solution will be optimal. Although today there is no universal criterion for assessing the applicability of a greedy algorithm for solving a specific problem, scientists have proved that it cannot contribute to finding a global extreme value in a set of optimization problems, e.g., in most scheduling problems. The desired algorithm may be iterative.

At the first step of the algorithm, it is rather logical to use a tractor (combine harvester) that can perform the considered mechanized work at the least cost. However, as mentioned above, one cannot consider agricultural operations one by one and optimize for each of them separately since operations constitute an interconnected set of works. In addition, when attaching tractors to operations, it is impossible to take into account their hourly productivity. This indirectly affects not only the fulfillment of constraints, but also the value of the objective function. For example, an expensive (in the sense of the price of one hour of work) combine harvester can perform a specific agricultural operation, albeit at great cost, but faster than a cheap but low-productivity machine. As a result, the operations may require fewer units of this brand, which may reduce the total costs.

Therefore, at the first step of the algorithm, for each tractor (j) and each mechanized work (i), it is necessary to determine the value (called the preference coefficient) for fixing a tractor brand for mechanized work. We denote the preference coefficient as k_{ij}. Since when choosing the most suitable fixing option, we strive to minimize costs, it is clear that it should be directly proportional to the hourly productivity and inversely proportional to the price of one hour of a tractor (combine) operation: $k_{ij} \sim p_{ij}/c_{ij}$.

We next pay attention to the fact that for the convenience of presenting information, one can choose any unit of measurement in order to achieve the necessary scale. It should be emphasized that in the calculation process, it is impossible to take into account the units of measurement of quantities. They can be different for each operation (t/h, pcs/h, ha/h, etc.), and this is of fundamental importance for the correct application of the developed algorithm. In order to ensure the compatibility of indicators in mathematical modeling, a normalization procedure is often used. In this case, the following equality may be used to determine the coefficients of respectability:

$$k_{ij} = \frac{p_{ij}}{\overline{p_i}} : \frac{c_{ij}}{\overline{c_i}}$$

To solve this problem heuristically, we propose the following iterative algorithm.

Step 1. Based on the given initial data, a matrix $\|k_{ij}\|$ of the preference coefficients is constructed.

Step 2. Determine the maximum element of the constructed matrix $\|k_{ij}\|$.

Step 3. For the selected tractor brand and the selected operation, we set the maximum possible duration of the working shift. After that, we calculate the preliminary required number of units of equipment. To do this, we use the following formula:

$$x_{i0j0} = \min\left\{\left[\frac{V_i^{(0)}}{D_t \cdot p_{i0j0} \cdot T_{\max}}\right] + 1,\ L_j^{(0)}\right\} \quad (17)$$

where the upper index corresponds to the number r of iterations (beginning from $r = 0$).

The meaning of the Formula (17) is to round the estimated number of tractors (combines) substantially. At the same time, the estimated number of fixed units of tractors of the brand cannot exceed the total number of such tractors at the disposal of the enterprise.

Then, it is possible to reduce the duration of the work shift to such a value that the entire amount of work on this agricultural operation is completed as follows:

$$y_{i0j0} = \min\left\{\frac{V_i^{(0)}}{D \cdot x_{i0j0} \cdot p_{i0j0}},\ T_{\max}\right\} \quad (18)$$

Equation (18) takes into account the production limit during the shift.

Step 4. There are two possible cases for this step.

- If $x_{i0j0} \cdot y_{i0j0} \cdot p_{i0j0} \cdot D = V_i$, then it is required to complete an analysis of the mechanized work and go back to step 2. It is only necessary to remove from the matrix of preference coefficients both the coefficient that was previously recognized as the maximum and those coefficients that were in the same row. It is also necessary to replace the value of the volume of mechanized work from V_i to $V_i^{(1)} = 0$.
- If $x_{i0j0} \cdot y_{i0j0} \cdot p_{i0j0} \cdot D < V_i$, then one should go back to step 2 of the algorithm, first removing the coefficient that was previously recognized as the maximum and replacing the value of the volume of the mechanized work by $V_i^{(1)} = V_i - x_{i0j0} \cdot y_{i0j0} \cdot p_{i0j0} \cdot D$

The above steps of the developed algorithm must be repeated until the equalities $V_1^{(m)} = V_2^{(m)} = \ldots = V_N^{(m)}$ are achieved at the last step m.

We have compared the result of the above heuristic algorithm with the result that can be obtained using the GAMS solver, which is one of the most advanced automated optimization tools. The relative deviation of the cost of the complex of agro-technical works from the optimal value found by the generalized reduced gradient method, for a conditional example, was less than 1%. Such a low error indicates that the proposed general schema and heuristic algorithm are of sufficiently high quality and suggests their possible application in solving a class of similar optimization problems.

6. Numerical Experiments and the Interpretation of the Obtained Results

We next apply the algorithm described in Section 5 for solving the problem of optimizing the composition and number of MTF used in a complex of mechanized operations in agricultural production to the agricultural enterprise "Novy Dvor-Agro", which is under the jurisdiction of "Grodno Azot" (Belarus).

To carry out the calculations, we considered the following characteristics of the MTF of the enterprise: the current composition of the MTF; the number of pieces of equipment involved in animal husbandry; the number of pieces of equipment requiring major repairs; the amount of mechanized work required for the production of crop products; the optimal agro-technical terms of the mechanized works; the production standards for a mechanized work; the storage locations of equipment; and the average travelling distance from the equipment storage location to the places of work.

For the calculations, we used one of the powerful multidimensional optimization tools known today, i.e., GAMS package (version 24.7). The MTF of the agricultural enterprise "Novy Dvor-Agro" is represented by a wide range of agricultural machines and equipment. Firstly, we identified the MT units which are used, in accordance with the technological needs, on livestock complexes and farms. The number of these machines is objective in nature and can change as the technology of keeping animals changes. Therefore, in the conducted experiment, it was set as a permanently fixed number throughout the planning period in such a way that the set of equipment is involved in both the crop and livestock production periods.

The composition of the MTF was optimized in the direction of crop production, while tractors and agricultural machines that were constantly involved in animal husbandry were not taken into account. Brief results of calculations performed using the computer models developed by the authors in the GAMS environment are presented in Table A1 (see Appendix A). As a result of the calculations, some agro-technical operations could not be performed under 100% optimal agro-terms with the specified cash composition of the MTF, and shortages of specific machines were identified. At the same time, the calculation was carried out for shift work conditions with shift durations of up to 9 h in busy periods. In addition, the coefficient of technical readiness of the equipment was taken into account: 0.85 for combine harvesters and 0.95 for the rest of the MTF equipment.

A failure to perform agricultural work according to the optimal agro-technical terms leads to significant decreases in the yield and quality of crops (up to 50% in the worst case), which leads to significant increases in costs per unit of production and, as a result, decreases in revenue and profit. Therefore, in the process of modeling, the initial and final timings of mechanized work were considered as deterministic values. Considering the specified cash composition of the MTF of the agricultural complex "Novy Dvor-Agro" and the requirement to optimize the agro-technical terms, the percentage completion of the required volume of mechanized works and the missing equipment are presented in Table A1 (see Appendix A).

7. Computational Results

In Table 1, it is shown that the farm lacks machines for certain operations as follows:

- Cultivators and plugging during the spring field work;
- Applications of mineral fertilizers and chemical weeding (throughout the year).

Table 1. Agricultural machines recommended to be purchased in addition to those available in the MTF to perform operations according to optimal agro-technical terms.

Type of Equipment	Equipment Brand	Deficit in Vehicles (Units)	
		For Single-Shift Work (With a Shift Duration of Up to 9 h during a Busy Period)	For Two-Shift Work (With a Shift Duration of 7 h Per Shift during a Busy Period)
Tractor	MTP-3522/3022	3	1
Cultivator	КПСМ-14	2	1
Sprayer	ОШ-2300	2	1
Baler	ПРФ-1.8	1	0
Fertilizer application machine	РМУ-800	1	0
Rake	MagnyumMk18	1	0

Table 1 also shows a selection of machines that are recommended to be purchased by the farm. At the same time, an additional calculation was carried out for the two-shift organization of the work of machine operators in intense periods.

The obtained results indicate that in addition to the equipment set that should be purchased, there is a surplus of machines on the farm, which may not be used if there is rational organization of labor and timely repair and maintenance of all equipment (see Table 2). If the coefficient of technical readiness of machines were lower than the calculated value, then all equipment would be fully utilized for the production of agricultural products.

Table 2. The equipment that remains unused under rational organization of the MT works.

Type of Equipment	Equipment Brand	Unit
Combine harvester	K3C-10K	1
Loader	Amkodor	1

In general, the agricultural enterprise "Novy Dvor-Agro" has a fairly balanced MT which allows it to perform more than 80% of mechanized agricultural work at the optim agro-technical conditions. Nevertheless, as evidenced by the calculations, the farm neec to purchase an additional number of energy-saturated MTZ-3022 tractors and MTZ-35 tractors (from one to three units). These tractors are needed, in particular, to ensu the preparation of the soil for sowing spring crops. In addition, the enterprise needs purchase one (or even two) cultivators and sprayers. It is also advisable to purchase or unit each of the following: a baler, a machine for mineral fertilizer application; and a rak When purchasing additional units of the equipment, one can buy either specific brands machines specified in Table 2, or their analogues (either domestic or foreign).

8. Discussions and Future Research

As a part of the further development of the proposed model and algorithm for op mizing the formation and use of the machine and tractor fleet of an agricultural enterpris it is possible to employ the mathematical method of mixed-integer linear programming. seems useful to develop an exact (or heuristic) algorithm that allows, on the basis of th optimal plan of a nonlinear problem, to build a valid integer plan that is as close as possib to the optimal one.

Of particular interest is the study of multi-criteria models for optimizing the machir and tractor fleet in agricultural production. As an alternative to the algorithm propose in Section 5, it is possible to develop algorithms based on new approaches and models schedule theory; see [22,23]. One of the most modern approaches for solving the proble of scheduling operations for a system of machines in field farming are algorithms base on neural networks. In particular, frameworks such as Opta-Planner (based on Jav syntax) and Pyomo (Python syntax) have proven themselves well in agricultural practic However, in such cases, much depends on the initial data, and the obtained solution quali from the mathematical point of view, is not optimal in the strict sense. Nevertheless, fc practical purposes, this is often sufficient, and the lower accuracy of the used algorithm compensated by its simplicity and implementation speed.

Of considerable interest is an approach based on simulation modeling. Such mode include a number of parameters (e.g., the productivity of machine and tractor units, th price of 1 h of work, the available amount of workable equipment, etc.) in the mathematic model in the form of random variables with a known probability distribution. A suitab probability distribution can be selected on the basis of the criteria of agreement known fro mathematical statistics based on the analysis of retrospective data (if any). Alternativel the probability distribution may be proposed by experts on the basis of their knowledg and ideas about the subject area.

Using the Monte Carlo method, it is possible to estimate the expected value and rang of fluctuations in the key endogenous variables of the mathematical model, as well as th objective function, which allows using a more balanced approach to the justification management decisions related to the management of a complex of mechanized works i field farming.

Interesting for further study is also the case of non-determinate deadlines for mec anized agricultural work. The delay of a certain operation may lead to crop losses an potential profits from the relevant agricultural products. However, at the same time, th may lead to resource savings. For example, it may not be necessary to purchase addition equipment for such operations as they are performed by the existing MT aggregates, albe in violation of the deadlines. Which of these scenarios is preferred is the question that the modified optimization model must answer.

9. Conclusions

In the course of this study, we developed the following method for optimizing the formation of the MTF of an agricultural enterprise for its subsequent use in field farming.

- At the first stage of this method, primary data on the functioning of the MTF of the agricultural enterprise are collected and processed. For example, calculations of the planned production rates and the cost of implementation of the MTF must be carried out. In addition, the permissible values of exogenous variables must be determined. In particular, the agro-terms of mechanized field work, and the available number of tractors and combines in the MTF are determined. It should be emphasized that with the exception of one loader and one combine harvester in the agricultural enterprise "Novy Dvor-Agro", all the machinery and equipment on both farms are fully involved in the production process. Therefore, it is necessary to update the existing equipment in time when 100% wear is reached.
- At the second stage, in order to develop reserves for improving efficiency on the basis of the economic and mathematical models presented above, the composition and structure of the MTF, as well as the schedule of its work during the planning period, are optimized. In the absence of an initial plan in the form of a current schedule for the work of the MTF, a heuristic algorithm for building an initial plan suitable for launching a model complex can be applied at this stage.
- At the third stage, a numerical solution obtained in the GAMS system is brought into the line with the integer requirement and checked for compliance with the constraints of the mathematical model. If necessary, the optimal plan is adjusted.
- At the fourth stage, on the basis of the modified optimal plan, a schedule for the implementation of the MT works for the planning period is constructed.
- The fifth stage consists of a comparison of the total costs for the agricultural operations of the MTF of the enterprise before and after optimization, with a breakdown into separate cost elements. The economic effect of the introduction of the proposed algorithm is estimated.

The developed method for optimizing the formation and use of the MTF of an agricultural enterprise in field cultivation that is proposed within the framework of this study can be successfully applied in managing the agro-industrial complex at the micro-level and meso-level. The process enables decision makers to optimize the schedule of the MTF for a given period, to draw up an optimal plan for the purchase of new equipment in terms of their total costs, and to identify unused equipment. The proposed model and algorithm can improve the comparative efficiency in the use of an enterprise's MTF. Optimization ensures a reduction in the cost of material resources, resulting in increased profitability of agricultural production.

Author Contributions: A.A.E.—formal analysis, methodology development, validation of the mathematical models, initial draft preparation; Y.N.S.—conceptualization, project administration, oversight and leadership responsibility for the research activity, planning and execution, substantive translation and editing, critical review; Y.S.B.—data collection, software application, implementation of the computer code and supporting algorithms, performing numerical experiments. All authors have read and agreed to the published version of the manuscript.

Funding: The research was funded by the Belarusian Republican Foundation for Fundamental Research, grant number Ф23РНФ-017.

Data Availability Statement: Not applicable.

Conflicts of Interest: The author declares no conflict of interest.

Appendix A. Computational Results Obtained for the Agricultural Enterprise "Novy Dvor-Agro"

Table A1. The percentage completion of the required mechanized work utilizing the specified cas composition of the MTF of the agricultural enterprise "Novy Dvor-Agro", optimal agro-technica terms, and missing equipment.

Mechanized Works	Unit of Measurement	Required Volumes of Works	Agricultural Terms		Percentage Execution with Available MTF	Composition of Unit	Number of Units That can Be Used (Actual)	Required Units	Unit Deficit
			Begining	Ending					
Application of mineral fertilizers	ha	8150	15 February	31 March	81.0	MTZ-1221+	3	3	
			A busy period of 20 days			PMY-8000, PMY-1,8	2	3	1
Loading of organic fertilizers	t	19,250	20 March		100.0				
Application of organic fertilizers	t	18,800	20 March		100.0				
Soil cultivation	ha	4200	20 March	30 April	63.1	MTP-3022+	2	3	1
						КПСМ-14	1	3	2
						MTP-3022+	3	3	
						KOH-2,8; AK-2,8	3	3	
			A busy period of 15 days			MTP 1523+ harrow	2	2	
						KPC-6+harrow	2	2	
						MTZ-1221+	2	2	
						КПС-4+борона	1	1	
Tillage	ha	2450	20 March	30 April	82.4	MTP-3522+	2	4	2
						PPO-8-40; PH-8	4	4	
						MTZ-82+	1	1	
						PLH-3-35	1	1	
Sowing of grain rapeseed	ha	2650	25 March		100.0				
Chemical protection works	ha	5400	25 April	30 June	57.0	POCA	2	2	
			A busy period of 20 days			MTZ-82+	3	3	
						OH-2300	1	3	2
Mowing	ha	2600	15 March	25 June	100.0				
Turning	ha	3000	15 March	25 June	100.0				
Selection of green mass with grinding	t	31,900	18 May		100.0				
Hay pressing	ha	230	24 May		100.0				
Application of mineral fertilizers	ha	5800	25 August	1 October	100.0				
Loading of organic fertilizers	t	20,000			100.0				
Application of organic fertilizers	t	18,000	25 August		100.0				
Soil cultivation	ha	3800	25 August	1 October	70.3	MTP-3022+	2	2	
						КПСМ-14	1	2	1
						MTP-3022+	3	3	
						KOH-2,8; AK-2,8	3	3	
						MTP 1523+	2	2	
						KPC-6+harrow	2	2	
						MTP-1221+	2	2	
						KPC-4+ harrow	1	1	

Table A1. *Cont.*

Mechanized Works	Unit of Measurement	Required Volumes of Works	Agricultural Terms		Percentage Execution with Available MTF	Composition of Unit	Number of Units That can Be Used (Actual)	Required Units	Unit Deficit
			Begining	Ending					
Tillage	ha	1750	25 August	1 October	100.0				
Sowing of grain rapeseed	ha	2420	1 September		100.0				
Chemical protection works	ha	4400	12 September	27 October	63.2	POCA	1	1	
						MTZ-82+	2	2	
						OIII-2300	1	2	1
Mowing	ha	2550	1 September	25 September	100.0				
Turning	ha	3000	1 September	25 September	93.7	MTP-82+	8	8	
						GVB-6.2; Evrotop-881; Volto-770; BBP-7.5; MagnyumMk18	7	8	1
Selection of green mass with grinding	t	30,000	10 September		100.0				
Hay pressing	ha	300	5 September		100.0				
Straw pressing	ha	1250	1 August	8 September	88.7	MTF-3022+	2	2	
						KUNH-870; GALLAZ651	2	2	
						MTF-82+	7	7	
						PRF-1.8	6	7	1
Grain harvesting	ha	2500	20 July		100.0				
Rapeseed harvesting	ha	200	27 June		100.0				
Rapeseed harvesting	ha	200	27 June		100.0				
Seed cleaning of various herbs	ha	150	15 July		100.0				

References

1. Durczak, K.; Ekielski, A.; Kozłowski, R.; Zelazinski, T.; Pilarski, K. A computer system supporting agricultural machinery and farm tractor purchase decisions. *Heliyon* **2020**, *6*, e05039. [CrossRef] [PubMed]
2. Gorodov, A.A.; Gorodova, L.V.; Fedorova, M.A. Optimizing the use of the machine and tractor fleet of an agricultural enterprise. *J. Krasn. State Agric. Univ.* **2014**, *9*, 3–11. (In Russian)
3. Vazquez, D.A.Z.; Fan, N.; Teegerstrom, T.; Seavert, C.; Summers, H.M.; Sproul, E.; Quinn, J.C. Optimal production planning and machinery scheduling for semi-arid farms. *Comput. Electron. Agric.* **2021**, *187*, 106288. [CrossRef]
4. Capitanescu, F.; Marvuglia, A.; Gutierrez, T.N.; Benetto, E. Multi-stage farm management optimization under environmental and crop rotation constraints. *J. Clean. Prod.* **2017**, *147*, 197–205. [CrossRef]
5. Pazova, T.H.; Shekihachev, Y.A.; Sohrokov, A.H. Optimization of the set of machine and tractors fleet. *Polythematic Online Electron. Sci. J. Kuban State Agrar. Univ.* **2012**, *75*, 113–116. (In Russian)
6. Kusnharev, L.I.; Dzuganov, V.B.; Dzuganov, A.V. Results of optimization of the machine-tractor park of farms and machine-technological stations. *Int. Sci. J.* **2013**, *4*, 13–18. (In Russian)
7. Toba, A.-L.; Griffel, L.M.; Hartley, D.S. Devs based modeling and simulation of agricultural machinery movement. *Comput. Electron. Agric.* **2020**, *177*, 105669. [CrossRef]
8. Li, J.; Li, T.; Yu, Y.; Zhang, Z.; Pardalos, P.M.; Zhang, Y.; Ma, Y. Discrete firefly algorithm with compound neighborhoods for asymmetric multi-depot vehicle routing problem in the maintenance of farm machinery. *Appl. Soft Comput. J.* **2019**, *81*, 105460. [CrossRef]
9. Hafezalkotob, A.; Hami-Dindar, A.; Rabie, N.; Hafezalkotob, A. A decision support system for agricultural machines and equipment selection: A case study on olive harvester machines. *Comput. Electron. Agric.* **2018**, *148*, 207–216. [CrossRef]
10. Camarena, E.A.; Gracia, C.; Sixto, J.M.; Cabrera, A. Mixed integer linear programming machinery selection model for multifarm systems. *Biosyst. Eng.* **2004**, *87*, 145–154. [CrossRef]

11. Bochtis, D.D.; Sorensen, C.G.C.; Busato, P. Advances in agricultural machinery management: A review. *Biosyst. Eng.* **2014**, *12* 69–81. [CrossRef]
12. Ahma, U.; Sharm, L. A review of best management practices for potato crop using precision agricultural technologies. *Sma Agric. Technol.* **2023**, *4*, 100220. [CrossRef]
13. Cao, R.; Li, S.; Ji, Y.; Zhang, Z.; Xu, H.; Zhang, M.; Li, M.; Li, H.; Zhou, J. Task assignment of multiple agricultural machine cooperation based on improved ant colony algorithm. *Comput. Electron. Agric.* **2021**, *182*, 105993. [CrossRef]
14. Cao, R.; Guo, Y.; Zhang, Z.; Li, S.; Zhang, M.; Li, H.; Li, M. Global path conflict detection algorithm of multiple agricultur machinery cooperation based on topographic map and time window. *Comput. Electron. Agric.* **2023**, *208*, 107773. [CrossRef]
15. Wang, Y.-J.; Huang, G.Q. A two-step framework for dispatching shared agricultural machinery with time windows. *Comp Electron. Agric.* **2022**, *192*, 106607. [CrossRef]
16. Volkova, E.; Smolyaninova, N. Trends in Russian exports and imports of agricultural machinery. *Transp. Res. Procedia* **2022**, *6* 1131–1138. [CrossRef]
17. Han, J.; Xiang, Q.; Zeng, B.; Lei, Y.; Luo, L. A multi-objective dynamic covering location problem for hierarchical agricultur machinery maintenance facilities. *Knowl.-Based Syst.* **2022**, *252*, 109462. [CrossRef]
18. Hu, Y.; Liu, Y.; Wang, Z.; Wen, J.; Li, J.; Lu, J. A two-stage dynamic capacity planning approach for agricultural machiner maintenance service with demand uncertainty. *Biosyst. Eng.* **2020**, *190*, 201–217. [CrossRef]
19. Han, J.; Zhang, J.; Zeng, B.; Mao, M. Optimizing dynamic facility location-allocation for agricultural machinery maintenanc using Benders decomposition. *Omega* **2021**, *105*, 102498. [CrossRef]
20. Cupial, M.; Szeląg-Sikora, A.; Niemiec, M. Optimisation of the machinery park with the use of OTR-7 software in context sustainable agriculture. *Agric. Agric. Sci. Procedia* **2015**, *7*, 64–69. [CrossRef]
21. Bang-Jensen, J.; Gutin, G.; Yeo, A. When the greedy algorithm fails. *Discret. Optim.* **2004**, *1*, 121–127. [CrossRef]
22. Werner, F.; Burtseva, L.; Sotskov, Y.N. Special issue on algorithms for scheduling problems. *Algorithms* **2018**, *11*, 87. [CrossRef]
23. Werner, F.; Burtseva, L.; Sotskov, Y.N. Special issue on exact and heuristic scheduling algorithms. *Algorithms* **2020**, *13*, 9. [CrossRe

algorithms

Article

Neural-Network-Based Quark–Gluon Plasma Trigger for the CBM Experiment at FAIR

Artemiy Belousov [1,2,*,†], Ivan Kisel [1,2,3,4,*], Robin Lakos [1,2] and Akhil Mithran [1,2,†]

1 Frankfurt Institute for Advanced Studies, 60438 Frankfurt am Main, Germany
2 Institute of Computer Science, J. W. Goethe University, 60325 Frankfurt am Main, Germany
3 GSI Helmholtzzentrum für Schwerionenforschung, 64291 Darmstadt, Germany
4 Helmholtz Forschungsakademie Hessen für FAIR, 64289 Darmstadt, Germany
* Correspondence: belousov@fias.uni-frankfurt.de (A.B.); i.kisel@compeng.uni-frankfurt.de (I.K.)
† These authors contributed equally to this work.

Abstract: Algorithms optimized for high-performance computing, which ensure both speed and accuracy, are crucial for real-time data analysis in heavy-ion physics experiments. The application of neural networks and other machine learning methodologies, which are fast and have high accuracy, in physics experiments has become increasingly popular over recent years. This paper introduces a fast neural network package named ANN4FLES developed in C++, which has been optimized for use on a high-performance computing cluster for the future Compressed Baryonic Matter (CBM) experiment at the Facility for Antiproton and Ion Research (FAIR, Darmstadt, Germany). The use of neural networks for classifying events during heavy-ion collisions in the CBM experiment is under investigation. This paper provides a detailed description of the application of ANN4FLES in identifying collisions where a quark–gluon plasma (QGP) was produced. The methodology detailed here will be used in the development of a QGP trigger for event selection within the First Level Event Selection (FLES) package for the CBM experiment. Fully-connected and convolutional neural networks have been created for the identification of events containing QGP, which are simulated with the Parton–Hadron–String Dynamics (PHSD) microscopic off-shell transport approach, for central Au + Au collisions at an energy of 31.2 A GeV. The results show that the convolutional neural network outperforms the fully-connected networks and achieves over 95% accuracy on the testing dataset.

Keywords: artificial neural network; multi-layer perceptron; convolutional neural network; heavy-ion experiment; compressed baryonic matter experiment; quark–gluon plasma

Citation: Belousov, A.; Kisel, I.; Robin, L.; Mithran, A. Neural-Network-Based Quark–Gluon Plasma Trigger for the CBM Experiment at FAIR. *Algorithms* **2023**, *16*, 344. https://doi.org/10.3390/a16070344

Academic Editor: Frank Werner

Received: 14 June 2023
Revised: 11 July 2023
Accepted: 12 July 2023
Published: 18 July 2023

1. Introduction

The upcoming heavy-ion physics experiment on compressed baryonic matter (CBM) at the Facility for Antiproton and Ion Research (FAIR) [1] is a fixed-target experiment designed to operate at extraordinarily high interaction rates. The combination of high-intensity beams with a high-rate detector system and a long beam time creates unparalleled conditions for the study of quantum chromodynamics (QCD) matter at the highest net-baryon densities achievable in a laboratory setting [2].

One of the main objectives of the CBM experiment is to explore the quark–gluon plasma (QGP) and its thermodynamic properties. The thermodynamic properties of a QCD system are expressed in terms of a (T, μ_B) phase diagram, where T is the temperature and μ_B is the baryonic chemical potential. The exploration of this complex phase diagram is still in its early stages. In particular, the high baryon-chemical potential region, marked by ($\mu_B > 500$ MeV), is of significant interest.

Engineered as a multipurpose tool, the CBM experiment will have the ability to detect hadrons, electrons, and muons in both elementary nucleon and heavy-ion collisions in the entire FAIR beam energy range. To execute high-precision, multi-differential measurements of rare processes, the experiment is designed to run at event rates from 100 kHz up to

10 MHz for several months annually [3]. Since it is challenging to generate a simple trigger signal for weakly decaying particles like hyperons and D-mesons, each event must be fully reconstructed. Furthermore, the decay topology needs to be identified online through fast algorithms. These algorithms will operate on a high-performance computing farm located at the GSI Green Cube [4]. At the planned CBM interaction rate of 10 MHz, one expects a data output rate of up to 1 TB/s from the detector's front-end electronics [5]. In order to optimize the storage cost, CBM requires a maximum archival rate of 3 GB/s. Therefore, there is a need to reduce the data output rate by a factor of at least 300 [6]. Thus, the experimental challenge is to identify and select (1/300 = 0.3%) rare events including complex decays in real time and discard the rest. Early classification, i.e., before data storage, will help with the efficient collection of important information from the collisions and storage of only the essential information. For this task, the CBM experiment has developed the First Level Event Selection (FLES) [7] package.

The FLES package of the CBM experiment can reconstruct the full event topology including the tracks of charged and short-lived particles. The FLES package consists of several modules (Figure 1): a track finder, a track fitter, a particle finder, and a physics analysis module. As input, the FLES package takes a simplified geometry of the tracking detectors and the hits created by charged particles crossing the detectors. The tracks of charged particles are reconstructed by the Cellular Automaton (CA) Track Finder. The Kalman Filter (KF)-based track fitter is used for a precise estimation of the track parameters. Short-lived particles, which decay before reaching the tracking detectors, can only be reconstructed via their decay products. The KF Particle Finder, based on the KFParticle package is used to find and reconstruct the parameters of short-lived particles by combining tracks of long-lived charged particles that have already been found. Finally, a quality assurance module allows for the control of the reconstruction quality at every stage. The FLES package is platform- and operating-system-independent. It will be used in the CBM experiment for online selection and offline analysis on a dedicated multi-core CPU/GPU farm.

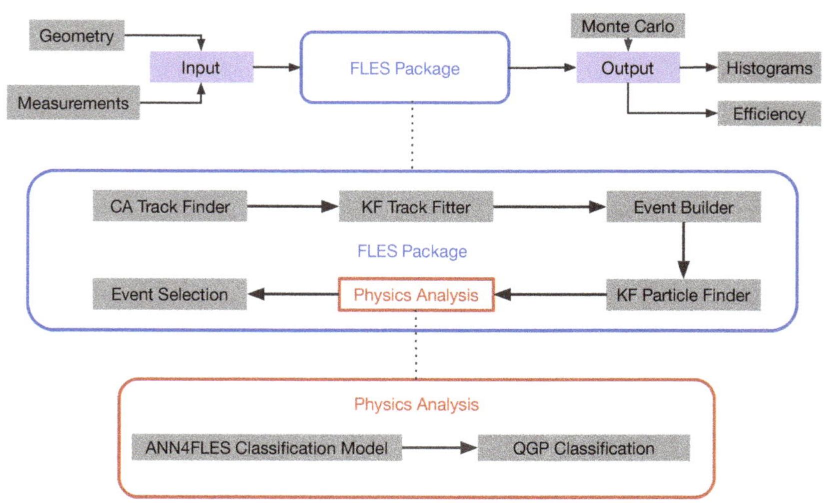

Figure 1. Block diagram of the FLES package with the tentative components of ANN4FLES, which will be used in the trigger for event selection.

A neural network for classification based on the ANN4FLES package, which receives information about reconstructed particles from the KF Particle Finder package, will be integrated into the physics analysis module of the FLES package (shown in red in Figure 1) and will then be used as a QGP trigger for event selection. Using the output from this neural network, in combination with the results from the FLES physics analysis module, the final event selection will be carried out within the FLES package.

In this paper, the possibility of using neural networks for the identification of collisions, more specifically collisions in which QGP was created, is investigated. Various models can generally be used to simulate the QCD phase transition in heavy ions. In this work, the simulation model used is a microscopic transport approach grounded in Parton–Hadron String Dynamics (PHSD) [8]. The simulation process accounting for QGP proceeds as follows: the collision volume is partitioned into grid cells. Inside each cell, collisions and hadronization occur in a manner that depends on the local energy density. This density is compared to a critical energy density threshold, which is equal to $\varepsilon_c = 0.5\ \mathrm{GeV/fm^3}$ [9]. Thus, in events where QGP is produced, it does not form throughout the entire collision volume. Instead, QGP arises only within specific cells where the local energy density surpasses the critical threshold. Therefore, as the collision energy increases, the number of these specific cells also grows, leading to an expansion in the volume of the QGP. Using this model, a dataset of QGP-aware and QGP-unaware simulations was created for training the neural networks.

2. Materials and Methods

2.1. Input Data

The dataset created with the PHSD model consists of 10,000 events, half of which contain quark–gluon plasma information, referred to as (QGP_{on}) and the other half without quark–gluon plasma information, referred to as (QGP_{off}). The data were simulated for central Au + Au collisions at a constant energy of 31.2 A GeV. This dataset is divided into 2 sets of 8000 and 2000 randomly selected events. The first set is used to train the neural network, and the second set is used for testing.

On average, each simulated collision produces around 1600 particles, most of which are quite rare. From all the particles recorded in the simulation, only 28 types of particles appear at least once in every 1000 events and were chosen as input features for the neural-network-based approaches. That way, it is possible to reduce the total size of the model as well as discard particles that are relatively less common and are assumed to have less impact on training. The remaining particles are produced too rarely to affect the trigger performance and might even be a hindrance in the training of the models. From the raw data for these 28 types of particles, the observables measured are the absolute value of momentum $|p|$, inclination angle or angle made by the momentum of the particle with respect to the positive direction of the beam axis θ, and azimuthal angle φ. This information is then entered into an array in such a way that the information for a single particle is split into 20 intervals for each of the observable, with the angle information divided into equal intervals and the absolute momentum value divided into 20 logarithmically spaced intervals. As most particles possess relatively small momentum, this enables the array to be more densely populated. So, the total length of the array comes out to be $28 \times 20 \times 20 \times 20$ for the complete 28 particles. Consequently, each event corresponds to a total of 22,400 input values or features which are the 28 different particles with each particle having a total of 8000 features from the 20 intervals for each of the $|p|$, θ, and ϕ bins. This flattened structure will be used as an input for the fully-connected networks. This can also be arranged as a 4D array, with dimensions $28 \times 20 \times 20 \times 20$, and serves as the input for the convolutional neural networks. The distribution of input information for the average over simulated events is shown in Figure 2.

On average, for the simulated dataset, nQGP collisions produce slightly more particles than QGP collisions. This can be seen clearly in the φ distribution (top right) in Figure 2. It should also be noted, from the top left panel of Figure 2, that more heavy strange baryons are created in QGP collisions. This strange enhancement is a signature of QGP formation [10].

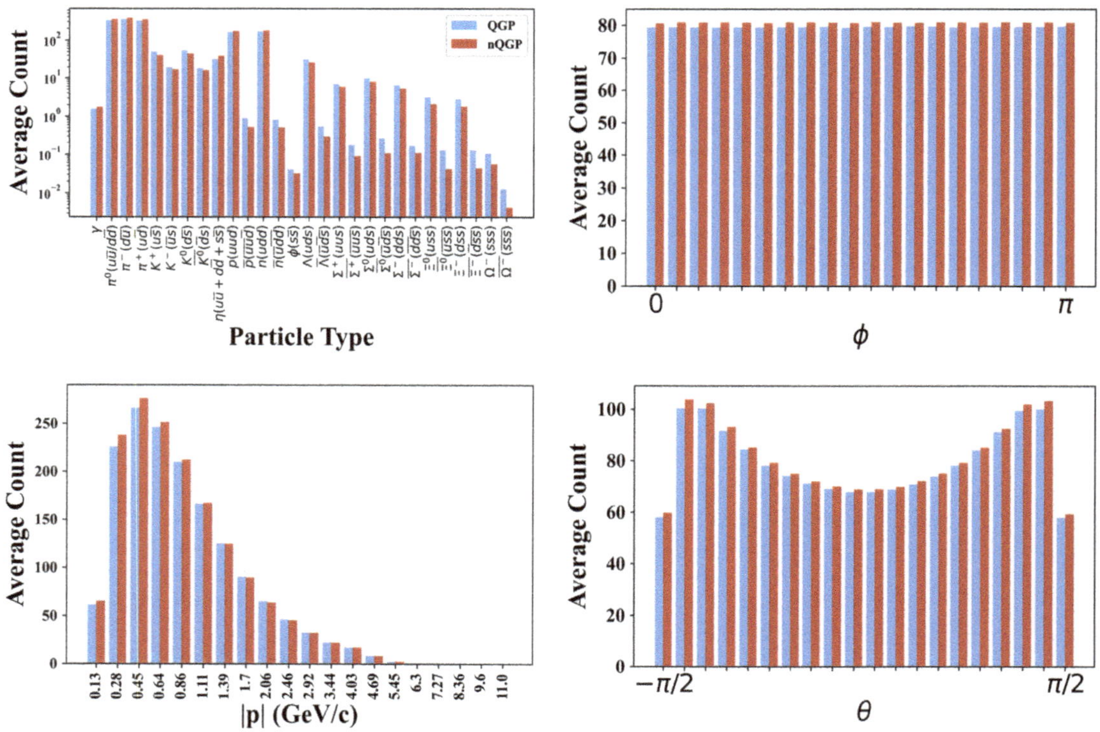

Figure 2. Average input distribution from simulated collisions. The panels in anti-clockwise ord from the top left show the distribution by particle type, by the absolute value of momentum $|p|$, b inclination angle θ and by azimuthal angle φ.

2.2. Neural Networks

Feedforward Neural Networks or MultiLayer Perceptrons (MLPs) [11] are amon the architectures used for classification in this study. Using MLP enables the constru tion of models that are easy to implement as well as to train. MLPs are very popula models for supervised learning and are commonly used for classification and regressio tasks [12]. A supervised learning procedure means that the network builds a model base on labeled data.

A MLP comprises three types of layers (input, hidden, and output) each with sever nonlinear computational units (also called neurons). The information flows from the inpu layer to the output layer through the hidden layer(s) [13]. Typically neurons from one laye are all connected to neurons in the adjacent fully-connected layers as shown in Figure The connection strengths are represented by weights in the computational process. Th weights can be thought of as the parameters of the function the neural network is tryin to approximate. The number of neurons in the input layer depends on the number predictor variables in the examples of the dataset, whereas the number of neurons in th output layer is the same as the number of target or true value variables in the exampl of the dataset. It can also be the number of variables required to produce the output fc the required task. These multi-layer connections along with the activation function enab such networks to approximate a large class of functions with a high degree based on th number of hidden units [14].

The primary operation in MLPs can be represented as:

$$\mathbf{a}_n = \mathbf{W}_n \cdot \mathbf{h}_{n-1} + \mathbf{b}_n$$

$$\mathbf{h}_n = F_A(\mathbf{a}_n)$$

where neurons in the n-th hidden layer are constructed from the neurons in the $(n-1)$-th, with 0-th layer being the input layer and the final layer being the output layer. Since every neuron in one layer is used to create a single neuron of the next layer, the corresponding weight matrix $\mathbf{W}_n$ would be $n_{l-1} \times n_l$ where n_{l-1} and n_l are the number of neurons in the $(n-1)$-th layer and n-th layer, respectively, see Figure 4. Here, $\mathbf{b}_n$ is the bias parameter for the n-th layer, which helps in learning an overall shift for the output and would have the same size as the number of neurons in that layer. F_A is the activation function that usually serves the purpose of introducing non-linearity to the network and increasing its representative capacity. $\mathbf{h}_n$ and $\mathbf{h}_{n-1}$ are neurons in the n-th and $(n-1)$-th layers, respectively.

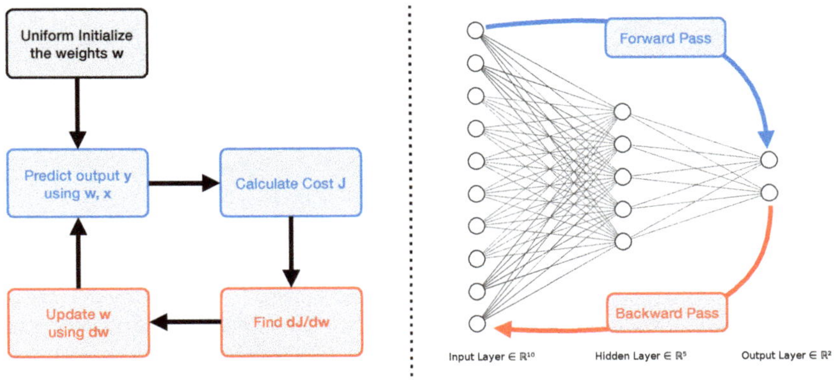

Figure 3. Structure of the fully-connected neural network used for QGP detection. The blue color is the forward propagation of information, and the red color is the backpropagation of information.

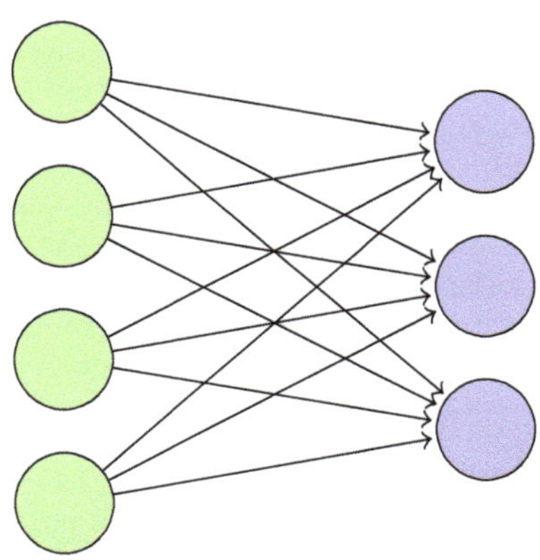

Figure 4. Each neuron in a fully-connected layer in a MLP is constructed from all the neurons of the previous layer. Each of the neurons in l-th layer, shown in purple, has connections or has input from every neuron in the $(l-1)$-th layer, shown in green.

The number of fully-connected hidden layers or network depth can be increased in an attempt to capture the optimal representational capacity of the network for this specific type of input and task that should be performed. A comparison of the performance of MLP models with different network depths for their architectures has been carried out by [15].

The other type of network used is the Convolutional Neural Network (CNN) [16 As compared to the MLPs explained above, these types of networks are more capable c capturing position-dependent features of the data. CNNs are commonly used for grid-lik data in multi-dimensional space. One of the popularly used examples of this is the objec detection or image recognition models, which utilize the grid-like arrangement of pixels i 2D space with usually color information as the third dimension. A similar correspondenc can be drawn to such image data with the input data used in this analysis. The datase used in this study can be viewed as a grid-like arrangement of three observables, namel ($|p|$), (θ), and (ϕ), of the most common particles in QGP and non-QGP events. The structur of the convolutional neural network used for QGP detection is shown in Figure 5.

CNNs are primarily based on the mathematical operation of the convolution [17 denoted by the operator $*$ and are generally defined as follows:

$$(f * g)(x) = \int_{-\infty}^{\infty} f(y)g(x-y)dy$$

where $f(x)$ and $g(x)$ are signals on the real line $\mathbb{R}$ for a 1D dataset. In general, as input dat are usually discrete signals/data in real-world applications, it is more suitable to use th discrete version of the above equation:

$$(f * g)[n] = \sum_{m=-\infty}^{\infty} f[m]g[n-m]$$

It is important to note that in CNNs, although the operation is termed as convolutio it is actually cross-correlation. Basically, in a CNN or for the cross-correlation operatio there will not be a flip of the filter as is required in typical convolutions. However, excep for this flip, both operations are identical.

CNNs have a local connection between specific regions in the input data and th corresponding units in the subsequent layer. In general, multiple filters can be applied t create a set of feature maps. Through the learning process, the filters are trained to captur abstract structural features of the data that help to match the desired output and reduce th corresponding cost function [18]. This makes them very suitable for classification tasks, a is the case for this analysis, but their applications extend to regression tasks as well.

With regards to practical implementation, there are also the benefits of parameter sha ing, which increase its efficiency, reduce the overall complexity of the network, and hel with overfitting issues. Some examples of possible applications of CNN in the field of part cle physics include regression tasks such as Pileup Mitigation in E_T^{miss} reconstruction [19 and classification tasks include quark–gluon jet discrimination [20].

In general, there can be three different types of convolution such as valid, same, an full convolutions. It depends on the size of the output feature map compared to the inpu feature map, such as if the output map is smaller (valid), same (same), or bigger (full) tha the input map.

An example of forward pass in convolutional layers is shown below, which shows th application of valid convolution with 2×2 kernel and 3×3 input map.

$$\begin{bmatrix} a & b & c \\ d & e & f \\ g & h & i \end{bmatrix} * \begin{bmatrix} p & q \\ r & s \end{bmatrix} = \begin{bmatrix} (a \cdot p) + (b \cdot q) + (d \cdot r) + (e \cdot s) & (b \cdot p) + (c \cdot q) + (e \cdot r) + (f \cdot s) \\ (d \cdot p) + (e \cdot q) + (g \cdot r) + (h \cdot s) & (e \cdot p) + (f \cdot q) + (h \cdot r) + (i \cdot s) \end{bmatrix}$$

It is very common to see a max-pooling layer either right after a convolution laye or after multiple ones. The main objective here is to extract the sharpest features of th input data. It also helps with reducing the dimension of the output feature map an computations. In the max-pooling layer, instead of matrix calculations in the convolutio operation above, the maximum element from the group of elements coinciding with th elements of the filter size is selected.

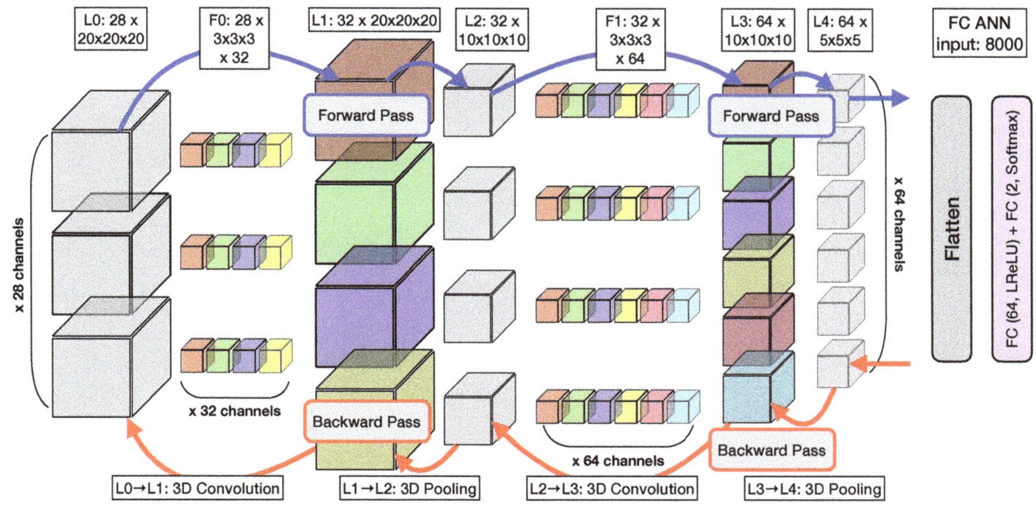

Figure 5. Structure of the convolutional neural network used for QGP detection. The blue color is the forward propagation of information, and the red color is the backpropagation of information. Each of the cubes can be represented as $L \times M \times N$ matrix and follow the forward pass operation.

In the case of 3D convolution, there will also be analogous calculations in the third dimension for both the kernel and input feature map such as shown in Figure 6a. This also applies to max-pooling in 3D as shown in Figure 6b. In the case of same convolution, as applied in this study, the input feature map will be padded with zeroes, called zero-padding, before applying the convolution in order to obtain an output feature map of the same dimension as the input feature map. Taking the above 2D convolution as an example again, the corresponding convolution operation in matrix multiplication can be expressed as follows:

$$\begin{bmatrix} 0 & 0 & 0 & 0 & 0 \\ 0 & a & b & c & 0 \\ 0 & d & e & f & 0 \\ 0 & g & h & i & 0 \\ 0 & 0 & 0 & 0 & 0 \end{bmatrix} * \begin{bmatrix} p & q \\ r & s \end{bmatrix} =$$

$$\begin{bmatrix} a \cdot s & a \cdot r + b \cdot s & b \cdot r + c \cdot s & c \cdot r \\ a \cdot q + d \cdot s & a \cdot p + b \cdot q + d \cdot r + e \cdot s & b \cdot p + c \cdot q + e \cdot r + f \cdot s & c \cdot p + f \cdot r \\ d \cdot q + g \cdot s & d \cdot p + e \cdot q + g \cdot r + h \cdot s & e \cdot p + f \cdot q + h \cdot r + i \cdot s & f \cdot p + i \cdot r \\ g \cdot q & g \cdot p + h \cdot q & h \cdot p + i \cdot q & i \cdot p \end{bmatrix}$$

In the above convolution, a zero-padding of width 1 is used to achieve a same convolution output. The backpropagation for such a convolution operation can be found using a similar convolution operation but changing the kernel and input depending on whether the gradient with respect to the weight matrix or the input gradient is required. The gradient with respect to the weight parameters is given as

$$\frac{\partial \mathbf{L}}{\partial \mathbf{W}} = \mathbf{X} * \frac{\partial \mathbf{L}}{\partial \mathbf{Y}}$$

which can be translated to the matrix form, when taking the 2D convolution without padding for the sake of matrix size, as (here it is a valid convolution because the output feature map is smaller than the input one):

$$\frac{\partial \mathbf{L}}{\partial \mathbf{W}} = \begin{bmatrix} \frac{\partial \mathbf{L}}{\partial p} & \frac{\partial \mathbf{L}}{\partial q} \\ \frac{\partial \mathbf{L}}{\partial r} & \frac{\partial \mathbf{L}}{\partial s} \end{bmatrix}$$
$$= \begin{bmatrix} a & b & c \\ d & e & f \\ g & h & i \end{bmatrix} * \begin{bmatrix} \frac{\partial \mathbf{L}}{\partial y_1} & \frac{\partial \mathbf{L}}{\partial y_2} \\ \frac{\partial \mathbf{L}}{\partial y_3} & \frac{\partial \mathbf{L}}{\partial y_4} \end{bmatrix}$$

and that for the input gradient the convolution in matrix form can be represented if th kernel is rotated and zero-padding is added to the output so that there is proper matchir of the kernel elements and output elements in the order where it appeared in the forwa pass convolution.

$$\frac{\partial \mathbf{L}}{\partial \mathbf{I}} = \begin{bmatrix} \frac{\partial \mathbf{L}}{\partial a} & \frac{\partial \mathbf{L}}{\partial b} & \frac{\partial \mathbf{L}}{\partial c} \\ \frac{\partial \mathbf{L}}{\partial d} & \frac{\partial \mathbf{L}}{\partial e} & \frac{\partial \mathbf{L}}{\partial f} \\ \frac{\partial \mathbf{L}}{\partial g} & \frac{\partial \mathbf{L}}{\partial h} & \frac{\partial \mathbf{L}}{\partial ci} \end{bmatrix}$$
$$= \begin{bmatrix} 0 & 0 & 0 & 0 \\ 0 & \frac{\partial \mathbf{L}}{\partial y_1} & \frac{\partial \mathbf{L}}{\partial y_2} & 0 \\ 0 & \frac{\partial \mathbf{L}}{\partial y_3} & \frac{\partial \mathbf{L}}{\partial y_4} & 0 \\ 0 & 0 & 0 & 0 \end{bmatrix} * \begin{bmatrix} s & r \\ q & p \end{bmatrix}$$

These equations involve computations of the gradients of the loss function **L** wi respect to the output feature map **Y**, the kernel **W**, and the input feature map **X** in th backward pass of 2D convolution using explicit matrix multiplication. See Figure 5 for 3 cube-like representation of the **Y**, **W**, and **X** matrices and the corresponding convolutio operations for the model used in this analysis.

2.3. Neural Network Models

For MLP networks (shown in Figure 7), a hidden layer with 64 fully-connected ne rons complemented by Leaky Rectified Linear Unit (LReLU) [21] activation function implemented. The number of neurons is determined empirically and remains constar to allow comparison of FC neural networks with varying numbers of layers. LReLU chosen for its performance, which is akin to the widely used Rectified Linear Unit (ReLU activation function, but it circumvents issues related to dead neurons [22]. For the learnin process, the adaptive moment estimation (ADAM) [23] algorithm is used to optimize th network parameters after each step. The ADAM algorithm updates exponential movin averages of the gradient (m_t) and the squared gradient (v_t), which themselves are estimat of the 1st moment (the mean) and the 2nd raw moment (the uncentered variance) of th gradient with the hyper-parameters β_1, β_2, which control the exponential decay rates c these moving averages with respective values 0.9 and 0.999. The values for α and ϵ a 0.001 and 10^{-8}, respectively [23].

The architecture of the CNN (shown in Figure 8) is composed of two three-dimension convolutional layers, each succeeded by a max-pooling layer, and two sequentially arrange fully-connected layers. The initial convolutional layer contains 32 filters of size $3 \times 3 \times$ with a zero-padding of $1 \times 1 \times 1$ and a stride of $1 \times 1 \times 1$, thus preserving the spati dimensions of the input. The convolution is then followed by a max-pooling operation wit a filter size of $2 \times 2 \times 2$ and stride of $2 \times 2 \times 2$, leading to a halving of the spatial dimensior The second convolutional layer consists of 64 filters of identical size and employs the sam padding and stride length as the preceding convolutional layer. It is subsequently followe by a max-pooling layer with an identical filter size and stride length to the previous poolin layer. The resulting $64 \times 5 \times 5 \times 5$ matrix is then flattened and fed into the fully-connecte layers with parameters mirroring those utilized in the MLP architectures.

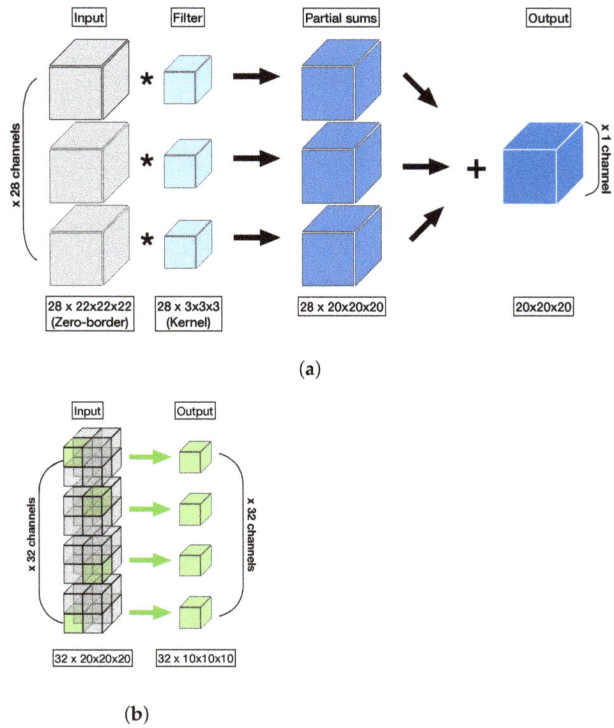

Figure 6. (**a**): 3D Convolution. An illustration of the three-dimensional convolution operation applied to the input layer using a single filter, composed of 28 kernels. This process transforms the 28 input channels into a singular output channel. The quantity of output channels directly corresponds to the number of filters used during the convolution. (**b**): 3D Pooling. An illustration of the three-dimensional pooling operation. Despite retaining the original number of channels, the data dimensions are halved. For instance, a $20 \times 20 \times 20$ cube is reduced to a $10 \times 10 \times 10$ cube through this process.

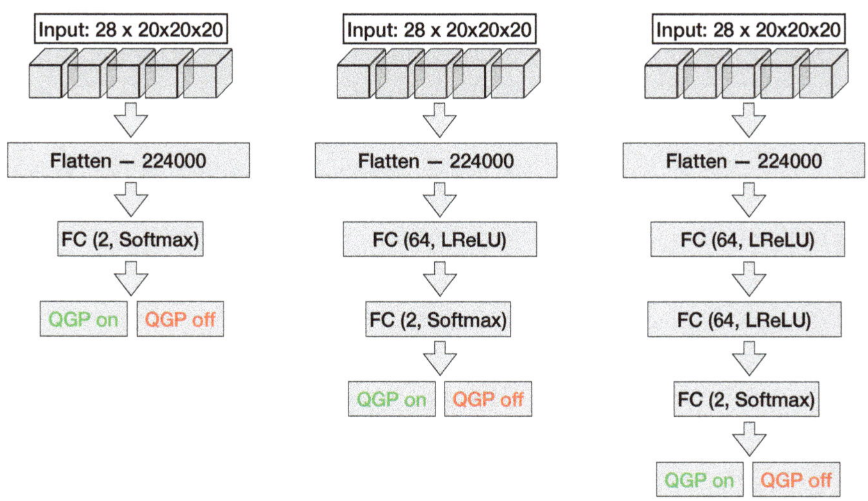

Figure 7. From left to right: structure of one-, two- and three-layer fully-connected neural networks used for QGP detection.

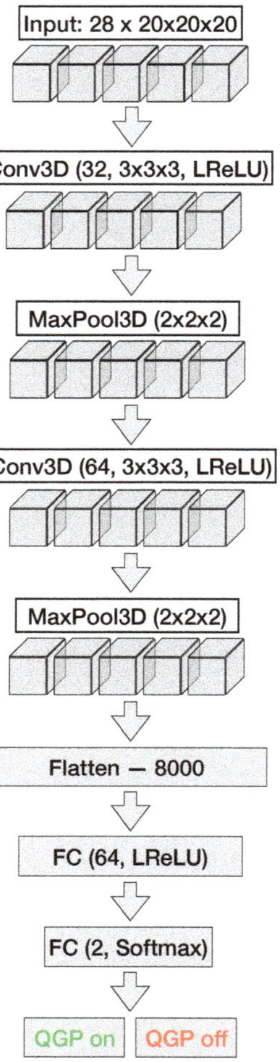

Figure 8. Structure of the convolutional neural network used for QGP detection. The network consists of two sets of convolution and max-pooling layers, followed by two fully-connected layers. After processing through the CNN, the final output matrix is fed into the fully-connected layers for further analysis and classification.

3. Results

Figure 9 compares the results for the same models implemented in ANN4FLES (shown in red) and PyTorch (shown in blue) for both training (represented by a dashed line) and testing (represented by a solid line) datasets.

The fully-connected networks show a maximum accuracy of around 80% for testing data for each of the three different depth configurations, namely 0, 1, and 2 hidden layers respectively. CNN, on the other hand, shows around 95% accuracy for its testing dataset. Another observation is the accuracy of CNN for the testing dataset is greater as compared to that of MLP by around 15%. This can be attributed to the grid-like ordering present in the input data and as mentioned earlier CNNs are more specialized in learning such grid-like data.

The comparative graphs also indicate that the mathematics used in the ANN4FLES package implementation agrees correctly with PyTorch. The small discrepancies in accuracy may be due to the use of different random seeds when initializing the weights in the two implementations. Since these weights are randomized, reproducing identical results is challenging.

Thus, although small deviations in accuracy are present due to the inherent randomness, the overall correlation between ANN4FLES and PyTorch implementation results reinforces the validity of ANN4FLES' mathematical foundations. This comparison shows that both ANN4FLES and PyTorch have an almost identical model for the classification task.

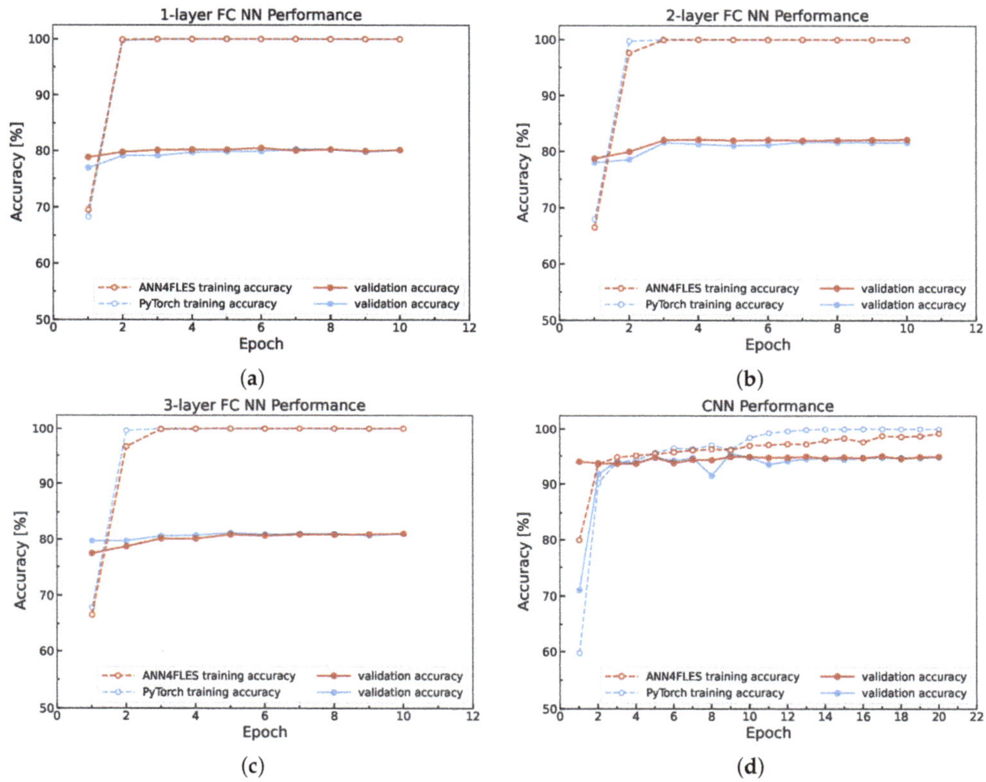

Figure 9. Results for same models implemented in ANN4FLES (red) and PyTorch (blue) for both training (dashed line) and testing (solid line) datasets. The accuracy for MLP models with 0 hidden layer ((**a**), Training and testing accuracy for MLP without hidden layers), 1 hidden layer ((**b**), Training and testing accuracy for MLP with 1 hidden layer) and 2 hidden layer ((**c**), Training and testing accuracy for MLP with 2 hidden layers) fits the training dataset well as the training accuracy reaches 100% as compared to the testing dataset where the accuracy saturates around 80%. For CNN ((**d**), Training and testing accuracy for CNN network) the generalization error is reduced compared to that of the MLP models and shows it is more capable of learning the right features for classification.

4. Conclusions

The results of this study indicate that the neural network classifiers manage to identify patterns in the raw data simulated using the transport model with and without a quark–gluon plasma (QGP) formation model. Among the four architectures tested, the CNN achieves the highest accuracy of approximately 95%. The potential of using neural network classifiers to identify QGP formation in heavy-ion collisions was shown. Moving forward, the ANN4FLES package will be integrated into the physics analysis module of the FLES package and will be used as a QGP trigger for event selection for the CBM experiment. Future work will continue to explore the performance of various neural network architectures within the ANN4FLES package across different types of input data. Another objective will be understanding the patterns these neural network classifiers learn and whether they match with our physics models.

Author Contributions: Conceptualization, A.B., I.K. and R.L.; Methodology, A.B. and I.K.; Softwa A.B., R.L. and A.M.; Validation, A.B. and I.K.; Formal analysis, A.B. and A.M.; Investigation, A.B. ar R.L.; Resources, I.K.; Data curation, I.K.; Writing—original draft, A.B., R.L. and A.M.; Writing—revie & editing, A.M.; Supervision, I.K.; Project administration, I.K.; Funding acquisition, I.K. All autho have read and agreed to the published version of the manuscript.

Funding: This work was partly supported by grants from Bundesministerium für Bildung ur Forschung grant number 01IS21092 and Helmholtz Forschungsakademie Hessen für FAIR, Darmsta Germany (HFHF Project ID: 2.1.4.2.5).

Conflicts of Interest: The authors declare no conflict of interest.

References

1. Sturm, C.; Stöcker, H. The Facility for Antiproton and Ion Research FAIR. *Phys. Part. Nucl. Lett.* **2011**, *8*, 865–868. [CrossRef]
2. Friman, B.; Höhne, C.; Knoll, J.; Leupold, S.; Randrup, J.; Rapp, R.; Senger, P. (Eds.) *The CBM Physics Book*, 1st ed.; Lecture Not in Physics; Springer: Berlin/Heidelberg, Germany, 2011; pp. 211–213.
3. Friese, V. Simulation and reconstruction of free-streaming data in CBM. In *Journal of Physics: Conference Series*; IOP Publishir Bristol, UK, 2011; Volume 331, p. 032008.
4. Schwarz, K.; Uhlig, F.; Karabowicz, R.; Montiel-Gonzalez, A.; Zynovyev, M.; Preuss, C. Grid Computing at GSI for ALICE ar FAIR-present and future. In *Journal of Physics: Conference Series*; IOP Publishing: Bristol, UK, 2012; Volume 396, p. 032097.
5. Friese, V.; CBM Collaboration. The high-rate data challenge: Computing for the CBM experiment. In *Journal of Physics: Conferen Series*; IOP Publishing: Bristol, UK, 2017; Volume 898, p. 112003.
6. Kisel, P. KF Particle Finder Package: Missing Mass Method for Reconstruction of Strange Particles in CBM (FAIR) and STA (BNL) Experiments. Ph.D. Thesis, Goethe University, Frankfurt am Main, Germany, 2023.
7. Kisel, I.; Kulakov, I.; Zyzak, M. Standalone first level event selection package for the CBM experiment. *IEEE Trans. Nucl. S* **2013**, *60*, 3703–3708. [CrossRef]
8. Cassing, W.; Bratkovskaya, E. Parton transport and hadronization from the dynamical quasiparticle point of view. *Phys. R* **2008**, *78*, 034919. [CrossRef]
9. Cassing, W.; Bratkovskaya, E. Parton–hadron–string dynamics: An off-shell transport approach for relativistic energies. *Nu Phys.* **2009**, *831*, 215–242. [CrossRef]
10. Koch, P.; Müller, B.; Rafelski, J. From Strangeness Enhancement to Quark–Gluon Plasma Discovery. *Int. J. Mod. Phys.* **201** *32*, 1730024. [CrossRef]
11. Taud, H.; Mas, J.; Multilayer Perceptron (MLP). *Geomatic Approaches for Modeling Land Change Scenarios*; Camacho Olmedo, M. Paegelow, M., Mas, J.F., Escobar, F., Eds.; Springer International Publishing: Cham, Switzerland, 2018; pp. 451–455.
12. Murtagh, F. Multilayer perceptrons for classification and regression. *Neurocomputing* **1991**, *2*, 183–197. [CrossRef]
13. Ramchoun, H.; Amine, M.; Idrissi, J.; Ghanou, Y.; Ettaouil, M. Multilayer Perceptron: Architecture Optimization and Trainir *Int. J. Interact. Multimed. Artif. Intel.* **2016**, *4*, 26–30. [CrossRef]
14. Hornik, K.; Stinchcombe, M.; White, H. Multilayer feedforward networks are universal approximators. *Neural Netw.* **198** 2, 359–366. [CrossRef]
15. Sergeev, F.; Bratkovskaya, E.; Kisel, I.; Vassiliev, I. Deep learning for Quark–Gluon Plasma detection in the CBM experiment. *I J. Mod. Phys.* **2020**, *35*, 2043002. [CrossRef]
16. O'Shea, K.; Nash, R. An Introduction to Convolutional Neural Networks. *arXiv* **2015**, arXiv:1511.08458
17. Dumoulin, V.; Visin, F. A guide to convolution arithmetic for deep learning. *arXiv* **2016**, arXiv:1603.07285.
18. Taye, M.M. Theoretical Understanding of Convolutional Neural Network: Concepts, Architectures, Applications, Futu Directions. *Computation* **2023**, *11*, 52. [CrossRef]
19. Convolutional Neural Networks with Event Images for Pileup Mitigation with the ATLAS Detector. 2019. Available onlir https://inspirehep.net/literature/1795222 (accessed on 13 June 2023)
20. Lee, J.S.H.; Park, I.; Watson, I.J.; Yang, S. Quark-Gluon Jet Discrimination Using Convolutional Neural Networks. *J. Korean Ph Soc.* **2019**, *74*, 219–223. [CrossRef]
21. Jiang, T.; Cheng, J. Target Recognition Based on CNN with LeakyReLU and PReLU Activation Functions. In Proceedings the 2019 International Conference on Sensing, Diagnostics, Prognostics, and Control (SDPC), Beijing, China, 15–17 August 201 pp. 718–722.
22. Dubey, A.K.; Jain, V. Comparative Study of Convolution Neural Network's ReLU and Leaky-ReLU Activation Functions. *Applications of Computing, Automation and Wireless Systems in Electrical Engineering*; Mishra, S., Sood, Y.R., Tomar, A., Eds.; Spring Singapore, 2019; pp. 873–880.
23. Kingma, D.P.; Ba, J. Adam: A Method for Stochastic Optimization. *arXiv* **2017**, arXiv:1412.6980.

algorithms

Article

Design of Cloud-Based Real-Time Eye-Tracking Monitoring and Storage System

Mustafa Can Gursesli [1,2], Mehmet Emin Selek [3], Mustafa Oktay Samur [4], Mirko Duradoni [2], Kyoungju Park [5], Andrea Guazzini [2,6] and Antonio Lanatà [1,*]

1 Department of Information Engineering, University of Florence, 50139 Florence, Italy; mustafacan.gursesli@unifi.it
2 Department of Education, Literatures, Intercultural Studies, Languages and Psychology, University of Florence, 50135 Florence, Italy; mirko.duradoni@unifi.it (M.D.); andrea.guazzini@unifi.it (A.G.)
3 Department of Mining Engineering, Istanbul Technical University, Istanbul 34467, Turkey; mehmeteminselek@gmail.com
4 Department of Electrical and Electronics Engineering, Bilgi University, Istanbul 34060, Turkey; oktaysamr@gmail.com
5 Department of Computer Science and Engineering, Chung-Ang University, Seoul 06974, Republic of Korea; kjpark@cau.ac.kr
6 Centre for the Study of Complex Dynamics, University of Florence, 50019 Sesto Fiorentino, Italy
* Correspondence: antonio.lanata@unifi.it

Abstract: The rapid development of technology has led to the implementation of data-driven systems whose performance heavily relies on the amount and type of data. In the latest decades, in the field of bioengineering data management, among others, eye-tracking data have become one of the most interesting and essential components for many medical, psychological, and engineering research applications. However, despite the large usage of eye-tracking data in many studies and applications, a strong gap is still present in the literature regarding real-time data collection and management, which leads to strong constraints for the reliability and accuracy of on-time results. To address this gap, this study aims to introduce a system that enables the collection, processing, real-time streaming, and storage of eye-tracking data. The system was developed using the Java programming language, WebSocket protocol, and Representational State Transfer (REST), improving the efficiency in transferring and managing eye-tracking data. The results were computed in two test conditions, i.e., local and online scenarios, within a time window of 100 seconds. The experiments conducted for this study were carried out by comparing the time delay between two different scenarios, even if preliminary results showed a significantly improved performance of data management systems in managing real-time data transfer. Overall, this system can significantly benefit the research community by providing real-time data transfer and storing the data, enabling more extensive studies using eye-tracking data.

Keywords: data management; cloud computing; RESTful API; eye tracking; web portal

Citation: Gursesli, M.C.; Selek, M.E.; Samur, M.O.; Duradoni, M.; Park, K.; Guazzini, A.; Lanatà, A. Design of Cloud-Based Real-Time Eye-Tracking Monitoring and Storage System. *Algorithms* **2023**, *16*, 355. https://doi.org/10.3390/a16070355

Academic Editor: Frank Werner

Received: 19 June 2023
Revised: 13 July 2023
Accepted: 23 July 2023
Published: 24 July 2023

1. Introduction

In recent decades, technology has become a crucial element of human life, leading to various innovative and convenient advancements across numerous fields, including health [1,2], entertainment [3,4], social media [5,6], physics [7,8], and chemistry [9,10]. While these innovations have positively impacted human life, they also demanded several technological requirements. These requirements, including computational power [11], Internet access [12], electricity [13], data [14], and other factors [15,16], have become increasingly crucial in both academia and industry sectors. Data and data management, in particular, became the center node for solving these technological challenges, and their relevance has been further increased by the growth of machine learning methods and AI applications [14,17,18].

However, despite the need for huge data, research applications still lack suitable and e fective data collection systems. Moreover, since many studies, especially those regardin a large part of the population, moved to mobile applications, real-time data became th strongest constraint to solve [19,20]. These conditions have led researchers to focus o improving and creating novel data collection systems to facilitate the technological advance in the research activity. These data collection systems are widely used in many studies o topics as different as brain signals [21], earthquakes [22], weather conditions [23], etc.

In this context, Representational State Transfer (REST), the most widely used wel based architecture in both the academic literature and industry, was introduced in 2000 as Ph.D. thesis by Roy Fielding [24] for leading the design and development of the architectur of an Internet-scale distributed hypermedia system. It facilitates the caching of component to reduce user-perceived latency, enforce security, and encapsulate legacy systems [24 REST employs the Hyper Text Transfer Protocol (HTTP) to enable communication betwee clients and servers. Its structure provides several advantages, including modifiability an statelessness, which enhance interoperability [25]. These advantages bring substantia benefits to the management of real-time data.

In addition to the solutions and limitations associated with real-time data managemen it is widely recognized that the real-time management of diverse data types present unique challenges due to their high density and rapid flow rates [26]. Eye-tracking dat in particular present this complexity due to their highly dynamic and rapidly changin nature [27–29]. Furthermore, an eye-tracking pattern is an indirect measure of the comple biological system behind it, which requires high-cost computational methods for analysi with models, creating a major problem for the smooth real-time streaming of data.

In this regard, eye tracking is a powerful research tool for studying various topic such as marketing [30], attention [31], perception [32], psychopathology [33], compute vision [34], and decision making [35,36]. Eye tracking provides insight into the neura mechanisms at the base of exploring strategies of visual stimuli [37]. The eye-trackin technology greatly advanced in recent years, achieving greater precision and accuracy, eve in real-world environments [34,38,39]. The history of eye tracking can be traced back t the late 1800s, with improvements in terms of comfort, wearability, and performance fo a long-time measure of eye movements [36,40,41]. Since then, there have been importan advancements that have led to the development of increasingly sophisticated eye-trackin systems [42–44].

Although physical eye-tracking devices have improved and become easier to us the real-world employment of these devices is still not widespread due to their hig cost [42–44]. This practical issue has prompted researchers to find different solution and many eye-tracking models using webcams have been developed [34,39,45]. Many o these models can be implemented locally on the user's devices and streamed to differen platforms via Internet and web servers. Researchers integrate their models into wel platforms to reach larger audiences and collect more data. Unfortunately, there is a gap i the literature regarding web-based streaming and storage systems that can be integrate with real-time eye-tracking models.

This study aims to introduce a system that allows the collection, processing, real time streaming, and storage of eye-tracking data with REST architecture implementatio The manuscript is structured as follows: In Section 1, data necessity, REST, real-time data and eye tracking are explained. Section 2 presents the materials and methods, the syste design, the Representational State Transfer, the application programming interface, Web Socket, the database server, Docker, WebGazer.js, the hardware implementation, and th experiment. In Section 3, the experimental results are detailed. Section 4 discusses th achieved experimental results compared with those presented in the literature. Lastl Section 5 provides a conclusion of the entire study and possible future research direction

2. Materials and Methods

The system's architecture consists of two software modules, i.e., the front-end and the back-end. The former is responsible for interfacing with the user, acquiring information, preprocessing, streaming live data, and transferring to the back-end. The latter is the invisible part and includes applications, servers, and databases. This section will display how our architecture articulates between these two modules. In our structure, three different interconnected platforms are designed to collect, process, stream, and store eye movements during an experimental session. These platforms are the experiment platform, the real-time results platform, and the database management platform (see Figure 1). The experiment and real-time results platforms are located in the front-end while the database management platform is located in the back-end. The front-end and back-end communicate through HTTP. Lastly, data gathered from this study were analyzed using Python Version 3.10.0 with Matplotlib library version 3.5.3. All details of the system and data flow are reported in the following sections.

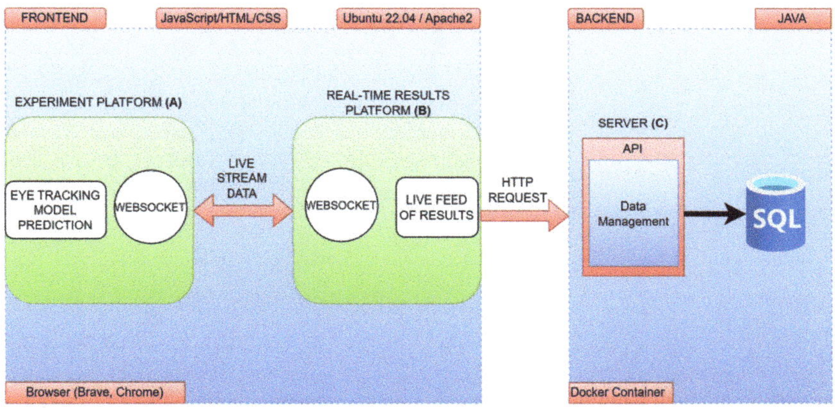

Figure 1. System design components: experiment platform (**A**), real-time results platform (**B**), and server (**C**).

2.1. System Design

The system is designed with three components under two main modules (see Figure 1). The experimental platform (A) and the real-time results platform (B) are in the front-end module. In the back-end module, there is a server (C) component. The front-end development uses JavaScript, HyperText Markup Language (HTML), and Cascading Style Sheets (CSS), which allows the creation of a user-friendly interface. This interface displays the live data stream and the evaluation report of the eye-tracking system. HTML5 video tags are used to display participant's live video stream.

The front-end is specifically designed to integrate the eye-tracking model and provide a clear presentation of its live results. Moreover, data transfer between the experiment platform (A) and real-time results platform (B) is carried out via WebSocket. Subsequently, these data are transmitted to the back-end server via an HTTP request and stored in the database. The front-end is the preferred implementation location for eye-tracking models to ensure a more robust privacy strategy. Since sensitive data, such as eye-tracking information, is processed in this system, the aim is to perform all computations exclusively on the computer being used, without involving external servers or sources. This strategic approach is motivated by the fact that various models, including eye-tracking models found in the literature, perform computations on snapshots captured by the user's webcam [46,47]. Processing these images on an external server is considered to introduce potential security vulnerabilities. Therefore, all computations are configured to take place only on the computer running the experiment, and only the results are transferred to other platforms and servers.

The back-end structure was built using Spring Boot, which is a framework of th Java language, providing a robust and scalable data processing and management platfor At the end of data collection on the front-end side, the collected data are sent to the bac end service by HTTP requests. The back-end service aims to process and manage da for database storage. In addition, the back-end provides a data management API th facilitates read and write operations to the SQL database.

Database management involves the use of an SQL database for the efficient storag and management of data. The database provides scalability and ease of retrieval an analysis of stored data. The back-end communicates with the database using Java Databa Connectivity (JDBC), a Java API designed to access and manage databases. This seamle integration enables effective data handling within the system. Dockerization plays major role in encapsulating the various components of the system. It involves separatir the front-end, back-end, and database into separate Docker containers. Each contain can be deployed independently, allowing for easy scalability based on the application needs. Dockerization also provides a secure and isolated environment for each componer ensuring the stability and security of the overall system.

The system flow can be briefly described as follows: The experiment platform (captures the eye movements and positions of the subject through an embedded mod converts them into coordinates, and sends them to the real-time results platform (B). The two platforms communicate with each other via WebSockets and provide a data flow b constantly listening to exchanged messages from A to B and vice versa. The eye-trackir model placed on the experimental platform initiates data collection and its results a then transmitted to a real-time results platform and streamed to the back-end via HTT requests. Following the end of the data collection session, the eye-tracking data, streame instantaneously on the real-time results platform (B), are sent via HTTP request to th Server (C), which constitutes the last stage of the data flow in the back-end (See Figure 2

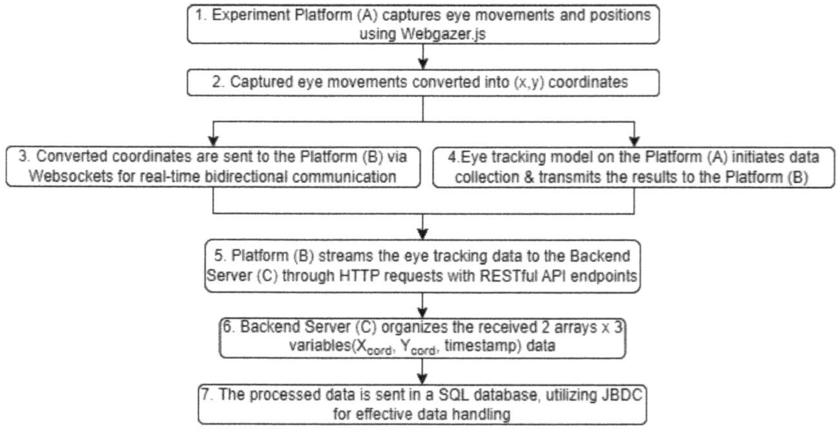

Figure 2. System flowchart.

2.2. Representational State Transfer (REST) and Application Programming Interface (API)

Representational State Transfer (REST) is designed to develop web services base on precise standards and limitations to grant an expandable and adaptable cross-da transaction over the Internet [24]. RESTful API (application programming interface) is a interpretation of the REST architecture that provides access to and actions on resourc using HTTP. In a RESTful API, the server does not store data about the user betwee requests; instead, each request has all the data the server needs to process it. RESTf APIs follow a set of constraints, such as client-server architecture and a consistent interfac among others, to ensure that they are reliable, scalable, and easy to maintain [48,49]. RES has become popular among developers due to its simplicity and flexibility. In additio

RESTful APIs have evolved into a standard for web services development and are actively used by many large companies such as Google, Twitter, etc.

2.3. WebSocket

WebSocket is a communication protocol pertaining to the application layer in the Transmission Control Protocol/Internet Protocol model (TCP/IP) [50]. Due to the popularity and prevalence of HTTP, WebSocket uses HTTP constructs for the initial connection between a client and a server [51] and provides persistent communication so that both the client and the server can send messages at any time. Compared to traditional real-time web communication, the WebSocket protocol saves a lot of network bandwidth and server resources, and the real-time performance is significantly improved [52]. It is helpful for real-time applications such as online games, financial trading platforms, eye tracking, and Internet of Things (IoT)-based applications that support server push technology [53,54].

2.4. Database Server (SQL)

The SQL (structured query language) is a fourth-generation declarative programming language for relational DBMSs (database management systems) and it is used to communicate with and manipulate databases [55]. The MySQL database stores and retrieves data via the REST API. The stored procedures and functions are designed as a security layer to perform operations that would receive queries from the API for SQL processing in the database [56].

There are many parameters to consider when evaluating database performance. In the next section, we will highlight the qualities that made SQL databases more suitable for this system over NoSQL databases. In particular, NoSQL databases outperform SQL databases regarding writing speed and scalability. NoSQL databases perform better when dealing with large scalability requirements and facilitating rapid data updates [57]. However, SQL databases better manage complex relationships and multiple client scenarios [57]. The characteristics of the SQL, structure, and capability to maintain data integrity make them suitable for scenarios involving relational data tables (such as the study carried out). Due to the anticipated availability of multiple user results and relational data in this system, the SQL database was chosen over NoSQL.

2.5. Docker

Docker is a technology that enables container virtualization, which can be compared to a highly efficient virtual machine due to its lightweight nature [58,59]. It is characterized by a modular architecture comprising multiple integral components that interact harmoniously to facilitate the process of "Containerization". These components are articulated as follows: At the core of Docker is the Docker Engine, which provides the runtime environment for containers [59]. Docker Images, read-only templates that serve as container building blocks, utilize a layered file system and copy-on-write mechanism for efficient image management [59]. When a Docker Image is instantiated, it becomes a Docker Container, which offers a lightweight and secure execution environment [59]. Docker Containers can be easily created, started, stopped, and deleted, providing flexibility in managing application instances [60]. To facilitate image sharing and distribution, Docker Registries, such as Docker Hub, host a vast collection of prebuilt images [61]. Additionally, organizations can establish private registries tailored to their specific image requirements [61]. The modular architecture of Docker, along with its components, enables scalable and flexible application deployment across various environments.

2.6. WebGazer.js

WebGazer.js is a JavaScript-based eye-tracking algorithm. This algorithm allows the real-time display of eye-gaze locations on the web using webcams on notebooks and mobile phones [39,62]. This tool aims to utilize eye-tracking systems, which are currently only used in controlled environments and experiments, to enable people to use them in their daily lives [39,62]. WebGazer.js consists of two core elements. These are a pupil detector and gaze estimator. The pupil detector detects the position of the eye and pupil through th webcam. At the same time, the gaze estimator uses regression analysis to estimate wher the individual is looking on the screen [39,62]. The gaze estimator applies a regressio analysis through a calibration based on mouse clicks and mouse movements. Moreove the pseudocode of WebGazer.js shows the algorithm details (See in Appendix A.1).

2.7. Hardware Implementation

In the system, three Docker virtual environments were used to perform experiment stream real-time eye movements, and store data. In order to carry out online experiment two separate physical AMD Central Processing Units (CPUs), 1 GB of Random Acces Memory (RAM), and 25 GB of Solid State Disk (SSD) hardware were used for the front-en where the eye-tracking model runs and for live feed eye-tracking data. Furthermore, to stor the data and manage the back-end, 2 physical Intel CPUs, 2 GB of RAM, and 25 GB of SSI hardware were used. The locations of the servers where the Dockers are used are locate in Frankfurt, Germany for online experiments. The local experiments were conducte with Intel i5 8600k CPUs and 16 GB of RAM. Lastly, in both systems, eye-tracking dat are collected in X and Y coordinates, while the data for time in seconds are stored i Year:Month:Day:Hour:Minute:Second:Millisecond.

2.8. Memory Management

Low-level programming languages, such as C, incorporate manual memory mar agement features like *malloc()* and *free()* [63]. Conversely, JavaScript handles memor allocation automatically during object creation and frees it when those objects are no longe in use, through a process known as garbage collection. "Garbage Collection" in JavaScrip plays a crucial role in determining which objects are necessary and which ones can b discarded [64]. It follows a cycle of memory release, where JavaScript identifies and mark objects that are no longer needed [65]. Specifically, within the *predictWebcam* function an the objects created within it, memory is allocated as required during each function cal Once the function produces an output, JavaScript performs the important task of markin and sweeping all the memory that will no longer be utilized, ensuring efficient memor management. In this system, we follow the garbage collection strategy.

2.9. Experiments

Experimental sessions were carried out to assess the reliability of the proposed systen architecture, comparing two different scenarios: local implementation (LI) and onlin implementation (OI). The local scenario involved configuring the system on the loca computer, while the online scenario consisted of configuring the system on the online serve

In order to measure the time delay of both scenarios (LI and OI), the timestamp of each platform were collected during a 100 s time window. The delay was calculate by subtracting the timestamp value of the experiment platform (A) from the timestam received on the real-time results platform (B) (B-A), (i.e., arrival time–starting time). It is o note that platform (A) sends data to platform (B) at the frequency of 1 HZ (see Figure 1). Th *Console.log()* function was used to visualize data in the experiment. Specifically, *Console.log(* is a function that allows the data given into the function to be seen outside the cod environment. This function allowed us to capture the precise timestamps indicating th arrival and starting time of data effectively.

Moreover, for the second experiment, 15 min of data were collected from the systen at one-second intervals to understand how the system affects memory usage and how i changes over time while the eye-tracking model is performing real-life computations in th experiment platform. A *logMemoryUsage()* function was used to record the memory usag measurements in real-time. Specifically, the *logMemoryUsage()* function can be used fo several purposes, such as analyzing the change in memory usage over time and detectin memory leaks or performance problems.

3. Results

In this study, a series of statistical analyses have been performed to evaluate the difference between the delays of LI and OI. In order to perform the analyses correctly, firstly, the Shapiro–Wilk test was applied to determine whether the delay data were normally distributed. According to the results of the Shapiro–Wilk test, both the LI delay data (Shapiro–Wilk test statistic = 0.370, $p < 0.05$) and the OI delay data (Shapiro–Wilk test statistic = 0.322, $p < 0.05$) did not fit a normal distribution. Time difference distributions are shown in Figure 3.

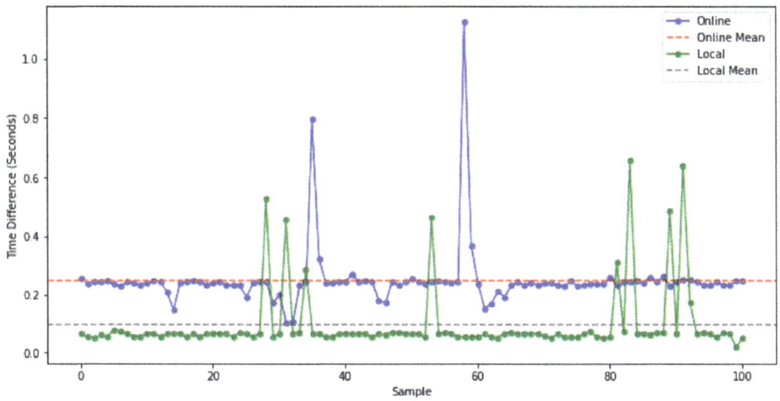

Figure 3. Comparison of time differences between the online and local systems.

Based on these results, it was concluded that parametric statistical tests could not be used and the Mann–Whitney U test, a non-parametric test, was preferred. The results of the Mann–Whitney U test showed a statistically significant difference between local and online latency (U = 794.0, $p < 0.05$). Table 1 shows the Mann–Whitney U test results.

Table 1. Mann-Whitney U test results regarding the local and online conditions.

Condition	U-Statistic	*p*-Value
Local vs. online	794.0	3.317643×10^{-25}

According to descriptive statistics, the MAD value for the LI delay was 0.004, the median value was 0.064, the minimum value was 0.020, and the maximum value was 0.660. Similarly, the MAD value for the OI delay was 0.006, the median value was 0.244, the minimum value was 0.101, and the maximum value was 1.123. All the results of the descriptive statistics are shown in Table 2.

Table 2. Descriptive statistics.

Condition	MAD	Median	Min	Max
Local	0.004	0.064	0.020	0.660
Online	0.006	0.244	0.101	1.123

These findings indicate that there is a statistically significant difference between LI and OI delays and that there is a significant difference in their performance.

In addition, analysis of the memory usage data revealed interesting results (see Table 3). The average increase between seconds was measured as 0.0037 MB. The average memory usage during the session was measured as 72.62 MB with a minimum of 63.74 MB, and the maximum memory usage was 83.62. The standard deviation of memory usage was calculated at 3.48 MB.

Table 3. Memory usage statistics.

Conditions	Memory (Megabyte (MB))
Average increase between seconds	0.0037
Average memory usage	72.62
Minimum memory usage	63.74
Maximum memory usage	83.62
Standard deviation	3.48

Figure 4 shows an initial low level of memory usage that increases over time, with steady increase over a period of time. Although there are occasional fluctuations, the a erage memory usage (red dashed line) is generally above the curve and shows a steadi increasing trend. These results show that the memory usage of the system varies over tin and reaches a stable level over a period of time.

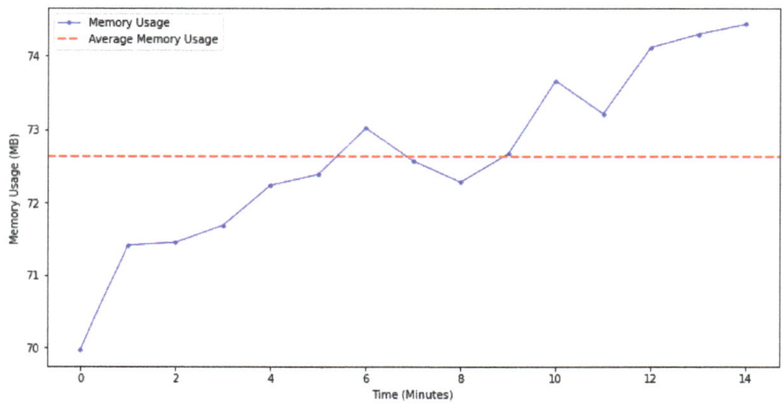

Figure 4. Diagram of memory usage: blue line, memory usage dynamic; red dotted line, memo usage average. Time axis is expressed in minutes.

4. Discussion

The demand for data has seen a substantial increase in recent years due to facto such as rapid technological advancements, growing interest in AI from both the priva sector and researchers, and the proliferation of diverse research in the literature [66–6 However, it is widely acknowledged that data collection systems, expected to keep up wi these demands, are facing limitations. This study aims to develop a system that facilitat the data collection process for various studies, particularly in the academic domain, whi simultaneously enabling the real-time observation and streaming of the collected data.

Presently, REST is extensively employed in academic research across various fields, i cluding case generation [70], methodologies [71], biological data [72], machine learning [7 etc. Furthermore, prominent companies, like Google, Amazon, Twitter, and Reddit, als utilize this architecture. As part of this study, REST enables the instantaneous streamin of the collected data. However, to avoid restricting researchers solely to Internet-base usage, the system incorporates the Dockerization technique, allowing for local implement tion. Consequently, tests were conducted in local and online (server-based) configuratior A significant difference was found between the time it took for the eye-tracking mod data to reach the results page in the locally configured system compared to the same sy tem configured online. Numerous performance bottlenecks, such as Internet latency [7 computer configuration [75], and server location [76], present considerable challenges th are difficult to mitigate. Although the latency experienced online is significantly high than that of the local configuration, it is believed that the experimental online latency is n substantial enough for users to discern [77] (the delay values are shown in Figure 3).

The system presented in this study, which is based on several different techniques, serves the purpose of the real-time streaming and storage of eye-tracking data. However, it is crucial to highlight the flexibility of the proposed system, which can be adapted for collecting and analyzing other data types in different experimental settings. Several studies in the literature use Docker technology to build cloud platforms and integrate them into a variety of experiments, similar to the approach used in this current study. The use of Docker technology allows for the integratation of AI and various models in studies. The system demonstrates a well-suited structure for numerous AI models in the literature. In particular, Shanti et al. (2022) successfully implemented facial emotion recognition using Convolutional Neural Networks [78]. In addition, Barillaro et al. (2022) presented a Deep Learning-based ECG signal classification model [79]. Similarly, Vryzas et al. (2020) focused on the task of speech emotion recognition, employing neural networks [80]. All these studies use models that are implemented using Docker technology and have substructures that can work in compatibility with the introduced system. Simultaneously, the system allows the real-time tracking of users' eye movements, enabling streaming over the Internet without being limited to a single task.

The memory consumption of the experimental system should also be highlighted. During the experiment, the memory consumption of the system slowly increased, putting a certain load on the computer used for the experiment. However, it is important to stress that this load is approximately 0.0037 MB per second and therefore does not have a noticeable impact on the overall performance. Nevertheless, in a scenario where the duration of the experiment is significantly longer, the potential load on the system should be carefully considered and the experiment should be structured to take this into account.

Furthermore, future studies need to examine a larger pool of participants and adopt more efficient memory management techniques. These improvements will contribute to a more thorough analysis of the system's capabilities and limitations, helping researchers to gain deeper findings and more reliable systems. Lastly, researchers should test the compatibility of the presented system with other structures and models, not only AI models (e.g., physiological data [81,82], and psychological tests [83,84]). In addition, the proposed architecture fosters strong collaboration between researchers adopting similar platforms, enabling an incredibly flexible data exchange and sharing. Data storage via the Internet is also expected to increase accessibility, thereby encouraging further research and discovery in various fields. However, it is important to recognize that for future implementations of this system, additional actions can be taken to increase the security of data storage. Examples of such actions include the integration of multi-factor authentication, one-time passwords, and other relevant security protocols [85,86].

5. Conclusions

This study reported on an approach to data collection and experimentation that demonstrates the intricacies of a multi-purpose system for both online and local applications. This study highlights the fundamental importance of data in scientific endeavors and calls for further exploration of alternative data collection techniques.

Author Contributions: Conceptualization, M.E.S., M.O.S., A.L., A.G., M.C.G., K.P. and M.D.; methodology, A.L. and M.C.G.; investigation, M.E.S., M.O.S., A.L. and M.C.G.; data curation, M.E.S., M.O.S. and M.C.G.; writing—original draft preparation, M.C.G., M.O.S., M.E.S. and M.D.; writing—review and editing, A.G., M.C.G., M.O.S., K.P. and A.L.; supervision, A.G., A.L., M.D., K.P., A.G. and A.L. are equally responsible for this study. All authors have read and agreed to the published version of the manuscript.

Funding: This research received no external funding.

Data Availability Statement: The data that support the findings of this study are available from the corresponding author, [A.L.], upon reasonable request.

Acknowledgments: Thanks to DigitalOcean (https://www.digitalocean.com/, accessed on 19 June 2023) and Oliver Mensah for providing us with servers for tests and various other experiments.

Conflicts of Interest: The authors declare no conflict of interest.

Appendix A

Appendix A.1. Pseudocode of WebGazer.js

Algorithm A1: Starting WebGazer

```
Function startWebGazer:
    Load WebGazer library;
    Set up video and canvas elements on the webpage;
```

Algorithm A2: Starting Calibration

```
Function startCalibration:
    Call initializeCalibration(), captureCalibrationData(), saveCalibrationData();
    Display calibration instructions to the user;
    Wait for the user to initiate the calibration process;
    Call saveCalibrationData() # Set and save calibration process;
```

Algorithm A3: Capturing Calibration Data

```
Function captureCalibrationData:
    Loop for a specified number of calibration points:;
        Display a calibration point on the screen;
        Wait for the user to focus their gaze on the calibration point;
        Store the recorded gaze data for the calibration point;
```

Algorithm A4: Saving Calibration Data

```
Function saveCalibrationData:
    Save the captured calibration data for future use;
    Call setCalibrationData();
```

Algorithm A5: Setting Calibration Data

```
Function setCalibrationData:
    Set previously saved calibration data;
```

Algorithm A6: Starting Gaze Tracking

```
Function startGazeTracking:
    Call initializeWebGazer();
    Call getGazeData();
    Begin real-time tracking of the user's gaze;
    Display the gaze position on the screen;
```

Algorithm A7: Stopping Gaze Tracking

```
Function stopGazeTracking:
    Stop tracking the user's gaze;
    Clear the displayed gaze position on the screen;
```

Algorithm A8: Getting Gaze Data

```
Function getGazeData:
    Retrieve the current gaze position data from the WebGazer library;
    Return the gaze data;
```

Algorithm A9: Example Usage

```
Function ExampleUsage:
    initializeWebGazer();
    startCalibration();
    captureCalibrationData();
    saveCalibrationData();
    // Later...;
    initializeWebGazer();
    loadCalibrationData();
    startGazeTracking();
    // During gaze tracking...;
    gazeData = getGazeData();
    // Utilize the gazeData for further processing or interaction;
```

References

1. Chaudhry, B.; Wang, J.; Wu, S.; Maglione, M.; Mojica, W.; Roth, E.; Morton, S.C.; Shekelle, P.G. Systematic review: Impact of health information technology on quality, efficiency, and costs of medical care. *Ann. Intern. Med.* **2006**, *144*, 742–752. [CrossRef] [PubMed]
2. Buntin, M.B.; Burke, M.F.; Hoaglin, M.C.; Blumenthal, D. The benefits of health information technology: A review of the recent literature shows predominantly positive results. *Health Aff.* **2011**, *30*, 464–471. [CrossRef] [PubMed]
3. Martucci, A.; Gursesli, M.C.; Duradoni, M.; Guazzini, A. Overviewing Gaming Motivation and Its Associated Psychological and Sociodemographic Variables: A PRISMA Systematic Review. *Hum. Behav. Emerg. Technol.* **2023**, *2023*, e5640258. . [CrossRef]
4. Rauterberg, M. Positive Effects of Entertainment Technology on Human Behaviour. In *Building the Information Society, Proceedings of the International Federation for Information Processing (IFIP) 18th World Computer Congress Topical Sessions, Toulouse, France, 22–27 August 2004* ; Jacquart, R., Ed.; Springer: Boston, MA, USA, 2004; pp. 51–58. [CrossRef]
5. Duradoni, M.; Spadoni, V.; Gursesli, M.C.; Guazzini, A. Development and Validation of the Need for Online Social Feedback (NfOSF) Scale. *Hum. Behav. Emerg. Technol.* **2023**, *2023*, e5581492.
6. Carr, C.T.; Hayes, R.A. Social media: Defining, developing, and divining. *Atl. J. Commun.* **2015**, *23*, 46–65. [CrossRef]
7. Kadish, K.M.; Ruoff, R.S. *Fullerenes: Chemistry, Physics, and Technology*; John Wiley & Sons: New York, NY, USA, 2000.
8. Nicollian, E.H.; Brews, J.R. *MOS (Metal Oxide Semiconductor) Physics and Technology*; John Wiley & Sons: New York, NY, USA, 2002.
9. Noll, W. *Chemistry and Technology of Silicones*; Elsevier: Amsterdam, The Netherlands, 2012.
10. Whistler, R.L.; BeMiller, J.N.; Paschall, E.F. *Starch: Chemistry and Technology*; Academic Press: New York, NY, USA, 2012; Google-Books-ID: pvAzqk2pAIsC.
11. Hwang, T. Computational power and the social impact of artificial intelligence. *arXiv* **2018**, arXiv:1803.08971.
12. Yaqoob, I.; Ahmed, E.; Hashem, I.A.T.; Ahmed, A.I.A.; Gani, A.; Imran, M.; Guizani, M. Internet of things architecture: Recent advances, taxonomy, requirements, and open challenges. *IEEE Wirel. Commun.* **2017**, *24*, 10–16. [CrossRef]
13. SG Andrae, A. New perspectives on internet electricity use in 2030. *Eng. Appl. Sci. Lett.* **2020**, *3*, 19–31.
14. Williams, P.H.; Margules, C.R.; Hilbert, D.W. Data requirements and data sources for biodiversity priority area selection. *J. Biosci.* **2020**, *27*, 327–338. [CrossRef]
15. Navajas, J.; Barsakcioglu, D.Y.; Eftekhar, A.; Jackson, A.; Constandinou, T.G.; Quiroga, R.Q. Minimum requirements for accurate and efficient real-time on-chip spike sorting. *J. Neurosci. Methods* **2014**, *230*, 51–64. [CrossRef]
16. Chaudhary, N.; Weissman, D.; Whitehead, K.A. mRNA vaccines for infectious diseases: Principles, delivery and clinical translation. *Nat. Rev. Drug Discov.* **2021**, *20*, 817–838. [CrossRef]
17. Vidgen, B.; Derczynski, L. Directions in abusive language training data, a systematic review: Garbage in, garbage out. *PLoS ONE* **2020**, *15*, e0243300.
18. Raupach, M.R.; Rayner, P.J.; Barrett, D.J.; DeFries, R.S.; Heimann, M.; Ojima, D.S.; Quegan, S.; Schmullius, C.C. Model–data synthesis in terrestrial carbon observation: Methods, data requirements and data uncertainty specifications. *Glob. Chang. Biol.* **2005**, *11*, 378–397. Available online: https://onlinelibrary.wiley.com/doi/pdf/10.1111/j.1365-2486.2005.00917.x (accessed on 19 June 2023). [CrossRef]

19. Farmer, A.; Gibson, O.; Hayton, P.; Bryden, K.; Dudley, C.; Neil, A.; Tarassenko, L. A real-time, mobile phone-based telemedici system to support young adults with type 1 diabetes. *Inform. Prim. Care* **2005**, *13*, 171–177. [CrossRef]
20. Gradl, S.; Kugler, P.; Lohmüller, C.; Eskofier, B. Real-time ECG monitoring and arrhythmia detection using Android-based mobi devices. In Proceedings of the 2012 Annual International Conference of the IEEE Engineering in Medicine and Biology Socie San Diego, CA, USA, 28 August–1 September 2012; IEEE: Piscataway, NJ, USA, 2012; pp. 2452–2455.
21. Teplan, M. Fundamentals of EEG measurement. *Meas. Sci. Rev.* **2002**, *2*, 1–11.
22. Boore, D.M.; Smith, C.E. Analysis of earthquake recordings obtained from the Seafloor Earthquake Measurement System (SEM instruments deployed off the coast of southern California. *Bull. Seismol. Soc. Am.* **1999**, *89*, 260–274. [CrossRef]
23. Xue, M.; Wang, D.; Gao, J.; Brewster, K.; Droegemeier, K.K. The Advanced Regional Prediction System (ARPS), storm-sca numerical weather prediction and data assimilation. *Meteorol. Atmos. Phys.* **2003**, *82*, 139–170. [CrossRef]
24. Fielding, R.T. *Architectural Styles and the Design of Network-Based Software Architectures*; University of California: Irvine, CA, USA, 20(
25. Costa, B.; Pires, P.F.; Delicato, F.C.; Merson, P. Evaluating a Representational State Transfer (REST) architecture: What is th impact of REST in my architecture? In Proceedings of the 2014 IEEE/IFIP Conference on Software Architecture, Sydney, Australi 7–11 April 2014; IEEE: Piscataway, NJ, USA, 2014; pp. 105–114.
26. Cho, G.Y.; Lee, S.J.; Lee, T.R. An optimized compression algorithm for real-time ECG data transmission in wireless network medical information systems. *J. Med. Syst.* **2015**, *39*, 1–8. [CrossRef]
27. Kroner, A.; Senden, M.; Driessens, K.; Goebel, R. Contextual encoder–decoder network for visual saliency prediction. *Neur Netw.* **2020**, *129*, 261–270. [CrossRef]
28. Skaramagkas, V.; Giannakakis, G.; Ktistakis, E.; Manousos, D.; Karatzanis, I.; Tachos, N.S.; Tripoliti, E.; Marias, K.; Fotiad D.I.; Tsiknakis, M. Review of eye tracking metrics involved in emotional and cognitive processes. *IEEE Rev. Biomed. Eng.* **202** *16*, 260–277. [CrossRef]
29. Black, M.H.; Chen, N.T.; Iyer, K.K.; Lipp, O.V.; Bölte, S.; Falkmer, M.; Tan, T.; Girdler, S. Mechanisms of facial emotion recognitic in autism spectrum disorders: Insights from eye tracking and electroencephalography. *Neurosci. Biobehav. Rev.* **2017**, *80*, 488–51 [CrossRef] [PubMed]
30. Wedel, M.; Pieters, R. A review of eye-tracking research in marketing. In *Review of Marketing Research*; Emerald Group Publishir Limited: Bingley, UK, 2017; pp. 123–147.
31. Srivastava, N.; Nawaz, S.; Newn, J.; Lodge, J.; Velloso, E.; Erfani, S.M.; Gasevic, D.; Bailey, J. Are you with me? Measurement Learners' Video-Watching Attention with Eye Tracking. In Proceedings of the LAK21: 11th International Learning Analytics an Knowledge Conference, Irvine, CA, USA, 12–16 April 2021; Association for Computing Machinery: New York, NY, USA, 202 pp. 88–98. [CrossRef]
32. Borys, M.; Plechawska-Wójcik, M. Eye-tracking metrics in perception and visual attention research. *Eur. J. Med. Technol. EJM* **2017**, *3*, 11–23.
33. Iacono, W.G.; Lykken, D.T. Eye Tracking and Psychopathology: New Procedures Applied to a Sample of Normal Monozygot Twins. *Arch. Gen. Psychiatry* **1979**, *36*, 1361–1369. [CrossRef]
34. Krafka, K.; Khosla, A.; Kellnhofer, P.; Kannan, H.; Bhandarkar, S.; Matusik, W.; Torralba, A. Eye Tracking for Everyone. Proceedings of the IEEE Conference on Computer Vision and Pattern Recognition, Las Vegas, NV, USA, 27–30 June 201 pp. 2176–2184.
35. Fiedler, S.; Glöckner, A. The Dynamics of Decision Making in Risky Choice: An Eye-Tracking Analysis. *Front. Psychol.* **2012**, *3*, 33 [CrossRef] [PubMed]
36. Holmqvist, K.; Nyström, M.; Andersson, R.; Dewhurst, R.; Jarodzka, H.; Van de Weijer, J. *Eye Tracking: A Comprehensive Guide Methods and Measures*; OUP: Oxford, UK, 2011.
37. Pfeiffer, U.J.; Vogeley, K.; Schilbach, L. From gaze cueing to dual eye-tracking: Novel approaches to investigate the neur correlates of gaze in social interaction. *Neurosci. Biobehav. Rev.* **2013**, *37*, 2516–2528. [CrossRef]
38. Duchowski, A.T. *Eye Tracking Methodology: Theory and Practice*; Springer: London, UK, 2017.
39. Papoutsaki, A.; Laskey, J.; Huang, J. SearchGazer: Webcam Eye Tracking for Remote Studies of Web Search. In Proceedings of th 2017 Conference on Conference Human Information Interaction and Retrieval, Oslo, Norway, 7–11 March 2017; p. 26. [CrossRe
40. Aslin, R.N.; McMurray, B. Automated Corneal-Reflection Eye Tracking in Infancy: Methodological Developments and Applic tions to Cognition. *Infancy* **2004**, *6*, 155–163. Available online: https://onlinelibrary.wiley.com/doi/pdf/10.1207/s15327078in06 2_1 (accessed on 19 June 2023). [CrossRef]
41. Marino, J. Reading Screens: What Eye Tracking Tells Us about the Writing in Digital Longform Journalism. *Lit. J. Stud.* **2016**, *8* , 138–14
42. Niehorster, D.C.; Hessels, R.S.; Benjamins, J.S. GlassesViewer: Open-source software for viewing and analyzing data from th Tobii Pro Glasses 2 eye tracker. *Behav. Res. Methods* **2020**, *52*, 1244–1253. [CrossRef]
43. Kortman, B.; Nicholls, K. Assessing for Unilateral Spatial Neglect Using Eye-Tracking Glasses: A Feasibility Study. *Occup. The Health Care* **2016**, *30*, 344–355.
44. Mele, M.L.; Federici, S. Gaze and eye-tracking solutions for psychological research. *Cogn. Process.* **2012**, *13*, 261–265. [CrossRe
45. Lu, F.; Sugano, Y.; Okabe, T.; Sato, Y. Head pose-free appearance-based gaze sensing via eye image synthesis. In Proceedings c the 21st International Conference on Pattern Recognition (ICPR2012), Tsukuba, Japan, 11–15 November 2012; pp. 1008–1011.
46. Xu, P.; Ehinger, K.A.; Zhang, Y.; Finkelstein, A.; Kulkarni, S.R.; Xiao, J. Turkergaze: Crowdsourcing saliency with webcam base eye tracking. *arXiv* **2015**, arXiv:1504.06755.

7. Papoutsaki, A.; Sangkloy, P.; Laskey, J.; Daskalova, N.; Huang, J.; Hays, J. WebGazer: Scalable Webcam Eye Tracking Using User Interactions. In Proceedings of the Proceedings of the Twenty-Fifth International Joint Conference on Artificial Intelligence (IJCAI'16), New York, NY, USA, 9–15 July 2016.
8. Wang, S.; Keivanloo, I.; Zou, Y. How do developers react to restful api evolution? In *Service-Oriented Computing: Proceedings of the 12th International Conference (ICSOC 2014), Paris, France, 3–6 November 2014*; Springer: Berlin/Heidelberg, Germany, 2014; pp. 245–259.
9. Richardson, L.; Ruby, S. *RESTful Web Services*; O'Reilly Media, Inc.: Sebastopol, CA, USA, 2008.
0. Berners-Lee, T.J. *Information Management: A Proposal*; Technical Report; CERN: Geneva, Switzerland, 1989.
1. Cassetti, O. Websockets and their integration in enterprise networks. *CiteSeerX* **2011** .
2. Hu, Y.; Cheng, W. Research and implementation of campus information push system based on WebSocket. In Proceedings of the 2017 12th International Conference on Intelligent Systems and Knowledge Engineering (ISKE), Nanjing, China, 24–26 November 2017; pp. 1–6. [CrossRef]
3. Soewito, B.; Christian; Gunawan, F.E.; Diana; Kusuma, I.G.P. Websocket to Support Real Time Smart Home Applications. *Procedia Comput. Sci.* **2019**, *157*, 560–566. [CrossRef]
4. Hale, M. Eyestream: An Open WebSocket-based Middleware for Serializing and Streaming Eye Tracker Event Data from Gazepoint GP3 HD Research Hardware. *J. Open Source Softw.* **2019**, *4*, 1620. [CrossRef]
5. Codd, E.F. A Relational Model of Data for Large Shared Data Banks. *Commun. ACM* **1970**, *13*, 377–387. [CrossRef]
6. Kern, C.; Kesavan, A.; Daswani, N. *Foundations of Security: What Every Programmer Needs to Know*; Apress: Berkeley, CA, USA, 2007.
7. Khan, W.; Kumar, T.; Zhang, C.; Raj, K.; Roy, A.M.; Luo, B. SQL and NoSQL Database Software Architecture Performance Analysis and Assessments—A Systematic Literature Review. *Big Data Cogn. Comput.* **2023**, *7*, 97. [CrossRef]
8. Anderson, C. Docker [Software engineering]. *IEEE Softw.* **2015**, *32*, 102-c3. [CrossRef]
9. Martin, J.P.; Kandasamy, A.; Chandrasekaran, K. Exploring the support for high performance applications in the container runtime environment. *Hum.-Centric Comput. Inf. Sci.* **2018**, *8*, 1–15. [CrossRef]
0. De Benedictis, M.; Lioy, A. Integrity verification of Docker containers for a lightweight cloud environment. *Future Gener. Comput. Syst.* **2019**, *97*, 236–246. [CrossRef]
1. Chamoli, S. Docker Security: Architecture, Threat Model, and Best Practices. In *Soft Computing: Theories and Applications: Proceedings of SoCTA 2020* ; Springer: Singapore, 2021; Volume 2, pp. 253–263.
2. Slim, M.S.; Hartsuiker, R.J. Moving visual world experiments online? A web-based replication of Dijkgraaf, Hartsuiker, and Duyck (2017) using PCIbex and WebGazer.js. *Behav. Res. Methods* **2022**, 1–19. [CrossRef]
3. Chen, X.; Slowinska, A.; Bos, H. Who allocated my memory? Detecting custom memory allocators in C binaries. In Proceedings of the 2013 20th Working Conference on Reverse Engineering (WCRE), Koblenz, Germany, 14–17 October 2013; IEEE: Piscataway, NJ, USA, 2013; pp. 22–31.
4. Pienaar, J.A.; Hundt, R. JSWhiz: Static analysis for JavaScript memory leaks. In Proceedings of the 2013 IEEE/ACM International Symposium on Code Generation and Optimization (CGO), Montreal, QC, Canada, 25 February–1 March 2013; IEEE: Piscataway, NJ, USA, 2013; pp. 1–11.
5. Degenbaev, U.; Eisinger, J.; Hara, K.; Hlopko, M.; Lippautz, M.; Payer, H. Cross-component garbage collection. *Proc. ACM Program. Lang.* **2018**, *2*, 1–24. [CrossRef]
6. Das, S.; Nayak, G.K.; Saba, L.; Kalra, M.; Suri, J.S.; Saxena, S. An artificial intelligence framework and its bias for brain tumor segmentation: A narrative review. *Comput. Biol. Med.* **2022**, *143*, 105273. [CrossRef] [PubMed]
7. Wilson, C. Public engagement and AI: A values analysis of national strategies. *Gov. Inf. Q.* **2022**, *39*, 101652. [CrossRef]
8. Lee, J.C.; Chen, X. Exploring users' adoption intentions in the evolution of artificial intelligence mobile banking applications: The intelligent and anthropomorphic perspectives. *Int. J. Bank Mark.* **2022**, *40*, 631–658. [CrossRef]
9. Dogan, M.E.; Goru Dogan, T.; Bozkurt, A. The use of artificial intelligence (AI) in online learning and distance education processes: A systematic review of empirical studies. *Appl. Sci.* **2023**, *13*, 3056. [CrossRef]
70. Arcuri, A. RESTful API automated test case generation. In Proceedings of the 2017 IEEE International Conference on Software Quality, Reliability and Security (QRS), Prague, Czech Republic, 25–29 July 2017; IEEE: Piscataway, NJ, USA, 2017; pp. 9–20.
71. Ehsan, A.; Abuhaliqa, M.A.M.; Catal, C.; Mishra, D. RESTful API testing methodologies: Rationale, challenges, and solution directions. *Appl. Sci.* **2022**, *12*, 4369. [CrossRef]
72. Miller, M.A.; Schwartz, T.; Pickett, B.E.; He, S.; Klem, E.B.; Scheuermann, R.H.; Passarotti, M.; Kaufman, S.; O'Leary, M.A. A RESTful API for access to phylogenetic tools via the CIPRES science gateway. *Evol. Bioinform.* **2015**, *11*, 43–48. [CrossRef]
73. Gossett, E.; Toher, C.; Oses, C.; Isayev, O.; Legrain, F.; Rose, F.; Zurek, E.; Carrete, J.; Mingo, N.; Tropsha, A.; et al. AFLOW-ML: A RESTful API for machine-learning predictions of materials properties. *Comput. Mater. Sci.* **2018**, *152*, 134–145. [CrossRef]
74. Briscoe, B.; Brunstrom, A.; Petlund, A.; Hayes, D.; Ros, D.; Tsang, J.; Gjessing, S.; Fairhurst, G.; Griwodz, C.; Welzl, M. Reducing internet latency: A survey of techniques and their merits. *IEEE Commun. Surv. Tutor.* **2014**, *18*, 2149–2196. [CrossRef]
75. Henning, J.L. SPEC CPU2000: Measuring CPU performance in the new millennium. *Computer* **2000**, *33*, 28–35. [CrossRef]
76. Charyyev, B.; Arslan, E.; Gunes, M.H. Latency comparison of cloud datacenters and edge servers. In Proceedings of the GLOBECOM 2020—2020 IEEE Global Communications Conference, Taipei, Taiwan, 7–11 December 2020; IEEE: Piscataway, NJ, USA, 2020; pp. 1–6.

77. Stetson, C.; Cui, X.; Montague, P.R.; Eagleman, D.M. Motor-sensory recalibration leads to an illusory reversal of action an sensation. *Neuron* **2006**, *51*, 651–659. [CrossRef]
78. Shanthi, N.; Stonier, A.A.; Sherine, A.; Devaraju, T.; Abinash, S.; Ajay, R.; Arul Prasath, V.; Ganji, V. An integrated approach fo mental health assessment using emotion analysis and scales. *Healthc. Technol. Lett.* **2022** , 1–11. [CrossRef]
79. Barillaro, L.; Agapito, G.; Cannataro, M. Edge-based Deep Learning in Medicine: Classification of ECG signals. In Proceedings o the 2022 IEEE International Conference on Bioinformatics and Biomedicine (BIBM), Las Vegas, NV, USA, 6–8 December 202 IEEE: Piscataway, NJ, USA, 2022; pp. 2169–2174.
80. Vryzas, N.; Vrysis, L.; Matsiola, M.; Kotsakis, R.; Dimoulas, C.; Kalliris, G. Continuous speech emotion recognition wit convolutional neural networks. *J. Audio Eng. Soc.* **2020**, *68*, 14–24. [CrossRef]
81. Shu, Y.S.; Chen, Z.X.; Lin, Y.H.; Wu, S.H.; Huang, W.H.; Chiou, A.Y.C.; Huang, C.Y.; Hsieh, H.Y.; Liao, F.W.; Zou, T.F.; et al. 26.1 4.5 mm^2 Multimodal Biosensing SoC for PPG, ECG, BIOZ and GSR Acquisition in Consumer Wearable Devices. In Proceeding of the 2020 IEEE International Solid-State Circuits Conference-(ISSCC), San Francisco, CA, USA, 16–20 February 2020; IEE Piscataway, NJ, USA, 2020; pp. 400–402.
82. Soufineyestani, M.; Dowling, D.; Khan, A. Electroencephalography (EEG) technology applications and available devices. *App Sci.* **2020**, *10*, 7453. [CrossRef]
83. Li, X.; Liu, Y.; Mao, J.; He, Z.; Zhang, M.; Ma, S. Understanding reading attention distribution during relevance judgement. I Proceedings of the 27th ACM International Conference on Information and Knowledge Management, Torino, Italy, 22–24 Octobe 2018; pp. 733–742.
84. Cox, W.M.; Fadardi, J.S.; Pothos, E.M. The addiction-stroop test: Theoretical considerations and procedural recommendation *Psychol. Bull.* **2006**, *132*, 443. [CrossRef]
85. Karie, N.M.; Kebande, V.R.; Ikuesan, R.A.; Sookhak, M.; Venter, H.S. Hardening SAML by Integrating SSO and Multi-Facto Authentication (MFA) in the Cloud. In Proceedings of the 3rd International Conference on Networking, Information Systems & Security, Marrakech, Morocco, 31 March–2 April 2020; pp. 1–6.
86. Bruzgiene, R.; Jurgilas, K. Securing remote access to information systems of critical infrastructure using two-factor authenticatio *Electronics* **2021**, *10*, 1819. [CrossRef]

algorithms

Article

Evolving Multi-Output Digital Circuits Using Multi-Genome Grammatical Evolution

Michael Tetteh [1,*], Allan de Lima [1], Jack McEllin [1], Aidan Murphy [2], Douglas Mota Dias [1] and Conor Ryan [1,*]

[1] Biocomputing and Developmental Systems Research Group, University of Limerick, V94 T9PX Limerick, Ireland; allan.delima@ul.ie (A.d.L.); jack.mcellin@ul.ie (J.M.); douglas.motadias@ul.ie (D.M.D.)
[2] School of Computer Science and Statistics, Trinity College Dublin, D02 PN40 Dublin, Ireland; amurph74@tcd.ie
* Correspondence: michael.tetteh@ul.ie (M.T.); conor.ryan@ul.ie (C.R.)

Abstract: Grammatical Evolution is a Genetic Programming variant which evolves problems in any arbitrary language that is BNF compliant. Since its inception, Grammatical Evolution has been used to solve real-world problems in different domains such as bio-informatics, architecture design, financial modelling, music, software testing, game artificial intelligence and parallel programming. Multi-output problems deal with predicting numerous output variables simultaneously, a notoriously difficult problem. We present a Multi-Genome Grammatical Evolution better suited for tackling multi-output problems, specifically digital circuits. The Multi-Genome consists of multiple genomes, each evolving a solution to a single unique output variable. Each genome is mapped to create its executable object. The mapping mechanism, genetic, selection, and replacement operators have been adapted to make them well-suited for the Multi-Genome representation and the implementation of a new wrapping operator. Additionally, custom grammar syntax rules and a cyclic dependency-checking algorithm have been presented to facilitate the evolution of inter-output dependencies which may exist in multi-output problems. Multi-Genome Grammatical Evolution is tested on combinational digital circuit benchmark problems. Results show Multi-Genome Grammatical Evolution performs significantly better than standard Grammatical Evolution on these benchmark problems.

Keywords: Grammatical Evolution; Multi-Genome; Evolvable Hardware; digital circuit design; Hardware Description Languages; SystemVerilog; combinational circuits

itation: Tetteh, M.; de Lima, A.; IcEllin, J.; Murphy A.; Dias, D.M.; yan, C. Evolving Multi-Output igital Circuits Using Multi-Genome rammatical Evolution. *Algorithms* 023, *16*, 365. https://doi.org/).3390/a16080365

cademic Editor: Frank Werner

eceived: 14 June 2023
evised: 25 July 2023
ccepted: 27 July 2023
ublished: 28 July 2023

1. Introduction

Evolvable Hardware (EWH) encompasses the application of evolutionary algorithms (EAs) to the design of re-configurable hardware and conventional circuits. Since its inception, circuits such as adders and multipliers have been evolved. Some EAs used in EHW include Genetic Algorithms, Genetic Programming (GP), Cartesian Genetic Programming, and Grammatical Evolution (GE). Confronting the field are two significant challenges: scalability of fitness evaluation and representation. The former deals with the required testing as circuit inputs increase (complex circuits). The latter, which is also a consequence of increasing inputs, requires longer chromosomes to represent individuals. Hence, due to the destructive nature of search operators (crossover and mutation), evolving circuits of such complexity is non-trivial.

Some existing approaches proposed to address the issue of representation scalability are decomposition [1,2] and more efficient genetic operators [3]. Existing decomposition approaches break complex circuits down into evolvable sub-circuits either via inputs [2] or outputs [1] and merge them into a complete circuit using varying strategies. Other research efforts have also been directed toward efficiently reducing the computational cost of circuit evaluation. Some of these include parallel implementations of EAs, using different representations for evaluation and, more recently, corner case testing, a wel known technique used in industry to reduce the amount of testing, combined with uniform sampling of training/testing cases [4].

A major benefit of GE's mapping process is the separation of the genotypic space fro the phenotypic space, which facilitates an unconstrained evolutionary search [5]. Whi there has been some suggestion that the low locality, i.e., the measure of the correlatio between neighbouring genotypes and their corresponding neighbouring phenotypes brin about an issue [6], other works [7–9] suggest genetic operations at the beginning regions GE's genome are destructive but may serve as a good region for genetic operations.

Generally, a multi-output problem requires modeling complex input-output rel tionships and/or inter-output dependencies. Multi-output problems requiring the simu taneous modeling of these relationships are very challenging to deal with [10]. Henc decomposing such problems into single-output problems and solving each using a singl output algorithm of choice may prove very challenging as such approaches do not consid inter-output correlations [10]. This paper proposes a Multi-Genome GE (MG-GE) fc solving multi-output or multi-target problems, such as circuit problems, efficiently. Eac genome encodes a solution to a single and unique output. Second, custom grammar synta rules are introduced to facilitate the evolution of inter-output correlations by evolutio Third, we speculate that using Multi-Genome (MG) reduces the destructive effect of genet operators by using a genome per output variable while benefiting from their ability t escape local optima. Fourth, MG-GE keeps track and stops the search for a solved outpu variable which is made available to all individuals in the population, thereby reducin the overall computational cost as evolution progresses. Finally, MG-GE is better suite for multi-output circuit problems than approaches that decompose such problems int single-output circuit problems using various decomposition techniques before merging th evolved sub-circuits into a complete circuit.

The contributions of this work are summarised as follows:

- We present a multi-genome implementation of GE better suited for tackling mult output problems;
- We adapt genetic operators, initialisation routine, and mapping mechanism an implement a wrapping operator well-suited for MG-GE;
- We introduce custom grammar syntax rules and a cyclic dependency-checking alg rithm that facilitates the evolution of inter-output dependencies;
- We investigate the performance of MG-GE with and without using our custom gran mar syntax rules on multi-output combinational circuit problems.

2. Background

2.1. Grammatical Evolution

GE is a GP variant that evolves programs in any arbitrary Backus–Naur form (BN compliant language. GE has been used in different application domains such as gam content design [11], architecture design [12], financial modelling [13], music [14] an software testing [15].Standard GE uses a single linear genome. The genome is a sequenc of codons (usually 8-bit unsigned numbers) that encode the genetic information of a individual. The corresponding phenotype is derived from a genome using a mapper. Th mapper requires a grammar, usually a subset of the target language, sufficient to evolv an optimal solution to a problem potentially. A valid phenotype is derived only when a non-terminal symbols have been re-written regarding terminal symbols (any term withou angle brackets). To expand a non-terminal into a string of terminals only, a derivatio formula (*codon*%num of productions) is applied. Each phenotype is evaluated using th defined fitness function. The fitness score returned by the fitness function is assigned as th individual's fitness.

BNF is a meta-syntax notation used for expressing grammars of formal language such as Context-Free Grammars (CFG). Grammars most commonly used within GE ar CFGs. A CFG denoted by G is defined by a quadrupled tuple $\{N, T, P, S\}$. N represents th set of non-terminal symbols which are enclosed within <>. For example, ⟨expr⟩ is a non-terminal symbol. Non-terminal symbols are placeholders and replaced by another symbol according to production rules. Production rules appear after the replacement symbol ::= on the right-hand side. All non-terminal symbols are replaced, or expanded, until they become terminal symbols. T represents the set of terminal symbols which are not enclosed within <>. For example, variable names and operators (e.g., +, −) of a programming language are considered terminals. P represents production rules which are alternatives or choices to replace a non-terminal and are separated by | symbol. S represents the start symbol which is part of N and serves as the initial symbol from which a legal sentence in the target language can be derived.

2.2. Multi-Output Problems

Multiple output or target variables characterise multi-output (also known as multi-target or multi-variate) problems. Multi-variate regression and multi-label classification are categories of multi-output problems. Multi-variate regression deals with the estimation of a single regression model which models how multiple independent and dependent variables are linearly related. Multi-variate regression is used in different domains such as economics and finance, health care, social sciences, environmental studies and market research. For example, in economics and finance multi-variate regression is used to investigate the factors that affect inflation rates, stock prices, housing prices and GDP growth rate. In multi-label classification, zero or multiple labels are required as output per input sample [16]. Gene classification in bio-informatics, text categorisation and image classification are real-world applications of Multi-label classification. These problems are challenging to deal with, mainly due to their multi-variate nature and possible dependencies between target variables [17].

Methodologies designed for tackling multi-output regression problems are categorised into two groups: *problem transformation* and *algorithm adaptation* methods [17]. Problem transformation methods transform multi-output problems into single-output problems, each uniquely solving one of the target variables using any single regression algorithm of choice [17]. Algorithm adaptation methods adapt existing single-target algorithms to handle multi-target problems [17]. Some advantages of the latter approach are better performance, better representation & interpretability, and computationally more efficiency compared to single-target methods [17].

2.3. Hardware Description Languages

Hardware Description Languages (HDLs) such as Verilog and VHDL are the de facto standard for circuit design in the industry due to several benefits [18]. Notable among these are the design of circuits at higher abstraction—Register Transfer Level (RTL), other than gate level [19]. Additionally, RTL designs are more interpretable, require less time to modify and easier to verify [20]. RTL designs employ programming constructs such as conditional statements, synthesisable for-loops, proceedural blocks, case statements, asynchronous and synchronous constructs to provide a human readable description of a circuit's behaviour. As a result, RTL designs must undergo logic synthesis where these high level descriptions of circuits are converted to basic building blocks such as logic gates (AND, NOT, NAND, NOR and XOR)and flip-flops (or storage elements). GE has successfully evolved complex and accurate multiplier, adder, and parity using SystemVerilog [4].

2.4. Related Work

Digital circuit designs like adders and multipliers require multiple output signals to be correct for their output to be accurate. Some of these output signals can be independent of one another, meaning that only a sub-section of an individual needs to be modified. These sub-modifications can be difficult for a classical GA with a single chromosome to perform as the genetic operators do not know how the modifications will affect the candidate design.

Multiple chromosomes have been used in various evolutionary hardware problems to tackle this problem. Cartesian Genetic Programming (CGP) is often used with gate-level evolutionary hardware problems as its column and row structure is ideal for connecting Boolean logic gates. Multiple codons in the chromosome are consumed when choosing a gate and its connections, which can lead to issues when performing crossover, as different gates can have a different number of connections. Slowik and Bialko [21] address this by using a multi-chromosome genome that groups the logic gates with their input connections. This allows for the crossover method only select crossover points that would not produce an unconnected input and thus produce only valid individuals.

Walker et al. [22] introduced a method called Multi-Chromosome CGP (MC-CGP) for Evolutionary Hardware. This approach uses a multi-chromosome where each chromosome is used in a separate CGP evolution to evolve a partial solution for a single output. When a solution is found for each output, they are then combined to produce the final solution. This approach allows the evolution to be performed in parallel but can produce redundant circuitry. To address this problem, Coimbra and Lamar [23] used a hybrid approach of running an MC-CGP followed by a standard CGP where the multi-chromosome is treated as a single chromosome. This approach allowed them to reduce the gate count of the evolved individuals significantly.

CGP is generally only employed at the gate-level and thus cannot enjoy the benefit of HDLs. Work that has looked at higher-level problems includes a multi-objective approach that was taken to evolve a Proportional-Plus-Derivative fuzzy logic controller. In this work, Baine [24] used four separate chromosomes to describe the input and output fuzzy sets for both the proportional and derivative parts of the controller. He found that the multi-chromosome approach converged around 20% faster than a single-chromosome approach.

In [25], standard Gene Expression Programming (GEP) is adapted to directly handle multi-target regression problems without resorting to any transformation or decomposition approaches. A multi-gene chromosome representation is adopted. An N-target regression problem requires a chromosome with N genes. Each gene codes a solution to a single and unique target variable. Hence, the number of genes contained in a chromosome is problem-dependent. Individual initialisation remains the same as in standard GEP but is subject to a metric that ensures an individual is only added to the initial population if its similarity compared to other individuals in the population is below a threshold. Three different transposition operators are used to transpose gene fragments within the same gene, between two genes (of the same chromosome), and move a gene to the beginning of the chromosome. Also, three recombination operators are used to create offspring. Tested on eight multi-target regression datasets in comparison to two other methods, Gene Expression Programming for Multi-target Regression (GEPMTR) significantly outperformed the two state-of-the-art methods in seven of the eight multi-target datasets employed.

These works show that using a multi-chromosome approach for multi-target problems can significantly help find solutions. In addition, it helps address the issue of locality that Grammatical Evolution can experience.

3. Proposed Approach: Multi-Genome GE

3.1. Problem Description

GE mapping process starts from a start symbol. Usually, the first rule's non-terminal is designated as the start symbol. For example in Figure 1, ⟨expr⟩ is the start symbol. GE iteratively expands or rewrites all non-terminals by using a modulus rule to select a production each time a choice needs to be made. This process continues until the sentence consists solely of terminals. In Figure 1, using the sample genome provided, the sentence $x + 5$ is obtained.

Assuming a mutation event affects the first codon, changing its value from 151 to 150, this means the first production ⟨var⟩ gets chosen after applying the mod rule ($150\%3 = 0$). As a result, the resultant sentence is now x after the mutation event. As described, a totally different phenotype is obtained after a simple codon alteration in GE's genome, with all potentially evolved building blocks lost after genetic operations. This phenomenon is referred to as *ripple effect*.

As mentioned earlier, multi-output problems require all outputs to be simultaneously evolved. Assuming a standard GE individual (single genome representation) solves two of the three output variables due to the ripple effect caused by genetic operators, solving the remaining output variable may be challenging. It is also computationally expensive as there is no mechanism in place to stop searching for output variables that other individuals in the population have successfully evolved. Furthermore, standard GE does not have the necessary functionality to evolve inter-target dependencies properly.

$$
\begin{aligned}
\langle\text{expr}\rangle &::= \langle\text{var}\rangle\ \texttt{(0)} \mid \langle\text{var}\rangle\langle\text{op}\rangle\langle\text{var}\rangle\ \texttt{(1)} \mid \langle\text{var}\rangle\langle\text{op}\rangle\langle\text{expr}\rangle\ \texttt{(2)} \\
\langle\text{var}\rangle &::= \texttt{x (0)} \mid \texttt{y (1)} \mid \texttt{constant (2)} \\
\langle\text{op}\rangle &::= \texttt{+ (0)} \mid \texttt{- (1)} \mid \times\ \texttt{(2)} \mid \texttt{/ (3)} \\
\langle\text{constant}\rangle &::= \texttt{0 (0)} \mid \texttt{1 (1)} \mid \texttt{2 (2)} \mid \texttt{3 (3)} \mid \texttt{4 (4)} \mid \texttt{5 (5)} \mid \texttt{6 (6)} \mid \texttt{7 (7)} \\
&\quad \mid \texttt{8 (8)} \mid \texttt{9 (9)}
\end{aligned}
$$

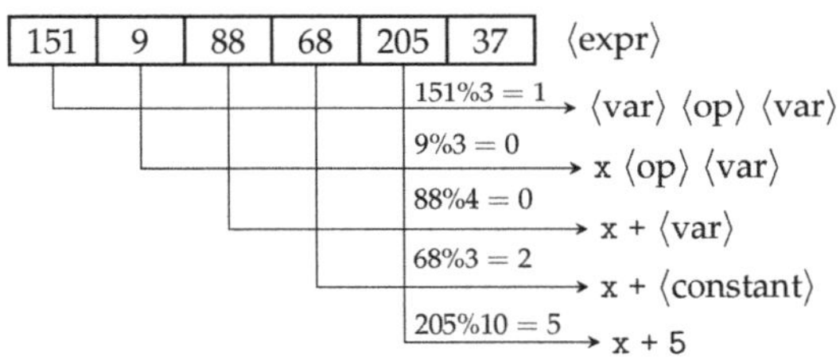

Figure 1. Grammatical Evolution Mapping Mechanism. The numbers enclosed in parenthesis after each production do not form part of the grammar but instead are shown for ease of interpretation and represent the production choice value.

3.2. Problem Formulation

Assuming a combinational circuit denoted as C has multiple inputs and outputs, the training/testing vectors for C can be denoted as $\{X_1 \cdots X_m\}$ and $\{Y_1 \cdots Y_n\}$ representing inputs and expected outputs respectively. Each circuit output in $\{Y_1 \cdots Y_n\}$ can depend on one to m input variables ($\{X_1 \cdots X_m\}$) as well as from zero to $n-1$ circuit outputs $\{Y_1 \cdots Y_n\}$; as far as no cyclic dependencies are formed between output variables in the case of combinational circuits. In certain instances, a circuit output may depend on one or more outputs as inputs.

Given that multi-output circuit problems (and multi-output problems in general) generally exhibit a more complex behaviour compared to a single-output circuit problem, evolving such circuits, especially at a low level of design—*gate-level*, using standard GE is intractable. To help cope with the challenges associated with evolving multi-output circuit problems using standard GE, a novel Multi-Genome GE is proposed.

3.3. Multi-Genome GE

MG-GE uses a multiple genome representation consisting of n genomes, where n represents the number of outputs or targets. Each genome evolves a circuit functionality that satisfies a single and unique circuit output. An example of a multi-genome for a multi-output problem with three output variables or target variables is shown in Figure 2. An output or target variable is a variable to be predicted by other variables.

A new genome representation requires suitable initialisation routines, mapping mechanisms, selection, replacement, wrapping mechanisms, and genetic operators. Furthermore, we introduce grammar design specifications which must be adhered to for proper parsing of the grammar to ensure the adapted initialisation routine and mapper algorithms wo properly. These adapted, and new operators are described in detail in subsequent sectior

234	32	112		
37	65	43	189	222
17	105	243	149	

Figure 2. A Multi-genome representation for an multi-output problem with three output variable

3.4. Grammar Design

In MG-GE, each genome is mapped to its output expression or subprogram to mod and predict its corresponding output variable. MG-GE requires a single grammar, just lik standard GE. However, custom grammar rules have been introduced and must be adhere to. There are two main custom rules: *output rule* and *output variable rule*. These rules a illustrated by a sample grammar in Figure 3. These custom rules allow for grammar rul to be annotated with required details which are parsed and used by the mapper, wrapp selection, initialisation and genetic operators.

```
        <stmts> ::= <tr1-output-1> <tr1-output-2> <tr1-output-3> <tr1-output-4>
 <tr1-output-1> ::= output_1 "=" <expr>;
 <tr1-output-2> ::= output_2 "=" <expr>;
 <tr2-output-3> ::= output_3 "=" <expr>;
 <tr2-output-4> ::= output_4 "=" <expr>;
  <tv1-outputs> ::= output_1 | output_2
  <tv2-outputs> ::= output_3 | output_4
         <expr> ::= <terminal> | <terminal> <op> <expr>
     <terminal> ::= a | b | <tv1-ouputs> | <tv2-outputs>
           <op> ::= & | ^ | ~^
```

Figure 3. MG-GE Sample Grammar.

An *output rule* (or *target rule*) is a rule that codes a solution to one of the output variabl in a multi-output problem. To define an output rule, the rule's name must be preceded b *tr* followed by an output group number. During the mapping process, whenever such rule is encountered, a sub-mapping process is spawned. For example, in Figure 3, there a four output rules: ⟨tr1-output-1⟩, ⟨tr1-output-2⟩, ⟨tr1-output-3⟩ and ⟨tr1-output-4⟩. Als in Figure 3, there are two groups of output variables: 1 and 2. In other words, there shoul be an output variable rule for each output group number as illustrated in Figure 3.

The purpose of the group numbers is to facilitate modelling dependencies betwee output variables while avoiding cyclic dependencies, which is very key for the evolutio of combinational circuit designs. Recall in Section 3.2, we stated there might exist d pendencies between outputs in some multi-output problems; hence, the group numbe allows outputs (represented by the output variable names as productions of output variabl rules) to be grouped to allow evolution to evolve the potential dependencies which ma exist between outputs belonging to the same group. For example, in combinational circu problems, there may exist dependencies between outputs, but we need to ensure ther exist no cyclic dependencies between these outputs. Failing to do so will result in circu synthesis tools synthesising memory elements to store past/present output values, whic render such a sequential circuit.

Illustrated in Listing 1 is an example of a program with an existing cyclic dependenc Assuming the program in Listing 1 is a combinational circuit design in SystemVerilog, bot outputs depend on each other, which will cause memory elements to be synthesised b circuit synthesis tools rendering the circuit a sequential circuit instead of a combination circuit. The cyclic dependency checker in Algorithm 3 is used to ensure that during th initialisation and mapping processes, such cyclic dependencies do not occur.

An output variable rule is defined by preceding the outputs group name by *tv* followe by the output group number (e.g., ⟨tv1-outputs⟩ and ⟨tv2-outputs⟩). Essentially, an outpu variable rule's productions are output variables (e.g., output_1 and output_2) as shown in Figure 3. Also, note that the exact order in which output rules are defined for each corresponding output variable must be followed when defining an output variable rule as observed in Figure 3. For implementation purposes, extra attributes (corresponding output rule) are used to differentiate these outputs (e.g., output_1 and output_2), which are terminals from other terminals in the grammar during initialisation and mapping processes. An output variable rule is how evolution evolves dependencies that may potentially exist between outputs. During the initialisation and mapping process of each output rule (in other words, when an output variable is being modelled), the cyclic dependency checker algorithm ensures only choices of output variables that do not cause cyclic dependency can be chosen whenever an output variable rule non-terminal is encountered. The cyclic dependency checker algorithm is described in Section 3.7.

Listing 1. A sample program with cyclic dependency.

```
...
        output_1  =  a  +  output_2;
        output_2  =  output_1  +  b
...
```

3.5. Initialisation

The initialisation of the multi-genome representation is dependent on the type of initialisation scheme required. In the case of random initialisation, each genome is randomly initialised. In other words, n number (n equals the number of outputs) of random initialisation events. However, sensible initialisation (SI) is preferred, as it creates diverse and valid individuals. SI is an adaptation of the ramped half-and-half GP initialisation scheme introduced by Koza [26]. To benefit from SI's desirable properties, we adapt sensible initialisation for use with the multi-genome representation. First, SI requires the grammar to be labelled. Each production of a rule is required to be labelled with the minimum depth to expand all non-terminals to terminals fully and whether or not the production is recursive or not. Each rule is then labelled recursive if any of its productions is recursive and the rule's minimum depth equals the minimum of the minimum depth of its productions. During initialisation, SI applies grow and full methods when constructing the derivation tree. When applying the Grow method, any production with a minimum depth less than the remaining depth is eligible for selection. The remaining depth is obtained by subtracting the current depth from the specified maximum depth. The full method behaves similarly, except recursive productions are preferable if the remaining depth can accommodate it.

During MG-GE SI, n genomes in the multi-genome will require n SI events. The start symbol for each SI event is an output rule. The order of definition of the output rules in the grammar determine which genome to use during initialisation. The first genome is initialised by fully mapping the first output rule encountered, including any other rules occurring before the first output rule. The $(n-1)th$ genome is initialised when the $(n-1)th$ rule is encountered. The nth genome is initialised with codons used to completely map the nth output rule encountered and any remaining rules appearing after the nth output rule. However, during the initialisation of an output rule, if an output variable rule is encountered, its corresponding dependency graph must be checked using the cyclic dependency checking algorithm to ensure only production choices not resulting in cyclic dependency are valid for selection. Recall from Section 3.4 productions of output variable rules are essentially output variable names.

3.6. Multi-Genome Mapping

MG consists of n genomes, where n equals the number of output variables that must be simultaneously predicted. Given that there are n genomes, the mapping process involves n sub-mapping processes. Each genome encodes a solution to a single and unique output or output variable. As mentioned in Section 3.4, the MG mapper requires a rule to be defined for each output variable termed *output rule*. Output rule non-terminals serve as the start symbols for the sub-mapping processes. The order of output rule definitions dictates whic genome to use during the sub-mapping process. The MG-GE mapping algorithm is show in Algorithm 1.

The algorithm uses the first genome in MG to map the first output rule encountere during the mapping process. In other words, the order of definition of the output rule dictates which genome in MG to use. In addition, if non-terminals exist before the first an last output rules during the mapping process, codons are consumed from the first genom Also, ideally, an output rule non-terminal must be used only once in the grammar.

MG-GE mapping process starts off by using the first genome, as can be seen on Line in Algorithm 1. Lines 7–10 check if the genome contains any codons and terminate the mapping process if empty, as this indicates an invalid individual. Otherwise, if th genome contains codons, the mapping process continues as normal. The sub-mappin process is spawned as shown on line 16 in Algorithm 1, which maps the first output rul encountered, including all prior non-terminals, as stated in the previous paragraph. Th sub-mapping process algorithm is shown in Algorithm 2. The sub-mapping algorithn is the same as the standard GE mapping process, with additional logic to accommodat the MG representation. The algorithm is recursive as it spawns a sub-mapping proces whenever it encounters an unmapped output rule non-terminal by checking the set o `mapped_output_rules`. Otherwise, it continues the mapping process consuming codon from the first genome (lines 13–18 in Algorithm 2). Lines 21–55 remain the same as standar GE mapping where symbols belonging to selected rule production are placed on a stack fo subsequent derivation steps. Wrapping events are checked and applied accordingly.

Algorithm 1: Multi-Genome GE Mapper

```
1  Require genome, grammar, wrap_operator, max_wraps;
2  Ensure multi_genome.size() > 1;
3  Function Map (multi_genome, grammar, wrap_operator, max_wraps)
4      genome.phenotype_valid ← true ;
5      genome_index ← 0;
6      genome ← multi_genome.genomeAt(index) ;
7      if genome is empty then
8          genome.phenotype ← empty string;
9          genome.phenotype_valid ← false;
10         genome.effective_size ← 0;
11     mapped_output_rules ← declare set;
12     //stores target rules that have been mapped;
13     phenotype ← empty string;
14     start_symbol ← grammar.getStartSymbol();
15     dependency_manager ← instantiate dependency_manager object ;
16     SubMap(start_symbol, mapped_output_rules, multi_genome, genome_index, phenotype,
         dependency_manager) ;
17     multi_genome.phenotype ← phenotype;
```

3.7. Cyclic Dependency Checking Algorithm

Algorithm 3 shows the pseudo-code for the cyclic dependency checking. A 2D matri is used as a graph to model the dependencies between each group of output variables. Fo each position i, j of matrix A, if $A[i,j] = 1$, it means that the output variable represented a position i depends on the output variable at position j. The function `UpdateGraphMatrix` i a recursive function, which has the inputs `M`, a square matrix with shape $n \times n$, and `pos`, th respective position to be updated. This function assigns 0 to the position `pos` in the matri `M`, but this assignment triggers subsequent updates in its consequence. Subsequent calls o this function are recursive to ensure the necessary updates are made to prevent cyclic de pendencies between output variables. For example, if output variable `a` depends on outpu variable `b`, then output variable `b` cannot depend on output variable `a`. Subsequently, an output variable which depends on output variable `b` cannot depend on output variable `a`

Algorithm 2: Output Rule Sub-Mapping

```
1  Function SubMap (start_symbol, mapped_outputs_rules, multi_genome, genome_index, phenotype,
     dependency_manager)
2    genome ← multi_genome[index];
3    {derivation_stack, is_wrapping } ← {stack, false} ;
4    {codon_index, effective_size} ← {0, 0} ;
5    if genome is empty then
6      return
7    derivation_stack ← push start_symbol ;
8    while derivation_stack not empty do
9      current_symbol ← derivation_stack.top();
10     derivation_stack.pop();
11     if current_symbol is TERMINAL then
12       phenotype ← append symbol ;
13     else if rule is OUTPUT_RULE and rule ∉ mapped_output_rules then
14       mapped_output_rules ← insert output_rule;
15       if mapped_output_rules.size() > 1 then
16         SubMap(current_symbol, mapped_output_rules, genome, mapped_outputs.size()-1,
             phenotype, dependency_manager) ;
17       else
18         goto Continue_Mapping_Process from line 20;
19     else
20       Continue_Mapping_Process:
21       rule ← grammar.GetRule(current_symbol);
22       production_choice ← 0;
23       if rule.productions.size() > 1 then
24         if codon_index == genome.length()-1 then
25           codon_index ← 0;
26           is_wrapping ← true
27         eligible_prods ← create vector to hold eligible productions
28         if not is_wrapping then
29           if current_rule == OUTPUT_RULE_VAR then
30             check if a dependency graph exists for this rule group else create one
31             eligible_prods ← retrieve valid output vars from dm
32             prod_choice ← genome[codon_index] % current_rule.prods.size();
33             if prod_choice not in eligible_prods then
34               randomly choose a prod from eligible_prods && modify codon value accordingly
35             update the dependency graph to reflect chosen output variable
36           else
37             for prod ∈ rule.prods do
38               if prod contains an output_var then
39                 if output_var has prods valid for selection then
40                   eligible_prods ← prod
41               else
42                 eligible_prods ← prod
43             prod_choice ← codon % rule.prods.size() ;
44             logic here same as from lines line 33 to line 34 highlighted in red
45         else
46           if current_rule == OUTPUT_RULE_VAR then
47             eligible_prods ← valid OUTPUT_RULE_VAR.prods
48           else
49             logic is the same as from line 37 to line 42 highlighted in blue
50           prod_choice ← invoke perfect wrapping operator;
51         if current_rule == OUTPUT_RULE_VAR then
52           update the dependency graph with chosen prod
53       selected_prod ← rule.prods[prod_choice];
54       for sym ∈ reverse(selected_prod.symbols) do
55         push prod_symbol onto derivation_stack;
56   {genome.phenotype, genome.effective_size} ← {phenotype,effective_size}
     genome.phenotype_validity ← true;
```

Algorithm 3: Cyclic Dependency Checking

```
Function UpdateGraphMatrix (M, pos_{x,y})
    M[pos_x, pos_y] ← 0;
    while i < n do
        if M[i, pos_y] = 1 then
            M ← UpdateGraphMatrix(M, [pos_x, i]);
        i++;
    return M;
Function FillMatrix (n, dependencies)
    M ← Initialise matrix;
    M[i,j] ← 0, where i = j;
    M[i,j] ← ✖, where i ≠ j;
    for pos in dependencies do
        if M[pos_x, pos_y] = 0 then
            raise error;
        else
            M[pos_x, pos_y] = 1;
            M = UpdateGraphMatrix(M, [pos_y, pos_x]);
            while i < n do
                if M[i, pos_y] = 0 then
                    M = UpdateGraphMatrix(M, [i, pos_x]);
                i++;
    return M;
```

The main function `FillMatrix` initialises an empty matrix M with shape $n \times n$. Sinc the variables cannot depend on themselves, the positions i, j, where $i = j$, are initialise with 0. The input `dependencies` is a list with the respective dependencies to be fille in the matrix. In the next step, the positions regarding each dependency are filled wit 1 (if possible), and the updates in consequence of that are made by calling the functio `UpdateGraphMatrix`.

3.8. Perfect Wrapping

Given that multiple output variables are evolving simultaneously, a partially mappe output rule will render the entire individual invalid, negatively impacting the evolutionar performance. This means performing genetic operations in MG-GE will record highe invalid individuals than standard GE. In other words, the higher the number of outpu variables in a multi-output problem, the higher the number of invalid individuals create by genetic operations.

To mitigate this effect, we implement a new wrapping operator called *perfect wrappin* Perfect wrapping requires the grammar rules and productions to be labelled with th minimal number of codons required to map fully. The perfect wrapping operator require a list of eligible productions as input. If the derived rule is an output variable rule, it corresponding dependency graph must be checked to determine its eligible production First, the list is populated with eligible productions which are non-recursive and require th minimum number of codons to expand fully. If the list is empty, then recursive production requiring the minimum number of codons to expand are considered. Second, the mod rul is applied to determine if the chosen production is part of the list of eligible productions. I not, one of the productions in the list is uniformly selected at random, and Equation (1 is used to generate a new codon to replace the current codon, which, when used with th mod rule, dictates the same choice. This process continues while codons are reused from the genome until a valid sentence is attained.

$$\text{new\_codon} = \text{random\_number} \,\%\left(\frac{\text{max\_codon\_value}+1}{\text{choices}}\right) \times \text{choices} + \text{chosen\_prod} \quad (1)$$

3.9. Selection

The selection operator implemented for MG-GE does not rely on the total aggregated fitness of all genomes in MG. This is because it is possible the worst-performing parent might have completely solved one of the output variables but will rarely or never be selected as a parent. Instead, a *pseudo-parent* is created by performing n number of selection events, where the best-performing genome per output variable is selected from the pool of potential parents. Any selection operator, such as tournament, lexicase, and roulette-wheel selections, can be used to select each genome.

For example, in a standard crossover event, two pseudo-parents are created and used to create two offspring. The selection process is illustrated in Figure 4.

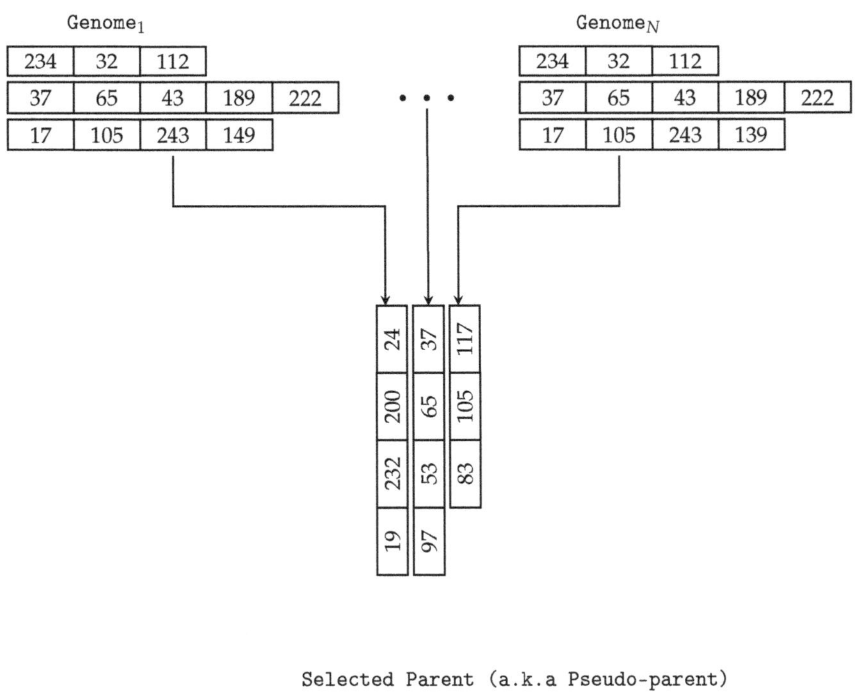

Figure 4. Multi-Genome Selection.

3.10. Well-formed Crossover and Mutation

Each genome in MG evolves a solution to a single and unique target variable. As a result, crossover operations occur between genomes that evolve the same output variable. Mutation operations are applied per genome in MG.

These genetic operations can be performed in several ways. Three types of events are currently implemented for genetic operation purposes. These include: *random single-event*, *binary mask-event* and *all-event*. In a random single event, only a single genome is randomly chosen for crossover and mutation. For a random single event, a binary mask of bit size equal to the number of genomes is randomly generated. All genomes in MG with bit positions in the binary mask whose bit values are one are chosen for mutation and crossover. In all-event, all genomes undergo genetic operations subject to the specified probability of these events occurring by the user.

3.11. Substitution Operator

In solving multi-output problems, there may exist inter-output dependencies as noted in Section 1. To facilitate the evolution of these dependencies, we introduced custom grammar rules as described in Section 3.4. Also, recall each genome in MG is meant to evolve a solution to a single unique output. Evolution is creative and can potentially exploit the inter-output dependency feature by using other sub-optimal output variable expressions as building blocks to solve another output perfectly. However, before extracting the solved output from an individual, if there exists a dependency on sub-optimal or optimal output variables, it is necessary to rewrite/substitute such output variables with their corresponding expression to obtain the final perfect expression for the solved output.

From Listing 2, assuming output variable `output_1` has completely been solved. Recall the best-evolved solution is a combination of the best-performing genome per output variable. Given that `output_1` is dependent on `output_2` and `output_2` is, in turn, dependent on `output_3`, if we extract `output_1` without recursively substituting output variables with their corresponding expressions to obtain an expression devoid of output variables, `output_1` will no longer be regarded as solved, as `output_2` and `output_3` are very likely to be different in the created best individual. Applying the substitution operator, we will obtain the solved expression devoid of any output variables as shown in Listing 3. Hence, the importance of the cyclic dependency checking algorithm is to ensure the substitution operator does not get stuck in a non-terminating loop as a result of cyclic dependency existing between output variables.

Listing 2. An individual that completely evolves the solution to *output_ 1 (50 out of 50 total cases).*

```
...
     output_1 = cos(x) + output_2 + output_2; (50/50)
     output_2 = output_3 + sin(y); (5/50)
     output_3 = 2^3 + 3; (1/50)
...
```

Listing 3. Final perfect output_ 1 statement after applying the substitution operator.

```
...
  1. output_1 = cos(x) + output_2 + output_2;
  2. output_1 = cos(x) + (output_3 + sin(y)) + (output_3 + sin(y));
  3. output_1 = cos(x) + ((2^3 + 3) + sin(y)) + ((2^3 + 3) + sin(y));
...
```

In Listing 3, a typical iteration of the substitution operator to rewrite the solved `output_1` variable before it is extracted. As can be observed from Listing 3, output variable `output_1` used output variable `output_2` twice which were replaced by the same expression at the end of the substitution operation. That is, in cases where an output variable uses another output variable multiple times will result in an increase in the size of the phenotype. In the case of digital circuits, such a scenario will increase the total number of gates required to realise the gate-level design of the circuit. However, this is a post-processing issue and is not addressed in this work.

3.12. Evolutionary Cycle

A steady-state EA is used to run the benchmark problems in this work. Unlike standard GE, where the best-performing individual is returned as the best-evolved solution, MG-GE creates its best individual by combining the best-performing genome for each output variable. However, when an output variable solution has been evolved, we perform substitution operations at the phenotype level described in Section 3.11. The function of the substitution operator is to rewrite an expression in terms of variables other than the output variables.

Once an output variable has been solved, its solution is made available to all individuals in the population, and evolution no longer searches for it. However, this functionality can be modified if required for evolution to continue the search but for solutions with additional desirable properties, such as shorter expressions.

4. Experiments

Two combinational benchmark problems are used in this work: *ripple carry adder* and *hamming code encoder*. Two instances of each problem are considered based on the number of inputs and outputs, Hamming Code (7,4) and (15,11) Encoders, and 5-bit + 5-bit and 10-bit + 10-bit Adders.

Experiments are conducted to investigate the performance of standard GE versus MG-GE on these benchmark problems. For each experiment, we design two grammars. The first grammar variant, which we refer to as Grammar with Output Variable Sharing, allows output variables to use other output variables as building blocks as long as no cyclic dependency between output variables is formed. This is achieved by the definition of Output Variable Rules as described in Section 3.4. In other words, Output Variable Rules, together with the cyclic dependency algorithm, are how MG-GE evolves inter-output dependencies that may exist. This feature is modelled in the grammar by adding the Output Variable Rule non-terminal to the ⟨expr-i⟩ rules as the last production (highlighted in both grammars). The second version of the grammar, which we refer to as Grammar with No-Output Variable Sharing, follows the same structure as the previous grammar but simply omits the Output Variable Rule. Hence, with this grammar variant, if inter-output dependency exists between two output variables, evolution will have to evolve the expression/functionality of the independent output variable.

We speculate that for problems with inter-output dependencies, the Grammar with Output Variable Sharing will perform better than the Grammar with No-Output Variable Sharing and vice versa.

4.1. Ripple Carry Adder

Adder circuits perform addition in digital electronic devices. There are several types of digital adders, such as ripple-carry, carry-save and carry-lookahead adders. In this work, we use the ripple-carry adder, as its operation follows elementary addition, which is ideal for exploiting the concept of output variable sharing.

Illustrated in Figure 5 is the elementary addition of two numbers. The addition operation starts from the last column (or the least significant numbers) and propagates any carry to the next least significant numbers up until the most significant numbers (first column). As can be observed, the $(n)th$ column addition depends/requires the carry from the $(n-1)th$ column addition. This problem can be modelled as an 8-output problem: four carry and four sum digits. Each sum digit (in other words, output) will require/depend on the carry from the previous addition stage as input. Without the inter-output dependency feature, each column addition to obtaining a sum digit will additionally require evolving the expression to generate the appropriate carry, taking into account all the carries propagated starting from the addition of the least significant digits of the addends.

$$\begin{array}{r} {\scriptstyle 1\,1\,1\ } \\ 8\,2\,3 \\ +\quad 9\,8\,9 \\ \hline 1\,8\,1\,2 \end{array}$$

Figure 5. Example of elementary addition.

4.2. Hamming Code Encoder

Hamming codes belong to the family of Linear Block Codes [27]. They are line error-correcting codes capable of detecting a single error and, at most, two errors but ca only correct one. For example, Hamming Code (7,4) Encoder encodes a 4-bit data wor into a 7-bit code word before transmission. It does so by generating and adding thre parity bits to the data word. Hamming Codes can be grouped into two categories base on the structure of the code words. These are *systematic* and *non-systematic* encodings. I systematic encoding, the data word and code word are separated while in non-systemati encoding, the data word and parity bits are interspersed. We adopt systematic encoding, a its structure is easier—data-word followed by the parity bits to obtain the code-word.

For example, the Hamming Code (7,4) Encoder can be modelled as a 3-output problem each output represents the redundant bit generated and added to the data word to obtai the code word. Each redundant bit is generated by applying bit operations to a unique se of specific bits in the data word. Therefore, no dependency exists between the outputs o the hamming code encoder. Hence, it is an ideal problem to explain the no-output variabl sharing concept as well as the performance of MG-GE on such problems.

4.3. Grammars

The grammars for the adder and hamming code encoder problems are shown i Listings 4 and 5, respectively. Both grammars are shown in a compressed form to sav space, with certain repetitive rules, production choices and symbols compressed. B repetitive, we mean rules with very similar, but not identical, definitions.

A repetitive rule with a similar definition has been compressed using the synta $\langle\text{tr1-sum-i}\rangle_{i=[1..n]}$ as shown in Listing 4. The same compression syntax has been applied t repetitive production choices and symbols and enclosed with curly braces where appropri ate.

Both grammars have been designed to use bitwise operators (i.e., gate-level design which makes the circuit problems more challenging to evolve from scratch. Each gramma is divided into two: *upper* and *lower* sections, separated by dashed lines. The upper sectio of the grammar contains the rules that need to be expanded. The lower section contain rules that define the fixed part of the circuit problem, such as the circuit interface. A expanded form of the grammar for the 5-bit + 5-bit Adder with Output and No-Outpu sharing are shown in Listings A1 and A2 respectively in the Appendix A.

Listing 4. N-bit + N-bit Adder Grammar.

```
        <stmts> ::= {<tr1-sum-i><tr1-cout-i>}n=5
                    {<tr1-sum-i+1><tr1-cout-i+1>}
                    ...
                    {<tr1-sum-i=n><tr1-cout-i=n>}
 <tr1-sum-i>i=[1..n] ::= sum[i] "=" <expr-i>; <nextline>
<tr1-cout-i>i=[1..n] ::= in_cout[i] "=" <expr-i>; <nextline>
    <expr-i>i=[1..n] ::= a[i] | b[i] | c_in
                   | (<expr-i><bitwise-op><expr-i>)
                   | <expr-i> <bitwise-op> <expr-i>
                   | <tv1-input>
<bitwise-op> ::= "&" | "|" | "^" | "~^"
 <tv1-input> ::= {sum[i = 1] | in_cout[i = 1]}
               | {sum[i = i+1] | in_cout[i = i+1]} | ...
               | {sum[i = n] | in_cout[i = n]}n=5
-------------------------------------------------------------------------
<output-stmt> ::= codeword " = {dataword,parity_bit};"<nextline>
   <nextline> ::= "\n"
```

Listing 5. Hamming Code (N,M) Encoder.

```
        <stmts> ::= <tr1-syndbit-i><tr1-syndbit-{i+1}> ···
        <tr1-syndbit-i = m>
<tr1-syndbit-i>i=[1..m] ::= parity_bit[i] " = " <expr>";" <nextline>
    <tv1-input> ::= parity_bit[1] | parity_bit[2] | parity_bit[3]
                  | parity_bit[4]
         <expr> ::= <input> | <input><bitwise-op><expr>
                  | <bitwise-neg>(<expr>)
        <input> ::= dataword[ <index> ] | <tv1-input>
 <index> ::= i | i+1 | ··· | k-1 | k=2^m - m - 1
   <bitwise-op> ::= & | "|" | ^
  <bitwise-neg> ::= ~
-------------------------------------------------------------------------
<output-stmt> ::= codeword " = {dataword,parity_bit};"<nextline>
   <nextline> ::= "\n"
```

4.4. Experimental Parameters

The experimental parameters for conducting the experiment are shown in Table 1. Preliminary experiments were conducted to tune these parameters. A population size of 1000 is used for all other experiments except the 10-bit + 10-bit Adder, which is a more challenging circuit to evolve. Down-sampled lexicase selection is used for each selection event. Down-sampled lexicase sub-samples training cases during the selection event, thereby reducing the total number of evaluations [28].

Table 1. Evolutionary Run Parameters. In bold are the default population sizes used for the actual experiments.

Parameter	Value	
Initialization	Sensible Initialization	
Selection	Down-sampled Lexicase Selection	
Crossover Rate	0.8	
Mutation Rate	0.01	
Replacement Rate	0.05	
Number of Runs	30	
Generations	100	
Mutation	All-events Well-formed Crossover	
Crossover	All-events Well-formed Crossover	
Wrapping Operator	Perfect Wrapping	
Population Size	1000	All other problems
	2000	10-bit + 10-bit Adder
Termination Condition	When mean, minimum and maximum fitness equals the maximum fitness or generation number equal specified generation number	

5. Results and Discussions

Figures 6, 7, 8 and 9 show the evolutionary performance for Hamming Code (7,4) Encoder, Hamming Code (15,11) Encoder, 5-bit and 10-bit adders using both grammar versions, respectively. The solid red line, dashed red line, solid black line, and dashed black line, are the mean best fitness across 30 independent runs for MG-GE using the Grammar with Output Variable Sharing, MG-GE using grammar with No-Output Variable Sharing, GE using Grammar with Output Variable Sharing, GE using grammar with No-Output Variable Sharing respectively. In Table 2, we summarise the number of independent runs for each experimental setup.

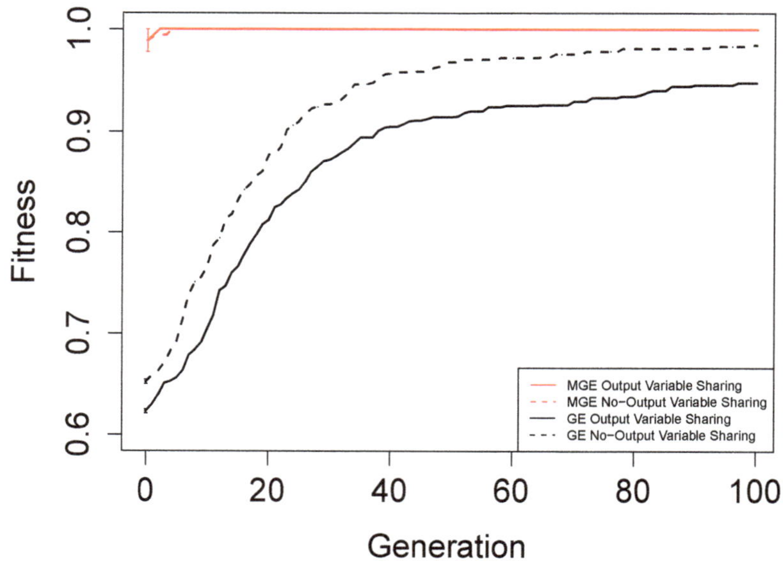

Figure 6. Mean average best across 30 independent runs for Hamming Code (7,4) using MG-GE and standard GE.

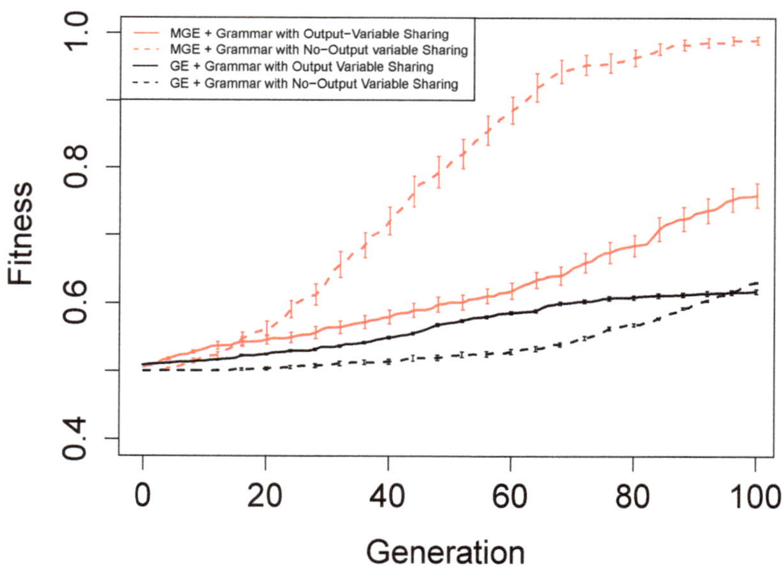

Figure 7. Mean average best across 30 independent runs for Hamming Code (15,11) using MG-GE and standard GE.

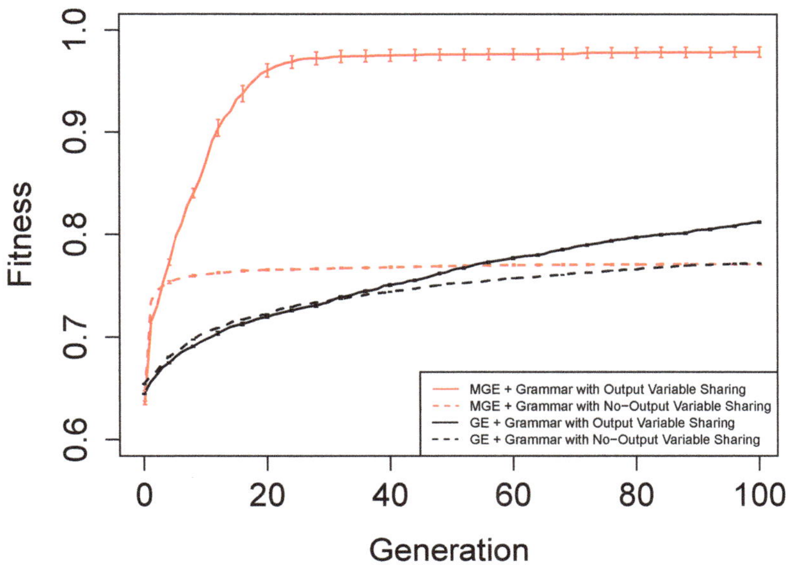

Figure 8. Mean average best across 30 independent runs for 5-bit + 5-bit Adder using MG-GE and standard GE.

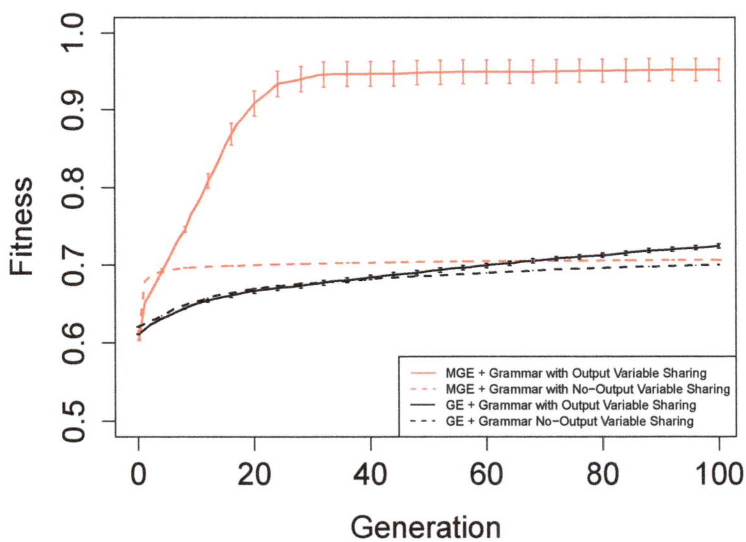

Figure 9. Mean average best across 30 independent runs for 10-bit + 10-bit Adder using MG-GE and standard GE.

Table 2. Success Rate On Benchmark Problems Out of 30 Independent Runs.

Problem	Standard GE		MG-GE	
	Output Variable Sharing	*No-Output Variable Sharing*	*Output Variable Sharing*	*No-Output Variable Sharing*
5-bit + 5-bit Adder	0	0	16	0
10-bit + 10-bit Adder	0	0	21	0
Hamming Code (7,4) Encoder	18	24	30	30
Hamming Code (15,11) Encoder	0	0	0	27

The benefits of the new genome representation can be observed from Figures 6– The experimental setups using MG-GE outperform GE when the same grammar varian are used except for the 5-bit + 5-bit adder in Figure 8, where both MG-GE and GE usin Grammar with No-Output Variable Sharing converge to similar final mean best fitnes However, MG-GE Grammar with No-Output Variable Sharing attains the final mean be fitness after a few generations. We also observe both MG-GE setups for the Hammin Code (7,4) Encoder in Figure 6 attain their final mean best fitness after a few generation This suggests evolution can perform quite well on relatively easier problems with no inte output dependencies when the least appropriate grammar is used (Grammar with Outpu Variable Sharing). Furthermore, MG-GE outperforms GE on all problems using the mo appropriate grammar variant.

We observe the experimental setup for MG-GE using the Grammar with Outpu Variable Sharing for the 5-bit + 5-bit and 10-bit + 10-bit adders recorded a success rate o 16/30 and 21/30, respectively, while all other setups recorded zero successful runs. This because the ripple-carry adder, which operates like elementary addition, propagates th carry bits from the previous bit addition stages to the last stage of bit addition. Henc designing the grammar to allow output variable sharing while ensuring no cyclic depe dency between output variables is formed ensures correct carry outputs are available fo the summation stages to use. As a result, the Grammars without Output Variable Sharin will require evolution to evolve the carry-out bit from the previous summation stage fo the current summation stage, rendering the problem more challenging to deal with.

On the Hamming Code (7,4) and Hamming Code (15,11) Encoder problems, MG-G with the Grammar with No-Output Variable Sharing obtained a success rate of 30/30 an 27/30, respectively. Using the Grammar with Output Variable Sharing, MG-GE obtaine zero successful runs. This is due to the fact that for the hamming code encoders, there exis no dependencies between the output variables. Therefore, using the grammar with Outpu Variable Sharing for a problem with non-existing inter-output dependencies impede evolutionary performance.

5.1. Limitations and Drawbacks of The Proposed Approach

Though MG-GE outperforms GE on multi-output problems, it is not without som limitations and drawbacks. Firstly, the Substitution Operator described in Section 3.11 ma not be universally applicable. Therefore, depending on the problem at hand, a new or modification of the substitution operator may be required. Secondly, the current outpu variable dependency feature (also known as output variable sharing) is very strict. Th output variables are only useful as dependencies to other output variables only when the completely solve their respective objective. In other words, an output variable is not use as input by another output variable if it has not attained the maximum fitness value. Thi may not be so beneficial for certain problems such as symbolic regression problems. Lastl the custom grammar syntax rules introduced require strict adherence and consequentl some minor errors may result in semantic errors which may be challenging to deal with.

6. Conclusions and Future Work

In this work, we presented a Multi-Genome Grammatical Evolution implementation and demonstrated that it is better suited for solving multi-output (or multi-target) problems than standard Grammatical Evolution. Genetic operators, mappers and initialisation routines have been adapted to work with the new genome representation. Custom grammar syntax rules, together with a cyclic dependency-checking algorithm, have been developed to facilitate the evolution of inter-output dependencies. A new wrapping operator called Perfect Wrapping has been developed to ensure every single Multi-Genome Grammatical Evolution mapping event creates a valid executable object.

Despite the success of Multi-Genome Grammatical Evolution on the benchmark circuit problems used, there are several open questions and further experiments that need to be conducted. For example, the best mutation and crossover events for the genetic operators adapted for Multi-Genome Grammatical Evolution need to be investigated. We need to develop more intelligent algorithms to help Multi-Genome Grammatical Evolution evolve very complex-output dependencies that may exist in other multi-output benchmark problems.

Furthermore, the limitations of output variable dependency feature mentioned in Section 5.1 needs to be improved to allow output variables that, when used by other output variables, contribute to increasing their fitness value.

Finally, Multi-Genome Grammatical Evolution has the potential to be applied to application domains other than the digital circuit domain. First, Multi-Genome Grammatical Evolution can be used to evolve the single dependent variable and several independent variables before performing multiple regression analysis to combine these variables to predict the target variable. Second, Multi-Genome Grammatical Evolution can be applied to multi-output classification problems. Finally, Multi-Genome Grammatical Evolution was applied to single-output problems that can be decomposed, however, Multi-Genome Grammatical Evolution should be applicable to multi-output problems. However, certain application domains may require several features of Multi-Genome Grammatical Evolution to be customised, such as the substitution operator and mapping mechanism.

Author Contributions: Conceptualization, M.T.; methodology, M.T. and C.R.; software, M.T. and A.d.L.; validation, M.T., C.R., A.M. and D.M.D.; formal analysis, M.T. and A.M.; investigation, M.T. and C.R.; resources, C.R.; data curation, M.T.; writing—original draft preparation, M.T., A.d.L. and J.M. writing—review and editing, C.R., D.M.D. and A.M.; visualization, M.T.; supervision, C.R.; project administration, M.T. and C.R.; funding acquisition, C.R. All authors have read and agreed to the published version of the manuscript.

Funding: The authors are supported by Research Grant 16/IA/4605 from the Science Foundation Ireland and by Lero, the Irish Software Engineering Research Centre. The fourth author is supported, in part, by Science Foundation Ireland grant 20/FFP-P/8818.

Institutional Review Board Statement: Not applicable.

Informed Consent Statement: Not applicable.

Data Availability Statement: Not applicable.

Conflicts of Interest: The authors declare no conflict of interest.

Appendix A

Listing A1. 5-bit + 5-bit Adder Grammar with Output Variable Sharing. Output variable sharing is enabled by making an output variable rule non-terminal a production of ⟨expr-*⟩ rules as highlighted in the grammar.

```
     <stmts> ::= <tr1-sum-1> <tr1-cout-1> <tr1-sum-2> <tr1-cout-2>
                 <tr1-sum-3><tr1-cout-3> <tr1-sum-4> <tr1-cout-4>
                 <tr1-sum-5> <tr1-cout-5>
 <tr1-sum-1> ::= sum[0] "="  <expr-1>";" <nextline>
<tr1-cout-1> ::= in_cout[0] "=" <expr-1>";" <nextline>
 <tr1-sum-2> ::= sum[1] "="  <expr-2>";" <nextline>
<tr1-cout-2> ::= in_cout[1]  "=" <expr-2>";" <nextline>
 <tr1-sum-3> ::= sum[2] "="  <expr-3>";" <nextline>
<tr1-cout-3> ::= in_cout[2] "=" <expr-3>";" <nextline>
 <tr1-sum-4> ::= sum[3] "="  <expr-4>";" <nextline>
<tr1-cout-4> ::= in_cout[3] "=" <expr-4>";" <nextline>
 <tr1-sum-5> ::= sum[4] "="  <expr-5>";" <nextline>
<tr1-cout-5> ::= in_cout[4] "=" <expr-5>";" <nextline>
    <expr-1> ::= a[0] | b[0] | c_in | <expr-1><bitwise-op><expr-1>
               | <expr-1><bitwise-op>(<expr-1>) | <tv1-input>
    <expr-2> ::= a[1] | b[1] | c_in | <expr-2><bitwise-op><expr-2>
               | <expr-2><bitwise-op>(<expr-2>) | <tv1-input>
    <expr-3> ::= a[2] | b[2] | c_in | <expr-3><bitwise-op><expr-3>
               | <expr-3><bitwise-op>(<expr-3>) | <tv1-input>
    <expr-4> ::= a[3] | b[3] | c_in | <expr-4><bitwise-op><expr-4>
               | <expr-4><bitwise-op>(<expr-4>) | <tv1-input>
    <expr-5> ::= a[4] | b[4] | c_in | <expr-5><bitwise-op><expr-5>
               | <expr-5><bitwise-op> (<expr-5>) | <tv1-input>
<bitwise-op> ::= & | "|" | ^ | ~^
<addend-idx> ::= 0 | 1 | 2 | 3 | 4
 <tv1-input> ::= sum[0] | in_cout[0] | sum[1] | in_cout[1] | sum[2]
               | in_cout[2] | sum[3] | in_cout[3] | sum[4]
               | in_cout[4]
--------------------------------------------------------------------
<begin-module> ::= "module adder(input logic [4:0] a, b, input
                   logic c_in, output logic [4:0] in_cout, output
                   logic [4:0] sum);" <nextline>
                   always @(*) begin <nextline><stmts><nextline>
                   end <nextline> <endmodule>
   <endmodule> ::= endmodule
    <nextline> ::= "\n"
```

Listing A2. 5-bit + 5-bit Adder Grammar without Output Variable Sharing.

```
      <stmts> ::= <tr1-sum-1> <tr1-cout-1> <tr1-sum-2> <tr1-cout-2>
                  <tr1-sum-3><tr1-cout-3> <tr1-sum-4> <tr1-cout-4>
                  <tr1-sum-5> <tr1-cout-5>
  <tr1-sum-1> ::= sum[0]  "="  <expr-1>";" <nextline>
 <tr1-cout-1> ::= in_cout[0]  "=" <expr-1>";" <nextline>
  <tr1-sum-2> ::= sum[1]  "="  <expr-2>";" <nextline>
 <tr1-cout-2> ::= in_cout[1]  "=" <expr-2>";" <nextline>
  <tr1-sum-3> ::= sum[2]  "="  <expr-3>";" <nextline>
 <tr1-cout-3> ::= in_cout[2]  "=" <expr-3>";" <nextline>
  <tr1-sum-4> ::= sum[3]  "="  <expr-4>";" <nextline>
 <tr1-cout-4> ::= in_cout[3]  "=" <expr-4>";" <nextline>
  <tr1-sum-5> ::= sum[4]  "="  <expr-5>";" <nextline>
 <tr1-cout-5> ::= in_cout[4]  "=" <expr-5>";" <nextline>
     <expr-1> ::= a[0] | b[0] | c_in | <expr-1><bitwise-op><expr-1>
                | <expr-1><bitwise-op>(<expr-1>)
     <expr-2> ::= a[1] | b[1] | c_in | <expr-2><bitwise-op><expr-2>
                | <expr-2><bitwise-op>(<expr-2>)
     <expr-3> ::= a[2] | b[2] | c_in | <expr-3><bitwise-op><expr-3>
                | <expr-3><bitwise-op>(<expr-3>)
     <expr-4> ::= a[3] | b[3] | c_in | <expr-4><bitwise-op><expr-4>
                | <expr-4><bitwise-op>(<expr-4>)
     <expr-5> ::= a[4] | b[4] | c_in | <expr-5><bitwise-op><expr-5>
                | <expr-5><bitwise-op> (<expr-5>)
 <bitwise-op> ::= & | "/" | ^ | ~^
 <addend-idx> ::= 0 | 1 | 2 | 3 | 4
  <tv1-input> ::= sum[0] | in_cout[0] | sum[1] | in_cout[1] | sum[2]
                | in_cout[2] | sum[3] | in_cout[3] | sum[4]
                | in_cout[4]
-----------------------------------------------------------------------
<begin-module> ::= "module adder(input logic [4:0] a, b, input
                   logic c_in, output logic [4:0] in_cout, output
                   logic [4:0] sum);" <nextline>
                   always @(*) begin <nextline><stmts><nextline>
                   end <nextline> <endmodule>
   <endmodule> ::= endmodule
    <nextline> ::= "\n"
```

References

1. Kalganova, T. Bidirectional incremental evolution in extrinsic evolvable hardware. In Proceedings of the Second NASA/DoD Workshop on Evolvable Hardware, Palo Alto, CA, USA, 15 July 2000; pp. 65–74. [CrossRef]
2. Stomeo, E.; Kalganova, T.; Lambert, C. Generalized Disjunction Decomposition for the Evolution of Programmable Logic Array Structures. In Proceedings of the First NASA/ESA Conference on Adaptive Hardware and Systems (AHS'06), Istanbul, Turkey, 15–18 June 2006; pp. 179–185. [CrossRef]
3. Hodan, D.; Mrazek, V.; Vasicek, Z. Semantically-Oriented Mutation Operator in Cartesian Genetic Programming for Evolutionary Circuit Design. In Proceedings of the 2020 Genetic and Evolutionary Computation Conference, GECCO '20, Cancún, Mexico, 8–12 July 2020; Association for Computing Machinery: New York, NY, USA, 2020; pp. 940–948. [CrossRef]
4. Tetteh, M.K.; Mota Dias, D.; Ryan, C. Evolution of Complex Combinational Logic Circuits Using Grammatical Evolution with SystemVerilog. In Proceedings of the Genetic Programming, Lille, France, 10–14 July 2021; Hu, T., Lourenço, N., Medvet, E., Eds.; Springer International Publishing: Cham, Switzerland, 2021; pp. 146–161.
5. O'Neill, M.; Ryan, C. Grammatical evolution. *IEEE Trans. Evol. Comput.* **2001**, *5*, 349–358. [CrossRef]
6. Rothlauf, F.; Oetzel, M. On the Locality of Grammatical Evolution. In Proceedings of the EuroGP, Budapest, Hungary, 10–12 April 2006.
7. Castle, T.; Johnson, C.G. Positional Effect of Crossover and Mutation in Grammatical Evolution. In Proceedings of the Genetic Programming, Istanbul, Turkey, 7–9 April 2010; Esparcia-Alcázar, A.I., Ekárt, A., Silva, S., Dignum, S., Uyar, A.Ş., Eds.; Springer: Berlin/Heidelberg, Germany, 2010; pp. 26–37.
8. Nicolau, M.; Agapitos, A. Understanding Grammatical Evolution: Grammar Design. In *Handbook of Grammatical Evolution*; Springer International Publishing: Cham, Switzerland, 2018; pp. 23–53. [CrossRef]
9. O'Neill, M.; Ryan, C.; Keijzer, M.; Cattolico, M. Crossover in Grammatical Evolution. *Genet. Program. Evolvable Mach.* **2003**, *4*, 67–93. [CrossRef]

10. Zhen, X.; Yu, M.; He, X.; Li, S. Multi-Target Regression via Robust Low-Rank Learning. *IEEE Trans. Pattern Anal. Mach. Int* **2018**, *40*, 497–504. [CrossRef] [PubMed]
11. Shaker, N.; Nicolau, M.; Yannakakis, G.N.; Togelius, J.; O'Neill, M. Evolving levels for Super Mario Bros using grammatic evolution. In Proceedings of the 2012 IEEE Conference on Computational Intelligence and Games (CIG), Granada, Spain, 11– September 2012; pp. 304–311. [CrossRef]
12. O'Neill, M.; McDermott, J.; Swafford, J.M.; Byrne, J.; Hemberg, E.; Brabazon, A.; Shotton, E.; McNally, C.; Hemberg, Evolutionary design using grammatical evolution and shape grammars: Designing a shelter. *Int. J. Des. Eng.* **2010**, *3*, 4– [CrossRef]
13. Grammatical Evolution. In *Biologically Inspired Algorithms for Financial Modelling*; Springer: Berlin/Heidelberg, Germany, 20 pp. 73–88. [CrossRef]
14. de la Puente, A.O.; Alfonso, R.S.; Moreno, M.A. Automatic Composition of Music by Means of Grammatical Evolution. *SIGA APL Quote Quad* **2002**, *32*, 148–155. [CrossRef]
15. Mariani, T.; Guizzo, G.; Vergilio, S.R.; Pozo, A.T. Grammatical Evolution for the Multi-Objective Integration and Test Ord Problem. In Proceedings of the Genetic and Evolutionary Computation Conference 2016, GECCO '16, Denver, CO, USA, 20– July 2016; Association for Computing Machinery: New York, NY, USA, 2016; pp. 1069–1076. [CrossRef]
16. Osojnik, A.; Panov, P.; Džeroski, S. Multi-label classification via multi-target regression on data streams. *Mach. Learn.* **20** *106*, 745–770. [CrossRef]
17. Borchani, H.; Varando, G.; Bielza, C.; Larrañaga, P. A survey on multi-output regression. *WIREs Data Min. Knowl. Discov.* **20** *5*, 216–233. [CrossRef]
18. Harris, S.; Harris, D. *Digital Design and Computer Architecture: ARM Edition*, 1st ed.; Morgan Kaufmann Publishers Inc.: S Francisco, CA, USA, 2015.
19. LaMeres, B.J. *Introduction to Logic Circuits & Logic Design with Verilog*; Chapter Verilog (Part 1); Springer International Publishi Berlin/Heidelberg, Germany, 2019; p. 157. [CrossRef]
20. *RTL Modeling with SystemVerilog For Simulation and Synthesis: Using SystemVerilog for ASIC and FPGA Design*; Sutherland HD Inc.: Tualatin, OR, USA, 2017.
21. Slowik, A.; Białko, M. Evolutionary Design and Optimization of Combinational Digital Circuits with Respect to Transistor Cou *Bull. Pol. Acad. Sci. Tech. Sci.* 2006, *54*, 4.
22. Walker, J.A.; Völk, K.; Smith, S.L.; Miller, J.F. Parallel Evolution Using Multi-Chromosome Cartesian Genetic Programming. *Gen Program. Evolvable Mach.* 2009, *10*, 417–445. [CrossRef]
23. Coimbra, V.; Lamar, M.V. Design and Optimization of Digital Circuits by Artificial Evolution Using Hybrid Multi Chromoso Cartesian Genetic Programming. In Proceedings of the Applied Reconfigurable Computing, Mangaratiba, Brazil, 22– March 2016; Lecture Notes in Computer Science; Bonato, V., Bouganis, C., Gorgon, M., Eds.; Springer International Publishi Berlin/Heidelberg, Germany, 2016; pp. 195–206. [CrossRef]
24. Baine, N. A Simple Multi-Chromosome Genetic Algorithm Optimization of a Proportional-plus-Derivative Fuzzy Logic Controll In Proceedings of the NAFIPS 2008—2008 Annual Meeting of the North American Fuzzy Information Processing Society, Ne York, NY, USA, 19–22 May 2008; pp. 1–5. [CrossRef]
25. Reyes, O.; Moyano, J.; Luna, J.; Ventura, S. A gene expression programming method for multi-target regression. In Proceedin of the International Conference on learning and optimization algorithms: Theory and applications, LOPAL '18, Rabat, Moroc 2–5 May 2018; ACM: New York, NY, USA, 2018; pp. 1–6.
26. Ryan, C.; Azad, R.M.A. Sensible Initialisation in Grammatical Evolution. In Proceedings of the GECCO 2003: Bird of a Feath Workshops, Genetic and Evolutionary Computation Conference, Chicago, IL, USA, 12–16 July 2003; Barry, A.M., Ed.; AAA Chigaco, IL, USA, 2003; pp. 142–145.
27. Miller, F.P.; Vandome, A.F.; McBrewster, J. *Hamming Code: Parity Bit, Two- out- of- Five Code, Hamming(7,4), Reed-Muller Co Reed-Solomon Error Correction, Turbo Code, Low- Density Parity-Check Code, Telecommunication, Linear Code*; Alpha Press: Lag Nigeria, 2009.
28. Hernandez, J.G.; Lalejini, A.; Dolson, E.; Ofria, C. Random Subsampling Improves Performance in Lexicase Selection. Proceedings of the Genetic and Evolutionary Computation Conference Companion, GECCO '19, Prague, Czech Republic, 13– July 2019; Association for Computing Machinery: New York, NY, USA, 2019; pp. 2028–2031. [CrossRef]

algorithms

MDPI

Article

A Neural-Network-Based Competition between Short-Lived Particle Candidates in the CBM Experiment at FAIR

Artemiy Belousov [1,2,†], Ivan Kisel [1,2,3,4,*,†] and Robin Lakos [1,2,*,†]

1 Frankfurt Institute for Advanced Studies, 60438 Frankfurt am Main, Germany; ar.belousov@gsi.de
2 Institute of Computer Science, J. W. Goethe University, 60629 Frankfurt am Main, Germany
3 GSI Helmholtz Centre for Heavy Ion Research, 64291 Darmstadt, Germany
4 Helmholtz Research Academy Hesse for FAIR, 60438 Frankfurt am Main, Germany
* Correspondence: i.kisel@compeng.uni-frankfurt.de (I.K.); lakos@fias.uni-frankfurt.de (R.L.)
† These authors contributed equally to this work.

Abstract: Fast and efficient algorithms optimized for high performance computers are crucial for the real-time analysis of data in heavy-ion physics experiments. Furthermore, the application of neural networks and other machine learning techniques has become more popular in physics experiments over the last years. For that reason, a fast neural network package called ANN4FLES is developed in C++, which will be optimized to be used on a high performance computer farm for the future Compressed Baryonic Matter (CBM) experiment at the Facility for Antiproton and Ion Research (FAIR, Darmstadt, Germany). This paper describes the first application of ANN4FLES used in the reconstruction chain of the CBM experiment to replace the existing particle competition between K_s-mesons and Λ-hyperons in the KF Particle Finder by a neural network based approach. The raw classification performance of the neural network reaches over 98% on the testing set. Furthermore, it is shown that the background noise was reduced by the neural network-based competition and therefore improved the quality of the physics analysis.

Keywords: artificial neural network; multi-layer perceptron; Kalman filter particle finder; heavy-ion experiment; compressed baryonic matter experiment

Citation: Belousov, A.; Kisel, I.; Lakos, R. A Neural-Network-Based Competition between Short-Lived Particle Candidates in the CBM Experiment at FAIR. *Algorithms* **2023**, 16, 383. https://doi.org/10.3390/a16080383

Academic Editor: Frank Werner

Received: 31 May 2023
Revised: 28 July 2023
Accepted: 8 August 2023
Published: 9 August 2023

1. Introduction

Over the last few years, the remarkable growth of machine learning and neural networks has had a profound impact across multiple scientific fields, redefining approaches to problem-solving and pushing the boundaries of scientific exploration [1]. The versatility and learning capacity of neural networks have positioned them as formidable tools in computational sciences, capable of addressing a broad spectrum of challenges across various domains. This includes, for instance, solving differential equations [2], and addressing forward and inverse problems involving nonlinear partial differential equations using physics-informed neural networks [3].

The predictive prowess of neural networks has resulted in models of outstanding accuracy. In fields like physics and computational science, these methodologies are offering new perspectives and solutions to longstanding challenges [4]. Particularly in particle physics, these methodologies permit applications at different stages of experiments, enabling entirely new approaches or complementing existing algorithms. This includes particle identification, trajectory reconstruction, event classification, and others [5,6].

This powerful interplay between computational science and particle physics will be prominently featured in the future heavy-ion experiment, Compressed Baryonic Matter (CBM), at the Facility for Antiproton and Ion Research (FAIR) [7]. This experiment will leverage advancements in neural networks for improved data analysis and interpretation. CBM is planned as a fixed-target experiment using the particle accelerator at FAIR. It will provide scientists with the ability to explore states of matter in regions of high baryonic densities at moderate temperatures [8] and will allow for the search for rare short-lived particles at unprecedented collision rates of up to 10 MHz [9].

In CBM, heavy ions (e.g., gold ions) will be accelerated to almost the speed of light to collide with a target (e.g., a thin plate of gold), to enforce a nucleus–nucleus collision that creates states of matter with extremely high density [10]. Under these conditions, a state known as Quark–Gluon Plasma can be produced. In this state, quarks and gluons are freed from their usual strong interactions within the plasma. After that phase, during hadronization, quarks combine into new particles that burst out of the central collision point (primary vertex) right into the detector setup.

Some of these newly formed particles decay almost immediately, either due to instability or interaction with other particles. At the point of decay, particles are generally referred to as mother particles, whereas the particles created during the decay are so-called daughter particles. The specific mother particles that decay almost immediately are called short-lived particles, and they can only be measured indirectly by the reconstruction of decays or decay chains, since they rarely reach any detector before. Then, the daughter particles' trajectories (tracks) are used and extrapolated to find the point of decay (secondary vertex), whereas their properties help to identify the decayed particle.

An efficient search for rare short-lived particles requires the already-mentioned high interaction rates of up to 10 MHz. This creates further computational challenges. At these interaction rates, it is not possible to store the data streams entirely, as they are produced with approximately 1 TB of data per second [11]. To reduce the amount of data that has to be stored, a reduction by approximately three orders of magnitude [12] is required and can be achieved by selecting only collisions (events) of physicists' interest. However, in CBM, there is no simple criteria for event selection, as the search for rare short-lived particles requires a full event reconstruction [13], including the reconstruction of decays and decay chains.

An algorithm package called First Level Event Selection (FLES) [14] is used to provide a full event reconstruction in real-time that allows selection of events of interest and, therefore, significantly reduces the amount of data that has to be stored on disk. The algorithms used for the experiment are tested and evaluated step by step using precise Monte Carlo simulated data. Thus, the true outcome of each event is known, and reconstructed particles can be matched with the corresponding simulated particles to allow a performance analysis. The reconstructed particle candidates are identified with a hypothesis, which can be tested and evaluated using simulated data. In real experiments, however, the comparison is not possible, which makes a detailed performance analysis a crucial step for a successful experiment. Therefore, the presented approach will use the already-established tools of the KF Particle Finder to measure the performance within the reconstruction chain of CBM.

The Kalman Filter (KF) Particle Finder is a package included in FLES, responsible for particle and decay reconstruction, including the reconstruction of mother particles. When mother particles are created, the type of particle and their properties are inferred by the properties of the daughter particles. Due to inaccuracies in the reconstruction of daughter particles, the reconstruction of multiple mother particle candidates is not uncommon. For that reason, the particles pass through a particle competition to find the best-fitting candidate. That way, the background noise produced by mistakenly created mother particles can be reduced.

The presented neural network approach is used to replace the existing particle competition of the KF Particle Finder. For each pair of mother particle candidates that would compete against each other, the neural network classifies the best-fitting mother particles based on their properties. The neural network solves the competition by classifying the most probable candidate out of both competitors. Previous work [15] already investigated a multi-layer perceptron-based approach, demonstrating that such models are generally capable of solving the problem with comparable results. The present work shows improvements in the particle competition by using a more complex model, including a different topology and hyper-parameters. The new model provides a raw classification performance with an error of less than 2% on the test set.

2. Materials and Methods

2.1. Particle Competition of K_s and Λ

The neutral particles K_s-mesons and Λ-hyperons serve as important indicators for the CBM experiment. K_s consists of a down-quark and a strange anti-quark, whereas Λ is build with an up-quark, down-quark and a strange quark. Theoretical predictions suggest that enhanced strangeness production (the production of strange, multi-strange or hyper-strange particles, that consist of one, two or three strange quarks or strange anti-quarks) is an indicator of deconfined matter [16], the Quark–Gluon Plasma. Both particles are abundantly created in the energy ranges of the experiment [15] and are therefore a reliable source of information. The two particles decay with the given probability BR (branching ratio) as follows:

$$K_s \rightarrow \pi^+\pi^- \qquad (\mathrm{BR}: 69.20 \pm 0.05\ \%),$$
$$\Lambda \rightarrow p\pi^- \qquad (\mathrm{BR}: 63.9 \pm 0.5\ \%),$$

(please see [17,18], respectively), and therefore both give a rise to negatively charged pions π^-. Moreover, all daughter particles of K_s and Λ are non-neutral and, therefore, can be measured by the detectors and reconstructed by the algorithms. The particle reconstruction procedure combines all possible daughter particles, resulting in the simultaneous creation of a "common" pion, which is a decay product for both, the Λ-hyperon and K_s-meson, leading to the creation of these two possible mother particles, even though only one exist in the Monte Carlo simulated data. As a result, Λ and K_s create background noise for each other, which will hinder the physical analysis of the particles using real experiment data. Performing a particle competition to decide for the best-fitting mother particles helps to reduce this physical background noise by removing the falsely created mother particle candidate.

The Kalman Filter (KF) Particle Finder [19] is an important package included in FLES, responsible for online reconstruction of short-lived particles and their decay chains. The package was updated recently by the Missing Mass method [20], and is now capable to reconstruct more than 150 different particle decays. Furthermore, it includes tools for performance measurements in the particle reconstruction process. The KF Particle Finder package reconstructs all possible mother particle candidates when a decay is recognized. Then, χ^2-cuts and a particle competition are applied to select the best-fitting reconstructed particles and to reject the others. The existing implementation of particle competition has several stages. One of the most important steps is the evaluation of particle candidates' reconstructed mass values. Here, the algorithm examines the reconstructed particles' masses of each pair of candidates (competitors), and checks if one is within 3σ range of the known mass distribution peak, the so-called Particle Data Group (PDG) (which refers to a global collaboration of particle physicists, who define standards and publish results within the scope of research) mass. If one of them is within the range, the mass distance to the respective particle's PDG mass is used to determine the best-fitting mother particle.

2.2. Data Extraction Using the KF Particle Finder Package

In CBM, the performance of algorithms within the FLES package is measured by a comparison of Monte Carlo simulated data and reconstructed results by the algorithm packages. Using this approach, the reconstruction efficiency and precision of each part of the package can be evaluated. The Monte Carlo data can be considered as the true outcomes of each event, allowing the application of supervised learning techniques. In the stage of the KF Particle Finder, when the particles and decay chains are reconstructed, they are matched with the corresponding Monte Carlo true particle. In this work, the Monte Carlo information of each matched particle is utilized to check if the reconstructed particle is a true K_s-meson or Λ-hyperon. If this is the case, the information of the correspondir reconstructed particle is extracted to build a dataset. In real experiments, Monte Carlo infc mation does not exist and, therefore, the neural network has to perform on reconstructe information and hypothesis only.

Overall, 25,000 events generated by the UrQMD model [21] were used in this wor A total of 12,000 events were used for training and testing, whereas 13,000 were used evaluate the network's performance in comparison to the existing approach. All events a central Au+Au collisions at 10 GeV energy, and therefore within the specifications of th CBM experiment. In general, the created generated particles are processed by a transpo engine (e.g., GEANT4 [22]) to simulate the particles flying through the detector syster including all relevant physics processes such as decays, scattering and interaction [23]. A this point, the whole event outcome is simulated, including all decay chains and trajectorie Afterward, the detector responses are generated, resulting in measurements (hits) th would also be produced by real experiment particles when they interact with a detector. Th hits are then used to reconstruct tracks and the KF Particle Finder is applied to reconstru short-lived particles and decays.

The first part of the dataset (12,000 events) is used to train and test the neural network a chitectures in the Artificial Neural Networks for First Level Event Selection (ANN4FLES) [2 standalone package. Here, a measurement for raw classification performance was obtaine by the accuracy and cross entropy loss values per epoch. This dataset was divided by 80:20 ratio for a training dataset and a testing dataset, respectively. Several fully-connecte neural network architectures and settings were tested by hand, where a multi-layer perce tron with three hidden layers with a peak accuracy of more than 98% on the test set wa finally chosen.

The second part of that data set, consisting of 13,000 events, is used for compariso of the neural network based approach and the existing particle competition within th KF Particle Finder. Hence, after training and testing, the pre-trained neural networks a evaluated, implemented in the KF Particle Finder package as a part of the reconstructio chain of the CBM experiment. That way, it is possible to use the tools for performanc measurement included in the KF Particle Finder, that are a well-established standard t evaluate the algorithms' performance in heavy-ion physics experiments.

2.3. *Performance Measurements in the KF Particle Finder Package*

When specific particles are investigated for physics analysis, it is important to achiev clean probes. Due to the large amount of particles (up to 1000) in a collision [25], ther are many tracks pointing to the collision point (primary vertex) and, thus, create a larg amount of possible track combinations. Due to the limited underlying detector resolutio and calculation inaccuracies of floating point representation in a computer system, it only possible to reconstruct all tracks and particle decays within an acceptable range c imperfection. In several cases, multiple tracks are within a defined error range, such tha uncertainties in the reconstruction can not be prevented. Some of the reconstructed particle tracks are real tracks that exist, others produce so-called combinatorial background, du to mismatched track segments in the reconstruction process. These can be found b comparison to the simulated data.

When using Monte Carlo simulated data, particles that were reconstructed and class fied correctly are called signals, whereas particles that were mistakenly reconstructed ar called ghosts, and misclassified particles are generally referred to as physical background for the respective other particles. The KF Particle Finder package produces histograms fc several parameters, such as particle's mass distribution, and separate histograms for eac of these categories. This allows a detailed analysis of the reconstruction performance whe working with simulated data.

Beside the histograms, metrics can be calculated based on it. These include th significance and the Signal/Background ratio (S/B ratio). The S/B ratio is just the amour of signal divided by the amount of background, which allows evaluation of the approache by showing if one or the other approach is rejecting more signal relative to the amount of rejected background. The significance expresses the relation of the signal peak in comparison to (lower) peaks produced by background. A significance of 1 indicates that the background peaks by fluctuation are as large as the signal and, therefore, in a real experiment, the peak would not be recognized as a different particle, as it has no difference to background fluctuations. Contrarily, a significance of 5 is considered a threshold to see a peak as a signal of a particle that should be investigated. However, since Λ and K_s are already well-known and parameters are usually set to find them with a high significance, the threshold for these particles is always achieved, even without competition. Nevertheless, a large reduction in significance should be investigated.

2.4. *Training and Testing Using ANN4FLES and PyTorch*

The C++ package ANN4FLES is designed for the fast and efficient creation of various neural network architectures and will be optimized for its usage within the full event reconstruction chain of the CBM experiment. In its current state, ANN4FLES includes architectures such as fully connected multi-layer peceptrons, convolutional neural networks, recurrent neural networks, graph neural networks, and more. Furthermore, it provides a graphical user interface for training, testing and fine-tuning of various hyperparameters without the need for additional programming, such that pre-trained neural networks can be easily exported to be used in CBM's FLES package.

In the present work, a Multi-Layer Perceptron (MLP) [26,27] is used to solve a classification problem between two possible mother particles in a competition based on their reconstructed properties. The ANN4FLES standalone package is used to create the neural networks for training and testing. Then, the chosen pre-trained network is included into the KF Particle Finder package and used in the particle competition to classify the competitors.

Since the previous work [15] already showed that a neural network can perform comparably to the existing competition of the KF Particle Finder, ANN4FLES is used for the first time within the KF Particle Finder package to implement a more complex neural network for this classification task (see Figure 1). ANN4FLES was tested on multiple well-known data sets and it was shown that ANN4FLES offered comparable results to other neural network packages, which makes one confident that the implemented mathematics in ANN4FLES are correct [24]. However, for comparison with a reference network implemented in PyTorch [28], the weights are initialized by the same uniform distribution method [29]. ADAM [30], with a learning rate of $\alpha = 0.003$ and default β_1, β_2, was chosen as a weight optimizer, whereas the selected activation functions are Leaky-ReLU for all hidden neurons and Softmax for the output layer. The loss was calculated using binary cross entropy and the training and testing phase was repeated over 100 epochs with a batch size of 50.

To find a well performing model and settings, different learning rates in the range of 0.001 and 0.005 were tested. The final results are accomplished by a network that was trained with a learning rate of 0.003, whereas lower learning rates performed almost equally, but larger learning rates tend to perform slightly worse. It is assumed that a larger learning rate does not allow for moving as deep into a minimum as with using lower rates, since it might overshoot the minimum slightly.

Besides the learning rates, different layer sizes and network depths were tested. Here, the main focus was set on finding a balance between network size and results. On the one hand, a more complex structure could lead to an even better performance. However, the raw classification performance is already good, such that much deeper networks were not tested yet. A deep neural network increases the amount of parameters and calculations, slowing the classification process and, therefore, has to be balanced with the fast algorithms required for the real-time event reconstruction in CBM. On the other hand, simpler architectures than the chosen one seem to perform worse, which indicates a less complex model is not capable of learning the patterns.

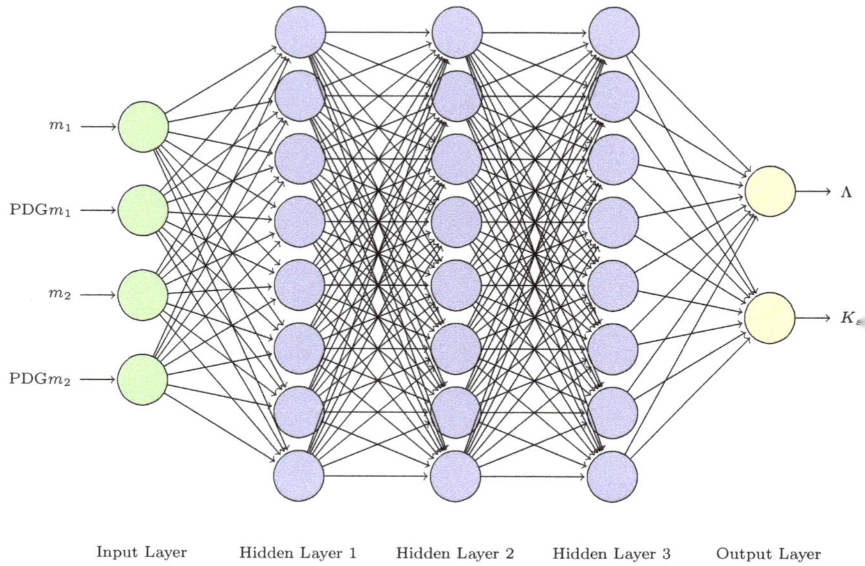

Figure 1. Multi-Layer Perceptron (MLP) topology used to classify K_s and Λ, using 3 hidden layer with 8 neurons each, hidden activation function Leaky-ReLU. Output layer consists of two neuron with Softmax activation and cross entropy loss.

3. Results

Particle Competition Based on Mass and PDG Mass

The MLP implemented using ANN4FLES provides a raw classification accuracy o up to 98.6% for the testing set (see Figure 2). An almost identically constructed neura network was implemented in PyTorch to ensure valid results. The PyTorch architectur provided equally high accuracy values and again confirmed the classification performanc of ANN4FLES.

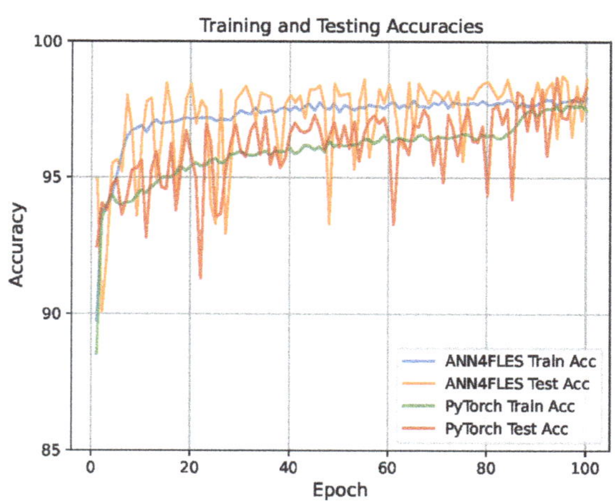

Figure 2. ANN4FLES and PyTorch accuracy for training and testing, using reconstructed mass and PDG mass over 100 epochs with a peak performance of 98.6% in the testing set. Both networks ANN4FLES and PyTorch, achieved high accuracy values on the testing set.

An error of only 1.4% on the testing set suggests that the classification performance of the more complex ANN4FLES architecture is more suitable to solve the task, since the error rate of the previous work is given with more than 10%. There are several possible reasons for the better results, such as the topology, different learning rate or the loss minimizing algorithm, which was Broyden–Fletcher–Goldfarb–Shanno (BFGS) [15,31,32] in the previous work. Furthermore, although the generators for simulated events should perform equally, further investigations are suggested, as previous work used the PHSD [33] model to generate data for the neural network training, testing and evaluation, whereas in the present work, UrQMD is the underlying model to generate event data.

In Figure 3, the total mass spectra histograms for K_s and Λ are shown. The results using KF Particle Finder without competition (black) and with the existing method (green) are visualized for comparison. The ANN4FLES approach is colored red, and one can see that it seems to reduce the number of entries over the whole range. In areas with larger distance to the peak, this is likely to be reduced background. Nevertheless, there is also a reduction in entries at the peak area for K_s, where a signal rejection can be the reason. In general, it reduces the amount of particles that were finally classified as K_s or Λ, respectively.

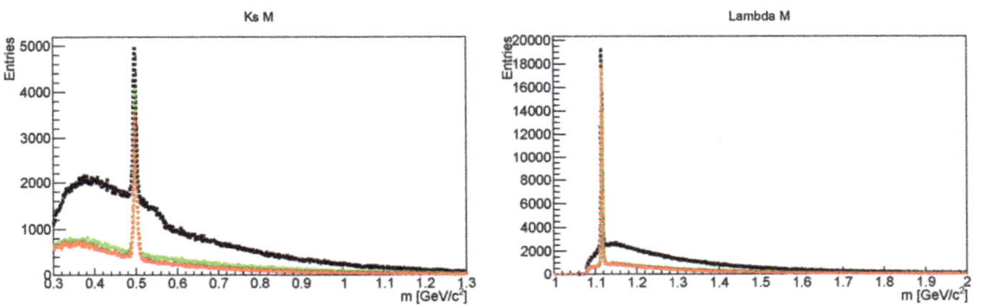

Figure 3. Histograms of mass spectra for K_s (**left**) and Λ (**right**). Comparison of no competition (black), the existing mother particle competition (green) and the competition by ANN4FLES (red).

Investigating the signal mass histograms in Figure 4 shows that, in both cases, a slight reduction in signal is indicated compared to running the KF Particle Finder without competition. For K_s, the ANN4FLES approach rejected slightly more signal compared to the existing method, whereas for Λ, the results are the other way around. Here, the existing method rejects more signal particles than ANN4FLES. Thus, one can assume that the largest part of rejected particles in Figure 3 is due to correctly rejected background.

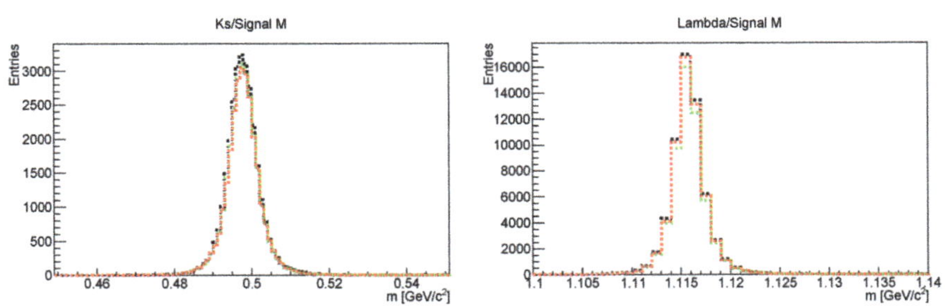

Figure 4. Histograms of signals for K_s (**left**) and Λ (**right**) masses. Comparison of no competition (black), the existing mother particle competition (green) and ANN4FLES (red).

In Figure 5, the background mass distribution is shown. Based on the histogram for Λ, it is difficult to see which competition approach is better. Both competitions reduce the background significantly but, around the peak, the existing method seems to perform better, since there is a clearly visible peak for ANN4FLES at Λ's PDG mass 1.116 GeV$/c^2$, whereas in the whole range, ANN4FLES seems to reduce the background slightly more. Moreover, there is a large peak of the existing method at $m < 1.11$ GeV$/c^2$, indicating less rejected background by the existing method compared to the neural-network-based approach. For Λ, this histogram indicates a tie between ANN4FLES and the existing method. However, evaluating K_s, there is no peak at the PDG mass of 0.493 GeV$/c^2$ by ANN4FLES. The neur network used seems to perform well in rejecting K_s background around the known ma peak, which, overall, increases the physics analysis for K_s. Furthermore, a competitic based on the mass is quite difficult, if the reconstructed mass of the background producir particle is within a range where it is expected for the respective investigated particle. The results show that the network is not only classifying by the distance to the mass distributic peak, as is performed in the existing method.

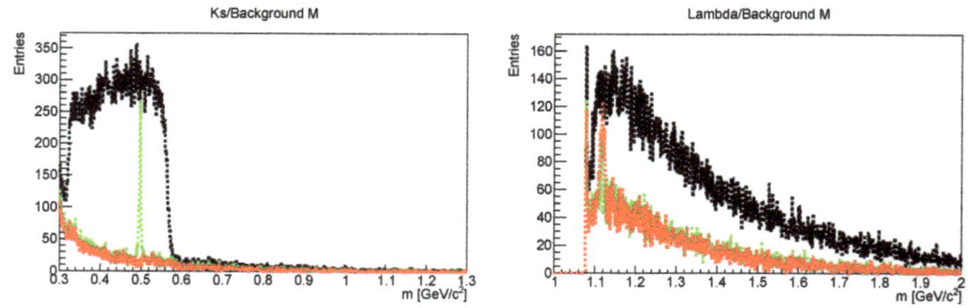

Figure 5. Histograms of background for K_s (**left**) and Λ (**right**) masses. Comparison of no competitic (black), the existing mother particle competition (green) and ANN4FLES (red).

In the ghost histograms (see Figure 6), ANN4FLES seems to be ahead in backgroun rejection in both cases Λ and K_s. Although, similar to the existing method, ANN4FLES ha a peak around the PDG mass bins, the existing method has more ghosts over the who range and within the peak area. Thus, the neural network rejects more ghost particles tha the default approach and, therefore, helps to reduce the mistakenly created mother partic candidates even more.

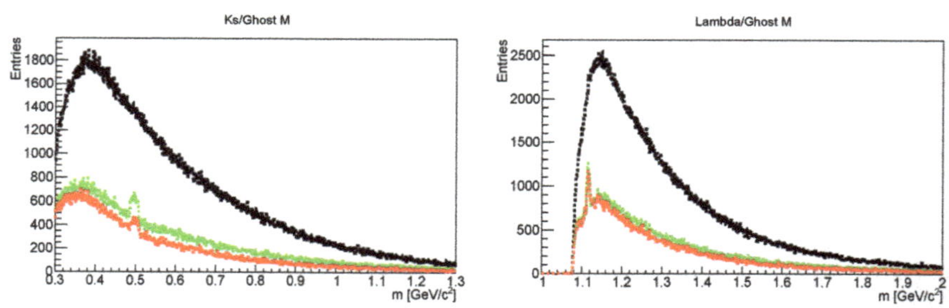

Figure 6. Histograms of ghosts for K_s (**left**) and Λ (**right**) masses. Comparison of no competitio (black), the existing mother particle competition (green) and ANN4FLES (red).

In general, the presented plots indicate a better performance of ANN4FLES by rejectin background particles. This can be confirmed by the S/B ratio and significance. In Figure the invariant mass spectra of $K_s = \pi^+\pi^-$ and $\Lambda = p\pi^-$ for the existing competition ar shown. With a significance of 149 and 213 for K_s and Λ, respectively, the clear signal is give in both cases using the existing competition of the KF Particle Finder. Additionally, the S/ ratio of 3.58 shows that the data visualized in the K_s-plot consists of almost four times mo signal than background, where it is over eight times more signal than background for Λ.

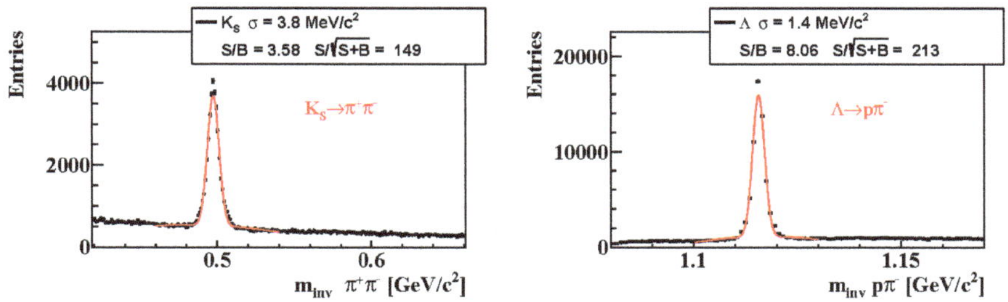

Figure 7. Invariant mass distributions of $K_s = \pi^+\pi^-$ and $\Lambda = \text{p}\pi^-$ for the existing competition, including signal–background ratio and significance.

The following results are achieved by the ANN4FLES approach (Figure 8). Comparing the S/B ratio for K_S, one can see that the ANN approach improved the value by around 16%. For Λ, however, the S/B ratio has been reduced by about 2%. Considering both particles, ANN4FLES has reduced the background successfully even further. However, for K_s, the significance was also decreased by about 3%, whereas the significance of Λ was increased by 1%. That indicates that even if the background was reduced successfully on average, the fluctuation in the background has been increased on average in comparison to the existing method. Nevertheless, both significance values are high enough to consider these particles as a clear signal, making the minor reduction negligible.

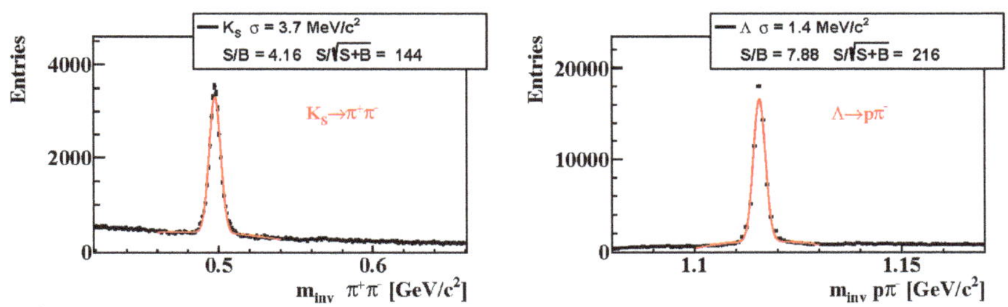

Figure 8. Invariant mass distributions of $K_s = \pi^+\pi^-$ and $\Lambda = \text{p}\pi^-$, including signal–background ratio and significance for the ANN4FLES approach.

4. Conclusions

Summarized, the ANN4FLES-based competition using reconstructed mass and PDG mass can perform comparably to the existing method. In general, using a more complex topology, it reduces background slightly better than the existing approach in the KF Particle Finder, even though the significance is decreased slightly on average. Especially, the amount of ghost particles were reduced almost over the whole range for both particles, and the background reduction around the PDG mass of K_s was strong, even though a similar model might show other results, depending on the learned features. The reason for a good background reduction is most likely that the existing competition is only based on the mass distance to the known PDG mass of a particle, whereas the neural network can also learn patterns between reconstructed mass and PDG mass that can be used to classify particles correctly.

The neural network approach is currently only classifying between Λ and K_s, whereas the existing method is furthermore cleaning the background by suppressing, for example, γ-decays and other cleanup methods. In the presented results, the network was not able to reject a particle entirely, hence neither classifying it as K_s nor Λ. The extension of the model by allowing either particle rejection or a classification between more particles that interact as background for each other, might require an increase of the underlying model complexity, but also can help to reduce the background even further.

The ANN4FLES package itself will now be improved with respect to its runtime for th planned applications in the real-time reconstruction chain of the future CBM experimen After these improvements, ANN4FLES will be integrated into the physics analysis modul of the FLES package.

Author Contributions: Conceptualization, I.K.; Methodology, A.B. and R.L.; Software, A.B. an R.L.; Validation, A.B. and R.L.; Investigation, A.B. and R.L.; Resources, A.B.; Data curation, A.B Writing original draft, A.B., I.K. and R.L.; Visualization, R.L.; Supervision, I.K.; Project administratio I.K.; Funding acquisition, I.K. All authors have read and agreed to the published version of th manuscript.

Funding: This research was partly supported by the Federal Ministry of Education and Researc (grant number 01IS21092), Germany, and Helmholtz Research Academy Hesse for FAIR (project II 2.1.4.2.5), Germany.

Conflicts of Interest: The authors declare no conflict of interest.

References

1. Jordan, M.I.; Mitchell, T.M. Machine learning: Trends, perspectives, and prospects. *Science* **2015**, *349*, 255–260. [CrossRef]
2. Tsoulos, I.G.; Gavrilis, D.; Glavas, E. Solving differential equations with constructed neural networks. *Neurocomputing* **200** *72*, 2385–2391. [CrossRef]
3. Raissi, M.; Perdikaris, P.; Karniadakis, G.E. Physics-informed neural networks: A deep learning framework for solving forwar and inverse problems involving nonlinear partial differential equations. *J. Comput. Phys.* **2019**, *378*, 686–707. [CrossRef]
4. LeCun, Y.; Bengio, Y.; Hinton, G. Deep learning. *Nature* **2015**, *521*, 436–444. [CrossRef]
5. Bourilkov, D. Machine and deep learning applications in particle physics. *Int. J. Mod. Phys.* **2019**, *34*, 1930019. [CrossRef]
6. Shlomi, J.; Battaglia, P.; Vlimant, J.R. Graph neural networks in particle physics. *Mach. Learn. Sci. Technol.* **2020**, *2*, 02100 [CrossRef]
7. Sturm, C.; Stöcker, H. The Facility for Antiproton and Ion Research FAIR. *Phys. Part. Nucl. Lett.* **2011**, *8*, 865–868. [CrossRef]
8. Friman, B.; Höhne, C.; Knoll, J.; Leupold, S.; Randrup, J.; Rapp, R.; Senger, P. (Eds.) *The CBM Physics Book*, 1st ed.; Lecture Note in Physics; Springer: Berlin/Heidelberg, Germany, 2011.
9. Ablyazimov, T.; Abuhoza, A.; Adak, R.; Adamczyk, M.; Agarwal, K.; Aggarwal, M.M.; Ahammed, Z.; Ahmad, F.; Ahmad, N Ahmad, S.; et al. Challenges in QCD matter physics –The scientific programme of the Compressed Baryonic Matter experiment a FAIR. *Eur. Phys. J. A* **2017**, *53*, 60. [CrossRef]
10. Friese, V. The CBM experiment at GSI/FAIR. *Nuclear Phys. A* **2006**, *774*, 377–386. [CrossRef]
11. Friese, V. Simulation and reconstruction of free-streaming data in CBM. *J. Phys. Conf. Ser.* **2011**, *331*, 032008. [CrossRef]
12. Agarwal, K. The Compressed Baryonic Matter (CBM) Experiment at FAIR–Physics, Status and Prospects. *Phys. Scr.* **2023**, *98*, [CrossRef]
13. Akishina, V. Four-Dimensional Event Reconstruction in the CBM Experiment. Ph.D. Thesis, J. W. Goethe University, Frankfur Germany, 2016.
14. Kisel, I.; Kulakov, I.; Zyzak, M. Standalone First Level Event Selection Package for the CBM Experiment. *IEEE Trans. Nucl. Sc* **2013**, *60*, 3703–3708. [CrossRef]
15. Banerjee, A.; Kisel, I.; Zyzak, M. Artificial neural network for identification of short-lived particles in the CBM experiment. *Int. Mod. Phys. A* **2020**, *35*, 2043003. [CrossRef]
16. Rafelski, J.; Müller, B. Strangeness Production in the Quark-Gluon Plasma. *Phys. Rev. Lett.* **1982**, *48*, 1066–1069. [CrossRef]
17. Zyla, P.A.; Barnett, R.M.; Beringer, J.; Dahl, O.; Dwyer, D.A.; Groom, D.E.; Lin, C.J.; Lugovsky, K.S.; Pianori, E.; Robinson, D.J.; et a Particle Data Group. *Prog. Theor. Exp. Phys.* **2020**, *2020*, 083C01.
18. Amsler, C.; Doser, M.; Antonelli, M.; Asner, D.; Babu, K.S.; Baer, H.; Band, H.R.; Barnett, R.M.; Beringer, J.; Bergren, E.; et a Particle Data Group. *Phys. Lett. B* **2008**, *667*, 1–6. [CrossRef]
19. Zyzak, M. Online Selection of Short-Lived Particles on Many-Core Computer Architectures in the CBM Experiment at FAI Ph.D. Thesis, J. W. Goethe University, Frankfurt, Germany, 2016.
20. Kisel, P. KF Particle Finder Package: Missing Mass Method for Reconstruction of Strange Particles in CBM (FAIR) and STA (BNL) Experiments. Ph.D. Thesis, Goethe University, Frankfurt, Germany, 2023.
21. Bleicher, M.; Zabrodin, E.; Spieles, C.; Bass, S.A.; Ernst, C.; Soff, S.; Bravina, L.; Belkacem, M.; Weber, H.; Stöcker, H. Relativisti hadron-hadron collisions in the ultra-relativistic quantum molecular dynamics model. *J. Phys. Nucl. Part. Phys.* **1999**, *25*, 185 [CrossRef]
22. Agostinelli, S.; Allison, J.; Amako, K.A.; Apostolakis, J.; Araujo, H.; Arce, P.; Asai, M.; Axen, D.; Banerjee, S.; Barrand, G.; et a Geant4—A simulation toolkit. *Nucl. Instrum. Methods Phys. Res. Sect. Accel. Spectrometers Detect. Assoc. Equip.* **2003**, *506*, 250–30 [CrossRef]
23. Friese, V.; for the CBM Collaboration. The high-rate data challenge: Computing for the CBM experiment. *J. Phys. Conf. Ser.* **2017** *898*, 112003. [CrossRef]

Senger, P.; Friese, V. *CBM Progress Report 2022*; Number CBM PR 2022; GSI: Darmstadt, Germany, 2022; p. 161.

Höhne, C.; Rami, F.; Staszel, P. The Compressed Baryonic Matter Experiment at FAIR. *Nucl. Phys. News* **2006**, *16*, 19–23. [CrossRef]

Rosenblatt, F. The perceptron: A probabilistic model for information storage and organization in the brain. *Psychol. Rev.* **1958**, *65*, 386–408. [CrossRef] [PubMed]

Rumelhart, D.E.; Hinton, G.E.; Williams, R.J. Learning internal representations by error propagation. *Parallel Distrib. Process.* **1986**, *1*, 318–363.

Paszke, A.; Gross, S.; Massa, F.; Lerer, A.; Bradbury, J.; Chanan, G.; Killeen, T.; Lin, Z.; Gimelshein, N.; Antiga, L.; et al. PyTorch: An Imperative Style, High-Performance Deep Learning Library. In *Advances in Neural Information Processing Systems 32*; Curran Associates, Inc.: Red Hook, New York, NY, USA, 2019.

torch.nn.Linear—PyTorch 1.9.0 Documentation. 2023. Available online: https://pytorch.org/docs/stable/generated/torch.nn.Linear.html (accessed on 30 March 2023).

Kingma, D.P.; Ba, J. Adam: A Method for Stochastic Optimization. In Proceedings of the 3rd International Conference for Learning Representations, San Diego, CA, USA, 7–9 May 2015.

Broyden, C. A new double-rank minimisation algorithm. Preliminary report. *Am. Math. Soc. Not.* **1969**, *16*, 670.

Fletcher, R. A new approach to variable metric algorithms. *Comput. J.* **1970**, *13*, 317–322. [CrossRef]

Cassing, W.; Bratkovskaya, E.L. Parton transport and hadronization from the dynamical quasiparticle point of view. *Phys. Rev. C* **2008**, *78*, 034919. [CrossRef]

algorithms

Article

A Hybrid Simulation and Reinforcement Learning Algorithm for Enhancing Efficiency in Warehouse Operations

Jonas F. Leon [1,2], Yuda Li [3], Xabier A. Martin [3], Laura Calvet [4], Javier Panadero [5] and Angel A. Juan [3,*]

1 Department of Computer Science, Multimedia and Telecommunication, Universitat Oberta de Catalunya, 08018 Barcelona, Spain; jofule@uoc.edu
2 Spindox España S.L., Calle Muntaner 305, 08021 Barcelona, Spain
3 Research Center on Production Management and Engineering, Universitat Politècnica de València, Plaza Ferrandiz-Salvador, 03801 Alcoy, Spain; yudali@upv.es (Y.L.); xamarsol@upv.es (X.A.M.)
4 Department of Telecommunications & Systems Engineering, Universitat Autònoma de Barcelona, 08202 Sabadell, Spain; laura.calvet.linan@uab.cat
5 Department of Computer Architecture & Operating Systems, Universitat Autònoma de Barcelona, 08193 Bellaterra, Spain; javier.panadero@uab.cat
* Correspondence: ajuanp@upv.es

Abstract: The use of simulation and reinforcement learning can be viewed as a flexible approach aid managerial decision-making, particularly in the face of growing complexity in manufacturir and logistic systems. Efficient supply chains heavily rely on steamlined warehouse operations, ar therefore, having a well-informed storage location assignment policy is crucial for their improveme The traditional methods found in the literature for tackling the storage location assignment proble have certain drawbacks, including the omission of stochastic process variability or the neglect interaction between various warehouse workers. In this context, we explore the possibilities combining simulation with reinforcement learning to develop effective mechanisms that allow for tl quick acquisition of information about a complex environment, the processing of that informatio and then the decision-making about the best storage location assignment. In order to test the concepts, we will make use of the FlexSim commercial simulator.

Keywords: warehouse operations; hybrid algorithms; simulation; reinforcement learning; optimizatic

Citation: Leon, J.F.; Li, Y.; Martin, X.A.; Calvet, L.; Panadero, J.; Juan, A.A. A Hybrid Simulation and Reinforcement Learning Algorithm for Enhancing Efficiency in Warehouse Operations. *Algorithms* **2023**, *16*, 408. https://doi.org/10.3390/a16090408

Academic Editor: Frank Werner

Received: 21 July 2023
Revised: 24 August 2023
Accepted: 25 August 2023
Published: 27 August 2023

1. Introduction

Manufacturing and logistic systems play a pivotal role in companies, serving a the backbone of their operations. Effective management of manufacturing and logist systems is crucial for meeting customer demand, reducing costs, improving operation efficiency, and gaining a competitive advantage in the market. In today's ever-evolvin landscape of manufacturing and logistic systems, characterized by increasing complexit and interdependencies, simulation has emerged as a powerful and versatile tool that ca significantly aid managerial decision-making [1]. Simulation serves as a powerful tool fc accurately modeling and analyzing intricate and dynamic systems that exhibit non-linea interactions. Among various simulation approaches, discrete-event simulation (DES) widely adopted across multiple industries. A plethora of commercial simulators such a Simio, AnyLogic, FlexSim, and others, as well as non-commercial ones like SimPy an Salabim, provide robust capabilities for DES modeling. The potential of these simulato can be greatly amplified by integrating them with advanced optimization or machir learning tools. Connecting DES platforms with external programming languages such a Python or R can enhance simulation modeling by leveraging additional mathematical an algorithmic capabilities, thereby enabling more sophisticated analyses and insights [2].

Reinforcement learning (RL) [3] is an increasingly popular field of machine learnin in artificial intelligence, which studies how intelligent agents ought to take actions in a environment with the aim of maximizing the cumulative reward. RL has plenty of applications in a wide range of fields such as natural language processing, image processing, recommendation systems, and marketing, among others. In the context of warehouse operations, RL can be used for various applications to optimize and automate tasks, improve efficiency, and reduce costs [4]. Some examples of RL applications in this context include inventory management (decisions on when to reorder, how much to reorder, and where to store items), order picking optimization (decisions on the most efficient routes for order picking), warehouse layout optimization (decisions on the arrangement of aisles, racks, and storage areas), autonomous guided vehicles routing, energy management (decisions on energy usage, such as scheduling equipment operations, adjusting temperature setpoints, and optimizing lighting), and quality control (decisions on item inspection based on factors such as item characteristics, inspection history, and inspection costs).

Combining advanced simulation environments and RL can be used for training an agent to find efficient policies that take into account realistic conditions such as those present in a warehouse. In this context, our work explores the potential of combining the well-established commercial simulation software FlexSim [5] and various RL implementations, programmed in Python [6]. FlexSim has several advantages that make it suitable for this project: *(i)* the focus on warehouse and manufacturing applications; *(ii)* the visual aspect, which facilitates the validation and also boosts managerial decision-making and insights by graphically showing the content of the model and the progress of the simulation; and *(iii)* the option to communicate with Python [7]. On the other hand, Python stands out as an open source, platform-independent, and general-purpose programming language. It offers plenty of comprehensive packages for data analysis, machine learning, scientific computing, and application development, among others. We present a case study where a dynamic version of the storage location assignment problem [8] is addressed. It illustrates the benefits and limitations of this approach and boosts a discussion on its potential in warehouse operations.

The work presented in this paper serves as a feasibility demonstration, in which the integration of two elements (namely, FlexSim and Python) that have not been previously documented as working together in scientific literature is showcased. This novel combination posed non-trivial challenges to the case study analyzed, i.e., learning from the realistic feedback of a commercial software implementation is not guaranteed. As reported in the related work section, the use of simplified simulation environments is a common approach, and consequently, the use of a more realistic model for the RL environment can be considered as the main contribution of this study. The second contribution is the resolution of a dynamic version of the storage location problem without using any prior knowledge and with a relatively small effort, at least for the validation instance considered. This problem, for a more realistic instance, is very difficult, or even intractable, using traditional methods. The study also covers a performance discussion, where the validation instance is scaled up, and the results are reassessed. The final contribution of this article is devoted to indicating where further research effort could go. In fact, this work can be seen as the first step in order to lay the ground for more advanced studies, in particular in the use of commercial simulation software in the context of digital twin optimization. The selection of a simplified case was carried out on purpose in order to be able to demonstrate its feasibility, to validate the effectiveness of the RL approach, and to provide a benchmark on the topic.

The rest of the paper is structured as follows. Section 2 reviews recent work on the combination of simulation and RL applied to warehouse operations. Afterward, Section 3 describes the algorithmic implementation for combining simulation and reinforcement learning. The case study is described in Section 4. Finally, Section 5 discusses open research lines in this area, while Section 6 highlights the most important findings and draws some conclusions.

2. Related Work

As the demand for fast and efficient warehouse operations continues to grow, there is a pressing need for advanced optimization techniques. In recent years, there has been an increasing number of publications on the use of RL and simulation related to warehouse operations (see Figure 1).

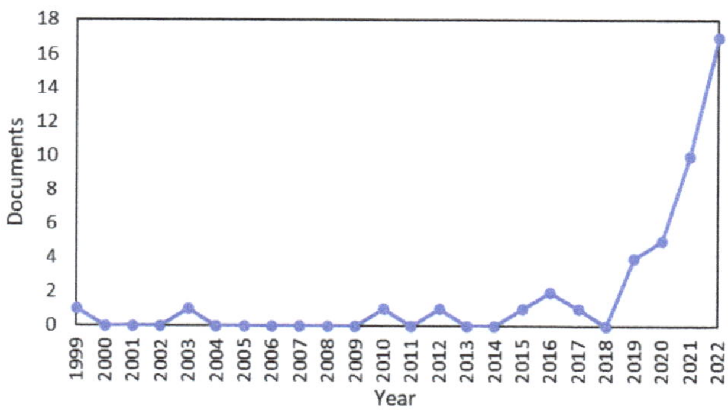

Figure 1. Documents by year in the Scopus database. Search query: "reinforcement learning", "simulation", and "warehouse" appear in the title, abstract, or keywords; the documents are either conference papers or articles; and the language is English. Information retrieved on 18 April 2023.

2.1. Early Work on RL with Simulation for Warehouse Operations

One of the first studies on the combination of simulation with RL was carried out by Kinoshita et al. [9], who proposed a novel approach for automated warehouse management using autonomous block agents with field intelligence. The field intelligence was developed through a RL process, allowing the agents to optimize the loading and ordering of crates. The simulation results demonstrated the adaptive process of field intelligence, mutual agent interactions, and the optimization of the automatic warehouse. Another early work was proposed by Rao et al. [10], which presented a simulation-based methodology for studying decentralized supply chain decision-making problems using stochastic game models. The authors used RL techniques to find near-optimal policies for non-zero sum stochastic games. The methodology was shown to be effective in capturing the short-term behavior of non-zero sum stochastic games, providing insights into the practical applications of inventory planning in warehouses. Later, focusing on large-scale data centers, Yan et al. [11] explored the application of RL in run-time scheduling to optimize energy consumption. By carefully optimizing RL algorithms, the authors demonstrated significant energy savings in IT equipment while maintaining performance. The study showcased the potential of RL in reducing operational costs and improving energy efficiency in warehouse data centers. In warehouse management problems, Estanjini et al. [12] presented a novel approximate dynamic programming algorithm. The algorithm utilized a least squares temporal difference learning method and operated on imperfect state observations. Simulation results confirmed the effectiveness of the algorithm in minimizing operating costs and outperforming existing heuristics in warehouse management. Similarly, Dou et al. [13] proposed a hybrid solution for intelligent warehouses, combining genetic algorithm-based task scheduling with RL-based path planning for multi-robot systems. The simulation results demonstrated the effectiveness of the proposed approach in optimizing travel time and overall system efficiency. The combination of simulation models with RL continued to advance with the work carried out by Rabe and Dross [14], which presented a decision support system (DSS) for logistics networks based on a data-driven discrete-event simulation model. The authors integrated RL into the DSS using SQL queries and a data warehouse to measure key performance indicators. The study provided a foundation for developing RL agents that can enhance decision-making in logistics networks. In another study, Wang et al. [15] proposed a novel incremental learning scheme for RL in dynamic environments where reward functions can change over time. The scheme aimed to adapt the optimal policy to accommodate environmental changes. The authors demonstrated the improved adaptability and applicability of RL in dynamic environments through simulation experiments in maze navigation and intelligent warehouse systems. In manufacturing scheduling, Drakaki and Tzionas [16] presented a method using Timed Colored Petri Nets and RL. The scheduling agent employed the Q-learning algorithm to search for optimal solutions. Through simulation experiments and performance evaluation, the proposed method showed promise in addressing manufacturing system adaptation and evolution in warehouse environments.

2.2. Applications of RL with Simulation in Warehouse Operations

Kono et al. [17] introduced an automatic policy selection method for transfer learning in RL, based on spreading activation theory. The proposed method enhanced the adaptability of RL algorithms in transfer learning. Simulation results validated the effectiveness of the proposed activation function and spreading sequence in automated policy selection. The combination also expanded to address specific tasks within warehouses with Li et al. [18], which focused on task selection in material handling and presented a deep reinforcement learning (DRL) methodology for autonomous vehicles in a warehouse context. The authors conducted simulation-based experiments to train and evaluate the capabilities of the proposed method. The results demonstrated the efficacy of the DRL approach for task selection in material handling scenarios. More recently, Sartoretti et al. [19] introduced PRIMAL, a framework that combined reinforcement and imitation learning to teach fully decentralized policies for multi-agent path-finding (MAPF) in warehouse automation. PRIMAL utilized demonstrations from an expert planner, reward shaping, and environment sampling during training. The framework scaled to different team sizes and world dimensions, enabling implicit coordination and reactive path planning. The study demonstrated the effectiveness of PRIMAL on randomized worlds with up to 1024 agents, highlighting its advantages over centralized planning approaches. Li et al. [20] presented a Deep Q-network (DQN)-based model for dispatching and routing autonomous mobile robots in warehouse environments. The DQN model outperformed traditional shortest travel distance rules by considering traffic conflicts, task completion makespan, and system mean time. Through discrete event simulation experiments, the study validated the effectiveness of the DQN model in improving task selection and performance in warehouse settings. Moreover, the integration of RL into supply chain control was explored by Barat et al. [21]. The authors proposed an RL controller trained through closed-loop multi-agent simulation. The framework aimed to maximize product availability while minimizing wastage under constraints. By combining RL with an actor-based multi-agent simulation, the study demonstrated the efficacy of the approach in controlling supply chain networks and optimizing warehouse operations. Another method was proposed by Sun and Li [22], which introduced an end-to-end path planning method for automated guided vehicles (AGVs) in intelligent logistics warehouses. This method utilized a DRL approach, combining visual image and LIDAR information. The algorithm employed a DQN with prioritized experience replay and a double DQN with the dueling architecture. Simulation experiments demonstrated the effectiveness of the proposed method in handling unknown and dynamic environments, improving AGV path planning in warehouses. Moreover, the challenge of learning decentralized policies for multi-robot tasks in warehouses was addressed by Xiao et al. [23]. The proposed approach was a macro-action-based decentralized multi-agent double deep recurrent Q-net (MacDec-MADDRQN). The method leveraged a centralized Q-net for action selection and allowed for centralized or decentralized exploration. The study demonstrated the advantages of the approach through simulation results, achieving near-centralized results and successful deployment of real robots in a warehouse task. Similarly, Yang et al. [24] proposed a DQN algorithm for multi-robot path planning in unmanned warehouse dispatching systems. The algorithm combined Q-learning, an empirical playback mechanism, and productive neural networks. The improved DQN algorithm showed faster convergence and better learning solutions for path-planning problems in multi-robot scenarios. Following the exploratic of reinforcement learning in warehouse management, Ushida et al. [25] presented a methc for transferring policies learned in simulation to real-world control of an Omni wheel rob in a warehouse environment. RL was used to acquire state-action policies for obstac avoidance and reaching a destination. The proposed method utilized transfer learnir to refine action control on real robots, addressing uncertainties in the real environme Experimental results validated the effectiveness of the acquired policy in a real-wor setting. In another multi-AVG scenario, Shen et al. [26] proposed the MAA3C algorith combining the A3C algorithm with an attention mechanism, for multi-AGV path plannir in warehouse environments. The algorithm incorporated advantages functions, entrop and both centralized and decentralized exploration. Simulation results demonstrated tl superiority of the MAA3C algorithm in terms of convergence and average reward, effe tively optimizing path planning and collaboration of multiple AGVs in warehouses. New and Alam [27] addressed task and motion planning (TAMP) in stochastic environmen The proposed method utilized MDPs and a DRL algorithm to synthesize high-level taski policies and low-level control policies for quad rotors in a warehouse setting. The methc achieved near-centralized results and efficiently accomplished tasks through physics-base simulations, highlighting the effectiveness of the approach. Similarly, Peyas et al. [28] pr sented the application of Deep Q-learning (DQL) to address navigation, obstacle avoidanc and space utilization problems in autonomous warehouse robots. The model was tested f single-robot and multi-robot cases, showcasing successful navigation, obstacle avoidanc and space optimization in warehouse environments through 2D simulation experimen Building upon automated warehouse systems, Ha et al. [29] presented a scheduling syste that utilized an AGV. The system incorporated a genetic algorithm (GA) for task schedulir and a Q-Learning algorithm for path planning. The introduction of a Collision Index (C based on AGV locations, in the GA's fitness function enhanced safety. The simulatior demonstrated the effectiveness of the CI in optimizing time, efficiency, and safety i an automated warehouse system. In the context of multi-robot tasks in warehouse Liu et al. [30] addressed multi-agent path finding (MAPF) in formation. The autho proposed a decentralized partially observable RL algorithm that used a hierarchical stru ture to decompose the task into unrelated sub-tasks. They introduced a communicatio method to facilitate cooperation among agents. Simulation experiments demonstrate the performance of their approach compared with other end-to-end RL methods, wi scalability to larger world sizes. Furthermore, Ushida et al. [31] focused on developing a autonomous mobile robot for warehouse environments. Five learning types were applie in a hybrid static and dynamic environment in simulations, with the aim of verifying tl effectiveness of these learning methods. The research laid the groundwork for learning i an actual machine and demonstrated the potential of RL for path planning and obstac avoidance. In a similar manner, Lee and Jeong [32] explored the application of RL tec nology for optimizing mobile robot paths in warehouse environments with automate logistics. The authors compared the results of experiments conducted using two bas algorithms and utilized RL techniques for path optimization. The findings contributed understanding the characteristics and differences of RL algorithms, providing insigh for future developments. Addressing the dynamic scheduling problem of order pic ing in intelligent unmanned warehouses, Tang et al. [33] proposed a hierarchical So Actor–Critic algorithm. The algorithm incorporated sub-goals and two learning level with the actor maximizing expected intrinsic reward and entropy. Experimental resul demonstrated the effectiveness of the proposed algorithm in improving multi-logistic AGV robots' collaboration and reward in sparse environments.

2.3. Advancements in RL with Simulation for Warehouse Operations

Li et al. [34] investigated the deployment of a Virtual Warehouse using Kubernete and Docker. The authors employed an RL algorithm to optimize the placement of th Virtual Warehouse, adapting to changing environmental conditions. Simulation mode ing was used to train the model and to obtain the optimal warehouse placement. The research highlighted the superiority of the RL algorithm in Kubernetes warehouse placement. DRL was another technique proposed by Ren and Huang [35], which presented an optimal path-planning algorithm for mobile robots in warehouses. The algorithm combined potential fields guidance with DRL to collect high-quality training data and to improve data efficiency. Simulation results demonstrated the successful navigation and obstacle avoidance capabilities of the DRL algorithm in warehouse environments. Similarly, Balachandran et al. [36] presented an autonomous navigation system for an autonomous mobile robot (AMR) in a warehouse environment. The system utilized a DQN algorithm trained with LIDAR-based robot models in a ROS Gazebo environment. The results demonstrated the successful navigation of the mobile robot in unknown environments through simulation and real-life experiments. Shifting the focus to transaction sequencing, Arslan and Ekren [37] focused on transaction sequencing in a tier-to-tier Shuttle-based Storage and Retrieval System (SBSRS). The authors proposed a DQL method to optimize the transaction selection of shuttles. By comparing the performance of DQL with heuristic approaches, such as first-come-first-serve (FIFO) and shortest process time (SPT) rules, the study demonstrated the advantages of DQL in reducing process time and improving the efficiency of the SBSRS. Continuing research in mobile robotic applications, Lewis et al. [38] addressed the challenge of autonomous navigation in mobile robotic applications. The authors proposed a novel approach that combined RL with object detection for collision-free point-goal navigation. The reward function was designed to grant rewards based on successful object detection with varying confidence levels. The results indicated significant improvements in point-goal navigation behavior compared with simpler reward function designs. In the context of task scheduling in automated warehouses, Ho et al. [39] focused on heterogeneous autonomous robotic (HAR) systems. The authors proposed a DRL-based algorithm using proximal policy optimization (PPO) to achieve optimal task scheduling. Additionally, a federated learning algorithm was introduced to enhance the performance of the PPO agents. Simulation results demonstrated the superiority of the proposed algorithm in terms of average queue length compared with existing methods. Later, Zhou et al. [40] addressed the order batching and sequencing problem in warehouses, a known NP-hard problem. The authors proposed an improved iterated local search algorithm based on RL to minimize tardiness. The algorithm incorporated an operator selecting scheme and adaptive perturbation mechanism to enhance global search ability. Extensive simulation experiments demonstrated the effectiveness and efficiency of the proposed approach compared with state-of-the-art methods. Similarly, Cestero et al. [41] presented Storehouse, a customizable environment for warehouse simulations designed to optimize warehouse management using RL techniques. The environment was validated against state-of-the-art RL algorithms and compared with human and random policies. The findings demonstrated the effectiveness of Storehouse in optimizing warehouse management processes. Choi et al. [42] focused on the cooperative path control of multiple AGVs in warehouse systems. The authors proposed a QMIX-based scheme that utilized cooperative multi-agent RL algorithms. Novel techniques, including sequential action masking and additional local loss, were introduced to eliminate collision cases and to enhance collaboration among individual AGVs. Simulation results confirmed the superiority of the proposed scheme in various layouts, highlighting the importance of cooperation among AGVs. Another approach was proposed by Elkunchwar et al. [43], which addressed the autonomous source seeking capability for small unmanned aerial vehicles (UAVs) in challenging environments. Inspired by bacterial chemotaxis, a simple gradient-following algorithm was employed for source seeking while avoiding obstacles. Real-time demonstrations showcased the success rate of the algorithm in navigating towards fire or light sources while maintaining obstacle avoidance. Moving to warehouse operations, Wang et al. [44] proposed a hybrid picking mode for real-time order picking in warehouse centers. Multiple picking stations were utilized to handle a large number of orders arriving at inconsistent quantities. The authors designed a RL algorithm called PRL to address the challenges of real-time order arrivals.

Numerical simulations demonstrated the algorithm's ability to handle a large number of o ders simultaneously and to improve picking efficiency. Similarly, Y. Ekren and Arslan [45 presented an RL approach, specifically Q-learning, for transaction scheduling in a shuttl based storage and retrieval system (SBS/RS). The proposed approach outperformed stati scheduling approaches, demonstrating its effectiveness in improving the performance c SBS/RS. Furthermore, Yu [46] focused on the logistics transportation scheduling of fres products. A DNQ algorithm based on a pointer network was proposed to solve the efficier logistics scheduling problem in fresh product distribution service centers. Simulatio experiments validated the algorithm's accuracy and stability, making it suitable for ac dressing complex logistics and transportation scheduling problems. Shifting to energ efficiency in mobile edge networks, Sun et al. [47] addressed this challenge by proposin an intelligent caching strategy based on DRL. The strategy utilized a DQN framework t design an intelligent content caching policy. By reducing duplicate content transmission between edge networks and a remote cloud, the proposed strategy significantly enhance the energy efficiency of mobile edge networks. Continuing the investigation of bridgin the gap between simulation and real environments, Ushida et al. [48] focused on propose a transfer learning method to improve the action control of an Omni wheel robot in rea environments. The effectiveness of the acquired policy was verified through experiment demonstrating the potential of sim-to-real transfer learning in supporting real-world appl cations of RL. Exploring the sparse reward problem in learning paths for multiple mobil robots in automated warehouses, Lee et al. [49] employed a multi-agent RL (MARL) ap proach. The proposed dual reward model incorporated complex actions and various route to enhance learning progress and to mitigate the sparse reward problem. Experiment conducted in a simulated automated warehouse environment validated the effectivenes and stability of the proposed reward model method. Liang et al. [50] focused on effectiv resource allocation in Industrial Internet of Things (IIoT) systems. A DQN-based schem was proposed to optimize bandwidth utilization and energy efficiency. The DQN mode utilized deep neural networks (DNNs) and Q-learning to select appropriate actions for im proving resource allocation. Simulation results demonstrated the efficacy of the propose scheme in enhancing both bandwidth utilization and energy efficiency compared witl other representative schemes. More recently, Guo and Li [51] presented an intelligent patl planning model for AGV-UAV transportation in smart warehouses using DRL. The mode utilized proximal policy optimization with covariance matrix adaptation (PPO-CMA) in th imitation learning and DRL networks. Simulation experiments conducted in warehousin scenarios validated the performance of the proposed model in optimizing transportatio routes for AGV-UAV collaboration. Finally, Yan et al. [52] introduced a methodology fo optimizing control strategies in vehicular systems using DRL. The methodology utilized variable-agent, multi-task approach and was experimentally validated on mixed autonom traffic systems. The study demonstrated the efficacy of the proposed methodology i improving control strategies, surpassing human driving baselines.

In Table 1, a classification of the studies presented in this section is provided. Th classification is conducted according to three different categories, namely, *(i)* whether th application is related to an improvement at the supply-chain or warehouse (macro) leve or the application is related to improvements to the navigation of robots or autonomou vehicles; *(ii)* whether the RL component makes use of DNNs; and *(iii)* whether the sim ulation component used is a dedicated simulation software. By "dedicated simulatio software", we refer herein to the use of a separate environment (third-party) in which th programmed RL algorithm interacts and learns from. This taxonomy allows for derivin some interesting insights about the context of the present study. There is an approximatel equal split between papers covering warehouse/supply chain and the autonomous vehicl navigation area. Also, approximately half of the papers make use of DNN, being nonethe less more common in the context of autonomous vehicle navigation. Finally, the use o dedicated simulation software is not commonly found in the literature, with only 20% o studies making use of it. The reasons are obviously the increased complexity of handlin the inter-software communication and the potentially richer environment from which the agent needs to learn, as exemplified in the present work with FlexSim.

Table 1. Taxonomical classification of the papers found in the literature review.

References	Warehouse /Supply Chain Management	AGV /Robot Motion	Use DNN	Dedicated Simulation Software
Kinoshita et al. [9]		✓		
Rao et al. [10]	✓			Arena
Yan et al. [11]	✓			
Estanjini et al. [12]	✓			
Dou et al. [13]	✓			
Rabe and Dross [14]	✓			SimChain
Wang et al. [15]		✓		
Drakaki and Tzionas [16]	✓		✓	
Kono et al. [17]		✓		
Li et al. [18]	✓		✓	
Sartoretti et al. [19]		✓		
Li et al. [20]		✓	✓	
Barat et al. [21]	✓			
Sun and Li [22]		✓	✓	
Xiao et al. [23]	✓		✓	
Yang et al. [24]		✓	✓	
Ushida et al. [25]		✓		
Shen et al. [26]		✓	✓	
Newaz and Alam [27]	✓		✓	CoppeliaSim
Peyas et al. [28]		✓	✓	
Ha et al. [29]		✓		
Liu et al. [30]		✓		
Ushida et al. [31]		✓	✓	
Lee and Jeong [32]		✓		
Tang et al. [33]	✓		✓	
Li et al. [34]	✓			CloudSim
Ren and Huang [35]		✓	✓	
Balachandran et al. [36]		✓	✓	Gazebo
Arslan and Ekren [37]	✓		✓	
Lewis et al. [38]		✓	✓	NVIDIA Isaac Sim
Ho et al. [39]	✓		✓	
Zhou et al. [40]	✓			
Cestero et al. [41]	✓		✓	
Choi et al. [42]		✓	✓	
Elkunchwar et al. [43]		✓		
Wang et al. [44]	✓			
Y. Ekren and Arslan [45]	✓			Arena
Yu [46]	✓		✓	
Sun et al. [47]	✓		✓	
Ushida et al. [48]		✓		
Lee et al. [49]		✓	✓	
Liang et al. [50]	✓		✓	
Guo and Li [51]		✓	✓	Unity
Yan et al. [52]		✓	✓	SUMO

3. Reinforcement Learning in FlexSim

In complex real-life warehouse environments, there are decisions that are oftentim made by humans, based on their current knowledge and their intuition. Some of the decisions could potentially be handled by so-called artificial intelligence. Let us consid a couple of examples: a worker might need to decide where to place a product in a intermediate storage area before the item can be processed by some equivalent worki stations or a worker needs to decide what product to pick up next from a given set orders. In both situations, the sheer amount of information and the interaction patterns be handled can easily surpass the capacity of a single human mind, resulting in inefficie processes. Therefore, if a RL agent is trained in order to make the right decisions such a complex contexts, it could enhance the efficiency of the overall warehouse syste Even though there are many applications that could benefit from this line of researc there are not many studies integrating simulation and RL algorithms in the context warehouse management and, in particular, to solve a dynamic version of the storag location assignment problem. Furthermore, to the best of the authors' knowledge, the are no studies in the literature that illustrate the combination of FlexSim and RL fo such purpose.

Being a simulation tool, FlexSim is not specifically designed to provide implement tions of particular RL algorithms developed in the scientific literature. Nonetheless, it straightforward to consider the possibility of using FlexSim as the environment in which e ternal RL agents train and learn. One of the main reasons to use FlexSim as an environme for RL is that it helps to create very detailed models of logistic environments very easi For instance, the daily operations of a large warehouse could be modelled with relative small effort and to a level of detail that would be difficult if they were to be modelled fro scratch using a generic programming language or an open source alternative. In order combine both software, a communication protocol is required between FlexSim and th outer world, so that an external program that executes a RL framework can incorpora a FlexSim simulation as a training environment. For that purpose, FlexSim allows co munication with external processes via sockets, using its internal programming languag FlexScript. In Figure 2, the classical state–action–reward RL scheme is adapted in order illustrate the methodology followed in this study. This is also shown in Algorithm 1, whe the reinforcement learning loop is repeated during t timesteps until the training finish This framework is generic and will allow us, in Section 4.3, to train and compare differe RL Models using the same FlexSim environment.

In line with the growing interest in this subject, in 2022, FlexSim released a versio of its software that simplifies the work of setting up FlexSim as an environment for R training. The software now contains a graphical user interface in which the differe elements required for training an RL algorithm can be easily set up, namely, the observatio space, the reward function, and the actions. The interface provided can communicate wit an external program, written in any programming language, which in turn is required have the corresponding functions or methods for exchanging messages with FlexSim.

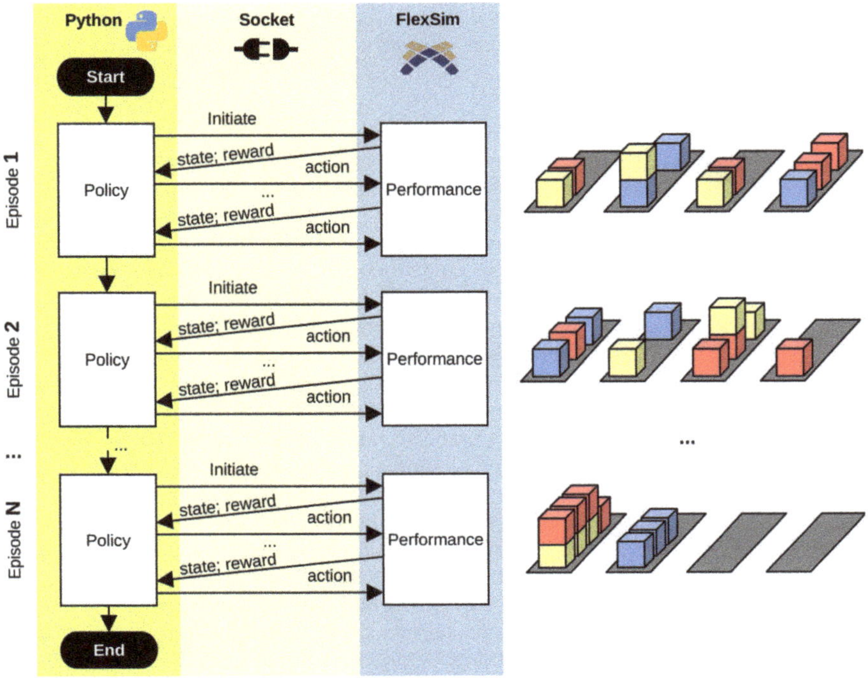

Figure 2. Schematic representation of the reinforcement learning framework implemented and simplified view of the use case.

Algorithm 1 Reinforcement learning framework.

Input: Environment, Agent
Output: Agent ▷ The trained Agent with the learned Policy
initialize($Agent$)
while $t \leq maxTimeStep$ **do** ▷ Equivalent to running $\sim N$ Episodes
  $s_t, r_t \leftarrow$ initialize($Environment$) ▷ Start a new Episode = instance of FlexSim
  while isFinished($Environment$) $\neq$ **true do**
    $Agent \leftarrow$ updatePolicy(s_t, r_t) ▷ Learning from current state and reward
    $a_t \leftarrow$ chooseAction($Agent, s_t$) ▷ Using the best available Policy
    $t+1 \leftarrow$ step($Environment, a_t$)
    $s_{t+1}, r_{t+1} \leftarrow$ observe($Environment$)
    $s_t, r_t \leftarrow s_{t+1}, r_{t+1}$
    $t \leftarrow t+1$
  close($Environment$)
return Agent
end

4. Case Study

This section provides a detailed description of the case study used to illustrate the application of RL algorithms in a FlexSim simulated environment. Firstly, the warehouse environment is explained, outlining the different elements contained in it and the configuration of the main RL components, namely, actions, observations, and rewards. After that, three different but well-known RL algorithms were trained within it, in order to observe the difference in performance. In order to do so, the case study is divided in a small validation instance and a larger performance instance. Finally, the outcomes of the RL training and a brief discussion on performance are presented. All implemented algorithms are coded in

Python and run on a Windows 10 operating system, with an i7-10750H CPU 2.60 GHz and 16 GB RAM. FlexSim version 22.1.2 was employed for the simulation model.

4.1. Use Case Description

The case study developed in this work is a simplified but dynamic version of a storage location assignment problem (SLAP), where items arrive at an entry point and have to be stored in different racks. In the most generic version, the goal of the SLAP is to define the optimal allocation for items in the available locations in a given warehouse, while considering the impact of this allocation on the handling cost or the storage space efficiency. The use of predefined policies (e.g., random, fixed, or class-based) is one of the most common approaches for dealing with the SLAP in a real-life warehouse context. In the version presented herein, the location assignment needs to be made upon the arrival of the items, as opposed to being predefined for the entire warehouse. This means that the problem is, in that sense, dynamic because the policy can change with time depending on the current status of the warehouse. The dynamism just described increases the difficulty of solving the SLAP, which could be arduous to solve using classic methods for warehouse optimization, such as metaheuristics. This type of dynamic problem, which requires real-time decision-making, could be potentially better addressed by employing either learnheuristics [53] or, as proposed in this paper, an RL agent that learns the policy to be applied given the status of the warehouse and the incoming items. In order to compensate for the additional difficulty of the use case problem definition, a minimalistic problem set-up will be considered, as shown in Figure 3.

The available locations of the warehouse are reduced to only four locations in which the incoming products can be placed. The rate at which the items arrive to the input point is fixed, and the type of products that arrive belong to four different categories (A, B, C, and D), depending on how frequently they are received in (or shipped out from) the warehouse. The movement frequency is assigned to the items according to a certain probability distribution, in particular, items of type A arrive and are requested with a 50% chance, items of type B arrive and are requested with 31% probability, items type C arrive and are requested with 13% probability, and items type D arrive and are requested with 6% probability. Furthermore, the capacity of the racks is limited to 50 items. This implies that given the relative position of the rack with respect to the input and output points, there are locations (racks) in the warehouse that are more convenient than others depending on the product type and the space available. Hence, the goal is to let an artificial intelligence autonomously learn what are the most convenient locations for the next arriving product given the current status of the warehouse. In order to verify if the artificial intelligence (i.e., the trained RL model) is actually learning the best possible policy, a couple of benchmark policies were defined. These are the random policy (Algorithm 2) and the greedy policy (Algorithm 3). In Section 4.5, the results of these policies are compared against the results from the RL framework shown in Algorithm 1.

This simplified setting has some advantages for the purposes of this work: *(i)* the time for training the algorithm can be reduced, since the FlexSim simulation can run to termination very quickly, allowing for more learning episodes to be employed; *(ii)* the number of factors influencing the evolution of the simulation is limited, so the decisions made by the RL agent can still be interpreted to a great extent by researchers and practitioners; *(iii)* the performance of policy obtained can be validated, given the fact that a very effective policy for this warehouse set-up is known beforehand, namely, a greedy policy; and *(iv)* a simple and well-defined warehouse scenario, for which the performance metric is easy to obtain, could be employed as a benchmark instance for future research efforts. On the last point, a FlexSim simulation environment could be added to a collection of environments used for validation and benchmarking of RL algorithms, such as the one available for the Python Gym library, which is presented below.

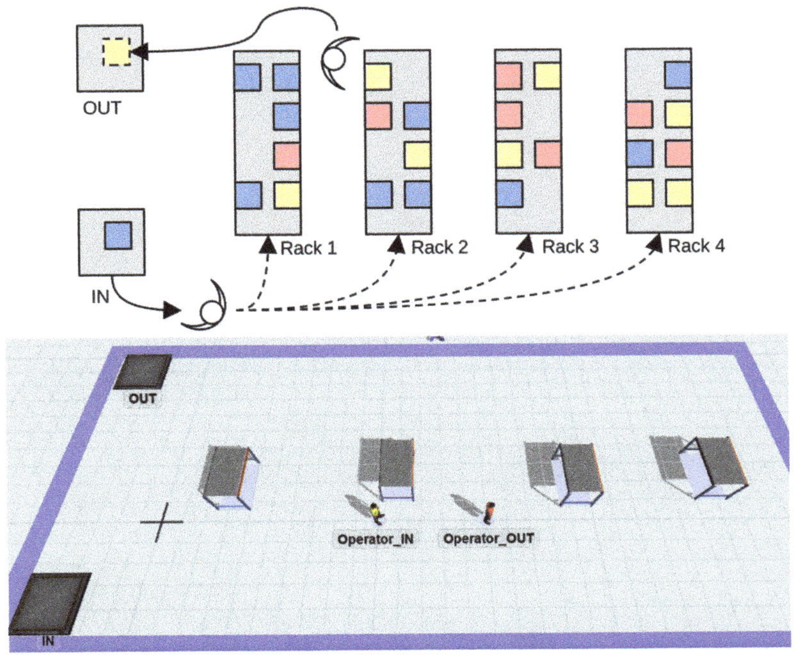

Figure 3. Schematic representation of the use case (**top**) and screenshot of the simulation set-up (**bottom**). It can be seen that the positions of the input (IN) and output (OUT) points make the first storage location the most appropriate for reducing the traveled distance of the operators, if no other restriction is considered.

Algorithm 2 Random policy.

Input: Item, Locations
Output: Location ▷ Location ∈ Locations to which the Item is assigned

while isAssigned($Item$) $\neq$ **true do**
  $k \leftarrow$ randomUniformBetween($1, count(Locations)$)
  $Location \leftarrow$ selectLocation($Locations, k$)
  if isFull($Location$) $=$ **true then**
    $Locations \leftarrow$ removeLocation($Locations, Location$)
  else
    $Location \leftarrow$ assignItem($Location, Item$)
return Location
end

Algorithm 3 Greedy policy.

Input: Item, Locations
Output: Location

while isAssigned($Item$) $\neq$ **true do**
  $k \leftarrow$ minDistance($Locations, Item$)
  $Location \leftarrow$ selectLocation($Locations, k$)
  if isFull($Location$) $=$ **true then**
    $Locations \leftarrow$ removeLocation($Locations, Location$)
  else
    $Location \leftarrow$ assignItem($Location, Item$)
return Location
end

4.2. Simulation Environment

In Figure 2 and in Algorithm 1, how the classical RL loop (action–state–rewa was embedded in a communication framework between the Python RL algorithm a the FlexSim environment is shown. The simulation model contained two pickers, o dedicated to the input activity and one dedicated to the output activity. Given that only o product is picked during each travel, there is no requirement for a specific routing poli Instead, the optimal route between the input or output point and the racks is determin using the A^* algorithm, avoiding collision with the various obstacles present (namely, rac and the other worker). To prevent overcomplicating the model, the rest of the paramete such as pickers' average speed or processing times, were left to the FlexSim default valu As described in Section 4.1, the action to be taken by the RL agent is the warehouse locati where to place the next item. This means that the action space is discrete and can take integer value between 1 and 4, representing each one of the four racks shown in Figure In order to learn from the environment, the current state of all the location are sent back observations to the learning agent. This means that the observation space is also discre consisting in the integer amount of product of each type per rack. The incoming item also sent as part of the observations. The observation of the environment status is ma every time that a new item arrives (set at a fixed interval), and the information of the ne item is also included in the observation, codified as an integer (type A = 1, type B = 2, etc Finally, the reward used for updating the RL policy is based on the distance workers ne to travel within the warehouse to position and retrieve the items. The objective functi or metrics used to evaluate and optimize SLAP can vary depending on the specific goa and requirements of the problem. Some common objective metrics include travel distan retrieval time, space utilization, and handling costs. In many studies reviewed by [the total travel distance is commonly employed as the objective metric. Hence, in th case study, we adopt the travel distance as the reward function for our RL algorithm In particular, the main driver for the reward is the inverse of the difference between th travelled distance in the current time step and the previous time step, so that a high reward is obtained when the difference is smaller. Following the classical RL notation, th formula for the selected reward can be expressed as follows:

$$r_t = R(s_t, s_{t-1}, a_{t-1}) = \frac{C}{d(a_{t-1}, s_t) - d(a_{t-1}, s_{t-1})}, \quad (\ $$

where r_t is the actual reward obtained at time-step t, which is a function R that depen on the current state s_t, the previous action a_{t-1}, and previous state s_{t-1}. The function calculated based on a constant C, which can be tuned to aid the learning, and the differen in total traveled distance d between current and previous state. We decided to refer th reward to the previous state and previous action in order to maintain the Markov propert and to ensure that the agent is learning within a Markov Decision Process where the curre state is dependent only upon the previous state and action.

4.3. Reinforcement Learning Implementations

Following the example provided by FlexSim on their web page (https://docs.flexsi com/en/22.1/ModelLogic/ReinforcementLearning/KeyConcepts/KeyConcepts.html, a cessed on 26 August 2023), the case study presented herein used the Python OpenAI Gy library [54] and the Stable-Baselines3 implementations of RL algorithms [55]. Gym is a open source Python library that provides a standard API to communicate between RL alg rithms and a collection of environments which simulate various real-world situations, i this case with FlexSim. Similarly, Stable-Baselines3 is a popular open source Python libra built on top of PyTorch, providing a collection of state-of-the-art RL algorithms. It is part the Stable-Baselines project, which aims to offer reliable and well-tested implementatio of various RL algorithms, making it easy for researchers and practitioners to experime with and apply these algorithms to their specific problems. Three different RL algorith from Stable-Baselines3 were employed in this paper: *(i)* Advantage Actor Critic (A2C), *(ii)* Proximal Policy Optimization (PPO), and *(iii)* Deep Q-Network (DQN) algorithms.

A2C is an on-policy reinforcement learning algorithm that combines elements of both policy gradient methods and value function approximation [56]. It involves training an actor (policy) network and a critic (value) network simultaneously. The actor is responsible for selecting actions, while the critic evaluates the value of state–action pairs. The advantage function, which represents how much better or worse an action is compared with the average action in a given state, plays a crucial role in A2C. During training, the actor network is updated using the policy gradient technique to maximize the expected cumulative reward. The critic network is updated to minimize the difference between the estimated value function and the actual cumulative reward. A2C often exhibits good sample efficiency and is relatively easy to implement compared with other algorithms. PPO is an on-policy RL algorithm that addresses some of the limitations of traditional policy gradient methods [57]. PPO optimizes the policy by iteratively updating it in a way that avoids large policy updates, which could lead to instability during training. The key idea behind PPO is to clip the objective function during optimization to prevent drastic changes in the policy. This clipping, referred to as the "surrogate objective", ensures that the updated policy remains close to the previous one. PPO also uses multiple epochs of mini-batch updates to improve data efficiency. DQN is an off-policy Q-learning algorithm that leverages deep neural networks to approximate the Q-function, which estimates the expected cumulative reward for each state–action pair [58]. DQN introduced the idea of using deep learning to represent the Q-function, allowing it to handle high-dimensional state spaces like images. The algorithm employs an experience replay buffer to store and sample transitions from past interactions with the environment. It uses a target network with delayed updates to stabilize the training process. During training, DQN minimizes the mean squared error between the Q-value predictions and the target Q-values, which are calculated using the Bellman equation.

4.4. Training Results

In the current study, the total number of time steps used for training the models was fixed to 200,000, and the simulation time of FlexSim model was fixed to 5000 s. In addition, all three different RL algorithm hyperparameters were set to the default values provided via Stable-Baselines3. In fact, the hyperparameters were left unmodified since a good performance was expected with the default hyperparameter values.

Figure 4 shows the average reward obtained during the training process for three different RL algorithms, where the horizontal and vertical axes represent the timesteps of the training process and the obtained average reward, respectively. Notice that for every RL algorithm, as the training time advances, the average reward tends to increase, finally reaching an average reward of around 85. This trend indicates that the agent has learned how to place items based on the received reward, until the reward cannot be further increased. The differences in learning behavior observed among the three RL algorithms can be attributed to the underlying design and optimization strategies of the algorithms. The A2C algorithm's behavior seems the most efficient, as in the initial phase of the training process, there is a very short descending trend in the average reward, corresponding to the exploration phase. Subsequently, as the training time advances, the average reward increases steadily, quickly reaching a plateau for the rest of the training process. Similarly, the PPO algorithm exhibits a short exploration phase in the initial training process, and as the training time advances, the average reward increases steadily. However, the average reward oscillates in the later stages of training, indicating that the PPO algorithm incorporates some exploration during the exploitation phase. In contrast, the DQN algorithm behaves somewhat differently from the other RL algorithms. The ample descending trend in the mean reward in the initial phase of the training process can be attributed to a long exploration phase, where the agent explores suboptimal actions and learns from its mistakes. Once it has collected sufficient data, the algorithm starts exploiting the learned Q-values and improves its performance. This is not surprising, a DQN is a value-based algorithm that learns to approximate the optimal Q-value functio using a deep neural network. This approach generally requires more training time tha A2C and PPO due to the algorithm's need to explore the state–action space to learn th optimal Q-values.

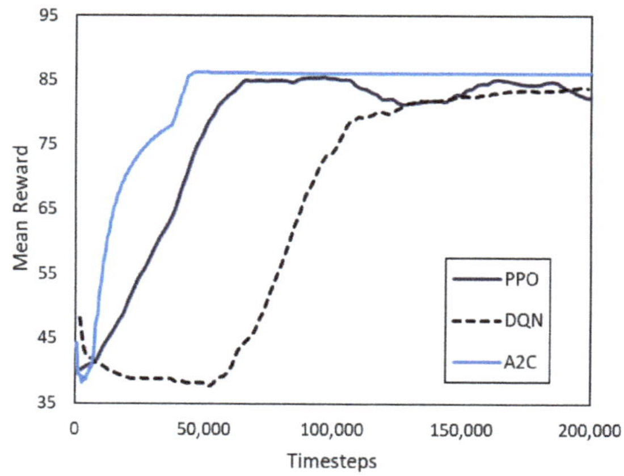

Figure 4. Comparison of the mean reward evolution during training for three different RL algorithm using the use case simulation as environment.

4.5. Validation Results

Table 2 show the main results obtained for the use case when applying the differen trained policies. The first metric evaluated is simply the distance traveled by the operators which is used as a reward for the learning, as explained above. The second one is th number of processed items during the time defined for each simulation episode. In orde to evaluate the productivity and efficiency of a warehouse (or any production system i general), a very common metric is the throughput, which evaluates the number of item processed per unit time. This is provided as the last metric in the table, which is equivalen to the number of items since the simulation time for each episode is fixed.

Table 2. Main results of the validation use case, comparing the different benchmark policies (random and greedy) against the RL agent learned policy (PPO, DQN, and A2C).

Policy	Distance Traveled (m)	Items Processed	Throughput (Items/min)
Random	7763	172	2.06
Greedy	6680	241	2.89
PPO	6801	241	2.89
DQN	6894	241	2.89
A2C	6676	241	2.89

The random policy (see Algorithm 2) can be considered the lower bound for evaluating the learning performance of the RL algorithm. On the other hand, the greedy policy (see Algorithm 3) can be used as a reference for the performance of the RL policies. This is because, if the available space within each rack is not limited, the greedy strategy is in fact the best possible strategy: the items would be placed and retrieved from the first rack minimizing the traveled distance. However, due to the fact that a restriction in the numbe of items per rack was introduced, the greedy strategy is not the best possible strategy. Th reason is that placing all items in the first rack regardless of their movement class (A, B C, and D) or the state of the racks could result in filling up the first rack and being forced to place less frequent incoming items further away, which then are to be retrieved from those far away positions. On the contrary, if some space is saved in the first rack for the less frequent items, they can be input and output directly from the first rack, reducing the overall travel distance. It can be seen that the results for the different RL policies match and, in the case of the A2C algorithm, even slightly improving those of the greedy policy. This means that the RL agents are indeed learning from the underlying structure of the problem and proposing a very competitive policy. For illustrative purposes, Figure 5 shows the graphical outputs of the simulation for the untrained (random) and the trained RL policy (PPO), so they can be compared visually. With this simple but effective use case, it is demonstrated that the use of standard RL libraries in combination with advanced simulation environments can be used for training an artificial intelligence to find efficient policies that take into account realistic conditions such as those present in a warehouse.

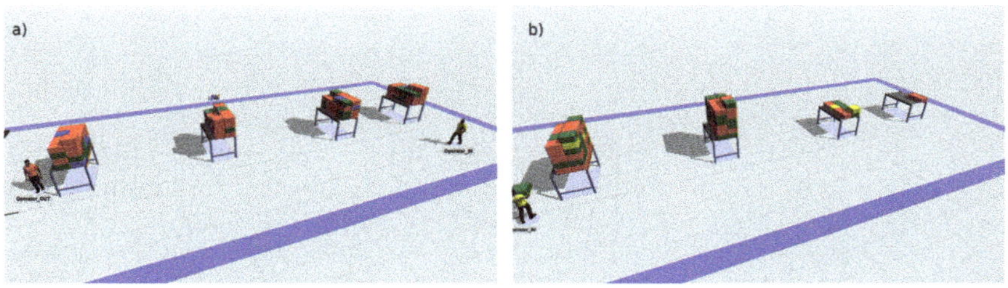

Figure 5. Screenshot of the result (**a**) when the random policy is used and (**b**) when the trained RL policy (PPO) is used. It can be seen that in (**a**) that products are stored without following an assignment logic (at random) in all four racks. In (**b**), most items are placed in the first two racks, resulting in a reduced overall travel distance for the operators.

4.6. Performance Discussion

In order to understand the implications of scaling up the validation use case in the algorithm's performance, an extended simulation instance was developed as shown in Figure 6. The RL training procedure described in Algorithm 1 was undertaken using the new instance and the RL implementations already presented in Section 4.3. It can be observed that the number of racks was doubled, from four to eight racks, which could represent a more realistic warehouse instance. The rest of the elements present in the simulation were kept the same (workers, input and output points, etc.) so that the impact of the increase in warehouse size can be fairly assessed. Also, the reward function defined in Equation (1) and the RL hyperparameters (learning rates, discount factors, etc.) were kept unmodified. It is important to note that the main aim of this section is not to compare the different RL implementation to find the "best" one but, rather, to showcase what there are the differences between them and how the algorithm performance was affected by the increase in size of the validation instance.

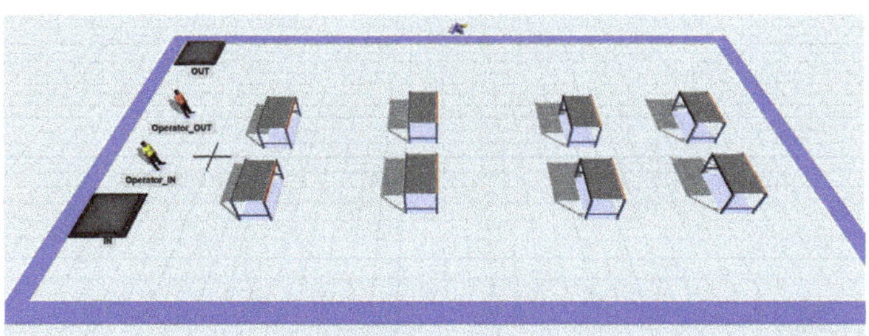

Figure 6. Screenshot of the simulation environment considered for evaluating the performance of the RL algorithm in bigger instances. The eight racks were distributed in two rows and four columns.

The three RL implementations presented in Section 4.3 were able to learn and provi very similar result in the extended instance. This meant that the different RL algorith "understood" the simulation environment context and maximized their expected reward the successive training episodes until the learning rate stabilized. Nonetheless, significa differences could be observed between the three different RL implementations in term of their learning profile, as it is shown in Figure 7, where the curves were normalized, i. scaled so that the values fall between 0 and 1. This adjustment was performed because t absolute value of the reward is not important (it depends on a constant and the distan covered according to Equation (1)); the critical aspect is to understand if the RL age is learning a policy that can provide good actions that can lead to increase in reward the following environment states. The normalization allows for comparing the learnir behavior across different instances, with potentially different distances between racks. It important to note that the computational effort is equivalent in both the validation use ca (four racks) and the performance use case (eight racks) simply because the length of t training is a parameter that can be adjusted. As in the validation case (see Section 4.4), t number of timesteps for training was set to 200,000.

One interesting result is the fact that both the DQN and the A2C algorithms display a very similar training behavior in both instances, suggesting that their learning profi was not significantly affected by the increased size of the warehouse. This is very like linked to the use of the default hyperparameters, which controls how the algorithm tra and learn from the simulation environment. A noticeable difference between both instanc for those RL algorithms are the "ripples" that can be observed in the eight-rack instan curves. These undulations on the curves could be interpreted as the increased difficul that the RL agent finds to the learning in the bigger instance, i.e., finding the best rack for given item given that the current status is not as simple due to the larger observational an action spaces and, hence, the learning progress is not as stable. On the other hand, the PP algorithm displayed a difference in behavior between both instances. In spite of the overa shape being very similar, the PPO algorithm in the eight-rack instance presents a delay about 50,000 timesteps, making the slope of learning progress much less steep. Also, t decrease in mean reward after reaching the plateau (signifying an exploratory phase of t training) is much deeper in the eight-rack instance for the same reasons provided for t uneven curves in the DQN and A2C algorithms. However, even if the learning curves a similar (or almost equivalent in the DQN and A2C implementations), this does not mea that the quality of the learning is the same as in the validation use case, as can be seen Table 3.

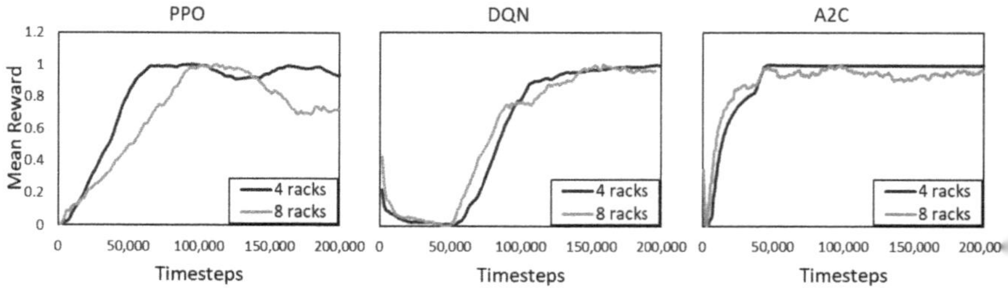

Figure 7. Comparison of the normalized mean reward evolution during training for the thr RL algorithms in both the validation environment (four racks) and the performance environme (eight racks).

Table 3. Main results of the extended use case, comparing the different benchmark policies (random and greedy) against the RL agent learned policy (PPO, DQN, and A2C).

Policy	Distance Traveled (m)	Items Processed	Throughput (Items/min)
Random	8813	172	2.06
Greedy	6663	241	2.89
PPO	8302	241	2.89
DQN	7084	241	2.89
A2C	8704	241	2.89

As in the validation use case (four racks), the RL agents managed to correctly allocate the incoming items, keeping the warehouse throughput at its optimal value, which is the same as the greedy heuristic (see Algorithm 3). Nonetheless, the final travelled distance is greater than that of the greedy heuristic in all cases (and, as expected, always smaller than the random heuristic), with the DQN implementation being the one that provided the best results in terms of distance. For the four-rack validation instance, the A2C implementation managed to find a policy that, while keeping the optimal throughput, also reduced the travelled distance with respect to the greedy heuristic (see Section 4.5). In the extended instance (eight racks), due to the increased observation and action space, finding such a favorable policy was much more complicated. In any case, this study demonstrates that the learning capacity is maintained for the proposed RL algorithm, even under significant modifications to the environment (i.e., doubling the number of racks). The impact in performance due to a change in the environment is not straightforward to quantify due to the number of factors involved, and the difference between different RL implementations. Furthermore, it is common practice in the RL community to treat each problem instance as a problem on its own, with the necessary parameter tuning and reward calibration to achieve a satisfactory learning. In our case, a careful comparison has been carried out by keeping all factors equal except the number of racks available (which was doubled), finding that the performance is maintained in terms of throughput, but that the travelled distance performance, measured as the difference between the algorithm result and the greedy algorithm result), dropped for all RL implementations. The greatest loss in performance was for the A2C algorithm, with a 31% reduction, followed by the PPO algorithm, with a 23% reduction. Finally, the DQN algorithm, with the use of deep neural networks and a longer exploratory phase, maintained performance, with only a 3% drop in performance.

5. Key Applications and Open Research Lines

Simulation has been increasingly used in warehouse operations. Some of the key applications include the following:

- Process Optimization: analyze and optimize various processes, such as receiving, put-away, picking, packing, and shipping. Managers can identify bottlenecks, test process changes, etc.;
- Layout and Design: design and optimize the layout, including the placement of racks, shelves, etc.;
- Resource Allocation: optimize the allocation of resources, such as labor, equipment, and space;
- Inventory Management: analyze and optimize inventory management strategies, such as reorder points, safety stock levels, and order quantities;
- Demand Forecasting: simulate demand patterns and forecast inventory requirements;
- Labor Planning and Scheduling: optimize labor planning and scheduling;
- Equipment and Automation: evaluate the impact of equipment and automation technologies, such as conveyor systems, automated guided vehicles, and robots.

The main applications of RL in warehouse operations include the following:

- Warehouse Management: optimize tasks such as inventory management, order picking, and routing;
- Autonomous Robots: train autonomous robots for tasks such as automated material handling, order fulfillment, and package sorting. Robots can learn how to navigate in complex warehouse environments, handle different types of items, and interact with other equipment and personnel;
- Resource Allocation: optimize the allocation of resources such as labor, equipment, and space;
- Energy Management: optimize energy consumption, which can have a significant impact on operational costs. For example, an agent can learn to control the usage of lighting, heating, and ventilation, based on occupancy, time of day, and other environmental factors;
- Safety and Security: for example, an agent can learn to detect and respond to safety hazards, such as obstacles in pathways, spills, or damaged equipment.

The combination of advanced simulation environments and RL represents a new field that remains to be completely explored. Here are a few promising research directions:

- Wider range of applications in warehouse operations. As manufacturing and logistics systems grow more complex and businesses seek to remain both competitive and sustainable, the increasing availability of data as well as new technologies through Industry 4.0 is expected to open up a wider range of applications in warehouse operations. This will give rise to a greater number of decision variables, objective functions, and restrictions.
- Emergence of DRL. DRL holds significant potential over traditional RL due to its ability to handle high-dimensional and complex state spaces through deep neural networks. DRL allows for more efficient and automated feature extraction, enabling the model to learn directly from raw data.
- Distributed and parallel techniques. Distributed and parallel RL can accelerate the learning process by allowing multiple agents to learn concurrently. Moreover, this approach can improve scalability, as it enables RL algorithms to handle larger and more complex state spaces. Finally, distributed and parallel RL can provide robustness and fault tolerance, as multiple agents can work in parallel, and failures or perturbations in one agent do not necessarily disrupt the entire learning process.
- Explicability. Explicability is important for building trust and acceptance of RL systems, as users may be hesitant to adopt decision-making systems that lack transparency and understanding. In addition, it can aid in understanding and diagnosing model behaviour, facilitating debugging, troubleshooting, and identifying potential biases or ethical concerns. Lastly, explicability can be crucial for compliance with regulatory requirements in domains where transparency and accountability are essential.
- Metaheuristics. Metaheuristics hold potential for various applications in RL. Firstly, they can be used for hyperparameter tuning in RL algorithms to optimize the performance of agents. Secondly, metaheuristics can be employed for policy search, where they can explore the policy space to find promising policies for RL agents. Lastly, they can aid in solving complex problems in RL with high-dimensional state and action spaces, where traditional RL algorithms may struggle, by providing effective search strategies for discovering good policies. The combination of RL with metaheuristics and simheuristics [59] is also an open challenge.

6. Conclusions

Simulation has emerged as a powerful tool for optimizing decision-making in warehouses, for instance, by analyzing and optimizing various processes, including receiving, put-away, picking, packing, and shipping. By creating virtual models of warehouses and simulating different scenarios, managers can identify bottlenecks and test process changes among others. In particular, the combination of simulation and RL offers a flexible approach for training intelligent agents in complex and dynamic environments, while mitigating challenges associated with replicating difficult or expensive scenarios in the real world. This paper showcases the integration of the FlexSim commercial simulator and the RL OpenAI Gym library in Python. Thus, we deliberately focus on a simplified version of the SLAP to highlight the connection between both components to demonstrate its feasibility. The effectiveness of the approach is validated through a set of experiments. However, enhancing the case study to reflect more complex and realistic scenarios is crucial for its broader applicability and relevance to practical settings.

Several avenues for future research can be identified, which could be categorized into three key domains: *(i)* enriching the SLAP modelization to describe more realistic and large-scale problems, showing that the combination of FlexSim with RL can handle these problems efficiently to deliver good performance in real-world contexts; *(ii)* conducting a more extensive series of experiments to compare various scenarios; and *(iii)* examining the performance of different RL algorithms and conducting sensitivity analyses to explore the impact of different algorithmic parameters.

Author Contributions: Conceptualization, J.F.L. and A.A.J.; methodology, J.F.L., Y.L. and X.A.M.; validation, L.C. and J.P.; writing—original draft preparation, J.F.L., Y.L., X.A.M., L.C. and J.P.; writing—review and editing, A.A.J.; supervision, A.A.J. All authors have read and agreed to the published version of the manuscript.

Funding: This work has been supported by the European Commission (SUN HORIZON-CL4-2022-HUMAN-01-14-101092612 and AIDEAS HORIZON-CL4-2021-TWIN-TRANSITION-01-07-101057294), FlexSim, Spindox, the Industrial Doctorate Program of the Catalan Government (2020-DI-116), and the Investigo Program of the Generalitat Valenciana (INVEST/2022/342).

Institutional Review Board Statement: Not applicable.

Informed Consent Statement: Not applicable.

Data Availability Statement: Not applicable.

Conflicts of Interest: The authors declare no conflicts of interest.

eferences

1. Zhang, L.; Zhou, L.; Ren, L.; Laili, Y. Modeling and Simulation in Intelligent Manufacturing. *Comput. Ind.* **2019**, *112*, 103123. [CrossRef]
2. Leon, J.F.; Li, Y.; Peyman, M.; Calvet, L.; Juan, A.A. A Discrete-Event Simheuristic for Solving a Realistic Storage Location Assignment Problem. *Mathematics* **2023**, *11*, 1577. [CrossRef]
3. Sutton, R.S.; Barto, A.G. *Reinforcement Learning: An Introduction*; MIT Press: Cambridge, MA, USA, 2018.
4. Yan, Y.; Chow, A.H.; Ho, C.P.; Kuo, Y.H.; Wu, Q.; Ying, C. Reinforcement Learning for Logistics and Supply Chain Management: Methodologies, State of the Art, and Future Opportunities. *Transp. Res. Part E Logist. Transp. Rev.* **2022**, *162*, 102712. [CrossRef]
5. Nordgren, W.B. FlexSim Simulation Environment. In Proceedings of the Winter Simulation Conference, San Diego, CA, USA, 8–11 December 2002; Chick, S., Sánchez, P.J., Ferrin, D., Morrice, D.J., Eds.; Institute of Electrical and Electronics Engineers, Inc.: Orem, UT, USA, 2002; pp. 250–252.
6. Van Rossum, G.; Drake, F.L. *Python 3 Reference Manual*; CreateSpace: Scotts Valley, CA, USA, 2009.
7. Leon, J.F.; Marone, P.; Peyman, M.; Li, Y.; Calvet, L.; Dehghanimohammadabadi, M.; Juan, A.A. A Tutorial on Combining Flexsim With Python for Developing Discrete-Event Simheuristics. In Proceedings of the 2022 Winter Simulation Conference (WSC), Singapore, 11–14 December 2022; Institute of Electrical and Electronics Engineers, Inc.: Singapore, 2022; pp. 1386–1400.
8. Reyes, J.; Solano-Charris, E.; Montoya-Torres, J. The Storage Location Assignment Problem: A Literature Review. *Int. J. Ind. Eng. Comput.* **2019**, *10*, 199–224. [CrossRef]
9. Kinoshita, M.; Watanabe, M.; Kawakami, T.; Kakazu, Y. Emergence of field intelligence for autonomous block agents in the automatic warehouse. *Intell. Eng. Syst. Through Artif. Neural Netw.* **1999**, *9*, 1129–1134.
10. Rao, J.J.; Ravulapati, K.K.; Das, T.K. A simulation-based approach to study stochastic inventory-planning games. *Int. J. Syst. Sci.* **2003**, *34*, 717–730. [CrossRef]
11. Yan, W.; Lin, C.; Pang, S. The Optimized Reinforcement Learning Approach to Run-Time Scheduling in Data Center. In Proceedings of the 2010 Ninth International Conference on Grid and Cloud Computing, Nanjing, China, 1–5 November 2010; pp. 46–51.

12. Estanjini, R.M.; Li, K.; Paschalidis, I.C. A least squares temporal difference actor-critic algorithm with applications to warehou management. *Nav. Res. Logist.* **2012**, *59*, 197–211. [CrossRef]
13. Dou, J.; Chen, C.; Yang, P. Genetic Scheduling and Reinforcement Learning in Multirobot Systems for Intelligent Warehous *Math. Probl. Eng.* **2015**, *2015*. [CrossRef]
14. Rabe, M.; Dross, F. A reinforcement learning approach for a decision support system for logistics networks. In Proceedings of t 2015 Winter Simulation Conference (WSC), Huntington Beach, CA, USA, 6–9 December 2015; pp. 2020–2032.
15. Wang, Z.; Chen, C.; Li, H.X.; Dong, D.; Tarn, T.J. A novel incremental learning scheme for reinforcement learning in dynam environments. In Proceedings of the 2016 12th World Congress on Intelligent Control and Automation (WCICA), Guilin, Chi 12–15 June 2016; pp. 2426–2431.
16. Drakaki, M.; Tzionas, P. Manufacturing scheduling using Colored Petri Nets and reinforcement learning. *Appl. Sci.* **2017**, *7*, 1 [CrossRef]
17. Kono, H.; Katayama, R.; Takakuwa, Y.; Wen, W.; Suzuki, T. Activation and spreading sequence for spreading activation poli selection method in transfer reinforcement learning. *Int. J. Adv. Comput. Sci. Appl.* **2019**, *10*, 7–16. [CrossRef]
18. Li, M.P.; Sankaran, P.; Kuhl, M.E.; Ganguly, A.; Kwasinski, A.; Ptucha, R. Simulation analysis of a deep reinforcement learni approach for task selection by autonomous material handling vehicles. In Proceedings of the 2018 Winter Simulation Conferen (WSC), Gothenburg, Sweden, 9–12 December 2018; pp. 1073–1083.
19. Sartoretti, G.; Kerr, J.; Shi, Y.; Wagner, G.; Satish Kumar, T.; Koenig, S.; Choset, H. PRIMAL: Pathfinding via Reinforcement a Imitation Multi-Agent Learning. *IEEE Robot. Autom. Lett.* **2019**, *4*, 2378–2385. [CrossRef]
20. Li, M.P.; Sankaran, P.; Kuhl, M.E.; Ptucha, R.; Ganguly, A.; Kwasinski, A. Task Selection by Autonomous Mobile Robots in Warehouse Using Deep Reinforcement Learning. In Proceedings of the 2019 Winter Simulation Conference, National Harbor, M USA, 8–11 December 2019; Institute of Electrical and Electronics Engineers, Inc.: National Harbor, MD, USA, 2019; pp. 680–68
21. Barat, S.; Kumar, P.; Gajrani, M.; Khadilkar, H.; Meisheri, H.; Baniwal, V.; Kulkarni, V. Reinforcement Learning of Supply Cha Control Policy Using Closed Loop Multi-agent Simulation. In *International Workshop on Multi-Agent Systems and Agent-Bas Simulation*; Lecture Notes in Computer Science (Including Subseries Lecture Notes in Artificial Intelligence and Lecture Notes Bioinformatics); Springer International Publishing: Cham, Switzerland, 2020; Volume 12025 LNAI, pp. 26–38.
22. Sun, Y.; Li, H. An end-to-end reinforcement learning method for automated guided vehicle path planning. In Proceedings the International Symposium on Artificial Intelligence and Robotics 2020, Kitakyushu, Japan, 1–10 August 2020; Volume 115 pp. 296–310.
23. Xiao, Y.; Hoffman, J.; Xia, T.; Amato, C. Learning multi-robot decentralized macro-action-based policies via a centralized q-net. Proceedings of the 2020 IEEE International Conference on Robotics and Automation (ICRA), Paris, France, 31 May–31 Augu 2020; pp. 10695–10701.
24. Yang, Y.; Juntao, L.; Lingling, P. Multi-robot path planning based on a deep reinforcement learning DQN algorithm. *CAAI Tra Intell. Technol.* **2020**, *5*, 177–183. [CrossRef]
25. Ushida, Y.; Razan, H.; Sakuma, T.; Kato, S. Policy Transfer from Simulation to Real World for Autonomous Control of an Om Wheel Robot. In Proceedings of the 2020 IEEE 9th Global Conference on Consumer Electronics (GCCE), Kobe, Japan, 13– October 2020; pp. 952–953.
26. Shen, G.; Ma, R.; Tang, Z.; Chang, L. A deep reinforcement learning algorithm for warehousing multi-agv path planning. Proceedings of the 2021 International Conference on Networking, Communications and Information Technology (NetCI Manchester, UK, 26–27 December 2021; pp. 421–429.
27. Newaz, A.A.R.; Alam, T. Hierarchical Task and Motion Planning through Deep Reinforcement Learning. In Proceedings of t 2021 Fifth IEEE International Conference on Robotic Computing (IRC), Taichung, Taiwan, 5–17 November 2021; pp. 100–105.
28. Peyas, I.S.; Hasan, Z.; Tushar, M.R.R.; Musabbir, A.; Azni, R.M.; Siddique, S. Autonomous Warehouse Robot using De Q-Learning. In Proceedings of the TENCON 2021–2021 IEEE Region 10 Conference (TENCON), Auckland, New Zealand, 7– December 2021; pp. 857–862.
29. Ha, W.Y.; Cui, L.; Jiang, Z.P. A Warehouse Scheduling Using Genetic Algorithm and Collision Index. In Proceedings of the 20 20th International Conference on Advanced Robotics (ICAR), Ljubljana, Slovenia, 6–10 December 2021; pp. 318–323.
30. Liu, S.; Wen, L.; Cui, J.; Yang, X.; Cao, J.; Liu, Y. Moving Forward in Formation: A Decentralized Hierarchical Learning Approa to Multi-Agent Moving Together. In Proceedings of the 2021 IEEE/RSJ International Conference on Intelligent Robots an Systems (IROS), Prague, Czech Republic, 27 September–1 October 2021; pp. 4777–4784.
31. Ushida, Y.; Razan, H.; Sakuma, T.; Kato, S. Omnidirectional Mobile Robot Path Finding Using Deep Deterministic Policy Gradie for Real Robot Control. In Proceedings of the 2021 IEEE 10th Global Conference on Consumer Electronics (GCCE), Kyoto, Japa 12–15 October 2021; pp. 555–556.
32. Lee, H.; Jeong, J. Mobile Robot Path Optimization Technique Based on Reinforcement Learning Algorithm in Warehou Environment. *Appl. Sci.* **2021**, *11*, 1209. [CrossRef]
33. Tang, H.; Wang, A.; Xue, F.; Yang, J.; Cao, Y. A Novel Hierarchical Soft Actor-Critic Algorithm for Multi-Logistics Robots Ta Allocation. *IEEE Access* **2021**, *9*, 42568–42582. [CrossRef]
34. Li, H.; Li, D.; Wong, W.E.; Zeng, D.; Zhao, M. Kubernetes virtual warehouse placement based on reinforcement learning. *Int. Perform. Eng.* **2021**, *17*, 579–588.

35. Ren, J.; Huang, X. Potential Fields Guided Deep Reinforcement Learning for Optimal Path Planning in a Warehouse. In Proceedings of the 2021 IEEE 7th International Conference on Control Science and Systems Engineering (ICCSSE), Qingdao, China, 30 July–1 August 2021; pp. 257–261.
36. Balachandran, A.; Lal, A.; Sreedharan, P. Autonomous Navigation of an AMR using Deep Reinforcement Learning in a Warehouse Environment. In Proceedings of the 2022 IEEE 2nd Mysore Sub Section International Conference (MysuruCon), Mysuru, India, 16–17 October 2022; pp. 1–5.
37. Arslan, B.; Ekren, B.Y. Transaction selection policy in tier-to-tier SBSRS by using Deep Q-Learning. *Int. J. Prod. Res.* **2022**. [CrossRef]
38. Lewis, T.; Ibarra, A.; Jamshidi, M. Object Detection-Based Reinforcement Learning for Autonomous Point-to-Point Navigation. In Proceedings of the 2022 World Automation Congress (WAC), San Antonio, TX, USA, 11–15 October 2022; pp. 394–399.
39. Ho, T.M.; Nguyen, K.K.; Cheriet, M. Federated Deep Reinforcement Learning for Task Scheduling in Heterogeneous Autonomous Robotic System. *IEEE Trans. Autom. Sci. Eng.* **2022**, 1–13. [CrossRef]
40. Zhou, L.; Lin, C.; Ma, Q.; Cao, Z. A Learning-based Iterated Local Search Algorithm for Order Batching and Sequencing Problems. In Proceedings of the 2022 IEEE 18th International Conference on Automation Science and Engineering (CASE), Mexico City, Mexico, 20–24 August 2022; pp. 1741–1746.
41. Cestero, J.; Quartulli, M.; Metelli, A.M.; Restelli, M. Storehouse: A reinforcement learning environment for optimizing warehouse management. In Proceedings of the 2022 International Joint Conference on Neural Networks (IJCNN), Padua, Italy, 18–23 July 2022; pp. 1–9.
42. Choi, H.B.; Kim, J.B.; Han, Y.H.; Oh, S.W.; Kim, K. MARL-Based Cooperative Multi-AGV Control in Warehouse Systems. *IEEE Access* **2022**, *10*, 100478–100488. [CrossRef]
43. Elkunchwar, N.; Iyer, V.; Anderson, M.; Balasubramanian, K.; Noe, J.; Talwekar, Y.; Fuller, S. Bio-inspired source seeking and obstacle avoidance on a palm-sized drone. In Proceedings of the 2022 International Conference on Unmanned Aircraft Systems (ICUAS), Dubrovnik, Croatia, 21–24 June 2022; pp. 282–289.
44. Wang, D.; Jiang, J.; Ma, R.; Shen, G. Research on Hybrid Real-Time Picking Routing Optimization Based on Multiple Picking Stations. *Math. Probl. Eng.* **2022**, *2022*, 5510749. [CrossRef]
45. Ekren, B.Y.; Arslan, B. A reinforcement learning approach for transaction scheduling in a shuttle-based storage and retrieval system. *Int. Trans. Oper. Res.* **2022**. [CrossRef]
46. Yu, H. Research on Fresh Product Logistics Transportation Scheduling Based on Deep Reinforcement Learning. *Sci. Program.* **2022**, *2022*, 8750580. [CrossRef]
47. Sun, S.; Zhou, J.; Wen, J.; Wei, Y.; Wang, X. A DQN-based cache strategy for mobile edge networks. *Comput. Mater. Contin.* **2022**, *71*, 3277–3291. [CrossRef]
48. Ushida, Y.; Razan, H.; Ishizuya, S.; Sakuma, T.; Kato, S. Using sim-to-real transfer learning to close gaps between simulation and real environments through reinforcement learning. *Artif. Life Robot.* **2022**, *27*, 130–136. [CrossRef]
49. Lee, H.; Hong, J.; Jeong, J. MARL-Based Dual Reward Model on Segmented Actions for Multiple Mobile Robots in Automated Warehouse Environment. *Appl. Sci.* **2022**, *12*, 4703. [CrossRef]
50. Liang, F.; Yu, W.; Liu, X.; Griffith, D.; Golmie, N. Toward Deep Q-Network-Based Resource Allocation in Industrial Internet of Things. *IEEE Internet Things J.* **2022**, *9*, 9138–9150. [CrossRef]
51. Guo, W.; Li, S. Intelligent Path Planning for AGV-UAV Transportation in 6G Smart Warehouse. *Mob. Inf. Syst.* **2023**, *2023*, 4916127. [CrossRef]
52. Yan, Z.; Kreidieh, A.R.; Vinitsky, E.; Bayen, A.M.; Wu, C. Unified Automatic Control of Vehicular Systems with Reinforcement Learning. *IEEE Trans. Autom. Sci. Eng.* **2023**, *20*, 789–804. [CrossRef]
53. Bayliss, C.; Juan, A.A.; Currie, C.S.; Panadero, J. A Learnheuristic Approach for the Team Orienteering Problem with Aerial Drone Motion Constraints. *Appl. Soft Comput.* **2020**, *92*, 106280. [CrossRef]
54. Beysolow T., II. *Applied Reinforcement Learning with Python: With OpenAI Gym, Tensorflow, and Keras*; Apress: New York, NY, USA, 2019.
55. Raffin, A.; Hill, A.; Gleave, A.; Kanervisto, A.; Ernestus, M.; Dormann, N. Stable-Baselines3: Reliable Reinforcement Learning Implementations. *J. Mach. Learn. Res.* **2021**, *22*, 1–8.
56. Mnih, V.; Badia, A.P.; Mirza, M.; Graves, A.; Lillicrap, T.; Harley, T.; Silver, D.; Kavukcuoglu, K. Asynchronous Methods for Deep Reinforcement Learning. In Proceedings of the International Conference on Machine Learning. PMLR, New York, NY, USA, 19–24 June 2016; pp. 1928–1937.
57. Schulman, J.; Wolski, F.; Dhariwal, P.; Radford, A.; Klimov, O. Proximal Policy Optimization Algorithms. *arXiv* **2017**, arXiv:1707.06347.
58. Mnih, V.; Kavukcuoglu, K.; Silver, D.; Graves, A.; Antonoglou, I.; Wierstra, D.; Riedmiller, M. Playing Atari With Deep Reinforcement Learning. *arXiv* **2013**, arXiv:1312.5602.
59. Rabe, M.; Deininger, M.; Juan, A.A. Speeding Up Computational Times in Simheuristics Combining Genetic Algorithms with Discrete-Event Simulation. *Simul. Model. Pract. Theory* **2020**, *103*, 102089. [CrossRef]

algorithms

MDPI

Article

A Multi-Objective Degree-Based Network Anonymization Method

Ola N. Halawi, Faisal N. Abu-Khzam * and Sergio Thoumi

Department of Computer Science and Mathematics, Lebanese American University, Beirut 1102 2801, Lebanon
ola.halawi@lau.edu (O.N.H.); sergio.thoumi@lau.edu (S.T.)
* Correspondence: faisal.abukhzam@lau.edu.lb

Abstract: Enormous amounts of data collected from social networks or other online platforms ar being published for the sake of statistics, marketing, and research, among other objectives. Th consequent privacy and data security concerns have motivated the work on degree-based dat anonymization. In this paper, we propose and study a new multi-objective anonymization approac that generalizes the known degree anonymization problem and attempts at improving it as a mor realistic model for data security/privacy. Our suggested model guarantees a convenient privacy leve based on modifying the degrees in a way that respects some given local restrictions, per node, suc that the total modifications at the global level (in the whole graph/network) are bounded by som given value. The corresponding multi-objective graph realization approach is formulated and solve using Integer Linear Programming to obtain an optimum solution. Our thorough experimenta studies provide empirical evidence of the effectiveness of the new approach, by specifically showin that the introduced anonymization algorithm has a negligible effect on the way nodes are clusterec thereby preserving valuable network information while significantly improving data privacy.

Keywords: data privacy; network data security; anonymization; degree-based anonymization

Citation: Halawi, O.N.; Abu-Khzam, F.N.; Thoumi, S. A Multi-Objective Degree-Based Network Anonymization Method. *Algorithms* **2023**, *16*, 436. https://doi.org/10.3390/a16090436

Academic Editor: Frank Werner

Received: 8 August 2023
Revised: 25 August 2023
Accepted: 27 August 2023
Published: 11 September 2023

1. Introduction

Among the available privacy-preserving techniques for network-based data, degre anonymization proves to be a practical tool in terms of conserving data utility and resistin re-identification attacks. It works by altering the set of edges of a graph so that nodes ar indistinguishable in terms of their degrees. Formally, a graph G is k-degree anonymou if, for every vertex v, there are at least $k-1$ other vertices with the same degree as v [1 This particular type of "hiding in the crowd" guarantees privacy, because an attacker ca identify an individual with a probability of at most $\frac{1}{k}$, where k is the anonymity/securit level desired by the data publisher.

Unfortunately, the above classical definition of degree anonymity is too restrictive Requiring at least k vertices to have the same degree, for each possible vertex degree could have a very high edge-modification cost in large networks. An alternative multi objective optimization approach is proposed in this paper. Our model sets restrictions or the number of added and deleted edges per vertex and relaxes the same-degree restrictior by setting a range parameter on the resulting degrees, so they would be required to b close enough, while not affecting the privacy level. Thus, it extends the real applicability o this type of network data anonymization. We formally define degree anonymization as a multi-objective optimization (or multi-parameterized) problem, as follows.

Multi-Parameterized Degree Anonymization

Given: An undirected graph $G = (V, E)$, positive constraint parameters a, d, a rang parameter t, and an anonymization parameter k.

Question: Can we obtain an anonymous graph $G' = (V, E')$ by adding at most a and deleting at most d edges per single vertex, so that, for each vertex v, we have at least $k-1$ other vertices whose degrees fall into the interval $[degree(v) - t, degree(v) + t]$?

The anonymization parameter k is assumed to be pre-defined by the user based on the desired anonymization level and the type of the given data.

The parameters a, d, and t are computed by the algorithm, as we propose in this paper, to deliver the least cost target solution. It is worth noting that adding local parameters or constraints, typically in graph modification problems, is known to have a notable positive effect on the problem's complexity, while improving the practicality of the model. This was noted in [2] in the context of (multi-parameterized) Cluster Editing, which inspired the above formulation and the work we present in this paper.

The above-proposed model is a generalization of the k-degree anonymization problem, which corresponds to the case where $t = 0$ and $a = d = |V| - 1$. We formulate the resulting graph realization problem as an Integer Linear Programming (ILP) problem. We test the utility of our approach by applying clustering on the initial graph and the modified one after performing our anonymization procedure. The comparison is based on measuring the symmetric difference between clusters. In addition, we compare some graph metrics before and after perturbation.

2. Preliminaries

We assume familiarity with basic graph theory terminology such as adjacency, vertex degree, and neighborhood, among others. Networks, or graphs, are often subject to attacks that are based upon some prior or presumed knowledge about the degrees of some targeted nodes. This is assumed to be one of the most significant types of attacks [3], since it could threaten individuals' privacy by inferring knowledge about the links to a node and the topology of the graph. Other types of attacks that rely on a priori knowledge of the neighborhood of a targeted node, or the corresponding induced subgraph, can be reduced down to knowledge about the degree of that targeted node.

To cope with the above threats, several methods for network data anonymization have been introduced based on the "hiding in the crowd" approach. Popular methods include clustering-based anonymization (see [4–6]) and degree-based anonymization, which we address in this paper. In general, the k-anonymity model aims at altering the structure of a given graph by adding and/or deleting edges or nodes such that each node in the resulting graph is similar to at least $k-1$ other nodes, in terms of a specific property [7,8]. The k-degree-anonymity approach specifies that nodes are indistinguishable by their degrees.

Each graph G can be represented by a sorted (often decreasing) sequence of the degrees of its vertices. We refer to this sequence by $D(G)$, being unique for G. The notion of the k-degree anonymity of a graph can, thus, be reduced to a transformation of its degree sequence into an anonymized one. We seek a minimal number of edge-editing operations.

Definition 1. *Generally, a degree sequence $D(G)$ is k-anonymous if every value in $D(G)$ is repeated at least $k-1$ times. Then, a graph G is k-degree anonymous if its degree sequence is k-anonymous.*

Our approach is divided into two parts. In the first, the descending degree sequence $D(G)$ is computed and anonymized to produce a degree sequence D'. In the second part, G' is constructed so that $D' = D(G')$. This latter procedure is known as graph realization, which we formulate as an ILP problem.

Previous Edge-Editing Methods

The first degree-based anonymization approach seems to be due to Liu and Terzi [9], who proposed a technique that modifies a given graph/network by adding/deleting a certain number of edges to generate a k-degree anonymous graph. While the work of Liu and Terzi is motivated by logical intuitions, they admit that additional work needs to carried out to develop theoretically and practically sound privacy models for graphs.

In some other attempts, the set of vertices is changed instead of the set of edges. F example, Chester et al. proposed an approach that generates new edges between auxilia and real nodes or between auxiliary nodes [10]. For unlabeled graphs, experiment results demonstrated that perturbing the set of vertices changes some important properti of a graph (such as how the nodes cluster) and weakens the "data accuracy" becau of the information loss. In [11], Casas-Roma et al. presented an algorithm for grap anonymization based on the univariate micro-aggregation. It works by modifying the s of edges, based on the univariate micro-aggregation method for data protection.

Another approach by Alavi et al., named the "GAGA Graph Anonymizer", w published in 2019 [12]. Their "Genetic Algorithm for Graph Anonymization" is claime to be the best solution for networks' protection because it overcomes all of the limitatio of other available solutions. Another genetic algorithm was presented in [13]. Genet algorithms, however, are known for their limitation in guaranteeing an optimal (or nea optimal) solution. Moreover, with the increase in problem size, especially with real larg networks, a genetic algorithm tends to slowly converge to a local minimum. In our wor we can achieve optimum solutions, modulo the various parameters, by employing an IL formulation of the problem.

Finally, Bazgan et al. [14] proved that the problem of degree anonymization via edg rotation is NP-Hard. In this problem, instead of deleting or adding edges and vertices, th objective is to find a minimum amount of "edge rotations" that make the graph k-degre anonymous.

3. Generating k-Anonymous Degree Sequences

We present an algorithm (namely Algorithm 1, below) that takes an original grap G and a privacy level k as input and starts by generating the descending ordered degre sequence $D(G)$ and copying it into the target degree sequence D', where the degre modifications are performed. We assume that the privacy level k is given. Otherwise, w compute a privacy level that is most suitable for G, based on the deviation of the degree in D. We leave a detailed description of this latter approach for future work. We apply vector-based approach that divides D' into chunks, or segments, of at least k nodes eac For every segment, we define the constraint parameters a and d, which correspond to th maximum number of edge additions and deletions per single vertex, respectively.

We set a as the absolute value of the difference between the first degree in each segme and the last one minus $2 * t$, and we set $d = a$ as a default value. The average degree i each part is calculated, and the node's degree that is the closest to the average will be set a the degree of the first node in that chunk in D'.

If the degree of the next node does not fall into the interval $[degree(v_1) - t, degree(v_1) +$ then we add, for that node, the required number of edges for its degree to belong to the abov interval. If the number of edges that have to be added exceeds the limit a, then we dele edges from the previous node and add edges to the second node within the allowed rang The algorithm will repeat the same process until D' is all covered.

3.1. Choosing k

As mentioned before, the anonymity value k is chosen based on the purpose o publishing the data and the desired privacy level. The larger the value of k, the mor resistant to attacks the data will be, but the more perturbation to the data set which will b performed. Hence, the challenge in deciding on the value of k is to keep the balance betwee maintaining privacy and utility simultaneously. The literature does not suggest any formul to set the value of k, other than by experimenting. In this paper, we suggest and apply statistical formula to decide on the privacy level that is the most convenient for each dat set, based on the distribution of the degrees of nodes. The formula is centered around th standard deviation of degrees of nodes. The standard deviation tells how the values in th degree sequence vector are spread out from the average. k is proportional to the standard deviation of degrees, which will have a good impact on data utility preservation. Formally:

$$k = \left\lceil \frac{\sigma}{\sqrt{n-1}} \right\rceil$$

where σ is the standard deviation of the values in D. To assure that the final value is a natural whole number, we take the ceiling of the calculated number. If the degrees are relatively close to each other, i.e., the difference between them is small, then our formula would suggest a small value for k, because the standard deviation is insignificant in this case. Working with a small k can guarantee the best solution in terms of utility because the data set does not need major alterations to be anonymized. However, if there is a vast difference between the degrees, i.e., their standard deviation is remarkable, then k would be too large to guarantee a good privacy level.

Algorithm 1: Multi-parameterized k-degree anonymization

```
Input: G = (V,E),k,t ;
Generate D(G); D' ⟵ D(G);
n ⟵ |V|; add ⟵ 1; delete ⟵ 1;
for i = 1; i < n; i = i + k do
    a ⟵ |D'[i] − D'[i + k − 1] − 2 * t|;
    d ⟵ a;
    avg ⟵ Average of degrees;
    j ⟵ Index of the closest node to avg;
    D'[i] ⟵ D'[j];
    lowerbd ⟵ D'[i] − t;
    upperbd ⟵ D'[i] + t;
    foreach z ∈ [i + 1, i + k] do
        if D'[z] ∉ [lowbd, upperbd] then
            changes ⟵ |lowerbd − D'[z + 1]|
            if changes ≤ a then
                while add ≤ changes do
                    D'[z + 1] ⟵ D'[z + 1] + add;
                    add + +;
                end
            end
            if changes > a then
                while delete ≤ d; add ≤ a AND D'[z] ≥ D'[z + 1] do
                    D'[z] ⟵ D'[z] − delete;
                    D'[z + 1] ⟵ D'[z + 1] + add;
                    add + +; delete + +;
                end
            end
        end
        D'[z + 1] ⟵ D'[z];
    end
end
return D'
```

3.2. Time Complexity

From a time-complexity standpoint, the worst-case scenario happens when there is a high standard deviation between the degrees of nodes, or when all nodes have different degrees. In this case, many edges will be affected to reach the anonymity level of k. For each node, we may have at most $k - t$ operations of edge addition and/or deletion. Therefore, the time complexity is $O(k * n)$. In the best case, on the other hand, there would be no significant divergence between the degrees of nodes, or the graph is nearly regular (al nodes have almost the same degree), and then the time complexity would be $O(n)$.

4. A Graph Realization Approach

In the second phase of the anonymization procedure, the output graph G' is con structed based on the target degree sequence D'. Recall that we aim to produce a grap that is k-anonymous by performing the least amount of perturbation to the topology an structure of G. The common practice is to remove edges incident on vertices that have t decrease their degrees, and add new edges to vertices that have to increase their degree without taking into consideration the major effect of graph re-construction on the topolog of the network. With this limitation in mind, we formally define "the realization" [15] as a optimization problem as follows:

Weighted Graph Realization
__Given:__ A graph G and a function $r : V(G) \rightarrow \mathbb{Z}$.
__Question:__ Is there a sequence of edge-editing operations that results in $G' = (V, E')$, suc that $\forall v \in V(G'), degree_{G'}(v) = degree_G(v) + r(v)$?

The realization procedure we propose begins by copying G into G', on which edg edits are performed. Then, it computes the vector of changes θ between D' and D, i.e $\theta = D' - D$. This vector is used to detect which nodes have to introduce or remove inciden edges. It can also be used to compute the anonymization cost. To further explicate, if $\theta[v]$ i negative, then $|\theta[v]|$ incident edges on v should be removed. However, if $\theta[v]$ is positive then $\theta[v]$ edges should be added to v. Each vertex will be labeled by its correspondin weight in θ.

ILP Formulation

We formulate this particular graph realization problem as an Integer Linear Program ming problem (ILP). For this purpose we use a binary variable $x_{i,j}$ for every pair of vertice i and j. The interpretation is that $x_{i,j} = 1$ if $\{i, j\}$ was added or deleted, otherwise $x_{i,j} =$ (This gives the following ILP formulation:

$$\text{Minimize} \sum_{u \in V, v \in V} x_{uv}$$

$$\text{Subject to:}$$

$$\sum_{ij \notin E} x_{ij} - \sum_{ij \in E} x_{ij} \geq w(i) - t$$

$$\sum_{ij \notin E} x_{ij} - \sum_{ij \in E} x_{ij} \leq w(i) + t$$

In other words, if the ILP solution assigns a value of 1 to x_{ij} and $\{i, j\}$ is not an edg (initially), then we add the edge $\{i, j\}$. On the other hand, if $\{i, j\}$ was an edge and $x_{ij} = 1$ then we remove the edge. Here, w is the weight of the vertex representing the number o edges that should be added or deleted.

5. Experimental Analysis

We implemented our multi-objective degree anonymization algorithm and ran multi ple tests using different graphs to assess its efficiency and, most importantly, its ability i preserving data utility. It was implemented in *Java*, and we used *CPLEX* for the realizatio algorithm. The tests were performed on an Intel(R) Core(TM) i7-7600U CPU @ 2.80 GH machine. Various values of k were tested while t was set to 2.

We compared our results with the ones presented in [16] for the algorithm of Liu an Terzi (k-Degree Anonymization: k-DA). We also compared our algorithm to the verte addition approach by Chester et al. [10], in which the anonymization process takes plac by adding fake vertices to the network and fake edges between these vertices, and betwee fake vertices and real ones, to attain the required k-anonymity level. Finally, we compare our results with Jordi-Casas et al.'s results in [11]. Their algorithm is based on the univariate micro-aggregation. It is available in two versions. The first, dubbed "NC", is based on the notion of neighborhood centrality, to decide which edges to delete. It tries to preserve the edges that are more relevant to the connectivity of the whole network than others. The second approach ("Rand") randomly selects edges to be removed. We used the authors' published results for comparison.

Real data sets were used for testing. The selected networks were obtained from the KONECT Project [17]. They are different in terms of topological, structural, and attribute properties. However, all of the graphs used are simple, unweighted, and undirected. The following were chosen:

- US politics book data (Polbooks-2004) [18] is a network of US politics' books where vertices represent books and an edge between two vertices implies that they are co-purchased frequently by the same buyers.
- Polblogs [19], which stands for political blog-sphere data, is a network that compiles data about links between US political blogs.
- GrQc [20] is a collaboration network that displays collaborations between authors and scientific papers in the field of General Relativity and Quantum Cosmology.
- American college football [21] is a network of American football games during Fall 2000. A vertex represents a playing team, and an edge between two teams means that they have played together.
- Erdos [17] network is a graph that shows a list of mathematician Paul Erdos' co-authors along with their respective co-authors.
- The Enron [22] email network covers all email communications within a dataset of around half a million emails.

The notion of data utility is not well-defined yet, so different authors have different approaches in quantifying data loss in a graph. In our work, we use the following graph structural measures to quantify and analyze information loss induced by the anonymization process:

- The largest eigenvalue of the adjacency matrix implies information about the diameter of a network and its cycles.
- The second smallest eigenvalue of the Laplacian matrix implies information about the tree structure of the graph. It shows if the communities separate efficiently or not.
- The average distance is the average of the shortest paths between all nodes in a network.
- The harmonic mean of the shortest distance is similar to the average distance; it is used to evaluate the connectivity of a network.
- Modularity measures the strength of the division of a network into clusters. High modularity values imply dense connections between the nodes of a graph.
- Transitivity is similar to the clustering coefficient; it detects the presence of loops near a vertex.
- Subgraph centrality measures the number of subgraphs a vertex takes part in, weighting them according to their size.

5.1. Empirical Results

We tested each dataset using the above-described algorithms in addition to our multi-parameterized model. We used the "Polbooks" network; it was not used to test the vertex addition algorithm, so we compared our multi-objective approach with Rand, NC, and kDA. We recorded the error induced by each algorithm on different utility measures. As shown in Figure 1, the Rand and NC algorithms surpass kDA, which induces a marginally less average error on the value of the transitivity measure. In general, NC outperforms Rand because it keeps essential edges in the network, which preserves the values of the measures to some extent. By comparing the average error produced by each algorithm, it is noticeable that our algorithm induces less noise and keeps the measures very close to their original values. Our results are shown for $k = 6$.

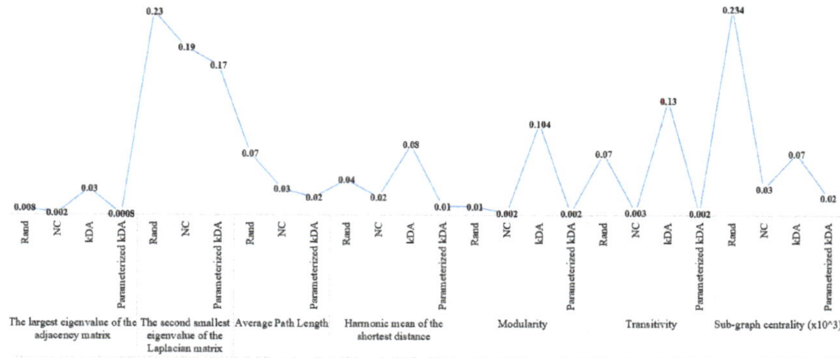

Figure 1. Polbooks experimental results.

We tested a larger network which is "Polblogs". According to Figure 2, Rand and N produced an average error that is less than that produced by vertex addition or kDA on a measures. kDA produced a remarkable deviation from the originally measured values. Th average error is 0.286 for NC and 0.291 for Rand, while it is 1.953 for kDA on the large eigenvalue of the adjacency matrix. Keeping eigenvalues close to their original value implies preserving cycles and the diameter of the network. Our approach outperforme Rand and NC by producing a smaller average error of around 0.213. Likewise, the verte addition algorithm produces a 0.043 average error on the harmonic mean of the shorte distance, while it is 0.0037 using our algorithm. Preserving the value of the harmon mean of the shortest distance implies preserving connectivity and path lengths. The sam analysis applies to other measures. Our results are shown for $k = 7$.

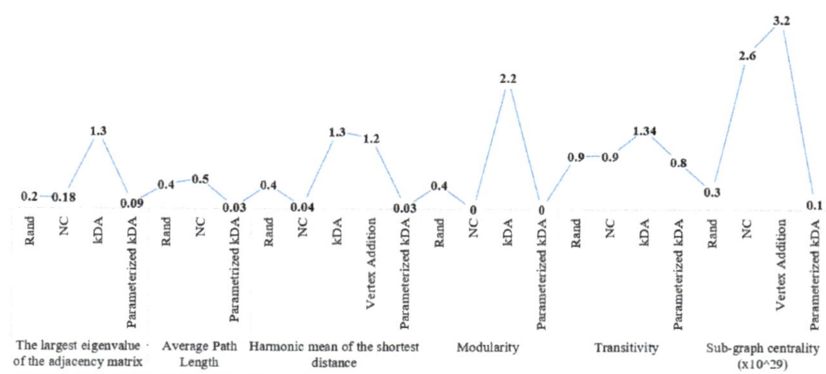

Figure 2. Polblogs experimental results.

For the GrQc graph, we show results for the same values of k as in [11], but bette results could be obtained when $k = 5$.

5.2. Clustering Analysis

To test the impact of the anonymization process on the topology of graphs and know edge extraction, we measure its effect on how data elements cluster. If the anonymizatio algorithm keeps almost the same clustered communities, then the topology of the origina graph is not affected much and the released graph would be useful for data mining applic tions. To compare the clusters of the original graph G and those of the anonymized graph G we need a certain measure of divergence. We used a precision index defined in [23], whic has a value between 0 and 1. A higher value implies that the clusters of G and G' are closer. value of 1 is obtained when the clusters of G and G' overlap completely. The correspondin experiments were implemented using R [24] and the results can be found in Table 1. The best algorithm is the one that has the highest precision index or the least precision error.

Table 1. The precision error produced by our approach versus that of NC on different data sets.

Network	Algorithm	Precision Error
American college football	NC	0.053
	Parameterized kDA	0.003
Erdos	NC	0.187
	Parameterized kDA	0.114
Enron	NC	0.121
	Parameterized kDA	0.081

According to [11], NC produces less precision error than Rand on most data sets. However, our multi-parameterized degree anonymization algorithm surpasses NC by notably minimizing the precision error. For the American college football network, our precision error is 43.39% less than that produced by NC. This is because, during the graph construction phase, we perform the minimum number of edge edits. As for Erdos, which is larger than the football network, our error is about 39% less than that of NC. Finally, we used the large network Enron to test the scalability of our algorithm. The corresponding average error produced is 33.05% less than that of NC.

6. Security Analysis

The essential features of our generalized multi-objective approach are the flexibility and practicality while applying the least modifications needed for a graph to be anonymous. Depending on the sensitivity of the data to be anonymized, the value of the parameter t differs, as it can be set to balance between privacy and utility. If we want to anonymize very sensitive data, then setting t to zero and applying our anonymization approach gives better results in terms of preserving data utility, compared to using traditional approaches. For each vertex, we are applying the minimum number of edge-editing operations. However, if the data are not critical enough, but the statistical information (for data mining purposes) is essential, we can assign a value for t that keeps the data utility as we can see in Table 2, where we present experimental results on the "GrQc" network when $t = 0$, versus those that are found in [11]. We measured the average error induced by each algorithm on the data utility measures for different k values. When, $t = 0$, parameterized kDA produced an average error that is 47% less than that produced by NC on the harmonic mean of the shortest path. For transitivity, our average error is 10% less than that of NC. Having this flexibility makes our approach a general umbrella for the existing algorithms, because we can preserve data utility and fine tune by setting the parameter t. Of course, our approach focused on enhancing the preservation of data utility without affecting privacy.

Table 2. Experimental results on the GrQc dataset using NC and our algorithm when $t = 0$.

Measure	Algorithm	Error
The largest eigenvalue of the adjacency matrix	NC	0.134
	Parameterized kDA	0.127
The second smallest eigenvalue of the Laplacian matrix	NC	0.242
	Parameterized kDA	0.223
Average path length	NC	0.097
	Parameterized kDA	0.09
Harmonic mean of the shortest distance	NC	0.15
	Parameterized kDA	0.08
Transitivity	NC	0.03
	Parameterized kDA	0.027
Sub-graph centrality	NC	0.757
	Parameterized kDA	0.754

To evaluate the robustness of our model in preserving privacy and security, we analyz and contradict the behavior of an intruder. If we consider the example of a medical data se where an intruder may have some information about a targeted individual like age, gende or address, among other things collected from external resources, then the (potentia intruder tries to match this information with nodes in the released network. Using ou constrained anonymization model to mask the data before releasing it has a better chanc of hindering the intruder from identifying his/her target, because the given informatio will be matched with many more individuals. To illustrate, if an individual in a networ has 500 links, and $t = 3$, then our approach can yield more vertices whose degrees fall i the interval $[497, 503]$. In practice, distinguishing between an individual with 500 links an another with 503 links is challenging. Furthermore, an intruder may try to link his/her priori information with released nodes and estimate the probability of correct matching In this context, a node is at risk if its identification probability exceeds a certain valu This probabilistic technique is particularly not helpful for identifying individuals in ou case, since we guarantee that many nodes have the same identification probability, whic obviously increases the intruder's uncertainty.

7. Conclusions and Future Work

We presented a generalized degree anonymization problem by adding constraint and bounds on the number of edge modifications, thereby relaxing the problem definitior which can extend its practicality and use in real applications. When applying degree-base anonymization, we have to use graph realization to obtain the resulting graph. An IL formulation has enabled us to compute the best possible solution by minimizing data los caused by edge modification operations. The main objective was to show the utility of th proposed k-anonymization model.

We considered simple unweighted undirected graphs, but this work can be extende to other types of graphs. Future work includes testing our approach on dynamic graph like online social networks where degrees vary with time, which requires adjusting th degree-anonymization solution. A possible approach would be to use a parameterized dy namic variant of the problem (see [25–27] for examples of studied parameterized dynami problems). It would also be interesting to modify our notion of degree-based anonymity t apply to distributed networks like intranets or communication networks.

Author Contributions: Conceptualization, O.N.H. and F.N.A.-K.; methodology, O.N.H. an F.N.A.-K.; validation, F.N.A.-K., O.N.H. and S.T.; formal analysis, F.N.A.-K. and O.N.H.; resource S.T.; data curation, O.N.H. and S.T.; writing—original draft preparation, O.N.H.; writing—reviev and editing, F.N.A.-K., O.N.H. and S.T.; supervision, F.N.A.-K. All authors have read and agreed t the published version of the manuscript.

Funding: This research received no external funding.

Data Availability Statement: Data available in a publicly accessible repository that does not is sue DOIs. Publicly available datasets were analyzed in this study. This data can be found here www.konect.cc (accessed on 26 August 2023).

Conflicts of Interest: The authors declare no conflict of interest.

References

1. Feder, T.; Nabar, S.; Terzi, E. Anonymizing Graphs. *CoRR* **2008**, arXiv:0810.5578.
2. Abu-Khzam, F.N. On the complexity of multi-parameterized cluster editing. *J. Discrete Algorithms* **2017**, *45*, 26–34. [CrossRef]
3. Arvind, N.; Vitaly, S. De-anonymizing Social Networks. In Proceedings of the 30th IEEE Symposium on Security and Privacy Oakland, CA, USA, 17–20 May 2009.
4. Aggarwal, G.; Panigrahy, R.; Feder, T.; Thomas, D.; Kenthapadi, K.; Khuller, S.; Zhu, A. Achieving Anonymity via Clustering *ACM Trans. Algorithms* **2010**, *6*, 1–19. [CrossRef]
5. Byun, J.W.; Kamra, A.; Bertino, E.; Li, N. Efficient k-Anonymization Using Clustering Techniques. In Proceedings of the Advance in Databases: Concepts, Systems and Applications, Bangkok, Thailand, 9–12 April 2007; Kotagiri, R., Krishna, P.R., Mohania, M Nantajeewarawat, E., Eds.; Springer: Berlin/Heidelberg, Germany, 2007; pp. 188–200.

Abu-Khzam, F.N.; Bazgan, C.; Casel, K.; Fernau, H. Clustering with Lower-Bounded Sizes—A General Graph-Theoretic Framework. *Algorithmica* **2018**, *80*, 2517–2550. [CrossRef]

Samarati, P. Protecting Respondents' Identities in Micro data Release. *IEEE Trans. Knowl. Data Eng.* **2001**, *13*, 1010–1027. [CrossRef]

Sweeney, L. k-anonymity: A model for protecting privacy. *Int. J. Uncertain. Fuzziness-Knowl.-Based Syst.* **2002**, *10*, 557–570. [CrossRef]

Liu, K.; Terzi, E. Towards identity anonymization on graphs. In Proceedings of the ACM SIGMOD Conferencem, Vancouver, BC, Canada, 10–12 June 2008; ACM: Vancouver, BC, Canada, 2008.

). Chester, S.; Kapron, B.M.; Ramesh, G.; Srivastava, G.; Thomo, A.; Venkatesh, S. Why Waldo befriended the dummy? k-Anonymization of social networks with pseudo-nodes. In Proceedings of the Social Network Analysis and Mining, Niagara Falls, ON, Canada, 25–28 August 2013; pp. 381–399.

. Casas-Roma, J.; Herrera-Joancomarti, J.; Torra, V. An Algorithm For k-Degree Anonymity On Large Networks. In Proceedings of the 2013 IEEE/ACM International Conference on Advances on Social Networks Analysis and Mining, Niagara Falls, ON, Canada, 25–28 August 2013; pp. 671–675. [CrossRef]

2. Alavi, A.; Gupta, R.; Qian, Z. When the Attacker Knows a Lot: The GAGA Graph Anonymizer. In Proceedings of the ISC, New York, NY, USA, 16–18 September 2019.

3. Casas-Roma, J.; Herrera-Joancomartí, J.; Torra, V. Evolutionary Algorithm for Graph Anonymization. *arXiv* **2013**, arXiv:1310.0229v2.

4. Bazgan, C.; Cazals, P.; Chlebíková, J. Degree-anonymization using edge rotations. *Theor. Comput. Sci.* **2021**, *873*, 1–15. [CrossRef]

5. Hakimi, S. On the realizability of a set of integers as degrees of the vertices of a simple graph. *J. SIAM Appl. Math.* **1962**, *10*, 496–506. [CrossRef]

6. Ying, X.; Pan, K.; Wu, X.; Guo, L. Comparisons of randomization and k-degree anonymization schemes for privacy preserving social network publishing. In *Workshop on Social Network Mining and Analysis*; ACM: New York, NY, USA, 2009; pp. 10:1–10:10.

7. Rossi, R.A.; Ahmed, N.K. The Network Data Repository with Interactive Graph Analytics and Visualization. In Proceedings of the Twenty-Ninth AAAI Conference on Artificial Intelligence, Austin, TX, USA, 25–30 January 2015.

3. Krebs, V. Social Network Analysis: An Introduction. 2013. Available online: http://www.orgnet.com/sna.html (accessed on 26 August 2023).

). Adamic, L.A.; Glance, N. The political blogosphere and the 2004 US election: Divided they blog. In Proceedings of the 3rd International Workshop on Link Discovery, Chicago, IL, USA, 21–24 August 2004; pp. 36–43.

). Leskovec, J.; Kleinberg, J.; Faloutsos, C. Graph evolution: Densification and shrinking diameters. *ACM Trans. Knowl. Discov. Data (TKDD)* **2007**, *1*, 2es. [CrossRef]

1. Girvan, M.; Newman, M.E. Community structure in social and biological networks. *Proc. Natl. Acad. Sci. USA* **2002**, *99*, 7821–7826. [CrossRef] [PubMed]

2. Leskovec, J.; Lang, K.J.; Dasgupta, A.; Mahoney, M.W. Community structure in large networks: Natural cluster sizes and the absence of large well-defined clusters. *Internet Math.* **2009**, *6*, 29–123. [CrossRef]

3. Cai, B.; Wang, H.; Zheng, H.; Wang, H. Evaluation repeated random walks in community detection of social networks. *Int. Conf. Mach. Learn. Cybern.* **2010**, *4*, 1849–1854.

4. R Core Team. *R: A Language and Environment for Statistical Computing*; R Foundation for Statistical Computing: Vienna, Austria, 2010. Available online: https://www.r-project.org/ (accessed on 26 August 2023).

5. Krithika, R.; Sahu, A.; Tale, P. Dynamic Parameterized Problems. *Algorithmica* **2018**, *80*, 2637–2655. [CrossRef]

5. Abu-Khzam, F.N.; Egan, J.; Fellows, M.R.; Rosamond, F.A.; Shaw, P. On the parameterized complexity of dynamic problems. *Theor. Comput. Sci.* **2015**, *607*, 426–434. [CrossRef]

7. Luo, J.; Molter, H.; Nichterlein, A.; Niedermeier, R. Parameterized Dynamic Cluster Editing. *Algorithmica* **2021**, *83*, 1–44. [CrossRef]

algorithms

MDPI

Article

HyperDE: An Adaptive Hyper-Heuristic for Global Optimization

Alexandru-Razvan Manescu and Bogdan Dumitrescu *

Department of Automatic Control and Computers, University Politehnica of Bucharest, 313 Spl. Independenț
060042 Bucharest, Romania; alexandru.manescu@stud.acs.upb.ro
* Correspondence: bogdan.dumitrescu@upb.ro

Abstract: In this paper, a novel global optimization approach in the form of an adaptive hyp heuristic, namely HyperDE, is proposed. As the naming suggests, the method is based on tl Differential Evolution (DE) heuristic, which is a well-established optimization approach inspired l the theory of evolution. Additionally, two other similar approaches are introduced for compariso and validation, HyperSSA and HyperBES, based on Sparrow Search Algorithm (SSA) and Bald Eag Search (BES), respectively. The method consists of a genetic algorithm that is adopted as a high-lev online learning mechanism, in order to adjust the hyper-parameters and facilitate the collaboratic of a homogeneous set of low-level heuristics with the intent of maximizing the performance of tl search for global optima. Comparison with the heuristics that the proposed methodologies are base on, along with other state-of-the-art methods, is favorable.

Keywords: global optimization; evolutionary algorithms; genetic algorithm; differential evolutio sparrow search; bald eagle search

1. Introduction

1.1. Problem

The problem under scrutiny is to find the global minimum of a function $f(x)$, wit $x \in \mathbb{R}^n$. Typically, the function has many variables and multiple local minima. The shap of the function is considered unknown, and we treat it as a black box; in particular, it is ir possible to apply analytical methods in order to determine the minimum; also, the gradie is not available.

1.2. State of the Art

Currently, there are a plethora of approaches, namely heuristics, that are able to searc the problem space for optimal solutions. An extensive list of heuristics can be found in [1 We enumerate a few that are considered representative by being the most cited: Partic Swarm Optimization (PSO) [2], Simulated Annealing (SA) [3], Ant Colony Optimizatio (ACO) [4], Artificial Bee Colony (ABC) [5], Harmony Search (HS) [6], Gravitational Searc Algorithm (GSA) [7], Firefly Algorithm (FA) [8]; many others have original traits. Thes methods intelligently evaluate the solution space, attempting to predict where the bes solution is located, considering the past discovered solutions. A partial exploration desired because the real world problems are complex; an exhaustive exploration is n feasible due to time and computational constraints. This being said, it is not guarantee that the heuristic has found the global optima at the end of the search.

The stochastic methods that are considered in this paper are enumerated below.

Firstly, inspired by the theory of evolution, we have the basic Differential Evolutio (DE) [9] algorithm along with two variants: the adaptive success-history based name SHADE [10] together with L-SHADE [11], which has additionally a linear population siz reduction strategy.

Citation: Manescu, A.-R.; Dumitrescu, B. HyperDE: An Adaptive Hyper-Heuristic for Global Optimization. *Algorithms* **2023**, *16*, 451. https://doi.org/10.3390/a16090451

Academic Editor: Frank Werner

Received: 14 August 2023
Revised: 14 September 2023
Accepted: 19 September 2023
Published: 20 September 2023

Inspired by the behavior of groups of individuals found in nature, such as animals and insects, there are various swarm optimization algorithms: Sparrow Search Algorithm (SSA) [12], Bald Eagle Search (BES) [13], Whale Optimization Algorithm (WOA) [14], Harris Hawks Optimization (HHO) [15], and Hunger Games Search (HGS) [16]. The conceptual contribution and the underlying metaphor of some of these algorithms may be questionable [17], but many of them have good practical behavior.

Inspired by concepts from mathematics, we have Chaos Game Optimization (CGO) [18], while Slime Mold Algorithm (SMA) [19] can be considered a bio-inspired search algorithm.

Most of the techniques listed above are not far from the state-of-the-art; other methods are not so recent but are well established. What is to be taken into consideration is that DE together with SHADE and LSHADE are considered the key contenders in our methodology validation, the other algorithms being less relevant.

Each enumerated method performs in a different manner, excelling at solving a particular subset of problems while not being appropriate for solving some other problems. Many of the available heuristics have hyper-parameters whose values affect the performance of the search, therefore being able to tailor the algorithm to the given problem. It often happens that the methods fail to converge to the global optima, remaining stuck in a locally optimal solution instead and struggling to find a balance between exploration and exploitation.

Regarding the development of hyper-heuristics, the field of study is relatively new, with an increase in publications on this subject over the last three–four years [20]. There are several methods available, such as approaches based on genetic programming [21], graph-based [22], VNS-based [23], ant-based [24], tabu search-based [25], greedy selection-based [26], GA-based [27], simulated annealing-based [28], and reinforcement learning-based [29]. Those are several relevant examples that initiated the domain in various directions.

More recent hyper-heuristics that merit attention could be a simulated-annealing-based hyper-heuristic [30], a reinforcement learning-based hyper-heuristic [31], a genetic programming hyper-heuristic approach [32], a Bayesian-based hyper-heuristic approach [33] and a very appealing, highly general approach for continuous problems [34].

None of the above resembles our proposed method; as revealed in [20], most of the hyper-heuristics are designed to be applied in different domains, problems such as scheduling, timetabling, constraint satisfaction, routing policies, not continuous problems as in our study. Unlike our method, the existent high-level procedures are usually not population-based and do not make use of parallelization.

1.3. Our Contribution

Our plan is to define an adaptive hyper-heuristic [35] for adjusting the hyper-parameters of a set of low-level heuristics, in an online manner, such as to maximize the performance in finding the global minimum.

A hyper-heuristic is a methodology that automates the selection, generation and adaptation of lower level heuristics in order to solve difficult search problems. Therefore, instead of exploring the problem space directly, it explores the space of possible heuristics.

Accordingly, our proposed method has two optimization layers:

- The high-level adaptive algorithm, which is variant of the genetic algorithm (GA), is responsible for the process of online learning of the hyper-parameters of the basic heuristics.
- The low-level optimization algorithm can be any optimization method characterized by a set of hyper-parameters that are tuned by the high-level algorithm. The low-level algorithm acts through agents that directly attempt to solve the optimization problem by exploring the solution space.

After an analysis that consisted of the evaluation of various heuristics, DE was selected as the main low-level agent in the context of the proposed optimization method. The combination of our variant of GA at the high-level and DE at the low-level is called HyperDE. Two other algorithms, SSA and BES, were also considered appropriate to serve as agents. The resulting methods are called HyperSSA and HyperBES, respectively. The three methods are similar in approach, sharing the same high-level procedure, but differing by which algorithms are adopted as agents.

Each of the above optimization algorithms that are used as agents presents a set of hyper-parameters that influence the performance of their search. The most important in this paper, DE, has the following hyper-parameters: F $\in [0,1]$, weighting factor; CR $\in [0,1]$, crossover rate; S $\in [0,5]$ (integer), index of the mutation strategy (See Section 2 for details). In the HyperDE algorithm, a population of DE instances is managed by our GA, which tunes the triplets (F, CR, S) in the attempt to improve the search compared to the case where a single triplet of hyper-parameters is used.

By this endeavor, it is expected to obtain a methodology that is more general in its applicability, adapting without intervention to the given problem, resulting in a superior average performance given a set of problems without additional effort from the human agent. We consider it to be one possible approach to deal with the "No Free Lunch" theorem [36] successfully.

The evaluation and analysis of the proposed hyper-heuristics in comparison with the other enumerated algorithms was conducted on 12 benchmark functions provided by CEC 2022 competition. We show that HyperDE has indeed the best average performance and Friedman rank, followed by L-SHADE, while HyperSSA and HyperBES demonstrate to be significant improvements over their counterparts.

1.4. Content

In Section 2, the Differential Evolution algorithm is briefly presented, as it represents an important part of the proposed method; also, in Section 3, we recall the principles of the BES and SSA algorithms. In Section 4, a short description of the genetic algorithm can be found, which is the second key component of our method. In Section 5, we give a thorough presentation of the proposed methodology, containing also algorithms and diagrams. Finally, in Section 6, the results of the proposed method in comparison with some other algorithms are presented. Section 7 contains the conclusion of the paper.

2. Differential Evolution Algorithm Overview

Differential Evolution algorithm (DE) [9,37] is a population-based optimization method inspired by the theory of evolution. The algorithm starts from a set of solutions that are gradually improved by using operators such as selection, mutation and crossover. There are many variants of the algorithm; we concentrate on the ones that do not have self-adaptive capabilities or an external history, considering several mutation strategies that are of interest.

The DE basic structure is given in Algorithm 1. The population of NP vectors is initialized randomly and then improved in $\text{iter}_{\max}$ iterations. In each iteration, each individual x_i can be replaced with a better one. A so-called donor vector is built with

$$v_i \leftarrow x_{r_1} + \mathrm{F} \cdot (x_{r_2} - x_{r_3}) \quad (1)$$

where $x_{r_1}, x_{r_2}, x_{r_3}$ are individuals chosen randomly; they are distinct one from each other and from x_i and F $\in [0,1]$ is a given weighting factor.

Then, a trial vector u_i is produced by crossover from x_i and the donor vector, with

$$u_{i,j} = \begin{cases} v_{i,j}, & \text{if } r_{i,j} \leq \mathrm{CR} \text{ or } j = j_{rand} \\ x_{i,j}, & \text{otherwise} \end{cases} \quad (2)$$

where $i = 1{:}\mathrm{NP}$, $j = 1{:}n$, $r_{i,j} \in U(0,1)$ is a uniformly distributed random number generated for each j and $j_{rand} \in 1:n$ is a random integer used to ensure that $u_i \neq x_i$ in all cases. The crossover rate CR $\in [0,1]$ dictates the probability with which the elements of the vector x are changed with elements of the donor vector.

Algorithm 1 Differential evolution algorithm

NP ← population size
F ← weighting factor
CR ← crossover probability
Initialize randomly all individuals x_i, i = 1:NP
t ← 0
while t < iter$_{max}$ **do**
  for $i = 1 :$ NP **do**
    Randomly choose $x_{r_1}, x_{r_2}, x_{r_3}$ from current population
    MUTATION: form the donor vector using the Formula (1)
    CROSSOVER: form trial vector u_i with (2)
    EVALUATE: if $f(u_i) \leq f(x_i)$, replace x_i with trial vector u_i
  end for
  t = t + 1
end while

To the two hyper-parameters that influence the behavior of the method (F and CR), we add a third, the integer S ∈ 0 : 5, representing the index of the mutation strategy. Among the many mutation operators that have been conceived and that can be an alternative to (1), in this paper we consider the following, singled out as "the six most widely used mutation schemes" in [37]:

0: "DE/rand/1" $v_i \leftarrow x_{r_1} + \mathrm{F} \cdot (x_{r_2} - x_{r_3})$, which is (1)
1: "DE/best/1" $v_i \leftarrow x_{best} + \mathrm{F} \cdot (x_{r_1} - x_{r_2})$
2: "DE/rand/2" $v_i \leftarrow x_{r_1} + \mathrm{F} \cdot (x_{r_2} - x_{r_3}) + \mathrm{F} \cdot (x_{r_4} - x_{r_5})$
3: "DE/best/2" $v_i \leftarrow x_{best} + \mathrm{F} \cdot (x_{r_1} - x_{r_2}) + \mathrm{F} \cdot (x_{r_3} - x_{r_4})$
4: "DE/current-to-best/1" $v_i \leftarrow x_i + \mathrm{F} \cdot (x_{best} - x_i) + \mathrm{F} \cdot (x_{r_1} - x_{r_2})$
5: "DE/current-to-rand/1" $v_i \leftarrow x_i + rand \cdot (x_{r_1} - x_i) + \mathrm{F} \cdot (x_{r_2} - x_{r_3})$

where the indexes r_1, r_2, r_3, r_4, r_5 are random integers that are all distinct, in the range 1:NP, and different from i; they are generated for each mutant vector. x_{best} represents the best individual from the current iteration.

Given the hyper-parameter or index S, the corresponding mutation strategy as defined above will be used by the DE agent, the algorithm remaining unchanged beyond that aspect. All the enumerated hyper-parameters will be manipulated by the genetic algorithm that will be presented.

3. Other Parameterized Heuristics

We briefly recall here information on two evolutionary algorithms that will be used, similarly with DE, as basic heuristics with which our hyper-heuristic works.

The Bald Eagle Search (BES) algorithm takes inspiration from the hunting behavior of bald eagles. The algorithm comprises three stages: selection of the search space, searching within the chosen space, and swooping.

In the selection stage, the eagles identify the best area within the search space where the maximum amount of food is available.

In the search stage, they scan the vicinity of the chosen space by spiraling and moving in various directions to look for prey.

During the swooping stage, the eagles move towards their target prey by shifting from their current best position. Overall, all points in the search space move towards the best point.

There are five hyper-parameters that need adjustment: $a \in [2, 20]$ (integer), determining the corner between point search in the central point; $R \in [0.1, 3]$, determining the number of search cycles; $\alpha \in [0.5, 3]$, controlling the changes in position; $c1 \in [0, 4]$ and $c2 \in [0, 4]$, increase the movement intensity of bald eagles towards the best and center points. Note that the above intervals are those recommended in the Python implementation from the library MEALPY [38] and we have used them. In the original work [1: the recommendations are $a \in [5, 10]$, $\alpha \in [1.5, 2]$, $R \in [0.5, 2]$, $c1, c2 \in [1, 2]$.

Sparrow search algorithm (SSA) [12] is a relatively new swarm optimization methc inspired by the behavior of sparrows, specifically by the group wisdom, foraging an anti-predatory behaviors. There are two types of sparrows, producers and scrounge The producers actively search for food while the scroungers exploit the producers b obtaining food from them. The roles are not fixed; an individual can shift from one foragir strategy to the other depending on its energy reserve. Each individual constantly tries avoid being located at the periphery of the group to be less exposed to danger. Additional when one or more birds detect danger, they will chirp, the whole group flying away fro the predator.

The hyper-parameters of SSA are ST $\in [0.5, 1]$, the alarm value; PD $\in [0, 1]$, the rat of producers; SD $\in [0, 1]$, the ratio of sparrows who perceive the danger. Note that in [1: PD and SD are integers between 1 and n. We modify them in fractions of n in order to b able to optimize them more easily in the genetic algorithm.

4. Genetic Algorithm Overview

Genetic algorithm (GA) is a well established population-based optimization metho inspired by the theory of evolution [39]. The approach is based on the Darwinian theo of survival of fittest in nature, adopting various biological-inspired operators such a crossover, mutation and fitness selection, operators that manipulate a set of chromosom representations. Algorithm 2 shows the basic GA structure.

Algorithm 2 Genetic Algorithm

$G \leftarrow$ the maximum number of iterations
$P_0 \leftarrow$ initial random population of individuals
$t \leftarrow 0$
while $t < G$ **do**
  Compute the fitness values of P_t
  $P_p \leftarrow$ Select the parent population from P_t
  $P_c \leftarrow$ Crossover individuals from parent population P_p
  $P_c \leftarrow$ Mutate individuals from offspring population P_c
  Compute the fitness values of P_c
  $P_{t+1} \leftarrow$ Obtain the next generation's population from P_t and P_c
  $t \leftarrow t + 1$
end while
return P_G

The algorithm starts by generating a random population of solutions P_0. The solutior are evaluated via obtaining the corresponding fitnesses. Based on the fitnesses, a subset c the current population P_t is selected as the parent population P_p. The crossover operator : applied on the individuals from P_p, obtaining a new set of solutions P_c that may also muta and are evaluated. At the end of the generation, the population of the next generation obtained based on P_t and P_c. This process is repeated for a number of G iterations, resultin in P_G, the final set of solutions to the problem.

In the HyperDE context, the chromosome associated with a DE instance is given b the hyper-parameters F, CR and S; for HyperSSA the genes are ST, PD and SD; while fc HyperBES we have as genes of the chromosome a, α, R, $c1$ and $c2$. We denote n_p as th number of hyper-parameters. The implementations of the basic GA operators are as follow Single-point crossover was used, meaning that the first c values of the hyper-paramete (in the order given above) are taken from the first parent and the remaining $n_p - c$ from th second parent, where c is a random integer between 0 and the number of hyper-paramete Mutation is implemented as the simple choice of a uniformly random real number (c integer, for S) in the interval of definition of each hyper-parameter. The fitness function will be described in the next section.

5. HyperDe Algorithm

As stated in Section 1.1, the goal is to find the minimum value of a function $f(x)$, with $x \in \mathbb{R}^n$. The proposed hyper-heuristic, HyperDE, works like many other global optimization algorithms, by generating tentative solutions. The modality in which the solution space is explored gives the specific of a method.

In the two-layer structure mentioned in Section 1.3, HyperDE adopts as a high-level algorithm a form of steady-state Genetic Algorithm (GA). The (hyper-)population in this context is composed of various instances of DE, each with different hyper-parameters. Therefore, HyperDE orchestrates the collaboration and execution in parallel of the DE agents, manipulating the hyper-parameters and generated solutions.

The proposed method is an adaptive hyper-heuristic, where the genetic algorithm plays the role of an online learning mechanism, adjusting the hyper-parameters of the agent ensemble and adapting to the state of the problem while exploring the solution space. Thus, there is a learning process based on the performance shown in the past of each particular DE agent, exploring also the space of heuristics by the means of the standard GA operators: selection, crossover and mutation. Ergo, the optimization is accomplished on two levels, simultaneously, searching primarily the space of possible DE instances, but also the actual space of solutions to the given problem, as depicted in Figure 1.

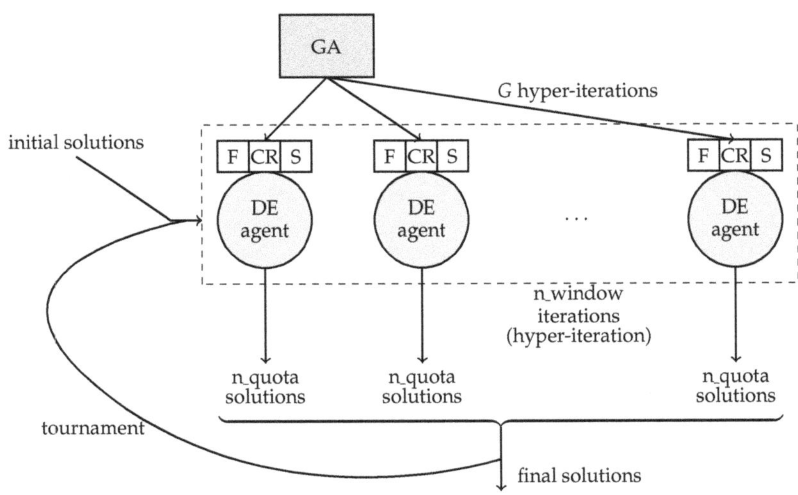

Figure 1. Structure of the proposed adaptive hyper-heuristic approach.

The algorithm manages the hyper-population of DE agents, named HP, which is initialized with random values of the hyper-parameters F, CR, S. It also maintains a solution population SP, also initialized at random.

In order to evaluate the hyper-population HP, the DE agents are executed in parallel for a number of n_window iterations. Each agent is responsible for the generation of n_quota solutions; in other words, each DE agent has n_quota individuals. Therefore, the entire hyper-population explores the problem space in a parallel manner, obtaining at the end a set of solutions. The history set of solutions for agent g is denoted H_g. The history H_g consists of n_window sets of solutions, each corresponding to an iteration executed by agent g. $H_{g,i}$ represents the set of solutions obtained by agent g at the end of iteration i, and has the size $|H_{g,i}|$ = n_quota.

In order to assign a fitness HF to each agent of HP, the obtained histories of solutions are utilized in the procedure AgentsFitness (Algorithm 3). For each window iteration

i, we compute the union O_i of the agents solutions set $H_{g,i}$ in that particular iteration. The obtained union O_i is sorted in ascending/descending order, depending on whether the problem to solve is one of minimization or maximization. Afterwards, a count is performed for each agent, counting how many of its solutions are found in the first third of the sorted union set, the count being then divided with $|O_i|/3$ for normalization. After the entire process, the average is computed over the entire window of iterations, thus obtaining the fitness value HF_g for each agent g.

Algorithm 3 Computation of the fitness function for all agents

---

procedure AGENTSFITNESS(HP, H, n_window)
  for each DE agent g in HP **do**
    $HF_g \leftarrow 0$
  end for
  for each iteration $i = 1 :$ n_window **do**
    $O_i \leftarrow \emptyset$
    for each DE agent g in HP **do**
      $O_i \leftarrow O_i \cup H_{g,i}$
    end for
    Sort in ascending/descending order by fitness the set O_i
    for each DE agent g in HP **do**
      $C_{g,i} \leftarrow$ Number of solutions from $H_{g,i}$ that are in the first third of set O_i
      $HF_g \leftarrow HF_g + \frac{C_{g,i}}{\text{n\_window} \cdot \frac{|O_i|}{3}}$
    end for
  end for
  return HF
end procedure

The above-described operations are used in Algorithm 4, which updates the solution population SP and computes the fitness HF by calling Algorithm 3. For each agent the current set of solutions SP is reduced firstly to half by random selection, after which the best n_quota solutions are retained. This set is the starting solution set for the agent in the next hyper-iteration, which consists of running the DE algorithm for n_window iterations. For the loop on the DE, agents can be executed in parallel. Finally, the procedure returns the union of the last sets of solutions of the entire ensemble of size $|HP| \cdot$ n_quota, which is the new set of solutions SP, and also the set containing the HF fitnesses associated with the agents.

Algorithm 5 gathers the main operations. The evaluation procedure, as described above in Algorithm 4, which also explores the problem space with DE agents, is executed in each hyper-iteration. Based on the obtained HF fitnesses of the agents, the ensemble of the next hyper-iteration HP_{t+1} is computed. This is accomplished by firstly retaining the best half of the hyper-population of agents. Then, $|HP|/2$ agents are randomly selected as parents in order to crossover and mutate (as described in Section 4), obtaining $|HP|/2$ new agents; along with the elite of $|HP|/2$ agents, they constitute the next hyper-generation. This process is sustained for G hyper-generations, or $G\cdot$n_window DE iterations.

As explained, besides the fitnesses of the agents, the set of solutions SP is also updated, representing the union of all sets of solutions produced by each agent in the last iteration of the execution window; or simply, the solutions to the problem obtained at the end of hyper-iteration t.

Algorithm 4 Evaluate and Explore algorithm

HP: hyper-population of DE agents
SP: solutions population
H_g: history of solutions of agent g
procedure EVALUATEANDEXPLORE(HP, SP, n_quota, n_window)
  for each DE agent g in HP **do**
    $S \leftarrow$ Select $\frac{|SP|}{2}$ random solutions from SP
    $S \leftarrow$ Retain the best n_quota solutions of set S
    $H_g \leftarrow$ solutions generated by the DE algorithm run for n_window iterations on population S
  end for
  $HF \leftarrow$ AGENTSFITNESS($HP, H,$ n_window)
  $SP \leftarrow \emptyset$
  for each DE agent g in HP **do**
    $SP \leftarrow SP \cup H_{g,n\_window}$
  end for
  return SP, HF
end procedure

Algorithm 5 HyperDE algorithm

$G \leftarrow$ the maximum hyper-generations
$HP_0 \leftarrow$ initial random hyper-population of SSA agents
$SP_0 \leftarrow$ initial random set of n_quota$\cdot|HP_0|$ solutions
n_quota $\leftarrow$ quota of solutions (number of sparrows) for each SSA agent
n_window $\leftarrow$ number of iterations for each SSA agent's execution
$t \leftarrow 0$
while $t < G$ **do**
  $SP_{t+1}, HF \leftarrow$ EVALUATEANDEXPLORE(HP_t,SP_t, n_quota, n_window)
  $HP_{t+1} \leftarrow$ Select the best $\frac{|HP_t|}{2}$ agents based on HF
  $P_p \leftarrow$ Select $\frac{|HP_t|}{2}$ agents for the parent population from HP_t
  $P_c \leftarrow$ Crossover agents from parent population P_p
  $P_c \leftarrow$ Mutate agents from offspring population P_c
  $HP_{t+1} \leftarrow HP_{t+1} \cup P_c$ (obtain population of next hyper-generation)
  $t \leftarrow t+1$
end while
return HP_G

We note that the above algorithm has a high degree of generality. It is written for DE agents, which are characterized by three hyper-parameters. However, the algorithm can be adapted to any other global optimization heuristic, with any (nonzero) number of hyper-parameters.

As examples, we implemented the HyperSSA and HyperBES algorithms. The methods resemble the HyperDE hyper-heuristic in most regards, differing just by what type of agents are used. We have as agents the time instances of SSA heuristics in one case and instances of BES heuristics in the other case. Since the top-level procedure is highly decoupled from the agent's inner workings, the algorithmic flows of the hyper-heuristics is the same as for HyperDE. We simply use the chromosomes presented in Section 3.

6. Results

The proposed adaptive hyper-heuristic methods are compared with 10 relatively new, state-of-the-art heuristics and well-established algorithms (including the basic heuristics that we employ: DE, BES, SSA), over a set of n_problems = 12 difficult problems, more exactly on the benchmarks provided by the CEC 2022 competition: (https://github.com/P-N-Suganthan/2022-SO-BO/blob/main/CEC2022%20TR.pdf, accessed on 18 September

2023). We have implemented our method in Python. The algorithms used for compariso listed in Table 1 (to be later explained), have been taken from the MEALPY library [3 implementation in Python. Our programs can be found at https://github.com/mening12 01/HyperHeuristica, accessed on 18 September 2023).

Our HyperDE hyper-heuristic is parameterized as follows: the number of hype iterations is $G = 40$, the evaluation window size is n_window $= 5$ iterations, the hype population has size $|HP| = 10$ (the number of DE instances, or agents), where each age has n_quota $= 20$ (the size of the solution population). In order for the comparison to b valid, the HyperDE hyper-heuristic along with the other methods should explore the sam number of solutions. We note that HyperDE performs $G \cdot$ n_window $= 200$ DE iteration and computes a population of $|HP| \cdot$ n_quota $= 200$ solutions per iteration, resulting i a total of $200 \cdot 200 = 40{,}000$ evaluated solutions. Therefore, the other methods will hav as parameters: the number of iterations to be executed $iterations = 200$, and the size o population $pop\_size = 200$; hence, the same volume of the solution space is explored at th end of execution. The other hyper-parameters specific to each method are set with defau values, as recommended by the literature.

Each heuristic is evaluated by computing the relative error as described in Algorithm The global minimum being known, the relative distance between the obtained result an the optimum is calculated.

For each problem, the heuristic in this case is evaluated n_tests = 60 times as describe averaging the relative error obtained in each evaluation. Finally, the average relative erro obtained on each problem is aggregated again, obtaining the final relative error that reflec the overall performance of that algorithm (smaller is better).

Algorithm 6 Evaluation, relative error

```
overall_error_sum ← 0
for each problem in n_problems do
    error_sum ← 0
    for each test in n_tests do
        best_solution ← heuristic(pop_size = 200, iterations = 200)
        if global_best ≠ 0 then
            relative_error ← (best_solution − global_best)/|global_best|
        else
            relative_error ← (best_solution − global_best)
        end if
        error_sum ← error_sum + relative_error
    end for
    overall_error_sum ← overall_error_sum + error_sum/n_tests
end for
final_error ← overall_error_sum/n_problems
```

As can be seen from Table 1, HyperDE has the minimal error on the selected sui of problems. We note also that HyperBES and HyperSSA perform better than their bas heuristics, BES and SSA.

Additionally, the Friedman ranking is computed, more precisely, the average ran over all the problems. The median was determined over the n_tests $= 60$ tests, for eac problem and method. If, for a particular problem, the difference between the medians fo two methods does not exceed 1×10^{-7}, then the two methods have the same rank, whic is the average of the corresponding ranks.

Table 1. Errors of the evaluated methods on the CEC problems.

Heuristic Name	Error
HyperDE	**0.045**
LSHADE	0.078
SHADE	0.085
HyperSSA	1.068
HyperBES	1.073
Chaos Game Optimization (CGO)	1.213
Whale Optimization Algorithm (WOA)	1.303
Sparrow Search Algorithm (SSA)	1.462
Slime Mold Algorithm (SMA)	1.741
Hunger Games Search (HGS)	1.795
Bald Eagle Search (BES)	2.068
Harris Hawks Optimization (HHO)	2.103
Differential Evolution (DE)	3.603

The results are given in Table 2 and show that HyperDE is the best from the entire suite of methods, at a significant distance from SHADE. Unlike in the error evaluation, SHADE is better then LSHADE. HyperBES preserves its fifth place, but HyperSSA falls down the ranking to tenth place, in particular below SSA.

Table 2. Friedman ranking of the evaluated methods on the CEC problems.

Heuristic Name	Rank
HyperDE	**1.875**
SHADE	2.680
LSHADE	3.097
Slime Mold Algorithm (SMA)	4.222
HyperBES	4.916
Sparrow Search Algorithm (SSA)	5.097
Differential Evolution (DE)	5.458
Chaos Game Optimization (CGO)	5.638
Whale Optimization Algorithm (WOA)	6.041
HyperSSA	6.208
Hunger Games Search (HGS)	6.791
Bald Eagle Search (BES)	8.166
Harris Hawks Optimization (HHO)	8.305

One aspect that is consistent in both evaluations is that HyperDE proves to behave remarkably well relative to the other algorithms, it being conclusive that our hyper-heuristic is the best performer in the given context.

The execution times of the top performing algorithms are given in Table 3. They were measured on a MacBook Air computer with an M1 chip having a max CPU clock rate of 3.2 GHz and 8 GB memory. Note that the implementation of our methods is purely sequential and does not take advantage of the inherent parallelism of the agents; also, the implementation is plain and does not use any speeding-up trick. So, as expected, HyperDE is more time-consuming than the simpler methods such as SHADE and LSHADE, due to the additional computations and manipulations. HyperDE is roughly 60–80% slower. HyperSSA and HyperBES do not seem that efficient; this is because of the agents that are used, which are not as fast as DE.

We reiterate that the number of function evaluations is the same for all methods; as long as the implementations are not fully optimized, this is the most important aspect in ensuring fairness of comparison. If the implementations would be equally well optimized for a specified computer, which is not an easy task, the results after a given time could be compared; even then, it may be argued that ideal conditions, like the inexistence of background processes, are nearly impossible to obtain. So, in these circumstances, we consider that our comparisons are reasonably fair.

Table 3. Average times of the best methods (in minutes).

Function	HyperDE	HyperSSA	HyperBES	LSHADE	SHADE
F1	4.09	6.61	10.72	2.43	2.34
F2	4.12	6.45	10.83	2.33	2.37
F3	4.29	7.16	11.39	2.36	2.37
F4	4.30	6.56	11.39	2.37	2.37
F5	4.20	6.51	11.09	2.34	2.32
F6	4.88	7.82	12.75	2.76	2.76
F7	5.41	6.71	14.22	3.17	3.22
F8	5.76	9.23	15.16	3.59	3.47
F9	4.51	7.26	11.87	2.62	2.65
F10	4.54	6.97	11.94	2.73	2.69
F11	4.76	7.42	12.48	2.80	2.82
F12	4.77	7.23	12.54	2.78	2.78

The convergence of the top five methods on the entire suite of problems is illustrated in Figures 2 and 3. The average over n_tests = 60 tests is shown, resulting in an average convergence curve, thus smoothing the stochastic behavior. The methods are executed for 200 iterations each, but only each fifth iteration is plotted in order to be aligned with the results of our hyper-heuristics, where the best result at the end of each hyper-iteration is shown.

It is visible that HyperDE converges nearest to the global minimum on four functions F2, F4, F6 and F7. For functions F1 and F3, HyperDE reaches about the same value as other methods, but it converges at the fastest rate. The convergence of HyperDE is more abrupt also on the other functions.

LSHADE and SHADE seem to take the lead on some of the other problems, not being drastically distant from our main method. HyperBES and HyperSSA are performing noticeably worse then the others. HyperBES is the most unimpressive on F1, F2, F3 and F11, while surpassing HyperSSA on F5, F6, F7, F8, F9, F10 and F12.

Box plots are shown in Figure 4, illustrating in more detail the distribution of the n_tests = 60 results of the algorithms. In most of the figures, the proposed method has a very reduced variance around the global optima, similarly to the other two DE variants. For F9, the variance is large while the median is aligned with the best result. In the F4 plot HyperDE has the lowest median, followed by the other two proposed hyper-heuristics. However, HyperSSA and HyperBES perform worse on the other problems, with fairly large variance and a median quite far from the best solution, not being very clear which is the best of the two.

In Table 4, we can see a comparison of the performance of the proposed optimization method, HyperDE, with the other three methods from the DE family. The performance metrics include the best solution found (Best), the mean solution obtained (Mean), and the standard deviation (Std. Dev) of the solutions.

As can be concluded, our method demonstrates an impressive performance, where it consistently outperforms the others in terms of the best solution. Regarding the mean, this is not always the case, as for F5, F8, F10, F11 and F12 the mean is slightly worse then for SHADE and LSHADE, while for F6 and F9 the inferiority is quite significant. Moreover, HyperDE achieves fairly low standard deviation values, indicating its reliability and ability to deliver stable and high-quality solutions.

Table 4. Method comparison for multiple problems.

Problem	Method	Best	Mean	Std. Dev
F1	HyperDE	300.0	300.0	3.11×10^{-14}
	SHADE	300.000000106882	300.0000004073815	2.43×10^{-7}
	LSHADE	300.0000001404671	300.00000041613555	2.21×10^{-7}
	DE	1235.4661553234967	4130.32659367826	1205.22
F2	HyperDE	400.00006692489313	405.7762007938934	3.18
	SHADE	400.3938197535978	407.5481893148344	2.13
	LSHADE	400.3851128433223	408.0876491551797	1.55
	DE	410.80352316352435	417.77563978207604	3.27
F3	HyperDE	600.0	600.0	2.08×10^{-14}
	SHADE	600.0	600.0	0.0
	LSHADE	600.0	600.0	0.0
	DE	600.0000112734627	600.0000363216427	1.05×10^{-5}
F4	HyperDE	800.0971590987756	800.29929127267	0.19
	SHADE	800.2721523050697	800.4602925668243	0.09
	LSHADE	800.2506108454668	800.397114829017	0.08
	DE	800.2004337865635	800.4850824190988	0.09
F5	HyperDE	900.0	900.0436061309064	0.11
	SHADE	900.0000000000498	900.0000000002758	1.74×10^{-10}
	LSHADE	900.0000000000752	900.0000000001007	5.35×10^{-12}
	DE	900.0308300706507	900.2115266993348	0.04
F6	HyperDE	1800.550008569961	2349.376836704244	1611.13
	SHADE	2527.2166249124543	3318.210953638849	515.35
	LSHADE	2448.651779056926	3156.2346074618913	433.08
	DE	18,245.220034908845	55,938.99918382257	23,898.85
F7	HyperDE	2001.494972244204	2020.428895032187	8.00
	SHADE	2023.69169017458	2028.6419318989665	1.74
	LSHADE	2014.5645721366564	2027.7440931323101	2.78
	DE	2024.5036568238922	2028.4449058504215	1.99
F8	HyperDE	2200.226924720861	2218.3297256215615	6.73
	SHADE	2209.5886930417746	2218.297973263973	4.32
	LSHADE	2208.325106401539	2217.383152114902	4.02
	DE	2230.0941806086953	2245.28243788769	9.28
F9	HyperDE	2300.0	2437.838567116613	174.83
	SHADE	2300.0001089307398	2300.0048868578	0.03
	LSHADE	2300.0001212533975	2300.0061751439484	0.03
	DE	2396.4069384108525	2646.9062600644074	60.17
F10	HyperDE	2598.5455167771906	2605.156197642855	25.86
	SHADE	2598.5468912550587	2598.5620204350707	0.07
	LSHADE	2598.5468210921954	2598.551948117506	0.00
	DE	2608.799360629708	2614.908013661977	3.19
F11	HyperDE	2600.0	2601.8934468491198	6.28
	SHADE	2600.0000050187055	2600.0000090069157	2.17×10^{-6}
	LSHADE	2600.0000049464516	2600.000009874206	2.98×10^{-6}
	DE	2607.8865627810346	2624.76104595252	4.06
F12	HyperDE	2863.76941226926	2865.838163178578	1.26
	SHADE	2821.118856642622	2864.1391105809807	5.62
	LSHADE	2864.224719298684	2864.904468801826	0.50
	DE	2866.84004856121	2867.9027213119152	0.50

Table 5 gives the results of the Wilcoxon signed-rank test. They show a statistical significant difference of HyperDE from the other methods on F1, as indicated by the e tremely low p-values (approximately 1.63×10^{-11}). This is also the case for F2, F4, F and F7, exhibiting fairly low *p*-values in comparison with the other three methods, where on F10, F11, and F12, our methodology is surpassed by the other two self-adaptive alg rithms. For F3, there is no significant difference between HyperDE and SHADE/LSHAD the p-value being large, 0.16; however, DE is clearly worse than HyperDE. This situatic is found for the other remaining problems (F5, F8, F9), where an actual winner cannot b proclaimed, except in comparison with the basic DE.

Table 5. Results of Wilcoxon signed-rank test.

Problem	Method	*p*-Value
F1	**HyperDE** vs. SHADE	1.63×10^{-11}
	HyperDE vs. LSHADE	1.63×10^{-11}
	HyperDE vs. DE	1.63×10^{-11}
F2	**HyperDE** vs. SHADE	1.41×10^{-4}
	HyperDE vs. LSHADE	3.50×10^{-7}
	HyperDE vs. DE	1.63×10^{-11}
F3	HyperDE vs. SHADE	0.16
	HyperDE vs. LSHADE	0.16
	HyperDE vs. DE	1.63×10^{-11}
F4	**HyperDE** vs. SHADE	3.78×10^{-7}
	HyperDE vs. LSHADE	1.27×10^{-5}
	HyperDE vs. DE	5.78×10^{-8}
F5	HyperDE vs. SHADE	0.44
	HyperDE vs. LSHADE	0.83
	HyperDE vs. DE	1.80×10^{-11}
F6	**HyperDE** vs. SHADE	5.11×10^{-8}
	HyperDE vs. LSHADE	1.86×10^{-8}
	HyperDE vs. DE	1.63×10^{-11}
F7	**HyperDE** vs. SHADE	1.66×10^{-10}
	HyperDE vs. LSHADE	2.71×10^{-9}
	HyperDE vs. DE	1.44×10^{-10}
F8	HyperDE vs. SHADE	0.20
	HyperDE vs. LSHADE	0.04
	HyperDE vs. DE	1.63×10^{-11}
F9	HyperDE vs. SHADE	0.12
	HyperDE vs. LSHADE	0.12
	HyperDE vs. DE	2.62×10^{-8}
F10	HyperDE vs. **SHADE**	7.20×10^{-10}
	HyperDE vs. **LSHADE**	7.20×10^{-10}
	HyperDE vs. DE	4.63×10^{-9}
F11	HyperDE vs. **SHADE**	4.20×10^{-6}
	HyperDE vs. **LSHADE**	4.20×10^{-6}
	HyperDE vs. DE	1.80×10^{-11}
F12	HyperDE vs. **SHADE**	1.50×10^{-5}
	HyperDE vs. **LSHADE**	9.35×10^{-6}
	HyperDE vs. DE	1.66×10^{-10}

In summary, the results suggest that HyperDE consistently outperforms or shows comparable performance to the other optimization methods on most of the problems.

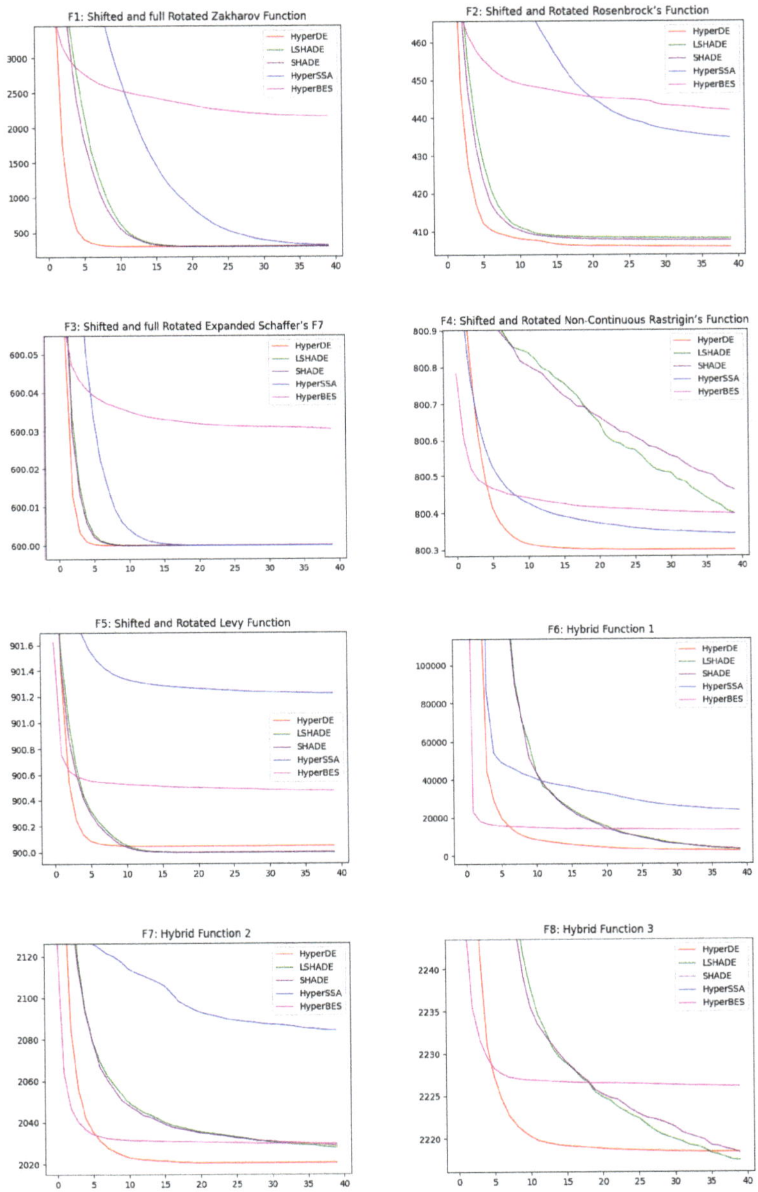

Figure 2. Overall convergence of the best methods.

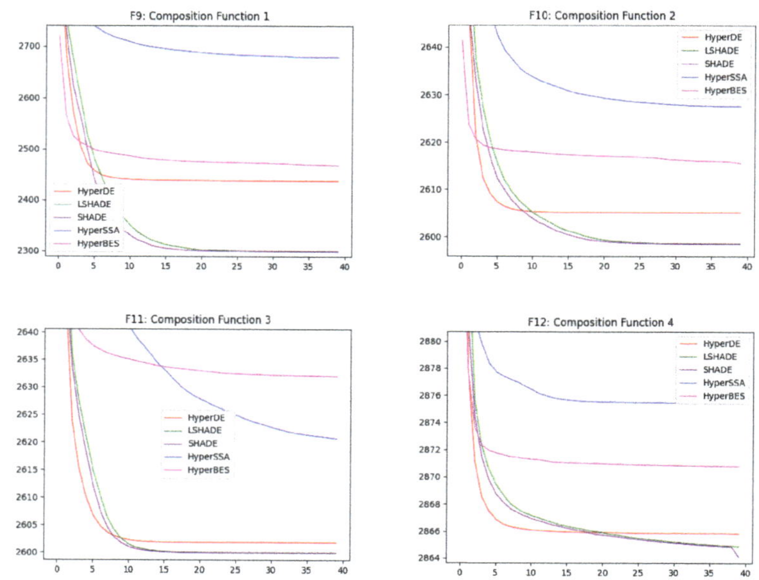

Figure 3. Overall convergence of the best methods.

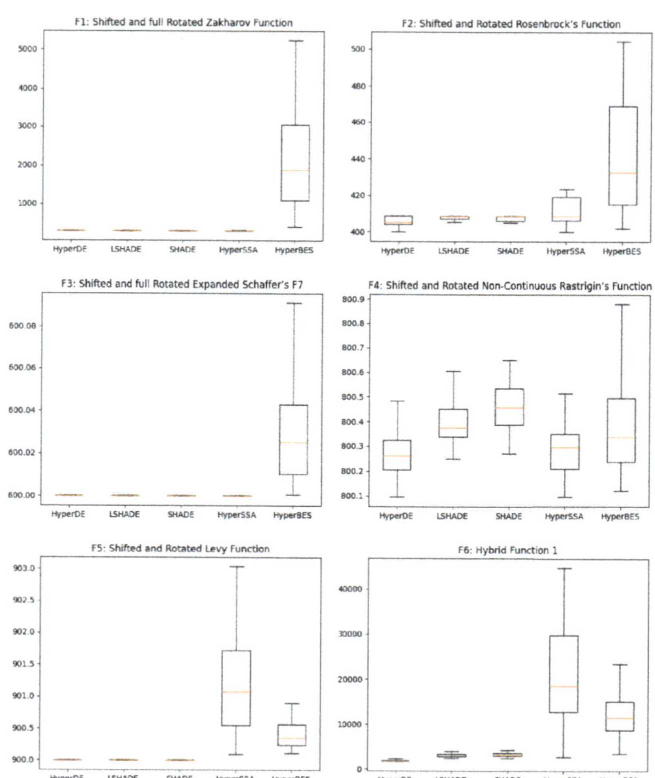

Figure 4. *Cont.*

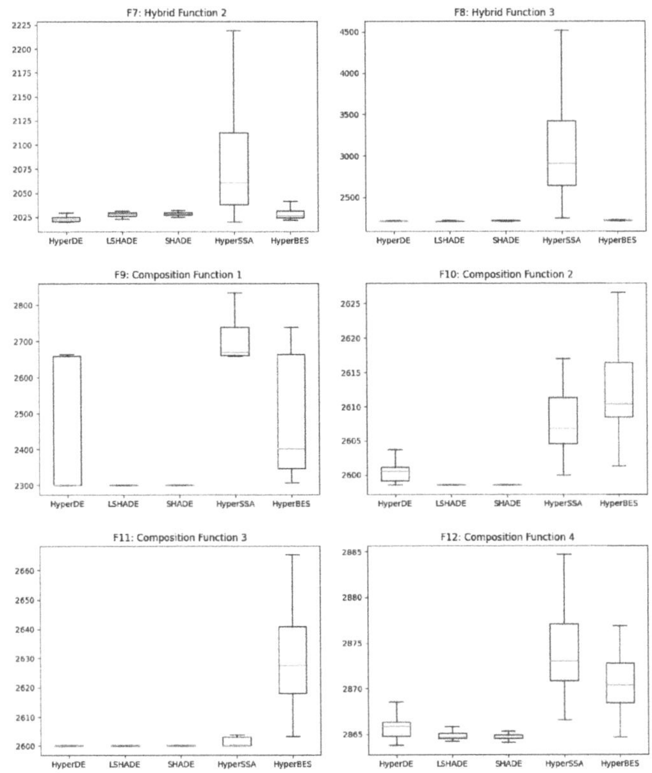

Figure 4. Box plots of the best methods.

7. Conclusions

In this paper, a novel search methodology for global optimization was proposed in the form of an adaptive hyper-heuristic based on the Differential Evolution algorithm along with two other similar approaches. These approaches are highly general in their applicability, having a low number of hyper-parameters that need no adjustments. It was shown that the performance of the main algorithm, HyperDE, is superior relative to the other existent heuristics, obtaining a smaller relative error and the best Friedman rank on a benchmark from the CEC competition. The other two methods are not to be ignored, showing a significant improvement over their counterparts.

There are many possible directions of future work. We plan to improve the efficiency of our implementation, possibly by trying to take advantage of its inherent parallelism. Extension of our technique to other performant heuristic that use a small number of hyper-parameters is envisaged. Also, we plan to compare our method with other methods that tune the hyper-parameters.

Author Contributions: Conceptualization, A.-R.M.; methodology, A.-R.M. and B.D.; software, A.-R.M.; validation, A.-R.M. and B.D.; writing—original draft preparation, A.-R.M.; writing—review and editing, A.-R.M. and B.D.; visualization, A.-R.M.; supervision, B.D. All authors have read and agreed to the published version of the manuscript.

Funding: This work was supported in part by a grant of the Ministry of Research, Innovation and Digitization, CNCS-UEFISCDI, project number PN-III-P4-PCE-2021-0154, within PNCDI III.

Data Availability Statement: No new data were created or analyzed in this study.

Conflicts of Interest: The authors declare no conflict of interest.

References

1. Ma, Z.; Wu, G.; Suganthan, P.N.; Song, A.; Luo, Q. Performance assessment and exhaustive listing of 500+ nature-inspire metaheuristic algorithms. *Swarm Evol. Comput.* **2023**, *77*, 101248. [CrossRef]
2. Kennedy, J.; Eberhart, R. Particle swarm optimization. In Proceedings of the ICNN'95-International Conference on Neur Networks, Perth, WA, Australia, 27 November–1 December 1995; IEEE: New York, NY, USA, 1995; Volume 4, pp. 1942–1948.
3. Kirkpatrick, S.; Gelatt, C.D., Jr.; Vecchi, M.P. Optimization by simulated annealing. *Science* **1983**, *220*, 671–680. [CrossRef]
4. Dorigo, M.; Birattari, M.; Stutzle, T. Ant colony optimization. *IEEE Comput. Intell. Mag.* **2006**, *1*, 28–39. [CrossRef]
5. Karaboga, D.; Basturk, B. A powerful and efficient algorithm for numerical function optimization: Artificial bee colony (AB algorithm. *J. Glob. Optim.* **2007**, *39*, 459–471. [CrossRef]
6. Geem, Z.W.; Kim, J.H.; Loganathan, G.V. A new heuristic optimization algorithm: Harmony search. *Simulation* **2001**, *76*, 60–6 [CrossRef]
7. Rashedi, E.; Nezamabadi-Pour, H.; Saryazdi, S. GSA: A gravitational search algorithm. *Inf. Sci.* **2009**, *179*, 2232–2248. [CrossRe
8. Yang, X.S. Firefly algorithms for multimodal optimization. In Proceedings of the International Symposium on Stochast Algorithms, Sapporo, Japan, 26–28 October 2009; Springer: Berlin/Heidelberg, Germany, 2009; pp. 169–178.
9. Storn, R.; Price, K. Differential evolution-a simple and efficient heuristic for global optimization over continuous spaces. *J. Glo Optim.* **1997**, *11*, 341. [CrossRef]
10. Tanabe, R.; Fukunaga, A. Success-history based parameter adaptation for differential evolution. In Proceedings of the 2013 IEE Congress on Evolutionary Computation, Cancun, Mexico, 20–23 June 2013; IEEE: New York, NY, USA, 2013; pp. 71–78.
11. Tanabe, R.; Fukunaga, A.S. Improving the search performance of SHADE using linear population size reduction. In Proceedin of the 2014 IEEE Congress on Evolutionary Computation (CEC), Beijing, China, 6–11 July 2014; IEEE: New York, NY, USA, 20 pp. 1658–1665.
12. Xue, J.; Shen, B. A novel swarm intelligence optimization approach: Sparrow search algorithm. *Syst. Sci. Control Eng.* **202** *8*, 22–34. [CrossRef]
13. Alsattar, H.A.; Zaidan, A.; Zaidan, B. Novel meta-heuristic bald eagle search optimisation algorithm. *Artif. Intell. Rev.* **202** *53*, 2237–2264. [CrossRef]
14. Mirjalili, S.; Lewis, A. The whale optimization algorithm. *Adv. Eng. Softw.* **2016**, *95*, 51–67. [CrossRef]
15. Heidari, A.A.; Mirjalili, S.; Faris, H.; Aljarah, I.; Mafarja, M.; Chen, H. Harris hawks optimization: Algorithm and applicatio *Future Gener. Comput. Syst.* **2019**, *97*, 849–872. [CrossRef]
16. Yang, Y.; Chen, H.; Heidari, A.A.; Gandomi, A.H. Hunger games search: Visions, conception, implementation, deep analysi perspectives, and towards performance shifts. *Expert Syst. Appl.* **2021**, *177*, 114864. [CrossRef]
17. Camacho-Villalón, C.L.; Dorigo, M.; Stützle, T. Exposing the grey wolf, moth-flame, whale, firefly, bat, and antlion algorithms: S misleading optimization techniques inspired by bestial metaphors. *Int. Trans. Oper. Res.* **2023**, *30*, 2945–2971. [CrossRef]
18. Talatahari, S.; Azizi, M. Chaos Game Optimization: A novel metaheuristic algorithm. *Artif. Intell. Rev.* **2021**, *54*, 917–100 [CrossRef]
19. Li, S.; Chen, H.; Wang, M.; Heidari, A.A.; Mirjalili, S. Slime mould algorithm: A new method for stochastic optimization. *Futu Gener. Comput. Syst.* **2020**, *111*, 300–323. [CrossRef]
20. Gárate-Escamilla, A.K.; Amaya, I.; Cruz-Duarte, J.M.; Terashima-Marín, H.; Ortiz-Bayliss, J.C. Identifying Hyper-Heuristic Trenc through a Text Mining Approach on the Current Literature. *Appl. Sci.* **2022**, *12*, 10576. [CrossRef]
21. Burke, E.K.; Hyde, M.R.; Kendall, G.; Ochoa, G.; Ozcan, E.; Woodward, J.R. Exploring hyper-heuristic methodologies with geneti programming. In *Computational Intelligence*; Springer: Berlin/Heidelberg, Germany, 2009; pp. 177–201.
22. Burke, E.K.; McCollum, B.; Meisels, A.; Petrovic, S.; Qu, R. A graph-based hyper-heuristic for educational timetabling problem *Eur. J. Oper. Res.* **2007**, *176*, 177–192. [CrossRef]
23. Hsiao, P.C.; Chiang, T.C.; Fu, L.C. A vns-based hyper-heuristic with adaptive computational budget of local search. In Proceeding of the 2012 IEEE Congress on Evolutionary Computation, Brisbane, Australia, 10–15 June 2012; IEEE: New York, NY, USA, 201 pp. 1–8.
24. Chen, P.C.; Kendall, G.; Berghe, G.V. An ant based hyper-heuristic for the travelling tournament problem. In Proceedings of th 2007 IEEE Symposium on Computational Intelligence in Scheduling, Honolulu, Hawaii, 1–5 April 2007; IEEE: New York, N USA, 2007; pp. 19–26.
25. Burke, E.K.; Kendall, G.; Soubeiga, E. A tabu-search hyperheuristic for timetabling and rostering. *J. Heuristics* **2003**, *9*, 451–47 [CrossRef]
26. Cowling, P.I.; Chakhlevitch, K. Using a large set of low level heuristics in a hyperheuristic approach to personnel scheduling. I *Evolutionary Scheduling*; Springer: Berlin/Heidelberg, Germany, 2007; pp. 543–576.
27. Han, L.; Kendall, G. Guided operators for a hyper-heuristic genetic algorithm. In Proceedings of the Australasian Joint Conferenc on Artificial Intelligence, Perth, Australia, 3–5 December 2003; Springer: Berlin/Heidelberg, Germany, 2003; pp. 807–820.
28. Bai, R.; Kendall, G. An investigation of automated planograms using a simulated annealing based hyper-heuristic. In *Metaheuri tics: Progress as Real Problem Solvers*; Springer: Berlin/Heidelberg, Germany, 2005; pp. 87–108.
29. Resende, M.G.; de Sousa, J.P.; Nareyek, A. Choosing search heuristics by non-stationary reinforcement learning. In *Metaheuristic Computer Decision-Making*; Springer: Berlin/Heidelberg, Germany, 2004; pp. 523–544.

30. Lim, K.C.W.; Wong, L.P.; Chin, J.F. Simulated-annealing-based hyper-heuristic for flexible job-shop scheduling. In *Engineering Optimization*; Taylor & Francis: Abingdon, UK, 2022; pp. 1–17.
31. Qin, W.; Zhuang, Z.; Huang, Z.; Huang, H. A novel reinforcement learning-based hyper-heuristic for heterogeneous vehicle routing problem. *Comput. Ind. Eng.* **2021**, *156*, 107252. [CrossRef]
32. Lin, J.; Zhu, L.; Gao, K. A genetic programming hyper-heuristic approach for the multi-skill resource constrained project scheduling problem. *Expert Syst. Appl.* **2020**, *140*, 112915. [CrossRef]
33. Oliva, D.; Martins, M.S. A Bayesian based Hyper-Heuristic approach for global optimization. In Proceedings of the 2019 IEEE Congress on Evolutionary Computation (CEC), Wellington, New Zealand, 10–13 June 2019; IEEE: New York, NY, USA, 2019; pp. 1766–1773.
34. Cruz-Duarte, J.M.; Amaya, I.; Ortiz-Bayliss, J.C.; Conant-Pablos, S.E.; Terashima-Marín, H.; Shi, Y. Hyper-heuristics to customise metaheuristics for continuous optimisation. *Swarm Evol. Comput.* **2021**, *66*, 100935. [CrossRef]
35. Burke, E.K.; Hyde, M.R.; Kendall, G.; Ochoa, G.; Özcan, E.; Woodward, J.R. A classification of hyper-heuristic approaches: Revisited. In *Handbook of Metaheuristics*; Springer: Berlin/Heidelberg, Germany, 2019; pp. 453–477.
36. Adam, S.P.; Alexandropoulos, S.A.N.; Pardalos, P.M.; Vrahatis, M.N. No free lunch theorem: A review. In *Approximation and Optimization: Algorithms, Complexity and Applications*; Springer: Berlin/Heidelberg, Germany, 2019; pp. 57–82.
37. Georgioudakis, M.; Plevris, V. A comparative study of differential evolution variants in constrained structural optimization. *Front. Built Environ.* **2020**, *6*, 102. [CrossRef]
38. Thieu, N.V.; Mirjalili, S. MEALPY: A Framework of The State-of-The-Art Meta-Heuristic Algorithms in Python. 2022. Available online: https://zenodo.org/record/6684223 (accessed on 18 September 2023).
39. Katoch, S.; Chauhan, S.S.; Kumar, V. A review on genetic algorithm: Past, present, and future. *Multimed. Tools Appl.* **2021**, *80*, 8091–8126. [CrossRef] [PubMed]

algorithms

MDPI

Article

Enhancing Cryptocurrency Price Forecasting by Integrating Machine Learning with Social Media and Market Data

Loris Belcastro *, Domenico Carbone, Cristian Cosentino, Fabrizio Marozzo * and Paolo Trunfio

Department of Informatics, Modeling, Electronics and Systems Engineering, University of Calabria, 87036 Rende, Italy; dcarbone@dimes.unical.it (D.C.); ccosentino@dimes.unical.it (C.C.); trunfio@dimes.unical.it (P.T.)

* Correspondence: lbelcastro@dimes.unical.it (L.B.); fmarozzo@dimes.unical.it (F.M.)

Abstract: Since the advent of Bitcoin, the cryptocurrency landscape has seen the emergence of severa virtual currencies that have quickly established their presence in the global market. The dynamic of this market, influenced by a multitude of factors that are difficult to predict, pose a challenge t fully comprehend its underlying insights. This paper proposes a methodology for suggesting when i is appropriate to buy or sell cryptocurrencies, in order to maximize profits. Starting from large set of market and social media data, our methodology combines different statistical, text analytics, an deep learning techniques to support a recommendation trading algorithm. In particular, we exploi additional information such as correlation between social media posts and price fluctuations, causa connection among prices, and the sentiment of social media users regarding cryptocurrencies. Severa experiments were carried out on historical data to assess the effectiveness of the trading algorithm achieving an overall average gain of 194% without transaction fees and 117% when considerin fees. In particular, among the different types of cryptocurrencies considered (i.e., high capitalizatior solid projects, and meme coins), the trading algorithm has proven to be very effective in predictin the price trends of influential meme coins, yielding considerably higher profits compared to othe cryptocurrency types.

Keywords: cryptocurrency; social media data; price prediction; trading recommendation; machin learning; deep learning

Citation: Belcastro, L.; Carbone, D.; Cosentino, C.; Marozzo, F.; Trunfio, P. Enhancing Cryptocurrency Price Forecasting by Integrating Machine Learning with Social Media and Market Data. *Algorithms* **2023**, *16*, 542. https://doi.org/10.3390/a16120542

Academic Editor: Frank Werner

Received: 1 November 2023
Revised: 23 November 2023
Accepted: 24 November 2023
Published: 27 November 2023

1. Introduction

Following the pioneering launch of Bitcoin by Satoshi Nakamoto, a multitude of vir tual currencies have seen notable increases in both their value and widespread acceptanc For instance, Ethereum and Litecoin emerged as prominent contenders, with Ethereum' smart contract capabilities driving its rapid ascent, while Litecoin focused on enhancin the transaction speed and scalability, making it a popular choice for everyday transaction Today, the cryptocurrency landscape boasts thousands of coins, many of which are char acterized by volatility and a lack of substantial projects [1]. Their value and volatility ar influenced by factors such as popularity obtained through word of mouth on social media For example, viral memes related to specific coins can drive a wave of interest, promptin people to invest based on the excitement generated by these online phenomena.

In recent years, the cryptocurrency market has witnessed extraordinary success, largel as a result of innovative marketing strategies adopted by exchange platforms [2]. These strategies, encompassing user-friendly interfaces and educational resources, have mad cryptocurrency investments more approachable, leading to a surge in market growth. More over, influential people have wielded their substantial social media presence to endors or critique cryptocurrencies through tweets and public statements, contributing to bot market volatility and a surge in public interest [3]. Based on the dynamic context of the cryptocurrency market, this paper delves into the analysis of factors that influence pric movements, mainly focusing on market dynamics and content published on social media

Our methodology involves predicting the cryptocurrency price movements by analyzing two large datasets: one comprising market data like prices and trading volumes for specific cryptocurrencies, and the other containing social media posts discussing these coins. These datasets were properly merged and analyzed using a set of statistical, text analytics, and deep learning techniques. Several studies have demonstrated substantial economic benefits for investors by leveraging machine learning predictions, which allow one to predict stock [4], equity risk [5], or bond [6] premiums, compared to a risk-free investments. In particular, in many cases, the use of machine learning techniques surpasses leading regression-based strategies, even doubling their effectiveness in certain cases, especially using decision trees and neural networks [7,8]. The goal of this methodology is to develop a trading recommendation algorithm that can identify optimal moments for buying and selling cryptocurrencies in order to maximize profits.

The proposed methodology is composed of different phases: data collection, data preprocessing, data enrichment, training machine learning models, and trading recommendation. To enhance the predictive capabilities of our methodology, we augmented these datasets with three additional features: (*i*) correlation between social media activities and cryptocurrency price fluctuations; (*ii*) causal connection among prices of cryptocurrencies, so as to consider how they influence each other and the impact that the most popular cryptocurrencies have on the broader market; and (*iii*) the sentiment of users about cryptocurrencies, obtained through a textual analysis of posts published on social media. Such datasets were used to train an long short-term memory (LSTM) model for predicting the prices of cryptocurrencies, supporting a trading recommendation algorithm capable of identifying and exploiting the direction in which the price of a cryptocurrency is moving (e.g., upward or downward trend). Unlike other existing works, our research supports price forecasting for different types of cryptocurrencies (i.e., high capitalization, solid projects, and meme coins), providing excellent market coverage. Our methodology stands out for its comprehensive analysis, encompassing a wide range of features to enhance cryptocurrency price forecasting. This includes evaluating correlations and causal connections among coins, as well as the detection of bot activities that can influence price predictions. Additionally, our solution extensively utilizes text analysis techniques on social media data to extract information about the popularity, overall market perception, and users' sentiment regarding specific cryptocurrencies.

Several experiments were carried out on historical data to assess the effectiveness of the trading algorithm. By investing in a selected set of cryptocurrencies, the trading algorithm achieved an overall average profit of 194% when transaction fees were not taken into account and 117% when transaction fees were considered. Focusing only on influential meme coins, the algorithm resulted in a very high profit of 902% with fees and 1258% without fees.

The structure of this paper is as follows. Section 2 discusses related work in the cryptocurrency field and provides a comparison between our methodology and existing research. Section 3 describes the proposed methodology. Section 4 discusses the achieved results. Finally, Section 5 concludes the paper.

2. Related Work

The cryptocurrency market has become a sector of growing interest, characterized by significant volatility and a wide variety of speculative activities. In this context, the accurate prediction of cryptocurrency prices has played a crucial role for investors, traders, and stakeholders in the financial industry. The use of machine learning and deep learning techniques has emerged as a research avenue to support cryptocurrency price predictions. In this section, we provide an overview of the existing related work, highlighting the most used approaches and challenges in cryptocurrency price forecasting.

Nowadays, the use of machine learning and deep learning techniques for price prediction is widespread [9–11]. Several studies have explored the application of neural networks, support vector machines, and other supervised learning models to predict cryptocurrency prices over time [12–14]. In particular, the use of methods such as long-short-term memo (LSTM) neural networks has shown particular promise in addressing time series challeng and identifying nonlinear patterns in price fluctuations [15–20]. Some works have exploite linear regression and random forest methods to analyze the model performance and pr itability of trading strategies [21,22]. Other studies have proposed novel models based c recurrent neural network (RNN) models, such as GRU, LSTM, and bi-LSTM, to achiev precise cryptocurrency price forecasts [23,24]. Such approaches have provided accura results and demonstrated their ability to detect complex dynamics, which can suppo trading decisions [25–27].

Other studies have explored the potential of employing text analysis on social med data to enhance the ability to predict cryptocurrency prices. Specifically, studies conducte by [28,29] have demonstrated that the sentiment analysis applied to social media posts ca offer valuable insights into understanding the dynamics behind price fluctuations. Th sentiment analysis of cryptocurrency-related tweets has mostly been conducted using too such as VADER [30] and TextBlob [31], both of which have proven their effectiveness i several related works [3,27,32].

Kim et al. [33] demonstrated that the utilization of on-chain data (i.e., data direct from the blockchain) can provide valuable insights into the dynamics of cryptocurrenc prices. Similarly, the analysis of on-chain data in conjunction with change point detectio methodologies has contributed to enhancing the accuracy of cryptocurrency price forecas and assisting investors in making more informed decisions [34,35].

Table 1 presents a comparison among the most recent works in the field of cryptocu rency price forecasting, which exploit different data and features. Specifically, each propose algorithm or methodology has been evaluated based on the following characteristics:

- *Price Trend (PT)*: identifying and exploiting the direction in which the price of cryptocurrency is moving (e.g., upward trend, downward trend).
- *Instant of Trading (IT)*: discovering the specific moment to buy/sell a cryptocurrenc
- *Publication Frequency (PF)*: exploiting social media data mentioning a particular cry tocurrency.
- *Impressions (I)*: evaluating the overall market sentiment or public perception about specific cryptocurrency.
- *Sentiment Analysis (SA)*: analyzing users' sentiments and opinions to gauge the ma ket's mood regarding a particular cryptocurrency.
- *Bot Analysis (BA)*: detecting the activities of bots on social media, as the posts the publish can influence the price prediction process.
- *Correlation among Coins (CC)*: measuring the relationship between the price movemen of different cryptocurrencies, such as correlation and causality.
- *Trading Indicators (TI)*: exploiting market metrics and signals used by traders to mak trading decisions, such as moving averages, relative strength index (RSI), movin average convergence divergence (MACD).
- *Deep Learning*: using deep learning approaches for price forecasting.
- *Type of Coins*: defining the type of cryptocurrencies considered for price predictio which can belong to the four categories discussed in Section 3.1, i.e., Solid Project (SP High Capitalization (HC), Influential Meme (IM), and Volatile Meme (VM) coins.

Our work stands out in the comparison due to its comprehensive analysis, encompas ing almost all available features. Unlike other works, our research supports price forecastin for different types of cryptocurrencies (HC, SP, and IM), providing excellent market co erage. We excluded support for Volatile Meme (VM) coins due to their unpredictabl and speculative nature, which makes them highly susceptible to market manipulatio In addition, we also discard posts with advertising content, often generated by bots fo promoting online trading platforms, which can disturb the price prediction process.

Table 1. Comparison among existing related works and their features.

Related Work	PT	TI	Social Media Data				Market Data		Deep Learning	Type of Coins
			PF	I	SA	BA	CC	TI		
Hitam et al. [12]	x	-	-	-	-	-	x	x	x	HC, SP
Abraham et al. [10]	x	-	-	-	x	-	-	-	-	HC
Lahmiri et al. [16]	x	-	-	-	-	-	-	x	x	HC
Vo et al. [28]	x	-	-	-	x	-	-	-	x	HC
Rathan et al. [25]	x	-	-	-	-	-	-	-	-	HC
Valencia et al. [9]	x	-	-	-	x	-	-	x	x	HC
Wołk [27]	x	-	x	x	x	-	-	-	x	HC, SP
Patel et al. [15]	x	-	-	-	-	-	-	-	x	-
Ioannis et al. [24]	x	x	-	-	-	-	x	x	x	-
Khedr et al. [13]	x	-	-	-	-	-	-	x	x	HC, SP
Jay et al. [14]	x	-	-	-	-	-	-	x	x	HC, SP
Poongodi et al. [18]	x	-	-	-	-	-	-	x	x	-
Mirtaheri et al. [26]	-	-	x	x	x	x	-	-	-	HC
Hamayel et al. [23]	x	-	-	-	-	-	-	-	x	HC
Tanwar et al. [34]	x	-	-	-	-	-	x	-	x	HC
Shahbazi et al. [35]	x	-	-	-	-	-	-	x	x	HC, SP
Kim et al. [33]	x	-	-	-	-	-	-	-	x	HC
Van Tran et al. [21]	x	x	-	-	-	-	x	x	-	HC, SP, IM
Ammer et al. [17]	x	x	-	-	-	-	x	x	x	HC, SP, IM, VM
Fleischer et al. [20]	x	x	-	-	-	-	x	x	x	-
Sun et al. [22]	x	x	-	-	-	-	-	-	-	HC, SP, IM
Sebastião et al. [29]	x	x	-	-	-	-	-	x	-	HC, SP
Lamon et al. [19]	x	-	-	-	x	-	-	-	-	HC
Our work	x	x	x	x	x	x	x	x	x	**HC, SP, IM**

3. Proposed Methodology

Our methodology aims to predict the price movements of cryptocurrencies through the examination of two large datasets: the first contains market data (e.g., prices and exchanged volumes) of a set of cryptocurrencies; and the second contains posts published on social media discussing such coins. These datasets have been combined and analyzed using different statistical analysis, text analysis, and deep learning techniques. The goal of the methodology is to define a trading algorithm capable of suggesting the moments in which to carry out sell-and-buy operations to maximize profits.

As illustrated in Figure 1, the methodology is composed of different phases: data collection, data preprocessing, data enrichment, training machine learning models, and trading recommendation. In the following, we discuss each phase in detail, highlighting the crucial and strategic decisions that characterize our methodology.

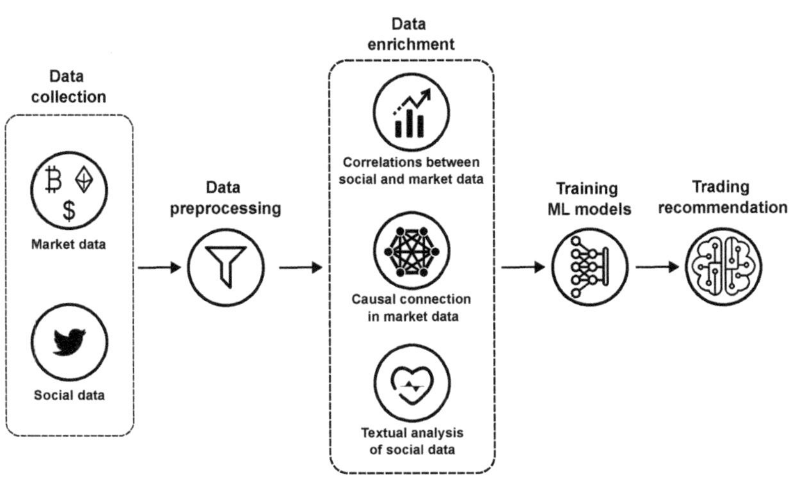

Figure 1. Execution flow of the proposed methodology.

To deal with such large and heterogeneous data, we leveraged Apache Spark to proces them efficiently. The use of such a framework for Big Data is widely adopted in the realn of Big Data analytics, enabling faster and more scalable data processing [36].

3.1. Data Collection and Preprocessing

In the data collection phase, we gather market and social media data related to selected group of cryptocurrencies. Our focus is on a heterogeneous set of representativ cryptocurrencies chosen from the most popular ones. As shown in Table 2, these cryptocu rencies have been categorized into four distinct categories based on their characteristics:

- *High Capitalization (HC)*: this category includes cryptocurrencies such as Bitcoin an Ethereum, which are highly popular and have a significant impact on the worl of cryptocurrencies.
- *Solid Project (SP)*: it includes cryptocurrencies backed by a robust project, althoug they may be less popular. Examples include Solana and Conflux, which form th foundation for various types of blockchains, as well as projects like The Sandbo which is associated with the metaverse and NFT-related initiatives.
- *Influential Meme (IM)*: it includes coins that do not rely on solid projects (i.e., mem coins). Despite their lower capitalization and the absence of substantial projects, the have a significant influence on the world of cryptocurrencies due to their history an popularity on social media.
- *Volatile Meme (VM)*: this category comprises cryptocurrencies created purely for spe ulative purposes, characterized by high volatility and substantial price fluctuation within short time periods.

Table 2. List of cryptocurrencies used for the analysis.

Category	Acronym	Cryptocurrencies
High Capitalization	**HC**	Bitcoin (BTC), Ethereum (ETH), Polygon (MATIC), Polkadot (DOT), Solana (SOL), Cosmos (ATOM), Stellar (XLM), Avalanche (AVAX), Tron (TRX), Litecoin (LTC)
Solid Project	**SP**	Conflux (CFX), Stacks (STX), Fantom (FTM), Quant (QNT) Loopring (LRC), The sandbox (SAND), Gala (GALA), Lido Dao (LDO), Cronos (CRON), Zilliqa (ZIL), Chiliz (CHZ), Neo (NEO), Vethor Token (VTHO), Bancor (BNT), The Graph (GRT)
Influent Meme	**IM**	Dogecoin (DOGE), Shiba Inu (SHIB), Decentraland (MANA)
Volatile Meme	**VM**	Babydoge Coin (BabyDoge), Floki (Floki), Catecoin (CATE), Dogelon Mars (ELON), Volt Inu v2 (VOLT), Dejitaru Tsuka (TSUKA), Kishu Inu (KISHU), Shiba Predator (SHIBAP), Pitbull (PIT), Akita Inu (AKITA)

For each coin considered, we collected historical data on market performance fron the CoinMarketCap website (https://coinmarketcap.com/, accessed on 1 November 2023 which provides information about price fluctuations (hourly, daily, weekly), market capi talization, daily traded amounts, and volumes of coins that are circulating in the marke Specifically, we gathered comprehensive market data for a selected group of cryptocurren cies spanning from January 2021 to March 2023. Cryptocurrency prices have been tracke over time in Tether (USDT), which is a stable coin designed to maintain a fixed 1:1 rati with the US dollar. The analysis of market data was of great use in evaluating some ke aspects of the relationships existing among the different cryptocurrencies, as discussed i the following.

Subsequently, the posts published by users talking about these coins were collecte on social media platforms. In particular, we collected a large set of tweets published i the considered period, using the Twitter APIs with a set of keywords associated with th considered coins. Each collected tweet contains specific attributes, including the timestam indicating when the tweet was posted, textual content, hashtags used, the author's user name, the number of followers, and a flag indicating the user's account verification status enhancing the reliability of the collected information. Furthermore, we decided to discard tweets with advertising content, for example, those generated for promotional purposes by online trading platforms, often utilizing bots, which frequently mention multiple cryptocurrencies in their text. Then, each post in the dataset has been modified by applying some common preprocessing operations, such as removing usernames and mentions, special characters, URLs, and so on.

The final datasets include the hourly market information of the coins under analysis and approximately 133 million tweets, which are used to extract valuable insights about popularity trends, price fluctuations, and users' investment behaviors.

3.2. Data Enrichment

After the preprocessing phase, our final datasets comprise detailed hourly market data and an extensive collection of tweets related to the selected cryptocurrencies. To enhance the predictive capabilities of our methodology, we augmented these datasets with three additional information, as detailed in the following sections. In Section 3.2.1, we analyzed the correlation between social media activities and cryptocurrency price fluctuations. Section 3.2.2 investigates how cryptocurrency prices influence each other, with a particular focus on the impact of well-known cryptocurrencies on the broader market. Finally, in Section 3.2.3, we examined the textual content of posts published by social media users, aggregating their expressed opinions about cryptocurrencies, so as to identify the sentiment and utilize it to improve the prediction of cryptocurrency prices.

3.2.1. Correlation between Social Media and Market Data

At this step, we started from the intuition that the information extracted from social media has a strong correlation with the price fluctuations of cryptocurrencies. For each considered cryptocurrency, we calculated some social engagement metrics (number of tweets, followers, likes, and retweets) to determine their correlation with the daily closing prices. In particular, we used both Pearson and Spearman correlation tests, which are statistical measures used to assess the relationships between variables. The Pearson correlation evaluates linear relationships between normally distributed time series data, while Spearman evaluates monotonic relationships between variables, which may not necessarily be linear. Given the nature of cryptocurrency prices and social data, both correlation measures were considered to provide a comprehensive understanding of the relationship among time series. For example, Figure 2 provides a view of the social metrics and price fluctuations of Shiba Inu, where the values have been normalized to make the chart more understandable and comparable.

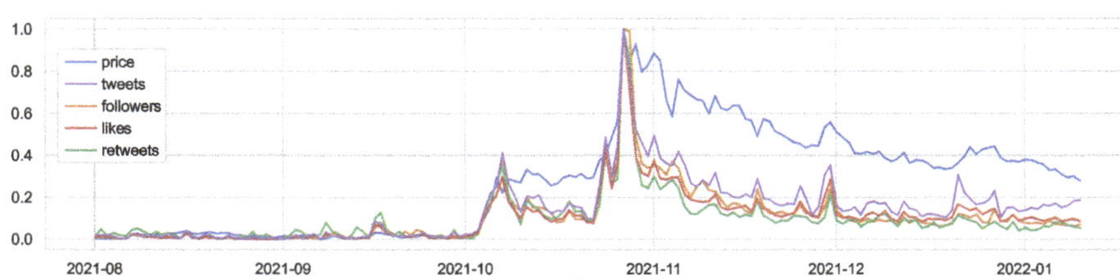

Figure 2. A five-month view of daily Twitter metrics and a closing price associated with Shiba Inu.

For all the cryptocurrencies considered, it has been verified that there is a strong correlation between the social metrics introduced above and the daily closing price. For example, Table 3 reports the Pearson and Spearman correlation coefficients of three meme coins (i.e., Shiba Inu, Floki, and CateCoin). As shown, the results indicate strong positive correlations between the tweet volume and cryptocurrency prices (ranging from 0.723 to 0.868 for Pearson and 0.841 to 0.909 for Spearman). The follower count exhibits moderate correlations, while likes and retweets show variable values, with Floki showing a strong correlation.

Table 3. Correlation coefficients between the price and social metrics for three meme coins (Shib Inu, Floki, and CateCoin).

	Shiba Inu		*Floki*		*CateCoin*	
Category	*Pearson*	*Spearman*	*Pearson*	*Spearman*	*Pearson*	*Spearman*
Tweets	0.723	0.841	0.868	0.909	0.797	0.880
Followers	0.659	0.761	0.523	0.858	0.320	0.751
Likes	0.752	0.849	0.896	0.913	0.414	0.854
Retweets	0.796	0.850	0.889	0.913	0.674	0.831

Finally, these correlation values are added as features to the dataset in order to us them for training a machine learning model.

3.2.2. Causal Connection in Market Data

In this phase, it was evaluated how the prices of the different cryptocurrencies consi ered influence each other. The underlying idea behind this analysis is that fluctuations i the prices of popular cryptocurrencies, such as Ethereum and Bitcoin, may causally affe the prices of other coins. Following the approaches used in [37,38], the Granger causalit test was employed to determine whether price variations in one cryptocurrency can b considered the cause of price changes in another coin.

The Granger causality test is used to determine whether a time variable X can b considered the cause of another time variable Y. During this test, the p-value, a widely use statistical concept for assessing evidence in support of or against a statistical hypothesi is computed using the *F-test*. Such a test involves two main steps. In the first ste two regression models are built: the first uses only past values of Y to predict its curre value, while the second model uses both past values of Y and X to predict the curre value of Y. In the second step, the goodness of fit of the two models is compared using statistical test. The test makes use of the following regression model:

$$y_t = \alpha_0 + \sum_{j=1}^{m} \alpha_j y_{t-j} + \sum_{j=1}^{m} \beta_j x_{t-j} + k_t$$

where: $alpha_0$ is the intercept term in the regression model; x_t represents the variab X at time t; y_t represents the variable Y at time t; β_j for $j = 1, \ldots, m$ are the regressio coefficients; and k_t represents the error at time t. This test is based on the null hypothesis

$$H_0 : \beta_1 = \beta_2 = \ldots = \beta_m = 0$$

when X causes Y, according to the Granger causality test, the null hypothesis is rejected.

Let us suppose that the null hypothesis represents the initial assumption that the pric variations of one cryptocurrency do not influence the price variations of another currenc The alternative hypothesis represents the hypothesis we want to support if the data provid sufficient evidence against the null hypothesis. The p-value is compared to a predefine level of significance, denoted by *alpha*, which represents the maximum probability o making an error, incorrectly rejecting the null hypothesis when it is true. If the p-valu is less than the level of significance *alpha* (typically 0.05), the null hypothesis is rejecte and it is concluded that the data provide statistical evidence in support of the alternativ hypothesis. In other words, it is believed that there is a significant effect or relationshi between the price variations of one cryptocurrency and that of another. Conversely, if th p-value is greater than *alpha*, there is not enough evidence to reject the null hypothesi and therefore, it cannot be stated that there is a significant effect or relationship betwee the price variations of the two currencies. For example, considering the cryptocurrenc Cosmos (ATOM), a cryptocurrency belonging to the solid project category, the Grange causality test indicated that its price is mostly influenced by Litecoin (LTC), as evidence by a p-value of 0.0102.

Considering a 3-day time window, p-values for each pair of cryptocurrencies have been calculated using hourly prices. Subsequently, for each cryptocurrency, the hourly price variations and exponential moving average of the price for the three cryptocurrencies that most influence that coin (i.e., the ones with the lowest p-value and those below the *alpha* level) were added to the final dataset.

3.2.3. Textual Analysis of Social Data

At this stage of the methodology, a textual analysis was carried out on the large dataset collected from social media. As discussed before, the dataset is a rich repository of posts authored by users who explicitly mention at least one of the cryptocurrencies under analysis. In particular, we analyzed the textual content of each post for determining its sentiment, categorizing it as either negative, positive, or neutral. In such a way, it is possible to assess the collective sentiment of social media users at any given moment with respect to a particular cryptocurrency. This insight is very important for predicting cryptocurrency price movements: a positive sentiment often heralds a potential price increase, while conversely, a negative sentiment can foreshadow a decline in value. Specifically, the sentiment analysis of cryptocurrency-related posts has been carried out using two different tools, VADER [30] and TextBlob [31], which have been used in many other related work [3,27,32].

VADER is a lexical-based model using an annotated lexicon of English words with sentiment valence scores. It also considers negations, intensity modulators, and word order for precise sentiment analysis. In contrast, TextBlob is a Python library for natural language processing that assigns polarity scores on a scale from -1 (very negative) to 1 (very positive) and provides a subjectivity score. Following the same approach used in [39], to improve the VADER lexicon and better adapt it to the cryptocurrency context, the scores of some terms in VADER have been redefined. In fact, in the context of cryptocurrencies, specific terms are commonly used to identify phenomena of considerable importance, but VADER identifies them as common terms. For example, the terms *buy*, *moon*, and *rocket* suggest that the price of a cryptocurrency is going to see a huge increase, but they have a neutral score according to the original VADER lexicon.

The information on the collective sentiment about the different cryptocurrencies has then been added to the final dataset, in order to provide additional training data for the machine learning model used to predict prices.

3.3. *Training Machine Learning Models*

In this phase, a wide set of machine learning algorithms have been evaluated to choose the best solution for predicting prices of cryptocurrencies, including ensemble regressor and neural network algorithms. Concerning ensemble regressors, we used: *Random Forest* [40], which exploits a forest of decision trees; *XGBoost* [41], which provides a parallel tree boosting; and *CatBoost* [42], which utilizes a categorical feature-aware boosting algorithm. As for neural networks, we employed the following algorithms: *Conv1D* [43], which is a one-dimensional convolutional neural network (CNN) architecture suitable for sequence data; *GRU* (Gated Recurrent Unit) [44], which is a specialized recurrent neural network (RNN) designed for handling long-range dependencies in sequential data; and *LSTM* [44], which is an RNN that is particularly effective in modeling complex patterns and relationships over extended sequences. In particular, using the hyperparameter values shown in Table 4, these algorithms have been trained using data collected during the period from January 2021 to December 2021, related to the cryptocurrencies listed in Table 2. Subsequently, the different models obtained were tested on data collected during the period ranging from January 2022 to March 2023.

Table 4. Hyperparameter values used for the algorithms under comparison.

Model	Hyperparameters
Random forest	max_features: $\sqrt{n}$; min_samples_split: 5; estimators: 300
XGBoost	eta: 0.01; gamma: 150; n_estimators: 100; subsample: 1
CatBoost	depth: 6; iterations: 200; learning_rate: 0.1; l2_leaf_reg: 0.2
Conv1D	conv1d_layer: [units: 256; kernel_size: 2; activation: ReLU]; flatten_layer: yes; dense_layer_1: [units: 8; activation: ReLU]; dense_layer_2: [units: 1; activation: linear]; optimizer: Adam; learning_rate: 0.0001; epoch: 200
GRU	gru_layer_units: 256; dense_layer_1: [units: 8; activation: ReLU]; dense_layer_2: [units: 1; activation: linear]; optimizer: Adam; learning_rate: 0.0001; epoch: 200
LSTM	lstm_layer_units: 32; lstm_layer_2_units: 64; dense_layer_1: [units: 8; activation: ReLU]; dense_layer_2: [units: 1; activation: linear]; optimizer: Adam; learning_rate: 0.0001; epoch: 200

Table 5 shows a comparative overview of the performance obtained by the differen machine learning models that have been tested. As shown, long short-term memory (LSTM appears to be the best-performing model among the ones listed. It has the lowest RMSE (0.003), MAE (0.002), and MAPE (1.2%), indicating that it predicts cryptocurrency prices with the smallest errors compared to the other models. Additionally, it has the highest R^2 value (0.97), suggesting that it explains a larger portion of the variance in the data, making it a strong choice for predicting cryptocurrency prices in this context. The results obtained are in line with what we expected. In fact, the benefits of LSTMs for cryptocurrency price prediction have been confirmed in other studies [45,46], which have highlighted that LSTMs are the best model for short-term price prediction.

Table 5. Performance comparison of the different machine learning algorithms in predicting cryptocurrency prices.

Model	Category	RMSE	MAE	R^2	MAPE
Random forest	Tree-based	0.085	0.055	0.75	5.2%
XGBoost	Tree-based	0.110	0.070	0.68	6.8%
CatBoost	Tree-based	0.025	0.035	0.92	1.7%
Conv1D	CNN	0.005	0.003	0.95	1.4%
GRU	RNN	0.004	0.002	0.96	1.3%
LSTM	RNN	**0.003**	**0.002**	**0.97**	**1.2%**

Taking into account such results, we used an architecture consisting of two LSTM layers, followed by two densely connected layers. The first two LSTM layers capture long term dependencies in the time sequence, while the subsequent dense layers handle data transformation and final prediction. Specifically, the first LSTM layer has been configured with 32 memory units, while the second one has been configured with 64 memory units The next densely connected layers exploit a rectified linear unit (ReLU) activation function which is commonly used to introduce nonlinearity into the neural network.

3.4. Trading Recommendation

The final phase of our methodology focused on defining a trading recommendation algorithm that exploits price predictions based on the LSTM model. The trading algorithm aims to suggest when is most appropriate to initiate trading operations (buy or sell) for a given cryptocurrency. To simplify the proposed heuristic, the algorithm invests the entire capital available in the account at each operation. However, in the future, less risky approaches could be studied, which involve better capital management in order to control losses. The algorithm takes into account some aspects:

- *Impact of commissions*: commission costs depend on the trading platform used, and thus, the algorithm is designed to take into account a certain percentage of the invested capital to be paid as transaction fees.
- *Identification of strong trends*: the algorithm implements a heuristic to limit the number of transactions, starting a new one only in the presence of a significant event. In this way, it is possible to avoid imprudent operations during phases of price uncertainty, with notable benefits in terms of profits.
- *Use of take-profit*: it leads the algorithm to close operations when the profit percentage exceeds a certain threshold.
- *Use of stop-loss*: it closes operations when the loss percentage exceeds a certain threshold.

It is worth noting that the algorithm is based on *future trading*, which allows traders to buy or sell cryptocurrencies at a predetermined price at a specified future date. This trading strategy enables traders to speculate on the price movements without owning the cryptocurrency. Specifically, traders can do two different types of trading operations: *shorting* a cryptocurrency or *going long* on a cryptocurrency. Shorting a cryptocurrency means betting that its price will decrease. Traders who short-sell borrow the cryptocurrency and sell it at the current price, hoping to buy it back later at a lower price, thus making a profit from the difference. On the contrary, going long on a cryptocurrency means betting that its value will rise, allowing traders to sell it later at a higher price and make a profit from the difference.

Algorithm 1 shows the pseudo-code of the *OpenTransaction* procedure, implementing the proposed trading algorithm that automates decisions on when to open and close operations based on the analysis of real and predicted prices. The algorithm receives the following parameters as input: a cryptocurrency C; a time E beyond which the execution of the trading algorithm ends; the loss percentage LV beyond which to activate the stop-loss procedure; the percentage gain PV beyond which to activate the take-profit procedure; a number D that indicates the time window (in days) for data used by the prediction model; a time W to wait before opening a trading operation; DB, the reference to the dataset containing aggregated social media and market information; $LSTM$, the trained neural network model for predicting prices; and a sleep time S between one completed operation and the next.

Algorithm 1 Pseudocode of the trading algorithm.

```
procedure OPENTRANSACTION(C,E, LV, PV, D, W, DB, LSTM, S)
    op ← null
    while now() < E do
        if op is null then
            previousData ← DB.getLastDaysData(C, D)
            P_p ← LSTM.predict(C, previousData)
            P_r ← getRealPrice(C)
            if intersect(P_r, P_p) then
                wait(W)                                   ▷ Safety waiting time
                if P_r > P_p then
                    op ← openSellOperation(C)             ▷ Betting against (or shorting) cryptocurrency C.
                else
                    op ← openBuyOperation(C)              ▷ Betting in favor of (or going long on) cryptocurrency C.
                end if
            end if
        else
            if op.isSell() then
                if hoursPredictedPriceGreaterThanReal(C) > W or checkStopLossOrTakeProfit(LV, PV) then
                    op.close()
                end if
            else
                if hoursRealPriceGreaterThanPredicted(C) > W or checkStopLossOrTakeProfit(LV, PV) then
                    op.close()
                end if
            end if
            if p.isClosed() then
                op.calculateProfit()
                op ← null
            end if
        end if
    end while
    return
end procedure
```

Given a reference cryptocurrency C, the algorithm initializes a variable op as nu which will be used to represent the current trading operation (line 2). Then, it initiates while loop that continues until the current time exceeds the specified duration E for tradir (line 3). If the op variable is null, indicating no active trading operation, then the algorith tries to start a new one.

To this end, it calculates the predicted and real prices for the cryptocurrency. I particular, the predicted price is given by the LSTM model based on the provide last D-days historical data (lines 5–6), while the real price is gathered from mark coin APIs (line 7). The algorithm checks whether the predicted price and real pri intersect (line 8), indicating a potential trading opportunity. After waiting a safe time W (line 9), aiming to avoid price retracements, the algorithm decides the type trading operation to perform. Price retracements represent temporary and relative short corrections within a growth or decline trend of a specific asset. They are commo phenomena in financial markets, including cryptocurrency markets, and can offer tradir and investment opportunities. Specifically, if the real price is greater than the predicte price, it starts a sell operation (lines 10–11), betting that the price will decrease (shorting Otherwise, it starts a buy operation (lines 12–13), betting that the price will rise (goin long). If op is defined, which means a trading operation is active, the algorithm star monitoring the prices of the cryptocurrency to establish whether the current operatio should be closed (lines 17–25). In particular, it checks whether the hours in which th predicted price exceeded the real price (or vice versa) have exceeded a given waitin time of W or if the stop-loss/take-profit condition is met. To close a sell operation, th algorithm checks whether, during the monitoring period (i.e., the period in which th operation is active), the predicted price P_r of the cryptocurrency always remained high than the real one or if the stop-loss/take-profit condition is met (lines 17–20). Similarly, close a buy operation, the algorithm checks whether the real price has always remaine higher than the predicted one for a time greater than W or if the stop-loss/take-prof condition is met (lines 21–25). If op has been closed, the profit (or loss) obtained from th trading operation is calculated (line 27); afterward, the variable op is set to null (line 2 to allow the start of a new trading operation.

Figure 3 illustrates how the trading algorithm operates, using the cryptocurrenc Shiba Inu as an example. As shown in Figure 3a, the first black vertical line (A) mark the point where the predicted price (P_p) intersects with the real price (P_r). Following th intersection, the real price consistently remains higher than the predicted price for the ne time W (depicted in orange). As there are no subsequent intersections during W, indicatin a stable downward trend, the algorithm suggests that a downward trend may be ongoin and starts a new shorting operation.

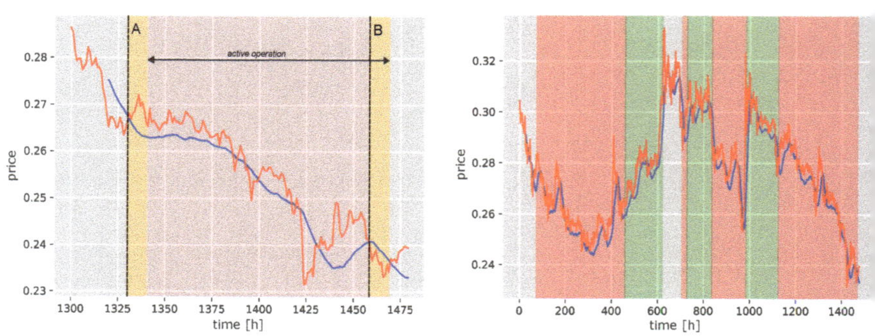

(**a**) Example of shorting operation.

(**b**) Operation opened in a period of two months fo Shiba Inu.

Figure 3. Example of how the trading algorithm works (the red line indicates the real price while th blue line indicates the predicted price).

At each subsequent intersection, the algorithm assesses whether it is advantageous to close the existing trading operation, observing a waiting period of W before making a decision. In the example, the second vertical black line (B) represents the intersection that leads to the closure of the operation. After B, the predicted price remains below the real price for a period W, suggesting a possible end of the downward trend. Consequently, the shorting operation is closed. The interval during which the algorithm kept the shorting operation open is represented by the red area.

Figure 3b illustrates the operations that have been initiated in two months of tests, using the cryptocurrency Shiba Inu. Specifically, the periods during which shorting operations were opened are highlighted in red, those in which long ongoing operations were opened and marked in green, while periods with no active operations were marked in gray.

4. Experimental Results

Several experiments were conducted on historical data to assess the effectiveness of the trading algorithm. Additionally, a phase of parameter tuning was carried out with the goal of identifying optimal values to maximize profits. The parameters assessed during this process included the take-profit (PV) and stop-loss (LV) percentages, as well as the duration of the safety interval before opening a trading operation (W), and the number of days for data used by the prediction model (D). In particular, after evaluating different values for such parameters, we identified the following optimal configurations: $PV = 12\%$, $LV = 8\%$, $W = 12$ h, and $D = 3$ days.

The training of the LSTM model has been carried out using a dataset spanning the period January 2021–December 2021, related to the cryptocurrencies listed in Table 2. Subsequently, we evaluated the obtained profits on data collected on a different period, ranging from January 2022 to March 2023. For our tests, among those listed in Table 2, we selected 28 coins in which to invest. In particular, we decided to invest exclusively in three categories of cryptocurrencies: high capitalization (HC), solid project (SP), and influential meme coin (IM). We decided not to invest in volatile meme coins (VM) due to their unpredictable nature, lack of fundamental value, and susceptibility to market manipulation, which can lead to significant financial losses. The evaluation was carried out starting from a virtual initial capital of USD 1000 for each cryptocurrency (USD 28,000 in total). Subsequently, the profits generated by the trading algorithm were evaluated, also taking into account the transaction fees of 1%. It is worth noting that fees are paid on each transaction, so the greater the number of open trading operations, the greater the amount paid.

The overall results of the algorithm are presented in Table 6, highlighting an overall gain of 194% when transaction fees are not taken into account, and of 117% when transaction fees are considered. Specifically, starting from an initial capital of USD 28,000, we obtained a final capital of USD 82,359 with no transaction fees and of USD 60,871 by considering fees. The trading algorithm proved to be extremely effective in predicting the price trend of influential meme (IM) coins, which appear to be significantly influenced by trends and popularity on social media. Specifically, trading on IM leads to a very high average profit of 902.48% with fees and 1257.96% without fees. However, it is worth noting that not all cryptocurrencies have produced profits, but some of them have experienced losses. In particular, fees have a significant impact on profits. As an example, in the case of BTC, the algorithm produced a loss of 14.91% with fees, while it produced a gain of 227.38% without fees. This phenomenon is due to the fact that the algorithm, in some situations, tends to open and close trading operations whose profit is not able to cover the cost of commissions. This is an aspect that will need to be better evaluated in the future, introducing additional operational constraints into the algorithm to address such situations. In some other cases (i.e., TRX and CHZ), the algorithm produced zero profits as no trading operations were carried out during the period considered. Finally, in some rare cases (e.g., SAND, GRT, and FTM), losses have occurred, both with and without fees. This behavior is most likely due to the fact that data collected for training were limited and did not provide the LSTM mode with sufficient predictive capabilities.

Table 6. Results obtained on selected cryptocurrencies categorized as high capitalization (HC), soli project (SP), and influential meme coin (IM).

Cryptocurrency	Acronym	Category	Profit % with Fees	Profit % without Fees
Bitcoin	BTC	HC	−14.91	+227.38
Ethereum	ETH	HC	+6.41	+16.35
Polygon	MATIC	HC	+164.55	+178.43
Polkadot	DOT	HC	−47.80	+28.13
Solana	SOL	HC	−33.56	−10.55
Cosmos	ATOM	HC	−42.27	+13.89
Stellar	XLM	HC	+40.01	+48.26
Avalanche	AVAX	HC	+23.26	+29.37
TRON	TRX	HC	0.00	0.00
Litecoin	LTC	HC	+10.58	+85.98
Conflux	CFX	SP	+112.46	+202.52
Stacks	STX	SP	+59.89	+109.21
Fantom	FTM	SP	−25.42	−22.88
Quant	QNT	SP	+74.17	+83.96
Loopring	LRC	SP	+3.73	+4.73
The Sandbox	SAND	SP	−80.04	−30.06
Gala	GALA	SP	+259.01	+297.28
Lido DAO	LDO	SP	−79.72	+85.95
Cronos	CRO	SP	−15.32	+5.68
Zilliqa	ZIL	SP	+38.22	+58.44
Chiliz	CHZ	SP	0.00	0.00
Neo	NEO	SP	+132.66	+240.80
VeThor Token	VTHO	SP	+26.57	+32.84
Bancor	BNT	SP	−7.44	−5.50
The Graph	GRT	SP	−25.37	−18.11
Dogecoin	DOGE	MCI	+27.68	+39.41
Shiba Inu	SHIB	MCI	+432.47	+771.74
Decentraland	MANA	MCI	+2247.29	+2962.72
Mean profit for HC coins			**+10.63**	**+61.72**
Mean profit for SP coins			**+31.56**	**+69.66**
Mean profit for IM coins			**+902.48**	**+1257.96**
Overall mean profit			**+117.40**	**+194.14**

5. Conclusions

In conclusion, the growing popularity and value of various cryptocurrencies, includ ing the emergence of meme coins like Dogecoin and Shiba Inu, have been driven by a combination of technological innovation and marketing strategies. In particular, socia media platforms and influential figures like Elon Musk have played key roles in shaping the cryptocurrency landscape. Our study has successfully identified the major factors influ encing cryptocurrency price fluctuations, with a primary emphasis on social media data By analyzing the correlation between tweet frequency, likes, retweets, and user popularity we revealed the significant impact of social media on cryptocurrency prices. Additionally we explored how high-cap cryptocurrencies can influence the broader market, especially meme coins, which are highly susceptible to external factors. Using a combination o different statistical analysis, text analysis, and deep learning techniques, we developed a methodology for predicting the price fluctuations of cryptocurrencies and suggesting the optimal moments for trading in order to maximize profits. In particular, we defined a trading recommendation algorithm that, exploiting price predictions provided by an LSTM model, leads to a total profit of 194% when transaction fees are not taken into accoun and of 117% when transaction fees are considered. Moreover, it proved highly effective in predicting the price trend of influential meme coins. Considering only such a category o coins, the algorithm resulted in a substantial average profit of 902% with fees and 1258% without fees. The proposed trading algorithm can serve as a powerful tool to optimize the trading strategies and maximize profits. Looking ahead, there is potential to further refine the algorithm by adopting a less risky capital management approach to better contro losses. This involves mitigating the risks associated with using the entire capital in each financial operation and minimizing the negative impact of trading commissions.

Author Contributions: All authors contributed to the structure of this article, providing critical feedback and helping to shape the research, analysis, and manuscript. D.C. and F.M. conceived the presented idea and organized the manuscript. C.C., L.B. and F.M. wrote the manuscript with contributions from all authors. D.C. implemented the programming examples. F.M. and P.T. were involved in planning the work and supervising and reviewing the structure and contents of the manuscript. All authors have read and agreed to the published version of the manuscript.

Funding: This research received no external funding.

Informed Consent Statement: Not applicable to this work.

Data Availability Statement: The market dataset was extracted using data from various cryptocurrencies, retrieved through the CoinMarketCap APIs (https://coinmarketcap.com/api/, accessed on 1 November 2023). In contrast, the social dataset was acquired by utilizing the Twitter API (https://developer.twitter.com/en/docs/twitter-api, accessed on 1 November 2023) to gather information related to cryptocurrency trends on the social media platform.

Conflicts of Interest: The authors declare no conflict of interest.

References

1. Härdle, W.K.; Harvey, C.R.; Reule, R.C. Understanding cryptocurrencies. *J. Financ. Econom.* **2020**, *18*, 181–208. [CrossRef]
2. Hashemi Joo, M.; Nishikawa, Y.; Dandapani, K. Cryptocurrency, a successful application of blockchain technology. *Manag. Financ.* **2020**, *46*, 715–733. [CrossRef]
3. Kraaijeveld, O.; De Smedt, J. The predictive power of public Twitter sentiment for forecasting cryptocurrency prices. *J. Int. Financ. Mark. Inst. Money* **2020**, *65*, 101188. [CrossRef]
4. Cakici, N.; Fieberg, C.; Metko, D.; Zaremba, A. Do Anomalies Really Predict Market Returns? New Data and New Evidence. *Rev. Financ. Forthcom.* **2023**, rfad025. [CrossRef]
5. Gu, S.; Kelly, B.; Xiu, D. Empirical asset pricing via machine learning. *Rev. Financ. Stud.* **2020**, *33*, 2223–2273. [CrossRef]
6. Bianchi, D.; Büchner, M.; Tamoni, A. Bond risk premiums with machine learning. *Rev. Financ. Stud.* **2021**, *34*, 1046–1089. [CrossRef]
7. Bali, T.G.; Beckmeyer, H.; Moerke, M.; Weigert, F. Option return predictability with machine learning and big data. *Rev. Financ. Stud.* **2023**, *36*, 3548–3602. [CrossRef]
8. Zhou, X.; Zhou, H.; Long, H. Forecasting the equity premium: Do deep neural network models work? *Mod. Financ.* **2023**, *1*, 1–11. [CrossRef]
9. Valencia, F.; Gómez-Espinosa, A.; Valdés-Aguirre, B. Price movement prediction of cryptocurrencies using sentiment analysis and machine learning. *Entropy* **2019**, *21*, 589. [CrossRef]
10. Abraham, J.; Higdon, D.; Nelson, J.; Ibarra, J. Cryptocurrency price prediction using tweet volumes and sentiment analysis. *SMU Data Sci. Rev.* **2018**, *1*, 1.
11. Branda, F.; Marozzo, F.; Talia, D. Ticket Sales Prediction and Dynamic Pricing Strategies in Public Transport. *Big Data Cogn. Comput.* **2020**, *4*, 36. [CrossRef]
12. Hitam, N.A.; Ismail, A.R. Comparative performance of machine learning algorithms for cryptocurrency forecasting. *Ind. J. Electr. Eng. Comput. Sci* **2018**, *11*, 1121–1128. [CrossRef]
13. Khedr, A.M.; Arif, I.; El-Bannany, M.; Alhashmi, S.M.; Sreedharan, M. Cryptocurrency price prediction using traditional statistical and machine-learning techniques: A survey. *Intell. Syst. Account. Financ. Manag.* **2021**, *28*, 3–34. [CrossRef]
14. Jay, P.; Kalariya, V.; Parmar, P.; Tanwar, S.; Kumar, N.; Alazab, M. Stochastic neural networks for cryptocurrency price prediction. *IEEE Access* **2020**, *8*, 82804–82818. [CrossRef]
15. Patel, M.M.; Tanwar, S.; Gupta, R.; Kumar, N. A deep learning-based cryptocurrency price prediction scheme for financial institutions. *J. Inf. Secur. Appl.* **2020**, *55*, 102583. [CrossRef]
16. Lahmiri, S.; Bekiros, S. Cryptocurrency forecasting with deep learning chaotic neural networks. *Chaos Solitons Fractals* **2019**, *118*, 35–40. [CrossRef]
17. Ammer, M.A.; Aldhyani, T.H. Deep learning algorithm to predict cryptocurrency fluctuation prices: Increasing investment awareness. *Electronics* **2022**, *11*, 2349. [CrossRef]
18. Poongodi, M.; Nguyen, T.N.; Hamdi, M.; Cengiz, K. Global cryptocurrency trend prediction using social media. *Inf. Process. Manag.* **2021**, *58*, 102708.
19. Lamon, C.; Nielsen, E.; Redondo, E. Cryptocurrency price prediction using news and social media sentiment. *SMU Data Sci. Rev.* **2017**, *1*, 1–22.
20. Fleischer, J.P.; von Laszewski, G.; Theran, C.; Parra Bautista, Y.J. Time Series Analysis of Cryptocurrency Prices Using Long Short-Term Memory. *Algorithms* **2022**, *15*, 230. [CrossRef]

21. Van Tran, L.; Le, S.T.; Tran, H.M. Empirical Study of Cryptocurrency Prices Using Linear Regression Methods. In Proceedings the 2022 RIVF International Conference on Computing and Communication Technologies (RIVF), Ho Chi Minh City, Vietna 20–22 December 2022; IEEE: Piscataway, NJ, USA, 2022; pp. 701–706.
22. Sun, J.; Zhou, Y.; Lin, J. Using machine learning for cryptocurrency trading. In Proceedings of the 2019 IEEE Internation Conference on Industrial Cyber Physical Systems (ICPS), Taipei, Taiwan, 6–9 May 2019; IEEE: Piscataway, NJ, USA, 201 pp. 647–652.
23. Hamayel, M.J.; Owda, A.Y. A novel cryptocurrency price prediction model using GRU, LSTM and bi-LSTM machine learnir algorithms. *AI* **2021**, *2*, 477–496. [CrossRef]
24. Livieris, I.E.; Pintelas, E.; Stavroyiannis, S.; Pintelas, P. Ensemble deep learning models for forecasting cryptocurrency time-seri *Algorithms* **2020**, *13*, 121. [CrossRef]
25. Rathan, K.; Sai, S.V.; Manikanta, T.S. Crypto-currency price prediction using decision tree and regression techniques. Proceedings of the 2019 3rd International Conference on Trends in Electronics and Informatics (ICOEI), Tirunelveli, India, 23– April 2019; IEEE: Piscataway, NJ, USA, 2019, pp. 190–194.
26. Mirtaheri, M.; Abu-El-Haija, S.; Morstatter, F.; Ver Steeg, G.; Galstyan, A. Identifying and analyzing cryptocurrency manipulatio in social media. *IEEE Trans. Comput. Soc. Syst.* **2021**, *8*, 607–617. [CrossRef]
27. Wołk, K. Advanced social media sentiment analysis for short-term cryptocurrency price prediction. *Expert Syst.* **2020**, *37*, e124 [CrossRef]
28. Vo, A.D.; Nguyen, Q.P.; Ock, C.Y. Sentiment analysis of news for effective cryptocurrency price prediction. *Int. J. Knowl. En* **2019**, *5*, 47–52. [CrossRef]
29. Sebastião, H.; Godinho, P. Forecasting and trading cryptocurrencies with machine learning under changing market conditior *Financ. Innov.* **2021**, *7*, 3. [CrossRef]
30. Hutto, C.; Gilbert, E. Vader: A parsimonious rule-based model for sentiment analysis of social media text. In Proceedings of tl International AAAI Conference on Web and Social Media, Ann Arbor, MI, USA, 1–4 June 2014; Volume 8, pp. 216–225.
31. Loria, S. textblob Documentation. *Release 0.16* **2018**, *2*, 269.
32. Pano, T.; Kashef, R. A complete VADER-based sentiment analysis of bitcoin (BTC) tweets during the era of COVID-19. *Big Da Cogn. Comput.* **2020**, *4*, 33. [CrossRef]
33. Kim, G.; Shin, D.H.; Choi, J.G.; Lim, S. A deep learning-based cryptocurrency price prediction model that uses on-chain da *IEEE Access* **2022**, *10*, 56232–56248. [CrossRef]
34. Tanwar, S.; Patel, N.P.; Patel, S.N.; Patel, J.R.; Sharma, G.; Davidson, I.E. Deep learning-based cryptocurrency price predictic scheme with inter-dependent relations. *IEEE Access* **2021**, *9*, 138633–138646. [CrossRef]
35. Shahbazi, Z.; Byun, Y.C. Improving the cryptocurrency price prediction performance based on reinforcement learning. *IEE Access* **2021**, *9*, 162651–162659. [CrossRef]
36. Belcastro, L.; Cantini, R.; Marozzo, F.; Orsino, A.; Talia, D.; Trunfio, P. Programming big data analysis: Principles and solutions. *Big Data* **2022**, *9*, 1–50. [CrossRef]
37. Al Guindy, M. Cryptocurrency price volatility and investor attention. *Int. Rev. Econ. Financ.* **2021**, *76*, 556–570. [CrossRef]
38. Aslanidis, N.; Bariviera, A.F.; López, Ó.G. The link between cryptocurrencies and Google Trends attention. *Financ. Res. Lett.* **202** *47*, 102654. [CrossRef]
39. Mardjo, A.; Choksuchat, C. HyVADRF: Hybrid VADER–Random Forest and GWO for Bitcoin Tweet Sentiment Analysis. *IEE Access* **2022**, *10*, 101889–101897. [CrossRef]
40. Breiman, L. Random forests. *Mach. Learn.* **2001**, *45*, 5–32. [CrossRef]
41. Chen, T.; Guestrin, C. Xgboost: A scalable tree boosting system. In Proceedings of the 22nd ACM SIGKDD Internation Conference on Knowledge Discovery and Data Mining, San Francisco, CA, USA, 13–17 August 2016; pp. 785–794.
42. Prokhorenkova, L.; Gusev, G.; Vorobev, A.; Dorogush, A.V.; Gulin, A. CatBoost: Unbiased boosting with categorical features. Proceedings of the Advances in Neural Information Processing Systems, Montreal, QC, Canada, 3–8 December 2018; Volume 3
43. Li, Z.; Liu, F.; Yang, W.; Peng, S.; Zhou, J. A survey of convolutional neural networks: Analysis, applications, and prospects. *IEE Trans. Neural Netw. Learn. Syst.* **2021**, *33*, 6999–7019. [CrossRef]
44. Hua, Y.; Zhao, Z.; Li, R.; Chen, X.; Liu, Z.; Zhang, H. Deep learning with long short-term memory for time series prediction. *IEE Commun. Mag.* **2019**, *57*, 114–119. [CrossRef]
45. Moustafa, H.; Malli, M.; Hazimeh, H. Real-time Bitcoin price tendency awareness via social media content tracking. Proceedings of the 2022 10th International Symposium on Digital Forensics and Security (ISDFS), Istanbul, Turkey, 6–7 June 202 IEEE: Piscataway, NJ, USA, 2022; pp. 1–6.
46. Maqsood, U.; Khuhawar, F.Y.; Talpur, S.; Jaskani, F.H.; Memon, A.A. Twitter Mining based Forecasting of Cryptocurrency usir Sentimental Analysis of Tweets. In Proceedings of the 2022 Global Conference on Wireless and Optical Technologies (GCWO Malaga, Spain, 14–17 February 2022; IEEE: Piscataway, NJ, USA, 2022; pp. 1–6.

algorithms

MDPI

Article

Compact Models to Solve the Precedence-Constrained Minimum-Cost Arborescence Problem with Waiting Times

Mauro Dell'Amico [1,2], Jafar Jamal [1] and Roberto Montemanni [1,2,*]

1 Department of Sciences and Methods for Engineering, University of Modena and Reggio Emilia, Via Amendola 2, 42122 Reggio Emilia, RE, Italy; mauro.dellamico@unimore.it (M.D.)

2 Interdepartmental Center En&Tech, University of Modena and Reggio Emilia, Capannone 19 Tecnopolo, Piazza Europa 1, 42122 Reggio Emilia, RE, Italy

* Correspondence: roberto.montemanni@unimore.it; Tel.: +39-0522-522-126

Abstract: The minimum-cost arborescence problem is a well-studied problem. Polynomial-time algorithms for solving it exist. Recently, a new variation of the problem called the Precedence-Constrained Minimum-Cost Arborescence Problem with Waiting Times was presented and proven to be $\mathcal{NP}$-hard. In this work, we propose new polynomial-size models for the problem that are considerably smaller in size compared to those previously proposed. We experimentally evaluate and compare each new model in terms of computation time and quality of the solutions. Several improvements to the best-known upper and lower bounds of optimal solution costs emerge from the study.

Keywords: arborescences; precedence constraints; mixed integer linear programming; constraint programming

Citation: Dell'Amico, M.; Jamal, J.; Montemanni, R. Compact Models to Solve the Precedence-Constrained Minimum-Cost Arborescence Problem with Waiting Times. *Algorithms* **2024**, *17*, 12. https://doi.org/10.3390/a17010012

Academic Editor: Frank Werner

Received: 2 December 2023
Revised: 23 December 2023
Accepted: 26 December 2023
Published: 27 December 2023

Correction Statement: This article has been republished with a minor change. The change does not affect the scientific content of the article and further details are available within the backmatter of the website version of this article.

1. Introduction

The *Minimum-Cost Arborescence* (MCA) problem asks to find a directed minimum-cost spanning tree (i.e., an arborescence) rooted at vertex r—the *root* of the arborescence—in a directed graph. Chu and Liu [1] and Edmonds [2] proposed the same polynomial time algorithm to solve the problem, independently from each other. A faster implementation was later proposed by Gabow and Tarjan [3], and a different polynomial time algorithm [4] that operates directly on the cost matrix was introduced by Bock [5].

Several variations of the MCA problem were introduced in the literature since its introduction. Given a directed graph with a resource associated to each of its vertices, the *Resource-Constrained Minimum-Weight Arborescence problem* aims at retrieving an arborescence with minimum total cost, with the additional constraint that outgoing arcs from each vertex have to have a cost at most equal to that of the resource of the vertex itself (Fischetti and Vigo [6]). Given a weighted directed graph $G = (V, A)$ with a vertex $r \in V$ identified as the root and an integer p, the *p-Arborescence Star problem* asks to identify a minimum-cost arborescence rooted at r. The arborescence spans the set of vertices $H \subseteq V\backslash\{r\}$ of size p, and there must be an assignment between each vertex $v \in V\backslash\{H \cup r\}$ and one of the vertices in H (Pereira et al. [7], Morais et al. [8], Hakimi [9]). Given a directed graph with a number assigned to each vertex, the *Restricted Fathers Tree problem* seeks a minimum-cost arborescence, with the constraint that each path between a vertex and the root has to touch vertices with ranking not lower than the vertex (Guttmann-Beck and Hassin [10]). Given a directed graph with a vertex r designed as the root and a set $A_v \subset V$ for every $v \in V\backslash\{r\}$ such that $r \in A_v$, the *Restricted Ancestors Tree problem* aims at finding a minimum-cost arborescence rooted at r, with the additional constraint that vertex i can be an ancestor of vertex j only when $i \in A_j$ (Guttmann-Beck and Hassin [10]). The *Minimum Spanning Tree Problem with Conflict Pairs* (Carrabs and Gaudioso [11]) is a variation of the classic *Minimum-Spanning Tree problem* (Kruskal [12]), characterized by an undirected graph and a set S

containing conflicting pairs of conflicting edges. The objective is to retrieve a minimum cost spanning tree with at most one edge from the pair in S. The *Capacitated Minimum Spanning Tree problem*, introduced in Gouveia and Lopez [13], is another variation, characterized by non-negative integer node demands q_j for each node $j \in V \backslash \{r\}$ and a budget Q for the sum of the weights in any root–leaf path. Further related problems can be found in Frieze and Tkocz [14], Fertin et al. [15], Eswaran and Tarjan [16], Li et al. [17], Kawatra and Bricker [18], Galbiati et al. [19], Bérczi et al. [20], Bang-Jensen [21], Yingshu et al. [22], Carrabs et al. [23], Darmann et al. [24] and Viana and Campêlo [25]. The *Sequential Ordering Problem*, introduced in Escudero [26], is relevant to the present study and can be described as follows. Given a weighted graph and a set of precedence constraints between vertex pairs and start and end vertices, the goal is to find a Minimum-Cost Hamiltonian Path that respects the precedence constraints. Solving algorithms can be found in Moon et al. [27], Balas et al. [28], Hernádvölgyi [29], Escudero et al. [30], Gambardella and Dorigo [31], Karan and Skorin-Kapov [32], Ascheuer et al. [33], Ascheuer et al. [34], Montemanni et al. [35] and Fiala Timlin and Pulleyblank [36]. The *Precedence-Constrained Minimum-Cost Arborescence* is an extension of the MCA problem first introduced in Dell'Amico et al. [37]. Precedence constraints have the following meaning. A precedence set R containing pairs of vertices is given. For each $(s, t) \in R$, if both vertices s and t are on a same path of the arborescence then vertex s has to be visited before vertex t. The optimization seeks to find an arborescence of minimum total cost such that all the precedence constraints are satisfied. Several models for the problem, all based on Mixed Integer Linear Programming (MILP), were proposed. We refer the interested reader to Chou et al. [38].

The *Precedence-Constrained Minimum-Cost Arborescence problem with Waiting Times* (PCMCA-WT)—which is the object of the current paper—was first introduced in Chou et al. [38], where the problem was shown to be $\mathcal{NP}$-hard through a reduction to the *Rectilinear Steiner Arborescence* problem (Shi and Su [39]), and different MILP models were proposed. The problem is about retrieving an arborescence where traveling times are present among vertices and temporal precedences relative to the time of visit have to be fulfilled among pairs of vertices. Waiting times at vertices are allowed to enforce such precedences, but these waiting times are accounted for in the objective function together with travel times. The optimization is to minimize such an objective function.

The organization of the paper is as follows. The PCMCA-WT is formally defined in Section 2. Section 3 describes a new family of compact models for the problem (characterized by a polynomial number of variables and constraints). Section 4 discusses the results of a vast experimental campaign where the new models are compared to those previously disclosed in the literature. Some conclusions are the content of Section 5.

The contributions of the paper can be summarized as follows:

- New models for the PCMCA-WT that are polynomial in size and are characterized by a substantially smaller memory footprint compared to the known models are introduced. This result is achieved by exploiting some theoretical properties emerging from the current study and previously unobserved.
- The new models are solved both with MILP and Constraint Programming (CP) solvers. The experimental results substantially improve the state of the art for the instances commonly adopted in the literature. Out of the 88 open instances from the literature, improved lower bounds are provided for 71 instances and improved upper bounds are provided for 80 instances. Finally, seven instances are closed for the first time.

2. Problem Description

The PCMCA-WT can be described according to the following definitions. A directed graph $G = (V, A, R)$ is given, with $V = \{1, \ldots, n\}$ being a set of vertices and $A \subseteq V \times V$ a set of arcs, with a non-negative cost c_{ij} associated with every arc $(i, j) \in A$. It represents the traversing time for that arc. The set $R \subset V \times V$ contains precedence relationships. Let d_j be the time step at which the flow enters vertex $j \in V$, with $d_r = 0$. For any $(s, t) \in R$ we impose $d_t \geq d_s$. This implies that the flow cannot enter vertex t before entering vertex s.

but it can wait at any vertex before servicing it. We define w_j as the waiting time at vertex $j \in V$, with $w_r = 0$. The waiting time at a vertex j that is visited after another vertex i in the current solution is defined as $w_j = d_j - (d_i + c_{ij})$. Given a vertex $r \in V$ being the root of the arborescence, the target of the optimization is to retrieve an arborescence T (with root r) that provides the lowest possible sum of the total cost plus the total waiting time.

An example of PCMCA-WT is provided in Figure 1. In the instance (top part of the figure), the precedence relationship $(1,3) \in R$ is represented as a dashed arrow, while in the bottom part of the figure, an optimal solution for the given instance is shown. The corresponding values of d_i and w_i are exposed near each vertex. The cost of the solution is 8 (obtained by adding the cost of the traversed arcs and the waiting times payed at vertices). In the example, observe the waiting time of 1 unit at vertex 3 ($d_1 = 4$, $d_3 = 3$ and $(1,3) \in R$).

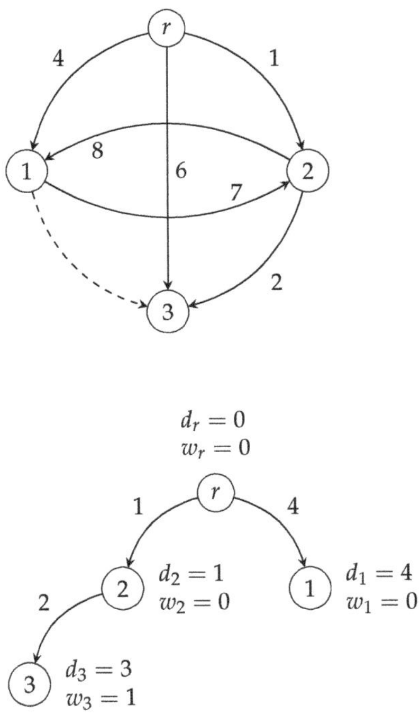

Figure 1. Instance of the PCMCA-WT problem and relative solution. The instance is depicted in the top of the figure, with its arc costs. The precedence relationship $(1,3) \in R$ is depicted through a dashed arrow. The bottom part of the figure depicts the optimal arborescence of cost 8.

3. New Compact Models

An MILP model for the PCMCA-WT that is polynomial in size was recently proposed in Chou et al. [38]. The model is based on a multicommodity flow formulation [40] that extends the flow conservation constraints in order to satisfy the precedence relationships between vertex pairs. However, the model suffers from computational limitations caused by the large number of variables and constraints, both in the order of $O(n^3)$. In this section, we derive two new models for the PCMCA-WT that are also polynomial in size. Compared to the previous models, the new ones use less variables and constraints for the description of the precedence relationships among pairs of vertices. This solves the memory issues that were encountered when using the multicommodity flow model originally introduced in [38], making compact models competitive against other solutions.

3.1. The Complete Model

We first define V^R as the set of vertices of V involved in at least one precedenc
relation as a head. Formally, $V^R = \{t \in V \mid \exists s \in V : (s,t) \in R\}$. Let x_{ij} be a binary variab
modeling if arc $(i,j) \in A$ is visited: $x_{ij} = 1$ if $(i,j) \in T$, and 0 otherwise. Let y_i be an integ
variable used to identify the position of vertex $i \in V$ along the only path of the arborescen
connecting the root r to vertex i itself. Let u^t_j be a binary variable with indices representir
vertex $j \in V$ and vertex $t \in V^R$. This variable will be used to model precedences. Let d_j b
a continuous variable containing entering time of the flow at vertex $j \in V$. Finally, let w_j b
a continuous variable modeling the time waited at vertex j before letting the flow enter th
node itself.

An MILP model for the PCMCA-WT is as follows.

$$
\begin{aligned}
\text{minimize} \quad & \sum_{(i,j)\in A} c_{ij}x_{ij} + \sum_{i\in V} w_i && && (1)\\
\text{subject to:} \quad & \sum_{(i,j)\in A} x_{ij} = 1 && \forall j \in V\setminus\{r\} && (2)\\
& y_i - y_j + 1 \leq n(1 - x_{ij}) && \forall (i,j) \in A : j \neq r && (3)\\
& u^t_s = 0 && \forall (s,t) \in R && (4)\\
& u^t_t = 1 && \forall t \in V^R && (5)\\
& u^t_j - u^t_i - x_{ij} \geq -1 && \forall t \in V^R, (i,j) \in A && (6)\\
& d_r = 0 && && (7)\\
& w_r = 0 && && (8)\\
& d_j \geq d_i - M + (M + c_{ij})x_{ij} && \forall (i,j) \in A && (9)\\
& w_j \geq d_j - d_i - M + (M - c_{ij})x_{ij} && \forall (i,j) \in A && (10)\\
& d_t \geq d_s && \forall (s,t) \in R && (11)\\
& x_{ij} \in \{0,1\} && \forall (i,j) \in A && (12)\\
& y_i \in \{0,1,\ldots,n-1\} && \forall i \in V && (13)\\
& u^t_j \in \{0,1\} && \forall t \in V^R, j \in V && (14)\\
& d_i \geq 0 && \forall i \in V && (15)\\
& w_i \geq 0 && \forall i \in V && (16)
\end{aligned}
$$

The objective function (1) minimizes the sum of the total travel and waiting time
as described in Section 2. The set of constraints (2) enforces that each vertex apart from th
root needs to have one incoming arc. Constraints (3) model subtour elimination and dictat
that any feasible solution cannot contain any cycles. The set of constraints (2) and (3) wor
together in order to enforce only solutions in the form of an arborescence rooted at vertex
Constraints (4), (5) and (6) regulate precedence constraints among the vertices visited i
a same branch of the tree. The logic behind these constraints will be explained in deta
in Section 3.1.1, entirely devoted to this purpose. Constraints (7) and (8) initialize th
distance traveled and the waiting time at the root r to 0. Constraints (9), activated once a
arc $(i,j) \in A$ is selected, force the arrival time at vertex j to be not lower than the arriva
time vertex i plus the travel time c_{ij}. Note that here and in the following set of constraint
M is an arbitrarily large constant. Constraints (10) push the waiting time at vertex j t
be no smaller than the the service time at vertex j minus the service time at vertex i plu
c_{ij}. Constraints (11) impose that the service time at vertex t cannot be smaller than th
service time at vertex s for all $(s,t) \in R$. This set of constraints, in conjunction with th
previous ones, regulates the value of the waiting times. Finally, constraints (12)–(16) defin
the domain of the variables.

The value of the large constant M, appearing in constraints (9) and (10), is an approx
mation by excess of the optimal cost of the problem. In our case, the solution cost of solvin

the instance as a Sequential Ordering Problem [34] using a nearest neighbor algorithm [41] is taken as the value of M. This is a valid upper bound for the optimal cost of a PCMCA-WT instance, being a valid solution for the Sequential Ordering Problem a simple directed path that includes all the vertices of the graph, with the constraint that t never precede s for all $(s,t) \in R$. This implies that $d_t \geq d_s$ for all $(s,t) \in R$.

The model proposed in this section has a considerably smaller memory footprint compared to the polynomial-size model proposed for the PCMCA-WT in [38]. In detail, the number of variables is reduced from $O(n^3)$ to $O(n^2)$. The number of constraints remains instead in the order of $O(n^3)$, although now the hidden multiplicative factor depends on the number of vertices involved in at least one precedence as a head, instead of all the vertices. This makes the number of constraints much smaller. All together, these improvements reduce substantially the memory footprint of the model, with great advantages for practical tractability.

3.1.1. The New Precedence Constraints

The approach proposed in this work to deal with precedences is similar to the idea originally introduced in Dell'Amico et al. [42] for the *Precedence-Constrained Minimum-Cost Arborescence* (PCMCA) problem. Constraints (4) and (5) impose the values of u_s^t and u_t^t to be 0 and 1, respectively, for all $(s,t) \in R$, and $t \in V : \exists (s,t) \in R$. On the other hand, the set of constraints (6) enforces that $u_j^t \geq u_i^t$ whenever arc $(i,j) \in A$ is selected to be part of the solution. These concepts together forbid any violation of precedence constraints along a same path of the solution arborescence T.

Figure 2 shows an example of how a precedence-violating path is detected using the set of constraints (6). In the figure, the range/value of variable u_j^t is written on the left of each vertex, and black arcs show the arcs that are part of the solution, while the red arcs show a precedence relationship $(s,t) \in R$. In the figure, constraints (6) enforce that u_1^t and u_2^t have to be greater than or equal to 1. However, once $u_s^t \geq 1$ is imposed through this logic, the constraint (4) relative to variable u_s^t is violated, rendering therefore the solution infeasible.

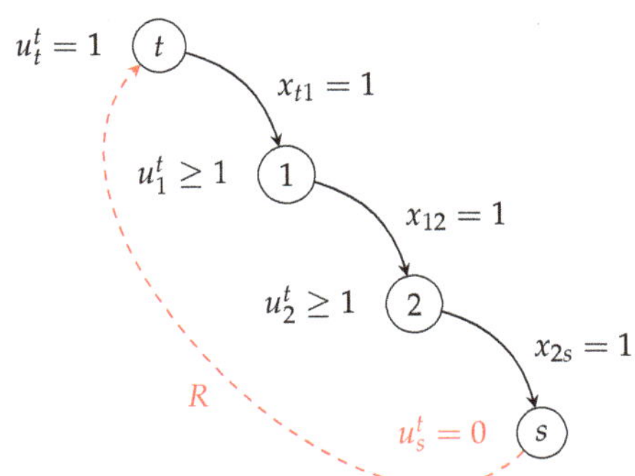

Figure 2. Example of how a precedence-violating path is detected using constraints (4)–(6).

3.2. The Reduced Model

It can be observed that by removing the set of constraints (4)–(6) from the model described in Section 3.1, the set of constraints (11) in general still enforces the precedence relationships between s and t with $(s,t) \in R$, apart from the following special case. A directed path that visits t before visiting s implies that $d_t \leq d_s$, which violates the set of constraints (11). However, the set of constraints (11) might fail to enforce a precedence relationship between s and t if a zero-cost path in G that reaches s from t exists. Therefore, variables u_j^t and constraints (4)–(6) need to be defined only for those t for which there exist at least an s for which $(s,t) \in R$ and a zero-cost path that connects t to s is available in G.

The identification of such pairs $(s,t) \in R$ for which a zero-cost path exists has, howeve to be performed in a preprocessing phase, adding some complexity to the overall proces The procedure we devised for the retrieval of such pairs will be detailed in Section 3.2.1.

The reduced set of constraints can be described formally as follows. Let $G_0 = (V_0, A_0, R$ be the graph obtained from G by considering only arcs with cost zero and the relevan nodes. Therefore, $A_0 = \{(i,j) \in A \mid c_{ij} = 0\}$ and $V_0 = \{i \in V \mid \exists j \in V : (i,j) \in$ A_0 or $(j,i) \in A_0\}$ (a node is considered relevant for the residual precedence constraint if it has at least an outgoing or incoming zero-cost arc). Let $SP_{ij} \subseteq A_0$ be a shortest pat that starts from i to j in G, and let $c(SP_{ij}) = \sum_{(k,l) \in SP_{ij}} c_{kl}$ be its cost. For each $t \in V^R$, le $V_0(t) = \{s \in V_0 \mid \exists\,(s,t) \in R \text{ with } c(P_{ts}) = 0\}$ be the set of vertices involved in a prece dence constraint with t as a head, and such that a zero-cost path from t to s exists. Finall let $V_0^R = \{t \in V^R \mid V_0(t) \neq \emptyset\}$ be the set of vertices involved as a head in at least on precedence constraint for which an inverse zero-cost path exists.

The *Reduced* model can be obtained from the *Complete* model described in Section 3. by substituting constraints (4)–(6) and (14) with the following specialized version of ther characterized by a reduced domain:

$$u_s^t = 0 \qquad \forall t \in V_0^R, s \in V_0(t) \tag{17}$$

$$u_t^t = 1 \qquad \forall t \in V_0^R \tag{18}$$

$$u_j^t - u_i^t - x_{ij} \geq -1 \qquad \forall t \in V_0^R, (i,j) \in A_0 \tag{19}$$

$$u_j^t \geq 0 \qquad \forall t \in V_0^R, j \in V_0 \tag{20}$$

Notice that the domain of the u variables is reduced according to (20).

Compared to the model introduced in Section 3.1, and given that zero-cost path are rare, the *Reduced* model uses less variables and constraints (although the theoretica complexity remains unchanged), thus further reducing the memory footprint. However, i might be characterized by a weaker linear relaxation due to the elimination of redundanc in the constraints, on top of having the burden of a preprocessing phase.

3.2.1. Selecting the Precedence Constraints involving a Zero-Cost Path

Zero-cost paths in G_0 that start from t and end in s for some $(s,t) \in R$ can be retrieve by running the procedure described in Algorithm 1.

Algorithm 1 Retrieve the Relevant Zero-Cost Paths from an Instance

1: Compute the shortest path SP_{ij} for each pair of vertices i, j of G_0
2: $V_0^R = \emptyset$
3: **for all** $t \in V_0$ **do**
4:     $V_0(t) = \emptyset$
5:     **for all** $s \in V_0 : (s,t) \in R$ **do**
6:         **if** $C(SP_{ij}) = 0$ **then**
7:             $V_0(t) = V_0(t) \cup \{s\}$
8:         **end if**
9:     **end for**
10:     **if** $V_0(t) \neq \emptyset$ **then**
11:         $V_0^R = V_0^R \cup \{t\}$
12:     **end if**
13: **end for**

Line 1 can be implemented by running the algorithm of Floyd-Warshall [43] to retriev the shortest path between each pair of vertices of a graph. The algorithm has a computa tional complexity of $O(n^3)$. Lines 2–13 scan the results to populate the sets $V_0(t)$, containin vertices involved in relevant zero-cost paths for each vertex $t \in V_0$, and the set V_0^R, with total computational complexity of $O(n^2)$. Therefore, the overall computational complexit of the procedure remains polynomial, in the order of $O(n^3)$. This guarantees negligible computation times for the graphs considered in the study and in real applications of the problem, for which n does not exceed 700.

3.3. Solving the New Models via Constraint Programming

Modern Constraint Programming solvers such as Google OR-Tools CP-SAT [44]—the one adopted for the present work—are able to solve compact MILP models efficiently [45]. In particular, these solvers are very effective in treating logical inferences that can be expressed effectively without the use of big-M coefficients (that weaken linear relaxations and consequently worsen solving times) in their syntax. The two MILP models discussed in Sections 3.1 and 3.2 use such a technique to describe the nonlinear relation between the variable x_{ij} and the set of variables $\{y_i, u_j^t, d_j, w_j\}$ in order to turn the constraints off whenever the value of x_{ij} is equal to zero. In this section, we will therefore manipulate the models previously introduced in order to transform the constraints involving big-Ms into logical inferences. Notice that this operation mentioned above is not strictly required, since CP-SAT is able to deal with big-M constraints natively, but according to some preliminary tests, using logical inferences enhances the performance of the solver. Conversely, MILP solvers such as CPLEX [46]—the one adopted for the present work—that are also able to treat logical inferences without big-M constraints present a strong degradation of the performances when big-M constraints are removed. For this reason, in the experiments reported in Section 4, we will use big-M constraints for the MILP solver and logical inferences for the CP solver.

Finally, it can be observed that CP solvers only accept integer-valued variables, which means that the value of the c_{ij}s should be discretized before being passed to the model in case they are not integer. See Montemanni and Dell'Amico [45] for a deeper traction.

In detail, the *Complete* model can be adapted by modifying constraints (3), (6), (9) and (10), which are substituted by the following ones:

$$x_{ij} \implies y_j = y_i + 1 \qquad \forall (i,j) \in A : j \neq r \tag{21}$$

$$x_{ij} \implies u_j^t \geq u_i^t \qquad \forall t \in V^R, (i,j) \in A \tag{22}$$

$$x_{ij} \implies d_j = d_i + w_j + c_{ij} \qquad \forall (i,j) \in A \tag{23}$$

Constraints (21) implement subtour elimination. The nonlinear relationship $y_j = (y_i + 1)x_{ij}$ is modeled by setting the value of y_j to $y_i + 1$ if $x_{ij} = 1$ (true). Technically, the logical implication is implemented through the *OnlyEnforceIf* construct of the CP-SAT solver [44]. Constraints (22) are the precedence-enforcing constraints that set the value of u_j^t to be greater than or equal to u_j^t if $x_{ij} = 1$ and model the nonlinear relationship $u_j^t \geq u_i^t x_{ij}$. Constraints (23) set the value of d_j to $d_i + w_j + c_{ij}$ if $x_{ij} = 1$. The set of constraints (23) deals therefore with the nonlinear relationship $(d_j - d_i - w_j - c_{ij})x_{ij} = 0$. Notice that the two constraints (9) and (10) are now combined in a single set of constraints.

Analogously, it is possible to obtain a version of the *Reduced* model based on logical inferences by changing constraints (3) to (21) and substituting constraints (19), (9) and (10) with the following new ones:

$$x_{ij} \implies u_j^t \geq u_i^t \qquad \forall t \in V_0^R, (i,j) \in A_0 \tag{24}$$

$$x_{ij} \implies d_j = d_i + w_j + c_{ij} \qquad \forall (i,j) \in A_0 \tag{25}$$

Notice that constraints (24) and (25) are the versions of (22) and (23) specialized to the reduced graph G_0 for what concerns zero-cost precedences and that constraints (25) cover again both the sets (9) and (10).

4. Computational Experiments

The experimental settings and conditions are described in Section 4.1 together with th instances adopted for the tests. The detailed results are instead presented and commente on in Section 4.2.

4.1. Experimental Settings

The computational experiments we present in order to position the proposed mo els within the existing literature are based on the benchmark instances of TSPLIB [47 SOPLIB [48] and COMPILERS [49]. All these datasets had originally been proposed fo the Sequential Ordering Problem, and they are commonly adopted in the PCMCA-W literature so far, see [38]. In total, the benchmark sets considered contain 116 instance with sizes ranging between 9 and 700 vertices (and an average of 248 vertices). Currentl the benchmark set has a total of 88 open instances (i.e., without a known optimal solution

The MILP solver adopted is CPLEX v12.8 [46] with standard settings. The CP solve used is OR-Tools v9.5 [44] CP-SAT, also run with standard settings. The computatio time of both solvers is limited to 1 h, while the preprocessing time required for the *Re duced* methods is not accounted for, being in the order of fractions of a second for all th instances considered.

The best-known solutions used as reference are those appearing in [38]. The valu reported is for each instance the best of the results achieved by the three models introduce there. This biases the comparison in favor of the old methods, since—according to the *N Free Lunch* Theorem [50]—taking the best of different approaches might give a substanti advantage. Among the three ideas disclosed in [38], the one improved in the present wor had shown some potential, however, it was the weakest of the set due to severe scalabilit issues (now solved, see Section 3). On the other hand, the results of [38] were obtaine on an Intel i7-8550U processor running at 1.8 GHz and with 8 GB of RAM, while the ne experiments are obtained on Intel Xeon Platinum 8375C running at 2.9 GHz and using u to 16 GB of RAM. This gives a hardware advantage to the new models, somehow balancin back the comparison. Notice that the newly proposed models are a direct improveme aiming at overcoming the crucial scalability of one of the three models of [38], makin computational fairness considerations less central, in our view.

4.2. Results

An aggregated summary of the results is presented in Table 1. The average optimalit gap across all the instances for which all the models were able to find a feasible/optim solution is reported under *Average optimality gap*. The average solution time among a the instances that were solved to optimality by all the models can be found under *Averag solution time*. The detailed results of each model can be found instead in Tables 2–4, whe the following data are reported for each instance. The name and size can be found i the columns with these names. The best-known bounds found in [38] are reported i the column *Best-Known* [38], where *LB* shows the best lower bound found, and *UB* th best-known solution. For each model, the following columns are displayed. The lower an upper bound can be found in the column with these names. The optimality gap, compute as $\frac{UB-LB}{UB}$, is reported in the column *Gap*. The solution time in seconds, which is reporte only for those instances that are closed in the given time, can be found in the column *Tim* Entries in bold indicate new best-known lower or upper bounds. Finally, the name of th instances for which optimality is proven for the first time in this work is highlighted i bold across the tables.

Comparing the average optimality gap of each model, it can be observed that the MIL solver run on the *Complete* model has an optimality gap of 0.206 on average (0.418 whe all the instances solved by the model are considered) but fails to solve two instances, as runs out of memory. The MILP solver on the *Reduced* model has an optimality gap o 0.153 on average (with a 25.7% improvement over the previous model) and an optimalit gap of 0.340 on average (an 18.7% improvement) across all the instances. The MILP solve on the *Reduced* model also runs out of memory on one instance. When considering the CP solver, the *Complete* model shows an optimality gap of 0.159 on average (with a 22.8% improvement), with an optimality gap of 0.157 on average across all the instances. However, the largest instances, with size larger than 200 or with a very dense precedence graph, are not solved, since the model runs out of memory due to the large number of constraints (19). When solving the *Reduced* model, the CP solver achieves an optimality gap of 0.122 on average (with a 40.7% improvement), with an optimality gap of 0.286 averaged across all the instances.

Table 1. Summary of the results achieved with each solver/model combination.

	MILP Solver		**CP Solver**	
	Complete Model	**Reduced Model**	**Complete Model**	**Reduced Model**
Average optimality gap	0.206	0.153	0.159	0.122
Average solution time	690.8	270.8	166.4	36.4
New best-known lower bounds	2	24	13	32
New best-known upper bounds	1	15	10	54
New optimal solutions	0	0	7	7

In terms of solution time, and comparing the instances that are optimally solved by all models (27 instances), using the MILP solver takes the *Complete* model to a solution time of 690.8 s on average, while the *Reduced* takes 270.8 s on average (with a 60.8% improvement). When the CP solver is used, the *Complete* model has a solution time of 166.4 s on average (with a 75.9% improvement), while solving the *Reduced* model takes 36.4 s on average (with a 94.7% improvement). Cross-comparing a same model when treated by the two different solvers, it emerges that generally the CP models outperform the MILP models on instances with medium to high density precedence graphs.

In terms of solution costs, the *Reduced* model solved by an MILP solver finds new best-known lower bounds for 24 out of 88 instances (27.3%) compared to the 2 retrieved by the *Complete* model solved by the same solver. Furthermore, the *Reduced* model finds new best-known upper bounds for 15 (17.1%) compared to the 1 only found by the *Complete* model. This indicates that the strength of the linear relaxation of the model is not drastically affected after removing a subset of the variables and constraints from the model. Furthermore, this shows that the *Reduced* model is generally easier to solve by the MILP solver adopted, and therefore the solver is able to find new bounds more frequently compared to solving the *Complete* model. When considering the CP solver, the *Reduced* model finds new best-known lower bounds for 32 (36.4%), while the *Complete* model finds new lower bounds for 13 (14.8%). For new best-known upper bounds, solving the *Reduced* model leads to new 54 new bests (61.4%), while solving the *Complete* model leads to 10 new bests (11.4%). This indicates that the *Reduced* model is generally more effective to solve by the CP solver when compared to the *Complete* model. Moreover, the use of the CP solver led to seven newly proven optimal solutions. In general, using the MILP solver seems to produce better lower bounds, while the CP solver is better at finding lower cost solutions.

In summary, the computational results show that the *Reduced* model generally outperforms the *Complete* model independently of the solver adopted. This is due to the fact that the *Reduced* model has a substantially smaller number of variables and constraints, giving an advantage to the solvers. Moreover, the CP solver performs better than the MILP solver in terms of the quality of the solutions, the average solution time and the average optimality gap. Furthermore, the CP solver finds new best-known lower/upper bounds for some instances.

Table 2. Computational results for TSPLIB instances.

Instance			MILP Solver								CP Solver							
			Complete Model				Reduced Model				Complete Model				Reduced Model			
Name	Size	Best-Known [38]	LB	UB	Gap	Time [s]	LB	UB	Gap	Time [s]	LB	UB	Gap	Time [s]	LB	UB	Gap	Time [s]
br17.10	18	[35, 44]	39	44	0.114	-	40	44	0.091	-	**44**	**44**	0.000	46.629	**44**	**44**	0.000	56.628
br17.12	18	[35, 44]	41	44	0.068	-	41	44	0.068	-	**44**	**44**	0.000	22.604	**44**	**44**	0.000	44.550
ESC07	9	1906	1906	1906	0.000	0.028	1906	1906	0.000	0.070	1906	1906	0.000	0.023	1906	1906	0.000	0.025
ESC11	13	2174	2174	2174	0.000	0.125	2174	2174	0.000	0.114	2174	2174	0.000	0.107	2174	2174	0.000	0.077
ESC12	14	1138	1138	1138	0.000	0.035	1138	1138	0.000	0.030	1138	1138	0.000	0.034	1138	1138	0.000	0.037
ESC25	27	1158	1158	1158	0.000	6.185	1158	1158	0.000	1.945	1158	1158	0.000	0.910	1158	1158	0.000	0.833
ESC47	49	747	747	747	0.000	59.760	747	747	0.000	22.153	747	747	0.000	3.886	747	747	0.000	2.708
ESC63	65	56	56	56	0.000	24.600	56	56	0.000	57.347	56	56	0.000	1.517	56	56	0.000	2.465
ESC78	80	1196	1196	1196	0.000	2410.483	1196	1196	0.000	257.609	1196	1196	0.000	100.511	1196	1196	0.000	18.971
ft53.1	54	4089	4089	4089	0.000	1764.235	4089	4089	0.000	2023.553	4089	4089	0.000	215.480	4089	4089	0.000	291.099
ft53.2	54	[4135, 4284]	4112	4317	0.047	-	**4161**	4334	0.040	-	4102	4284	0.042	-	4103	4284	0.042	-
ft53.3	54	[4623, 5457]	4746	5425	0.125	-	**4799**	**5279**	0.091	-	4493	60	0.161	-	4508	5484	0.178	-
ft53.4	54	[5657, 6439]	5922	**6420**	0.078	-	**5923**	**6420**	0.077	-	5338	6502	0.179	-	5357	**6420**	0.166	-
ft70.1	71	[33,128, 33,298]	32,777	33,308	0.016	-	32,827	33,308	0.014	-	32,669	33,472	0.024	-	33,101	33,298	0.006	-
ft70.2	71	[33,357, 34,450]	33,057	33,977	0.027	-	33,089	33,916	0.024	-	32,938	**33,670**	0.022	-	32,897	**33,670**	0.023	-
ft70.3	71	[33,914, 42,732]	34,152	38,546	0.114	-	**34,423**	38,351	0.102	-	33,825	36,939	0.084	-	33,813	**36,932**	0.084	-
ft70.4	71	[36,517, 40,404]	36,737	39,145	0.062	-	**36,850**	38,771	0.050	-	33,825	**36,939**	0.084	-	35,664	39,843	0.105	-
rbg048a	50	[261, 264]	260	265	0.019	-	259	264	0.019	-	**263**	**263**	0.000	9.442	**263**	**263**	0.000	25.294
rbg050c	52	225	225	225	0.000	863.662	225	225	0.000	36.673	225	225	0.000	2.575	225	225	0.000	1.234
rbg109	111	[354, 414]	354	426	0.169	-	**366**	407	0.101	-	357	488	0.268	-	359	**401**	0.105	-
rbg150a	152	[447, 541]	447	511	0.125	-	461	**509**	0.094	-	**463**	591	0.217	-	461	517	0.108	-
rbg174a	176	[446, 580]	452	601	0.248	-	**463**	**553**	0.163	-	457	571	0.200	-	461	572	0.194	-
rbg253a	255	[477, 773]	523	1252	0.582	-	**532**	**718**	0.259	-	-	-	-	-	527	722	0.270	-
rbg323a	325	[926, 4035]	981	10,111	0.903	-	974	2466	0.605	-	-	-	-	-	**1009**	**1891**	0.466	-
rbg341a	343	[681, 3800]	764	9313	0.918	-	761	2907	0.738	-	-	-	-	-	**780**	**1457**	0.465	-
rbg358a	360	[706, 3296]	950	11,528	0.918	-	755	2453	0.692	-	-	-	-	-	**788**	**1150**	0.315	-
rbg378a	380	[649, 2759]	672	10,242	0.934	-	648	2191	0.704	-	-	-	-	-	**678**	**1126**	0.398	-
kro124p.1	101	[32,858, 35,231]	32,651	37,120	0.120	-	32,630	36,099	0.096	-	32,504	34,100	0.047	-	32,561	**33,962**	0.041	-
kro124p.2	101	[33,190, 37,956]	32,886	42,573	0.228	-	33,006	39,931	0.173	-	32,764	37,074	0.116	-	32,799	**35,860**	0.085	-
kro124p.3	101	[34,217, 53,988]	33,813	54,183	0.376	-	34,005	46,764	0.273	-	33,561	43,910	0.236	-	33,488	**42,416**	0.210	-
kro124p.4	101	[39,413, 55,187]	39,969	58,944	0.322	-	39,333	53,456	0.264	-	38,433	50,910	0.245	-	37,676	**49,590**	0.240	-
p43.1	44	[2827, 4470]	2660	4085	0.349	-	2656	3955	0.328	-	**2860**	**3955**	0.277	-	2851	3990	0.285	-
p43.2	44	[2826, 4275]	991	4450	0.777	-	2705	4210	0.357	-	2856	**4160**	0.313	-	**2870**	4180	0.313	-

Table 2. *Cont.*

Instance			MILP Solver								CP Solver							
			Complete Model				Reduced Model				Complete Model				Reduced Model			
Name	Size	Best-Known [38]	LB	UB	Gap	Time [s]	LB	UB	Gap	Time [s]	LB	UB	Gap	Time [s]	LB	UB	Gap	Time [s]
p43.3	44	[2864, 5375]	1067	5015	0.787	-	1383	4440	0.689	-	**2966**	4450	0.333	-	2897	**4255**	0.319	-
p43.4	44	[3101, 4900]	2995	5035	0.405	-	**3125**	4605	0.321	-	3090	**4495**	0.313	-	3094	4620	0.330	-
prob.100	100	[674, 1008]	668	2125	0.686	-	**677**	741	0.086	-	666	784	0.151	-	667	**738**	0.096	-
prob.42	42	171	171	171	0.000	396.458	171	171	0.000	230.506	171	171	0.000	79.667	171	171	0.000	34.245
ry48p.1	49	[13,371, 13,722]	13,114	14,272	0.081	-	13,200	**13,670**	0.034	-	13,036	**13,670**	0.046	-	13,061	**13,670**	0.045	-
ry48p.2	49	[13,508, 14,659]	13,299	14,415	0.077	-	13,336	**14,305**	0.068	-	13,216	**14,305**	0.076	-	13,185	**14,305**	0.078	-
ry48p.3	49	[14,371, 16,326]	13,882	16,193	0.143	-	13,994	15,840	0.117	-	13,764	15,546	0.115	-	13,728	**15,477**	0.113	-
ry48p.4	49	[17,339, 19,649]	17,162	19,744	0.131	-	17,180	19,583	0.123	-	16,550	19,837	0.166	-	16,483	**19,495**	0.155	-
Average					0.158	552.557			0.167	263.000			0.103	37.184			0.128	36.782

Table 3. Computational results for SOPLIB instances.

Instance			MILP Solver								CP Solver							
			Complete Model				Reduced Model				Complete Model				Reduced Model			
Name	Size	Best-Known [38]	LB	UB	Gap	Time [s]	LB	UB	Gap	Time [s]	LB	UB	Gap	Time [s]	LB	UB	Gap	Time [s]
R.200.100.1	200	29	29	29	0.000	18.394	29	29	0.000	6.017	29	29	0.000	28.271	29	29	0.000	31.403
R.200.100.15	200	[505, 1271]	497	1431	0.653	-	525	1033	0.492	-	381	1864	0.796	-	**589**	**979**	0.398	-
R.200.100.30	200	[669, 2011]	686	3252	0.789	-	774	**1761**	0.560	-	451	3001	0.850	-	**838**	1871	0.552	-
R.200.100.60	200	[8070, 18,761]	8760	17,004	0.485	-	**8861**	16,930	0.477	-	6018	31,561	0.809	-	8440	**16,197**	0.479	
R.200.1000.1	200	887	887	887	0.000	1288.092	887	887	0.000	15.635	887	887	0.000	649.979	887	887	0.000	26.0915
R.200.1000.15	200	[6665, 16,496]	6769	16,336	0.586	-	6895	**12,601**	0.453	-	5318	25,196	0.789	-	**7231**	12,812	0.436	-
R.200.1000.30	200	[9340, 30,351]	9937	23,226	0.572	-	**10,512**	**22,781**	0.539	-	7381	38,410	0.808	-	10,120	23,249	0.565	-
R.200.1000.60	200	[10,508, 23,748]	11,399	21,706	0.475	-	**12,042**	21,993	0.452	-	6666	28,522	0.766	-	10,665	**19,934**	0.465	
R.300.100.1	300	13	13	13	0.000	37.352	13	13	0.000	35.012	13	13	0.000	205.731	13	13	0.000	56.4263
R.300.100.15	300	[625, 12,903]	660	6958	0.905	-	669	2259	0.704	-	-	-	-	-	**811**	**2056**	0.606	-
R.300.100.30	300	[948, 3767]	1008	6790	0.852	-	1102	3163	0.652	-	-	-	-	-	**1157**	**2590**	0.553	-
R.300.100.60	300	[824, 3005]	919	4732	0.806	-	949	1954	0.514	-	-	-	-	-	**991**	**1865**	0.469	-
R.300.1000.1	300	715	715	715	0.000	3187.049	715	715	0.000	64.683	715	715	0.000	257.074	715	715	0.000	71.6789
R.300.1000.15	300	[7213, 112,424]	7607	110,366	0.931	-	7832	**24,047**	0.674	-	-	-	-	-	**8768**	29,423	0.702	-
R.300.1000.30	300	[10,385, 40,457]	11,179	53,835	0.792	-	12,071	40,863	0.705	-	-	-	-	-	**12,269**	**31,618**	0.612	-
R.300.1000.60	300	[9413, 30,655]	10,180	38,212	0.734	-	10,275	25,323	0.594	-	-	-	-	-	**10,408**	**21,623**	0.519	-

Table 3. *Cont.*

Instance			MILP Solver								CP Solver							
			Complete Model				Reduced Model				Complete Model				Reduced Model			
Name	Size	Best-Known [38]	LB	UB	Gap	Time [s]	LB	UB	Gap	Time [s]	LB	UB	Gap	Time [s]	LB	UB	Gap	Time [s]
R.400.100.1	400	6	6	376	0.984	-	6	6	0.000	995.137	6	6	0.000	726.057	6	6	0.000	97.3851
R.400.100.15	400	[729, 47,117]	781	35,044	0.978	-	856	22,767	0.962	-	-	-	-	-	**963**	**3591**	0.732	-
R.400.100.30	400	[780, 7243]	911	39,022	0.977	-	1010	26,438	0.962	-	-	-	-	-	**1084**	**3061**	0.646	-
R.400.100.60	400	[731, 5545]	837	3309	0.747	-	861	2652	0.675	-	-	-	-	-	**966**	**2069**	0.533	-
R.400.1000.1	400	780	780	780	0.000	161.021	780	780	0.000	124.990	780	780	0.000	208.525	780	780	0.000	90.9555
R.400.1000.15	400	[7760, 501,543]	8357	85,878	0.903	-	9083	85,878	0.894	-	-	-	-	-	**9976**	**35,160**	0.716	-
R.400.1000.30	400	[10,076, 95,523]	11,030	127,290	0.913	-	11,783	127,290	0.907	-	-	-	-	-	**12,337**	**57,272**	0.785	-
R.400.1000.60	400	[8103, 55,950]	9360	65,615	0.857	-	9877	36,662	0.731	-	-	-	-	-	**9954**	**22,376**	0.555	-
R.500.100.1	500	3	3	3	0.000	2157.743	3	3	0.000	1881.297	3	3	0.000	2333.235	3	3	0.000	112.086
R.500.100.15	500	[924, 11,452]	964	11,452	0.916	-	1018	11,452	0.911	-	-	-	-	-	**1250**	**5508**	0.773	-
R.500.100.30	500	[773, 12,225]	849	16,963	0.950	-	976	14,273	0.932	-	-	-	-	-	**1099**	**4841**	0.773	-
R.500.100.60	500	[669, 8427]	840	49,105	0.983	-	840	6357	0.868	-	-	-	-	-	**931**	**2723**	0.658	-
R.500.1000.1	500	297	297	297	0.000	97.473	297	297	0.000	85.459	297	297	0.000	85.281	297	297	0.000	77.4382
R.500.1000.15	500	[8420, 107,776]	8949	107,776	0.917	-	9461	107,776	0.912	-	-	-	-	-	**10,628**	**45,356**	0.766	
R.500.1000.30	500	[10,431, 181,835]	11,799	156,359	0.925	-	**12,694**	156,359	0.919	-	-	-	-	-	12,576	**57,330**	0.781	
R.500.1000.60	500	[7094, 33,260]	**8233**	112,466	0.927	-	8192	45,696	0.821	-	-	-	-	-	6559	**20,465**	0.680	-
R.600.100.1	600	[1, 379]	1	55	0.982	-	1	55	0.982	-	**1**	**1**	0.000	2710.470	**1**	**1**	0.000	2182.18
R.600.100.15	600	[670, 5949]	714	5931	0.880	-	845	4044	0.791	-	-	-	-	-	**938**	**2443**	0.616	-
R.600.100.30	600	[873, 12,875]	945	18,932	0.950	-	**1099**	18,932	0.942	-	-	-	-	-	740	**6467**	0.886	-
R.600.100.60	600	[751, 7893]	**838**	26,732	0.969	-	778	25,214	0.969	-	-	-	-	-	538	**2494**	0.784	-
R.600.1000.1	600	322	322	322	0.000	352.202	322	322	0.000	140.645	322	322	0.000	127.397	322	322	0.000	103.378
R.600.1000.15	600	[10,181, 121,877]	10,753	121,877	0.912	-	**10,915**	121,877	0.910	-	-	-	-	-	9401	**65,039**	0.855	-
R.600.1000.30	600	[10,151, 151,010]	11,352	190,145	0.940	-	**12,431**	190,145	0.935	-	-	-	-	-	9356	**48,775**	0.808	-
R.600.1000.60	600	[7604, 87,770]	7962	256,464	0.969	-	**8162**	75,269	0.892	-	-	-	-	-	6908	**42,652**	0.838	-
R.700.100.1	700	2	-	-	-	-	-	-	-	-	2	2	0.000	1649.486	2	2	0.000	619.22
R.700.100.15	700	[799, 6561]	815	14,478	0.944	-	**972**	5718	0.830	-	-	-	-	-	655	**2759**	0.763	-
R.700.100.30	700	[762, 20,281]	896	6960	0.871	-	**983**	4218	0.767	-	-	-	-	-	588	**2531**	0.768	-
R.700.100.60	700	[516, 9030]	538	7033	0.924	-	**555**	1854	0.701	-	-	-	-	-	383	**1598**	0.760	-
R.700.1000.1	700	[611, 621]	611	616	0.008	-	611	616	0.008	-	**611**	**611**	0.000	592.107	**611**	**611**	0.000	368.139
R.700.1000.15	700	[4636, 147,321]	4375	147,321	0.970	-	**5136**	7145	0.281	-	-	-	-	-	2787	**6315**	0.559	-
R.700.1000.30	700	[4303, 50,000]	4477	32,742	0.863	-	**4827**	6981	0.309	-	-	-	-	-	2658	**6115**	0.565	-
R.700.1000.60	700	[2857, 15,579]	2942	8534	0.655	-	**2997**	5842	0.487	-	-	-	-	-	1913	**5357**	0.643	-
Average					0.689	912.416			0.577	372.097			0.268	797.801			0.492	319.698

Table 4. Computational results for COMPILERS instances.

Instance			MILP Solver								CP Solver							
			Complete Model				Reduced Model				Complete Model				Reduced Model			
Name	Size	Best-Known [38]	LB	UB	Gap	Time [s]	LB	UB	Gap	Time [s]	LB	UB	Gap	Time [s]	LB	UB	Gap	Time [s]
gsm.153.124	126	[246, 313]	257	312	0.176	-	269	**311**	0.135	-	278	317	0.123	-	**280**	**311**	0.100	-
gsm.444.350	353	[2103, 2873]	2294	4878	0.530	-	2405	4856	0.505	-	-	-	-	-	**2456**	4310	0.430	-
gsm.462.77	79	[396, 488]	402	478	0.159	-	402	477	0.157	-	**419**	474	0.116	-	418	**465**	0.101	-
jpeg.1483.25	27	87	87	87	0.000	26.041	87	87	0.000	18.556	87	87	0.000	1.194	87	87	0.000	1.071
jpeg.3184.107	109	[489, 684]	506	656	0.229	-	510	715	0.287	-	**518**	718	0.279	-	517	692	0.253	-
jpeg.3195.85	87	[22, 25]	17	25	0.320	-	17	25	0.320	-	**23**	25	0.080	-	22	25	0.120	-
jpeg.3198.93	95	[172, 204]	180	188	0.043	-	180	**188**	0.043	-	**181**	**188**	0.037	-	**181**	**188**	0.037	-
jpeg.3203.135	137	[600, 750]	602	980	0.386	-	618	751	0.177	-	**629**	913	0.311	-	626	750	0.165	-
jpeg.3740.15	17	33	33	33	0.000	1.523	33	33	0.000	0.839	33	33	0.000	0.157	33	33	0.000	0.095
jpeg.4154.36	38	90	90	90	0.000	556.798	90	90	0.000	60.924	90	90	0.000	1.272	90	90	0.000	1.764
jpeg.4753.54	56	164	164	164	0.000	2753.752	164	164	0.000	1790.269	164	164	0.000	15.342	164	164	0.000	16.877
susan.248.197	199	[736, 1184]	792	1978	0.600	-	802	1370	0.415	-	**805**	1361	0.409	-	780	1320	0.409	-
susan.260.158	160	[564, 876]	568	937	0.394	-	573	938	0.389	-	596	991	0.399	-	**598**	897	0.333	-
susan.343.182	184	[591, 862]	617	798	0.227	-	622	**776**	0.198	-	**636**	1043	0.390	-	632	792	0.202	-
typeset.10192.123	125	[280, 415]	274	429	0.361	-	282	**379**	0.256	-	293	385	0.239	-	292	387	0.245	-
typeset.10835.26	28	[99, 112]	99	111	0.108	-	100	112	0.107	-	**110**	**111**	0.009	-	109	**111**	0.018	-
typeset.12395.43	45	[143, 146]	140	146	0.041	-	141	146	0.034	-	**146**	**146**	0.000	2181.942	**146**	**146**	0.000	2780.121
typeset.15087.23	25	97	97	97	0.000	60.502	97	97	0.000	29.118	97	97	0.000	0.477	97	97	0.000	0.318
typeset.15577.36	38	125	125	125	0.000	286.210	125	125	0.000	43.164	125	125	0.000	2.116	125	125	0.000	1.713
typeset.16000.68	70	[77, 80]	66	81	0.185	-	66	80	0.175	-	**79**	80	0.013	-	71	80	0.113	-
typeset.1723.25	27	60	60	60	0.000	590.577	60	60	0.000	86.068	60	60	0.000	4.013	60	60	0.000	3.469
typeset.19972.246	248	[1325, 1929]	1422	3562	0.601	-	1452	2509	0.421	-	1519	2961	0.487	-	**1525**	2804	0.456	-
typeset.4391.240	242	[1093, 1412]	1108	2595	0.573	-	1137	2476	0.541	-	1149	2511	0.542	-	**1154**	1905	0.394	-
typeset.4597.45	47	[150, 155]	150	154	0.026	-	151	154	0.019	-	**154**	**154**	0.000	209.659	**154**	**154**	0.000	128.916
typeset.4724.433	435	[2460, 3433]	-	-	-	-	2673	6131	0.564	-	-	-	-	-	**2679**	7194	0.628	-
typeset.5797.33	35	113	113	113	0.000	851.490	113	113	0.000	28.504	113	113	0.000	0.547	113	113	0.000	0.574
typeset.5881.246	248	[1305, 1700]	1378	2258	0.390	-	1396	2426	0.425	-	**1406**	2385	0.410	-	1394	2084	0.331	-
Average					0.206	640.862			0.191	257.180			0.154	241.672			0.161	293.492

5. Conclusions

This work introduced new models for the Precedence-Constrained Minimum-Cost Arborescence Problem with Waiting-Times that are polynomial in size and are characterized by a smaller memory footprint with respect to the polynomial-sized models previously proposed in the literature. A first model is based on a new set of variables to model precedences. The number of variables and constraints are further reduced, at the price of a preprocessing phase, in a second model. The two models are solved both by Mixed Integer Linear Programs and Constraint Programming solvers. The computational results show that the model characterized by the need of preprocessing outperforms the other one. Furthermore, the Constraint Programming solver achieves the best overall results in terms of both optimality gap and solution time. However, the Mixed Integer Linear Programming solver generally finds better lower bound estimates on the instances. Finally, the models proposed were able to close 7 new instances that were previously open, to provide improved lower bounds for 71 instances, and to find improved upper bounds for 80 instances, out of a total of 88 open instances.

Future work should cover aspects such as robustness of the approaches and the addition to the models of other realistic constraints. Given the progress on the solvers, new instances should be also introduced in order to extend the study on scalability of the different models. Finally, a deeper analysis of the characteristics of the instances that mainly affect the different approaches presented should be in order.

Author Contributions: Conceptualization, J.J., R.M. and M.D.; methodology, J.J.; software, J.J.; validation, J.J. and R.M.; formal analysis, J.J., R.M. and M.D.; investigation, J.J. and R.M.; resources, R.M.; data curation, J.J.; writing—original draft preparation, J.J. and R.M.; writing—review and editing, R.M. and M.D.; visualization, R.M. All authors have read and agreed to the published version of the manuscript.

Funding: This research received no external funding.

Data Availability Statement: The instances used in the paper are available from the literature.

Conflicts of Interest: The authors declare no conflicts of interest.

References

1. Chu, Y.J.; Liu, T. On the shortest arborescence of a directed graph. *Sci. Sin.* **1965**, *14*, 1396–1400.
2. Edmonds, J. Optimum branchings. *J. Res. Natl. Bur. Stand.* **1967**, *71*, 233–240. [CrossRef]
3. Gabow, H.N.; Galil, Z.; Spencer, T.; Tarjan, R.E. Efficient algorithms for finding minimum spanning trees in undirected and directed graphs. *Combinatorica* **1986**, *6*, 109–122. [CrossRef]
4. Chou, X.; Gambardella, L.M.; Montemanni, R. A tabu search algorithm for the probabilistic orienteering problem. *Comput. Oper. Res.* **2021**, *126*, 105107. [CrossRef]
5. Bock, F. An algorithm to construct a minimum directed spanning tree in a directed network. *Dev. Oper. Res.* **1971**, 29–44.
6. Fischetti, M.; Vigo, D. A branch-and-cut algorithm for the resource-constrained minimum-weight arborescence problem. *Netw. Int. J.* **1997**, *29*, 55–67. [CrossRef]
7. Pereira, A.H.; Mateus, G.R.; Urrutia, S. Branch-and-cut algorithms for the p-arborescence star problem. *Int. Trans. Oper. Res.* **2022**, *29*, 2374–2400. [CrossRef]
8. Morais, V.; Gendron, B.; Mateus, G.R. The p-arborescence star problem: Formulations and exact solution approaches. *Comput. Oper. Res.* **2019**, *102*, 91–101. [CrossRef]
9. Hakimi, S.L. Optimum distribution of switching centers in a communication network and some related graph theoretic problems. *Oper. Res.* **1965**, *13*, 462–475. [CrossRef]
10. Guttmann-Beck, N.; Hassin, R. On two restricted ancestors tree problems. *Inf. Process. Lett.* **2010**, *110*, 570–575. [CrossRef]
11. Carrabs, F.; Gaudioso, M. A Lagrangian approach for the minimum spanning tree problem with conflicting edge pairs. *Networks* **2021**, *78*, 32–45. [CrossRef]
12. Kruskal, J.B. On the shortest spanning subtree of a graph and the traveling salesman problem. *Proc. Am. Math. Soc.* **1956**, *7*, 48–50. [CrossRef]
13. Gouveia, L.; Lopes, M.J. The capacitated minimum spanning tree problem: On improved multistar constraints. *Eur. J. Oper. Res.* **2005**, *160*, 47–62. [CrossRef]
14. Frieze, A.M.; Tkocz, T. A Randomly Weighted Minimum Arborescence with a Random Cost Constraint. *Math. Oper. Res.* **2022**, *47*, 1664–1680. [CrossRef]

5. Fertin, G.; Fradin, J.; Jean, G. Algorithmic Aspects of the Maximum Colorful Arborescence Problem. In *Theory and Applications of Models of Computation*; TAMC 2017; Springer: Cham, Switzerland, 2017; pp. 216–230.
6. Eswaran, K.P.; Tarjan, R.E. Augmentation problems. *SIAM J. Comput.* **1976**, *5*, 653–665. [CrossRef]
7. Li, J.; Liu, X.; Lichen, J. The constrained arborescence augmentation problem in digraphs. In Proceedings of the 2017 3rd IEEE International Conference on Computer and Communications (ICCC), Chengdu, China, 13–16 December 2017; pp. 1204–1209.
8. Kawatra, R.; Bricker, D. Design of a degree-constrained minimal spanning tree with unreliable links and node outage costs. *Eur. J. Oper. Res.* **2004**, *156*, 73–82. [CrossRef]
9. Galbiati, G.; Gualandi, S.; Maffioli, F. On minimum changeover cost arborescences. *Lect. Notes Comput. Sci.* **2011**, *6630*, 112–123.
0. Bérczi, K.; Fujishige, S.; Kamiyama, N. A linear-time algorithm to find a pair of arc-disjoint spanning in-arborescence and out-arborescence in a directed acyclic graph. *Inf. Process. Lett.* **2009**, *109*, 1227–1231. [CrossRef]
1. Bang-Jensen, J. Edge-disjoint in- and out-branchings in tournaments and related path problems. *J. Comb. Theory—Ser. B* **1991**, *51*, 1–23. [CrossRef]
2. Li, Y.; Thai, M.; Wang, F.; Du, D.Z. On the construction of a strongly connected broadcast arborescence with bounded transmission delay. *IEEE Trans. Mob. Comput.* **2006**, *5*, 1460–1470.
3. Carrabs, F.; Cerulli, R.; Pentangelo, R.; Raiconi, A. Minimum spanning tree with conflicting edge pairs: A branch-and-cut approach. *Ann. Oper. Res.* **2021**, *298*, 65–78. [CrossRef]
4. Darmann, A.; Pferschy, U.; Schauer, J. Determining a Minimum Spanning Tree with Disjunctive Constraints. In *Algorithmic Decision Theory*; Springer: Berlin/Heidelberg, Germeny, 2009; pp. 414–423.
5. Viana, L.A.d.C.; Campêlo, M. Two dependency constrained spanning tree problems. *Int. Trans. Oper. Res.* **2020**, *27*, 867–898. [CrossRef]
6. Escudero, L. An inexact algorithm for the sequential ordering problem. *Eur. J. Oper. Res.* **1988**, *37*, 236–249. [CrossRef]
7. Moon, C.; Kim, J.; Choi, G.; Seo, Y. An efficient genetic algorithm for the traveling salesman problem with precedence constraints. *Eur. J. Oper. Res.* **2002**, *140*, 606–617. [CrossRef]
8. Balas, E.; Fischetti, M.; Pulleyblank, W. The precedence-constrained asymmetric traveling salesman polytope. *Math. Program.* **1995**, *68*, 241–265. [CrossRef]
9. Hernádvölgyi, I. Solving the sequential ordering problem with automatically generated lower bounds. In *Operations Research Proceedings 2003*; Springer: Berlin/Heidelberg, Germany, 2004; pp. 355–362.
0. Escudero, L.; Guignard, M.; Malik, K. A Lagrangian relax-and-cut approach for the sequential ordering problem with precedence relationships. *Ann. Oper. Res.* **1994**, *50*, 219–237. [CrossRef]
1. Gambardella, L.; Dorigo, M. An ant colony system hybridized with a new local search for the sequential ordering problem. *INFORMS J. Comput.* **2000**, *12*, 237–255. [CrossRef]
2. Karan, M.; Skorin-Kapov, N. A branch and bound algorithm for the sequential ordering problem. In Proceedings of the MIPRO, 2011 Proceedings of the 34th International Convention, Opatija, Croatia, 23–27 May 2011; pp. 452–457.
3. Ascheuer, N.; Escudero, L.; Grötschel, M.; Stoer, M. A cutting plane approach to the sequential ordering problem (with applications to job scheduling in manufacturing). *SIAM J. Optim.* **1993**, *3*, 25–42. [CrossRef]
4. Ascheuer, N.; Jünger, M.; Reinelt, G. A branch & cut algorithm for the asymmetric traveling salesman problem with precedence constraints. *Comput. Optim. Appl.* **2000**, *17*, 61–84.
5. Montemanni, R.; Smith, D.H.; Gambardella, L.M. Ant colony systems for large sequential ordering problems. In Proceedings of the IEEE Swarm Intelligence Symposium (SIS), Honolulu, HI, USA, 1–5 April 2007; pp. 60–67.
6. Fiala Timlin, M.; Pulleyblank, W. Precedence constrained routing and helicopter scheduling: Heuristic design. *Interfaces* **1992**, *22*, 100–111. [CrossRef]
7. Dell'Amico, M.; Jamal, J.; Montemanni, R. A mixed integer linear program for a precedence-constrained minimum-cost arborescence problem. In Proceedings of the 8th International Conference on Industrial Engineering and Applications (Europe), Online, 8–11 January 2021; pp. 216–221.
8. Chou, X.; Dell'Amico, M.; Jamal, J.; Montemanni, R. Precedence-Constrained Arborescences. *Eur. J. Oper. Res.* **2022**, *307*, 575–589. [CrossRef]
9. Shi, W.; Su, C. The rectilinear Steiner arborescence problem is NP-complete. *SIAM J. Comput.* **2005**, *35*, 729–740. [CrossRef]
0. Wang, I.L. Multicommodity network flows: A survey, Part I: Applications and Formulations. *Int. J. Oper. Res.* **2018**, *15*, 145–153.
1. Hurkensa, C.A.J.; Woeginger, G.J. On the nearest neighbor rule for the traveling salesman problem. *Oper. Res. Lett.* **2004**, *32*, 1–4. [CrossRef]
2. Dell'Amico, M.; Jamal, J.; Montemanni, R. Compact Models for the Precedence-Constrained Minimum-Cost Arborescence Problem. In Proceedings of the 2022 The 6th International Conference on Intelligent Traffic and Transportation (ICITT), Paris, France, 25–27 September 2022; IOS Press: Amsterdam, The Netherlands, 2023; pp. 112–126.
3. Floyd, R. Algorithm 97: Shortest Path. *Commun. ACM* **1962**, *5*, 345. [CrossRef]
4. Google. Google OR-Tools. 2023. Available online: https://developers.google.com/optimization (accessed on 20 November 2023).
5. Montemanni, R.; Dell'Amico, M. Solving the Parallel Drone Scheduling Traveling Salesman Problem via Constraint Programming. *Algorithms* **2023**, *16*, 40. [CrossRef]
6. IBM. IBM CPLEX Optimizer. 2023. Available online: https://www.ibm.com/products/ilog-cplex-optimization-studio/cplex-optimizer (accessed on 20 November 2023).

47. Reinelt, G. TSPLIB–A travelling salesman problem library. *ORSA J. Comput.* **1991**, *3*, 376–384. [CrossRef]
48. Montemanni, R.; Smith, D.H.; Rizzoli, A.E.; Gambardella, L.M. Sequential ordering problems for crane scheduling in po terminals. *Int. J. Simul. Process Model.* **2009**, *5*, 348–361. [CrossRef]
49. Shobaki, G.; Jamal, J. An exact algorithm for the sequential ordeing problem and its application to switching energy minimizatic in compilers. *Comput. Optim. Appl.* **2015**, *61*, 343–372. [CrossRef]
50. Wolpert, D.; Macready, W. No Free Lunch Theorems for Optimization. *IEEE Trans. Evol. Comput.* **1997**, *1*, 67. [CrossRef]

algorithms

MDPI

Article

Ensemble Heuristic–Metaheuristic Feature Fusion Learning for Heart Disease Diagnosis Using Tabular Data

Mohammad Shokouhifar [1,*], Mohamad Hasanvand [2], Elaheh Moharamkhani [3,4] and Frank Werner [5,*]

1 Department of Electrical and Computer Engineering, Shahid Beheshti University, Tehran 1983969411, Iran
2 Department of Computer Engineering, University of Mohaghegh Ardabili, Ardabil 5619911367, Iran; mohamadhasanvand5691@gmail.com
3 Department of Computer Engineering, Institute of Higher Education Saeb, Abhar 3697345619, Iran; elaheh.moharamkhani@uoh.edu.iq
4 IRO, Computer Science Department, University of Halabja, Halabja 46018, Iraq
5 Faculty of Mathematics, Otto-von-Guericke University, 39016 Magdeburg, Germany
* Correspondence: m_shokouhifar@sbu.ac.ir (M.S.); frank.werner@ovgu.de (F.W.)

Abstract: Heart disease is a global health concern of paramount importance, causing a significant number of fatalities and disabilities. Precise and timely diagnosis of heart disease is pivotal in preventing adverse outcomes and improving patient well-being, thereby creating a growing demand for intelligent approaches to predict heart disease effectively. This paper introduces an ensemble heuristic–metaheuristic feature fusion learning (EHMFFL) algorithm for heart disease diagnosis using tabular data. Within the EHMFFL algorithm, a diverse ensemble learning model is crafted, featuring different feature subsets for each heterogeneous base learner, including support vector machine, K-nearest neighbors, logistic regression, random forest, naive bayes, decision tree, and XGBoost techniques. The primary objective is to identify the most pertinent features for each base learner, leveraging a combined heuristic–metaheuristic approach that integrates the heuristic knowledge of the Pearson correlation coefficient with the metaheuristic-driven grey wolf optimizer. The second objective is to aggregate the decision outcomes of the various base learners through ensemble learning. The performance of the EHMFFL algorithm is rigorously assessed using the Cleveland and Statlog datasets, yielding remarkable results with an accuracy of 91.8% and 88.9%, respectively, surpassing state-of-the-art techniques in heart disease diagnosis. These findings underscore the potential of the EHMFFL algorithm in enhancing diagnostic accuracy for heart disease and providing valuable support to clinicians in making more informed decisions regarding patient care.

Keywords: heart disease diagnosis; ensemble learning; feature selection; heuristics; metaheuristics; Pearson correlation coefficient (PCC); grey wolf optimizer (GWO)

Citation: Shokouhifar, M.; Hasanvand, M.; Moharamkhani, E.; Werner, F. Ensemble Heuristic–Metaheuristic Feature Fusion Learning for Heart Disease Diagnosis Using Tabular Data. *Algorithms* **2024**, *17*, 34. https://doi.org/10.3390/a17010034

Academic Editors: Roberto Montemanni and Günther Raidl

Received: 27 October 2023
Revised: 18 December 2023
Accepted: 12 January 2024
Published: 14 January 2024

1. Introduction

Currently, a person's workload has significantly increased as a result of more work. There is a great likelihood that the person will get heart disease as a result of this terrible situation, which cannot be avoided [1–3]. Heart diseases are brought on by a reduction in the amount of blood circulating to the brain, heart, lungs, and other vital organs. The most prevalent and least serious kind of cardiovascular illness is congestive heart failure. Blood is transported to the heart by blood veins in the human anatomy. Defective heart valves, which can cause heart failure, are one of the additional causes of heart disease. Anesthesia may also be present together with upper abdominal muscle pain, which is a characteristic indication of heart illness. It is advised to reduce blood pressure, lower cholesterol, and exercise frequently to reduce the risk of heart disease. Angina pectoris, dilated cardiomyopathy, stroke, and congestive heart failure are among the conditions most closely associated with heart disease. As a result, it is important to keep an eye on indicators of cardiovascular disease and speak with medical professionals [4–6].

Cardiovascular diseases are one of the most prevalent causes of global mortality, and their diagnosis and prediction have consistently posed substantial challenges due to their dynamic nature. Risk factors contributing to the elevated risk of heart disease encompass age, gender, smoking habits, family medical history, cholesterol levels, poor dietary choices, high blood pressure, obesity, physical inactivity, and alcohol consumption. Additionally, hereditary factors like high blood pressure and diabetes heighten susceptibility to heart disease. Certain risk factors can be influenced by individual choices. In conjunction with the aforementioned risk factors, lifestyle decisions, such as dietary patterns, sedentary behavior, and obesity, are recognized as significant contributors [7–9]. Heart conditions manifest in various forms, including myocarditis, angina pectoris, congestive heart failure, cardiomyopathy, congenital heart disease, and coronary heart disease. Manual calculations to assess the likelihood of heart disease based on these risk factors are intricate, necessitating the adoption of computer-assisted techniques for efficient and accurate evaluation [10].

Machine learning is effective for a wide range of problems. Utilizing the values of independent variables to predict the value of a dependent variable is one use for this technique. Since the healthcare industry has huge data resources that are challenging to manage manually, it is an application area for data mining. Even in wealthy nations, heart disease has been found to be one of the leading causes of death. The hazards are either not recognized or are not recognized until much later, which is one of the causes of fatalities from heart disease. Machine learning techniques, on the other hand, can be helpful in overcoming this issue and enabling early risk prediction [11].

In this study, we introduce an advanced method for detecting and predicting heart disease patients using ensemble learning, feature selection, and heuristic–metaheuristic optimization. The presented method has two stages. In the first stage, we utilize a combined heuristic–metaheuristic feature selection algorithm based on the Pearson correlation coefficient (PCC) and the grey wolf optimizer (GWO), called the PCC–GWO, to increase the accuracy and performance of each machine learning model. In the second stage, a heterogeneous ensemble learning model is applied to generate the final outputs based on the aggregation of the opinion of the different base learners. As a result, the following significantly contribute to this evolved diagnosis model of heart disease:

- The introduction of an advanced ensemble heuristic–metaheuristic feature fusion learning (EHMFFL) algorithm as a robust model in predicting heart diseases;
- The construction of a heterogeneous ensemble learning model for heart disease diagnosis comprising seven base learners: support vector machine (SVM), K-nearest neighbors (KNNs), logistic regression (LR), random forest (RF), naive bayes (NB), decision tree (DT), and eXtreme Gradient Boosting (XGBoost) techniques;
- The presentation of a combined heuristic–metaheuristic algorithm (called PCC–GWO) to select an optimal feature subset for each machine learning model, separately. In the PCC–GWO model, at first, the PCC is used to calculate an importance score for each feature. Then, these scores are used as heuristic knowledge to guide the search process of the GWO for obtaining the best achievable feature subset;
- The analysis of the relationships between different variables within the cardiovascular datasets using a correlation heat map (CHM), and the evaluation of the performance of the EHMFFL algorithm using different measures: accuracy, precision, recall, F1 score, specificity, and the receiver operating characteristic (ROC);
- The successful development of the EHMFFL algorithm in MATLAB R2022b for heart disease prediction using the Cleveland and Statlog datasets, respectively.

The rest of this paper is organized as follows: In the Section 2, we examine related works. The Section 3 provides details on the two datasets used in this paper. The proposed EHMFFL algorithm is introduced in the Section 4. The results are provided and assessed in the Section 5 and, finally, concluding remarks are presented in the Section 6.

2. Literature Review

In this section, we delve into the realm of machine learning, ensemble learning, and deep learning techniques. Machine learning methods for classification are widely adopted across various industries, and researchers are continually working on advancing their categorization capabilities. One such approach is ensemble learning, which can be either homogeneous or heterogeneous. Early techniques, such as bootstrap aggregating (bagging) [12] and boosting [13], exemplify the power of ensemble learning, often leading to improved classification performance when implemented. In addition to these, various strategies have been explored by researchers, including methods like majority voting, to effectively combine multiple classifiers or partitions for enhanced results.

2.1. *Machine Learning Approaches*

Miao and Miao [14] underscored the critical significance of early detection and diagnosis of coronary heart disease (CHD), a leading global cause of mortality. To facilitate the training and evaluation of diverse deep neural network (DNN) architectures, including convolutional neural networks and recurrent neural networks, they curated a comprehensive dataset comprising 303 patients and 14 clinical attributes, encompassing factors like age, gender, and cholesterol levels. Their results demonstrated that the proposed DNN models outperformed established methods like logistic regression and decision trees, showcasing high accuracy in CHD detection. Furthermore, feature importance analysis revealed that age, maximum heart rate, and ST segment depression, were the three most critical variables for predicting CHD.

Vijayashree and Sultana [15] introduced a machine learning framework designed for feature selection in heart disease classification, leveraging an enhanced particle swarm optimization (PSO) algorithm in conjunction with an SVM classifier. The innovative PSO algorithm, crafted with the unique blend of a hybrid mutation operator, velocity clamping, and adaptive inertia weight, aimed to overcome the limitations of conventional PSO methods. Evaluating the framework using the Cleveland heart disease dataset, the results showcased its superiority over alternative feature selection techniques. Notably, the framework exhibited a high degree of accuracy in classifying heart disease, underscoring its potential for improving the accuracy and effectiveness of heart disease diagnosis.

Waigi et al. [16] presented a study focused on predicting the risk of heart disease by employing advanced machine learning techniques. The research explores innovative approaches to risk assessment in cardiovascular health, utilizing a diverse range of machine learning algorithms. By leveraging extensive data and applying advanced analytics, the study aims to enhance the accuracy and effectiveness of heart disease risk prediction. This work contributes to the field of cardiovascular medicine and underscores the potential of machine learning in improving heart disease risk assessment and patient care.

Tuli et al. [17] presented HealthFog, a smart healthcare system that used ensemble deep learning techniques for the autonomous diagnosis of cardiac illnesses in an integrated Internet of Things (IoT) and fog computing environment. The system was able to effectively diagnose heart illnesses by processing real-time data from numerous sensors and devices, including blood pressure monitors and electrocardiogram (ECG) devices. The HealthFog system's patient monitoring module, data preprocessing module, feature extraction and selection module, and classification module, were all covered in the authors' full architecture presentation. The findings demonstrated that the HealthFog system performed better than other current systems in terms of precision and timeliness.

Jindal et al. [18] focused on heart disease prediction through the application of numerous algorithms, including KNNs, LR, and RF. Their research explores the utilization of these algorithms to enhance the accuracy of heart disease risk assessment and prediction. By leveraging advanced data analytics and machine learning techniques, the study aims to contribute to the field of cardiovascular medicine and improve the effectiveness of heart disease prediction, potentially leading to better patient care.

Sarra et al. [19] reported on a study that used machine learning and statistical analys to increase the precision of heart disease prediction. They chose the most importa candidate features from a list of candidate features using the two statistical models. On th basis of the chosen features, they then applied a support vector machine to create predictic models. According to the findings, the two statistical models and the SVM combinatio had the highest level of success in predicting heart disease.

Aliyar Vellameeran and Brindha [20] introduced a new type of deep belief netwo (DBN) for diagnosing heart disease utilizing IoT wearable medical devices that was su ported with optimal feature selection. The main objective of the study was to train th DBN model by analyzing and selecting the most important features from a big datas The proposed method was evaluated using actual data gathered from wearable medic devices connected to the Internet of Things, and it has shown promising results in correct identifying heart disease.

2.2. Ensemble Learning Approaches

In the case of ensemble learning models, Latha and Jeeva [21] examined the effectiv ness of several machine learning techniques, including support vector machines, decisio trees, and random forests. They contrasted the distinct methods with an ensemble metho that brought these models together. The results showed that the ensemble method ou performed the individual algorithms in terms of prediction accuracy, sensitivity, an specificity. The study also emphasized the importance of feature selection in raising th model's accuracy.

Ali et al. [22] have innovated a smart healthcare monitoring system designed t integrate multiple clinical data sources for accurate heart disease prediction. This syste employs a combination of deep learning models, outperforming traditional methods i terms of accuracy. A standout feature of this system is its real-time patient data monitorin capability, facilitating timely intervention and heart disease prevention. By incorporatin ECG readings, blood pressure, body temperature, and other pertinent clinical factors, th system provides precise cardiac illness prognosis.

Shorewala [23] delved into the realm of coronary heart disease early detection, wit a specific focus on harnessing the potential of ensemble methods. They pinpointed th most effective approach for early disease detection by rigorously analyzing a spectru of models and algorithms, including DT, RF, SVM, KNNs, and artificial neural network (ANNs). The results underscore the superiority of ensemble approaches, which seamless integrate multiple algorithms, yielding the highest accuracy in disease prediction. Th research highlights the significance of ensemble techniques in enhancing early detectio capabilities for coronary heart disease.

Ghasemi Darehnaei et al. [24] introduced an approach known as swarm intelligenc ensemble deep transfer learning (SI-EDTL), designed for the task of multiple vehic detection in images captured by unmanned aerial vehicles (UAVs). This method combine the power of swarm intelligence algorithms and deep transfer learning to enhance th accuracy of vehicle detection in UAV imagery. The research demonstrated the effectivenes of SI-EDTL, offering a solution for the challenging task of detecting multiple vehicle in aerial images, which has significant applications in fields such as surveillance an autonomous navigation.

Shokouhifar et al. [25] have presented a novel approach for accurately measurin arm volume in patients with lymphedema. This method utilized a three-stage ensembl deep learning framework empowered by swarm intelligence techniques. By combinin the power of deep learning and swarm intelligence, the research aimed to enhance th precision of arm volume measurement, which is crucial in the diagnosis and manageme of lymphedema. The proposed model demonstrated promising results, showcasing it potential to improve healthcare outcomes for individuals with lymphedema by providin more accurate and reliable measurements of arm volume.

2.3. Feature Selection Algorithms

There are also various feature selection techniques applied for the enhancement of prediction accuracy in heart diseases. For example, Nagarajan et al. [26] introduce a feature selection and classification model tailored for the prediction of heart disease. The research explores advanced techniques for selecting relevant features and enhancing the accuracy of heart disease prediction. Their results showed that this technique can efficiently improve the effectiveness of early detection and risk assessment for heart disease, potentially benefiting both patients and healthcare providers.

Al-Yarimi et al. [27] presented a heart disease prediction model using supervised learning techniques. The focus of their study was on feature optimization, where they employ discrete weights to enhance the accuracy of heart disease prediction models. By selecting and assigning weights to relevant features, the research aims to improve the efficiency and precision of predictive models in diagnosing heart disease.

Ahmad et al. [28] conducted a comparative investigation on the optimal medical diagnosis of human heart disease using machine learning techniques. They specifically examined the impact of sequential feature selection, comparing its inclusion with conventional machine learning approaches that do not employ this feature selection method. The research aimed to enhance the efficiency and accuracy of heart disease diagnosis through the identification of the most relevant features. They provided some insights into the utility of sequential feature selection in improving the performance of machine learning-based heart disease diagnostic models.

Pathan et al. [29] proposed an analysis to assess the influence of feature selection on the accuracy of heart disease prediction. The study specifically focused on understanding how different feature selection techniques could enhance or affect the accuracy of predictive models for heart disease. By investigating the impact of feature selection, the research aimed to optimize the heart disease prediction model.

Zhang et al. [30] developed a heart disease prediction model that combines feature selection methods with deep neural networks. The research focused on optimizing the feature selection process to enhance the accuracy of heart disease prediction. By utilizing deep neural networks, they achieved more efficient results for diagnosing heart disease, which resulted in the development of diagnostic tools for heart disease diagnosis.

2.4. Our Contributions Compared with the Literature

This paper addresses a significant gap in the existing literature by introducing an innovative EHMFFL algorithm for heart disease diagnosis using tabular data. The EHMFFL approach stands out by seamlessly integrating ensemble learning and feature fusion into a comprehensive framework. The EHMFFL algorithm not only leverages an ensemble of base learners, including SVM, KNNs, LR, RF, NB, DT, and XGBoost techniques, but it also combines the advantages of heuristic–metaheuristic approaches for the selection of a specific feature subset for each base learner within the ensemble learning model. The hybridization of the PCC as a heuristic knowledge source with the metaheuristic-driven GWO sets our combined PCC–GWO feature selection algorithm apart.

3. Data Gathering

In our analysis, we utilize two well-established datasets on cardiac illnesses sourced from the University of California's Irvine Machine Learning Repository, specifically the Cleveland and Statlog datasets [31,32]. Table 1 details the attributes common to both datasets, with the final attribute serving as an indicator of a person's heart disease status. To gain deeper insights into the feature distribution, we present Figures 1 and 2, which illustrate the relationship between the maximum heart rate and age, as well as the distribution of the remaining 12 features, respectively.

Table 1. Description of the attributes in the datasets.

Feature	Description	Type	Values
Age	Age of the patients	Numeric	Years
Sex	Gender of the patients	Categorial	M, F
Ca	Number of major vessels	Categorial	0–4
Chol	Serum cholesterol	Numeric	mg/dL
Exang	Exercise induced angina	Categorial	Yes = 1, No = 0
Cp	Chest pain type	Categorial	Male = 1, Female = 0
Oldpeak	ST depression induced by exercise relative to rest	Numeric	0–6.2
Fbs	Fasting blood sugar	Categorial	mg/dL
Restecg	Resting electrocardiographic	Categorial	0, 1, 2
Thal	Normal; Fixed defect; Reversible defect	Categorial	0, 1, 2, 3
Thalach	Maximum heart rate achieved	Numeric	71–202
Slope	Slope of the peak exercise ST segment	Categorial	0, 1, 2
Trestbps	Resting blood pressure	Numeric	94–200
Num	Heart disease status	Categorial	Yes/No

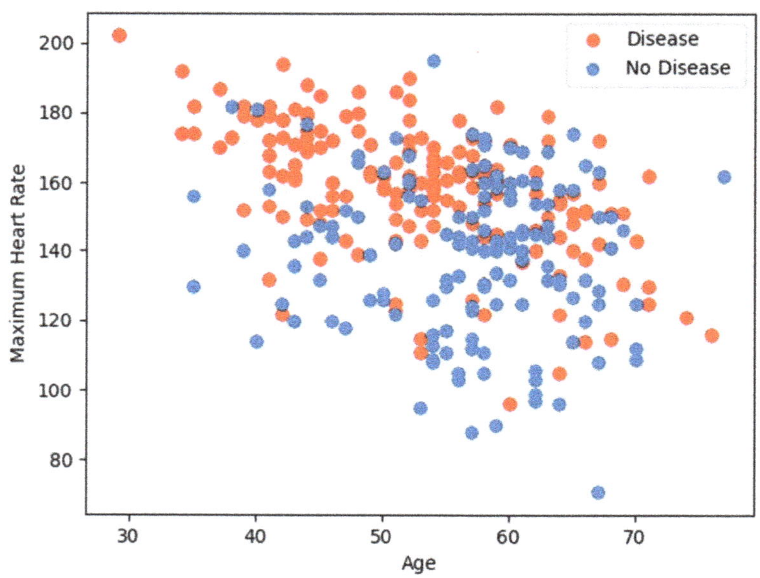

Figure 1. Maximum heart rate versus age.

The Cleveland dataset comprises medical records from individuals who underwent heart disease evaluations at the Cleveland Clinic Foundation in the late 1980s, containing 303 instances, each representing a patient, and encompassing 13 features, including critical factors like age, gender, blood pressure, cholesterol level, chest pain presence, and results from various medical tests. This dataset has played a pivotal role in the development and testing of machine learning algorithms aimed at predicting cardiac disease.

The Statlog dataset, part of a dataset collection, consists of 270 instances (patients) with 13 attributes, including age, gender, blood pressure, cholesterol, fasting blood sugar, and various electrocardiography (ECG) and exercise stress test readings. Originally sourced from the Cleveland Clinic Foundation, this dataset has been widely employed in studies related to machine learning algorithms for medical diagnosis. The primary objective is to enable physicians to make more informed treatment decisions by accurately identifying patients based on their feature values.

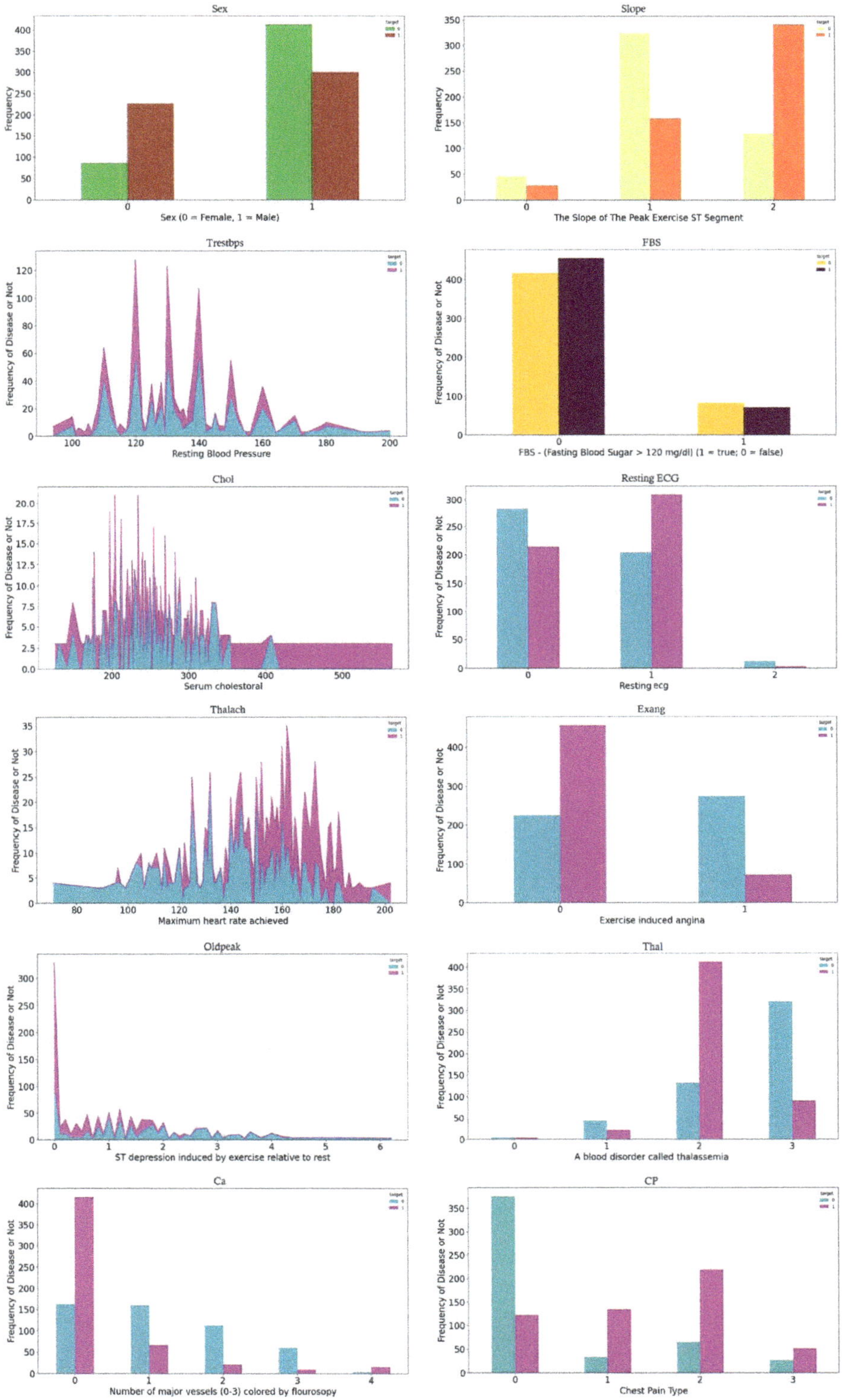

Figure 2. Distribution of all the features.

4. Proposed EHMFFL Algorithm

The proposed EHMFFL algorithm represents a heterogeneous ensemble learning framework, featuring seven base learners, namely SVM, KNNs, LR, RF, NB, DT, and XGBoost techniques. To optimize the performance of each machine learning model, a combined heuristic–metaheuristic algorithm known as the PCC–GWO is performed on each base learner, separately. Initially, the PCC method is employed to calculate the feature importance scores, serving as critical heuristic knowledge for guiding the GWO in selecting the most effective features for the heart disease diagnosis. Subsequently, the tuned machine learning models (SVM, KNNs, LR, RF, NB, DT, and XGBoost) are employed to create the final ensemble learning model. The subsequent sections provide a detailed account of the feature selection process using the PCC–GWO algorithm and the comprehensive classification process with the tuned EHMFFL model.

4.1. Feature Selection Using PCC–GWO

Feature selection is a crucial step in machine learning, particularly when dealing with datasets with high dimensionality. Its primary objective is to streamline the dataset by reducing its dimensionality, thereby identifying the most relevant features that contribute significantly to predictive accuracy, while discarding irrelevant or noisy attributes. This process not only enhances computational efficiency, but also minimizes redundancy among the selected features. Feature selection is essential in various domains, including text categorization, data mining, pattern recognition, and signal processing [33], where it aids in improving model performance by focusing on the most informative attributes and discarding superfluous ones.

Feature selection poses a challenging problem, acknowledged as non-deterministic polynomial hard (NP-hard) [34], making exact (exhaustive) search methods impractical due to their computational complexity and time requirements. Therefore, heuristic and metaheuristic algorithms and their hybridizations become essential in this context [35]. When crafting a metaheuristic algorithm for an NP-hard problem, a delicate balance between exploration and exploitation must be carefully maintained to optimize search algorithms [36]. The GWO is recognized in the literature for its adeptness in striking the right equilibrium between exploration and exploitation. Simultaneously, the PCC stands out as a swift heuristic method for identifying and eliminating highly correlated features [37]. Hence, we have chosen to employ PCC and GWO as the heuristic and metaheuristic components of our integrated PCC–GWO feature selection algorithm. This strategy aims to harness the advantages of both methods concurrently, combining the speed of heuristic-based PCC with the precision of metaheuristic-driven GWO to enhance the feature selection process.

Algorithm 1 outlines the PCC–GWO feature selection approach, offering a hybrid method for selecting an optimal feature subset for each base learner within the ensemble learning model. Initially, the algorithm employs the PCC method to compute an importance score for each feature. Subsequently, these scores serve as heuristic knowledge to guide the GWO during the search process. To achieve this, the importance scores are normalized within the range of [0, 1], and a roulette wheel selection method is utilized to choose features for each grey wolf within the initial population generation procedure. The subsequent sections delve into the specifics of the PCC–GWO algorithm, encompassing both the PCC and GWO phases, facilitating a comprehensive understanding of the feature selection process.

Algorithm 1. Feature selection using PCC–GWO algorithm.

Input:
Full heart disease dataset
Output:
Optimal Feature Subset for Machine Learning Model
Heuristic Feature Selection: Calculation of Importance Scores using PCC:

For (i = 1: *Number of Features*)
Calculation of the correlation of feature i with the class: CC_i
Calculation of the correlation of feature i in relation to the other features: CF_i
Calculation of the PCC importance score of feature i: $IS_i = CC_i/CF_i$
End For

Metaheuristic Feature Selection: Final Feature Subset Selection using GWO:
$t = 0$ (*Initial Population*)
For (s = 1: *PopSize*)
for (i = 1: *Number of Features*)
Calculation of the probability of feature i in solution s using Equation (3)
Deciding to select or decline feature i using roulette wheel selection
end for
Calculation of the fitness of each grey wolf s using Equation (4)
End For
Considering the best solution as alpha wolf: X_α
Considering the second best solution as beta wolf: X_β
Considering the third best solution as delta wolf: X_δ
For (t = 1: *MaxIter*)

% *Population Updating*

for each grey wolf s
Updating a, A_i, and C_i, r_{Ai}, and r_{Ci}.
Calculation of updating factor towards alpha grey wolf using Equation (13)
Calculation of updating factor towards beta grey wolf using Equation (14)
Calculation of updating factor towards delta grey wolf using Equation (15)
if ($|Ai| \geq 1$)
Updating the wolf s using search for prey by Equation (16)
elseif ($|Ai| < 1$)
Updating the wolf s using attacking prey by Equation (16)
end if
end for

% *Fitness Evaluation*

for (s = 1: *PopSize*)
Calculation of the fitness of each grey wolf s using Equation (4)
End for
Updating the best solution as alpha wolf: X_α
Updating the second best solution as beta wolf: X_β
Updating the third best solution as delta wolf: X_δ
End For

Return X_α as the optimized feature subset

4.1.1. Calculating the Importance Score of Features Using PCC

The PCC is a measure of the degree and direction of a relationship between two variables [38]. The PCC values vary from −1 to +1. A value of zero shows that there is no correlation between the two variables, while values near −1 or +1 suggest that there is a strong association between the two variables. The PCC is determined by:

$$r_{x,y} = \frac{\sum (x_i - \overline{x})(y_i - \overline{y})}{\sqrt{\sum (x_i - \overline{x})^2 \sum (y_i - \overline{y})^2}}, \tag{1}$$

where $\overline{x}$ and $\overline{y}$ are the means of the two variables x and y, respectively. Moreover, x_i denotes the i-th value of the variable x, and y_i denotes the i-th value of the variable y.

By computing the correlation coefficient between each feature and the target variable, the method identifies the most informative features for an accurate classification. Then, by considering the correlation of each feature with respect to all the other features in the dataset, the method identifies redundant or highly correlated features that may not provide much additional information. The selection status of each feature is then determined based on a threshold value derived from its correlation coefficients. Finally, the GWO algorithm is used to repeat the selection process multiple times, and the feature subset with the highest fitness value is selected as the final solution. This method provides an effective way to identify and select the most valuable features in high-dimensional datasets, leading to improved predictive accuracy and better performance of machine learning models. The overall operation of PCC can be summarized as follows:

(1) The correlation coefficient of each feature i with the class is computed as CC_i;
(2) The correlation coefficient of each feature i in relation to the other features is calculated as CF_i;
(3) The importance score of each feature i can be calculated as $IS_i = CC_i/CF_i$.

Concerning the PCC, if the value of IS_i is greater than a specific threshold TH ($IS_i > TH$), the feature i is selected; otherwise, it is not chosen. However, in the proposed combined PCC–GWO algorithm, the importance scores obtained by the PCC are used to guide the search process of the GWO for achieving a better level of convergence.

4.1.2. Feature Subset Selection Using GWO

The GWO was originally introduced by Mirjalili et al. [39]. It is based on the hunting behavior and social order of grey wolves found in nature. The social hierarchy of grey wolves is described by four types of wolves, which are the following:

- Alpha (α): the finest solution;
- Beta (β): the second best solution;
- Delta (δ): the third best solution;
- Omega (ω): the rest of the grey wolves.

Similar to other metaheuristic algorithms, the GWO initiates its search procedure by creating an initial population of viable solutions. Subsequently, it undergoes iterative phases, comprising a fitness assessment and population adaptation, until it fulfills a predefined stopping condition, such as reaching a specific number of iterations.

Representation of Feasible Solutions: The encoding of a feasible solution X (i.e., a grey wolf) is depicted in Figure 3. If the quantity of the i-th variable is equal to 1, the feature i is selected by the grey wolf; otherwise, it is not picked. Consequently, a value of 1 is used to represent the feature subset's scope, which is expressed as follows:

$$X(i) = \begin{cases} 1 & if\ feature\ i\ is\ selected \\ 0 & otherwise \end{cases} . \quad (2)$$

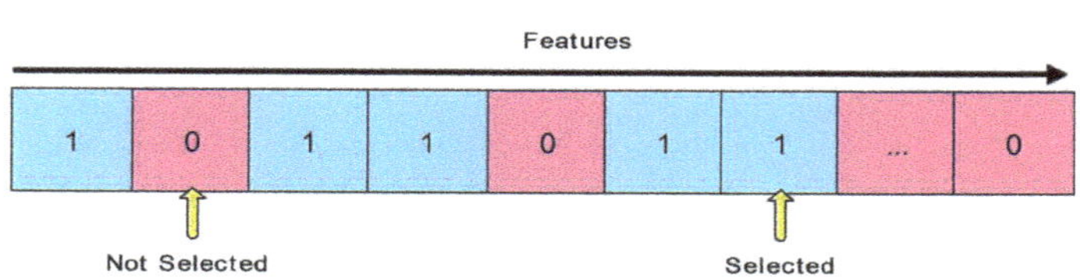

Figure 3. Representation of a feasible solution.

Initial Population Generation: As mentioned above, the original GWO algorithm starts its search process with a random population of grey wolves. However, in the proposed combined PCC–GWO algorithm, the importance scores of the features obtained by the PCC are utilized to generate a set of near-optimal initial solutions for the GWO. To achieve this purpose, at first the normalized importance score for each feature i is calculated and, then, the probability of feature i to be selected in each solution (grey wolf) s can be expressed using the roulette wheel selection method, as follows:

$$NIS_i = \frac{IS_i - \min(ISs)}{\max(ISs) - \min(ISs)}. \tag{3}$$

Fitness Evaluation: The original dataset is separated into train and test datasets. The train dataset is considered for the optimization procedure via the GWO by means of K-fold cross-validation. However, the test dataset is unseen for the final evaluation of the generalizability of the trained model. The following is the fitness function of the GWO to assign the quality of each solution, which aims to be maximized:

$$\text{maximize } Fitness = \left(\mu \times accuracy + (1-\mu) \times \frac{Number\,of\,all\,features}{Number\,of\,selected\,features}\right), \tag{4}$$

where *accuracy* is the total accuracy of the base learner using the validation dataset, and μ is a parameter ($0 < \mu < 1$) that determines the relative importance of accuracy and the number of selected features on the fitness value. The higher μ, the higher impact of *accuracy* on the fitness value. We consider $\mu = 0.99$ to ensure that high-accuracy solutions are achieved, while the number of features in the second rank is minimized.

Population Updating: At every iteration of the GWO, after the fitness evaluation of all the wolves, the first three best wolves, α, β, and δ, are in charge of leading the optimizer's hunting process, while ω simply obeys and follows them. Encircling, hunting, and attacking are the three well-organized steps that the GWO does during the optimization process. The following equations were used to determine the encircling process:

$$\vec{D} = \left|\vec{C} \cdot \vec{X}_p(t) - \vec{X}(t)\right|, \tag{5}$$

$$\vec{X}(t+1) = \vec{X}_p(t) + \vec{A} \cdot \vec{D}, \tag{6}$$

where t indicates the number of iterations, X represents the location vector of the wolf, and X_p represents the location vector of the prey. Moreover, A and C represent the vector coefficients expressed as follows:

$$\vec{A} = 2\vec{a} \cdot \vec{r}_1 - \vec{a}, \tag{7}$$

$$\vec{C} = 2 \cdot \vec{r}_2, \tag{8}$$

Where [0, 1] is a random range for the vectors r_1 and r_2, and the elements within the vector a start at 2 and fall linearly to 0 during the execution of the algorithm, as follows:

$$\vec{a} = 2 - t \cdot \frac{2}{MaxIter}, \tag{9}$$

where *MaxIter* denotes the maximum number of iterations.

The GWO keeps the top three solutions (α, β, and δ) obtained so far and compels ω to modify their placements in order to follow them. As a result, a series of equations that run for each search candidate is used to simulate the GWO hunting process. To achieve this, at first, the parameters of D for alpha, beta, and delta wolves are expressed as follows:

$$\vec{D}_\alpha = \left|\vec{C}_1 \cdot \vec{X}_\alpha - \vec{X}\right|, \tag{10}$$

$$\vec{D}_{\beta} = \left| \vec{C}_2 \cdot \vec{X}_{\beta} - \vec{X} \right|, \quad (11)$$

$$\vec{D}_{\delta} = \left| \vec{C}_3 \cdot \vec{X}_{\delta} - \vec{X} \right|, \quad (12)$$

Then, the moving vectors of the grey wolf X towards the alpha, beta, and delta wolv can be calculated as Equations (12)–(14), respectively. Finally, the movement of the gre wolf X is obtained through the aggregation of the three moving vectors according Equation (15).

$$\vec{X}_1 = \vec{X}_{\alpha} - A_1 \cdot (\vec{D}_{\alpha}), \quad (13)$$

$$\vec{X}_2 = \vec{X}_{\beta} - A_2 \cdot (\vec{D}_{\beta}), \quad (14)$$

$$\vec{X}_3 = \vec{X}_{\delta} - A_3 \cdot (\vec{D}_{\delta}), \quad (15)$$

$$\vec{X}(t+1) = \frac{\vec{X}_1 + \vec{X}_2 + \vec{X}_3}{3}. \quad (16)$$

4.2. *Ensemble Learning Model*

Ensemble learning is a technique for improving the performance of a classifier. It an efficient classification strategy that combines a weak classifier with a strong classifi to improve the effectiveness of the weak learner [40]. The proposed EHMFFL algorith utilizes the ensemble technique to improve the accuracy of the SVM, KNNs, LR, R NB, DT, and XGBoost base learners for diagnosing heart disease. When compared to single classification, the goal of integrating numerous learning models is to achieve bett performance with more robustness. Figure 4 illustrates how ensemble learning is used improve heart disease diagnosis using these seven base learners.

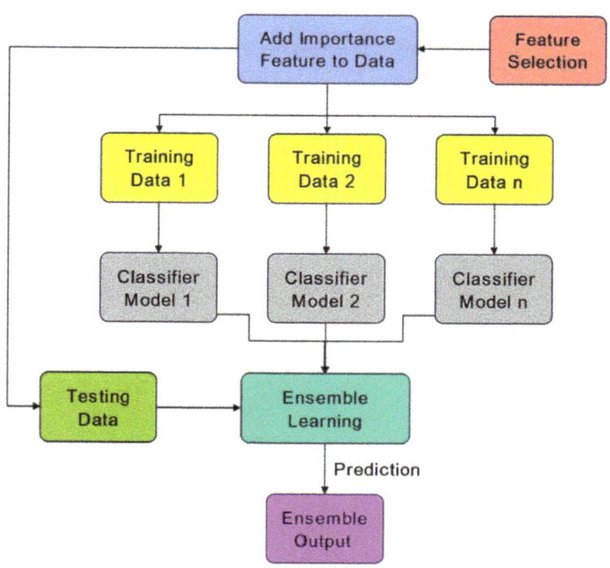

Figure 4. The proposed ensemble learning model.

Finally, using a weighted averaging method, we predict heart disease using eac dataset. The weights of the different base learners are adjusted so that each learner wit a higher accuracy has a higher weight in the ensemble learning model. The algorithm involves separately predicting each class and, then, using a weighted function to combine the outcomes. In contrast to hard voting with an equal chance for each base learner, each prediction receives a weight, and the final results are combined by computing the weighted average. More specifically, the weight of base learner b is proportional to its normalized accuracy using the validation dataset against all the base learners within the ensemble model.

5. Evaluation and Findings

This section offers a comprehensive view of the performance metrics and results obtained in our study. All simulations were meticulously conducted on a PC, featuring an Intel i7 CPU with 2.6 GHz and 16 GB of RAM, and executed on MATLAB R2022b within the Windows 10 environment. Table 2 provides a snapshot of the parameter set applied to the GWO algorithm, facilitating a clearer understanding of the experimental setup. In the following, we evaluate the performance of the proposed EHMFFL algorithm against the seven base learners, as well as the state-of-the-art techniques.

Table 2. Parameter settings for the GWO.

Parameter	Value
Number of grey wolves (PopSize)	30
Number of iterations (MaxIter)	100
Search domain	{0, 1}
Solution dimension	No. Features

5.1. Performance Metrics

In this paper, each dataset was split into 80% and 20% to train and test the datasets. The train dataset (using K-fold cross-validation with K = 10) was applied to optimize the model, while the test dataset was used to assess the generalizability of the tuned model on new unseen data samples. Considering the true positive (TP), true negative (TN), false positive (FP), and false negative (FN), we utilized different performance measures to evaluate the performance of the different techniques:

- True positive (TP): the number of correctly identified positive instances inside the desired class;
- True negative (TN): the number of correctly identified negative instances outside the desired class;
- False positive (FP): the number of incorrectly predicted positive samples when the actual target was negative;
- False negative (FN): the number of incorrectly predicted negative samples when the actual target was positive.

Accuracy: Occurs when the proportion of occurrences correctly classified by the classification learner equals the proportion of correctly predicted samples to the total number of examples, which can be calculated as follow:

$$\text{Accuracy} = \frac{TP + TN}{TP + FP + TN + FN}. \tag{17}$$

Precision: It is one of the performance indicators that will be used to determine how many correct positive forecasts were made. So, precision measures the minority class's accuracy; then, the ratio of correctly predicted positive instances divided by the total number of positive cases predicted is utilized to compute it, using:

$$\text{Precision} = \frac{TP}{TP + FP}. \tag{18}$$

Recall: It is a measurement that quantifies the proportion of actual positive predictions correctly identified out of all potential positive predictions. Unlike precision, which considers the correctly predicted positives relative to all positive predictions, recall focuses on the positives that were overlooked. Essentially, it signifies the extent to which the positive class is comprehensively captured, which is calculated as follows:

$$\text{Recall} = \frac{TP}{TP + FN}. \quad (19)$$

F1 score: In an ideal classifier, we aim for both accuracy and recall to be maximized, equating to values of one. This optimal scenario indicates that both the FP and FN are reduced to zero, highlighting the classifier's ability to make accurate and comprehensive predictions; ultimately, minimizing errors in both positive and negative classifications. As a result, we need a statistic that takes precision and recall into account. The F1 score is a precision and recall-based measure that is defined as follows:

$$\text{F1-score} = \frac{2 \times \text{Precision} \times \text{Recall}}{\text{Precision} + \text{Recall}}. \quad (20)$$

Specificity: It is the proportion of true negative samples to all actual negative samples, which indicates the ratio of the projected presence to the total samples with heart disease presence. The specificity is expressed as follows:

$$\text{Specificity} = \frac{TN}{TN + FP}. \quad (21)$$

5.2. Experimental Findings

As mentioned above, 80% of each dataset were used for the training of the proposed model, while the remaining 20% of the data samples were kept unseen for the validation of the tuned model. More specifically, 61 and 54 data samples were used to test the proposed model and compare it with the other techniques using the Cleveland and Statlog datasets, respectively. The obtained confusion matrix by the proposed EHMFFL algorithm using both datasets can be seen in Figure 5.

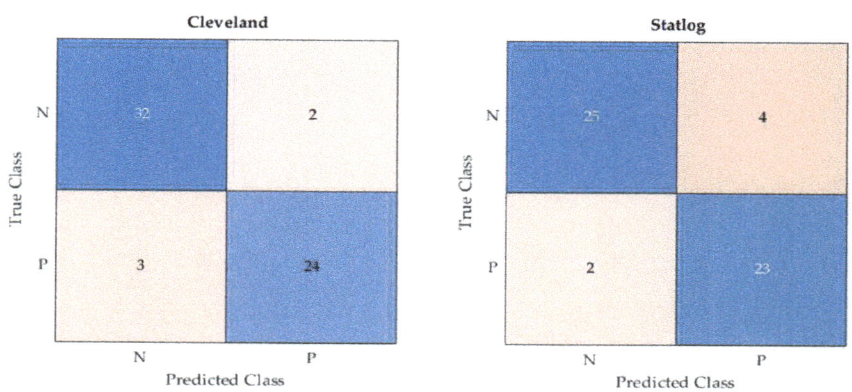

Figure 5. Confusion matrix of the proposed EHMFFL algorithm using the Cleveland and Statlog datasets.

To find the effectiveness of the proposed ensemble EHMFFL algorithm against the base learners, a comparison of various performance measures using the test data samples from the Cleveland and Statlog datasets is provided in Tables 3 and 4, respectively. While some algorithms may display higher performance than the EHMFFL algorithm on a measure, the proposed method outperforms all the techniques on average for both datasets.

Figures 5 and 6 show the accuracy of the EHMFFL algorithm using various methods. The EHMFFL algorithm surpasses all other methods, as illustrated in Figures 6 and 7.

Table 3. Comparison of the EHMFFL algorithm with existing methods using the Cleveland dataset.

Algorithms	Accuracy	Precision	Recall	Specificity	F1 Score
LR	85.2	90.3	82.4	88.9	86.2
DT	82	84.8	82.4	81.5	83.6
RF	90.2	96.7	85.3	96.3	90.6
NB	85.2	87.9	85.3	85.2	86.6
SVM	86.9	88.2	88.2	85.2	88.2
KNNs	83.6	87.5	82.4	85.2	84.8
XGBoost	88.5	96.6	82.4	96.3	88.9
EHMFFL (Proposed)	91.8	91.4	94.1	88.9	92.8

Table 4. Comparison of the EHMFFL algorithm with existing methods using the Statlog dataset.

Algorithms	Accuracy	Precision	Recall	Specificity	F1 Score
LR	79.6	80	82.8	76	81.4
DT	81.5	85.2	79.3	84	82.1
RF	84.4	86.2	85.5	76	87.4
NB	77.8	79.3	79.3	76	79.3
SVM	83.3	81.3	89.7	76	85.2
KNNs	80.8	84.5	78.9	83	81.6
XGBoost	85.2	88.9	82.8	88	85.7
EHMFFL (Proposed)	88.9	92.6	86.2	92	89.3

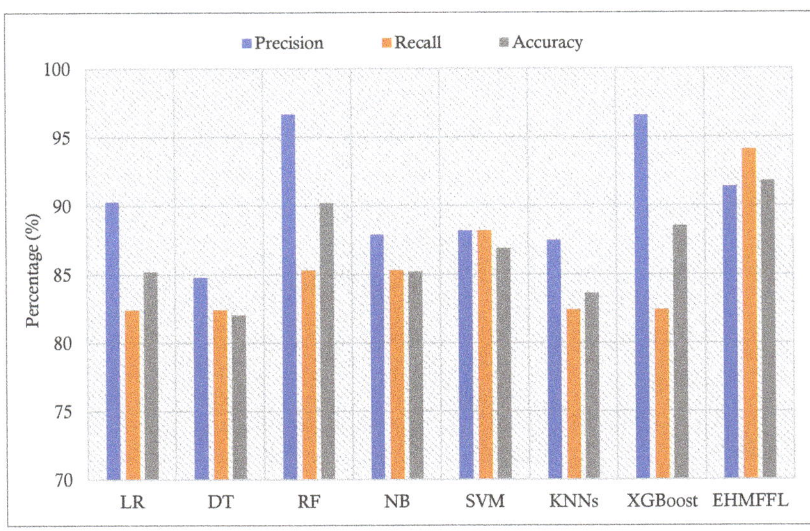

Figure 6. Comparison of the results of different methods using the Cleveland dataset in terms of precision, recall, and accuracy.

According to the different performance metrics for various classification techniques using the Cleveland dataset, the EHMFFL algorithm outperforms all the base learners with an accuracy of 91.8%, a precision of 91.4%, a recall of 94.1%, an F1 score of 92.8%, and a specificity of 88.9. This shows that the EHMFFL algorithm is the most effective and efficient method for the supplied dataset. Other algorithms also perform well in some cases, with accuracies ranging from 82% to 90.2%. When comparing the other algorithms, RF is the best base learner with an accuracy of 90.2% and, then, XGBoost and SVM with accuracies of

88.5% and 86.9% are in the next in order. Also, based on the results in Table 4, the EHMFF algorithm exceeds all other algorithms with an accuracy score of 88.9%. After the EHMFF algorithm, XGBoost, RF, and SVM, obtained better results than the other base learners wi accuracy scores of 85.2%, 84.4%, and 83.3%, indicating that these three methods are th most accurate base learners, the same as observed for the Cleveland dataset. The resul show that the EHMFFL algorithm again shines out in terms of all the performance metric on average.

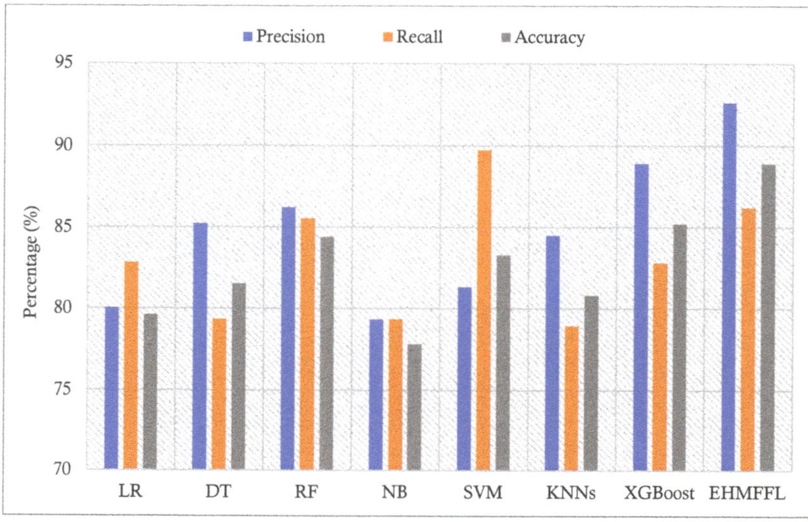

Figure 7. Comparison of the results of different methods using the Statlog dataset in terms c precision, recall, and accuracy.

5.2.1. Running Time Analysis

To assess the trade-off between enhanced performance and time-consuming cost i the proposed EHMFFL algorithm, we conducted a comprehensive analysis comparin its running time with the seven base learners and an ensemble model utilizing all th original features for each base learner, named "Ensemble" in Table 5. Our findings, detaile in Table 5, delineate the offline training/tuning phase and the online test phase tim comparisons for both datasets. The offline time for each base learner signifies its individu training time, while for the Ensemble model, it represents the total training duration of th seven base learners within the model. Conversely, in our EHMFFL model, this duratio encapsulates the time for feature selection via the PCC–GWO algorithm and training th base learners with the reduced feature subsets.

Table 5. Comparison of the running time (in seconds) of the different techniques.

Algorithms	Offline Training/Tuning Phase		Online Test Phase	
	Cleveland Dataset	Statlog Dataset	Cleveland Dataset	Statlog Dataset
LR	0.01	0.01	0.02	0.02
DT	0.13	0.12	0.03	0.03
RF	0.74	0.7	0.08	0.07
NB	0.12	0.14	0.04	0.04
SVM	0.21	0.23	0.06	0.07
KNNs	0.08	0.07	0.03	0.02
XGBoost	0.86	0.83	0.1	0.09
Ensemble	2.3	2.2	0.17	0.16
EHMFFL (Proposed)	142	137	0.13	0.13

Analysis of Running Time in Offline Training/Tuning Phase: Table 5 indicates that the Ensemble model, leveraging all the original features for each base learner, approximately accumulates the total time consumption of the training phase for individual base learners, given their sequential training approach. However, the huge increase in the running time of the EHMFFL algorithm, compared to the Ensemble model, primarily stems from the implementation of the time-intensive PCC–GWO feature selection algorithm for selecting an appropriate feature subset for each base learner. Notably, these processes are confined to the offline model's tuning and do not affect the test phase time.

Analysis of Running Time in Online Test Phase: In the online test phase, both the Ensemble and EHMFFL models exhibit slightly higher time consumption than the single base learners. As the test phase operations occur in parallel, the cumulative time of the base learners is not entirely additive for these models. While the Ensemble model shows around a 70% increase compared to the most time-consuming base learner (i.e., XGBoost), the EHMFFL model, owing to the PCC–GWO feature selection, presents reduced response times for the base learners compared to the Ensemble model. As a result, the online time of the EHMFFL algorithm exhibits a 24% and 19% reduction when using the Cleveland and Statlog datasets, respectively.

Despite the significant increase in the offline running time of the EHMFFL model caused by the combined heuristic–metaheuristic PCC–GWO feature selection algorithm, the implementation of PCC–GWO yields a reduction in the online processing time when compared to the Ensemble model encompassing all the original features.

5.2.2. Analysis of the Correlation Heat Map (CHM)

This section presents the CHM, illustrating the relationships between different variables within the cardiovascular data for both the Cleveland and Statlog datasets. Figures 8 and 9 display these CHMs, where each column signifies a specific variable, and each row visualizes its correlations with other variables. The numerical values within the tables convey the strength and direction of these correlations, which can span from −1, indicating a perfect inverse correlation, to 1, representing a perfect positive correlation. This visual representation offers valuable insights into the interplay among the dataset variables and their potential impacts on heart disease prediction.

In Figure 8, the CHM of the Cleveland dataset illustrates the comparisons among various variables. These variables include age, gender, blood pressure (trestbps), cholesterol level (chol), fasting blood sugar (fbs), electrocardiogram results (restecg), maximum heart rate achieved (thalach), exercise-induced angina (exang), ST depression induced by exercise relative to rest (oldpeak), the number of major vessels colored by fluoroscopy (ca), type of chest pain (cp), and slope of the peak exercise ST segment (slope). Additionally, the presence of two types of thalassemia, indicated as thal and thal2, are considered. The values within the matrix fall within the −1 to 1 range, where positive values signify a positive correlation, negative values indicate a negative correlation, and a value of 0 denotes no discernible correlation between the variables. Analysis of the CHM for the Cleveland dataset reveals the following insights:

- The first section of the matrix compares age, sex, and blood pressure. The correlation between age and blood pressure is weakly positive (0.28), while the correlation between sex and blood pressure is weakly negative (−0.098);
- The second section compares cholesterol and blood sugar. Cholesterol and blood sugar have a weakly negative correlation (−0.057);
- The third section compares restecg, thalach, exang, and oldpeak. The resting electrocardiogram results (restecg) and exercise-induced angina (exang) have a weakly positive correlation (0.14), while the maximum heart rate achieved during exercise (thalach) has a weakly negative correlation (−0.044) with ST depression induced by exercise relative to rest (oldpeak);
- The fourth section compares the number of major vessels colored by fluoroscopy (ca) with the other variables. There is a weakly positive correlation between ca and age (0.12), and a weakly positive correlation between ca and cholesterol (0.097);
- The fifth section compares the different types of chest pain (cp) and their correlations with the other variables. Chest pain type 0 (cp_0) has a weakly positive correlation with ca (0.14), while chest pain type 1 (cp_1) has a weakly negative correlation with thal2 (−0.15). Chest pain type 2 (cp_2) has a weakly positive correlation with fbs (0.084), and chest pain type 3 (cp_3) has a weakly positive correlation with age (0.048);
- The final section of the matrix compares the slope of the peak exercise ST segment (slope) and the two types of thalassemia (thal and thal2). There is a weakly positive correlation between slope and thal2 (0.18), and a weakly negative correlation between slope and thal (−0.42).

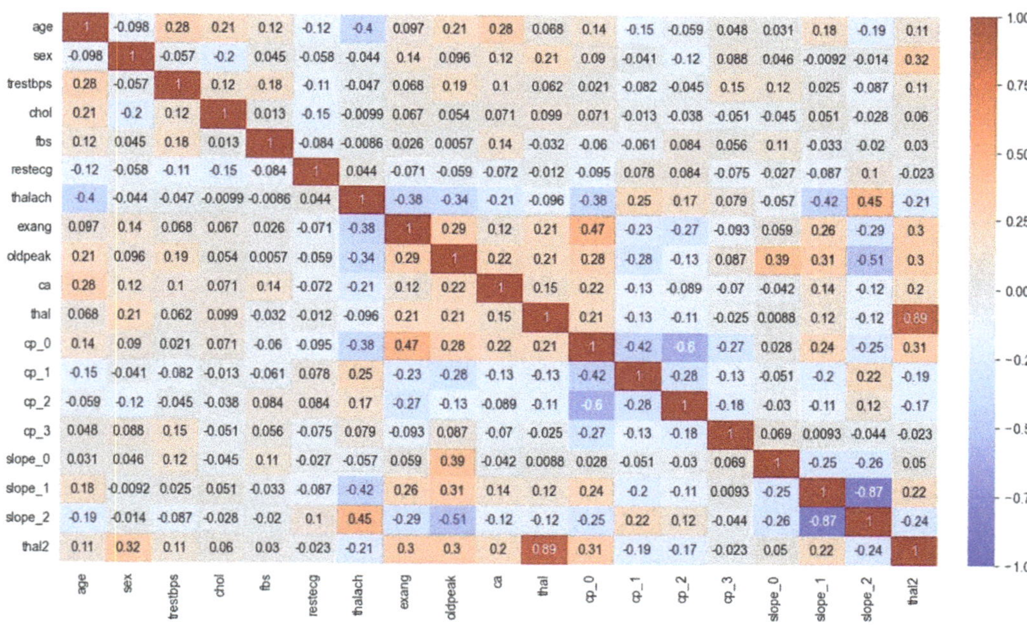

Figure 8. CHM analysis for the Cleveland dataset.

Also, according to the results of the CHM analysis for the Statlog dataset in Figure 9, it can be understood that:

- The values in the matrix represent the correlations between each pair of variables. A positive value indicates a positive correlation (as one variable increases, so does the other), while a negative value indicates a negative correlation (as one variable increases, the other decreases);

- For example, we can see that age is highly negatively correlated with itself (correlation coefficient of −1.00), since it is impossible for someone's age to be negatively correlated with their own age. Sex is negatively correlated with BP and positively correlated with cholesterol levels. We can also see that the ST depression is positively correlated with exercise-induced angina, thallium stress test results, and chest pain types 3 and 4;
- Some notable correlations include a positive correlation between age and BP (r = 0.27), a negative correlation between age and max HR (r = −0.4), and a positive correlation between chest pain type 3 and ST depression (r = 0.35). There also appear to be some negative correlations between certain variables, such as sex and chest pain type 3 (r = −0.26) and slope of ST 3 and thal2 (r = −0.24).

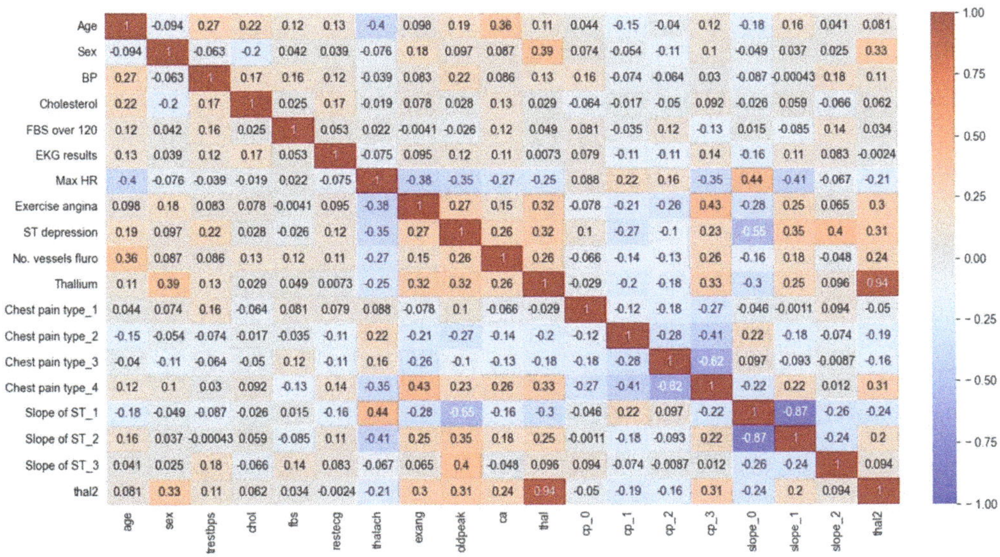

Figure 9. CHM analysis for the Statlog dataset.

5.2.3. Analysis of the Receiver Operating Characteristic (ROC)

In Figures 10 and 11, we present the ROC curves, which illustrate the performance of various heart disease prediction models, encompassing the seven base learners within our ensemble learning model, the EHMFFL algorithm as a whole, and random classification. These curves showcase the trade-off between sensitivity and specificity at different decision thresholds. To gauge the diagnostic value of these tests, we calculate the area under the ROC curve (AUC), where a larger AUC signifies a more effective test. According to the obtained results, the EHMFFL algorithm outperforms all the other compared techniques, achieving AUC values of 0.95 for the Cleveland dataset and 0.88 for the Statlog dataset, underscoring its superior predictive capability in heart disease diagnosis.

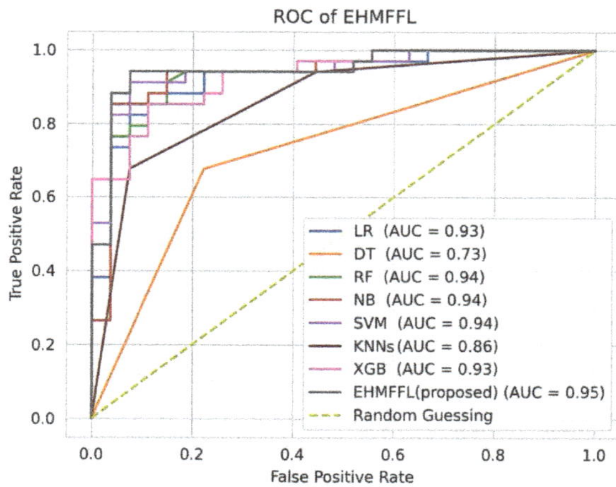

Figure 10. Analyzing the ROC curves of the different techniques using the Cleveland dataset.

5.3. Comparison with Existing Techniques

In this section, we conduct a comparative analysis of the EHMFFL algorithm again three existing heart disease diagnosis methods. Since the EHMFFL algorithm utilizes heuristic–metaheuristic-driven feature selection algorithm (i.e., PCC–GWO) embedded i an ensemble learning model, we considered the machine learning approach based on LR b Jindal et al. (2021) [18] (referred to as ML), an ensemble of different machine learning mo els, including DT, RF, SVM, KNNs, and ANN, developed by Shorewala (2021) [23] (referre to as EL), and a sequential heuristic feature selection method by Ahmad et al. (2022) [2 (referred to as FS). We assess the precision, recall, and accuracy of the different method as depicted in Figures 12 and 13, for the Cleveland and Statlog datasets, respectively. Th results in Figure 12 indicate that the EL model outperforms the EHMFFL algorithm i terms of recall when using the Cleveland dataset. A similar trend is observed in Figure 1 for the Statlog dataset, where the FS method excels in achieving the highest recall amon all the techniques. However, when considering overall performance and emphasizin accuracy as the main metric, the proposed EHMFFL model demonstrates its superiorit over all the compared techniques for both datasets, underscoring its effectiveness in hea disease diagnosis.

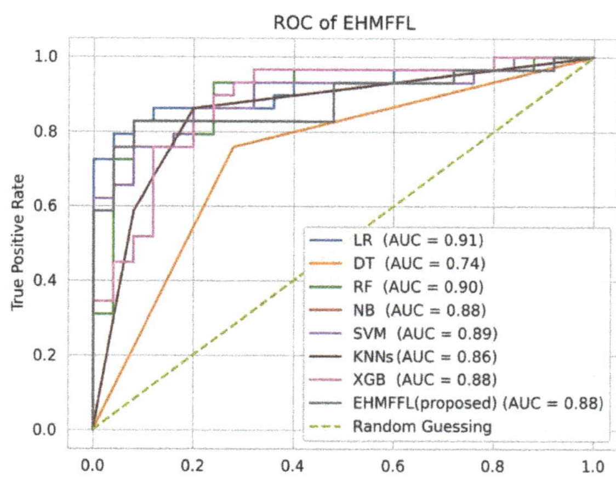

Figure 11. Analyzing the ROC curves of the different techniques using the Statlog dataset.

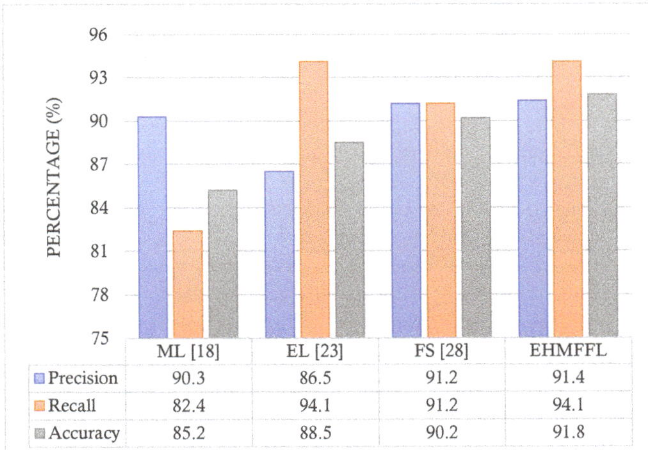

Figure 12. Comparison of the results of the EHMFFL algorithm with the existing techniques using the Cleveland dataset.

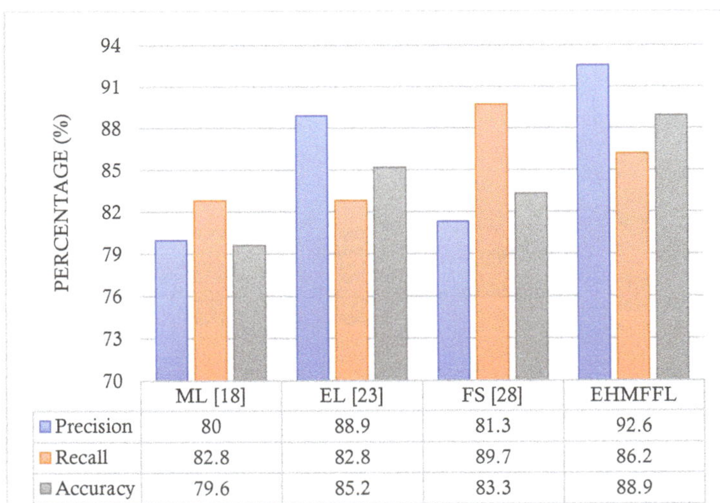

Figure 13. Comparison of the results of the EHMFFL algorithm with the existing techniques using the Statlog dataset.

6. Conclusions

In this study, we have introduced an ensemble heuristic–metaheuristic feature fusion learning (EHMFFL) algorithm, as a powerful tool for heart disease diagnosis using tabular data. The EHMFFL algorithm's first phase employed a hybrid feature selection approach, combining heuristic-based PCC and metaheuristic-driven GWO techniques through the innovative PCC–GWO method. This approach effectively selects the essential features for each machine learning model, facilitating the construction of a robust predictive model through ensemble learning. We evaluated the performance of the EHMFFL algorithm using the Cleveland and Statlog datasets. With an accuracy rate of 91.8% for the Cleveland dataset and 88.9% for the Statlog dataset, our method outperformed the base learners and state-of-the-art approaches. These outcomes highlight the potential of our strategy to elevate cardiac disease prediction accuracy and support healthcare professionals in making more informed patient care decisions.

In implementing the EHMFFL algorithm, the choice of classical machine learning methods within the ensemble model was driven by their inherent benefits related to the utilized datasets in this paper. Classical models offer superior interpretability crucial for comprehending feature influences, especially conspicuous with straightforward attributes. Their efficiency in handling smaller datasets, computational simplicity, and lower risk of overfitting in scenarios with limited samples, outweigh the potential gains from deep learning techniques, particularly considering the simplicity of the provided features. However, if we encounter larger datasets with intricate patterns, the utilization of deep learning techniques becomes imperative. Looking ahead, expanding the application of the EHMFFL algorithm to larger-scale datasets with complex features and more extensive sample sizes stands as a key future endeavor. An appealing prospect is to use deep neural networks integrated with metaheuristic-driven ensemble learning techniques, employing deep networks as base learners within the ensemble model. This amalgamation holds the promise of creating resilient systems adept at deciphering intricate heart disease data streams. Additionally, the integration of real-time patient data streams and the development of a user-friendly interface remain pivotal avenues, promising transformative healthcare tools for timely disease detection and proactive intervention. Furthermore, we plan to explore further enhancements to the proposed algorithm by delving into more advanced feature selection methods and metaheuristic algorithms, continually striving to optimize diagnostic accuracy and efficiency in healthcare.

Author Contributions: Conceptualization, M.H. and E.M.; Data curation, M.H. and E.M.; Formal analysis, M.S. and F.W.; Investigation, M.H. and E.M.; Methodology, M.H., E.M. and M.S.; Resources, M.H. and E.M.; Software, M.H. and E.M.; Supervision, M.S. and F.W.; Validation, M.S. and F.W.; Writing—original draft, M.H. and E.M.; Writing—review and editing, M.S. and F.W. All authors have read and agreed to the published version of the manuscript.

Funding: This research received no external funding.

Data Availability Statement: The data used in the study are available from the authors and can be shared upon reasonable request.

Conflicts of Interest: The authors declare no conflicts of interest.

References

1. Das, S.; Sharma, R.; Gourisaria, M.K.; Rautaray, S.S.; Pandey, M. Heart disease detection using core machine learning and deep learning techniques: A comparative study. *Int. J. Emerg. Technol.* **2020**, *11*, 531–538.
2. Hasan, T.T.; Jasim, M.H.; Hashim, I.A. FPGA design and hardware implementation of heart disease diagnosis system based on NVG-RAM classifier. In Proceedings of the 2018 3rd Scientific Conference of Electrical Engineering (SCEE), Baghdad, Iraq, 19–20 December 2018; IEEE: Piscataway, NJ, USA, 2018; pp. 33–38.
3. Rahman, A.U.; Saeed, M.; Mohammed, M.A.; Jaber, M.M.; Garcia-Zapirain, B. A novel fuzzy parameterized fuzzy hypersoft set and riesz summability approach based decision support system for diagnosis of heart diseases. *Diagnostics* **2022**, *12*, 154[illegible] [CrossRef] [PubMed]
4. Javid, I.; Alsaedi AK, Z.; Ghazali, R. Enhanced accuracy of heart disease prediction using machine learning and recurrent neural networks ensemble majority voting method. *Int. J. Adv. Comput. Sci. Appl.* **2020**, 11. [CrossRef]
5. Muhsen, D.K.; Khairi TW, A.; Alhamza NI, A. Machine learning system using modified random forest algorithm. In Proceedings of the Intelligent Systems and Networks (ICISN 2021), Hanoi, Vietnam, 19 March 2021; Springer: Singapore; pp. 508–515.
6. Mastoi QU, A.; Wah, T.Y.; Mohammed, M.A.; Iqbal, U.; Kadry, S.; Majumdar, A.; Thinnukool, O. Novel DERMA fusion technique for ECG heartbeat classification. *Life* **2022**, *12*, 842. [CrossRef] [PubMed]
7. Nahar, J.; Imam, T.; Tickle, K.S.; Chen YP, P. Computational intelligence for heart disease diagnosis: A medical knowledge driven approach. *Expert Syst. Appl.* **2013**, *40*, 96–104. [CrossRef]
8. Lee, H.G.; Noh, K.Y.; Ryu, K.H. Mining biosignal data: Coronary artery disease diagnosis using linear and nonlinear features of HRV. In Proceedings of the Emerging Technologies in Knowledge Discovery and Data Mining: PAKDD 2007 International Workshops, Nanjing, China, 22–25 May 2007; Revised Selected Papers 11. Springer: Berlin/Heidelberg, Germany, 2007; pp. 218–228.
9. Sudhakar, K.; Manimekalai, D.M. Study of heart disease prediction using data mining. *Int. J. Adv. Res. Comput. Sci. Softw. Eng.* **2014**, *4*, 1157–1160.
10. Khazaee, A. Heart beat classification using particle swarm optimization. *Int. J. Intell. Syst. Appl.* **2013**, *5*, 25. [CrossRef]

1. Xing, Y.; Wang, J.; Zhao, Z. Combination data mining methods with new medical data to predicting outcome of coronary heart disease. In Proceedings of the 2007 International Conference on Convergence Information Technology (ICCIT 2007), Gwangju, Republic of Korea, 21–23 November 2007; IEEE: Piscataway, NJ, USA, 2007; pp. 868–872.
2. Breiman, L. Bagging predictors. *Mach. Learn.* **1996**, *24*, 123–140. [CrossRef]
3. Schapire, R.E.; Singer, Y. Improved boosting algorithms using confidence-rated predictions. In Proceedings of the 11th Annual Conference on Computational Learning Theory, Madison, WI, USA, 24–26 July 1998; pp. 80–91.
4. Miao, K.H.; Miao, J.H. Coronary heart disease diagnosis using deep neural networks. *Int. J. Adv. Comput. Sci. Appl.* **2018**, *9*, 1–8. [CrossRef]
5. Vijayashree, J.; Sultana, H.P. A machine learning framework for feature selection in heart disease classification using improved particle swarm optimization with support vector machine classifier. *Program. Comput. Softw.* **2018**, *44*, 388–397. [CrossRef]
6. Waigi, D.; Choudhary, D.S.; Fulzele, D.P.; Mishra, D. Predicting the risk of heart disease using advanced machine learning approach. *Eur. J. Mol. Clin. Med* **2020**, *7*, 1638–1645.
7. Tuli, S.; Basumatary, N.; Gill, S.S.; Kahani, M.; Arya, R.C.; Wander, G.S.; Buyya, R. HealthFog: An ensemble deep learning based Smart Healthcare System for Automatic Diagnosis of Heart Diseases in integrated IoT and fog computing environments. *Future Gener. Comput. Syst.* **2020**, *104*, 187–200. [CrossRef]
8. Jindal, H.; Agrawal, S.; Khera, R.; Jain, R.; Nagrath, P. Heart disease prediction using machine learning algorithms. *IOP Conf. Ser. Mater. Sci. Eng.* **2021**, *1022*, 012072. [CrossRef]
9. Sarra, R.R.; Dinar, A.M.; Mohammed, M.A.; Abdulkareem, K.H. Enhanced heart disease prediction based on machine learning and $\chi 2$ statistical optimal feature selection model. *Designs* **2022**, *6*, 87. [CrossRef]
0. Aliyar Vellameeran, F.; Brindha, T. A new variant of deep belief network assisted with optimal feature selection for heart disease diagnosis using IoT wearable medical devices. *Comput. Methods Biomech. Biomed. Eng.* **2022**, *25*, 387–411. [CrossRef] [PubMed]
1. Latha CB, C.; Jeeva, S.C. Improving the accuracy of prediction of heart disease risk based on ensemble classification techniques. *Inform. Med. Unlocked* **2019**, *16*, 100203. [CrossRef]
2. Ali, F.; El-Sappagh, S.; Islam, S.R.; Kwak, D.; Ali, A.; Imran, M.; Kwak, K.S. A smart healthcare monitoring system for heart disease prediction based on ensemble deep learning and feature fusion. *Inf. Fusion* **2020**, *63*, 208–222. [CrossRef]
3. Shorewala, V. Early detection of coronary heart disease using ensemble techniques. *Inform. Med. Unlocked* **2021**, *26*, 100655. [CrossRef]
4. Ghasemi Darehnaei, Z.; Shokouhifar, M.; Yazdanjouei, H.; Rastegar Fatemi SM, J. SI-EDTL: Swarm intelligence ensemble deep transfer learning for multiple vehicle detection in UAV images. *Concurr. Comput. Pract. Exp.* **2022**, *34*, e6726. [CrossRef]
5. Shokouhifar, A.; Shokouhifar, M.; Sabbaghian, M.; Soltanian-Zadeh, H. Swarm intelligence empowered three-stage ensemble deep learning for arm volume measurement in patients with lymphedema. *Biomed. Signal Process. Control.* **2023**, *85*, 105027. [CrossRef]
6. Nagarajan, S.M.; Muthukumaran, V.; Murugesan, R.; Joseph, R.B.; Meram, M.; Prathik, A. Innovative feature selection and classification model for heart disease prediction. *J. Reliab. Intell. Environ.* **2022**, *8*, 333–343. [CrossRef]
7. Al-Yarimi FA, M.; Munassar NM, A.; Bamashmos MH, M.; Ali MY, S. Feature optimization by discrete weights for heart disease prediction using supervised learning. *Soft Comput.* **2021**, *25*, 1821–1831. [CrossRef]
8. Ahmad, G.N.; Ullah, S.; Algethami, A.; Fatima, H.; Akhter SM, H. Comparative study of optimum medical diagnosis of human heart disease using machine learning technique with and without sequential feature selection. *IEEE Access* **2022**, *10*, 23808–23828. [CrossRef]
9. Pathan, M.S.; Nag, A.; Pathan, M.M.; Dev, S. Analyzing the impact of feature selection on the accuracy of heart disease prediction. *Healthc. Anal.* **2022**, *2*, 100060. [CrossRef]
0. Zhang, D.; Chen, Y.; Chen, Y.; Ye, S.; Cai, W.; Jiang, J.; Xu, Y.; Zheng, G.; Chen, M. Heart disease prediction based on the embedded feature selection method and deep neural network. *J. Healthc. Eng.* **2021**, *2021*, 6260022. [CrossRef] [PubMed]
1. Heart Disease. UCI Machine Learning Repository. Available online: https://doi.org/10.24432/C52P4X (accessed on 1 August 1989).
2. Statlog (Heart). UCI Machine Learning Repository. Available online: https://doi.org/10.24432/C57303 (accessed on 13 February 1993).
3. Jensen, R. Combining Rough and Fuzzy Sets for Feature Selection. Ph.D. Thesis, University of Edinburgh, Edinburgh, UK, 2005.
4. Seyyedabbasi, A. Binary Sand Cat Swarm Optimization Algorithm for Wrapper Feature Selection on Biological Data. *Biomimetics* **2023**, *8*, 310. [CrossRef] [PubMed]
5. Shokouhifar, M.; Sohrabi, M.; Rabbani, M.; Molana SM, H.; Werner, F. Sustainable Phosphorus Fertilizer Supply Chain Management to Improve Crop Yield and P Use Efficiency Using an Ensemble Heuristic–Metaheuristic Optimization Algorithm. *Agronomy* **2023**, *13*, 565. [CrossRef]
6. Sohrabi, M.; Zandieh, M.; Shokouhifar, M. Sustainable inventory management in blood banks considering health equity using a combined metaheuristic-based robust fuzzy stochastic programming. *Socio-Econ. Plan. Sci.* **2023**, *86*, 101462. [CrossRef]
7. Xie, W.; Li, W.; Zhang, S.; Wang, L.; Yang, J.; Zhao, D. A novel biomarker selection method combining graph neural network and gene relationships applied to microarray data. *BMC Bioinform.* **2022**, *23*, 303. [CrossRef]
8. Pearson, K. Contributions to the mathematical theory of evolution. *Philos. Trans. R. Soc. Lond. A* **1894**, *185*, 71–110.
9. Mirjalili, S.; Mirjalili, S.M.; Lewis, A. Grey wolf optimizer. *Adv. Eng. Softw.* **2014**, *69*, 46–61. [CrossRef]

40. Grover, P.; Chaturvedi, K.; Zi, X.; Saxena, A.; Prakash, S.; Jan, T.; Prasad, M. Ensemble Transfer Learning for Distinguishin Cognitively Normal and Mild Cognitive Impairment Patients Using MRI. *Algorithms* **2023**, *16*, 377. [CrossRef]

algorithms

Article

Efficient Time-Series Clustering through Sparse Gaussian Modeling

Dimitris Fotakis [1], Panagiotis Patsilinakos [1], Eleni Psaroudaki [1,*] and Michalis Xefteris [2]

1 School of Electrical and Computer Engineering, National Technical University of Athens, 15780 Zografou, Greece; fotakis@cs.ntua.gr (D.F.); patsilinak@mail.ntua.gr (P.P.)
2 LIP6, Sorbonne Université, CNRS, F-75005 Paris, France; michail.xefteris@lip6.fr
* Correspondence: epsaroudaki@mail.ntua.gr; Tel.: +30-210-772-1550

Abstract: In this work, we consider the problem of shape-based time-series clustering with the widely used Dynamic Time Warping (DTW) distance. We present a novel two-stage framework based on Sparse Gaussian Modeling. In the first stage, we apply Sparse Gaussian Process Regression and obtain a sparse representation of each time series in the dataset with a logarithmic (in the original length T) number of inducing data points. In the second stage, we apply k-means with DTW Barycentric Averaging (DBA) to the sparsified dataset using a generalization of DTW, which accounts for the fact that each inducing point serves as a representative of many original data points. The asymptotic running time of our Sparse Time-Series Clustering framework is $\Omega(T^2/\log^2 T)$ times faster than the running time of applying k-means to the original dataset because sparsification reduces the running time of DTW from $\Theta(T^2)$ to $\Theta(\log^2 T)$. Moreover, sparsification tends to smoothen outliers and particularly noisy parts of the original time series. We conduct an extensive experimental evaluation using datasets from the UCR Time-Series Classification Archive, showing that the quality of clustering computed by our Sparse Time-Series Clustering framework is comparable to the clustering computed by the standard k-means algorithm.

Keywords: time series; clustering; Dynamic Time Warping; sparse Gaussian processes

Citation: Fotakis, D.; Patsilinakos, P.; Psaroudaki, E.; Xefteris, M. Efficient Time-Series Clustering through Sparse Gaussian Modeling. *Algorithms* **2024**, *17*, 61. https://doi.org/10.3390/a17020061

Academic Editor: Frank Werner

Received: 24 December 2023
Revised: 24 January 2024
Accepted: 25 January 2024
Published: 30 January 2024

1. Introduction

A time series is a sequence of observations measured successively in time. Time series are usually classified as dynamic data because their observed values evolve over time. Typical examples of time series include financial and sales data, stock prices, weather data, energy production and consumption data, biomedical measurements and biometrics data, sensor data, and mobility data through GPS detectors. As the computational and data storage capabilities increase, more (and much larger) time-series datasets become available, and the demand for efficiently processing them and using them to support forecasting and decision-making grows. Hence, in the last couple of decades, efficient processing of time series has become one of the most important and intriguing tasks in modern algorithms and data science (see, e.g., the long list of references in [1,2] for many diverse examples of time-series applications and may different approaches to efficient time-series processing and analysis).

Computational tasks of interest related to time series include regression and prediction [3], forecasting [4], and clustering [2,5]. In this work, we focus on efficient clustering of relatively long time series (with at least a few hundred data points, see also Table 1), using the very popular (but also computationally demanding) Dynamic Time Warping (DTW). Clustering time series is an important (and a daunting) computational task. On the one hand, it can be easily applied to a wide range of contexts and settings (see, e.g., ([2], Table 1)), due to its unsupervised nature. If successfully applied, it naturally leads to the discovery of interesting patterns that evolve. However, time-series data are inherently high-dimensional and complex. Even determining the similarity of two time series admits many different viewpoints (see, e.g., the very long list of dis(similarity) measures in ([2], Tables 2 and 3)), with most dis(similarity) measures being computationally demanding. For example, computing (or approximating) the DTW distance of two time series requires quadratic time in their length, making it time-consuming for time series with more than a few thousand observations.

1.1. Clustering Time Series: Approaches and Related Work

Due to its practical significance and its applications to many different fields, there is a vast literature on efficient clustering of time series following several different approaches (e.g., hierarchical, density-based, grid-based, shape-based, feature-based, model-based) and using various dis(similarity) measures (see, e.g., the long list of references in [2,5,6]). Moreover, time-series clustering can be used as a subroutine in other data mining algorithms, such as rule discovery and indexing (see, e.g., [7] and the references therein).

At the conceptual level, there are two main formulations for time-series clustering [5]: correlation-based online clustering, where time series are clustered in real time based on their correlation; and offline clustering, where a time-series dataset is partitioned into k clusters based on a distance function that quantifies how much two time series agree with each other. There are three main different approaches to time-series similarity, namely shape-based, feature-based, or model-based [6]. In feature-based approaches, a selection of static features is extracted from each time series, and similarity reflects the proximity of the time series in the feature space. In model-based approaches, each time series is approximated by an appropriate model (e.g., by selecting appropriate parameters for a particular function form), and similarity reflects the proximity of the time series in the space of the model parameters. In this work, we focus on shape-based clustering, where the raw time series is considered, and similarity reflects how well the shapes of two time series agree with each other.

In offline shape-based clustering, the choice of the distance function is of key importance (and comprises a major challenge). The majority of shape-based time-series clustering methods are based on Dynamic Time Warping (DTW), where the distance of two time series is computed with respect to an optimal alignment of their data points (see, e.g., [8–10] and their references for the key properties and many applications of DTW). DTW is regarded as one of the most robust and accurate distance functions for time series because, in a natural, versatile, and robust way, DTW deals with differences in the time reference, the length, the time scale and/or the observation frequency of the time series at hand. However, due to the requirement for an optimal alignment of the data points, computing DTW of two time series with length T requires $O(T^2)$ time (Regarding the computational complexity of DTW, we refer an interested reader to [11], where a (large) constant factor nearly linear time approximation algorithm for the closely related edit distance is presented. Moreover, the related work section of [11] outlines a significant volume of work on the computational complexity of computing the edit distance either exactly or approximately). Thus, DTW becomes computationally expensive for time series with more than a few hundred data points. There has been a significant volume of previous work aiming at computationally efficient methods for shape-based time-series clustering with the DTW distance by managing to put aside the quadratic computational burden of computing (or approximating) DTW (see, e.g., the relevant references in [2,5,6]).

Moreover, there is previous work on sparse representation methods for time series and computationally efficient time series clustering. An interesting approach relevant to our work is that of Adaptive Piecewise Constant Approximation (APCA) [12]. APCA aims to approximate a time series using a set of constant-value segments with varying lengths such that the total reconstruction error is minimal. The approach of Iorio et al. [13] is also conceptually similar to ours. They model a time series using P-spline smoothers and then cluster the functional objects, as summarized by the optimal spline coefficients, using the *k*-means algorithm and the DTW distance. Their experimental evaluation approach is also based on the Adjusted Rand Index (ARI) of the resulting clusterings.

1.2. Contribution

In this work, following an approach conceptually similar to that of [12,13], we present and evaluate experimentally a novel two-stage framework for shape-based time-series clustering with the widely used Dynamic Time Warping (DTW) distance. However, instead of constant-value segments of varying length [12] or *P*-spline smoothers [13], we resort to the richer and better-behaved space of Sparse Gaussian Processes for time-series simplification. More specifically, to mitigate the burden of DTW computation, we first use Sparse Gaussian Process Regression (SGPR) to obtain a sparse representation of each time series in the dataset, using a logarithmic (in the original length T) number of inducing data points. We then apply the k-means algorithm to the sparsified time series with an appropriate generalization of DTW. As with most previous work on the topic and for simplicity, we focus on univariate time series in the presentation and the experimental evaluation of our approach, with the understanding that extension to time series with d-dimensional observations is straightforward.

As in [12,13], our key insight is to regard each time series as a noisy realization of a functional form. To identify the function that best fits the time series at hand, we apply regression to the space of Gaussian Processes. A *Gaussian Process* (GP) is a stochastic process such that the joint distribution of every finite collection of its random variables is a multivariate Gaussian distribution [14]. Gaussian Processes extend the notion of multivariate Gaussian distributions to infinite dimensions (and thus, to distributions over functions) and are fully characterized by a mean function and a covariance (or kernel) function (see also Section 3). Building on this intuition, *Gaussian Process Regression* (GPR) applies the standard Bayesian regression approach to the space of Gaussian Processes. GPR aims to identify an optimal set of parameters for the mean function and the kernel function from a relatively small set of observations and then use the resulting Gaussian Process to predict the data point values at other points in time.

Gaussian Process Regression is conceptually simple and has many nice theoretical properties (see also Section 3.3). In practice, however, GPR can only deal with regression tasks of moderate size (with at most a few thousand data points) due to its cubic running time. As a result, several sparse approximation methods have been proposed to extend the practical applicability of GPR (see, e.g., [15] and the references therein). In this work, we resort to Sparse Gaussian Process Regression (SGPR) [16]. SGPR uses a small number of carefully selected inducing points to obtain a sparse approximation to the actual Gaussian Process with a small number of inducing data points (see also Section 3.4 and [17]). (Sparse) Gaussian Process Regression can potentially approximate any continuous target function, with the use of appropriate kernel functions, see, e.g., in [17,18]. Hence, our approach does not make use of any (implicit or explicit) assumptions on the nature of the time series.

In our *Sparse Time-Series Clustering* framework, we use SGPR and approximate a time series of length T with a sparse time series consisting of $\Theta(\log T)$ inducing points. Then, we cluster the resulting sparse dataset using the k-means algorithm with a generalization of DTW, which accounts for the fact that each inducing point serves as a representative of many original data points (see also Section 2.2). In the implementation of k-means, we use the DTW Barycentric Averaging (DBA) algorithm [19] to update the cluster representatives in each iteration.

The running time of our Sparse Time-Series Clustering framework is $O(NT\log^2 T + INk\log^2 T)$, where the first term accounts for the time complexity of Sparse Gaussian Process Regression with $\Theta(\log T)$ inducing points and the second term accounts for the running time of k-means with the DTW distance, running for a maximum of I iterations when applied to N sparse time series with $\Theta(\log T)$ inducing points each. The running time of applying the k-means algorithm to the original dataset with N time series of length T each is $O(INkT^2)$. Therefore, the asymptotic running time of our Sparse Time-Series

Clustering framework is $\Theta(\max\{T^2/\log^2 T, IkT/\log^2 T\})$ times faster than the asymptot running time of directly applying k-means to the original dataset. Intuitively, the improve asymptotic running time of our framework is due to improved running time for computir DTW from $\Theta(T^2)$ in the original data to $\Theta(\log^2 T)$ in the sparsified data.

In addition to speeding up k-means, by computing a sparse representation of th original data set, Sparse Gaussian Process Regression tends to smoothen outliers an particularly noisy parts of the original time series, thus resulting in clusterings that a more robust to noisy observations and of higher quality.

We conduct an extensive experimental evaluation of our Sparse Time-Series Clusterir framework on the datasets of the University of California (UCR) Time-Series Classificatic Archive [20] (see Section 5). The main finding is that Sparse Time-Series Clustering, with logarithmic number of inducing points, computes clusterings with Adjusted Rand Inde (ARI, see Section 2.3) comparable to the ARI of a baseline clustering, computed by applyir the standard k-means algorithm to the original datasets (see Table 3). As for the runnin time, k-means runs significantly faster when applied to the sparsified dataset (see Figure The most computationally demanding step of our framework is the modeling step, whe we apply Sparse Gaussian Process Regression. For large datasets, the total running tim of our framework is faster than applying k-means to the original dataset (see Table Moreover, there are datasets for which we did not manage to run the standard k-mear algorithm in our computational infrastructure, while our Sparse Time-Series Clusterin framework produces good quality clusterings in reasonable running time (see Table We should also note that the modeling step may run offline, once per time series, with i sparse approximation stored for any future use, and is perfectly parallelizable.

1.3. Organization

In Section 2, we introduce the generalization of DTW used in our framework an the Adjusted Rand Index (ARI), used to evaluate the quality of clusterings. Section gives a brief introduction to Gaussian Processes, Gaussian Process Regression, and Spars Gaussian Process Regression. Our framework of Sparse Time-Series Clustering and it main properties are presented in Section 4. The experimental setting and the key finding of our experimental evaluation are presented in Section 2.3. We briefly summarize ou work and conclude with some directions for future work in Section 6.

2. Notation and Preliminaries

A *univariate time series* X of length T is a sequence $X = ((x_1, t_1), (x_2, t_2), \ldots, (x_T, t_T$ of pairs where each $x_i \in \mathbb{R}$ is a data point and each $t_i \in \mathbb{R}$, with $0 \leq t_1 < t_2 < \cdots t_T$, is th point in time when x_i is observed.

2.1. Time-Series Clustering

Given a set $\mathcal{X} = \{X_1, \ldots, X_N\}$ of N time series, a *k-clustering* of $\mathcal{X}$ is a partitioning c $\mathcal{X}$ into k sets (or *clusters*) $\mathcal{X}_1, \ldots, \mathcal{X}_k \subseteq \mathcal{X}$ such that similar time series are assigned to th same set (see also ([2], Definition 1)).

In this work, we mostly focus on time series with the same number T of data point and on *shape-based clustering*, where we aim to maximize the similarity of time series in th same cluster (or to maximize the dissimilarity of time series in different clusters). Shap based clustering is defined with respect to a shape-based *dissimilarity* (or *distance*) functio $d : \mathcal{X} \times \mathcal{X} \to \mathbb{R}_{\geq 0}$, which is symmetric, i.e., $d(X, Y) = d(Y, X)$ for all $X, Y \in \mathcal{X}$, an satisfies $d(X, X) = 0$ for all $X \in \mathcal{X}$, but in the context of our work, may not satisfy th triangle inequality. We say that a dissimilarity function d satisfies the *triangle inequality* if fc all $X, Y, Z \in \mathcal{X}$, $d(X, Z) \leq d(X, Y) + d(Y, Z)$. If a dissimilarity function is symmetric, ha $d(X, X) = 0$ for all $X \in \mathcal{X}$, and satisfies the triangle inequality, we say that d is a distanc function. For simplicity and clarity, we abuse the terminology and refer to dissimilarit functions d that may not satisfy the triangle inequality as distance functions. We focu on the widely used Dynamic Time Warping (DTW) distance (cf. Section 2.2), which is symmetric but does not satisfy the triangle inequality.

Given a distance function $d : \mathcal{X} \times \mathcal{X} \to \mathbb{R}_{\geq 0}$, a k-shape-based clustering (or k-clustering, for brevity) is a partitioning $\mathcal{X}$ into k clusters $\mathcal{X}_1, \ldots, \mathcal{X}_k \subseteq \mathcal{X}$, where each cluster $\mathcal{X}_j$ is associated with a representative time series C_j (which may or may not belong to $\mathcal{X}_j$), with the closest representative of each time series $X \in \mathcal{X}_j$ being C_j, i.e.,

$$\mathcal{X}_j = \left\{ X \in \mathcal{X} : d(X, C_j) = \min_{i \in [k]} \{d(X, C_i)\} \right\}, \tag{1}$$

such that the total clustering cost, defined as

$$\mathrm{Cost}(\mathcal{X}, k) = \sum_{j=1}^{k} \sum_{X \in \mathcal{X}_j} d(X, C_j), \tag{2}$$

is minimized.

2.2. *Distance Functions*

There is a very long list of possible distance functions among time series (see, e.g., ([2], Table 3)). In this work, we focus on a prominent representative of shape-based distance functions for time series, the Dynamic Time Warping (DTW) distance. For completeness, we first introduce the simpler Euclidean distance for time and then present DTW as an elastic generalization of it.

2.2.1. Euclidean Distance

The *Euclidean distance* [21] is a so-called *lockstep* distance, which can be applied only if two time series have the same number of data points, i.e., the same length. The Euclidean distance $L_2(X, Y)$ of two time series X and Y with T data points each is simply the L_2 norm of the L_2 distances between the corresponding data points (see also Figure 1a). Namely,

$$L_2(X, Y) = \sqrt{\sum_{i=1}^{T} (x_i - y_i)^2} \tag{3}$$

A generalization of the Euclidean distance, usually referred to as the *Minkowski distance* for time series, can be obtained by taking the L_p norm of the L_p distances between the corresponding data points (instead of the L_2 norm of the L_2 distances in (3)), for some fixed $p \geq 1$ or $p = \infty$. The main advantages of the Euclidean distance are that (i) it is simple and intuitive, and (ii) it can be computed in linear time in the size of the input. However, the Euclidean distance fails to deal with slight time shifts and/or periodical changes in the sampling frequency of the time series.

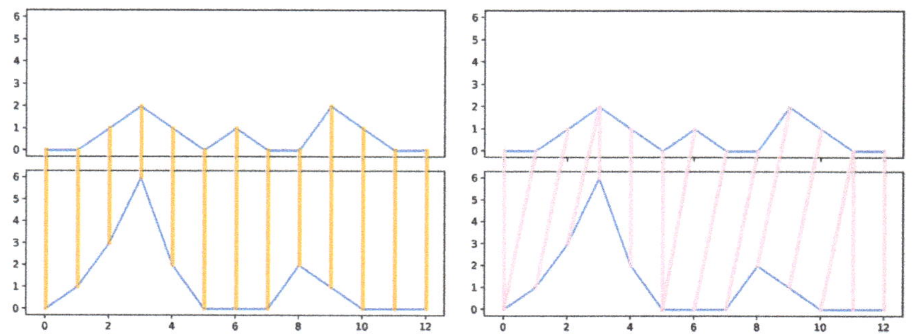

(**a**) Euclidean distance. (**b**) DTW distance.

Figure 1. Simple example outlining the difference between the Euclidean distance in (**a**) and the Dynamic Time Warping (DTW) in (**b**) for time series.

2.2.2. Dynamic Time Warping Distance

The *Dynamic Time Warping* (DTW) distance is a so-called *elastic* distance, which can deal with time series of different lengths, different sampling frequencies, and different time alignments. DTW seeks an optimal alignment (or warping) of the data points of two time series X and Y that minimizes the resulting pairwise Euclidean distance of the corresponding data points. DTW is regarded as one of the most robust and accurate distance functions for time series and has been extensively used in practice (see, e.g., [8–10,22] and the references therein).

The optimal alignment of two time series X and Y, with $X = ((x_1, t_1), \ldots, (x_T, t_T))$ and $Y = (y_1, \tau_1), \ldots, (y_V, \tau_V))$, which is used for the computation of DTW, is a sequence $W = ((T_1, V_1), \ldots, (T_l, V_l))$ with $l \leq T + V$ index pairs that aligns the data points of X and Y such that (i) $(T_1, V_1) = (1, 1)$ and $(T_l, V_l) = (T, V)$, i.e., the first and the last points of X and Y are aligned with each other; (ii) every point of X (resp. Y) is aligned with at least one point of Y (resp. X); and (iii) for every two consecutive index pairs (T_ℓ, V_ℓ), $(T_{\ell+1}, V_{\ell+1})$, $(T_\ell - T_{\ell+1}, V_\ell - V_{\ell+1}) \in \{(0,1), (1,0), (1,1)\}$, i.e., the alignment sequence is increasing and without cross-alignments (see also Figure 1b).

Then, the DTW distance of two time series X and Y is defined as:

$$D(X, Y) = \min_{X\text{-}Y \text{ warping } W} \sqrt{\sum_{(T_\ell, V_\ell) \in W} (x_{T_\ell} - y_{V_\ell})^2} \tag{4}$$

We note that DTW is symmetric and satisfies $D(X, X) = 0$, but it does not satisfy the triangle inequality. The square of DTW can be computed in quadratic time $\Theta(TV)$, using dynamic programming based on the recursion below, which is similar to the recursion used for computing the Edit Distance of two strings:

$$D(X[i], Y[j]) = \begin{cases} \sum_{\ell=1}^{j} (x_1 - y_\ell)^2 & \text{if } i = 1 \\ \sum_{\ell=1}^{i} (x_\ell - y_1)^2 & \text{if } j = 1 \\ (x_i - y_j)^2 + & \\ \min\{D(X[i-1], Y[j-1]), D(X[i-1], Y[j]), D(X[i], Y[j-1])\} & \text{otherwise} \end{cases}$$

where $X[i] = ((x_1, t_1), \ldots (x_i, t_i))$ denotes the prefix of X consisting of X's first i data points and $Y[j] = ((y_1, \tau_1), \ldots (y_j, \tau_j))$ denotes the prefix of Y consisting of Y' first j data points.

We should note that the definition of DTW sometimes restricts the maximum number of data points that can be aligned with a single one, which leads to faster computation and possibly better practical results (see also [23]).

In this work, we focus on a generalization of DTW, referred to as β-DTW, for some fixed parameter $\beta \geq 0$, where the distance between two aligned data points (x_i, t_i) and (y_j, t_j) is computed as:

$$\delta_\beta((x_i, t_i), (y_j, t_j)) = (x_i - y_j)^2 + \beta(t_i - t_j)^2, \quad (5)$$

instead of simply $(x_i - y_j)^2$. Then, β-DTW is computed by the dynamic programming above by replacing the distance function $(x_i - y_j)^2$ with the more general $\delta_\beta((x_i, t_i), (y_j, t_j))$.

For $\beta = 0$, we obtain the standard DTW. As β grows larger, β-DTW penalizes the alignment of data points observed at quite different points in time. Using a moderate value of β proves useful in our Sparse Time-Series Clustering framework because the inducing points used for time-series representation can be located by Sparse Gaussian Process Regression at very different points in time. In fact, the locations of the inducing points highly depend on the shape and the variance of the regressed time series at different time intervals. Hence, the second term in $\delta_\beta(\cdot)$ serves to penalize significant differences in how two time series evolve. Moreover, as β increases above a certain (instance-dependent) threshold, β-DTW becomes a lockstep distance and essentially coincides with the Euclidean distance.

2.3. Evaluation Criteria of Sparse Time-Series Clustering

We focus on shape-based clustering, where the clustering algorithm seeks to minimize $\text{Cost}(\mathcal{X}, k)$, with $\mathcal{X}$ being a set of time series to be partitioned into a predefined number k of clusters. $\text{Cost}(\mathcal{X}, k)$ is given by (2), with respect to the β-DTW distance for every instance. To this end, we apply the k-means algorithm with the β-DTW distance for some fixed parameter $\beta \geq 0$, and the DTW Barycenter Averaging (DBA) algorithm [19] for updating the cluster representatives in each iteration. For each dataset $\mathcal{X}$, k-means is applied to the original time series in $\mathcal{X}$ and to the time series consisting of the inducing points placed by Sparse Gaussian Process Regression (SGPR) applied to each time series in $\mathcal{X}$.

A ground truth clustering is available for all our instances $(\mathcal{X}, k)$. Therefore, to evaluate the performance of our approach, we resort to the *Adjusted Rand Index* (ARI), an extensively used extrinsic clustering metric quantifying how much the clustering computed by our algorithm overlaps with the ground truth clustering. For completeness, we briefly define the Rand Index (RI) and the Adjusted Rand Index (ARI) below.

2.3.1. Rand Index

The *Rand Index* (RI) [24] quantifies the similarity of two clusterings (i.e., the ground truth clustering and the clustering computed by the algorithm) by counting the number of "correct" pairs of data points, which are both assigned either to the same or to different clusters in the two clusterings. More precisely, RI is defined as

$$\text{RI} = \frac{2\,(\text{SS} + \text{DD})}{n(n-1)},$$

where n is the number of data points (and $n(n-1)/2$ is the total number of data point pairs) and $\text{SS} + \text{DD}$ is the number of "correct" pairs. Specifically, SS (resp. DD) is the number of pairs of data points that belong to the same cluster (resp. to different clusters) in both clusterings. By definition, $\text{RI} \in [0, 1]$. However, the threshold above which RI values are considered satisfactory strongly depends on the number of clusters k, with a completely random (and oblivious to the cluster sizes) clustering achieving an expected RI of $1/k$ against any given clustering.

2.3.2. Adjusted Rand Index

The *Adjusted Rand Index* (ARI) [25,26] is essentially a normalization of RI so that random clustering obtains an ARI equal to 0. A simple and natural way to define ARI is

$$\mathrm{ARI} = \frac{\mathrm{RI} - \mathbb{E}[\mathrm{RI}]}{1 - \mathbb{E}[\mathrm{RI}]}, \tag{6}$$

where $\mathbb{E}[\mathrm{RI}]$ is computed over all random clusterings with given cluster sizes compared against the ground truth clustering. (6) defines ARI as the fraction by which the RI of the computed clustering (against a fixed ground truth clustering) outperforms the RI of random clustering (with given cluster sizes, against the same ground truth clustering).

An equivalent definition of ARI is given in ([27], Section 2):

$$\mathrm{ARI} = \frac{2\,(\mathrm{SS}\cdot\mathrm{DD} - \mathrm{SD}\cdot\mathrm{DS})}{(\mathrm{SS}+\mathrm{SD})(\mathrm{SD}+\mathrm{DD}) + (\mathrm{SS}+\mathrm{DS})(\mathrm{DS}+\mathrm{DD})}, \tag{7}$$

where SS (resp. DD) is the number of pairs of data points that belong to the same cluster (resp. to different clusters) in both clusterings and DS (resp. SD) is the number of pairs of data points they belong to different clusters (resp. to the same cluster) in the ground truth clustering and to the same cluster (resp. to different clusters) in the clustering computed by the algorithm.

A perfect agreement among two clusterings is denoted by ARI $= 1.0$, while an essentially random clustering is denoted by ARI $= 0.0$. ARI can take negative values, denoting clusterings with an unusually high number of discordant data point pairs. However, correcting for $\mathbb{E}[\mathrm{RI}]$ in (6) implies that ARI values do not explicitly depend on the number of clusters.

2.3.3. Evaluation

In this work, we resort to ARI to quantify the performance of the clusterings computed by our framework. More precisely, for every instance $(\mathcal{X}, k)$, with a set $\mathcal{X}$ of time series to be partitioned into a predefined number k of clusters, we calculate the ARI for the clustering computed by k-means on the original instance $(\mathcal{X}, k)$ and on the instance obtained by applying SGPR to the time series in $\mathcal{X}$.

Comparing the ARI of the two clusterings indicates the performance loss (or sometimes benefit) due to the sparsity of $\mathcal{X}$'s representation in our framework. Moreover, we use the *spread* and the *average difference* (which can be gain or loss), computed with respect to the ARI of the two algorithms on a family of instances, as a summary indicator of the performance of our Sparse Time-Series Clustering framework.

2.3.4. Average and Spread Difference of Two Clustering Methods

To compare two clustering methods for multiple instances, we need to aggregate the difference in ARI values of the two methods across all instances. To this end, we use the average difference and the second moment of the difference of the two methods' ARI values.

The *average difference* quantifies the average performance gain (or loss) of a clustering method against another one with respect to their ARI values across multiple instances:

$$\mathrm{Diff}_{(1,2)} = \sum_{i=1}^{N} \frac{\mathrm{ARI}^1(i) - \mathrm{ARI}^2(i)}{N} \tag{8}$$

We usually refer to $\mathrm{Diff}_{(1,2)}$ as $\mathrm{Gain}_{(1,2)}$, if $\mathrm{Diff}_{(1,2)} > 0$, as $\mathrm{Loss}_{(1,2)}$, if $\mathrm{Diff}_{(1,2)} < 0$.

The *spread* corresponds to the second moment of the difference between the ARI values of two clustering methods across multiple instances:

$$\text{Spread} = \sum_{i=1}^{N} \frac{(\text{ARI}^1(i) - \text{ARI}^2(i))^2}{N} \tag{9}$$

where $\text{ARI}^1(i)$ (resp. $\text{ARI}^2(i)$) denotes the ARI value of algorithm 1 (resp. 2) for instance i and N is the total number of instances.

3. Gaussian Process Regression for Time Series

A typical approach to dealing with a sequence of individual data points, such as a time series, boils down to inferring a continuous function that approximately describes the entire sequence. There are a few popular approaches in this direction depending on the prior information about the model and on the complexity of the data itself (see, e.g., [28]).

If a time series can be described (or can be approximated) by a relatively simple function (i.e., a polynomial of degree d), we may use parametric fitting to estimate the function's unknown parameters from a few data points. Then, interpolation, or *regression*, can be used to essentially fill in the space between data points and to create a continuous function representation of the time series, which can be used as a way to predict new or hidden data points, as well as to reduce the size and the complexity of the time series representation. In the context of time series, we may regard regression as a supervised learning problem, where we wish to learn a continuous mapping f from the time domain to the domain of data points, given a relatively simple class of functions to select from (i.e., polynomials of degree d) and a relatively small set of data points.

Although regression may sound natural and practically appealing, in most practical applications, time series cannot be reasonably approximated by a fixed class of relatively simple functions. Hence, in this work, we resort to (sparse) *Gaussian Process Regression* (GPR), a general approach relying on minimal assumptions about the nature of the time series.

GPR is a Bayesian nonparametric approach to regression, where instead of calculating a probability distribution over the finite set of parameters of a specific functional form, we calculate a probability distribution over all admissible functions that best approximates the time series at hand. In the following paragraphs, we briefly present the main ingredients of sparse Gaussian Process Regression (see also [14,29] for elaborate introductions to Gaussian Processes and their applications).

3.1. Gaussian Processes for Time Series

At a conceptual level, a *Gaussian Process* extends the notion of multivariate Gaussian distributions to infinite dimensions (and thus, to distributions over functions). Formally, a Gaussian Process is a stochastic process $(Z_1, \ldots, Z_t, \ldots)$ such that the joint distribution of every finite collection $(Z_{t_1}, \ldots, Z_{t_k})$ of its random variables is a *multivariate Gaussian distribution* ([14], Definition 2.1).

For this work, it is convenient to regard a Gaussian Process model as a probability distribution over continuous functions (or over time series). For simplicity and since in this work we mostly deal with real-valued time series, where the observed data points $x_i \in \mathbb{R}$, we restrict our attention to regression over functions that map points in time to real data points. Starting with the special case where a time series is evaluated in a fixed number n of points in time, for any n-dimensional vectors $\vec{x} = (x_1, \ldots, x_n)$ and $\vec{t} = (t_1, \ldots, t_n) \in \mathbb{R}^n$, a n-variate Gaussian distribution $\mathcal{N}(m(\vec{t}), k(\vec{t}, \vec{t}))$ determines the probability that the observed data points $(x_1, \ldots, x_n)$ at times $(t_1, \ldots, t_n)$ are drawn from a n-variate Gaussian distribution with mean function $m : \mathbb{R} \to \mathbb{R}$ and covariance function (a.k.a. *kernel* function) $k : \mathbb{R} \times \mathbb{R} \to \mathbb{R}$. In fact, given a time series $X = (\vec{x}, \vec{t})$, we want to compute a $m(\vec{t}) = (m(t_1), \ldots, m(t_n))$ and positive semidefinite covariance matrix $K = (k(t_i, t_j))_{i,j \in [n]}$) maximizing the probability that the observed data point vector $\vec{x}$ is drawn the n-variate Gaussian distribution $\mathcal{N}(m(\vec{t}), k(\vec{t}, \vec{t}))$.

The notion of a Gaussian Process naturally extends the idea of a n-variate Gaussian distribution to arbitrary dimensions, which allows us to regress over continuous functions and time series. A Gaussian process is defined by a *mean function* $m : \mathbb{R} \to \mathbb{R}$ and a *kernel function* $k : \mathbb{R} \times \mathbb{R} \to \mathbb{R}$. The mean function $m(\cdot)$ determines the expected value $m(t)$ of a data point $x_t \in \mathbb{R}$ at any time t. The kernel function $k(\cdot,\cdot)$ quantifies the correlation $k(t,t')$ between the observed data points x_t and $x_{t'}$ at any two times t and t'. We let $f \sim \mathcal{GP}(m,k)$ denote that the time series described by the function $f : \mathbb{R} \to \mathbb{R}$ (i.e., the values of the data points are $f(t)$ at all times t) follows a Gaussian Process $\mathcal{GP}$ with mean function m and kernel function k.

The mean function m determines the average value of data points over time and is usually normalized to 0 over the entire time horizon. The kernel function k determines the shape of the time series modeled by the Gaussian Process, in the sense that if two points in time t and t' are highly correlated (e.g., because t and t' are neighboring points in time, or because we expect that the observed data points at t and t' should be close to each other), the kernel function should favor time series f with similar values $f(t)$ and $f(t')$.

3.2. *Kernel Functions for Time Series*

Kernel functions play a central role in Gaussian Process Regression because they incorporate the information (and our assumptions) about the smoothness and the degree of correlation between data points in the time series that we aim to approximate. The kernel function $k : \mathbb{R} \times \mathbb{R} \to \mathbb{R}$ maps any two points in time t and t' to a real number that quantifies the expected similarity between the observed data points x_t and $x_{t'}$. In any finite dimensions n, the covariance matrix K of the corresponding n-variate Gaussian is computed by evaluating the kernel function $k(t,t')$ over all n^2 pairs of points t and t' in time. The kernel function should ensure that the resulting covariance matrix is always positive semidefinite.

A kernel function k is *stationary*, if for any two points in time t and t' and any translation u, it holds that $k(t,t') = k(t+u, t'+u)$. Specifically, the covariance $k(t,t')$ of any two points in time t and t' only depends on $t - t'$ and is invariant under translation. If the covariance $k(t,t')$ of any two points in time t and t' only depends on their distance $|t - t'|$, we say that the kernel function is *isotropic*. In the following, we discuss two widely used stationary (and isotropic) kernel functions, the *Radical Basis Function* (RBF) kernel and the *Matérn* kernel (see also ([14], Chapter 4)).

3.2.1. The Radial Basis Function Kernel

The Radial Basis Function (RBF) kernel (a.k.a. the Gaussian kernel or the Squared Exponential kernel) is defined as:

$$k_{\mathrm{RBF}(s,\ell)}(t,t') = s^2 \exp\left(-\frac{(t-t')^2}{2\ell^2}\right) \tag{10}$$

In (10), k has two hyperparameters: the *scale factor* s, which quantifies the deviation to the mean value m of a function f drawn from the corresponding Gaussian Process; and the *length scale* ℓ, which quantifies the strength of the correlation between the data points $f(t)$ and $f(t')$ of two points in time at distance $|t - t'|$. Gaussian Process Regression with the RBF kernel corresponds to Bayesian linear regression with an infinite number of basis functions. Due to its nice properties (see, e.g., ([14], Sections 4.2 and 4.3)), RBF has become the default kernel function in practical applications.

3.2.2. The Matérn Kernel

The class of Matérn kernels is a generalization of RBF kernels with an additional hyperparameter ν, which controls the smoothness of the kernel function. A Matérn kernel is defined as:

$$k_{M(s,\ell,\nu)}(t,t') = \frac{s^2 2^{\nu-1}}{\Gamma(\nu)} \left(\frac{\sqrt{2\nu}|t-t'|}{\ell} \right)^{\nu} K_{\nu}\left(\frac{\sqrt{2\nu}|t-t'|}{\ell} \right), \quad (11)$$

where $\Gamma(\cdot)$ is the gamma function and $K_\nu(\cdot)$ is the modified Bessel function of the second kind. Larger values of ν result in smoother approximated time series, while as ν grows to ∞, the Matérn kernel becomes equivalent to the RBF kernel. We note that the cases where $\nu = 3/2$ and $\nu = 5/2$ have nice closed forms ([14], (4.17)) and are of special interest to practical applications. In this work, we use the Matérn kernel for $\nu = 3/2$.

3.3. *Gaussian Process Regression*

Gaussian Process Regression (GPR) applies the standard Bayesian regression approach to Gaussian Processes. In Bayesian regression, we first compute a posterior distribution on the parameters of an admissible functional form (e.g., polynomials of degree d) based on some prior information about these parameters (if available) and on the available data points. This is extended to a predictive posterior distribution, i.e., a distribution on the values of unseen data points, which is derived from the prior distribution on the parameters of the admissible functional form.

In our setting, we are given a time series $X = ((x_1, t_1), \ldots, (x_n, t_n))$ with n data points and aim to compute a posterior Gaussian Process, which provides a probability distribution over unseen data points $x(t)$ at any point in time t. We assume that each data point $x_i = f(t_i) + \epsilon_i$, where $f : \mathbb{R} \to \mathbb{R}$ is a latent function (for which do not make any particular assumptions) and $\epsilon_i \sim \mathcal{N}(0, \sigma^2)$ is an independent sample drawn from a white noise process with standard deviation σ.

For the Bayesian regression process, we make the standard assumption that the data are normalized to 0 over the entire time horizon. Hence, we consider Gaussian Processes with a zero-mean function, i.e., with mean function $m(t) = 0$ for all points in time t. Then, the prior distribution is a n-variate Gaussian distribution conditioned on the input time series $X = ((x_1, t_1), \ldots, (x_n, t_n))$. Specifically, the distribution of $\vec{x}$ conditional on $\vec{t}$ is:

$$\vec{x} \,|\, \vec{t} \sim \mathcal{N}(0, k_\theta + \sigma^2), \quad (12)$$

where $k_\theta : \mathbb{R} \times \mathbb{R} \to \mathbb{R}$ is a kernel function (e.g., an RBF kernel or a Matérn kernel) with hyperparameters θ and $\vec{x} = (x_1, \ldots, x_n)$ are noisy values sampled from the latent function $f : \mathbb{R} \to \mathbb{R}$ at times $\vec{t} = (t_1, \ldots, t_n)$. Due to noise, the covariance matrix of $\mathcal{N}$ is $\tilde{K}_{\theta,\sigma} = K_\theta + \sigma^2 I$, where $K_\theta = (k_\theta(t_i, t_j))_{i,j \in [n]}$ is the positive semidefinite covariance matrix computed by applying the kernel function k_θ to $\vec{t}$, σ is the standard deviation of the white noise, and I is the identity matrix.

The hyperparameters θ of the kernel function k_θ and the standard deviation of the observation noise σ are optimized based on the input time series $X = ((x_1, t_1), \ldots, (x_n, t_n))$. Hyperparameter optimization in (12) corresponds to a non-convex optimization problem, which is typically solved through gradient-based optimization techniques, such as Adam [30] and L-BFGS [31]. The running time is typically cubic, and the space requirement is typically quadratic in the size of the input data, i.e., $O(n^3)$ and $O(n^2)$ for time and space, respectively, with the computational complexity dominated by the time required to invert the covariance matrix $\tilde{K}_{\theta,\sigma}$.

We use the resulting posterior Gaussian Process $\mathcal{GP}(0, k_\theta)$ in order to estimate the values of m data points $\vec{x}' = (x'_1, \ldots, x'_m)$ observed at times $\vec{t}' = (t'_1, \ldots, t'_m)$, assuming that the values x'_j are sampled from the same latent function $f : \mathbb{R} \to \mathbb{R}$ used for X and thus, the joint distribution of $\vec{x}$ and $\vec{x}'$ is given by $\mathcal{GP}(0, k_\theta)$.

Therefore, the joint distribution of $\vec{x}$ and $\vec{x}'$ is an $(n+m)$-variate Gaussian distrib tion obtained by applying the Gaussian Process $\mathcal{GP}(0, k_\theta)$ to time vectors $\vec{t}$ and $\vec{t}'$. Th covariance matrix $K_\theta(\vec{t}, \vec{t}')$ is a positive semidefinite $(n+m) \times (n+m)$ matrix with th following form:

$$K_\theta(\vec{t}, \vec{t}') = \begin{bmatrix} K_\theta(\vec{t}, \vec{t}) + \sigma^2 I & K_\theta(\vec{t}, \vec{t}') \\ K_\theta(\vec{t}', \vec{t}) & K_\theta(\vec{t}', \vec{t}') \end{bmatrix},$$

where the covariance (sub)matrix $K_\theta(\vec{a}, \vec{b})$ is defined as $K_\theta(\vec{a}, \vec{b}) = (k_\theta(a_i, b_j))_{a_i \in \vec{a}, b_j \in \vec{b}}$.

Conditioning on X and its posterior distribution $\mathcal{N}(0, k_\theta + \sigma^2)$, we obtain the Gaussia predictive distribution of $\vec{x}'$. Specifically, we obtain that the values of the data points follow a m-variate Gaussian distribution with mean value vector $\vec{m}'$ and covariance matr K' as given below:

$$\vec{m}' = K_\theta(\vec{t}', \vec{t})(K_\theta(\vec{t}, \vec{t}) + \sigma^2 I)^{-1} \vec{x} \quad (1$$

$$K' = K_\theta(\vec{t}', \vec{t}') - K_\theta(\vec{t}', \vec{t})(K_\theta(\vec{t}, \vec{t}) + \sigma^2 I)^{-1} K_\theta(\vec{t}, \vec{t}') \quad (1$$

We note that the predicted mean value of $\vec{x}'$ in (13) is a linear combination of the inp values $\vec{x}$. Equivalently, one can obtain the mean value of each x'_j as a linear combinatio $\sum_{i=1}^{n} \alpha_j k_\theta(t_i, t'_j)$, with coefficients $\vec{\alpha} = (K_\theta(\vec{t}, \vec{t}) + \sigma^2 I)^{-1} \vec{x}$. We also note that the covarianc matrix in (14) does not directly depend on the input values $\vec{x}$ (but it depends on the poin in time $\vec{t}$ when these values are observed). We refer the interested reader to ([14], Section 2. for more details on Gaussian Process Regression.

3.4. Sparse Gaussian Process Regression

From a conceptual viewpoint, Gaussian Process Regression (GPR) is versatile an elegant, with a simple conceptual structure and many desirable theoretical propertie In practice, however, GPR can only deal with regression tasks of moderate size, with a most a few thousand input data points, due to the cubic time complexity required fo computing the posterior and the predictive posterior distributions. As a result, severa sparse approximation methods have been proposed to make GPR practically applicab to settings with a medium to large number of input data points (see, e.g., [15,17] and th references therein). These sparse GPR methods aim to represent the underlying Gaussia Process using a much smaller set of m, with $m \ll n$, inducing points, which can be learne so that they are highly informative about the actual posterior Gaussian Process. Spars GPR methods achieve a time complexity of $O(m^2 n)$ and a space complexity of $O(m^2 + n$ for approximating the posterior and the predictive posterior Gaussian Processes.

A standard approach to optimizing the sparse Gaussian Process is by minimizing i Kullback–Leibler (KL) divergence to the actual (and possibly intractable) Gaussian Proces In general, optimal (with respect to the KL divergence) sparse Gaussian processes do no have a closed form (as, e.g., happens with the predictive Gaussian process in (13) and (14) Then, Variational Inference (VI) can be used to approximate the actual posterior with variational distribution.

In this work, we use the *Variational Free Energy* (VFE) framework (a.k.a. *Sparse Gau sian Process Regression* (SGPR)), introduced by Titsias [16]. SGPR uses a small number c carefully selected inducing points, along with variational inference, to obtain a low-ran approximation (with respect to the KL divergence) to the actual Gaussian Process. In SGP the total number m of inducing points is chosen in advance so that the overall time an space complexity are acceptable. Their locations in time and their values are optimize so that more inducing points are located at time intervals where the time series exhibits more complex behavior (see also Figure 2).

Other approaches to sparse GPR include treating inducing point selection as a conti uous optimization problem [32] and online approaches where the sparse Gaussian Proces is iteratively trained by processing each input individually [33,34]. We refer the intereste reader to [17] for an elaborate treatment of Sparse Gaussian Process Regression.

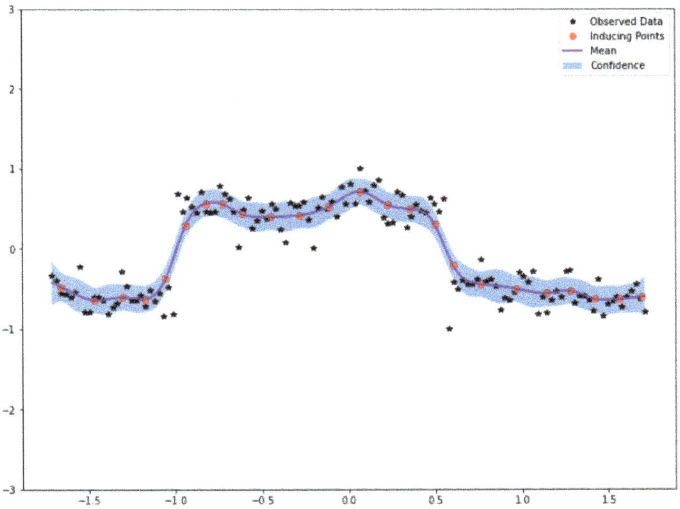

Figure 2. Sparse Gaussian Process Regression (SGPR) uses a predetermined number of inducing points (red dots) to compute a sparse approximate representation of a given time series (black stars).

4. The Sparse Time-Series Clustering Framework

The *Sparse Time-Series Clustering* (STSC) framework consists of two stages, as outlined in Algorithm 1. The input instance consists of $(\mathcal{X}, k)$, where $\mathcal{X}$ is a set of N time series to be partitioned into k clusters. The first stage is to approximate each time series $X_j \in \mathcal{X}$ with a sparse time series X'_j consisting of m inducing data points by applying Sparse Gaussian Process Regression (see Section 4.1 and Algorithm 2). The second stage is to cluster the reduced instance $(\{X'_1, \ldots, X'_N\}, k)$ using the k-means algorithm with the β-DTW distance, for some fixed parameter $\beta \geq 0$, and the DTW Barycenter Averaging (DBA) algorithm (see Section 4.2 and Algorithm 3). The outcome of the second stage is a tuple with k representative time series, which define a k-clustering of the reduced dataset $\{X'_1, \ldots, X'_N\}$ (and the corresponding k-clustering for the original dataset $\mathcal{X}$) by (1).

Algorithm 1 Sparse Time-Series Clustering Framework

Input : Instance $\mathcal{X} = (X_1, \ldots, X_N)$ with N time series, number of clusters k
Output: k cluster representatives $(C_1, \ldots, C_k)$ (which k-cluster $\mathcal{X}$ into $(\mathcal{X}_1, \ldots, \mathcal{X}_k)$.

`framework`$(\mathcal{X}, m, \text{seed})$:
  for $j \in [N]$ **do**
    $X'_j \leftarrow$ `modeling`(X_j, m) {$\triangleright$ SGPR with m inducing points on each X_j $\triangleleft$}
  end for
  $(C_1, \ldots, C_k) \leftarrow$ `clustering`$(\{X'_1, \ldots, X'_N\}, k, \text{seed})$
  {$\triangleright$ k-means clustering of reduced instance $\triangleleft$}
  return $(C_1, \ldots, C_k)$

Algorithm 2 Modeling through Sparse Gaussian Process Regression

Input : time series $X = ((x_1, t_1), \ldots, (x_T, t_T))$, number of inducing points m
Output: approximate time series $X' = ((x'_1, \tau_1), \ldots, (x'_m, \tau_m))$ with m inducing points

`modeling` $(X = ((x_1, t_1), \ldots, (x_T, t_T)), m)$:
  model $\leftarrow$ `train_SGPR`(X, m)
  {$\triangleright$ apply SGPR for the given number m of inducing points $\triangleleft$}
  $(x'_1, \tau_1), \ldots, (x'_m, \tau_m)) \leftarrow$ `extract_induced_points`(model, m)
  return $X' = ((x'_1, \tau_1), \ldots, (x'_m, \tau_m))$

Algorithm 3 k-Means Clustering

```
Input : dataset 𝒳 = (X_1, ... X_N) with N time series, number k of clusters,
        seed for initialization
Output: 𝒞 = (C_1, ..., C_k) with k cluster representatives
clustering (𝒳, k, seed):
   for j ∈ [k] do
      r ← random_generator(seed, N)
      {▷ randomly choose initial cluster representatives ◁}
      C_j^(0) ← X_r
   end for
   for i ∈ [100] do
      (C_1^(i), ..., C_k^(i)) ← DBA(𝒳, k, (C_1^(i−1), ..., C_k^(i−1)))
      {▷ update representatives with DBA ◁}
      if (C_1^(i), ..., C_k^(i)) ≈ (C_1^(i−1), ..., C_k^(i−1)) then
         break {▷ k-means converged to a k-clustering ◁}
      end if
   end for
   return (C_1, ..., C_k)
```

In the following (and unless stated otherwise), we consider a dataset $\mathcal{X} = \{X_1, \ldots, X_N$ of N univariate time series, where each time series $X = ((x_1, t_1), \ldots, (x_T, t_T)) \in \mathcal{X}$ consists of T data points. We assume that all time series in the same dataset have the same length T (nevertheless, our framework can be applied to datasets with time series of different lengths without any modification).

4.1. Modeling through Sparse Gaussian Process Regression

In this stage, we apply the framework of Sparse Gaussian Process Regression, as outlined in Section 3, in order to obtain a sparse approximation $X' = (x'_1, \tau_1), \ldots, (x'_m, \tau_m))$ of each time series $X = ((x_1, t_1), \ldots, (x_T, t_T))$ in the original dataset $\mathcal{X}$ (see also Algorithm 2

We use the Variational Free Energy (VFE) (a.k.a. Sparse Gaussian Process Regression (SGPR)) approach, outlined in Section 3.4, using the Matérn kernel with parameter $\nu = 3/2$ Each time series $X = ((x_1, t_1), \ldots, (x_T, t_T))$ is approximated by a sparse time series $X' = ((x'_1, \tau_1), \ldots, (x'_m, \tau_m))$ with $m \ll T$ inducing data points.

A logarithmic (in length T of the original time series) number of inducing points suffices for a reasonably good approximation of the original time series. More specifically we use $m = \gamma \log_2 T$, for $\gamma \in \{1, 2, 3, 4, 5\}$ (and with the resulting number rounded to the closest integer), in our experimental evaluation. Thus, the time complexity of this step is $O(T \log^2 T)$, and the space required is $O(T + \log^2 T)$.

4.2. Clustering Stage

The second and final stage of our framework is to partition the dataset $\mathcal{X}' = (X'_1, \ldots, X'_N$ consisting of N sparse time series with m inducing points each, into k-clusters using the k means algorithm for time series, with the DTW Barycenter Averaging (DBA) algorithm [19 used for updating the cluster representatives in each iteration of k-means.

We apply k-means with the β-DTW distance, defined in Section 2.2, with $\beta = \frac{\alpha T}{m}$. We use $\alpha \in \{0, 10^{-4}, 10^{-3}, 10^{-2}\}$ in our experimental evaluation. The intuition behind setting β to a multiple of T/m is that we expect that each inducing point serves as a representative of approximately T/m points, with increasing density of inducing points in time intervals where the time series exhibits more complex behavior. Hence, we want to (mildly) penalize with a multiple of T/m cases where different time series exhibit a high density of inducing points in distant time intervals.

The time complexity of k-means with the β-DTW distance and the DBA algorithm for updating the cluster representatives is $\Theta(INkm^2) = O(INk \log^2 T)$, where I is the number of iterations and $O(m^2)$ is the time required to compute the β-DTW distance between a pair of sparse time series, and $\Theta(Nkm^2T) = \Theta(Nk\log^2 T)$ is the time complexity of a single iteration of k-means. In our experimental evaluation, we run k-means and DBA for a maximum of $I = 100$ iterations.

4.3. Time Complexity

The overall time complexity of our Sparse Time-Series Clustering framework is $\Theta(NT\log^2 T + INk\log^2 T)$, where the first term corresponds to the time complexity of the Sparse Gaussian Process Regression with $m = \Theta(\log T)$ inducing points and the second term corresponds to the running time of k-means with the β-DTW distance when applied to N sparse time series with $m = \Theta(\log T)$ inducing points each. As expected, the running time of our framework crucially depends on the number m of inducing points.

In our experimental evaluation, we compute a baseline clustering by applying Algorithm 3. The overall time complexity for computing a baseline clustering with k-means on the original dataset with N time series of T data points each is $\Theta(INkT^2)$.

Therefore, the asymptotic running time of our Sparse Time-Series Clustering framework is about $\Theta(\max\{T^2/\log^2 T, IkT/\log^2 T\})$ times faster than the asymptotic running time of directly applying k-means to the original dataset. Intuitively, the asymptotic running time of our framework is $\Omega(T^2/\log^2 T)$ times faster than the standard k-means because the improved running time for computing DTW from $\Theta(T^2)$ in the original data to $\Theta(\log^2 T)$ in the sparsified data.

5. Experimental Evaluation

5.1. Datasets

The University of California (UCR) Time-Series Classification Archive [20] is one of the most widely used and the largest labeled time-series data archives for classification, consisting of 128 datasets. Each dataset is divided into training and test data and is accompanied by performance indicators of several algorithms with different parameter settings. In this work, we use the univariate datasets of the UCR archive in order to support the claim that our Sparse Time-Series Clustering (STSC) framework leads to clusterings with respect to the β-DTW distance of similar (or even improved) quality (compared against applying k-means to the original datasets), but with significantly improved running time. Baseline results are available for most of the UCR datasets in [22]. Nevertheless, we chose to run the baseline k-means algorithm on all the datasets used for experimental evaluation. For the scope of this work, we focused on univariate datasets and omitted datasets for which, due to computational power considerations, we were not able to run the k-means algorithm with DTW metric (see Section 5.6 for more details).

The datasets used in our experimental evaluation are synthetic, semi-synthetic, or real and originate from various domains. Each dataset is univariate and contains from 40 to 5000 time series. Although the time series within each dataset have the same length, the length varies across datasets, ranging from 60 to 1882. A concise summary of these datasets is provided in Table 1, including information such as the number of time series, the number of clusters, the length of each time series, and dataset type.

Table 1. Dataset Description.

Dataset	Size	Length	No. of Classes	Type
Adiac	781	176	37	IMAGE
ArrowHead	211	251	3	IMAGE
Beef	60	470	5	SPECTRO
BeetleFly	40	512	2	IMAGE
BirdChicken	40	512	2	IMAGE
Car	120	577	4	SENSOR
CBF	930	128	3	SIMULATED
Coffee	56	286	2	SPECTRO
Computers	500	720	2	DEVICE
CricketX	780	300	12	MOTION
CricketY	780	300	12	MOTION
CricketZ	780	300	12	MOTION
DiatomSizeReduction	322	345	4	IMAGE
DistalPhalanxOutlineAgeGroup	539	80	3	IMAGE
DistalPhalanxCorrect	876	80	2	IMAGE
DistalPhalanxTW	539	80	6	IMAGE
Earthquakes	461	512	2	SENSOR
ECG200	200	96	2	ECG
ECGFiveDays	884	136	2	ECG
FaceAll	2250	131	14	IMAGE
FaceFour	112	350	4	IMAGE
FacesUCR	2250	131	14	IMAGE
FiftyWords	905	270	50	IMAGE
Fish	350	463	7	IMAGE
GunPoint	200	150	2	MOTION
Ham	214	431	2	SPECTRO
Herring	128	512	2	IMAGE
InsectWingbeatSound	2200	256	11	SENSOR
ItalyPowerDenand	1096	24	2	SENSOR
LargeKitchenAppliances	750	720	3	DEVICE
Lightning2	121	637	2	SENSOR
Lightning7	143	319	7	SENSOR

Table 1. *Cont.*

Dataset	Size	Length	No. of Classes	Type
Meat	120	448	3	SPECTRO
MedicalImages	1141	99	10	IMAGE
MiddlePhalanxOutlineAgeGroup	554	80	3	IMAGE
MiddlePhalanxOutlineCorrect	891	80	2	IMAGE
MiddlePhalanxTW	553	80	6	IMAGE
MoteStrain	1272	84	2	SENSOR
OliveOil	60	570	4	SPECTRO
OSULeaf	442	427	6	IMAGE
PhalangesOutlinesCorrect	2658	80	2	IMAGE
Plane	210	144	7	SENSOR
ProximalPhalanxOutlineAgeGroup	605	80	3	IMAGE
ProximalPhalanxOutlineCorrect	891	80	2	IMAGE
ProximalPhalanxTW	605	80	6	IMAGE
RefrigerationDevices	750	720	3	DEVICE
ShapeletSim	200	500	2	SIMULATED
ShapesAll	1200	512	60	IMAGE
SmallKitchenAppliances	750	720	3	DEVICE
SonyAIBORobotSurface1	621	70	2	SENSOR
SonyAIBORobotSurface2	980	65	2	SENSOR
Strawberry	983	235	2	SPECTRO
SwedishLeaf	1125	128	15	IMAGE
Symbols	1020	398	6	IMAGE
SyntheticControl	600	60	6	SIMULATED
ToeSegmentation1	268	277	2	MOTION
ToeSegmentation2	166	343	2	MOTION
Trace	200	275	4	SENSOR
TwoLeadECG	1162	82	2	ECG
TwoPatterns	5000	128	4	SIMULATED
Wine	111	234	2	SPECTRO
WordSynonyms	905	270	25	IMAGE
Worms	258	900	5	MOTION

5.2. Experimental Setting

Both our Sparse Time-Series Clustering framework and the baseline, which applies k-means to the original datasets, are implemented in Python. For the application of k-means to the sparse (resp. the original) dataset, we use β-DTW (resp. the standard DTW) and DBA for updating the cluster representatives in each iteration. We use the GPyTorch library [35] for the implementation of Sparse Gaussian Process Regression and the Tslearn package [36] for the implementation of k-means. Our experiments run on an Intel(R) Xeon(R) Silver 4210 CPU (2.20 GHz) with 16 GB of RAM.

5.3. Parameter Selection and Tuning

We run our experiments with a logarithmic (in the length T of the original time series) number m of inducing points. More specifically, we run our experiments with $m = \gamma \log_2 T$ (rounded to the closest integer), for $\gamma \in \{1,2,3,4,5\}$. For the Sparse Gaussian Process Regression, we choose a constant-mean prior for the Gaussian Process and use the Matérn kernel with parameter $\nu = 1.5$. We use Adam [30] to optimize the parameters of SGPR. We use a learning rate of $1/10$ for optimizing the parameters of the Gaussian Process (i.e., the hyperparameters of the Matérn kernel and the standard deviation of the noise) and a learning rate of $1/(10\gamma)$ for optimizing the locations of the inducing points. For the initialization of SGPR's inducing point location optimization, we divide the time horizon of the dataset into m equally sized intervals. Thus, we avoid ending up with quite different inducing point locations for different initializations, which may happen due to the non-convexity of SGPR's objective and its sensitivity to different initializations.

We should highlight that SGPR's objective function is highly sensitive to Adam' learning rate. If the learning rate is too large, we end up with inducing points outside th time horizon of the original time series, while if the learning rate is too low, the learnin becomes local, and inducing points tend to reflect the behavior of the time series in small interval around them. Hence, we had to carefully select the learning rates for ou experiments, with the value of 1/10 proven to be a good and consistent choice. A summar of the parameters used in the experimental evaluation, with a short description of their rol and their values, can be found in Table 2.

Table 2. Collection of parameters (with their role in our approach) and their corresponding value used in experimental evaluation. We recall that T denotes the length of the time series, N is th number of time series in the instance, and k is the number of clusters.

Parameter	**Algorithm—Role**	**Value**
learning rate	Adam, parameter optimization SGPR	$1/10$
learning rate	Adam, optimization of inducing point locations in SGPR	$1/(10\gamma)$, for $\gamma \in \{1,2,3,4,5\}$
ν	Matérn kernel, SGPR	$3/2$
m	# inducing points in SGPR	$\gamma \log_2 T$, for $\gamma \in \{1,2,3,4,5\}$
α	$(\alpha T/m)$-DTW distance for clustering	$\in \{0, 10^{-4}, 10^{-3}, 10^{-2}\}$
I	max # iterations of k-means and DBA	100

For the k-means algorithm, we use the β-DTW distance with $\beta = \alpha T/m$ (whic we often denote $(\alpha T/m)$-DTW), for $\alpha \in \{0, 10^{-4}, 10^{-3}, 10^{-2}\}$ and the DTW Barycente Averaging (DBA) [19] for updating the cluster representatives in each iteration. We ru k-means and DBA for a maximum of 100 iterations each.

We execute 10 runs of Algorithm 1 for each sparse dataset and each parameter comb nation (we have 5 choices for γ times 4 choices for α, which makes 12 different paramete combinations for each dataset), showcasing the average CPU time and the average Ad justed Rand Index (ARI) against the ground truth clustering provided in the UCR archiv In each run, the initial set of k cluster representatives is chosen randomly. Nevertheless, th seeds were predefined for each run to ensure reproducibility and facilitate fair comparison between different methods.

To assess our approach against the standard k-means, we opted to compute a baselin ARI for each original dataset from scratch by executing 10 runs of Algorithm 3 for each o them with the standard DTW distance (with $\beta = 0$). As for the sparse case, the initial se of k cluster representatives is chosen randomly with predefined seeds. For each origina dataset, we logged the average CPU time and the average Adjusted Rand Index (ARI against the ground truth clustering. Therefore, we ensure consistent initialization and CPU time reporting across all runs, facilitating a comprehensive comparison and evaluation o run times.

5.4. Dataset Level Assessment

Our experimental evaluation indicates that Algorithm 1 (Sparse Time-Series Cluster ing), with sufficiently many (but still logarithmic in T) inducing points and for relativel small values of α in $(\alpha m/T)$-DTW, computes clusterings with ARI metrics quite simila to the ARI metrics of the baseline, computed by applying Algorithm 3 (i.e., standard k means) to the original datasets. However, the asymptotic running time of Algorithm 1 i $\Omega(T^2/\log^2 T)$ times faster than the asymptotic running time of Algorithm 3.

Following the practices described in [22], in our experimental evaluation, we repor the average ARI score over 10 runs of Algorithms 1 and 3 and also rank the performanc (according to the average ARI in decreasing order) of Algorithms 1 and 3 with differen parameter configurations in all the datasets of Table 1. A comprehensive summary of th average ARI and the average rank for each method (over all Table 1 UCR datasets for each parameter configuration) can be found in Table 3.

Table 3. Summarized ARI averages for different parameter configurations. The average relative order of the results achieved by each algorithm is reported in parentheses. ARI values for each dataset are reported in Table A1 (where $\alpha = 0$) and in Table A2 (where we report average ARI over all different values of $\alpha \in \{0, 10^{-4}, 10^{-3}, 10^{-2}\}$) in Appendix A.

		$(\alpha T/m)$-DTW				
Parameter α	**Baseline**	**$1 \cdot \log T$**	**$2 \cdot \log T$**	**$3 \cdot \log T$**	**$4 \cdot \log T$**	**$5 \cdot \log T$**
0	0.249 (2.524)	0.173 (4.270)	0.222 (3.683)	0.217 (3.492)	0.220 (3.762)	0.225 (3.270)
10^{-4}	0.249 (2.587)	0.175 (4.365)	0.222 (3.746)	0.217 (3.635)	0.220 (3.635)	0.226 (3.032)
10^{-3}	0.249 (2.746)	0.172 (4.508)	0.213 (3.841)	0.214 (3.317)	0.215 (3.444)	0.224 (3.143)
10^{-2}	0.249 (2.762)	0.162 (4.381)	0.196 (4.127)	0.210 (3.476)	0.215 (3.492)	0.228 (2.762)
best	0.249 (3.254)	0.193 (4.238)	0.238 (3.810)	0.238 (3.333)	0.243 (3.333)	0.252 (3.032)
mean	0.249 (2.556)	0.171 (4.413)	0.213 (3.857)	0.215 (3.556)	0.217 (3.587)	0.226 (3.032)

In each of the first four lines of Table 3, we compare the average ARI of the standard k-means (baseline) with the average ARI of our framework for a different number of inducing points while maintaining the parameter α in $(\alpha T/m)$-DTW constant. In the fifth (resp. the sixth) line, we take the best (resp. the mean) ARI over all values of α, for each different number of inducing points $\gamma \log_2 T$, for $\gamma \in \{1, 2, 3, 4, 5\}$.

In Table 3, we observe that average ARI values improve as the number of inducing points increases (for every fixed value of α, see also the spread diagrams in Figure 3, where we use $\alpha = 10^{-4}$). Moreover, for $m \leq 4 \log_2 T$ inducing points, average ARI values slightly deteriorate as the value of α increases (see also the spread diagrams in Figure 4, where we use $m = 2 \log_2 T$), while for $m = 5 \log_2 T$ inducing points, average ARI values marginally improve as α increases (see also the spread diagrams in Figure 5, where we use $m = 5 \log_2 T$). We note that as the number m of inducing points increases, $(\alpha T/m)$-DTW becomes less sensitive in an increase in α. Then, a combination of many inducing points and $\alpha \in [10^{-3}, 10^{-2}]$ produces quite satisfactory results (see also the spread diagrams in Figure 5c,d. For $m = 5 \log_2 T$ inducing points, keeping the best ARI over all values of α for each dataset gives clusterings of marginally better quality on average compared against the clusterings produced by the standard k-means algorithm (see the best ARI for $m = 5 \log_2 T$ in the best line of Table 3 and the spread diagram in Figure 5e). On the other hand, even for $m = 5 \log_2 T$ inducing points, any fixed value of α results in clusterings of slightly worse quality on average compared against the clusterings produced by the standard k-means algorithm (see the mean ARI for $m = 5 \log_2 T$ in the mean line of Table 3 and the spread diagram in Figure 5f).

Even though it allows for conclusions that are informative and easy to grasp, averaging ARI results across different datasets (and possibly across different parameter configurations) is inadequate for a comprehensive evaluation of the proposed framework for Sparse Time-Series Clustering. A particularly poor or particularly good performance in specific datasets for certain parameter configurations may significantly affect the average ARI, potentially leading to misleading conclusions (notice also the standard deviations in Table A2). A characteristic example is the TwoPatterns dataset (see the corresponding rows in Tables A1 and A2), where the standard k-means achieves an average ARI of 0.870, while the average ARI of our framework for different numbers of inducing points (where average is taken across all values of α) ranges from 0.304 to 0.825 (see the corresponding row in Table A1 and the large standard deviations in the corresponding row of Table A2).

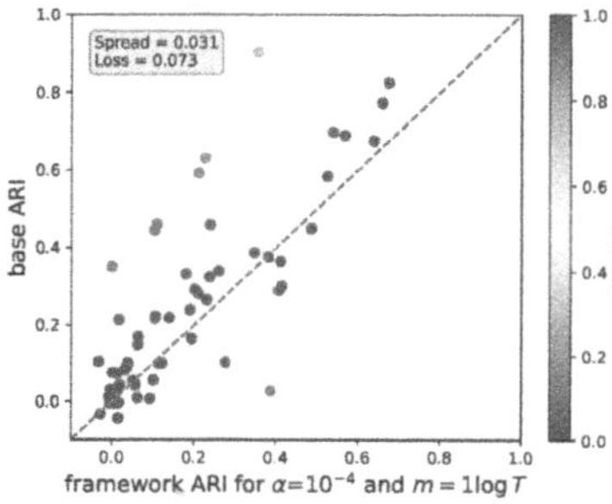

(**a**) ARI spread with $m = \log_2 T$ (loss = 0.073, spread = 0.031).

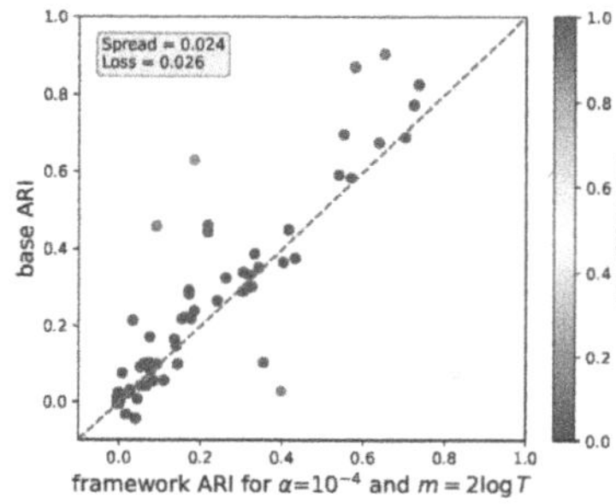

(**b**) ARI spread with $m = 2\log_2 T$ (loss = 0.026, spread = 0.024)

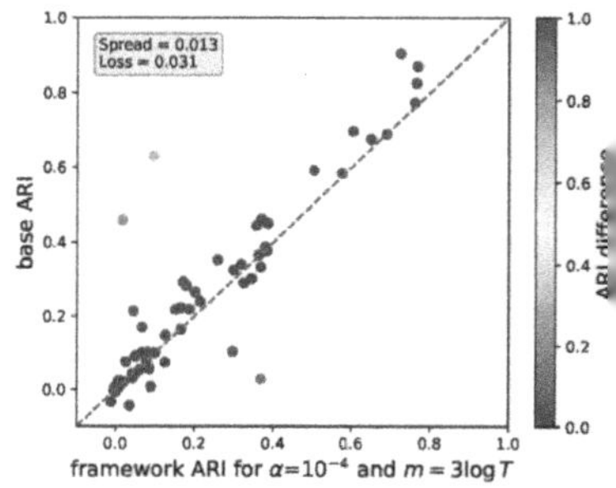

(**c**) ARI spread with $m = 3\log_2 T$ (loss = 0.031, spread = 0.013).

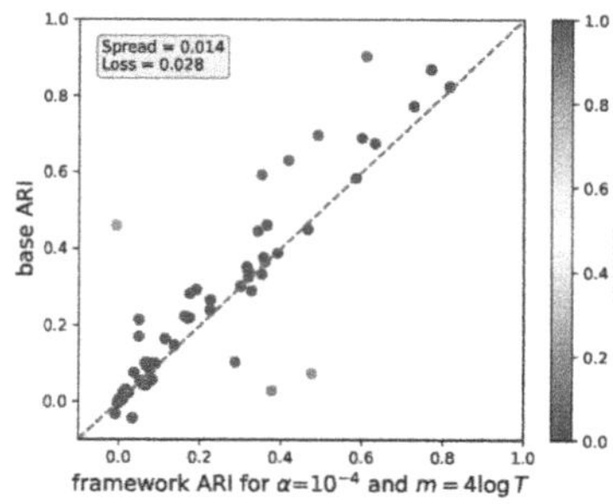

(**d**) ARI spread with $m = 4\log_2 T$ (loss = 0.028, spread = 0.014).

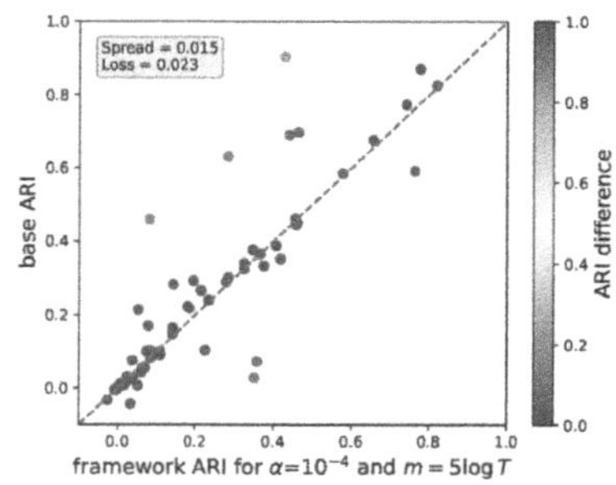

(**e**) ARI spread with $m = 5\log_2 T$ (loss = 0.023, spread = 0.015).

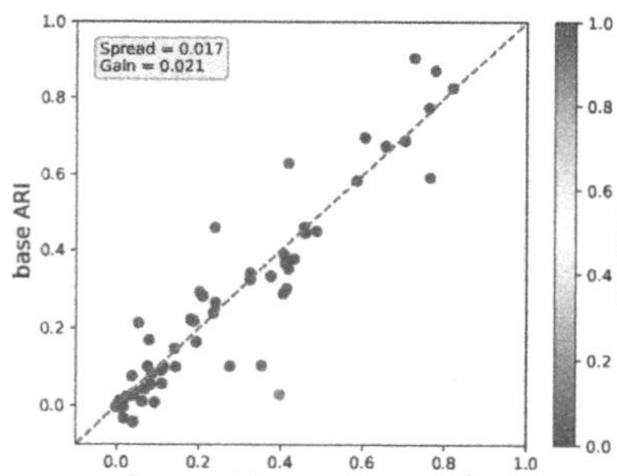

(**f**) Best ARI spread (gain = 0.021, spread = 0.017).

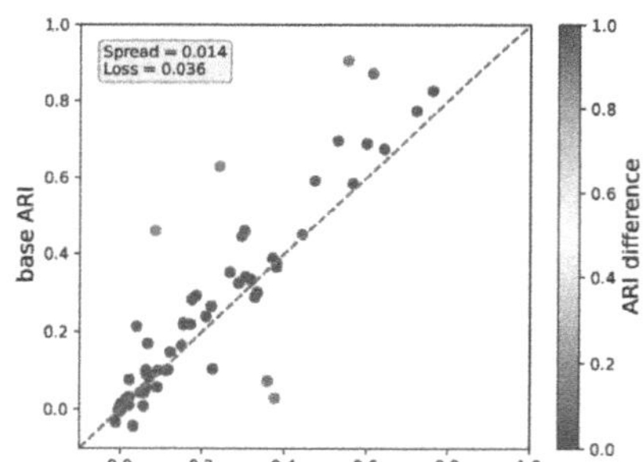

(**g**) Mean ARI spread (loss = 0.036, spread = 0.014).

Figure 3. Spread diagrams with comparative ARI results of Algorithm 1 against Algorithm 3 wi $(10^{-4}T/m)$-DTW and $m = \gamma \log_2 T$ inducing points, for $\gamma \in \{1,2,3,4,5\}$. The spread and the averag loss of the sparse framework are reported in the caption and in the upper left corner. We observe slight improvement in clustering quality as the number of inducing points increases. We observe small average gain in (**f**), where we keep the best ARI, and a small average loss in (**g**), where we tak the mean ARI in each dataset (both across all values of $\gamma \in \{1,2,3,4,5\}$).

To provide a more detailed picture of the quality of clusterings produced by ou framework for different datasets and how they compare against the clustering produce by the standard k-means, in Appendix A, we present in Table A1 the average ARI for eac dataset for the baseline and our framework with $m = \gamma \log_2 T$ inducing points, for eac value of $\gamma \in \{1,2,3,4,5\}$ and $\alpha = 0$, where average ARI is taken across all 10 runs for bot the standard k-means and our framework. In Table A2, we present the same informatio for all datasets along with the standard deviation computed across all 10 runs (for standard k-means) and all 10 runs and all different values of $\alpha \in \{0, 10^{-4}, 10^{-3}, 10^{-2}\}$. The information in Table A2 demonstrates the importance of careful (and possibly dependent on the parameters of the datasets) tuning. Nevertheless, the mean (across all different datasets and all values of α) loss of our framework for $5\log_2 T$ inducing points is small, and keeping the best clustering for each dataset results in a small improvement in the average clustering quality of Algorithm 1 compared against the standard (and way more time demanding) k-means.

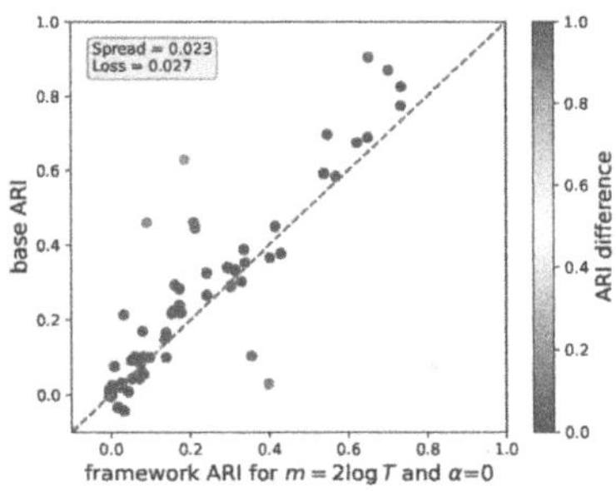

(**a**) ARI spread with $\alpha = 0$ (loss = 0.027, spread = 0.023).

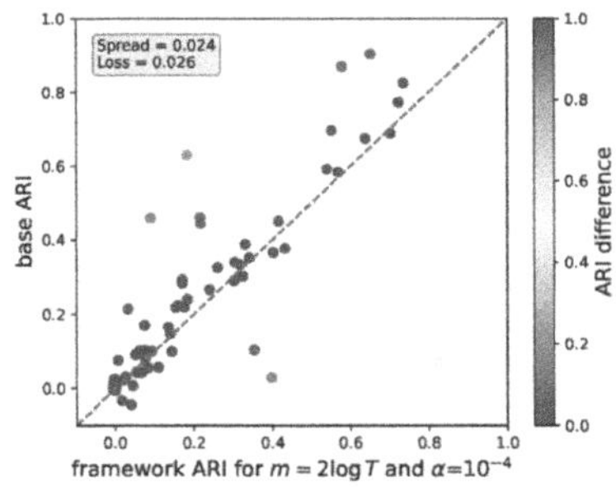

(**b**) ARI spread with $\alpha = 10^{-4}$ (loss = 0.026, spread = 0.024).

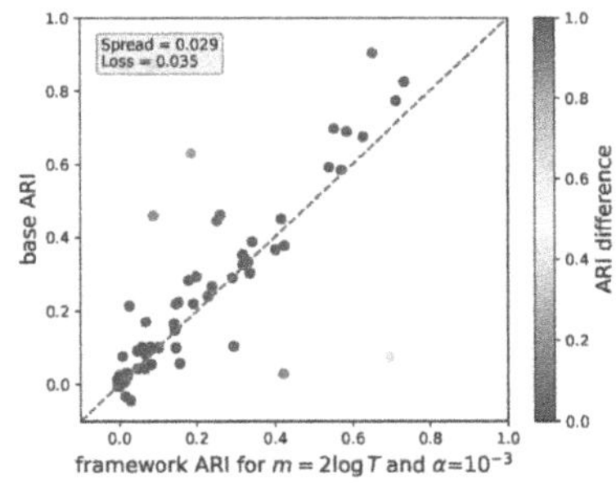

(**c**) ARI spread with $\alpha = 10^{-3}$ (loss = 0.035, spread = 0.029).

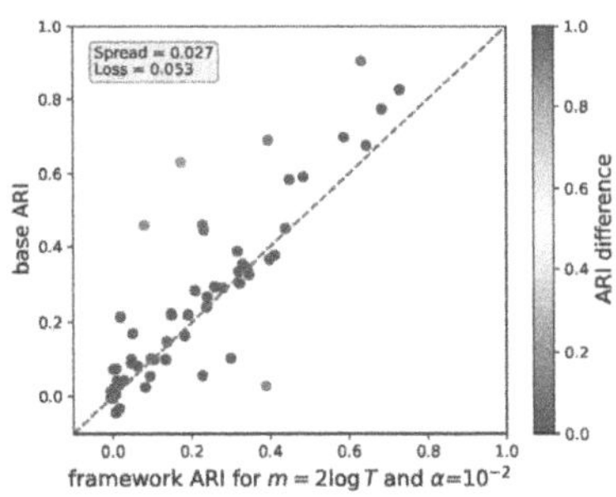

(**d**) ARI spread with $\alpha = 10^{-2}$ (loss = 0.053, spread = 0.027).

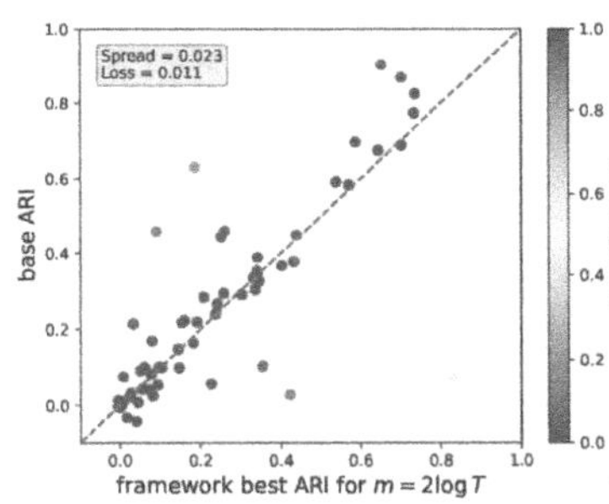

(**e**) Best ARI spread (loss = 0.011, spread = 0.023).

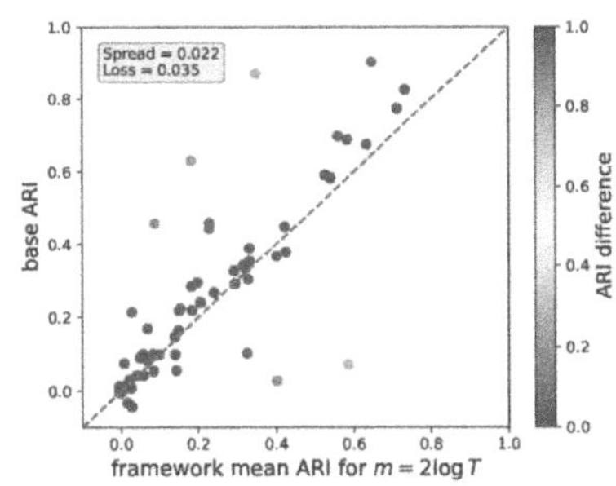

(**f**) Mean ARI spread (loss = 0.035, spread = 0.022).

Figure 4. Spread diagrams with comparative ARI results of Sparse Time-Series Clustering against standard k-means overall datasets for the $(\alpha T/m)$-DTW distance, with different values of $\alpha \in \{0, 10^{-4}, 10^{-3}, 10^{-2}\}$ and with $m = 2\log_2 T$ inducing points. The average spread and the average loss of the sparse framework are reported in the caption and on the upper left corner of each plot. We observe a slight deterioration in clustering quality as α increases and a small average loss in (**e**) and (**f**), where we keep the best ARI and the mean ARI in each dataset (both across all values of $\alpha \in \{0, 10^{-4}, 10^{-3}, 10^{-2}\}$).

5.5. Computational Efficiency

As noted in Section 4.3, an important contribution of our work is that the combined computational complexity of our Sparse Time-Series Clustering framework is $O(NT\log^2 T + INk\log^2 T)$, where I is the iterations of k-means, N is the number of time series in the dataset and T is their length, compared against a running time of $O(INkT^2)$ of the standard k-means algorithm applied to the original dataset. Next, we evaluate the running time and the CPU utilization of our framework in practice. .

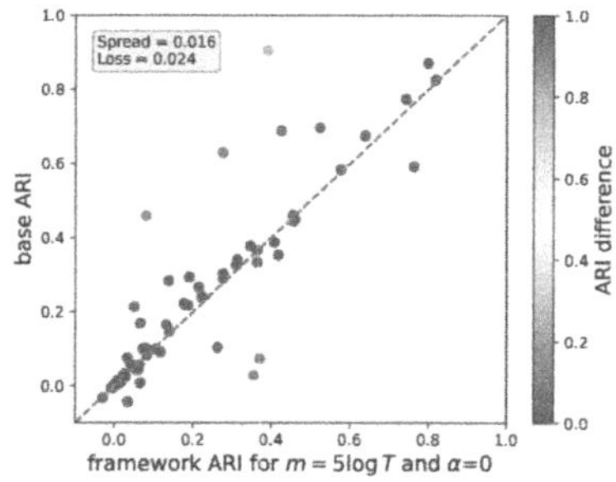

(**a**) ARI spread with $\alpha = 0$ (loss = 0.024, spread = 0.016).

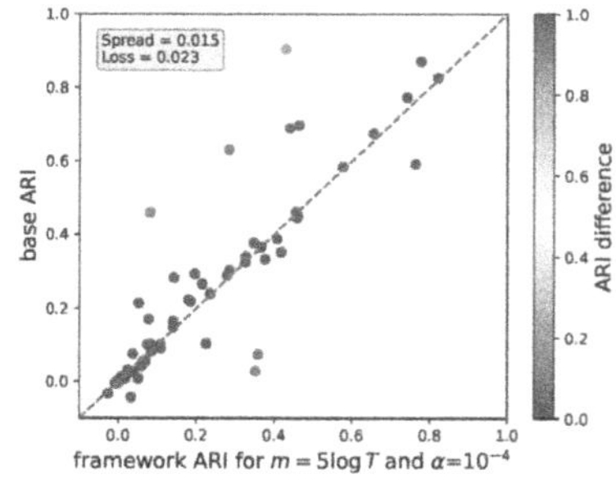

(**b**) ARI spread with $\alpha = 10^{-4}$ (loss = 0.023, spread = 0.015).

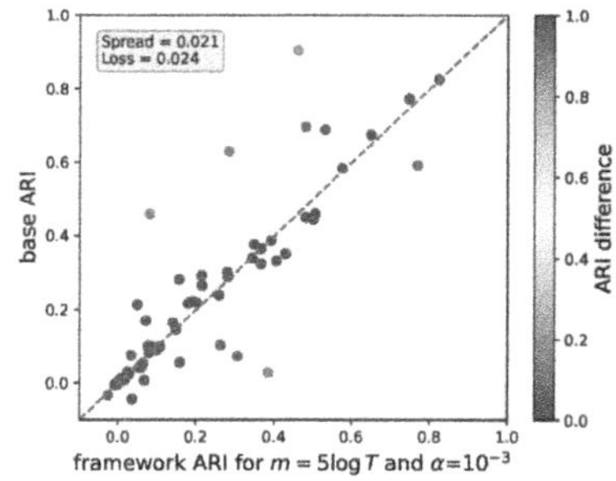

(**c**) ARI spread with $\alpha = 10^{-3}$ (loss = 0.024, spread = 0.021).

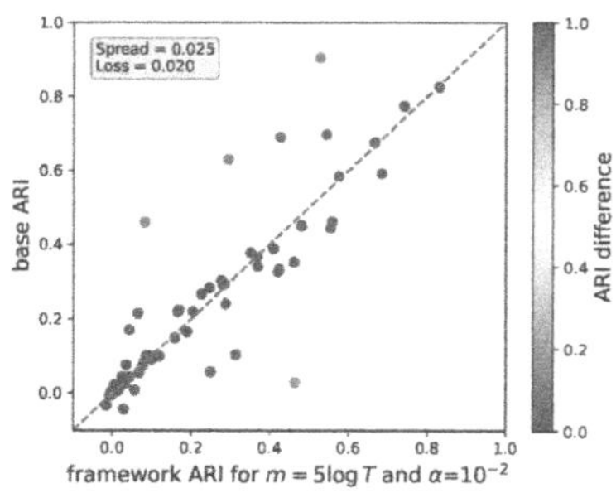

(**d**) ARI spread with $\alpha = 10^{-2}$ (loss = 0.025, spread = 0.020).

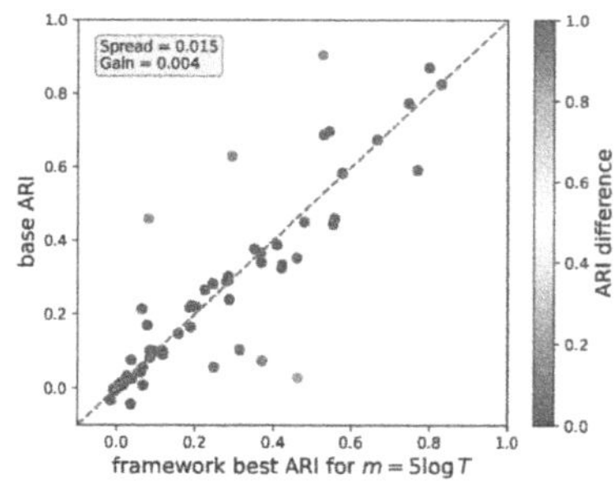

(**e**) Best ARI spread (gain = 0.004, spread = 0.015).

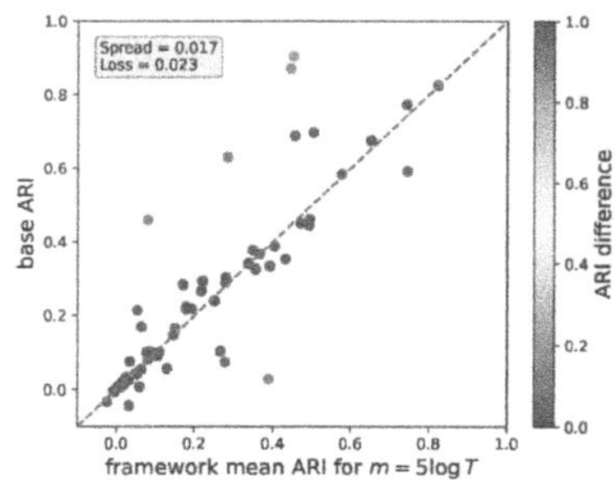

(**f**) Mean ARI spread (loss = 0.023, spread = 0.017).

Figure 5. Spread diagrams with comparative ARI results of Sparse Time-Series Clustering against standard k-means overall datasets for the $(\alpha T/m)$-DTW distance, with different values of $\alpha \in \{0, 10^{-4}, 10^{-3}, 10^{-2}\}$ and with $m = 5\log_2 T$ inducing points. The average spread and the average loss of the sparse framework are reported in the caption and on the upper left corner of each plot. In contrast to the case where $m = 2\log_2 T$, in Figure 4, with $m = 5\log_2 T$ inducing points, we observe a stable clustering quality, and even a slight improvement, as α increases. This behavior is attributed to the fact that larger m makes $(\alpha T/m)$-DTW less sensitive to an increase in α. We also observe a small average gain in (**e**), where we keep the best ARI, and a small average loss in (**f**), where we take the mean ARI in each dataset (both across all values of $\alpha \in \{0, 10^{-4}, 10^{-3}, 10^{-2}\}$).

Table 4 displays the CPU utilization times for our framework and standard k-means on all datasets. Specifically, we provide the following metrics: T_k is the CPU utilization time of the standard k-means algorithm applied to the original dataset; T_a is the CPU utilization time of the modeling phase, where Sparse Gaussian Process Regression is applied, in steps 4–6 of Algorithm 1; and T_b is the CPU utilization time of the k-means algorithm in step 7 of Algorithm 1, where Algorithm 3 is applied to the sparse time series produced by the Sparse Gaussian Process Regression. Moreover, $T_a + T_b$ is the total CPU utilization of our method, $(T_a + T_b)/T_k$ indicates the CPU utilization overhead due to the modeling process (which dominates the running time of our framework); T_k/T_b quantifies how much slower k-means become when applied to the original dataset compared against the same algorithm applied to the sparsified dataset; and T_a/N is the average running time of the modeling phase (Sparse Gaussian Process Regression) per time series in the particular dataset.

Table 4. CPU Utilization time of the standard k-means algorithm and the modeling and the clustering phase of Algorithm 1. T_k denotes the CPU utilization time of the standard k-means algorithm in the original dataset; T_a denotes the CPU utilization time of the modeling phase; and T_b denotes the CPU utilization time of the clustering phase. $T_a + T_b$ is the total CPU utilization of our method, $(T_a + T_b)/T_k$ indicates the CPU utilization overhead due to the modeling process; T_k/T_b quantifies how much slower k-means becomes when applied to the original dataset compared against the same algorithm applied to the sparsified dataset; and T_a/N is the average running time of the modeling phase per time series in the particular dataset.

Dataset	T_k	T_b	T_a	$\frac{T_k}{T_b}$	$\frac{(T_a+T_b)}{T_k}$	$\frac{T_a}{N}$
Adiac	809.606	117.040	5468.717	6.9	6.9	7.002
ArrowHead	449.036	5.795	1473.779	77.5	3.3	6.985
Beef	237.538	1.238	460.083	191.9	1.9	7.668
BeetleFly	91.529	0.609	289.232	150.3	3.2	7.231
BirdChicken	152.857	0.660	312.412	231.6	2.0	7.810
Car	350.987	2.881	968.850	121.8	2.8	8.074
CBF	127.093	45.560	5959.039	2.8	47.2	6.408
Coffee	100.512	0.798	383.234	126.0	3.8	6.843
Computers	1448.839	12.139	2334.388	119.4	1.6	4.669
CricketX	2457.813	62.977	5748.995	39.0	2.4	7.371
CricketY	1731.068	61.845	5792.806	28.0	3.4	7.427
CricketZ	1628.689	62.495	5524.100	26.1	3.4	7.082
DiatomSizeReduction	702.399	8.619	2606.539	81.5	3.7	8.095
DistalPhalanxOutlineCorrect	42.445	14.438	5711.787	2.9	134.9	6.520
DistalPhalanxOutlineAgeGroup	22.358	10.411	3348.379	2.1	150.2	6.212
DistalPhalanxTW	32.310	19.760	3462.503	1.6	107.8	6.424
Earthquakes	764.784	17.812	3897.637	42.9	5.1	8.455
ECG200	10.045	4.051	1430.853	2.5	142.8	7.154
ECGFiveDays	193.677	26.262	5910.736	7.4	30.7	6.686
FaceAll	681.338	267.684	13,986.357	2.5	20.9	6.216
FaceFour	174.810	2.035	583.206	85.9	3.3	5.207
FacesUCR	656.559	168.009	9845.755	3.9	15.3	4.376
FiftyWords	3719.422	110.433	4634.011	33.7	1.3	5.120
Fish	1401.001	14.399	3173.496	97.3	2.3	9.067
GunPoint	204.587	3.420	1606.681	59.8	7.9	8.033
Ham	498.690	5.834	2085.700	85.5	4.2	9.746
Herring	393.123	2.633	972.268	149.3	2.5	7.596
InsectWingbeatSound	8642.398	137.208	8987.362	63.0	1.1	4.085
ItalyPowerDemand	48.611	26.104	6500.469	1.9	134.3	5.931
LargeKitchenAppliances	3391.768	19.276	2969.682	176.0	0.9	3.960
Lightning2	280.387	3.525	1002.119	79.6	3.6	8.282
Lightning7	266.726	4.853	1057.223	55.0	4.0	7.393
Meat	140.371	2.340	1162.826	60.0	8.3	9.690
MedicalImages	193.023	82.434	7299.850	2.3	38.2	6.398
MiddlePhalanxOutlineAgeGroup	22.883	11.684	3700.447	2.0	162.2	6.680
MiddlePhalanxOutlineCorrect	40.408	15.421	5762.425	2.6	143.0	6.467
MiddlePhalanxTW	41.743	20.060	3480.027	2.1	83.8	6.293
MoteStrain	213.246	50.299	7216.290	4.2	34.1	5.673
OliveOil	63.692	0.953	534.073	66.8	8.4	8.901
OSULeaf	2005.386	21.865	3731.238	91.7	1.9	8.442
PhalangesOutlinesCorrect	151.922	47.915	14,683.742	3.2	97.0	5.524
Plane	12.636	4.129	1233.003	3.1	97.9	0.584
ProximalPhalanxOutlineCorrect	28.106	13.378	5230.995	2.1	186.6	24.910
ProximalPhalanxOutlineAgeGroup	21.364	12.143	3819.305	1.8	179.3	6.313
ProximalPhalanxTW	33.438	19.141	3490.010	1.7	104.9	3.917
RefrigerationDevices	2699.834	16.155	2965.134	167.1	1.1	4.901
ShapeletSim	291.462	5.064	1651.373	57.6	5.7	2.202
ShapesAll	9397.260	132.630	4991.169	70.9	0.5	24.956

Table 4. *Cont.*

Dataset	T_k	T_b	T_a	$\frac{T_k}{T_b}$	$\frac{(T_a+T_b)}{T_k}$	$\frac{T_a}{N}$
SmallKitchenAppliances	1683.222	18.953	3321.628	88.8	2.0	2.768
SonyAIBORobotSurface1	34.634	15.644	3655.760	2.2	106.0	4.874
SonyAIBORobotSurface2	71.301	25.905	6676.567	2.8	94.0	10.751
Strawberry	1183.540	23.964	7845.866	49.4	6.6	8.006
SwedishLeaf	224.676	67.156	5367.119	3.3	24.2	5.460
Symbols	4984.632	43.091	9755.276	115.7	2.0	8.671
SyntheticControl	26.540	16.777	3758.807	1.6	142.3	3.685
ToeSegmentation1	464.657	8.339	1931.603	55.7	4.2	3.219
ToeSegmentation2	263.977	4.073	1176.577	64.8	4.5	4.390
Trace	225.796	4.452	1505.905	50.7	6.7	9.072
TwoLeadECG	115.038	33.520	7091.992	3.4	61.9	35.460
TwoPatterns	767.798	313.861	28,274.694	2.4	37.2	24.333
Wine	51.230	1.493	831.680	34.3	16.3	0.166
WordSynonyms	3179.780	61.514	3889.850	51.7	1.2	35.044
Worms	1540.641	9.298	2799.553	165.7	1.8	3.093
mean	982.337	37.214	4401.955	53.8	40.0	8.095

We observe that k-means runs from 1.6 (in very small datasets) up to 230 times faste when applied to the sparsified dataset (compared against the k-means algorithm applied the original instance, see also Figure 6). The speed-up is due to the improved running tim for computing DTW from $\Theta(T^2)$ in the original data to $\Theta(\log^2 T)$ in the sparsified data. A expected, the speed-up becomes more apparent when it comes to datasets with time-serie length T above a few hundred. On average, k-means runs more than 50 times faster whe applied to the sparsified dataset than when applied to the original one.

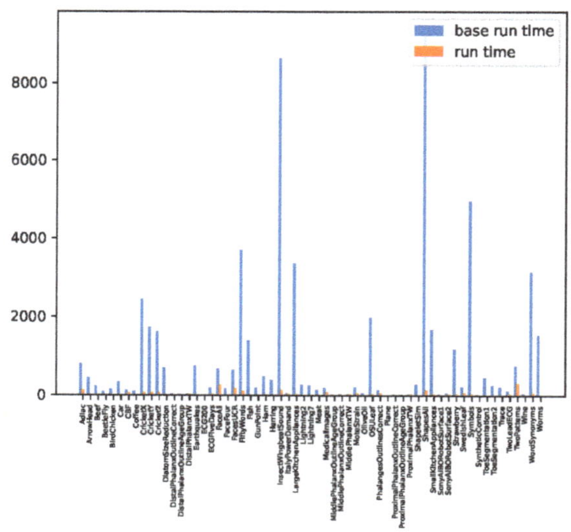

Figure 6. CPU utilization time comparison of the k-means algorithm applied to the original datase (blue bars) and to the sparsified data sets (orange bars). k-means on the sparsified instance can ru up to 230 times faster than k-means on the original instance.

On the other hand, the computational overhead of Sparse Gaussian Process Regre sion becomes quite high, compared against the running time of the standard k-mean algorithm, when Algorithm 1 is applied to datasets of small to moderate size (and wit time series of small to moderate length). However, for datasets with larger sizes an longer time series, such as InsectWingbeatSound (with 2200 time series of length 256 each), RefrigerationDevices and LargeKitchenAppliances (both with 750 time series of length 720 each), the benefits of the significantly improved asymptotic computational complexity of our framework become apparent. In these datasets, the total $T_a + T_b$ running time of our framework is practically identical to the total running time of the standard *k*-means. For some larger datasets, such as ShapesAll (with 1200 time series of length 512 each), the total $T_a + T_b$ running time of our framework is half the total running time of the standard *k*-means. Moreover, there are datasets, such as ElectricDevices (with about 16,500 time series of length 96 each), where our framework is able to run successfully in our computational infrastructure and to produce clusterings with average ARI higher than that reported in [22], while it is impossible to successfully run the standard *k*-means algorithm due to the quadratic computational complexity of DTW and/or the large size of the dataset (see also Table 5 and Section 5.6).

Table 5. ARI results for the ElectricDevices dataset consisting of 16637 time series of length 96 each. The best ARI computed by the standard *k*-means in [22] is 0.19, while our framework achieves a best ARI of 0.21, which is 10% larger than that reported in [22].

Parameter a	$1 \cdot \log T$	$2 \cdot \log T$	$3 \cdot \log T$	$4 \cdot \log T$	$5 \cdot \log T$
0	0.18	**0.19**	0.18	0.17	0.17
$\mathbf{10^{-4}}$	**0.21**	0.18	0.18	**0.19**	**0.19**
$\mathbf{10^{-3}}$	0.14	**0.20**	0.18	0.18	0.18
$\mathbf{10^{-2}}$	0.04	0.12	**0.21**	0.18	**0.20**

In a nutshell, we observe that the total CPU utilization of our framework becomes comparable to that of applying *k*-means to the original data for datasets with NT^2 ranging from 10^8 to $3 \cdot 10^8$, while the benefits of our framework's significantly improved asymptotic computational complexity become apparent for datasets with NT^2 larger than $4 \cdot 10^8$. On the other hand, if we focus on *k*-means only, for datasets with T at most 100, applying *k*-means to sparsified datasets is about 10–20 times faster than its application to the original data. As T grows larger to 200–400, the speed-up factor of *k*-means increases to 60–80, and reaches values above 120–150 for a time-series length T above 600.

As an additional note regarding the high computational overhead due to Sparse Gaussian Process Regression, we should mention that (i) SGPR could run offline, independently of *k*-means (or any other shape-based time-series clustering algorithm) and only once per time series, with the resulting sparse time series stored for any future use; and (ii) that one could arrange for SGPR to run in parallel (and completely independently) for each different time series, which would result in a completion time about two orders of magnitude faster, without increasing the total CPU utilization.

5.6. Empirical Results: Time and Memory Considerations

As mentioned in Section 5.1, we excluded certain UCR univariate datasets from our experimental evaluation, because it was impossible to successfully run the standard *k*-means algorithm on the original dataset in our computational infrastructure)and [22] does not provide running time estimations for the UCR datasets). The application of *k*-means to those datasets was terminated either due to memory issues, because of the very large size $\Theta(NT)$ of the dataset, or due to running time exceeding two days without completing a single run of *k*-means.

Nevertheless, using our Sparse Time-Series Clustering framework, we managed to obtain results for those datasets successfully, demonstrating its usefulness. For example, Table 5 reports the ARI achieved by our framework for the ElectricDevices dataset, a very large dataset consisting of 16637 time series of length 96 each and $k = 7$ clusters (this is one of the datasets for which we could not run *k*-means with the original time series in our computational infrastructure). We note that the best ARI is obtained by *k*-means with the original data, and the standard DTW distance is 0.19, as reported in [22].

6. Discussion and Future Work

Our proposed framework, as we demonstrated in Section 5, has competitive results to the standard k-means algorithm for time-series clustering. In our comprehensive evaluation, we highlight the significant advantages of our framework in clustering quality, CPU utilization, and memory requirements, especially for larger datasets and for time series of moderate to large lengths.

The bottleneck of our method in terms of CPU utilization is the modeling phase. We underline that this step is completely independent for each time series; hence, it can be parallelized, reducing the total running time of our framework. Moreover, SGPR can be run once as an offline step, with its results stored for any future use. The modeling step allows us to significantly reduce the memory requirements for the clustering step since the time-series representation is logarithmic in the length of the original time series, making the clustering step feasible in huge datasets (with a large number of long time series) for the popular, but computationally demanding, DTW distance.

The extensive evaluation of our framework, including additional metrics, has been made accessible on GitHub, providing a comprehensive resource for researchers. This transparency ensures the reproducibility of results and facilitates further exploration and validation. The reported CPU utilization times comprise an important addition to the thus far assessment of time-series clustering methods.

Moving forward, there are several promising directions for future work. First, an in-depth exploration of the tuning process is warranted to establish a correlation between the nature of the dataset and the optimal parameter selection of the framework. This understanding could lead to refined configurations, enhancing the effectiveness of the proposed framework across diverse datasets and applications.

Additionally, the incorporation of different alignment distances in our framework presents an intriguing direction of research. For instance, Frechét distance [37] and Wasserstein distance [38], which can be used in time-series clustering, come with computational challenges. Therefore, our framework, with the reduction of the time-series length, may allow the efficient application of these distances in time-series clustering to longer univariate time-series.

Last but not least, the extension of our framework to handle multivariate time series is a natural direction for future work. The ability to effectively analyze and model complex multi-dimensional time-series data expands the range of potential applications across diverse domains.

Author Contributions: Conceptualization, D.F.; Methodology, D.F., P.P., E.P. and M.X.; Software, E.P. and M.X.; Validation, E.P. and M.X.; Investigation, D.F., P.P., E.P. and M.X.; Data curation, M.X.; Writing—original draft, P.P., E.P. and M.X.; Writing—review & editing, D.F. and E.P.; Visualization, E.P.; Supervision, D.F.; Funding acquisition, D.F. All authors have read and agreed to the published version of the manuscript.

Funding: This work was supported by the Hellenic Foundation for Research and Innovation (H.F.R.I.) under the "First Call for H.F.R.I. Research Projects to support Faculty members and Researchers and the procurement of high-cost research equipment grant", project BALSAM, HFRI-FM17-1424. A significant part of this work was made while Michalis Xefteris was a student at the National Technical University of Athens.

Data Availability Statement: The source code, the datasets, and more results with additional parameter configurations and for clustering quality indicators other than ARI can be found in https://github.com/pseleni/ts_clustering (accessed on 25 January 2024).

Conflicts of Interest: The authors declare no conflicts of interest.

Appendix A. Tables with Detailed ARI and Results

Table A1. ARI of UCR datasets for Algorithm 3 (the baseline computed by standard k-means) and Algorithm 1 (Sparse Time-Series Clustering) with standard DTW (i.e., $\beta = 0$) and number of inducing points $m = \gamma \log_2 T$, for every $\gamma \in \{1,2,3,4,5\}$. The best ARI achieved is marked in bold. In parenthesis, we report the relative order of the corresponding ARI among the six ones reported, from 1 (best) to 6 (worst). In the last line, we report the average ARI (and the average relative order) for each column across all datasets.

Dataset	Baseline	$1 \cdot \log T$	$2 \cdot \log T$	$3 \cdot \log T$	$4 \cdot \log T$	$5 \cdot \log T$
Adiac	**0.266** (1)	0.229 (3)	0.242 (2)	0.201 (6)	0.227 (4)	0.214 (5)
ArrowHead	0.165 (2)	**0.195** (1)	0.139 (4)	0.163 (3)	0.111 (6)	0.132 (5)
Beef	0.100 (2)	**0.115** (1)	0.097 (3)	0.078 (6)	0.090 (4)	0.083 (5)
BeetleFly	0.091 (2)	0.036 (6)	0.051 (4)	0.048 (5)	0.079 (3)	**0.118** (1)
BirdChicken	0.010 (4)	**0.062** (1)	0.002 (6)	0.022 (2)	0.010 (5)	0.018 (3)
Car	0.102 (2)	**0.277** (1)	0.081 (4)	0.082 (3)	0.063 (6)	0.078 (5)
CBF	**0.689** (1)	0.511 (5)	0.650 (2)	0.641 (3)	0.584 (4)	0.426 (6)
Coffee	0.592 (2)	0.210 (6)	0.539 (3)	0.503 (4)	0.352 (5)	**0.763** (1)
Computers	0.043 (5)	0.023 (6)	0.052 (3)	0.052 (4)	**0.065** (1)	0.058 (2)
CricketX	**0.218** (1)	0.106 (6)	0.153 (5)	0.157 (4)	0.167 (3)	0.187 (2)
CricketY	**0.219** (1)	0.138 (6)	0.177 (4)	0.185 (2)	0.169 (5)	0.179 (3)
CricketZ	**0.223** (1)	0.109 (6)	0.156 (5)	0.167 (3)	0.162 (4)	0.177 (2)
DiatomSizeReduction	**0.904** (1)	0.355 (6)	0.652 (3)	0.729 (2)	0.610 (4)	0.391 (5)
DistalPhalanxOutlineCorrect	0.001 (2)	−0.003 (6)	**0.001** (1)	−0.001 (5)	−0.001 (4)	−0.001 (3)
DistalPhalanxOutlineAgeGroup	0.366 (3)	0.396 (2)	**0.402** (1)	0.363 (5)	0.360 (6)	0.365 (4)
DistalPhalanxTW	0.302 (4)	**0.423** (1)	0.330 (3)	0.343 (2)	0.300 (5)	0.277 (6)
Earthquakes	−0.043 (6)	0.027 (5)	0.033 (2)	0.027 (4)	0.030 (3)	**0.034** (1)
ECG200	0.100 (5)	0.117 (2)	**0.139** (1)	0.100 (4)	0.080 (6)	0.107 (3)
ECGFiveDays	0.008 (5)	**0.091** (1)	0.043 (4)	0.045 (3)	0.002 (6)	0.066 (2)
FaceAll	**0.461** (1)	0.072 (6)	0.209 (5)	0.367 (3)	0.358 (4)	0.455 (2)
FaceFour	0.352 (2)	0.001 (6)	0.339 (3)	0.277 (5)	0.316 (4)	**0.419** (1)
FacesUCR	0.445 (2)	0.070 (6)	0.212 (5)	0.353 (3)	0.342 (4)	**0.456** (1)
FiftyWords	**0.325** (1)	0.210 (6)	0.241 (5)	0.274 (4)	0.299 (3)	0.311 (2)
Fish	**0.283** (1)	0.204 (2)	0.172 (4)	0.179 (3)	0.169 (5)	0.138 (6)
GunPoint	−0.004 (3)	**0.026** (1)	−0.005 (6)	−0.003 (2)	−0.004 (4)	−0.005 (5)
Ham	0.032 (2)	−0.004 (6)	0.027 (3)	**0.045** (1)	0.023 (5)	0.024 (4)
Herring	**0.013** (1)	−0.007 (6)	−0.005 (5)	0.003 (4)	0.007 (3)	0.007 (2)
InsectWingbeatSound	0.057 (4)	0.079 (2)	**0.081** (1)	0.066 (3)	0.045 (5)	0.043 (6)
ItalyPowerDemand	**0.004** (1)	0.000 (6)	0.001 (3)	0.001 (4)	0.001 (5)	0.002 (2)
LargeKitchenAppliances	**0.170** (1)	0.065 (4)	0.080 (2)	0.065 (5)	0.051 (6)	0.066 (3)
Lightning2	0.025 (2)	0.008 (5)	0.003 (6)	0.008 (4)	0.017 (3)	**0.029** (1)
Lightning7	**0.293** (1)	0.197 (2)	0.162 (6)	0.169 (5)	0.190 (4)	0.190 (3)
Meat	**0.630** (1)	0.225 (4)	0.186 (5)	0.095 (6)	0.418 (2)	0.277 (3)
MedicalImages	**0.101** (1)	0.039 (6)	0.060 (5)	0.062 (4)	0.066 (3)	0.073 (2)
MiddlePhalanxOutlineAgeGroup	0.388 (4)	0.337 (5)	0.336 (6)	0.405 (2)	0.392 (3)	**0.408** (1)
MiddlePhalanxOutlineCorrect	−0.005 (6)	**0.025** (1)	0.000 (3)	0.000 (2)	−0.002 (4)	−0.003 (5)
MiddlePhalanxTW	0.290 (5)	**0.382** (1)	0.303 (4)	0.323 (3)	0.326 (2)	0.278 (6)
MoteStrain	0.029 (6)	0.386 (2)	**0.398** (1)	0.364 (4)	0.372 (3)	0.357 (5)
OliveOil	**0.459** (1)	0.238 (2)	0.090 (3)	0.017 (5)	−0.007 (6)	0.081 (4)
OSULeaf	**0.148** (1)	0.064 (6)	0.136 (3)	0.128 (5)	0.132 (4)	0.139 (2)
PhalangesOutlinesCorrect	0.006 (5)	**0.012** (1)	0.001 (6)	0.006 (4)	0.010 (3)	0.010 (2)
Plane	**0.825** (1)	0.665 (6)	0.734 (5)	0.770 (4)	0.815 (3)	0.818 (2)
ProximalPhalanxOutlineCorrect	0.055 (4)	0.051 (6)	**0.082** (1)	0.062 (3)	0.053 (5)	0.064 (2)
ProximalPhalanxOutlineAgeGroup	0.450 (4)	**0.486** (1)	0.416 (5)	0.385 (6)	0.465 (2)	0.461 (3)
ProximalPhalanxTW	0.377 (4)	0.380 (3)	**0.431** (1)	0.384 (2)	0.355 (5)	0.347 (6)
RefrigerationDevices	**0.076** (1)	0.002 (6)	0.008 (5)	0.026 (4)	0.040 (2)	0.033 (3)
ShapeletSim	**0.006** (1)	−0.003 (5)	−0.003 (6)	−0.001 (4)	0.002 (3)	0.004 (2)
ShapesAll	**0.340** (1)	0.247 (6)	0.294 (5)	0.315 (2)	0.313 (4)	0.314 (3)

Table A1. *Cont.*

Dataset	Baseline	$1 \cdot \log T$	$2 \cdot \log T$	$3 \cdot \log T$	$4 \cdot \log T$	$5 \cdot \log T$
SmallKitchenAppliances	**0.214** (1)	0.014 (6)	0.032 (5)	0.045 (4)	0.049 (3)	0.051 (2)
SonyAIBORobotSurface1	**0.697** (1)	0.535 (4)	0.548 (3)	0.599 (2)	0.487 (6)	0.524 (5)
SonyAIBORobotSurface2	0.104 (5)	−0.033 (6)	**0.355** (1)	0.295 (3)	0.300 (2)	0.263 (4)
Strawberry	−0.033 (6)	−0.029 (5)	**0.016** (1)	−0.011 (3)	−0.011 (2)	−0.029 (4)
SwedishLeaf	0.333 (4)	0.180 (6)	0.314 (5)	**0.367** (1)	0.356 (3)	0.364 (2)
Symbols	**0.675** (1)	0.642 (3)	0.622 (6)	0.658 (2)	0.639 (4)	0.639 (5)
SyntheticControl	**0.773** (1)	0.633 (6)	0.733 (4)	0.756 (2)	0.728 (5)	0.743 (3)
ToeSegmentation1	0.022 (4)	0.005 (6)	0.022 (3)	**0.027** (1)	0.027 (2)	0.021 (5)
ToeSegmentation2	0.043 (5)	0.063 (2)	**0.071** (1)	0.041 (6)	0.056 (4)	0.059 (3)
Trace	0.584 (2)	0.526 (6)	0.570 (5)	0.574 (4)	**0.585** (1)	0.577 (3)
TwoLeadECG	0.074 (5)	0.011 (6)	**0.817** (1)	0.138 (4)	0.519 (2)	0.371 (3)
TwoPatterns	**0.870** (1)	0.304 (6)	0.702 (5)	0.825 (2)	0.813 (3)	0.799 (4)
Wine	−0.004 (3)	−0.005 (5)	−0.005 (4)	−0.002 (2)	**−0.002** (1)	−0.007 (6)
WordSynonyms	**0.240** (1)	0.169 (6)	0.172 (5)	0.202 (4)	0.221 (3)	0.223 (2)
Worms	**0.083** (1)	0.031 (6)	0.074 (5)	0.079 (4)	0.080 (3)	0.082 (2)
	0.249 (2.524)	0.173 (4.270)	0.222 (3.683)	0.217 (3.492)	0.220 (3.762)	0.225 (3.270)

Table A2. Average ARI (and standard deviation) of UCR datasets for Algorithm 3 (the baseli computed by standard k-means) and Algorithm 1 (Sparse Time-Series Clustering) with numb of inducing points $m = \gamma \log_2 T$, for $\gamma \in \{1,2,3,4,5\}$ and $(\alpha m/T)$-DTW. Averages and standa deviations are computed over ARI values of 10 different runs (for the baseline) and ARI values of 1 different runs for each different value of $\alpha\{0, 10^{-4}, 10^{-3}, 10^{-2}\}$ for the sparse framework. The be average ARI is reported in bold. In parenthesis, we report the relative order of the correspondir average ARI among the six ones reported, from 1 (best) to 6 (worst). In the last line, we report th average ARI (and the average relative order) for each column across all datasets.

Dataset	Baseline	$1 \cdot \log T$	$2 \cdot \log T$	$3 \cdot \log T$	$4 \cdot \log T$	$5 \cdot \log T$
Adiac	**0.266 ± 0.017** (1)	0.234 ± 0.005 (3)	0.240 ± 0.001 (2)	0.201 ± 0.001 (6)	0.227 ± 0.002 (4)	0.217 ± 0.005 (5)
ArrowHead	0.165 ± 0.058 (3)	**0.204 ± 0.011** (1)	0.149 ± 0.019 (5)	0.178 ± 0.026 (2)	0.135 ± 0.031 (6)	0.150 ± 0.022 (4)
Beef	0.100 ± 0.032 (2)	**0.114 ± 0.001** (1)	0.099 ± 0.004 (3)	0.086 ± 0.008 (6)	0.091 ± 0.006 (4)	0.086 ± 0.005 (5)
BeetleFly	0.091 ± 0.068 (2)	0.033 ± 0.005 (6)	0.049 ± 0.003 (5)	0.060 ± 0.014 (4)	0.072 ± 0.004 (3)	**0.106 ± 0.008** (1)
BirdChicken	0.010 ± 0.027 (3)	**0.058 ± 0.004** (1)	0.002 ± 0.000 (6)	0.010 ± 0.010 (4)	0.004 ± 0.006 (5)	0.018 ± 0.001 (2)
Car	0.102 ± 0.045 (2)	**0.286 ± 0.016** (1)	0.083 ± 0.008 (5)	0.092 ± 0.013 (3)	0.081 ± 0.024 (6)	0.088 ± 0.015 (4)
CBF	**0.689 ± 0.143** (1)	0.443 ± 0.107 (6)	0.583 ± 0.116 (2)	0.582 ± 0.105 (3)	0.543 ± 0.071 (4)	0.456 ± 0.043 (5)
Coffee	0.592 ± 0.243 (2)	0.217 ± 0.012 (6)	0.526 ± 0.024 (3)	0.498 ± 0.011 (4)	0.360 ± 0.008 (5)	**0.745 ± 0.035** (1)
Computers	0.043 ± 0.028 (3)	0.018 ± 0.005 (6)	0.041 ± 0.018 (4)	0.041 ± 0.018 (5)	**0.055 ± 0.022** (1)	0.050 ± 0.015 (2)
CricketX	**0.218 ± 0.030** (1)	0.108 ± 0.003 (6)	0.151 ± 0.003 (5)	0.152 ± 0.005 (4)	0.170 ± 0.005 (3)	0.179 ± 0.009 (2)
CricketY	**0.219 ± 0.028** (1)	0.136 ± 0.005 (6)	0.184 ± 0.007 (5)	0.199 ± 0.014 (2)	0.185 ± 0.014 (4)	0.192 ± 0.011 (3)
CricketZ	**0.223 ± 0.017** (1)	0.111 ± 0.004 (6)	0.154 ± 0.004 (5)	0.163 ± 0.007 (4)	0.164 ± 0.002 (3)	0.179 ± 0.008 (2)
DiatomSizeReduction	**0.904 ± 0.114** (1)	0.355 ± 0.001 (6)	0.647 ± 0.009 (3)	0.730 ± 0.009 (2)	0.619 ± 0.042 (4)	0.452 ± 0.050 (5)
DistalPhalanxOutlineCorrect	0.001 ± 0.001 (2)	−0.003 ± 0.001 (6)	**0.001 ± 0.000** (1)	−0.001 ± 0.000 (5)	−0.001 ± 0.000 (4)	−0.001 ± 0.000 (3)
DistalPhalanxOutlineAgeGroup	0.366 ± 0.138 (4)	**0.416 ± 0.013** (1)	0.401 ± 0.001 (2)	0.363 ± 0.001 (5)	0.360 ± 0.002 (6)	0.367 ± 0.001 (3)
DistalPhalanxTW	0.302 ± 0.030 (4)	**0.405 ± 0.025** (1)	0.328 ± 0.006 (3)	0.337 ± 0.007 (2)	0.296 ± 0.005 (5)	0.279 ± 0.003 (6)
Earthquakes	−0.043 ± 0.005 (6)	0.009 ± 0.012 (5)	0.027 ± 0.012 (3)	0.026 ± 0.010 (4)	**0.035 ± 0.008** (1)	0.033 ± 0.003 (2)
ECG200	0.100 ± 0.073 (5)	0.132 ± 0.020 (2)	**0.141 ± 0.005** (1)	0.106 ± 0.011 (4)	0.092 ± 0.011 (6)	0.110 ± 0.005 (3)
ECGFiveDays	0.008 ± 0.010 (5)	**0.084 ± 0.011** (1)	0.026 ± 0.019 (4)	0.074 ± 0.020 (2)	0.002 ± 0.000 (6)	0.060 ± 0.007 (3)
FaceAll	0.461 ± 0.040 (2)	0.099 ± 0.016 (6)	0.228 ± 0.020 (5)	0.387 ± 0.020 (3)	0.385 ± 0.028 (4)	**0.494 ± 0.042** (1)
FaceFour	0.352 ± 0.121 (2)	0.013 ± 0.019 (6)	0.332 ± 0.009 (4)	0.272 ± 0.009 (5)	0.335 ± 0.024 (3)	**0.432 ± 0.018** (1)
FacesUCR	0.445 ± 0.055 (2)	0.097 ± 0.015 (6)	0.228 ± 0.015 (5)	0.375 ± 0.023 (3)	0.368 ± 0.031 (4)	**0.492 ± 0.040** (1)
FiftyWords	0.325 ± 0.047 (4)	0.245 ± 0.025 (6)	0.291 ± 0.042 (5)	0.326 ± 0.045 (3)	0.346 ± 0.042 (2)	**0.356 ± 0.043** (1)
Fish	**0.283 ± 0.034** (1)	0.214 ± 0.009 (2)	0.182 ± 0.015 (5)	0.200 ± 0.030 (3)	0.189 ± 0.021 (4)	0.171 ± 0.044 (6)
GunPoint	−0.004 ± 0.003 (3)	**0.014 ± 0.011** (1)	−0.005 ± 0.000 (6)	−0.004 ± 0.001 (2)	−0.004 ± 0.001 (4)	−0.005 ± 0.000 (5)
Ham	0.032 ± 0.025 (2)	−0.004 ± 0.000 (6)	0.021 ± 0.006 (5)	**0.045 ± 0.001** (1)	0.028 ± 0.008 (3)	0.025 ± 0.001 (4)
Herring	**0.013 ± 0.015** (1)	−0.007 ± 0.001 (6)	−0.005 ± 0.001 (5)	0.004 ± 0.001 (4)	0.010 ± 0.004 (2)	0.008 ± 0.001 (3)
InsectWingbeatSound	0.057 ± 0.008 (6)	0.128 ± 0.043 (5)	**0.143 ± 0.055** (1)	0.139 ± 0.070 (2)	0.133 ± 0.077 (3)	0.130 ± 0.081 (4)
ItalyPowerDemand	0.004 ± 0.002 (2)	**0.008 ± 0.015** (1)	0.002 ± 0.001 (3)	0.001 ± 0.001 (5)	0.001 ± 0.000 (6)	0.002 ± 0.000 (4)
LargeKitchenAppliances	**0.170 ± 0.078** (1)	0.061 ± 0.004 (4)	0.068 ± 0.011 (2)	0.060 ± 0.009 (5)	0.047 ± 0.003 (6)	0.064 ± 0.013 (3)
Lightning2	0.025 ± 0.016 (2)	0.021 ± 0.027 (4)	0.021 ± 0.035 (3)	0.020 ± 0.019 (5)	0.012 ± 0.003 (6)	**0.032 ± 0.004** (1)
Lightning7	**0.293 ± 0.044** (1)	0.232 ± 0.038 (2)	0.197 ± 0.038 (6)	0.206 ± 0.039 (5)	0.209 ± 0.023 (4)	0.221 ± 0.038 (3)
Meat	**0.630 ± 0.183** (1)	0.222 ± 0.007 (4)	0.182 ± 0.005 (5)	0.098 ± 0.003 (6)	0.415 ± 0.007 (2)	0.285 ± 0.006 (3)
MedicalImages	**0.101 ± 0.018** (1)	0.031 ± 0.015 (6)	0.056 ± 0.006 (5)	0.065 ± 0.004 (4)	0.067 ± 0.001 (3)	0.078 ± 0.005 (2)
MiddlePhalanxOutlineAgeGroup	0.388 ± 0.077 (4)	0.364 ± 0.027 (5)	0.331 ± 0.010 (6)	0.393 ± 0.013 (2)	0.392 ± 0.001 (3)	**0.404 ± 0.007** (1)
MiddlePhalanxOutlineCorrect	−0.005 ± 0.000 (6)	**0.011 ± 0.008** (1)	−0.000 ± 0.000 (3)	−0.000 ± 0.001 (2)	−0.003 ± 0.000 (4)	−0.003 ± 0.000 (5)
MiddlePhalanxTW	0.290 ± 0.104 (5)	**0.396 ± 0.011** (1)	0.294 ± 0.010 (4)	0.326 ± 0.003 (2)	0.324 ± 0.005 (3)	0.280 ± 0.001 (6)

Table A2. *Cont.*

Dataset	Baseline	$1 \cdot \log T$	$2 \cdot \log T$	$3 \cdot \log T$	$4 \cdot \log T$	$5 \cdot \log T$
MoteStrain	0.029 ± 0.005 (6)	0.385 ± 0.009 (4)	**0.402 ± 0.012** (1)	0.383 ± 0.017 (5)	0.399 ± 0.025 (2)	0.389 ± 0.045 (3)
OliveOil	**0.459 ± 0.145** (1)	0.238 ± 0.000 (2)	0.087 ± 0.004 (3)	0.017 ± 0.000 (5)	−0.008 ± 0.001 (6)	0.081 ± 0.000 (4)
OSULeaf	**0.148 ± 0.023** (1)	0.067 ± 0.005 (6)	0.139 ± 0.003 (3)	0.126 ± 0.002 (5)	0.136 ± 0.004 (4)	0.147 ± 0.007 (2)
PhalangesOutlinesCorrect	0.006 ± 0.001 (3)	0.004 ± 0.005 (5)	0.004 ± 0.003 (6)	0.006 ± 0.000 (4)	0.010 ± 0.000 (2)	**0.010 ± 0.000** (1)
Plane	**0.825 ± 0.147** (1)	0.671 ± 0.008 (6)	0.733 ± 0.003 (5)	0.767 ± 0.006 (4)	0.808 ± 0.008 (3)	0.823 ± 0.004 (2)
ProximalPhalanxOutlineCorrect	0.055 ± 0.003 (4)	0.052 ± 0.000 (6)	**0.085 ± 0.005** (1)	0.063 ± 0.002 (3)	0.053 ± 0.000 (5)	0.065 ± 0.001 (2)
ProximalPhalanxOutlineAgeGroup	0.450 ± 0.108 (4)	**0.477 ± 0.010** (1)	0.422 ± 0.010 (5)	0.380 ± 0.009 (6)	0.463 ± 0.004 (3)	0.471 ± 0.010 (2)
ProximalPhalanxTW	0.377 ± 0.119 (3)	0.373 ± 0.010 (4)	**0.425 ± 0.008** (1)	0.379 ± 0.009 (2)	0.358 ± 0.003 (5)	0.349 ± 0.002 (6)
RefrigerationDevices	**0.076 ± 0.032** (1)	0.003 ± 0.002 (6)	0.008 ± 0.000 (5)	0.026 ± 0.001 (4)	0.039 ± 0.002 (2)	0.035 ± 0.002 (3)
ShapeletSim	**0.006 ± 0.011** (1)	−0.002 ± 0.001 (5)	−0.003 ± 0.000 (6)	−0.002 ± 0.001 (4)	−0.000 ± 0.002 (3)	0.002 ± 0.002 (2)
ShapesAll	**0.340 ± 0.027** (1)	0.265 ± 0.013 (6)	0.316 ± 0.018 (5)	0.334 ± 0.019 (4)	0.337 ± 0.021 (3)	0.338 ± 0.021 (2)
SmallKitchenAppliances	**0.214 ± 0.024** (1)	0.021 ± 0.007 (6)	0.028 ± 0.006 (5)	0.043 ± 0.002 (4)	0.052 ± 0.003 (3)	0.054 ± 0.006 (2)
SonyAIBORobotSurface1	**0.697 ± 0.051** (1)	0.423 ± 0.178 (6)	0.560 ± 0.016 (3)	0.599 ± 0.010 (2)	0.498 ± 0.016 (5)	0.503 ± 0.032 (4)
SonyAIBORobotSurface2	0.104 ± 0.081 (5)	−0.007 ± 0.043 (6)	**0.325 ± 0.029** (1)	0.321 ± 0.027 (2)	0.302 ± 0.011 (3)	0.266 ± 0.031 (4)
Strawberry	−0.033 ± 0.003 (6)	−0.017 ± 0.016 (4)	**0.016 ± 0.001** (1)	−0.012 ± 0.001 (3)	−0.009 ± 0.002 (2)	−0.024 ± 0.005 (5)
SwedishLeaf	0.333 ± 0.041 (4)	0.171 ± 0.012 (6)	0.321 ± 0.007 (5)	0.375 ± 0.008 (3)	0.376 ± 0.022 (2)	**0.392 ± 0.023** (1)
Symbols	**0.675 ± 0.103** (1)	0.641 ± 0.015 (5)	0.633 ± 0.009 (6)	0.667 ± 0.015 (2)	0.646 ± 0.026 (4)	0.652 ± 0.010 (3)
SyntheticControl	**0.773 ± 0.126** (1)	0.594 ± 0.074 (6)	0.713 ± 0.019 (5)	0.751 ± 0.013 (2)	0.730 ± 0.004 (4)	0.743 ± 0.002 (3)
ToeSegmentation1	0.022 ± 0.018 (2)	0.004 ± 0.002 (6)	0.017 ± 0.008 (5)	**0.025 ± 0.016** (1)	0.021 ± 0.012 (3)	0.018 ± 0.008 (4)
ToeSegmentation2	0.043 ± 0.049 (5)	0.047 ± 0.018 (4)	**0.058 ± 0.017** (1)	0.042 ± 0.011 (6)	0.050 ± 0.016 (3)	0.054 ± 0.007 (2)
Trace	**0.584 ± 0.116** (1)	0.489 ± 0.053 (6)	0.540 ± 0.052 (5)	0.561 ± 0.014 (4)	0.584 ± 0.001 (2)	0.576 ± 0.001 (3)
TwoLeadECG	0.074 ± 0.014 (5)	0.009 ± 0.005 (6)	**0.585 ± 0.341** (1)	0.098 ± 0.055 (4)	0.342 ± 0.196 (2)	0.278 ± 0.119 (3)
TwoPatterns	**0.870 ± 0.032** (1)	0.131 ± 0.119 (6)	0.348 ± 0.296 (5)	0.447 ± 0.352 (3)	0.448 ± 0.347 (2)	0.445 ± 0.347 (4)
Wine	−0.004 ± 0.004 (3)	−0.005 ± 0.000 (5)	−0.005 ± 0.000 (4)	−0.003 ± 0.001 (2)	**−0.002 ± 0.000** (1)	−0.007 ± 0.000 (6)
WordSynonyms	0.240 ± 0.016 (3)	0.190 ± 0.016 (6)	0.206 ± 0.028 (5)	0.236 ± 0.030 (4)	0.247 ± 0.028 (2)	**0.251 ± 0.025** (1)
Worms	**0.083 ± 0.020** (1)	0.028 ± 0.003 (6)	0.070 ± 0.006 (5)	0.081 ± 0.002 (3)	0.080 ± 0.004 (4)	0.082 ± 0.002 (2)
	0.249 (2.556)	0.171 (4.413)	0.213 (3.857)	0.215 (3.556)	0.217 (3.587)	0.226 (3.032)

References

1. Fu, T.C. A Review on Time-Series Data Mining. *Eng. Appl. Artif. Intell.* **2011**, *24*, 164–181.
2. Aghabozorgi, S.; Shirkhorshidi, A.S.; Wah, T.Y. Time-series clustering—A decade review. *Inf. Syst.* **2015**, *53*, 16–38. [CrossRef]
3. Hung, J.L.; Wang, M.C.; Wang, S.; Abdelrasoul, M.; Li, Y.; He, W. Identifying at-risk students for early interventions—A time-series clustering approach. *IEEE Trans. Emerg. Top. Comput.* **2015**, *5*, 45–55. [CrossRef]
4. Bandara, K.; Bergmeir, C.; Smyl, S. Forecasting across time series databases using recurrent neural networks on groups of similar series: A clustering approach. *Expert Syst. Appl.* **2020**, *140*, 112896. [CrossRef]
5. Kotsakos, D.; Trajcevski, G.; Gunopulos, D.; Aggarwal, C.C. Time-Series Data Clustering. In *Data Clustering: Algorithms and Applications*; Data Mining and Knowledge Discovery Series; CRC Press: Boca Raton, FL, USA; Taylor and Francis Group: Abingdon, UK, 2014; Volume 15, pp. 357–380.
6. Warren Liao, T. Clustering of time series data—A survey. *Pattern Recognit.* **2005**, *38*, 1857–1874. [CrossRef]
7. Gunopulos, D.; Das, G. Time series similarity measures and time series indexing. In Proceedings of the SIGMOD Conference, Santa Barbara, CA, USA, 21–24 May 2001; p. 624.
8. Kate, R.J. Using dynamic time warping distances as features for improved time-series classification. *Data Min. Knowl. Discov.* **2016**, *30*, 283–312. [CrossRef]
9. Rakthanmanon, T.; Campana, B.; Mueen, A.; Batista, G.; Westover, B.; Zhu, Q.; Zakaria, J.; Keogh, E. Searching and mining trillions of time series subsequences under dynamic time warping. In Proceedings of the 18th ACM SIGKDD International Conference on Knowledge Discovery and Data Mining (KDD), Beijing, China, 12–16 August 2012; pp. 262–270.
10. Tan, C.W.; Webb, G.I.; Petitjean, F. Indexing and classifying gigabytes of time series under time warping. In Proceedings of the SIAM International Conference on Data Mining, Houston, TX, USA, 27–29 April 2017; pp. 1–10.
11. Andoni, A.; Nosatzki, N.S. Edit Distance in Near-Linear Time: It's a Constant Factor. In Proceedings of the 61st IEEE Annual Symposium on Foundations of Computer Science (FOCS 2020), Durham, NC, USA, 16–19 November 2020; pp. 990–1001.
12. Keogh, E.; Chakrabarti, K.; Pazzani, M.; Mehrotra, S. Locally Adaptive Dimensionality Reduction for Indexing Large Time Series Databases. In Proceedings of the 2001 ACM SIGMOD International Conference on Management of Data, Santa Barbara, CA, USA, 21–24 May 2001; SIGMOD '01, pp. 151–162. [CrossRef]
13. Iorio, C.; Frasso, G.; D'Ambrosio, A.; Siciliano, R. Parsimonious time series clustering using P-splines. *Expert Syst. Appl.* **2016**, *52*, 26–38. [CrossRef]
14. Rasmussen, C.E.; Williams, C.K.I. *Gaussian Processes for Machine Learning (Adaptive Computation and Machine Learning)*; The MIT Press: Cambridge, MA, USA, 2005.
15. Leibfried, F.; Dutordoir, V.; John, S.; Durrande, N. A tutorial on sparse Gaussian processes and variational inference. *arXiv* **2020**, arXiv:2012.13962.
16. Titsias, M. Variational Learning of Inducing Variables in Sparse Gaussian Processes. In Proceedings of the Twelth International Conference on Artificial Intelligence and Statistics, Clearwater Beach, FL, USA, 16–18 April 2009; van Dyk, D., Welling, M., Eds.; Proceedings of Machine Learning Research; Hilton Clearwater Beach Resort: Clearwater Beach, FL, USA, 2009; Volume 5, pp. 567–574.

17. Quiñonero-Candela, J.; Ramussen, C.; Williams, C. Approximation methods for Gaussian process regression. In *Large-Scale Kern Machines*; MIT Press: Cambridge, MA, USA, 2007; pp. 203–223.
18. Micchelli, C.A.; Xu, Y.; Zhang, H. Universal Kernels. *J. Mach. Learn. Res.* **2006**, *7*, 2651–2667.
19. Petitjean, F.; Ketterlin, A.; Gançarski, P. A global averaging method for dynamic time warping, with applications to clusterin *Pattern Recognit.* **2011**, *44*, 678–693. [CrossRef]
20. Dau, H.A.; Keogh, E.; Kamgar, K.; Yeh, C.C.M.; Zhu, Y.; Gharghabi, S.; Ratanamahatana, C.A.; Yanping; Hu, B.; Begum, N.; et a The UCR Time Series Classification Archive. 2018. Available online: https://www.cs.ucr.edu/~eamonn/time_series_data_2018 (accessed on 25 January 2024).
21. Faloutsos, C.; Ranganathan, M.; Manolopoulos, Y. Fast subsequence matching in time-series databases. *ACM Sigmod Rec.* **199** *23*, 419–429. [CrossRef]
22. Javed, A.; Lee, B.S.; Rizzo, D.M. A benchmark study on time series clustering. *Mach. Learn. Appl.* **2020**, *1*, 100001. [CrossRef]
23. Paparrizos, J.; Gravano, L. Fast and accurate time-series clustering. *ACM Trans. Database Syst. (TODS)* **2017**, *42*, 1–49. [CrossRe
24. Rand, W.M. Objective criteria for the evaluation of clustering methods. *J. Am. Stat. Assoc.* **1971**, *66*, 846–850. [CrossRef]
25. Morey, L.C.; Agresti, A. The measurement of classification agreement: An adjustment to the Rand statistic for chance agreemen *Educ. Psychol. Meas.* **1984**, *44*, 33–37. [CrossRef]
26. Hubert, L.; Arabie, P. Comparing Partitions. *J. Classif.* **1985**, *2*, 193–218. [CrossRef]
27. Vinh, N.X.; Epps, J.; Bailey, J. Information theoretic measures for clusterings comparison: Is a correction for chance necessary In Proceedings of the 26th Annual International Conference on Machine Learning, Montreal, QC, Canada, 14–18 June 200 pp. 1073–1080.
28. Chatterjee, S.; Simonoff, J.S. *Handbook of Regression Analysis*; John Wiley & Sons: Hoboken, NJ, USA, 2013.
29. Wang, J. An intuitive tutorial to Gaussian processes regression. *Comput. Sci. Eng.* **2023**, 1–8. [CrossRef]
30. Kingma, D.P.; Ba, J. Adam: A method for stochastic optimization. *arXiv* **2014**, arXiv:1412.6980.
31. Liu, D.C.; Nocedal, J. On the limited memory BFGS method for large scale optimization. *Math. Program. B* **1989**, *45*, 503–52 [CrossRef]
32. Snelson, E.; Ghahramani, Z. Sparse Gaussian processes using pseudo-inputs. In *Advances in Neural Information Processing System 18*; MIT Press: Cambridge, MA, USA, 2006; pp. 1257–1264.
33. Csató, L.; Opper, M. Sparse online Gaussian processes. *Neural Comput.* **2002**, *14*, 641–668. [CrossRef]
34. McIntire, M.; Ratner, D.; Ermon, S. Sparse Gaussian Processes for Bayesian Optimization. In Proceedings of the UAI, New York NY, USA, 25–29 June 2016.
35. Gardner, J.R.; Pleiss, G.; Bindel, D.; Weinberger, K.Q.; Wilson, A.G. GPyTorch: Blackbox Matrix-Matrix Gaussian Process Inferenc with GPU Acceleration. In Proceedings of the Advances in Neural Information Processing Systems, Montreal, QC, Canada, 3– December 2018.
36. Tavenard, R.; Faouzi, J.; Vandewiele, G.; Divo, F.; Androz, G.; Holtz, C.; Payne, M.; Yurchak, R.; Rußwurm, M.; Kolar, K.; et a Tslearn, A Machine Learning Toolkit for Time Series Data. *J. Mach. Learn. Res.* **2020**, *21*, 1–6.
37. Driemel, A.; Krivošija, A.; Sohler, C. Clustering time-series under the Fréchet distance. In Proceedings of the Twenty-Seventh Annual ACM-SIAM Symposium on Discrete Algorithms, SIAM, Arlington, VA, USA, 10–12 January 2016; pp. 766–785.
38. Muskulus, M.; Verduyn-Lunel, S. Wasserstein distances in the analysis of time-series and dynamical systems. *Phys. D Nonlinea Phenom.* **2011**, *240*, 45–58. [CrossRef]

MDPI
St. Alban-Anlage 66
4052 Basel
Switzerland
www.mdpi.com

Algorithms Editorial Office
E-mail: algorithms@mdpi.com
www.mdpi.com/journal/algorithms

www.ingramcontent.com/pod-product-compliance
Lightning Source LLC
Chambersburg PA
CBHW061619220926
51850CB00005B/543
9783725806416